Antique Maps
of the
British Isles

David Smith

B T Batsford Ltd, London

To my Mother and the memory of my Father

'Curiosity to visit as much of my native country as I had opportunity excited a desire to know all that related to its topographical antiquities. The scarcity of descriptions by the pen or pencil soon appeared not so great as former lists represented it. A diligent inquiry after every article of this kind, which some notwithstanding must have escaped, produced the catalogue I now present to those whose pursuits are congenial to my own. If a catalogue of the authors or artists of Great Britain be interesting to their countrymen, some account of those who have traced its topographical antiquities to their source may not be unworthy their notice. We are naturally inclined to think what is of importance to ourselves deserves to be accounted so to others. These Anecdotes have informed and amused the collector:—if they only amuse the readers I shall not be absolutely condemned; if they inform them, my passion for British antiquities becomes a zeal to serve the public'.

From the Preface to Richard Gough, *Anecdotes of British Topography or, an historical account of what has been done for illustrating the Topographical Antiquities of Great Britain and Ireland*, 1768

© David Smith 1982
First published 1982

ISBN 0 7134 1694 7

Typeset by Keyspools Ltd, Golborne, Lancs. and printed in Great Britain by
Butler & Tanner Ltd
Frome, Somerset

for the publishers
B. T. Batsford Ltd
4 Fitzhardinge Street
London W1H 0AH

Contents

List of Illustrations

The reference numbers are given after the plate number for maps covered in the detailed analyses of Chapter VII. Illustrations reproduced by permission of the British Library: note the Library's press-mark in brackets after the attribution.

Colour plates
A 'Anglia', by Christopher Saxton, 1579
B 'The Kingdome of Scotland', by John Speed, 1610
C 'Irelande', by Baptista Boazio, 1599
D 'Cambriae Typus Auctore Humfredo Lhuydo', published by Abraham Ortelius, 1573–80

Black and white illustrations
1 England and Wales, by Sebastian Munster, c.1578
2 Cumberland, by John Speed, 1676
3 Buckingham and Bedford, by Jan Jansson, 1646
4 Cambridgeshire, by Emanuel Bowen, 1751
5 'Ila Insula ex Aebudarum majoribus una', by Joan Blaeu, 1654
6 East Lothian, by John Adair, c.1736
7 Orkney Islands, by Archibald Fullarton, c.1857
8 Ireland, by Abraham Ortelius, 1574
9 Kildare, by John Noble & James Keenan, 1752
10 British Isles, by Martin Waldseemuller, 1513
11 Somerset, by Robert Morden, 1695 (detail)
12 'A plan of London and its environs', published by Samuel Lewis, 1833 (detail)
13 Birmingham, published by Charles Knight, 1850 (detail)
14 Staffordshire, by Joseph Browne, 1682
15 Jersey and Guernsey, by Alain Manesson Mallet, 1683
16 Ulster and Leinster, by Antonio Zatta, 1778
17 'A Map of the Levels in Lincoln Shire . . .', by William Stukeley, 1723
18 'A Map of Hemlingford Hund.', by Henry Beighton, 1729
19 'A Map of the Hundreds of Barstable, Rochford & Dengy', engraved by Thomas Bowen, 1762–68
20 'A Map of the Hundred of Little and Lesnes, and the Hundred of Dartford and Wilmington', published by Edward Hasted, c.1780
21 Ordnance Survey Sheet No. 1. Brentwood, c.1835
22 'Plan of the Baynards Estate in the County of Surrey', lithographed by G. E. Mudeley, 1832
23 'Billingsgate Ward and Bridge Ward', by Benjamin Cole, 1760
24 'Nordovicum', by Braun & Hogenberg, c.1590
25 Kingston upon Hull, engraved by Isaac Taylor, 1796
26 Colchester, from Morant's *Essex*, c.1768
27 Colchester, by Cole & Roper, 1805
28 Glasgow, by John Dower, c.1830 (detail)
29 Waterford, by William Richards & Bernard Scalé, 1764
30 'Manchester and its environs', by Edward Baines, 1824
31 'Environs of London', by W. Schmollinger, 1837
32 Slipcase cover of 'Mogg's New Map of Steam Navigation', 1837
33 Andover to 'Crookhorn', by John Ogilby, 1675 (detail)
34 'Crookhorn' to Weymouth, by Bowen & Owen, 1720
35 The road 'through Ryegate', by Charles Smith, 1800

Acknowledgments

A work of this nature is essentially a tiny link in a chain of expanding knowledge. It is, on the one hand, a synthesis of existing knowledge and, on the other, hopefully, a platform for future work on the subject. As such it owes an immense debt to the scholarship of others.

Firstly, I must acknowledge the foundations laid by the great pioneers and developers of carto-bibliography; in particular, Richard Gough, Sir Herbert George Fordham, Thomas Chubb, E. G. Box, Harold Whitaker, Edward Lynam, Raymond Lister and R. A. Skelton.

Like John Speed before me, 'I haue put my sickle into other mens corne'. I wish to acknowledge with gratitude the encouragement, and authorization to quote and draw material from the works, of the following: Roger Baynton-Williams; John Booth; Philippa Glanville of the Museum of London; Dr Brian Harley of the University of Exeter; Professor Paul D. A. Harvey of the University of Durham; Donald Hodson, particularly for access to his comprehensive listing of English county map and atlas holdings; Ralph Hyde of the Guildhall Library; D. G. Moir of the Royal Scottish Geographical Society; Elizabeth M. Rodger of Glasgow University Library; R. V. Tooley; and Sarah Tyacke of the British Library. I should also like to express my gratitude to the late Professor Harry Thorpe and the late Dr Gordon Wyatt, and to the authors of the many other invaluable printed works on the subject.

I am grateful to the following publishers for permission to use material from their publications: Barracuda Books for *Maps of Bucks*; Bell & Hyman for *Collecting Old Maps and Globes*; Collins Publishers for *British Maps & Mapmakers*; David & Charles for *The Royal English Atlas*; Eason & Son for *Irish Maps*; Map Collector Publications for *London Map Sellers 1660–1720*, particularly for the advertisements from the *London Gazette*; Shire Publications for *Discovering Antique Maps*; and the University of Chicago Press for *Maps* and *Five Centuries of Map Printing*.

In the preparation of this work, I have received the willing co-operation of numerous libraries, museums and individuals who have offered research facilities and provided information. Without this co-operation, the book could not have been written. I thank all who have generously helped, but must make special mention of the staffs of: the Map Library of the British Library, with special thanks to Yolande Hodson; the Royal Geographical Society, particularly for direct access to the collection and notes of Sir H. G. Fordham; Birmingham Reference Library; Bodleian Library, Oxford; Brotherton Library, University of Leeds; Cambridge University Library; Central Library, Cardiff; National Library of Ireland; Lancashire Record Office; National Library of Scotland, with special thanks to Margaret Wilkes; St Albans Central Library; National Library of Wales; and Warwickshire County Record Office. I am also indebted to Dr John Andrews of Trinity College, Dublin, Clive Burden, and Charles Meacock of the London College of Printing for information freely given.

Some illustrations have been kindly supplied by Ivan Deverall, Ben Hardisty, Stanley Gibbons Antiquarian, Richard Miller, Jason Musgrave and Richard Nicholson. Thanks are due to Simon Mills and Richard Wight for their photographic work and to Celia Goyns and Wendy Holden for the tedious task of typing the manuscript.

Many others have contributed to the success of this work through their interest, co-operation and goodwill. I am particularly indebted to Samuel Carr of B. T. Batsford Ltd who had faith in the idea when many fainter hearts had none. Richard Miller, Jason Musgrave and Dr Iain Taylor patiently considered many ideas and offered much helpful advice and information, and were, throughout, enthusiastic supporters.

Finally, I wish to express my gratitude to my wife for her fortitude and help during the lengthy preparation of this work; it was her present of a Cary of 'Glocestershire' that sparked the interest and she has rued the day ever since!

Needless to say, all errors and omissions are entirely my own responsibility. Inevitably, the wide compass of this work leaves much to be desired and nobody can be more aware of its inadequacies than I!

The superscript numerals in the text refer to the Notes at the end of the book (pages 233–34).

Preface

As my interest in British antique maps developed and my collection grew, I became increasingly frustrated by, on the one hand, the lack of readily accessible information on the subject, and, on the other, the apparent arbitrariness of dealers' map identifications and datings. There seemed to be so many unanswered questions and so many unidentified maps, and what information there was, was scattered amongst a very wide range of publications. Other collectors were experiencing the same frustrations. Gradually the resolve grew to produce in one book all the basic information required by the serious collector of British antique maps. That resolve developed into a major research project.

This book is designed to fulfil several functions. Firstly, it provides a general background to the development of map production and British mapping, and points the direction for readers who wish to delve deeper into any aspect of the subject. Secondly, it gives detailed descriptions of the maps themselves as an aid to identification. And, thirdly, it offers an exhaustive breakdown of the issues of each map series to help in dating maps once they have been identified. It is hoped that the evidence supporting this analysis will eventually be gathered into an accessible form for reference. The book also discusses the range of maps available and catalogues collections and dealers.

The extent of the coverage was a vexatious problem. Eventually the criteria evolved that the maps covered should be both available and within the finances of the average collector. Examples of all the maps covered by the detailed analyses have been offered for sale during the past year at less than £100 each (1980 prices!)—even rare maps appear on the market cheaply, often because they are unrecognized![1] Such has been the increase in map prices that the four most celebrated map series of Britain are now beyond the pocket of the average collector; thus, Saxton, Speed, Blaeu and Jansson have been denied detailed analysis, although, of course, their importance in the development of British mapping is recognized. Other rare and expensive series have also been excluded; however, these maps are superbly documented elsewhere, and the collector in search of information will find himself well provided for. The coverage usually ends at about 1845, since later maps are not yet widely stocked by dealers, but issues of some maps covered have been recorded beyond that date (usually until they underwent some major change). Marine and coastal charts have been excluded since they are a specialised study in their own right.

It is hoped that this work will facilitate the accurate identification and dating of British antique maps and will also place them within the wider context of the evolution of map production and the mapping of the British Isles.

David A. Smith
Bexley. January 1981.

A Chronology of Cartographers, Engravers and Publishers

Monarchs	Flourished	Events
The Tudors:	1534–94d. Gerard Mercator	1536: Dissolution of the monasteries
1509–47:	1551–68d. Humphrey Lhuyd	1536: Wales combined with England
Henry VIII	1564–98d. Abraham Ortelius	
1547–53:	1569–1606 Christopher Saxton	
Edward VI	1580b.–1661d. Robert Gordon	1579: Christopher Saxton's atlas
1553–58:	1590–1610 Timothy Pont	1590: Timothy Pont surveys Scotland
Mary I	1591–1611d. Jodocus Hondius	
1558–1603:	1592–98 Philip Symonson	
Elizabeth I	1592–1630d. John Bill	
	1593–1626d. John Norden	1593: Parliament establishes the statute mile
	1598–1635 William Kip	
	1599–1618 John Sudbury	
	1599–1638d. Willem Janszoon Blaeu	
	1599–c.1646d. Pieter van den Keere	
	1602–3 William Smith	
The Stuarts:	c.1603–40d. George Humble	
1603–25:	1607–46 William Hole	1607: Camden's *Britannia* with maps by Kip & Hole
James I	1610–29d. John Speed	
	1611–57d. Henricus Hondius	1611: Speed's *Theatre*
	1612–22 Michael Drayton	
	1616–64d. Jan Jansson	
	1622–73d. Thomas Jenner	
1625–49:	1623b.–87d. Sir William Petty	1634: Louis XIII decrees the Ile de Fer as the prime meridian of longitude
Charles I	1629–52 William Web	
	1635–54d. Mathew Simons	
	1640–59 William Humble	c.1637: Draining of the Fens
	1641–65d. Peter Stent	1641: Irish rebellion
	1646–73d. Joan Blaeu	1642: Civil War
	1659–93 Thomas Bassett	1653: Act of Satisfaction
1660–85:	1660–67 Roger Rea, the elder	1654: Blaeu's atlas of Scotland
Charles II	& younger	1657: Post Office of England established
	1660–97 John Seller	1660: Restoration
	1660–1705d. Richard Blome	
	c.1661 Rutger Hermannides	1663: Turnpike Act
	1665–98 Abel Swale	
	1666–76d. John Ogilby	1666: Great Fire of London
	1666–1707 John Overton	
	1666–1711 Richard Chiswell	
	1667–96 Moses Pitt	
	1667–1701 Francis Lamb	
	1669–1703d. Robert Morden	
	1670–1700 Richard Palmer	1672: Destruction of the Blaeu premises
	1675–90 William Morgan	
	1676–1718 John Garrett	1676: Prime meridian of London first used
	1681–93 Capt. Greenvile Collins	
	1681–c.1715d. Peter Schenk	

	1681–c.1720d. Gerard Valck	
	1681–1728 Awnsham Churchill	
	1681–1722d. John Adair	
	1683–1700 Philip Lea	
1685–1688:	1683–1714 Thomas Bowles I	1685: Sir William Petty's *Hiberniae Delineatio*
James II	1688–1712 Christopher Browne	
1688–1702:	1688–1732d. Herman Moll	
William III and	1689–c.1713 Sutton Nicholls	
Mary II (1688–	1690–1714 John Churchill	
94)	1702–40 John Senex	
1702–14:	1702–58 George Bickham	
Anne	1707–37 George Willdey	1707: Union with Scotland
	1707–44 Philip Overton	
The House of	1707–49 Henry Overton	
Hanover:	c.1712–24 Thomas Taylor	1712: Duty on imported maps
1714–27:	c.1714–c.1762 Thomas Bowles II	1714: Longitude Act
George I	1719–45 Thomas Badeslade	1718: Thomas Taylor's *The Principality of*
	1719–54 Thomas Gardner	*Wales*
	c.1720 John Owen	
	1720–67 Emanuel Bowen	
	1720–77 John Bowles	
	1723–58 William Henry Toms	1725: Moll's atlas of Scotland
1727–60:	1729–55 John Tinney	
George II	1730–64 Thomas Bakewell	1731: Sextant invented independently by John
	1732–71d. Thomas Jefferys	Hadley and Thomas Godfrey
	1732–75 Richard William Seale	
	1734–44 John Cowley	1734: Copyright Act introduced
	1734–62d. John Rocque	
	1735–64d. James Dodsley	
	1738–76 Thomas Kitchin	
	1744–64d. Robert Dodsley	
	1745–81 John Hinton	1745: Jacobite rising
	1745–94 Robert Sayer	
	c.1746 Samuel Simpson	
	1746–70d. Richard Baldwin	1747–55: Military Survey of Scotland
	c.1748 Thomas Osborne	
	1750–87 John Gibson	
	1750–90 Joseph Ellis	
	1754–93d. Carington Bowles	
	1754–94 John Lodge	
	1757–97 Antonio Zatta	
1760–1820:	1760–87 Bernard Scalé	1759: Royal Society of Arts £100 award for
George III	1760–90d. Thomas Bowen	large-scale county maps
	c.1765 Benjamin Donn	
	1766–79 G. Rollos	1760: Chronometer invented by John Harrison
	1766–1809 John Andrews	
	1768–81 Capt. Andrew Armstrong	1763: Jesse Ramsden invents the graduating
	c.1769 P. Russell	engine leading to the development of the
	c.1770 Andrew Dury	theodolite
	1770–1812 Robert Laurie	
	1770–1811 Capt. Daniel Paterson	
	1771–91 Mostyn John Armstrong	
	1771–1823 William Faden	
	1772–1813 John Ainslie	1773: General Turnpike Act
	1775–77 Andrew Skinner	
	1775–77 George Taylor	
	1776–1812 Daniel Lizars	1776: American War of Independence

1776–1820 John Luffman   1776: Bridgewater Canal
1778–c.1818 Alexander Hogg   1778: Grand Trunk Canal
1780–93d. John Murray
1780–1801 Thomas Conder
1780–1824 Benjamin Baker
1781–1814d. John Stockdale
c.1783–1835d. John Cary
c.1784 George Augustus Walpoole   1784: Hounslow Heath baseline
c.1786–1820 Thomas Brown
c.1790 John Aikin   1790: Forth-Clyde Canal
c.1791 John Harrison   1791: Ordnance Survey established
1794–1818d. James Whittle   1794: Prime meridian of Greenwich first used
1795–1824d. Samuel John Neele   1795: Hydrographic Office established
1799–c.1821 Thomas Dix   1798: Alois Senefelder invents lithography
1800–52 Charles Smith
1801–10 John Roper   1801: General Enclosure Act
1802–10 George Alexander Cooke   1801: Act of Union with Ireland
                                      1801: Publication of the first Ordnance Survey
                                      maps
c.1803 R. Butters
1803–16 Robert Rowe
c.1804 William Green
1804–35 Edward Langley
1806–10 H. Cooper
1806–34 William Darton
1807–74 Adam Black   1807: Geological Society of London founded
c.1808 Benjamin Pitts Capper
1808–26 Edward Mogg
1809–c.1839 Joseph Phelps
c.1810 G. Cole
1810–20 James Wallis
1810–21 Robert Miller
1814–c.1835 John Thomson
1815–39 William Smith
1816–20 Joseph Nightingale
1817–34 Christopher & John Greenwood
1818–26 John Wood
1818–36d. James Robins
1818–60 Sidney Hall
c.1819 James Dugdale
1819–36 William Lewis
1819–36 James Wyld Senior
1820–30: 1820–30 Josiah Neele
George IV 1820–28 Orlando Hodgson
1820–42 Samuel Leigh
1822–26 George & John Grierson
1822–42 Thomas Moule
c.1823 G. & W. B. Whittaker
1823–76 George Frederick Cruchley
c.1824 George Carrington Gray   1824: Act for the Uniformity of Measures
1824–28 William Ebden
1824–35 Andrew Bryant
1825–35 John Lothian   1825: Stockton-Darlington Railway
1825–46 James Pigot   1825: Telford's Menai Bridge
1826–71d. Alexander Keith Johnston
1828–57 Henry Teesdale
1830–37: c.1830 John & Charles Walker   1830: Liverpool-Manchester Railway
William IV 1830–34 T. L. Murray   1830: Royal Geographical Society

1830–50 Society for the Diffusion of Useful
   Knowledge
1830–87 James Wyld Junior
c.1831 R. Creighton
c.1831 Samuel Lewis
c.1832 Lt. Robert Kearsley Dawson   1832: First Reform Act
  1832–70 Archibald Fullarton
c.1833 James Duncan
c.1833 William Pinnock
c.1833 John Gorton
  1834–74 Charles Black   1835: Municipal Corporations Act
  1835–60 Thomas Dugdale   1836: Tithe Commutation Act

1837–1901:   c.1838 John Dower   1838: London–Birmingham Railway
Victoria
  1839–53 William Blackwood
  1840–50 Alfred Adlard
  1841–65 Joshua Archer
  1842–45 Fisher, Son & Co.
c.1845 'Reuben Ramble'
c.1847 Thomas Johnson
  1847–59 Isaac Slater
c.1850 John Tallis
  1850–58 Henry George Collins   1851: Great Exhibition
c.1850 William Colling Hobson
c.1852 Benjamin Clarke
c.1852 William Orr
  1858–84d. Edward Weller   1867: Second Reform Act

A Table of Measurement

	Inches	Feet	Yards	Rods/ Poles/ Perches	Chains	Furlongs	Miles	Metric Equivalent
1 Barleycorn	0.33	0.027						0.85 cm
1 Inch	1	0.083	0.027	0.005				2.56 cm
1 Link	7.92				0.01			20.28 cm
1 Foot	12	1	0.33	0.06				30.72 cm
1 Yard	36	3	1	0.18	0.045			92.16 cm
1 Pace	approx.	approx.	approx.					approx.
(i.e. 2 steps)	60	5	1.66					1.54 m
1 Rod/Pole/Perch	198	16.5	5.5	1	0.25	0.025		5.05 m
1 Chain	792	66	22	4	1	0.1	0.0125	20.18 m
1 Furlong	7,920	660	220	40	10	1	0.125	201.8 m
1 Mile	63,360	5,280	1,760	320	80	8	1	1.62 km

N.B. Rods/Poles/Perches varied between 9 and 26 feet before being standardised at 16.5 ft.

Conversion of old to new British currency:
Old: £1 = 20s. (shillings) = 240d. (pence); New: £1 = 100p.
   i.e. 1s. = 5p.; 2.4d. = 1p.

Introduction

Any map, no matter when or why it was prepared, is a child of its times. It reflects not only the geographical knowledge of its period but also the artistic fashions and the state of cartographic technology. Antique maps are a unique synthesis of geography, art, economics, history, science and technology, which has been appreciated and collected for centuries. Each generation of map-makers built on the experience and knowledge of earlier generations and the history of cartography is one of increasing accuracy and content replacing fanciful decoration. Gradually surveying methods were improved, reliable instruments developed, measurement units standardised, and longitude determined more precisely, so that both distance and direction came to be represented more accurately on the map. Commercial map-makers also necessarily had to consider their market, for they had to earn a living like other businessmen; consequently, the demands of consumers and the need to generate finance and support exerted a potent influence on map design and development.

Inevitably older maps are less accurate than modern maps; in fact, they are often totally misleading. Since surveying was always expensive, map-makers usually prepared their maps from existing material rather than original surveys. This was standard practice despite the constant claims of originality and accuracy; the Greenwoods, for example, went as far as advertising for local maps to help them prepare their large-scale county series. Consequently, even the first editions of maps often conveyed outdated information which continued to be presented as the state of current geographical knowledge through subsequent issues. John Speed's maps, for instance, were issued for about 160 years, thus perpetuating errors dating from the first edition. In copying Saxton, Speed queried an unnamed village on the former's map of Wiltshire by labelling it 'Quare' on his drawing, intending to check the name. However, this was overlooked and the note was engraved on the copper-plate and appeared on Speed's map. The unfortunate village remained as 'Quare' (or 'Quaere' when copied incorrectly by the Dutch!) on the maps of Blaeu, Jansson, Blome, Morden and others, until finally correctly named as North Burcombe by Emanuel Bowen 145 years later[2]. In a later age Joseph Lindley and William Crosley happily copied John Rocque's large-scale map of Surrey, published c.1768, for their map of the same county of April 1793. Correspondence refers to 'the alterations occasioned by the copying of Rocque'; however, in this case, use of such an outdated source brought '. . . discredit . . . on the Map . . .' and Lindley later, rather uncharitably, passed the blame for the heavy use of Rocque's material onto the deceased Crosley. This practice of preparing maps from the material of earlier publishers thus held back the development of geographical knowledge.

Maps had been produced for centuries on clay tablets, mosaic floors, sheepskin, vellum, silk and linen, but it was the invention of printing that brought them into wide circulation. An 'original' map is not an individual work of art, for an unknown number of copies would have been printed from a woodblock, copper or steel plate, or stone; it is, rather, a limited edition, for original printings were small and the survival rate was low. Nevertheless, a rich choice is available and few other types of antiques can boast of a ready supply of seventeenth-, eighteenth- and nineteenth- century examples. Antique maps are a healthy investment field and are still comparatively underpriced, often surprisingly so, for they rarely command the high prices enjoyed by other art works simply because they were produced in numbers. They offer a fascinating, yet relatively inexpensive, interest to anyone with a sense of history and a love of cartography.

I The Development of British Cartography

Map production has always flourished in the wake of accelerated economic and social development and the growth of sea power; and has declined at times of quiescence. Thus, Italy was the first nation to lead cartographically, followed by Holland from the late sixteenth century and France from the mid-seventeenth century; in each case, cartographers responded to commercial prosperity and maritime power. It was only from the end of the eighteenth century that England came to the forefront as the world's leading cartographic nation.

Cartographic progress was spasmodic, with periods of stagnation juxtaposed with periods of rapid development which introduced new techniques that came into use side-by-side with traditional methods. It was all too easy to plagiarise earlier work, and the commercial risks of map production persuaded map-makers to adopt a cautious approach to new developments. Cartographers, thus, resisted change and, although technical improvements were known, they often chose to continue with tried and trusted methods and ideas. Even when the mathematical revolution in surveying could no longer be ignored, its techniques diffused in an uneven fashion, with many practitioners clinging to outmoded practice.

In time, the British maritime monopoly, resulting from the Revolutionary and Napoleonic wars, combined with the success of both commercial and military enterprises, created a suitable climate for the flowering of British cartography, with London becoming the centre of universal cartographic progress. In the meantime, however, British cartography was freed from its continental ties, and map-makers, stimulated by the frequent fear of invasion and consequent defence requirements, and by commercial opportunity, energetically mapped the countryside and cities of the British Isles. They also made major contributions to the development of cartographic science and knowledge using the mass of information generated by maritime expansion.

Select Bibliography

CHUBB, T.: *The Printed Maps in the Atlases of Great Britain and Ireland 1579–1880. A bibliography.* (1927; reprinted 1974)

CRONE, G. R., CAMPBELL, E. M. J., SKELTON, R. A.: 'Landmarks in British Cartography'. (*GJ*, 128; 1962)

EDEN, P. (ED.): *Dictionary of Land Surveyors and Local Cartographers of Great Britain and Ireland 1550–1850.* (1975–79)

FORDHAM, SIR H. G.: *Hand-List of Catalogues and Works of Reference relating to Carto-Bibliography and Kindred Subjects for Great Britain and Ireland 1720 to 1927.* (1928)

FREEMAN, M. J. AND LONGBOTHAM, J.: *The Fordham Collection: A Catalogue.* (Historical Geography Research Series; 1981)

HUMPHREYS, A. L.: *A Handbook to County Bibliography, being a Bibliography of Bibliographies relating to the Counties and Towns of Great Britain and Ireland.* (1917; reprinted 1974)

MACLEOD, M. N.: 'Evolution of British Cartography'. (*Endeavour*; 1974)

PUBLIC RECORD OFFICE: *Maps and Plans in the Public Record Office, I. British Isles c.1410–1860.* (1967)

SHIRLEY, R.W.: *Early Printed Maps of the British Isles 1477–1650. A Bibliography.* (MCC; 1973–74; reprinted (1980)

SKELTON, R. A.: *County Atlases of the British Isles, 1579–1703. A Bibliography.* (1970; reprinted 1978)

ENGLAND AND WALES

The modern mapping of England and Wales dates from Sebastian Munster's edition of Ptolemy's *Geographia Universalis* produced in Basle in 1540. The accuracy of the outline was gradually improved on other sixteenth-century maps of the British Isles (Fig. 1), particularly those of George Lily (1546) and Gerard Mercator (1564); but the best representation was produced by Humphrey Lhuyd for the 1573 *Additamentum* to Abraham Ortelius's *Theatrum Orbis Terrarum*, first published in 1570.

The sixteenth century also saw the first tentative steps towards the mapping of inland areas. In

1 England and Wales by Sebastian Munster, c.1578. *By courtesy of Ivan R. Deverall*

response to the reorganization of property ownership following the dissolution of the monasteries in 1536 and the Tudor enclosure movement, an increasing number of land surveyors produced local plans, not only of rural areas but also of a few provincial towns. Tudor England was particularly suited to the development of a national cartography. In comparison with the fourteenth and fifteenth centuries, the Tudor age was both peaceful and prosperous, stimulating the growth of national consciousness and energetic exploration. Stable political conditions combined with scientific and commercial progress to create a climate in which the cartographic demands of navigators, explorers, landowners and businessmen could be satisfied. Increasingly maps were required for property assessment, taxation, communication development, administration and, particularly, for strategic planning; and, consequently, the practice of

mapping Britain as a single unit gave way to regional mapping using the county as the basic division. The spread of printing, the development of the engraving arts, and a general intellectual awakening, stimulated demand from a growing acquisitive landed gentry establishing itself on confiscated monastic lands.

It was a professional land surveyor who carried English cartography into a new era by producing maps of inland areas which could, at last, challenge the accuracy of the sea charts produced from the wealth of information supplied by seamen. Christopher Saxton, a professional 'land-meater', surveyed England and Wales for nine years in order to prepare the first national atlas of England and Wales, published in 1579; a development which established a tradition of county mapping which was to continue until the establishment of the Ordnance Survey. Saxton's survey also established the practice of funding by patronage, for he was supported by Thomas Seckford, an eminent lawyer and civil servant, who, through his influence, stimulated official interest in the project. The Privy Council issued orders for the continuation of the survey in 1575 and 1576 and Lord Burghley used proof copies of the maps for tactical and defensive planning.

The late sixteenth and early seventeenth centuries witnessed an expansion of map production. John Norden mapped a few counties, introducing roads and triangular distance tables detailing the distances between towns; but his ambitious scheme for a series of county histories was doomed by his inability to interest a sponsor, and his advanced techniques were adopted only later by other map-makers. Other important Tudor works included Ralph Agas's maps of Cambridge, London and Oxford; Richard Lyne's plan of Cambridge; John Hooker's plan of Exeter; Philip Symonson's map of Kent; and William Smith's few 'Anonymous' county maps. These works were to be copied by cartographers until the mid-eighteenth century and, indeed, the second county atlas of England and Wales, published in 1607 in William Camden's *Britannia*, was simply a reduction of Saxton's and Norden's maps by Kip and Hole. The culmination of Tudor cartographic advance was the publication of John Speed's magnificent *Theatre of the Empire of Great Britaine* in 1611 (Fig. 2), marking the high point of native development to this time, and the moment at which it lost its momentum. The early and middle seventeenth century saw little further advance with map-makers content to copy Saxton, Norden, Smith

2 Cumberland by John Speed, 1676. *By courtesy of Stanley Gibbons Antiquarian*

and Speed, or simply even to satisfy demand by reprints from their original copper-plates. Even the stimulus of the Civil Wars failed to generate new survey work and military demand was satisfied by reworking existing plates.

English map-makers were largely reliant upon continental engravers and it was standard practice to have the plates engraved in Holland where the map trade was better established. Following the successful examples of Ortelius and Mercator, the great rival firms of Blaeu and Jansson grew to dominate world map production with their extensive world atlases. Although the Dutch produced the most beautifully engraved and sensitively decorated of English maps (Fig. 3), the geographical content was simply a repeat of the work of earlier cartographers, particularly Speed. The firms of Blaeu, Hondius and Jansson dominated the European market, but their grip was loosened as other map-makers, often their own past apprentices, established independent businesses. Plates passed from firm to firm through

inheritance or purchase; thus, Jansson's plates were inherited by his sons-in-law who subsequently sold them at auction to Pieter Schenk & Gerard Valk; and Braun & Hogenberg's passed to Frederik de Wit. Despite the Dutch industry's long domination, it suffered a spectacular decline in its fortunes and the consequent weakening of the established link provided an incentive to growth for the infant English industry.

The Elizabethan surveys, and the contemporary maps derived from them, were increasingly inadequate for the demands of quickening economic development. Agricultural advances and the beginnings of a national infrastructure drew attention to the deficiencies of existing maps and induced some publishers to try to modify outdated plates. The Great Fire of London of 1666 destroyed much of the map trade's stock and, thus, intensified the need for new surveys. Restoration England, perhaps spurred by Charles II's own interest in maps, was ripe for cartographic advance and production increased

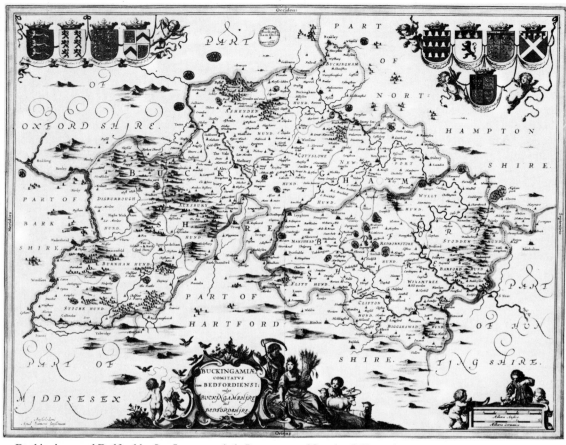

3 Buckingham and Bedford by Jan Jansson, 1646. *By courtesy of Stanley Gibbons Antiquarian*

rapidly, with a growth in the number of map-makers operating in London. Several publishers projected new county atlases before 1700, but only Richard Blome and Robert Morden could nurse their projects to fruition. Blome readily acknowledged his plagiarism from earlier sources; but Morden, Ogilby and others were producing the first original material for many years. There was a new emphasis on scientific improvements, encouraged by Charles II's founding of the Royal Observatory at Greenwich, the production of Halley's meteorological and magnetic charts, and the passing of the Longitude Act offering a reward to anyone 'who shall discover longitude at sea'. New surveys of individual counties were carried out by John Seller, John Oliver, Robert Plot, John Ogilby, and others; longitude was measured from the London meridian; distance measurement was standardised; and marine hydrography revived. A major innovation of the late

seventeenth century was the road atlas, initiated by John Ogilby's brilliantly conceived strip road maps published in his *Britannia* of 1675. This immensely practical delineation of the roads marked the beginning of a new stage of transport development; the expansion of trade and industry depended on a parallel expansion of transport facilities, particularly roads, and henceforth map-makers considered them important features.

The techniques of British cartographers had generally lagged behind those of their European contemporaries. However, native map-makers progressively shed the continental influence and developed their own style and techniques, aided by the imposition of a duty on imported maps in 1712 and an influx of skill and experience brought by European cartographers who settled in London. Advances in geography, geodesy, hydrography and surveying were exploited to meet demands for greater accuracy; and the traditional rich embellishment, which had been used to compensate for the poverty of geographical information, was steadily reduced to allow more detail. However, these changes did not occur overnight, for the diffusion of knowledge and the adoption of new techniques was a slow process.

The first half of the eighteenth century saw little improvement, in fact, in the quality of maps produced. There was little originality and, in terms of development, the period was uneventful. Old plates continued to be reworked and re-issues of Saxton, Speed and others remained in use; new engraved plates dispensed with much of the rich decoration of earlier styles but introduced little compensatory additional information. The delicate ships, monsters and figures were replaced by the copious topographical and historical notes of Bowen and Kitchin or the marginal antiquities of Herman Moll. A few new features were introduced, more maps were printed, and they became cheaper, but, generally, map-makers in Britain lagged behind continental rivals, with only Moll attempting to incorporate continental advances into his poorly designed maps. The representation of roads made little progress with Bowen, Gardner and Senex content to produce pocket versions of Ogilby's *Britannia*, and the many county map-makers, such as Ellis and Kitchin, happy to copy from earlier sources. British maps continued to be inaccurate; Richard Gough, writing in 1780, commented that: 'Notwithstanding the assertions of Bowen and Kitchin and other modern map-makers, that their maps are formed from actual new surveys, there is scarce a single one which does not abound with faults'. However, although this criticism applied to most county atlases of the period, there was, in contrast, work of unprecedented quality being produced by an ever increasing number of energetic local land surveyors who were introducing new techniques.

As the agrarian revolution gathered momentum, land was enclosed at an accelerating pace and new agricultural methods were introduced. These changes stimulated the demand for large-scale surveys both for practical use and the gentleman's library. As the volume of traffic grew, so the demand for more accurate road maps increased. Technical advance in cartographic and surveying methods allowed larger scales than ever before to be used, over greater areas, to show the details of land use, industry and settlement. The expansion of maritime influence spurred these cartographic advances, and commercial expansion created secure employment for the surveyor. The proliferation of dedications to the landed gentry and the naming of their estates and houses illustrates the close relationship between the wealthy and the surveyor, and the importance of patronage. Accurate maps were increasingly required by the armed forces, government departments and land agents; and, thus, surveyors built up experience and techniques in the surveying of estates, properties and communications which brought about a cartographic advance without parallel elsewhere. The vital encouragement for the production of large-scale maps came from the Royal Society of Arts which offered awards for large-scale county maps in an effort to raise the standards of British cartography. Such was the prestige of these awards, that most major map-makers of the late eighteenth and early nineteenth centuries were involved, to some extent, in the production of county maps at a minimum scale of 1 inch to 1 mile. The few winners included Thomas Jefferys, John Cary and the Greenwood brothers, but the overall effect was to stimulate widespread improvements in map production and develop a new refined style reflecting the solid prosperity of the period. Greater attention was paid to communications, and maps began to note distances between towns and from London, or other major cities, and even to comment on the state of repair of the roads.

By the last years of the eighteenth century London had become the unquestioned cartographic centre of the world, with a massive production of fine atlases, charts, maps and plans. Despite the popularity of the 1 inch scale, the early nineteenth century was a period of prolific output for smaller scale county atlases, road books, gazetteers, guides and directories, produced to satisfy the demands of an exploding economy. Generally, however, the advances of the large-scale maps were not reflected at the smaller scales, for most map-makers continued to rely on earlier sources. Fortunately, a new source of data was, by this stage, developing rapidly. The Ordnance Survey, which grew indirectly from the great military survey of Scotland, began its triangulation under the superintendence of William Roy and published its first maps in 1801. The Survey's influence was twofold: firstly, it established an austere, uniform style, devoid of decoration and individuality; and secondly, its national series of triangulation tables provided exact basic information which map-makers increasingly utilised in their

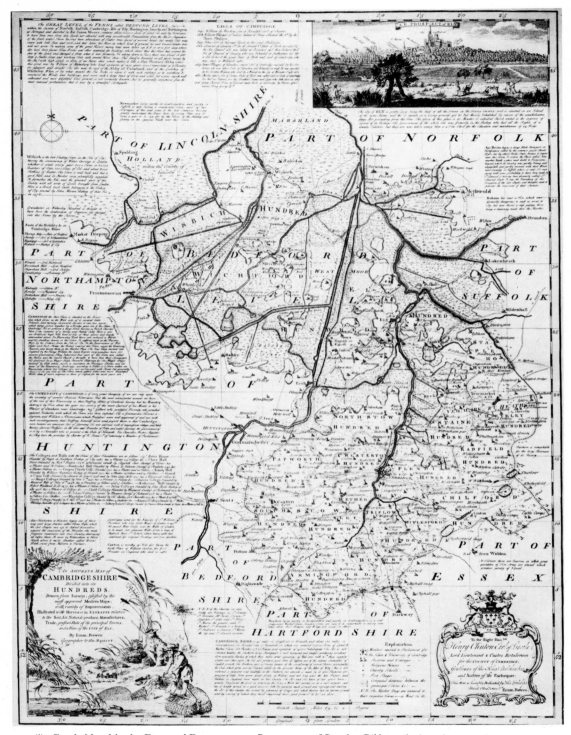

4 14(i): Cambridgeshire by Emanuel Bowen, 1751. *By courtesy of Stanley Gibbons Antiquarian*

work. Maps published by both public and private sectors became progressively stereotyped, designed to be severely practical. Technological developments also wrought changes in map design; techniques of colour printing improved, allowing a greater production of thematic maps using overprinted colour, and the introduction of lithography, and, later, photography, reduced the use of traditional map-making skills so that, generally, in the mid-nineteenth century, production declined in quality, until the new, cheap mass production techniques were perfected.

Select Bibliography

ENGLAND:

BRUCE MAYNE, L.: 'Maps from Saxton to Royal Ordnance'. (*Amateur Historian*, Vol. 1, No. 12; 1954)

HARLEY, J. B.: 'The re-mapping of England 1750–1800'. (*IM*, 19; 1965)

MORGAN, V.: 'The cartographic image of "the country" in early modern England'. (*Trans. of the Royal Historical Society*, 5th series, Vol. 26; 1979)

RICHESON, A. W.: *English land measuring to 1800: Instruments and Practices*. (1966)

TAYLOR, E. G. R.: *Late Tudor and Early Stuart Geography 1583–1650*. (1934)

TAYLOR, E. G. R.: *The Mathematical Practitioners of Tudor and Stuart England*. (1954)

THROWER, N. J. W.: *The Compleat Plattmaker. Essays on chart and mapmaking in England in the 17th and 18th centuries*. (1978)

TYACKE, S. AND HUDDY, J.: *Christopher Saxton and Tudor map-making*. (British Library Series, No. 2; 1980)

WALTERS, B.: 'Engraved Maps from the English Topographies c.1660–1825'. (*CJ*, 7; 1970)

WHITAKER, H.: *The Harold Whitaker Collection of County Atlases, Road Books and Maps presented to the University of Leeds. A catalogue*. (1947)

WALES:

BOOTH, J.: *Antique Maps of Wales*. (1977)

DAVIES, M.: *Wales in Maps*. (1951)

EVANS, O.C.: *Maps of Wales and Welsh cartographers*. (MCC, 13; 1964)

NORTH, F. J.: *Maps, their history and uses, with special reference to Wales*. (1933)

NORTH, F. J.: 'The Map of Wales before 1600 A.D.'. (*ACs.*, 90; 1935)

SCOTLAND

Scotland was first represented on Ptolemy's map of Great Britain by the spectacular error of orienting it twisted over to the right. This was corrected only in Bernardus Sylvanus's edition of 1511 when it was shown in its correct upright position.

Mercator's 1564 map of the British Isles gave a truer representation of Scotland which was used as the basis for the first separate map of Scotland produced by Abraham Ortelius in the 1573 *Additamentum*. This, and maps by Bishop John Leslie in 1578 and Nicolas de Nicolay in 1583, were superseded by Gerard Mercator's single-sheet map of Scotland first issued in the 1595 edition of his *Atlas*. The maps of Mercator and Ortelius were to provide the outlines copied by all cartographers, including Hole, Blome, Speed, and Blaeu (in 1635), before Blaeu's new map was published in 1654.

Although the outline of Scotland was now represented fairly accurately, there was no attempt to delineate the inland areas in any detail, until a major breakthrough in Scottish cartography was brought about by one man, Timothy Pont, working alone. His surveys provided the basis of all Scottish maps until the end of the seventeenth century. Amazingly, between about 1580 and 1600, Pont surveyed 'on foot right through the whole of this kingdom as no-one before him had done', but, unfortunately, his great work was never brought to publication due to 'the greed of printers & booksellers', and only his map of 'the Shyres

5 'Ila Insula ex Aebudarum majoribus una' by Joan Blaeu, 1654. *By courtesy of Stanley Gibbons Antiquarian*

Lothian and Linlitquo', engraved by Jodocus Hondius, was ever published. However, Pont's rudimentary manuscripts were adapted, redrawn, and added to by Robert Gordon of Straloch and his son, James, so that they could be used by Blaeu to produce the first national atlas of Scotland. Volume 5 of the *Theatrum Orbis Terrarum, sive Atlas Novus*, published in 1654 with subsequent editions in Dutch, Latin, French and Spanish, contained three general maps, 36 regional maps based on the surveys of Timothy Pont, three by Robert Gordon, one by James, and six without attribution (Fig. 5). It superseded all earlier maps of Scotland and became the source for both British and European map-makers for the next 100 years. In fact, the resulting curved outline of the north coast and the inaccurate shape of Lewis were not corrected until Bryce and Mackenzie carried out their surveys between 1741 and 1750.

John Adair's attempt to produce more accurately surveyed maps (Fig. 6) was initially doomed to failure due to lack of resources. Fortunately,

however, his manuscripts of the Scottish coasts and some counties, surveyed by rudimentary triangulation at the end of the seventeenth century, were used by Herman Moll for his 'The North Part of Britain called Scotland' of 1714, which marked a definite improvement in the outline, by breaking away from those of Mercator and Gordon. Moll's county atlas of 1725 was also a breakthrough, for not only was it the first since Blaeu's of 1654, but it was also the first ever to mark roads in Scotland.

The mapping of Scotland was catapulted into a new era by military exigencies. From 1725, General Wade was constructing military roads from Inverness to the south, necessitating new surveys; but the major impetus came from the Jacobite rebellion of 1745. It was clear that the existing mapping of Scotland, particularly of the Highlands, was quite inadequate for the troop movements necessary to quell the rebel clans, and, thus, the Military Survey of Scotland was initiated under Colonel Watson, the Quartermaster-General of Scotland, in 1747. The Survey, mainly conducted by William Roy, initially

6 East Lothian by John Adair, c.1736. *By permission of the British Library (K.49.88)*

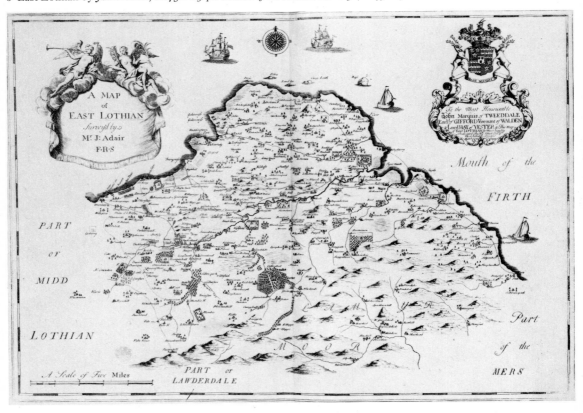

Watson's clerk but later his deputy and a founder of the Ordnance Survey, was started in the Fort Augustus area and was mainly completed by 1754. However, these military surveys were not actually made available to other cartographers until 1805 when Aaron Arrowsmith was allowed to use their data (in addition to all the coastal charts, county maps and local surveys by that time available) for his detailed and accurate quarter-inch map of Scotland.

Increased interest in the mapping of Scotland was reflected in new survey work and the production of new maps: the north coast was properly surveyed by Alexander Bryce between 1741 and 1743; John Laurie published his map of the Lothians in 1745; Elphinstone, Bowen and Overton produced new maps of Scotland; and Murdoch Mackenzie produced a trigonometrical survey of the Orkneys and Lewis in 1750. This crop of new data contributed to the production of James Dorret's much improved map of Scotland of 1750 which was to be the standard map, copied by Armstrong, Bowles, Cary and Kitchin, amongst others, for the next 40 years, until superseded by John Ainslie's map of 1789. Another significant development was the publication of the first pocket atlas of Scotland, possibly designed for the military market, by Thomas Kitchin in 1749.

The interest in large-scale mapping, encouraged by the Royal Society of Arts, spread to Scotland from the mid-eighteenth century. Between 1772 and 1783, John Ainslie produced five large-scale county maps, plus coastal surveys, a large plan of Edinburgh, and an accurate map of the whole country on nine sheets, at a scale of 4 miles to the inch, which was to become the standard reference map of Scotland for a period. Four other counties were covered at the large-scale by Andrew & Mostyn Armstrong, and others by local land surveyors. Mostyn Armstrong used the results of these surveys to prepare his reduced county maps published as the *Scotch Atlas* in 1777. This data was also used for the preparation of John Stockdale's map on the scale of 3.5 miles to the inch, (the largest map of Scotland published prior to the work of the Ordance Survey), and of William Faden's map, but both were quickly rendered obsolete by Aaron Arrowsmith's map of 1807 which standardized the outline of Scotland for the next 50 years.

The early nineteenth century was a period of lively activity for Scottish cartographers and publishers. Thomas Brown, John Lothian, W. Murphy and William Blackwood produced county

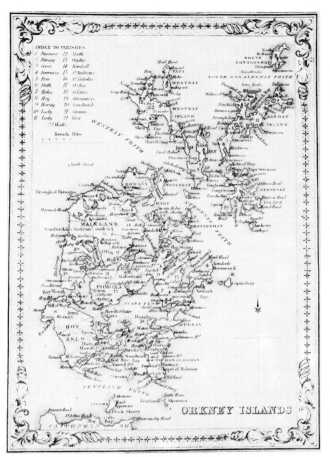

7 44(ii): Orkney Islands by Archibald Fullarton, c.1857.
Photograph: Mills-Wight Studio

atlases in c.1807, 1827, 1832 and 1838 respectively; but the finest atlas of Scotland was John Thomson's folio production issued in parts from 1820. Numerous single sheet maps were produced and towards the middle of the century, maps were published not only in atlases, but also in gazetteers, guide books and travelling companions by Archibald Fullarton, Adam & Charles Black, and many others.

Select Bibliography

The Mapping of Scotland. (IVth International Conference on the History of Cartography; 1971)

ADAMS, I. H.: *Scottish Record Office: Descriptive List of Plans.* 2 vols. (1966 and 1970)

ADAMS, I. H.: 'The Scottish Record Office Plan Collection'. (*CJ*, 4; 1967)

ADAMS, I. H.: 'Large-scale Manuscript Plans in Scotland'. (*Jour. of the Soc. of Archivists*, 3; 1967)

CASH, C. G.: 'The First Topographical Survey of Scotland'. (*SGM*, 17; 1901)

EDINBURGH UNIVERSITY LIBRARY: *The Development of Mapping in Scotland. Exhibition of maps and atlases in Edinburgh University Library.* (1973–4)

INGLIS, H. R. G.: 'Early Maps of Scotland and their Authors'. (*SGM*, 34; 1918)

MITCHELL, SIR A. AND CASH, C. G: 'A Contribution to the Bibliography of Scottish Topography'. (*Scottish Historical Soc. Pub.* 2nd Series, 15; 1917)

MOIR, D. G.: *The Early Maps of Scotland.* (3rd. ed.; Royal Scottish Geog. Soc.; 1973)

MOIR, D. G. AND SKELTON, R. A.: 'New light on the first atlas of Scotland'. (*SGM*, 84; 1968)

SHEARER, J. E.: *Old Maps and Map-makers of Scotland.* (1905)

SKELTON, R. A.: 'The Military Survey of Scotland, 1747–55.' (*SGM*, 83; 1967)

STONE, J. C.: 'The Preparation of the Blaeu Maps of Scotland: a Further Assessment.' (*SGM*, 86; 1970)

TAYLOR, A. B.: 'Some additional Early Maps of Scotland.' (*SGM*, 77; 1961)

IRELAND

Ireland was first represented by Ptolemy on his map of the British Isles, initially printed in Bologna in 1477. Improved maps were produced by George Lily from 1546, Ortelius from 1573 (Fig. 8), and Mercator from 1595. Mercator's map was copied by Hole in 1607 for William Camden's *Britannia*, and by Coronelli in 1695; but it was John Speed who produced the first detailed maps of Irish regions for the fourth book of his *Theatre*. Speed's material came partly from the pioneering surveys of Robert Lythe of c.1570 and Francis Jobson of c.1590, and his mapping of Ireland was a great improvement on earlier maps, since it represented the north coast more accurately. His maps were copied by con-

8 Ireland by Abraham Ortelius, 1574. *By courtesy of Ivan R. Deverall*

tinental cartographers including Blaeu, Jansson, De Wit, and Sanson.

The Elizabethan period was one of piecemeal surveying and map-making in Ireland as the English government and landowners attempted to delineate an unfamiliar land. There was little progress in the century following the publication of Speed's maps, but many official outline 'plantation' surveys of landholdings were produced, usually at about 6 inches to the mile, to facilitate land transfers and clarify ownership. These 'plantation' surveys, at best covering only a barony or a parish, which were produced from the Elizabethan settlement of Munster to the beginning of the eighteenth century, were sometimes combined to create maps of regions, provinces and even the whole of Ireland, with unsurveyed areas left blank.

The major breakthrough in the mapping of Ireland came in the seventeenth century through William Petty's 'Down Survey' which led to the publication of *Hiberniae Delineatio*, the first atlas of Ireland, in 1685. His maps were more accurate than any before and quickly superseded all others, being copied by map-makers at home and abroad virtually until the issue of the Ordnance Survey.

Land development created demands for local surveys which stimulated a countrywide growth of professional land surveying, the only cartographic enterprise sustained in Ireland for any period of time. Consequently, estate maps, usually notable for their dearth of information, were produced in quantities, often with lavish decoration.

Two atlases were published in the eighteenth century: Herman Moll's rare county atlas of 1728 and the similar, charming, *Hibernian Atlas* of 1775 by Bernard Scalé, who emigrated to Ireland in the mid-eighteenth century. Another transient emigré was John Rocque, who worked for six years in Dublin producing some large-scale county maps, town plans, and estate surveys. Between them, Scalé and Rocque pushed the techniques of Irish cartography forward by their sophisticated approach to both land use representation and decoration.

The first large-scale map produced by native cartographers was the 1 inch to 1 mile map of Kildare, published in 1752, by John Noble & James Keenan (Fig. 9). The spread of affluence, signified by the proliferation of country estates and mansions, created a demand for such large-scale maps, and other counties were covered during the following decades and the early nineteenth century. The country's roads were adequately mapped for the first time by George Taylor & Andrew Skinner in 1777; and George Grierson, a prominent Dublin publisher, issued the first atlas of Ireland produced solely by Irishmen in about 1818. With this rare exception, small-scale maps of Ireland tended to be published from London and the Continent, and the lack of a native industry sadly reduced the range of maps produced.

The pressures of a growing population forced an increased official interest in Ireland, generating a plethora of official maps covering a wider field than found in many other countries. This range of production was greatly simplified from 1824 when the Ordnance Survey established itself in Phoenix Park, Dublin, and took over many of the themes. The activities of the Ordnance Survey, particularly between 1829 and 1858, stimulated cartography generally in Ireland. As the nineteenth century progressed, there was a considerable increase in the production of maps of Ireland, with the series by Alfred Adlard and Samuel Lewis prominent.

Select Bibliography
ANDREWS, J. H.: *Ireland in maps.* (1961)

ANDREWS, J. H.: 'Ireland in maps: a bibliographical postscript'. (*Irish Geography*, 4; 1962)

ANDREWS, J. H.: 'The French school of Dublin land surveyors'. (*Irish Geography*, 5; 1967)

ANDREWS, J. H.: *Introduction to* 'Hiberniae Delineatio' *by Sir William Petty, and* 'Geographical Description of ye Kingdom of Ireland' *by Sir William Petty and F. Lamb.* (1969)

ANDREWS, J. H.: *Notes on Boazio's map of Ireland.* (1970)

ANDREWS, J. H.: *Irish Maps.* (Irish Heritage Series, 18; 1978)

ANDREWS, M. C.: 'The Map of Ireland 1300–1700'. (*Belfast Nat. Hist. and Philosophical Soc.*; 1923)

BONAR LAW, A.: *Three hundred years of Irish printed maps.* (1972)

DUNLOP, R.: '16th-Century Maps of Ireland'. (*English History Review*; 1905)

HAYES-MCCOY, G. H.: *Ulster and other Irish Maps.* (1964)

LYNAM, E. W.: 'Boazio's Map of Ireland'. (*British Museum Quarterly*, Vol. 2, No. 2; 1937)

WESTROPP, T. J.: 'Early Italian Maps of Ireland from 1300 to 1600'. (*Proc. of the Royal Irish Academy*, 30; 1913)

9 (Overleaf) Kildare by John Noble & James Keenan, 1752. *By permission of the British Library (Maps 12170(3))*

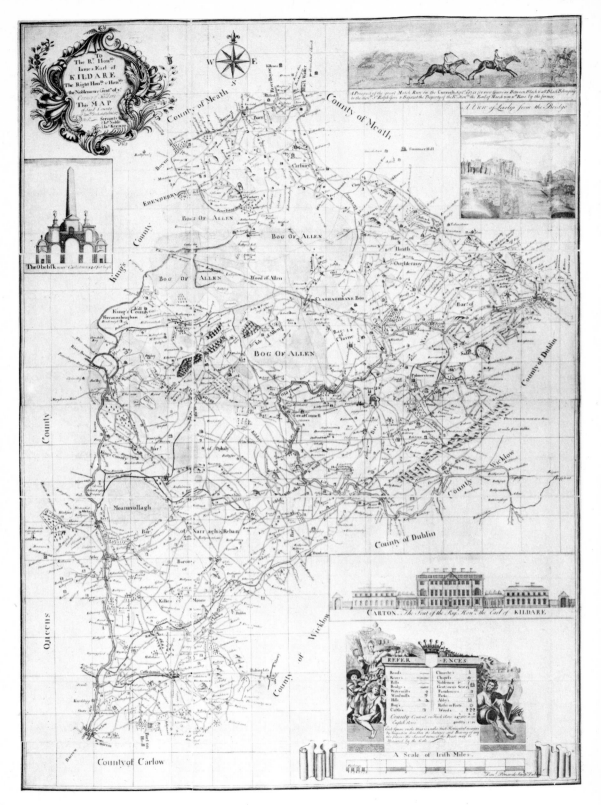

A MAP of the County of KILDARE

TO The Rt. Honble. James, Earl of KILDARE The Right Honble. & Honble. the Noblemen & Gentry of ye County of Kildare. This MAP of said County is humbly dedicated by their most Obedient humble Servants the Noble the Kennan

The Obelisk near Castletown 140 feet high.

A Prospect of the great Match Run on the Curragh Septr. 1751 for 1000 Guineas Between Black & all Black Belonging to the Hon.ble. J. Ralph Gore & Bajazet the Property of the Rt. Hon.ble. the Earl of March won ye Race by the former.

A View of Leixlip from the Bridge

CARTON...The Seat of the Rt. Honble. the Earl of KILDARE

REFERENCES
Roads
Rivers
Rills
Bridges
Watermills
Windmills
Hills
Bogs
Castles
Churches
Chapels
Noblemen &c.
Gentlemens Seats
Farmhouses
Parks
Abbey
Raths or Forts
Woods

County of Meath
County of Dublin
County of Wicklow
County of Carlow
Kings County
Queens County
BOG OF ALLEN
Wood of Allen
Edenderry
Moanavollagh

A Scale of Irish Miles.

30

II Map Production

THE HISTORY OF MAP PRODUCTION

The history of map production is one of the application of advancing technology to the problem of how to represent the map-maker's data with ever-greater accuracy and flexibility.

The earliest printed maps were woodcuts (Fig. 10) produced from wooden blocks which were carved in relief with the features to be shown standing above the block surface. Blank areas were cut away, leaving the raised mirror image of the map to be inked before being impressed on paper damped to increase ink absorbence. There were several inherent disadvantages in printing from wood-blocks: (1) the woodcut had only black and white tones; (2) the relief carving was laborious and time

consuming; (3) the woodblock could only be altered by cutting out a section and inserting a new carved piece; and (4) it was difficult to engrave satisfactory lettering in the wood. In order to improve lettering on woodcuts, metal type letters were set into the block so that type and map could be printed in one operation. However, the natural inadequacies of the coarse woodcut doomed it to die out in map production as intaglio printing using the copper-plate developed.

Copper-plate engraving was developed and popularised by Italian map-makers; the first edition of Ptolemy from copper plates was printed as early as 1477 in Bologna, but it was only from the mid-sixteenth century that woodcuts were totally

10 British Isles from Ptolemy's *Geography*, edited and published by Jacobus Ezler & Georgius Ubelin of Strasburg; woodblock engraving by Martin Waldseemuller, 1513. *By courtesy of Stanley Gibbons Antiquarian*

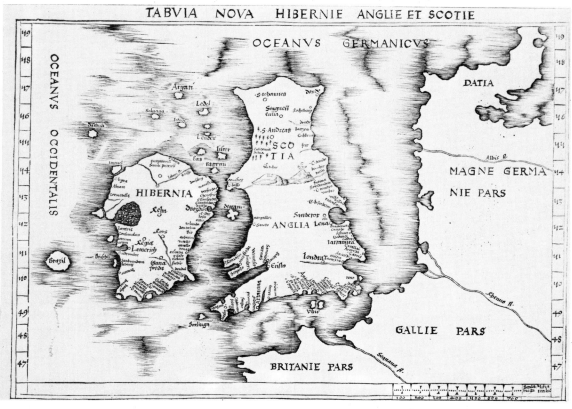

superseded. The greater flexibility of engraving on the soft copper offered possibilities of finer representation and greater precision. Printing from copper plates allowed some of the disadvantages of the woodcut to be overcome: (1) the engraver could vary the ink tones by differing groove depths and could achieve delicate and intricate representations of the geographer's detail by stippling, shading and fine line-work; (2) he could work faster than the wood engraver, thus compensating for the greater cost of copper and the more expensive printing process; (3) the copper plate was easily revised by scraping out the engraved lines and tapping the inaccurate areas from behind to create a flat surface that could be re-engraved; thus, publishers were able to revise maps regularly to keep them up-to-date; and (4) the flowing movement of the burin could create elegant lettering and subtle decoration. (Evidence suggests that copper plates were occasionally also engraved by stone, probably flint, to produce a different tone for such features as hills).

In the intaglio process, the detail was cut into the copper plate, which was then inked so that the incised grooves were filled with ink. Surplus ink was wiped from the surface, thus contributing to plate wear, and the map was printed under pressure onto damped paper, producing slightly raised ink lines. As the cleaning and re-inking process was repeated for each map printed, the engraving inevitably eventually began to wear and lose its sharpness.

Although a map plate might be signed by an engraver, there is no guarantee that he engraved the whole plate. Obviously the talents of the master craftsman were required for the detailed, delicate work, the difficulty of which was increased by the need to engrave in reverse to produce a mirror image of the desired design; but there was also much simple engraving work, such as the repetitive border design or the stamping of conventional symbols with a punch, that could be undertaken by the less skilled journeymen and apprentices employed by most large workshops, (John Rocque, for example, employed ten draughtsmen and engravers in his London shop). Such assistants would be trained in the master's style and might even specialize in the engraving of a particular feature such as a compass indicator, scale or simple shading (Fig. 11).

Copper sheets needed to be about 3 mm (0.1 in.) thick—'fully as thick as an half-crown'—in order to be sufficiently rigid for printing. Unfortunately, however, both the copper itself and the engraving process were expensive. In the 1650s an unengraved

copper plate, measuring 265 × 310 mm (10.6 × 12.5 in.) cost the then substantial sum of 9s. 6d. 'The cost of producing an engraved plate was considerable, and it varied with both the size of the plate and the complexity of the map. Gregory King charged John Adams £26 8s. to engrave two plates. Petty's *Ireland* cost £1,000 to be engraved in 1675 in Amsterdam. In 1742, Emanuel Bowen indicated that a plate 69.0 × 56.0 cm (27¼ × 22⅛ in.) would cost £10 10s. for '... close work, such as the map of England ...' and £3 10s. for '... open work such as sea charts of ye coast'.[3]

In an effort to keep costs to the minimum, engravers worked on plates only fractionally larger than the maps to be engraved, with the result that the indentation created by the pressure of the plate pressing into the paper (the plate-mark) appeared very close to the map border. As production costs were reduced, larger plates were used and generally the further the plate-mark from the border, the later the map. When cheaper steel plates replaced copper in the mid-1820s, even larger plates were used with the plate-mark often several inches from the border and sometimes even lost entirely due to cropping during binding.

Any engraved plate will show signs of wear with use, but because copper is much softer than either wood or steel, copper plates are particularly prone to wear, with the sharp lines beginning to blur and becoming heavily inked, and the fine detail beginning to disappear, after only as few as 300 impressions. The life of a plate depended on the depth of engraving and the amount of fine detail, but plates were often kept in use despite serious wear. Fine detail might be seriously worn after 800 to 1,000 impressions but the plate was still serviceable for up to 3,000 or 4,000 copies; in 1607, for example, it was estimated that careful use would produce 1,000 impressions from a plate, but the Ordnance Survey, in 1902, considered that: 'A copperplate with fine work upon it will generally give about 500 good impressions'. Life could be very much prolonged by retouching worn areas or by major re-engraving of the plate in an effort to revise and update it. Cost-conscious publishers in a highly competitive business often succumbed to the temptation to print from out-dated plates while they still had life. Efforts to revamp old plates often produced anachronistic combinations of old and new data as some detail or ornamentation was erased, often leaving traces, and replaced by more up-to-date information; Philip Lea, for instance,

11 Somerset by Robert Morden, 1695 (detail)
12 69(i): 'A plan of London and its environs' published by Samuel Lewis, 1833 (detail)

reworked Christopher Saxton's plates of c.1577 for his atlas of 1694 by revising some of the obsolete information and adding inset town plans and heraldry.

Some plates had a remarkably long life (e.g. some of Speed's were used from 1611 to 1770), but eventually all plates became unsuitable for further re-engraving and had to be scrapped. Some were cut into pieces and used as packing material for presses[4], and others were simply sold as scrap: 'the plates of "The Royal English Atlas" were sold in October 1825 as old copper at 11d. a pound; the plates of the "The Large English Atlas" were sold at the same time for 1s. a pound.'[5]

From about 1820, steel plates began to replace copper (Pigot's maps of c.1826–30 were the first county series to be printed from steel plates). The change was commercially attractive to map-makers for the harder metal was cheaper, and allowed many more impressions to be taken before signs of wear started to appear. Further attractions were that the steel-plates required no change in printing methods but allowed even finer line-work and more delicate representation of light and shade than copper (Fig. 12).

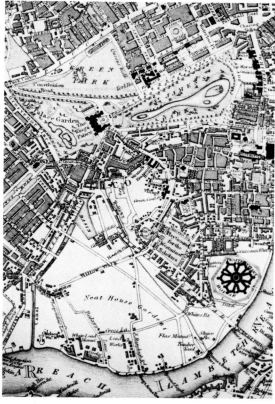

From the mid-nineteenth century, both copper and steel plate printing were being replaced by the cheaper and faster new process of stone lithography invented in 1796 by Alois Senefelder. This process depended on the fact that oil and water do not mix. A design was drawn in reverse with a greasy pencil on a flat stone (limestone) surface, which was then prepared with acid and water so that oil-based lithographic ink would adhere only to the drawn lines and not to the other areas of the stone. When the stone was inked, impressions of the design could be taken in the normal way in a printing press.

Alternatively the design could be drawn on a special transfer paper which could then be pressed onto the prepared stone to transfer the design; or it could be passed to the transfer paper directly from an existing engraved plate, thus producing the finest lithographic reproduction of all. Although most engraved plates were used for both direct intaglio printing and lithographic transfers, (so that the same map might be produced by both methods), an increasing number of plates were engraved specifically for lithographic transfer only.

Lithographic printing was attractive to the publisher for it suffered no plate wear and, therefore, there was no need regularly to rework the engraving. Moreover, the design on the stone was easily altered and revised, and publishers were more inclined to undertake adjustments and up-dating. Many nineteenth-century lithographed maps show extensive changes from edition to edition with titles, scales, north points, etc., redesigned or moved, and detail added from other engraved plates or by hand. Consequently, some lithographed maps bear little resemblance to the original plate, and the history of some maps is further complicated by the fact that not only was the lithographic stone altered during the life of a map but so too was the engraved plate. However, plate alterations would then continue to appear unless specifically erased and re-engraved, whereas transfer alterations would appear only on maps printed from that particular stone preparation.

The flexibility of lithography opened up new avenues for commercial exploitation. Information, particularly concerning railway development, could be up-dated at frequent intervals; small issues of thematic maps could be produced to emphasize selected data; and lithographic transfers of an area could be taken from a map of a larger area or the whole country and could then be adapted by the addition of a border, title, scale, north point, and so on, and by the removal of unwanted detail (Fig. 13).

The advantages of lithography were quickly realised by the War Office which used the process to prepare army maps, initially for the Peninsular War of 1808–14, and more generally from the 1820s. Although chromolithography was used to print coloured surveys and estate maps from the 1840s, it

13 Birmingham; a plan lithographed from the inset 'Plan of Birmingham and its environs' on the Birmingham plan published by the Society for the Diffusion of Useful Knowledge. Published by Charles Knight, 1850 (detail). *Photograph: Mills-Wight Studio*

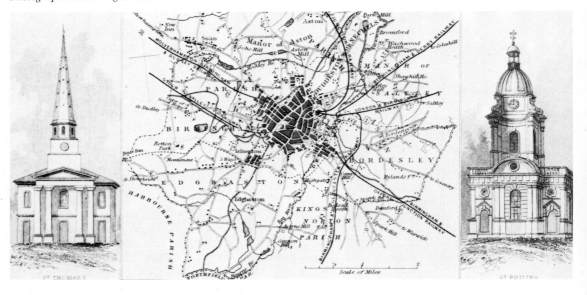

was the exhibits on colour printing at the Great Exhibition of 1851 that opened the eyes of commercial map publishers to the potential of the coloured inks that could be used in lithography. Most maps of the second half of the nineteenth century were produced by the new process and, consequently, few were hand-coloured.

The major differences between lithographed maps and those printed from engraved plates were that the former were absolutely flat with no raised ink lines, and that there was no indented plate-mark caused by the pressing of the plate into the paper. Generally, impressions tend to be duller and less attractive than those taken directly from plates, lacking the sharp clarity of the latter.

The combination of the camera with the lithographic process to create photo-lithography enabled transfers to be made at altered sizes, and it became possible to enlarge and reduce maps in the transfer process. An unfortunate by-product of this new process was technological unemployment amongst map engravers, for their skills were now obsolete and the craft died out rapidly.

The first step in the printing of a map was to take a trial impression to check that all was correct. These 'proofs' were often taken before assistants had added simple detail and the impressions were in an unfinished state. Like aberrant stamps, these 'proof' copies are much sought after.

The 'state' of a plate or transfer defines its condition at the time of printing; subsequent modifications are referred to as 'second state', 'third state', and so on. It is not usually known how many copies were printed for each issue of a map but editions of up to 1,000 to 2,000 copies are recorded; Richard Blome, for example, listed 800 subscriptions for his *Britannia* in 1670.[6] Commercially-minded publishers exploited every opportunity of using engraved plates to the full; impressions could be published many years after the original engraving and map issues are often incorrectly dated because there was no change in the detail of the map. When no alterations were made, maps can, at least, often be placed in chronological order by the state of wear of the engraving, by evidence of retouching or re-engraving, or by the appearance of cracks or fractures which may subsequently be repaired.

Select Bibliography
Engraving:
BRITISH MUSEUM: *A guide to the processes and schools of engraving.* (1923)

COLVIN, SIR S.: *Early engraving and engravers in England, 1545–1695.* (1905)

GRENACHER, F.: 'The Woodcut map'. (*IM*, 24; 1970)

HIND, A. M.: *An Introduction to a History of Woodcut, with a Detailed Survey of Work done in the Fifteenth Century.* (1935; reprinted 1963)

HIND, A. M.: *Engraving in England in the Sixteenth and Seventeenth Centuries. Part I. The Tudor period.* (1952); *Part II. The reign of James I.* (1955)

HIND, A. M.: *A history of engraving and etching.* (3rd ed; 1923)

LYNAM, E. W.: 'Flemish Map Engravers in England in the 16th Century'. (*Marine*, 3; 1943; reprinted in *The Mapmaker's Art*)

Printing:
CRONE, G. R.: 'The Evolution of Map Printing'. (*Printing*—A Supplement Published by The Times on the Occasion of the 10th International Printing Machinery and Allied Trades Exhibition; 1955)

FORDHAM, M.: 'A note on maps and printing'. (*Book-Collectors' Quarterly*, 4; 1934)

MUMFORD, I.: 'Lithography, photography and photozincography in English map production before 1870'. (*CJ*, 9; 1972)

OLDFIELD, M.: 'Five Centuries of Map Printing'. (*British Printer*; 1955)

SKELTON, R. A.: 'Early Maps and the Printer'. (*Printing Review*, 16; 1951)

SKELTON, R. A.: 'The Early Map Printer and His Problems'. (*Penrose Annual*, 57; 1964)

TWYMAN, M.: *Lithography 1800–1850, the techniques of drawing on stone in England and France and their application in works of topography.* (1970)

WAKEMAN, G.: 'Lithography, photography and map printing' in *Aspects of Victorian Lithography.* (1970)

WOODWARD, D. (ED.): *Five Centuries of Map Printing.* (1975)

PAPER

Most printed maps were printed on paper, but there were exceptions; fine copies might be produced on vellum, and copies on silk and cotton cloth are also known. Paper is often a useful aid for roughly dating a map, since advancing technology improved production processes and the quality of the resulting paper. Although the accurate dating of paper is a complex skill, frequent handling of examples will build up knowledge and experience and most collectors develop an instinct for the age of paper. An obvious dating aid is the watermark which appears as a translucent pattern when the paper is held up to the light, but this is not necessarily present and, in any case, it dates only the manufacture of the paper and not its use for the printing of the map.

Early paper was manufactured from pulp made from rags; the finer the rag-cloth used, the finer the paper produced. The sheets of paper were formed by covering a grid of thin wires in a tray with pulp of the desired paper thickness and allowing the liquid to drip away. The sheets were then pressed between felt to remove any remaining water and dried. Papermakers added an identification symbol to the wire grid by incorporating a design of soldered wire which was embedded, along with the marks of the grid, in the pulp as it dried forming the thinner translucent images. When the paper is viewed against the light, this watermark and the grid lines, usually a series of parallel lines just over an inch apart, can be clearly seen.

Towards the late eighteenth century, paper manufacturing methods advanced and machine-made paper slowly came into use. Whereas the earlier hand-made paper was coarse and of uneven thickness, the new paper was more uniform, with a finer, smooth surface texture. Although the grid marks disappeared from much paper, some producers continued to imitate the earlier hand-made papers with line impressions and most continued to incorporate a watermark. From the early nineteenth century, bleached paper came into use and, henceforth, maps were printed on much whiter paper.

The largest paper sheet that early printing machines could satisfactorily handle was approximately 600 × 750 mm (24 × 30 in.) and this came to be the largest standard size on which atlases were based. For larger maps, the publisher would have the map printed from several engraved plates and the resulting sheets would be joined; however, advancing technology eventually supplied map-makers with larger sheets. For example, in the production of his map of Scotland, Aaron Arrowsmith was able to use special paper produced by 'Fourdrinier's Patent Machinery, thus avoiding the numerous junctions, which too often injure the appearance of good Maps, when printed on many Sheets'. For smaller maps, the standard sheet could be divided along its longest edge thus:

(i) without division: folio

(ii) divided twice making four sheets: quarto: 4to: $4°$
(iii) divided again to make eight sheets: octavo: 8to: $8°$
(iv) divided to make 12 sheets: duodecimo: 12mo: $12°$
(v) divided to make 16 sheets: sextodecimo: 16mo: $16°$.

The sheets, often considerably trimmed, were then usually bound into the atlas folded in half, so that the actual page size halved one of the sheet's dimensions. A protective paper guard was glued along the centre-fold so that it could be sewn into the binding without damaging the map, and without obscuring information along the centre-fold. Sometimes, however, maps were printed on a full sheet and bound into the atlas without folding, with the full sheet as the page; in this case, their sizing is sometimes referred to as 'large' folio, quarto, etc. It was also possible to subdivide the folio sheet irregularly by dividing either edge into a suitable fraction of the whole and, in this case, their size is referred to as 'long' or 'oblong' quarto, etc.

Select Bibliography

AKERS, B.: 'History of Paper Making'. (*MC*; Dec. 1978)

AKERS, B.: 'The History of Watermarks'. (*MC*; March 1979)

CLARKE, R. V.: 'The Use of Watermarks in Dating Old Series One-Inch Maps'. (*CJ*, 6; 1969)

CHURCHILL, W. A.: *Watermarks in paper in Holland, England, France, etc. in the XVII and XVIII centuries.* (1935)

HEAWOOD, E.: 'The Use of Watermarks in Dating Old Maps and Documents'. (*GJ*, 63; 1924) Reprinted in: Lister, R.: *How to Identify Old Maps and Globes.*

HEAWOOD, E.: 'Sources of English Paper-Supply'. (*The Library*, Series 4, Vol. 10; 1930)

HEAWOOD, E.: *Watermarks, mainly of the 17th and 18th centuries.* (1950)

SHORTER, A. H.: *Paper making in the British Isles.* (1971)

SHORTER, A. H.: *Paper mills and paper makers in England 1495–1800.* (1957)

COLOUR

With the exception of a few isolated experiments in colour printing, maps were printed in black and white only. Until the development of colour lithography from about 1840, colour was added to maps by hand and map colouring was a highly skilled, specialised profession. A surprising number of maps were offered for sale both coloured and plain at an appropriate price differential; for example, Badeslade & Toms's *Chorographia Britanniae* of 1742 was sold 'Price in Sheets 5ˢ Bound 6ˢ Bound & Coloured 12ˢ'; John Gibson's *Counties of England and Wales* of 1759 was advertised at 'Price 4s, bound in Calf, 5s 6d with maps colour'd ...'; Pigot & Co.'s *British Atlas* of 1831 was 'Price, with Coloured Maps, neatly made up in boards £2 10s. od. Extra Coloured, and the maps mounted on Cloth £4 0s. od ...'; and the large-scale county maps of the late eighteenth and early nineteenth centuries usually cost an extra five shillings for colouring. The great advantage of a coloured map is that it is easier to read and understand than a plain black and white map. It is also, of course, more attractive.

Much early colour is extremely fine and maps with splendid contemporary colouring are desirable and sought after. The height of the colourist's art was achieved in the seventeenth century with the domination of map production by Dutch and Flemish map-makers. The great map publishing houses, like those of Blaeu and Jansson, either employed their own colourists or placed the work with independent specialists (Abraham Ortelius, for example, was an early freelance colourist before turning to atlas publication). The profuse baroque decoration of the period allowed the production of superbly hand-coloured atlases. However, not all maps were coloured; Speed, for instance, issued his maps uncoloured and it is unusual to find them with original colour; the only ones coloured being prepared by special request. As baroque style succumbed to the spread of rococo, colouring became less flamboyant and colour disappeared from cartouches and vignettes and was used more sparingly on the map face. Since colour was an important selling point, every effort was made to choose suitable colours and to apply them in an attractive style, and this commercial consideration caused colouring to reflect the artistic fashions of the day, with the bright elaboration of the early seventeenth century giving way to the refined, lighter, subtle colouring of the late seventeenth and early eighteenth centuries, and then gradually evolving into the austere functionalism of the early nineteenth century.

Although most early colour is of high quality, some was obviously undertaken 'on-the-cheap', often by employing children on piece work, and is crude, inappropriate, and, sometimes, inaccurate. The small children suitable for such boring and repetitive colouring work often suffered blindness at an early age due to years of eye straining work in badly lit workshops, and even in the late nineteenth century the Ordnance Survey employed 13- and 14-year-old boys to colour large-scale maps at a wage of sixpence to a shilling a day. Such young, unskilled labour could not faithfully follow the reference copies coloured by the master illumineurs and, consequently, much fine engraved detail was obscured by the crude application of thick colour. Another source of poor colouring was the encouragement of amateur colourists by some publishers in the eighteenth and early nineteenth centuries by advertising the delights of home colouring as 'agreeable amusements' for the family.

Early colourists followed the colouring conventions of manuscript maps, and a generally accepted code evolved with: hills usually brown, but occasionally green; woodland, estates and parks green; rivers blue; sea either in outline blue or an overall pale blue wash; roads yellow or brown; and cities and towns red. Boundaries were generally coloured with a different colour on each side of the boundary line, but there were several approaches adopted according to the period, colourist and cartographer: (1) entire divisions were coloured by a pale wash colouring with or without the boundary being marked by a thin pen line, (2) boundary lines were simply marked by a thin pen line, (3) each side of the line was coloured by a narrow band of consistent colour, and (4) each side of the line was coloured by a wider band of colour gradually fading as the distance from the boundary increased. Coats-of-arms were coloured correctly and any other decoration, such as vignettes, cartouches, and decorative borders, when not left plain or partially plain, was coloured naturally at the colourist's discretion.

Following the Civil War, books on the subject of map colouring began to appear, thus helping to standardize colouring; although, clearly, conventions were seen only as guide-lines for there are wide variations between examples. It is also clear that great care was taken to achieve the correct tones, and the imported constituents made an intriguing if insignificant contribution to Britain's growing international trade. Most original colours have retained their brilliance and original condition to the present time, but greens which were made from verdigris have a tendency to rot through paper, causing it to become brittle and disintegrate; whole sections outlined in green have been known to fall out of maps, but the problem largely disappears with maps coloured after about 1700.

Often draughtsmen would provide an indication of the correct colouring of important subjects, such as heraldry, by using reference letters or different patterns of shading. The commonest codings were:

Colour	Reference Letters	Shading
Silver (Argent)	a, A	Plain, no shading
Gold (Or)	o, or, O	Dotted
Red (Gules)	g, G	Vertical lines
Blue (Bleu)	b, B (sometimes also A for Azure)	Horizontal lines
Purple	p, P	Diagonal lines from bottom left to top right
Black (Sable)	s, sa, S	Cross hatched grid formed by horizontal and vertical hatching
Green (Vert)	v, V	Diagonal lines from bottom right to top left

John Speed, for example, provided the coding for colourists on his maps, but many cartographers did not, and it is not difficult to imagine the colourist's consternation at being presented, for instance, with Robert Plot's map of Staffordshire with its 246 (a later issue had 248) heraldic arms to be coloured with little guidance (Fig. 14). Inevitably, mistakes were frequent. Colourists often mistook coasts for boundaries, rivers for coasts, and so on; the Dutch managed to reverse blue and red in their colouring of heraldry; and the Blaeu colourists incorrectly coloured the Arms of the Prince of Wales with gold lions on a red shield.

Strong, uncoloured, early impressions are best left in their original state, but later copies, which may be weak or faint, can be enhanced and strengthened by modern colouring. Generally, only the purists among today's collectors prefer their maps in the original plain uncoloured state, and thus the profession of map colourist still exists and many original maps are skilfully coloured in the style and colours of their period and cartographer. Obviously most collectors will prefer to have maps with original colour, but modern colouring is often so good that even experts can find difficulty in distinguishing between original and modern. Basically you should like the colouring of your maps, and a little experience will soon show those which have been coloured by unknowledgeable 'amateurs'. When in doubt, it is wise to assume that colouring is modern, for few dealers can resist the commercial temptations of making maps more saleable!

Map colouring underwent its technical revolution from the mid-nineteenth century with the introduction of colour lithography which eventually rendered the map colourist redundant. No longer did colour have to be applied by hand; instead uniform flat colour could be produced mechanically, but the new process was only slowly adopted and power driven lithographic machines producing coloured maps were not general until the 1880s.

Select Bibliography
CAYLEY, H.: 'On the Colouring of Maps'. (*Proc. of the Royal Geog. Soc.*, 1; 1879)

SKELTON, R. A.: 'Colour in Mapmaking'. (*GM*, 32; 1960)

SURVIVAL OF MAPS
By their very nature maps have a high mortality rate. They are particularly vulnerable to time and it is certain that only a small percentage, perhaps only 25–30% of those originally printed, have survived to the present day.

Maps are practical items. They are produced for soldiers, sailors, engineers, travellers, investors and scholars. Many maps simply did not survive harsh practical use or were discarded when more 'up-to-date' versions were published or when they had outlived their usefulness.

Map supplies have also been ravaged by the effects of war and fire. It is impossible to even guess at losses caused by war, particularly from the unprecedented mass devastation of the Second World War, which, for instance, destroyed some of the British Library's collection. In the past, destruction of premises by fire was a far commoner occurrence than it is today. For example, on 22 February 1672, the great map printing house of the Blaeus in Amsterdam burned down, apparently as a result of apprentices carelessly drying firewood, with loss of equipment, stock and some of the copper

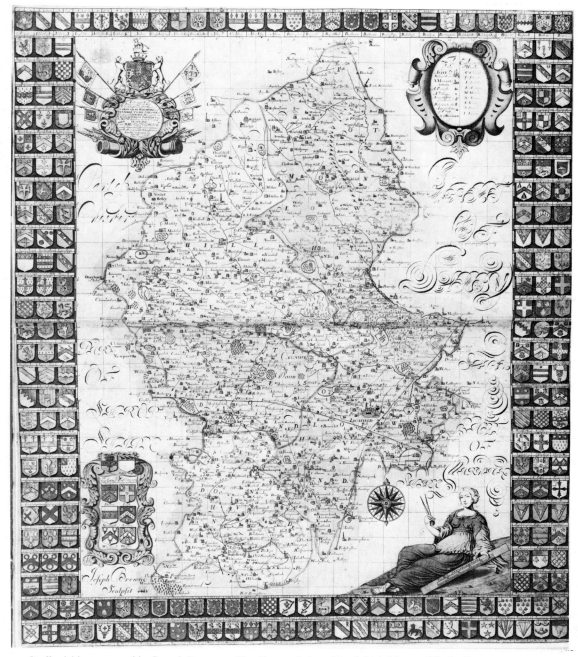

14 Staffordshire engraved by Joseph Browne, 1682. *By permission of the British Library (K.38.36)*

plates. This fire destroyed the sheets for a ten-volume Spanish edition of the *Atlas Major* which was then in preparation; thus making it a rare item today. (Copies of the maps from French or Dutch editions of the atlas are sometimes found with sheets of Spanish letterpress pasted over the original text). Similarly: John Rocque's stock and Whitehall premises were destroyed, together with neighbouring buildings, in 1750; on 17 January 1820, John Cary's premises at 181, Strand, and his younger brother's instrument-making business next door, were completely gutted when fire spread from a neighbouring boot and shoe-makers, rumoured due to an accident 'attributable to the gas', (although most of the copper-plates survived, the premises were razed and there was a substantial loss of stock); and in the Edinburgh fire of 15–17 November 1824, James Kirkwood's business at 19, Parliament Square was ravaged.

On a grander scale, the Great Fire of London of 1666—'from Pudding Lane to Pie Corner'—decimated the Newgate–Old Bailey–St Paul's area, the centre of the book, map and print trade, including, incidently, the printing and publishing business of John Ogilby, leaving him with a capital of only £5! Samuel Pepys was told that 'there is above £150,000 of books burned; all the great booksellers almost undone …'—including both already printed maps and plates (probably including Saxton's plates of Devon and Northumberland which had certainly disappeared by the c.1689 issue of Saxton's atlas by Philip Lea). Maps printed in the few years before the Great Fire tend to be in short supply today; the 1662 issues of both John Speed's atlas and Pieter van den Keere's 'Miniature Speed' atlas, for instance, are much rarer than most other editions. In advertising their edition of Speed's atlas in 1675, Bassett & Chiswell refer to the loss: '. . . the greatest part of an Impression, then newly Printed, being destroyed by the late dreadful Fire, 1666'.[7] The Great Fire was also disruptive in the sense that it interfered with production plans; for example, editions of both Saxton's and Speed's atlases planned in 1665 before the Fire were never published.

Other maps and atlases have simply been lost—Samuel Pepys's diary, for instance, describes the loss of his 1625 edition of Speed and other atlases when he moved his possessions in September 1666 in the face of the Great Fire—'. . . mighty troubled, and even in my sleep, at my missing four or five of my biggest books—Speed's Chronicle—and Maps, and the two parts of the Waggoner, and book of Cards . . .'. (However, happily the books were later found on this occasion!)

Many atlases were splendidly produced and were expensive—often very expensive by today's standards. They were aimed at the rich market presented by the aristocracy and the wealthy, who adorned their library shelves with these fine volumes. This has kept many maps in pristine condition, protected from the discolouration and brittleness caused by exposure to air and light, and protected from the damage caused by constant handling.

Generally, it is these maps, preserved in fine volumes, that are found in the finest condition. Maps from smaller atlases, particularly traveller's guides and children's texts, which were, in any case, more easily lost than the large tomes, were in regular use and tend, often, to be somewhat battered. It was common practice to print maps of the larger counties, such as Yorkshire and Norfolk, on larger sheets which folded into the atlas. These larger sheets were particularly prone to damage and are rarely found without tears. Sheet maps were frequently produced without the protection of a binding cover and were, consequently, often badly damaged. When maps were laid on linen they were less vulnerable to damage but the containing slipcase was easily mislaid. The large wall maps had the lowest survival rate of all because they were subjected to assault from the widest combination of damaging agents—light, temperature and humidity changes, and frequent handling.

There is little direct evidence of the number of maps actually printed from the original plate, block or stone, but it is certain that a high proportion of this number have been lost, damaged or destroyed over the centuries and the surviving few, therefore, represent true 'limited editions'.

SOURCES OF MAPS

Maps originate from a variety of sources. The majority of maps found will come from the many atlases of the British Isles published with county, provincial and regional maps. However, also available are a mass of other maps which were produced as separate sheets or in a multitude of other works. Many world atlases contained national, regional, county and town maps, as did encyclopaedias and other reference works, and gazetteers, street directories, histories, periodicals and guide books. The geographical grammars, such as Herman Moll's *A System of Geography* of 1701 or Emanuel Bowen's *A Complete System of Geography* of 1747, which proliferated from the eighteenth century, usually contained some maps of the British Isles. Other sources of maps, particularly around the middle of the eighteenth century, were the popular literary periodicals which published cartographical works: e.g.:

(i) *The Gentleman's Magazine and Historical Chronicle.*   fl.1736–75

(ii) *The London Magazine; or Gentleman's Monthly Intelligencer.* fl.1747–60

(iii) *The Universal Magazine of Knowledge and Pleasure.* fl.1747–97

(iv) *The General Magazine of Arts and Sciences.* fl.1755–64

(v) (a) *The Universal Museum, or Gentleman's & Ladies Polite Magazine of History, Politicks and Literature.* fl.1762–64

(b) *The Universal-Museum and Complete Magazine of Knowledge and Pleasure.* fl.1765–70

(vi) *The Political Magazine and Parliamentary, Naval, Military and Literary Journal.* fl.1782–90

The first half of the nineteenth century was a period of considerable popularity for the topographical engraving. The resulting illustrated books, such as Francis Grose's lavishly illustrated *Antiquities of England and Wales* and Brayley & Britton's *Beauties of England and Wales* often contained sets of county maps in addition to their engraved views.

Important sources of maps and plans were the commercial directories which developed as a result of the growing markets for goods and services. Businessmen required ever more detailed and comprehensive information on sources of supply, potential markets, competitors, transport facilities and postal services. Commercial directories were produced from the early days of the Industrial Revolution, but it was only in the nineteenth century that many included maps and plans. The heyday of Victorian prosperity generated the production of great national directories, such as those of Pigot & Co., which often contained finely engraved maps.

Maps originating from a county atlas usually have a clear bibliographical identity and chronology, which allows them to be identified and dated fairly exactly. However, it is a very different and difficult task to identify exactly and date maps and plans that have been removed from many other publications and, all too often, they are attributed incorrectly.

CAMDEN'S *BRITANNIA*

Special mention must be made of William Camden's famous antiquarian work *Britannia*, which traced the history of Britain from pre-Roman times until the middle of the sixteenth century, for it was an important vehicle for the publication of county maps. The *Britannia* was first published in 1586, but the first five editions contained only a general map. However, the sixth, the last edition published by Camden himself in 1607, contained a series of county maps reduced mainly from Saxton by William Kip and William Hole. These maps were reissued in the editions of 1610 and 1637, before being replaced in 1695 by the county series of Robert Morden which had been engraved by Sutton Nicholls and John Sturt. Morden's maps remained in use until 1789, when they were replaced in turn by John Cary's folio maps for Gough's edition of the *Britannia*. Camden's work was so popular that abridged versions containing county maps were produced by Pieter van den Keere in 1607, John Bill in 1626, John Seller in 1701, and Samuel Tymms in c.1842; and, containing general and regional maps only, by Regner Vitellius, published by Blaeu, in 1639.

Select Bibliography

KLEIN, C. M.: *A Checklist of Maps in Eighteenth-Century British Periodicals* (forthcoming)

NORTON, J. E.: *Guide to the National & Provincial Directories of England & Wales, excluding London, published before 1856.* (1950)

III Conventional Signs

Early manuscript maps represented features pictorially as seen from ground level. This convention was adopted on the first printed maps but gradually representation evolved through the bird's-eye view to the vertical viewpoint, and pictorial symbols gave way to geometrical signs. Pictorial symbolism was used until the eighteenth century and was, in fact, developed and elaborated as the possibilities of copper engraving were exploited in the cause of greater decoration. The growth of scientific agriculture, power-based industry, new forms of transport, and popular democracy created a need for an ever-increasing variety of signs which were used to draw ever-finer distinctions of representation. While the delineation of natural features remained generally unchanged, new signs proliferated to indicate rapidly changing economic and social circumstances, and influences from estate surveying and from Europe were introduced by John Rocque and others to distinguish land features and use in greater detail. These new influences weaned map-makers away from the old habits of pictorial representation and they began to develop geometrical signs and techniques to represent features in plan. This changed approach gathered momentum during the eighteenth century but some of the old-style pictorial representations, nevertheless, remained in use until the early nineteenth century.

RELIEF

The representation of relief was a thorny problem for early cartographers since they were unable to devise a satisfactory means of depicting the height and dimensions of relief features. While the representation of drainage, vegetation, communications and settlement became increasingly accurate, only the most obvious relief features were shown, and many map-makers made no attempt to show relief at all accurately.

The conventions of medieval manuscript maps led early map-makers to adopt the 'mole-hill': a pictorial representation of a hill as a hummock, usually shaded on the eastern side. Some map-makers, such as Saxton and Speed, attempted to indicate relative heights, producing grossly exaggerated mountains far out of proportion to the rest of the map; but, generally, cartographers contented themselves with using a standard symbol to indicate hilly country. No indication of gradient or height was given and there was no attempt to show the relief profile of the land; individual hills simply rose above an apparently flat surface. This anachronistic use of pictorial symbols on what was essentially a plan was only gradually superseded from about 1680 by the representation of hills in plan.

Attempts to show relief in plan established a new and significant convention for, at last, the area covered by a relief feature could be mapped accurately. The features were seen from above, with unshaded summits and slopes indicated by shading varying in density according to steepness. This new convention initially led to what have been described as 'hairy caterpillars', with map-makers using the technique to engrave long, narrow ranges of hills which bore little resemblance to the actual ground plan. However, the demands of greater accuracy induced refinements of hachuring technique, and John Rocque's work, in particular, increased the effectiveness of the technique and popularised its use. Although some nineteenth-century maps have much of their detail obscured by over-enthusiastic shading, this hachuring technique developed into a delicate and subtle means of representing the fine details of local relief, culminating in the first three-dimensional representation of landscape on the early Ordnance Survey maps.

However, relief representation by hachuring was unsatisfactory in that it still did not indicate height. Although spot heights had been occasionally used on earlier maps, the first British map to mark altitudes above sea level was Christopher Packe's 1743 chart of East Kent; however, the general use of the spot height had to await development by the Ordnance Survey. Similarly, the contour method of linking points of equal height or depth, the most effective method of relief representation, was first used by the

Dutch hydrographer Cruquius in 1729 to chart the Merwede estuary, but this, too, awaited development by the Ordnance Survey in the nineteenth century.

Select Bibliography
HORNER, A.: 'Some examples of the representation of height data on Irish maps before 1750, including an early use of the spot-height method'. (*Irish Geography*, 7; 1974)

JONES, Y.: 'Aspects of Relief Portrayal on 19th Century British Military Maps'. (*CJ*, 11; 1974)

WOODLAND, PARK AND COUNTRY ESTATE

The convention of depicting woodland by tree symbols dates from manuscript maps and all early maps indicated wooded areas by groups of tree symbols, sometimes casting a shadow to the east. In the sixteenth and seventeenth centuries, these symbols were somewhat randomly scattered about the map, but as agriculture expanded and the demands of iron smelting and ship-building reduced the great forests in the eighteenth century, wooded areas became more clearly defined and their boundaries were marked with greater accuracy. From the mid-eighteenth century, smaller, more carefully distributed tree symbols were engraved to indicate woodland areas.

The steady spread of enclosure under the Tudors created the need for a symbol to represent the landholdings of the nobility and gentry, and Christopher Saxton established the convention of representing estates as an area enclosed by a paling fence. The agrarian and industrial revolutions and expanding commerce created wealth which, in a period of no direct taxation, was transformed into ostentatious real estate, thus creating a demand for a finer delineation of property on maps. The representation of country houses, parks and estates was intended not only to designate land-use, but also to curry favour with the wealthy in the hope that they would provide a ready market for the map; many cartographers ingratiated themselves even further by actually noting the names of owners beside their houses or parks.

SETTLEMENT

The limitations of wood-block carving necessarily kept settlement symbols simple, and early woodcut maps generally marked settlements either as crude representations of castles and other buildings, or simply as small, plain circles. The greater artistic potential of copper engraving allowed the introduction of more complex and decorative representation, and the decline of mediaeval fortifications led to the replacement of the castle symbol by a church or a tower, sometimes casting a shadow to the east. Early profile representations of major towns evolved sometimes into a bird's-eye perspective with buildings shown in elevation on a flat ground plan; but generally towns were still shown by profile engravings of great buildings and towered cities. In contrast, villages were represented only by a church or tower with a circle at the door marking the village centre, and churchless hamlets by only the circle. Unfortunately, these detailed, delicate engravings were often crudely obliterated by careless, contemporary colouring and the fine craftsmanship was thus obscured. As yet, few cartographers attempted to devise any classification of town symbols to indicate variations in size and importance; in any case, with the exception of the small circles, the symbols were hopelessly out of scale. Such pictorial symbols continued in use until the late seventeenth century when there began a gradual transition to representation in plan.

Following the lead of John Ogilby & William Morgan, map-makers began to represent large towns in plan as blocks of buildings within a simple street pattern, but maintained a compromise for smaller towns and villages by showing these as rows of buildings in elevation alongside roads in plan. Villages and hamlets continued to be shown by pictorial representations of churches and towers, and by the small circles; and the country houses of the nobility and gentry were also shown in elevation. Asterisks were often appended to towns to indicate the numbers of members returned to Parliament.

From the mid-eighteenth century, complete representation in plan superseded the earlier pictorial symbols apart from the churches, towers, and country houses. It has been suggested[8] that these latter symbols were kept in elevation in the hope of generating subscriptions and patronage from the clergy and gentry and, in fact, with increasing accuracy, the general symbol for country houses declined in use on larger-scale maps in favour of specific representations of each individual house.

After about 1800, map-makers moved towards a standardised representation of settlements in plan and it was the influence of the Ordnance Survey that finally removed the last vestiges of pictorial representation as its conventions and symbols were adopted, and all kinds of buildings were shown by symbol or in plan.

COAST AND SEA

The sea was a frightening force to early cartographers and was, consequently, represented, until the mid-sixteenth century, by a forbidding combination of tempests, monsters and shipwrecks. Although sea areas were populated with ships, monsters and mythical figures for another 200 years, the actual representation of sea and coast evolved through several distinct forms, most of which tended to reappear on maps of later periods. The effective differentiation of land and sea was a major concern of cartographers and, for this reason, ships and sea-monsters remained as decoration, for they were the clearest means of distinction. Before it eventually disappeared from the seas, this marine decoration gradually became more naturalistic, with: the ships up-dated to the designs of the day; monsters becoming more recognizable as whales, dolphins and fish; and the mythical nymphs and tritons omitted.

The engraving of sea areas by stippling (i.e. in a fine dot pattern) became common in the sixteenth century, sometimes in conjunction with short, horizontal hatching along the coastline. An attractive, but rather overbearing, shading style, which was adopted by such British map-makers as Bill and Speed, was developed by the refugee European engravers, particularly Jodocus Hondius, in the early seventeenth century, representing the sea as 'watered silk' (moiré).

Engravers began to leave sea areas blank from about 1630, although coastlines often retained the easily engraved horizontal hatching. In the late eighteenth century this hatching was intensified in length and density, and was used in this heavy form on maps for another century.

From about 1730, cartographers, such as Thomas Kitchin, began popularising the use of form lines, resembling a receding series of waves, parallel to the shore, growing fainter and further apart as the distance from the shore increased. These became the commonest method of shading coasts during the late eighteenth and nineteenth centuries and were adopted by the Ordnance Survey.

SCALE

The linear scale, like the north point, has an essential function on a map; but for the early map-maker it offered another possibility for decoration and is sometimes an attractive feature. Often it was set within a cartouche of contemporary design, with those of the seventeenth-century Dutch cartographers particularly ornamental with local figures, or cherubs holding measuring instruments. A common design element decorating the scale was a pair of dividers surmounting the cartouche or scale bar. However, as map-makers adopted a plainer, more functional approach in the late eighteenth and nineteenth centuries, scales tended to eschew ornamentation.

Differences of accepted mile length induced some cartographers to omit scales; Norden, for example, excluded a linear scale because of the mile's variation; and others, such as Morden with his great, 'midle' and small miles, included several scale bars to take account of local or national mile variations.

Scales sometimes define distance in terms of degrees of latitude and this inevitably varied according to the length of the mile used. The adoption of the statute mile by John Ogilby in 1675 helped to standardise the measurement at $69\frac{1}{2}$ miles to the degree (first used by Senex in 1721), but prior to this the English 'computed' mile was generally put at 60 miles to the degree. Scotland used the earlier measurement of 48 to 50 miles to the degree, and the Irish mile measured '$54\frac{1}{2}$ & 34 Poles to a Degree'.

Despite the general adoption of the statute mile following Ogilby's work, variations still occurred from time to time: John Adair, for instance, reckoned the measurement at 72 miles to a degree.

DISTANCE

The statute mile (also known as 'the measured mile' and 'the dimensurated mile') was established for London and Westminster in 1593, by Act of Parliament, as eight furlongs (1760 yards); but prior to this date, various local mile lengths, or 'customary' miles (also known as 'computed', 'vulgar computed', and 'reputed' miles), were used, and these local interpretations continued in use for at least another 100 years. Local miles were usually longer than the statute mile, and consequently local distances gave a shorter mileage than statute distances. John Ogilby complained that 'the Vulgar Computation ... in some Parts near equals, in others, answers only 3 quarters, and sometimes but Two Thirds of the Dimensuration' (i.e. of the measurement in statute miles) and a 1617 commentary noted that: 'a common English mile makes one and halfe Italian, but towards the north, and in some particular places of England the miles are longer, among which the Kentish mile is proverbially held to be extraordinarily long'.

The old English mile seems to have averaged 1,500 paces, i.e. about 11 furlongs. Mile length on Christopher Saxton's maps varied from about 1,925 yards to about 2,728 yards; Sir Charles Close[9] calculated that the map of Hampshire was drawn on a local mile length of 2,140.6 yards (i.e. 9.73 furlongs; 1.216 statute miles) and Dr Harry Thorpe[10] demonstrated that the local mile length on the map of Warwickshire averaged 2,164.8 yards (i.e. 9.84 furlongs; 1.23 statute miles). Old milestones still standing in Yorkshire in the early years of the twentieth century gave a value of 2,442 yards for the old mile[11] (i.e. 11.1 furlongs; 1.385 statute miles). Dr Thorpe also showed how the mile might vary in length within a relatively small area; calculating from Henry Beighton's map of Warwickshire of 1728 that between Warwick and Coventry a local mile averaged 10 furlongs, between Warwick and Birmingham 12 furlongs, and between Nuneaton and Atherstone about 15 furlongs.[12]

Such was the confusion and variation that some map-makers gave more than one scale in an attempt to clarify distances; Robert Morden's Warwickshire, for instance, gave scales of great (2,420 yards; 11 furlongs; 1.37 statute miles), middle (2,200 yards; 10 furlongs; 1.25 statute miles), and small (1,980 yards; 9 furlongs; 1.12 statute miles) miles, while his Shropshire gave scales of measured (1,760 yards) and computed (2,640 yards; 12 furlongs; 1.5 statute miles) miles. Thus, local miles showed a considerable variation, generally falling between about 1,600 yards and about 2,700 yards. As a further complication, both Scotland and Ireland had their own generally accepted lengths for the mile, with the Scottish mile being about 1,980 yards and the Irish mile about 2,240 yards.

However, the statute mile was adopted by John Ogilby for his influential road atlas *Britannia* of 1675, and other cartographers gradually followed his lead and dispensed with the old 'customary' miles. The spread of the postal service from London in the seventeenth and eighteenth centuries encouraged the acceptance of a standardised length for the mile which was finally established by the Act for the Uniformity of Measures in 1824.

Select Bibliography
CLOSE, SIR C.: 'The Old English Mile'. (*GJ*, 76; 1930)

NORTH POINT

The accepted convention was that maps were oriented with north to the top, but this was not always the case and a different orientation was often adopted in order to make better use of limited space. The indication of the cardinal points offered map-makers another opportunity for decoration and many north points are extremely ornamental. Compass designs were generally developed from three basic patterns: the cruciform, the circle and the star; in contrast, some maps had no north point or simply a note of the cardinal points at the edge of the map or within the border. The commonest form for the north indicator was the fleur-de-lys, although the arrowhead pointer was increasingly used on smaller maps, and east was often marked by a small cross, possibly because of its religious association.

OTHER SYMBOLS

In addition to the standard symbols relevant to any age, maps are covered with a variety of symbols representing the social and economic life of the period. Seventeenth-century maps depict growing industrialism with symbols for wind and water mills, iron forges, lime kilns and so on, and illustrate the social environment with gallows, stocks, maypoles and cockpits. In contrast, the nineteenth-century equivalents are canals, gasworks and railways; and public baths, workhouses and board schools. The modern symbol of crossed swords for a battle site evolved from the seventeenth-century convention of representing such sites by tents or fighting armies.

IV Decoration

Map-makers decorated their maps to fill empty space left by insufficient knowledge or preparation, and to give them a competitive edge over rivals. The blank areas between map detail and frame, the title, the dedication, the scale, the imprint, the sea, the signature, and the frame itself, all offered opportunities for embellishment and ornamentation. Naturally the style of decoration reflected the artistic fashions of the period: the pageantry of Saxton and Speed was followed, in turn, by the voluptuous baroque harmony of Blaeu and Jansson, the light rococo elegance of Bowen and Kitchin, the austere functionalism of Cary and Smith, and the revivalist Victorian romanticism of Moule.

As knowledge increased and the technique of map-drawing and production developed, more and more geographical information was represented on maps and extraneous ornamentation was progressively reduced. Decoration was gradually subordinated to topographical information and became concentrated in more confined areas as cartographers channelled their efforts towards greater accuracy and detail.

Select Bibliography

LYNAM, E. W.: *The Mapmaker's Art.* (1953)

LYNAM, E. W.: 'Period ornament, writing and symbols on maps, 1250–1800.' (*GM*, 18; 1945–6; reprinted in *The Mapmaker's Art.*)

LYNAM, E. W.: 'The Development of Symbols, Lettering, Ornament and Colour on English Maps'. (*British Records Assoc.*, 4; 1939)

SKELTON, R. A.: 'Decoration and Design in Maps Before 1700'. (*Graphis*, 7; 1951)

LETTERING

Generally, lettering was only used on the map face where there was no available symbol, and its objective was to present information as legibly and succinctly as possible. Lettering was usually engraved so that it could be read without turning the map, with the exception of river names which were engraved along the river's course. However, the title and the blank areas beyond the map detail offered opportunities for the use of lettering as decoration, and ornamental calligraphy reflecting the fashions of the period often filled all available space.

The age of woodcut production offered little scope for ornamental lettering since the carving of letters in relief from the wooden block was a laborious and crude process. The use of copper plates gave the engraver greater flexibility and he was able to use his graver virtually as a pen to produce flowing lettering. Henceforward, a variety of lettering styles was used on maps, with a tendency to a more conservative, less flamboyant style as cartography developed and blank areas surrounding map detail diminished. Increasingly, lettering became more utilitarian, resembling the type-printing of books, but continued to be graded in style to indicate different categories of subject. The magnificent swash lettering of the seventeenth century, with its exuberant flourishes and sweeping tails, was designed to fill unwanted space, but, inevitably, it was destined to disappear from the map face as ornamentation became less extravagant and map-makers concentrated on content and accuracy.

Select Bibliography

HEAL, SIR A.: *The English writing-masters and their copy-books, 1570–1800.* (1931)

OSLEY, A. S.: *Mercator: a monograph on the lettering of maps.* (1969)

OSLEY, A. S.: 'Calligraphy—a Cartographic Tool?'. (*IM*, 24; 1970)

CARTOUCHE

The most prominent decorative feature on early maps was the cartouche: an ornamental panel containing the title, key, dedication, scale or signature. The difficulties of relief carving of woodblocks necessarily kept the cartouches of woodcut maps plain and simple, but the ease of copper engraving allowed the development of cartouche style and many were highly ornamental and elaborate.

Sixteenth- and early seventeenth-century maps favoured cartouche designs based on the natural raw materials of the day: leather and wood. Designs represented strapwork of interwoven leather and formal wooden fretwork, with curling ends and projections respectively. Some of the larger maps, for instance those of Speed, decorated these formal frames with heraldic shields, drapery, shells, fish, fruit and flowers, and the ubiquitous cherubs who peopled maps for almost 200 years with their garlands and surveying instruments. Throughout the seventeenth century a variation of the strapwork design resembling scrolled plasterwork was commonly found, as for example on some of the maps of Richard Blome and John Ogilby.

As the seventeenth century developed, cartouche design became more naturalistic, displaying local inhabitants engaged in their crafts and pastimes, allegorical and classical figures, animals, and masses of flowers and fruit. This baroque style reached the height of its development on the maps of Blaeu and Jansson, but towards the end of the century its influence weakened and cartouches, as for example those of Robert Morden, became smaller and less elaborate. Other cartouches, such as some of John Seller's, simply presented the title on a scalloped shell or a suspended drape of tasselled brocade.

In the 1740s, the influence of rococo style spread from France and became general on British maps. The effect was to produce light, elegant cartouches placing the title within delicate wreaths of scrolling, foliage and flowers, or within a rural scene, sometimes depicting local crafts and products. These fanciful scenes were most splendidly presented on the large maps of Emanuel Bowen and Thomas Kitchin. The romantic influence made itself felt by the introduction of classical ruins and spreading trees into the designs.

The late eighteenth and the nineteenth centuries witnessed the decline of decoration on maps and the ornamental cartouche virtually disappeared, with titles being presented in plain panels or without any surround. Decoration concentrated on finely engraved vignettes; and titles, particularly on the larger-scale maps, tended to rely on attractive combinations of lettering styles for their ornamentation. The major exception to the plain approach of Cary, Smith, the Ordnance Survey, and other contemporary cartographers, was the return to elaborately decorated cartouches by Thomas Moule.

BORDER

Maps are traditionally surrounded by a border which frames the irregular shape of the map. This border can not only, itself, be utilised for decoration, but also often creates blank areas between map and frame which can be used for further ornamentation and information. Cartographers filled these unused areas with decorative cartouches, dedications, scales, compasses and vignette views, and, in the case of Emanuel Bowen, Thomas Kitchin, and others, with descriptive notes on history and topography.

Border decoration was related to the style of the period, with the most elaborate borders being found on the maps of the late sixteenth and seventeenth centuries. The borders of the Saxton/Speed period mainly resemble the mouldings of picture frames, whilst the Dutch cartographers, notably Blaeu, sometimes created their borders of vignette views, plans and figures (however, their British county maps have plain-ruled borders only). Map-makers often used their borders to present the heraldic arms of families and institutions; John Speed's magnificent map of Cambridge displayed the 24 arms of the university, its colleges and founder, the dukes of York and the earls of Cambridge and Chester; Robert Plot's 1682 map of Staffordshire incorporated 233 heraldic shields into its border; and John Harris's 1719 map of Kent was framed with 118 shields.

However, as map-making became more scientific and less decorative, cartographers increasingly used the border to show only latitude and longitude by a double inner borderline graduated into degrees and minutes. There were variations on this functional approach: many nineteenth-century maps adopted some adaptation of the Ordnance Survey's 'piano-key' style, and there were occasional throwbacks to early decorative styles, particularly in the period of Victorian romanticism.

LONGITUDE

The standardisation of longitude measurements was a particularly troublesome aspect of cartographic development, for, unlike latitude which has the poles and the equator as its natural bases, longitude must be measured from an arbitrary base, or prime, meridian. Various prime meridians, often chosen only for nationalistic reasons, were used as the basis of longitude measurement: Pope Alexander VI established, in 1494, a demarcation line between Spanish and Portuguese lands 370 leagues west of the Cape Verde Islands for Catholics, but Protestants adopted Ptolemy's meridian passing through the Canary Islands or that through St Michael, the largest island of the Azores, which gave London a longitude of 25° 54′ E; Blaeu, Jansson and Ortelius measured their longitude from the Isla del Fuego in the Cape Verde Islands, but later adopted a base line through the Canaries; and in 1636 Louis XIII decreed that all French maps would adopt the meridian of Ferro, the most westerly of the Canary Islands, making Paris 20° E, and this became the accepted base for the calculation of longitude on French maps until the end of the eighteenth century. Clearly there was much confusion amongst geographers. British maps generally used the vague Atlantic meridian, originally adopted since it was the edge of the known world, which varied between the Azores and the Canaries.

However, increasing dissatisfaction with the inaccuracy of longitude calculation induced Charles II to establish the Royal Observatory at Greenwich in 1675, and this focused the attention of British cartographers on London as the basis for longitude measurement. (However, the *Gentleman's Magazine*, as late as 1748, was still urging British map-makers to adopt 'general meridians thro' Britain ... as had been done in France'.) John Seller's 1676 map of Hertfordshire was the first to adopt a prime meridian passing through London; subsequently this was positioned more precisely through St Paul's Cathedral which was chosen in preference to Greenwich itself probably because of the public interest in its rebuilding by Christopher Wren following the destruction caused by the Great Fire of 1666. Some maps also adopted the marking of time variations from the meridian in order to facilitate the calculation of local time, and this form of graduation, which generally died out about 1725, is found particularly on the maps of Robert Morden. Some map-makers increased confusion by using different prime meridians in the same set of maps, and national or local chauvinism or flattery sometimes caused prime meridians to be taken through other British capitals or county towns. Some maps even reverted to earlier conventions; Gough, for example, records Thomas Jefferys' criticism of John Elphinstone's 1745 map of Scotland: '... The making his longitude from Paris preferable to London is a gross absurdity in a map representing part of an island where London is the metropolis'.

Although the Greenwich meridian had occasionally been used, it was the triangulation for the maps of the Ordnance Survey, started in 1784, that concentrated attention on a prime meridian passing through the Observatory. John Cary's use of it on his sectional *New Map of England and Wales, with part of Scotland*, published in 1794, established the Greenwich meridian, and, henceforth, it was used on all British maps. The Greenwich meridian was proposed for international use in 1883, agreed in 1884, and finally formally adopted as the prime meridian for all maps at the 1911 conference for the international map of the world.

Select Bibliography

MASKELYNE, N.: 'Concerning the latitude and longitude of the Royal Observatory at Greenwich'. (*Philosophical Trans*, 77; 1787)

PERRIN, W. G.: 'The Prime Meridian'. (*Mariners' Mirror*, 13; 1927)

HERALDRY

Maps have always been decorated with the heraldic arms of nations, provinces, counties, towns, institutions and families, and changes in dedications and arms sometimes provide a useful means of differentiating editions. Many maps display the Royal Arms; for example: the original issue of Saxton's maps displayed the arms of Elizabeth I supported by a lion and a dragon, but the Saxton/Kip maps of Camden's *Britannia* and John Speed's maps, published during the reign of James I, replaced the English dragon with the Scottish unicorn; later the 'Civil War Issue' of Saxton's plates by William Web in 1645 substituted the arms of Charles I.

Cartographers financed by a patron might include his family arms; thus, the maps of Saxton bore the arms of Sir Thomas Seckford; and, often, they would attempt to raise subscriptions by selling dedications, or simply use the display of coats-of-arms to flatter and, thus, generate support and a potential market for the project. Often, having agreed to purchase a dedication, would-be subscribers backed out of their commitment; alternatively map-makers might miscalculate the number of dedications that could be sold; consequently, for both these reasons, maps are found with blank shields which had been worked into the map design but could not be filled.

VIGNETTE

Vignettes have long been used to decorate maps and to illustrate the nature of important buildings and towns, or the scenery and activities of a particular area. Views of cathedrals and palaces and 'prospects' of towns embellished the maps of the seventeenth and eighteenth centuries, with the vignettes of Bowen & Kitchin's *Large English Atlas* and *Royal . . .* outstanding; but it was the nineteenth century which saw the vignette develop as the dominating decorative feature of the map in a period of generally austere style. Refinements in the techniques of copper engraving and the development of steel engraving allowed the production of delicate, subtle vignettes composed by accomplished artists. The maps and plans of Darton, Fullarton, Greenwood, Langley, Moule, Pigot, Tallis and others, draw a detailed and fascinating picture of early nineteenth-century Britain.

IMPRINT

Inscriptions giving publication details of a map provide vital evidence for identification and dating. The owner of a plate controlled the publication of the maps because only he could give permission for impressions to be taken from that plate, and only he could authorise the sale of the resulting maps. The owner frequently stated his authority in an imprint or privilege statement, and, naturally, if ownership of the plate changed through sale or succession, so the inscription was often altered. The publisher's imprint gave details of who the map was printed for and, often, who had authority to sell it. Sometimes the owner would feel insufficiently protected and would apply for a letters patent which would give him copyright privilege for a stated number of years. Christopher Saxton received a royal letters patent from Elizabeth I in 1577 for a period of ten years; in 1608 George Humble was granted a 21-year royal privilege to print and sell John Speed's atlas; and Charles II granted John Seller 30 years' copyright protection for his planned sea atlases in 1672.

However, by the early eighteenth century, plagiarism had become so rife that Parliament was forced to provide stronger protection. There was much copying of other map-makers' works without acknowledgement, and, consequently, in 1734 Parliament passed an act 'for the Encouragement of the Arts of Designing, Engraving & Etching Historical & other Prints by vesting the Properties thereof in the Inventors and Engravers'. Copyright protection lasted for 14 years and maps now usually bore the imprint 'Published as the Act directs', or some variation, with the date 'of first publishing' and 'the name of the Proprietor'. The penalties for stealing another's work were very severe: pirated plates had to be given up to the 'inventor or engraver' and a fine of five shillings was charged for each print from the plates in the culprit's possession. Specific coverage of 'Map, chart or Plan' only came in a further Act of 1767 which doubled the period of protection to 28 years, and the consolidating Act of 1777 allowed actions for breach of copyright to be brought in which damages were assessed by jury.

V The Map Trade

THE HISTORY OF THE MAP TRADE

Map-sellers in Britain before the early years of the seventeenth century depended on imported supplies, particularly from Holland, for there was no native production. English cartographers were usually forced to send their drafts overseas for engraving: only eight of Saxton's 35 maps, engraved between 1574 and 1579, were signed by Englishmen, and Speed's maps of 1611–12 were engraved by Jodocus Hondius in Amsterdam.

However, the influx of engravers, such as Pieter van den Keere and Jodocus Hondius, from the Netherlands in the later years of the sixteenth century, injected technical knowledge and trading experience into the embryonic English trade which had been initiated by the few English engravers and the first London print-sellers John Sudbury and his nephew George Humble. Sudbury & Humble's publication of John Speed's atlas in 1611 was an immediate success, stimulating a demand which was satisfied until the Civil War by reprints of Speed's maps and, indeed, the older maps of Saxton, Norden, Symonson and others, and by the import of the new maps by Blaeu and Jansson. Sudbury retired in 1618 and Humble seems to have enjoyed a virtual monopoly of London map publication until his death in 1640.

The close relationship with the Dutch trade continued because maps were imported in quantity, and it was commercially sensible to use existing plates and supplies rather than engrave new maps. Dutch publishers maintained offices in London and there was a free flow of technical information and supplies. From 1640 the trade became more competitive, particularly during the Civil Wars and the Commonwealth, with the establishment of several important new map-selling businesses. George Humble's son, William, continued to sell Speed's maps until 1659, but the major map publishers were: Peter Stent, who energetically bought up the stock of other map-sellers; Thomas Jenner, whose Puritan sympathies persuaded him to diversify from print selling to map publishing to aid the Commonwealth armies; and Robert Walton. Military considerations also probably account for the frequent reissues of Speed's maps, the resurrection of Saxton's, and the imports of Blaeu's and Jansson's.

The post-Restoration period from 1660 witnessed a further growth in the infant English map trade, with a proliferation of both engravers and map-sellers. The London map trade, which in effect was the national map trade, concentrated in two areas: one around St Paul's Churchyard, Newgate and Cheapside, and the other in and around Cornhill; but signs were already apparent of the later eighteenth-century spread westwards with the establishment of some dealers in Holborn, Fleet Street and the Charing Cross area following the Great Fire of 1666. However, despite this expansion, publishing still tended to be concentrated in relatively few hands for the financial commitment of atlas production was too substantial for most. John Overton acquired Stent's stock and, in turn, passed his stock in 1707 to his son Henry; in this way, the map plates of Speed, Norden and others were kept in production long after their original publication. Philip Lea (c.1689–1694) [and later: George Willdey (c.1732), the Bowles family (c.1733–53), Thomas Jefferys (c.1755), and Cluer Dicey (c.1770)] republished Saxton's plates and John Garrett reissued Jenner's, but some new publishers such as John Seller, Robert Morden, and John Ogilby & William Morgan were turning their attention to the production of fresh surveys.

The resurgence of interest in native production was intensified in 1712 by the imposition of a 30% duty on imported maps which gave a substantial competitive advantage to home producers, and effectively severed the established connection with the map producers of Europe. Increasing demand generated capital for the map trade, and, as the eighteenth century progressed, the traditional flow of trade was actually reversed and English maps began to be exported to the Continent.

An unusual feature of the map trade in the

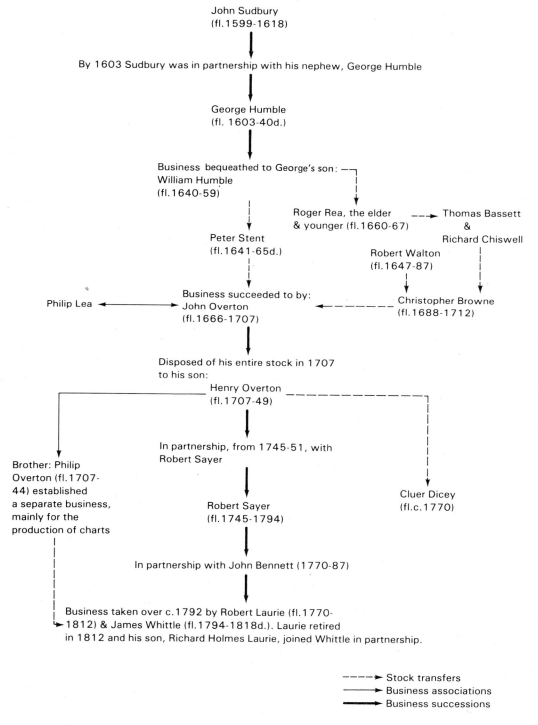

John Sudbury
(fl.1599-1618)

By 1603 Sudbury was in partnership with his nephew, George Humble

George Humble
(fl. 1603-40d.)

Business bequeathed to George's son:
William Humble
(fl.1640-59)

Roger Rea, the elder
& younger (fl.1660-67)

Thomas Bassett
&
Richard Chiswell

Peter Stent
(fl.1641-65d.)

Robert Walton
(fl.1647-87)

Philip Lea

Business succeeded to by:
John Overton
(fl.1666-1707)

Christopher Browne
(fl.1688-1712)

Disposed of his entire stock in 1707
to his son:

Henry Overton
(fl.1707-49)

Cluer Dicey
(fl.c.1770)

In partnership, from 1745-51, with
Robert Sayer

Brother: Philip
Overton (fl.1707-
44) established
a separate business,
mainly for the
production of charts

Robert Sayer
(fl.1745-1794)

In partnership with John Bennett (1770-87)

Business taken over c.1792 by Robert Laurie (fl.1770-
1812) & James Whittle (fl.1794-1818d.). Laurie retired
in 1812 and his son, Richard Holmes Laurie, joined Whittle in partnership.

----→ Stock transfers
———→ Business associations
━━━━▶ Business successions

Business relationships in the London map trade

51

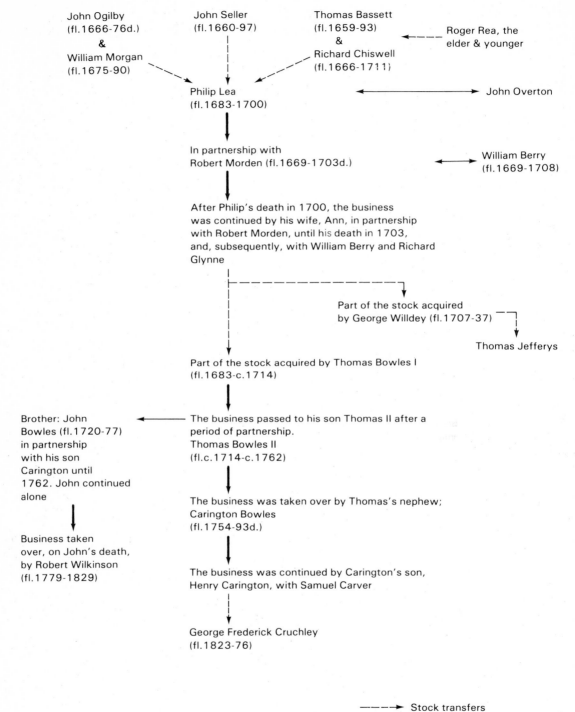

John Ogilby
(fl.1666-76d.)
&
William Morgan
(fl.1675-90)

John Seller
(fl.1660-97)

Thomas Bassett
(fl.1659-93)
&
Richard Chiswell
(fl.1666-1711)

Roger Rea, the
elder & younger

Philip Lea
(fl.1683-1700)

John Overton

In partnership with
Robert Morden (fl.1669-1703d.)

William Berry
(fl.1669-1708)

After Philip's death in 1700, the business
was continued by his wife, Ann, in partnership
with Robert Morden, until his death in 1703,
and, subsequently, with William Berry and Richard
Glynne

Part of the stock acquired
by George Willdey (fl.1707-37)

Thomas Jefferys

Part of the stock acquired by Thomas Bowles I
(fl.1683-c.1714)

Brother: John
Bowles (fl.1720-77)
in partnership
with his son
Carington until
1762. John continued
alone

The business passed to his son Thomas II after a
period of partnership.
Thomas Bowles II
(fl.c.1714-c.1762)

Business taken
over, on John's death,
by Robert Wilkinson
(fl.1779-1829)

The business was taken over by Thomas's nephew;
Carington Bowles
(fl.1754-93d.)

The business was continued by Carington's son,
Henry Carington, with Samuel Carver

George Frederick Cruchley
(fl.1823-76)

- - - - → Stock transfers
——— → Business associations
━━━ → Business successions

Business relationships in the London map trade

eighteenth century was the involvement of women, for business was very much a male preserve. When Philip Lea died in 1700, his business was carried on by his wife, Ann, firstly in partnership with Robert Morden, until his death in 1703, and, subsequently, by herself or in partnership with Richard Glynne. Mary Ann Rocque published maps for her husband, John, and carried on his business after his death in 1762; James Ainslie's wife carried on his business in Edinburgh after his death, and Mary Senex continued her husband's from his death in 1740; and Andrew Dury's wife and Elizabeth Beighton both acted as publishers of maps produced by their husbands.

Publishing relationships were often extremely complex, with publishers grouping together into joint-stock enterprises or partnerships for particular projects or periods. Stock was continually being taken over or inherited, and plates issued solely with changed publisher's imprints; this picture was further complicated by the fact that many publishers were also surveyors, draughtsmen, engravers and map-sellers who worked not only for themselves but also for others.

The trade continued to be dominated by a relatively few businesses: the Overton brothers were associated with Robert Sayer, who was in partnership with John Bennett from 1770 until 1787; Sayer's business was, in turn, taken over about 1792 by Laurie & Whittle who, thus, acquired many of the Overtons' plates. Thomas Bowles bought up some of the stocks of Robert Morden, Philip Lea, and John Seller and built a successful business on this foundation, allowing him to pass it on, via his son Thomas, to his nephew Carington, and retire to the rural delights of Stoke Newington.

On a lesser scale, Emanuel Bowen and Thomas Kitchin were periodically associated in the mid-eighteenth century, passing, at least, some of their stocks to Emanuel's son, Thomas. The Dodsley brothers, Robert and James, published maps from about 1735, and the immigrant Rocque family were also active, despite somewhat precarious business methods.

Another important business succession was the passing of Thomas Jefferys' business at Charing Cross to William Faden on the former's death in 1771, and subsequently in 1823 to James Wyld

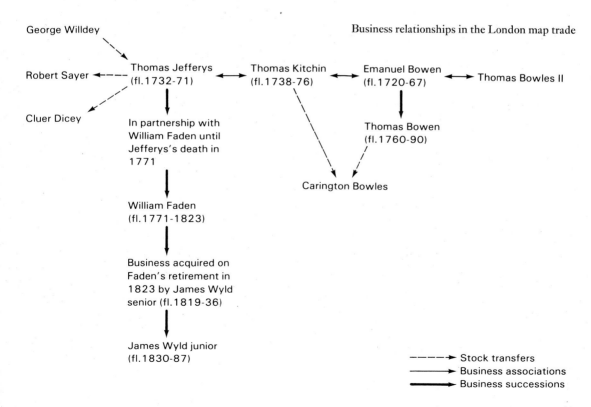

Business relationships in the London map trade

----> Stock transfers
——> Business associations
━━━▶ Business successions

senior, the 'Geographer Royal', and then to his son, James the younger. However, the most prolific and arguably greatest map producer and publisher of the late eighteenth and early nineteenth centuries was John Cary, who established his business in 1783 after a long apprenticeship under the engraver William Palmer. Cary's business subsequently passed to his sons, George and John, and later to George Frederick Cruchley, who had learnt his trade working for the Arrowsmith firm.

The relative decline in the demand for expensive, elaborately decorated maps, as the total map market grew, created opportunities for the satisfaction of the cheaper end of the market. Consequently, in the early nineteenth century, there were many smaller publishing and engraving businesses in London which, in aggregate, made a significant contribution to the map trade. Fine maps were produced from the establishments of Edward Mogg, James Reynolds, James Pigot, Charles Smith, Henry Teesdale, and many others. Publishers were serviced by numerous engravers, such as Joshua Archer, Sidney Hall, and the Neele family ('Engraving in general …

performed with neatness and expedition'), who frequently exploited opportunities to publish their own maps as well.

The London map trade was very much the British map trade, for the narrowness of local markets restricted development in Scotland and Ireland to the work of purely local publishers and land surveyors. National markets were served from London and it was customary for provincial maps and atlases to be produced with a London imprint. Local trade in Ireland naturally centred on Dublin, with the Grierson family particularly prominent; in contrast, Scotland did eventually succeed in developing Edinburgh as a national centre of the map trade.

Increasing prosperity and the late eighteenth-century explosion of Scottish culture created a demand for books and maps, fed by a growing number of publishers and engravers. Initially small maps were engraved only to illustrate books—firstly, based on James Dorret's maps of 1750 and 1751, and, later, on the new county maps, on John Ainslie's map of 1789, and on Aaron Arrowsmith's

Business relationships in the London map trade

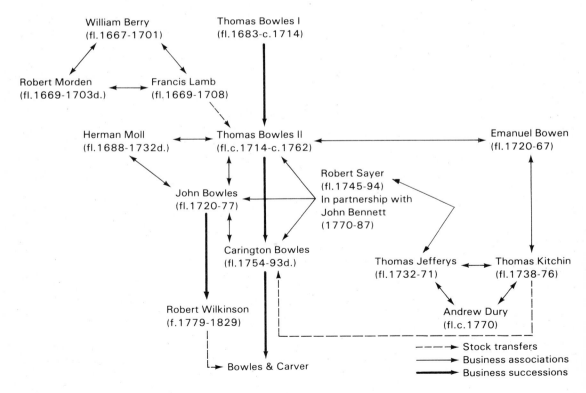

of 1807. However, by the late eighteenth and early nineteenth centuries, Edinburgh publishing houses were producing virtually all Scottish national atlases; these emanated from the establishments, mainly concentrated in 'The Bridges' area, of Thomas Brown, William Blackwood, Adam & Charles Black, John Lothian and others, and, later in the century, from Archibald Fullarton, the Bartholomew family, and Gall & Inglis.

Select Bibliography

ARBER, E. (ED.): *The Term Catalogues, 1668–1709.* (3 vol; 1903)

MACKERROW, R. B.: *A dictionary of printers and booksellers . . . 1557–1640.* (1910)

PLOMER, H. R.: *A dictionary of the booksellers and printers . . . 1641–1667.* (1907)

PLOMER, H. R.: *A dictionary of the printers and booksellers . . . 1668 to 1725.* (1922)

PLOMER, H. R., BUSHNELL, G. H. and DIX, E. R. MCC: *A dictionary of the printers and booksellers . . . 1726 to 1775.* (1932)

TYACKE, S. J.: 'Map-sellers and the London map trade c.1650–1710'. (in Wallis, H. and Tyacke, S. J. (eds.): *My head is a map*; 1973)

TYACKE, S. J.: *London Map-sellers 1660–1720.* (1978)

FINANCING MAP PRODUCTION

The engraving and printing of maps was expensive, for funds had to be raised for surveying, engraving, machine time, materials, overheads, colouring, and, sometimes, binding. John Seller's projected English atlas was costed at one shilling a mile for the survey, copper plates at about £1 5s. each, or £8 for the engraving of each county, and 100 town plans at £1 each. Aaron Arrowsmith's map of Scotland cost 'before I was in possession of the first impression (Five Hundred Copies)' ... 'in Copper, Engraving, Paper, Printing and Colouring, £2,050, including about £100 lost by a cancelled plate ...'.

Naturally, publishers were reluctant to commit themselves to such heavy expenditure without some guaranteed market, and every effort was made to generate support before laying out too much capital. The high cost of a new survey often encouraged publishers to plagiarise earlier work and to re-issue old stock long out-of-date. Thus, difficulties of finance exerted a conservative influence on map production and held back the representation of up-to-date information. Despite the perpetual claims to modernity and to the use of 'actual survey' material, most areas were surveyed only infrequently and maps would be prepared from the last available survey, which might well be more than 100 years old. As Richard Gough complained in 1780: 'as to the several sets of county maps professing to be drawn from the latest observations, they are almost invariable copies of those that preceded them'. There was no legal hindrance to such plagiarism, for the only copyright protection available in the sixteenth and seventeenth centuries was a privilege granted for a limited number of years, usually less than ten; and only in 1734 was statutory copyright protection enacted by Parliament.

These commercial risks induced publishers to adopt various tactics to raise funds and push sales. In the sixteenth and early seventeenth centuries, cartographers depended on the support of patrons for finance. Christopher Saxton was funded by Thomas Seckford, John Speed by Sir Fulke Greville, and Robert Morden by Thomas Goddard, but John Norden's *Speculum Britanniae* failed because he was unable to interest a sponsor. Later, publishers issued: prospectuses; subscriber copies; special, large, elaborate versions; and extra copies for securing orders from others; in an effort to stimulate the market. They also charged fees for incorporating dedications to the local nobility and the family arms of the gentry. Some publishers received grants, authorised by the monarch, from the Treasury (generally in the form of money payment but alternatively sometimes as a licence allowing relief or exemption from customs-duty payable on imported paper or books and maps needed in the preparation of an atlas), or sometimes from the City; and others sold off unwanted book stocks, sometimes by lottery, in order to raise cash; e.g., 'Mr. Ogilby's Lottery of Books opens on Monday the 25th instant, at the Old Theater, between Lincolns-Inn-Fields and Vere-Street; where all persons concerned may (if they please) repair to take a View of the Volumes, and put in their Money.'[13]

Often, costs were so extensive that publishers were forced into partnership and joint-stock arrangements in order to spread the risks of production and increase the number of retail outlets available and, even then, it was often necessary to publish by instalments as the capital came to hand. The need for substantial capital resources tended to concentrate production and stocks in relatively few hands, and map publishing came, increasingly, to be conducted by a small number of important, inter-connected, publishing houses. The imprints of these constantly changing business associations often provide a simple means of dating map issues.

However, the principal means of raising working capital was by the practice of soliciting advance subscriptions, which remained in use until the early nineteenth century. The familiarity of the system guaranteed, at least, some regular contributors from the ranks of the wealthy, and publishers energetically canvassed potential sources of funds. A frequently used 'carrot' was the promise of a dedication or the family arms engraved on the map itself. Richard Blome was particularly adept not only at selling such dedications for the original engraving of his maps, but also at finding alternative patrons at a later date, perhaps when the flow of funds from the first source had dried up; his maps are not only found with re-engraved dedications, but also with new dedications simply pasted over the old. Maps sometimes merely listed subscribers' names; but others, particularly in the eighteenth century, were a riot of heraldry with the coats-of-arms of the subscribers dominating the maps themselves; the map of Hertfordshire of c.1724 by John Warburton, Joseph Bland and Payler Smith, for example, sported a lavish 841 coats-of-arms! (Warburton's maps are sometimes found both with and without such heraldry since arms were sometimes printed on separate strips for pasting around the map outside the frame.) Even when the fashion for heraldry and dedications died out in the late eighteenth century, map-makers continued to flatter the vanity of potential subscribers and purchasers by giving prominence to the representation and naming of their country houses and estates, and sometimes this was the only information up-dated for later issues.

An obvious problem was that too few subscribers could be recruited to cover costs and that the project would have to be abandoned, thus disappointing early subscribers. John Seller failed to raise sufficient at 40s. per head for his projected *Atlas Anglicanus* and Moses Pitt's desperate advertisement in the *London Gazette* of 3–7 July 1679 suggests the subsequent demise of his projected *English Atlas*: '... those Gentlemen; that have Subscribed; or will Subscribe, immediately Pay their Forty shillings to Dr Yates, Principle of Brazen Nose Colledge in Oxen, or M. Pitt at the Angel in St Pauls Church-yard, for which they will have a Receipt, or else their names will not be Printed in the Preface of the said Book, and likewise loose the

Advantage of the subscription, and any that desire their Coat of Arms on any plate, shall be kindly used by the said Mr Pitt.'

Atlas production was always a precarious business. Often publishers had to canvas official grants to cover the deficit caused by an excess of expenditure over revenue; Taylor & Skinner, for example, had to be supported by the Commissioners for Forfeited Estates because the subscriptions for their *Survey and Maps of the Roads of North Britain* totalled less than £1,050 as against costs of £1,433. Other publishing businesses simply over-extended themselves to the point of bankruptcy: Thomas Jefferys' business failed in 1766 probably due to his commitment to winning the Royal Society of Arts' award, and John Thomson was forced to petition for bankruptcy in 1830 because he could not meet the expenses of his *Atlas of Scotland*.

Select Bibliography

CLAPP, S. L.: 'The subscription enterprises of John Ogilby and Richard Blome'. (*Modern Philology*, 30; 1932–33)

TAYLOR, E. G. R.: 'The English Atlas of Moses Pitt, 1680–83'. (*GJ*, 95; 1940)

ADVERTISING

Advertising was an essential component of the map marketing process. Since magazines and newspapers developed significantly only in the late seventeenth century, publishers had to devise alternative methods of placing their wares before the public.

Some early maps were advertised by handbills which solicited subscriptions by being distributed or displayed in such suitable public places as St Paul's Cathedral. These handbills gradually evolved into the grand prospectuses of the eighteenth and nineteenth centuries which were so fundamental to the funding of map production; a Greenwood prospectus, for example, extolled the virtues of their county maps which used 'every means to join superior elegance with minutest accuracy'.

Publishers also sometimes built in the supply details of their stock by specifying retail outlets and other works available for sale. George Willdey's maps, for instance, were obtainable at his 'Great Toy Spectacle, China Ware and Print Shop the Corner of Ludgate Street near St Paul's'; Herman Moll used the issue of his Irish atlas to advertise the availability of his 'fifty new and correct Maps of England and Wales' and 'His Set of thirty-two new and correct Maps of Scotland ... never done before ...'; and Darton & Son used the covers of their folding maps to present their 'Maps of the English Counties Just Published' to the public. A natural extension of such advertising was the production of stock catalogues by publishers. The earliest English map-seller's catalogue known was issued by Robert Walton as early as 1655, but it was only later that it became standard practice for map-sellers to issue them. Mary Senex, for instance, issued 'A Catalogue of Globes Maps, etc. made by the late John Senex FRS, and continues to be sold, etc.' when she carried on the business after her husband's death, and William Faden's catalogue of about 1822 listed over 300 maps, atlases, plans, charts and globes. For the relatively short period 1655–1720 alone, 29 map-sellers' catalogues are known.

However, the most important advertising media for the map-seller were the newspapers and trade catalogues where details of proposals and progress could be announced. Advertisements would give details of the project, the names of the undertakers, their addresses and other information, including prices; and, as projects advanced successfully, map-sellers would publish progress reports and, sometimes, record favourable customer reactions. Some sellers even used their advertisements to criticize their commercial rivals; John Overton, for example, established his superiority over Robert Walton by claiming that he had 'more than ten time the Choice and stock that RW hath, though he vapors that he is the oldest man'. (Walton, however, gave as good as he got in this particular exchange of acrimony, describing much of Overton's catalogue as 'utterly false'!).

Major advertising media of the late seventeenth and early eighteenth centuries were the *Term Catalogues* which were produced quarterly from 1668 to 1709, corresponding with the law terms, by the stationers Robert Clavell and John Starkey, as trade journals for London booksellers. After John Ogilby's attempts to raise finance for his projected *English Atlas* in 1668, most map-sellers followed suit by advertising their stock and projects in the *London Gazette*. This newspaper was a major vehicle for map-selling until the Stamp Act of 1712 drastically reduced its advertisements by placing a duty of one shilling on each entry. Although this effectively killed off much map advertising in the *Gazette*, other newspapers, such as the *London Evening Post*, later developed to take its place as important showcases for map publishers. (Other newspapers carrying map and atlas advertisements included: *The Morning Chronicle*, *The General Advertiser*, *The Evening Post*, *The Gazetteer and New Daily Advertiser*, *The Whitehall Evening Post*, *The Public Advertiser*, *The Daily Courant*, *The Flying Post*, *Mist's Weekly Journal*, *The Post-Man*, *The Daily Journal*, *The Daily Post*, *The London Journal*, *Fog's Weekly Journal*, and *Lloyd's Evening Post*).

VI Types of Maps

MAPS OF THE BRITISH ISLES, THE NATIONS, AND REGIONS

Not only were general maps of the British Isles and their constituent nations produced in most county atlases, but they were also generally published in the vast mass of atlases of Europe and the world that appeared during the same period. Consequently, there is a far wider range of these general maps available than there is of county maps; and many fine cartographers, ranging from Ortelius, Mercator and Sanson to Arrowsmith, Tallis and Wyld,[14] published general maps but no county maps. The shapes of the British Isles and their nations and islands offered considerable scope for decoration and many maps, particularly of French and Dutch origin, were highly ornamented, reflecting the artistic style of the period (Fig. 15).

There are many maps of the individual nations available, but England was more comprehensively covered than the others, and Wales tended to be included with England rather than being mapped separately. Wales, in fact, was particularly difficult to map in the sixteenth and seventeenth centuries for it was a backward and remote area where English was rarely spoken. Even native map-makers contented themselves with preparing only general maps of North and South Wales, and this precedent was often followed even in the nineteenth century. Much the same problem existed for Scotland and Ireland, and, indeed, parts of highland England, and accurate maps generally date only from a later period than those of lowland England.

Some cartographers produced regional maps — for example, regional maps of England and Wales, Scotland and Ireland were published in the third part of Mercator's *Atlas* in 1595,[15] and both Keere and Zatta produced maps of the regions of Scotland and Ireland (Fig. 16). Some, such as Saxton, Jansson and Keere, sometimes grouped a number of counties together, thus producing a map of a region rather than an individual county; and after, as in the case of Petrus Bertius, Franz von Reilly or Michel Perrot, these regional maps, apart from a few maps of single

15 Jersey and Guernsey by Alain Manesson Mallet, 1683. *Photograph: Mills-Wight Studio*

counties, are their only maps of Britain.

A popular regional study was the mapping of drainage areas, in particular the Fenlands of Cambridge, Lincoln and Norfolk (Fig. 17). Interest was stimulated by the encouragement of James I; by the great engineering works of Cornelius Vermuyden, a Dutchman engaged by the Earl of Bedford; and by the Act of 1649 for the Draining of the Great Level of the Fens. Dutch involvement in the draining of the Fens led Henricus Hondius first to map the area in 1632. The map was re-issued by

16 Ulster and Leinster by Antonio Zatta, 1778. *By courtesy of Ivan R. Deverall*

Jansson, and Schenk & Valk, and copied by Blaeu for his famous 'Regiones Inundatae': The Fens continued to be mapped as a distinct region until the nineteenth century and Sir H. G. Fordham[16] has listed 25 specific maps of them. Other areas, such as the lakes of Cumbria or Killarney, were generally not so well covered, but were, nevertheless, often mapped as distinct regions.

A surprising variety of regional maps is available.

COUNTIES

From the Elizabethan inception of British printed maps until the alternative approach of the Ordnance Survey, the county was the traditional unit chosen for regional representation, and the county atlas was the standard medium of publication. Since detail beyond the county boundary was shown only incidentally or as an essential supplement, and the varying shapes of the counties only partially filled the rectangular copper-plate, map-makers had blank space available for decoration, and county maps are, therefore, often highly ornamented and extremely attractive. Most counties were covered by a proliferating number of maps, some with several variant states, from the late sixteenth and early

seventeenth centuries to the mid-Victorian period (Donald Hodson, for example, catalogued 112 distinct printed maps of Hertfordshire published before 1845, excluding variants).

County cartography evolved through several phases of development. The pioneering Tudor surveyors, such as Christopher Saxton, John Norden, William Smith, Philip Symonson and John Speed, laid the foundations of county map-making until the late seventeenth century, for no new surveys were undertaken and their maps were simply reprinted without significant revision, or were copied by other map-makers. Despite the increased scientific awareness of the Restoration period, few new surveys were produced, but the increasing dissatisfaction with the inadequacies of the out-dated Tudor surveys eventually forced a major breakthrough, with counties scientifically surveyed by triangulation and mapped on the large-scale of 1 inch to 1 mile. Before the Ordnance Survey started publishing its maps commercially, virtually all Britain had been re-surveyed by private cartographers. Inevitably, the influence of the Tudor cartographers continued as their maps were drawn from throughout the first half of the eighteenth century; but eventually new surveys, promoted and encouraged by the Royal Society of Arts' premiums for original county surveys, gradually ousted these old sources.

Large-scale maps and surveys produced a profound improvement in the smaller scale county maps. The standard practice was to create an apparently new map by plagiarising several sources, and commercial map-makers were always searching for cost-cutting means of avoiding original surveys. Just as the large-scale map-makers incorporated material from local maps, estate plans, and canal and railway proposals, so the commercial atlas producers from Bowen and Kitchin to Cary and Smith edited the large-scale surveys and increasingly derived material from the Ordnance Survey. County maps were also published in a variety of guides and gazetteers which supplemented the more expensive atlases and often managed to keep costs low by transferring the maps lithographically from existing plates. However, not all planned county series were successfully completed; some, such as that of William Tunnicliff in the late eighteenth century, faltered after a promising start, and others, such as Robert Plot's ambitious project, hardly got under way.

In addition to the series of county maps, some

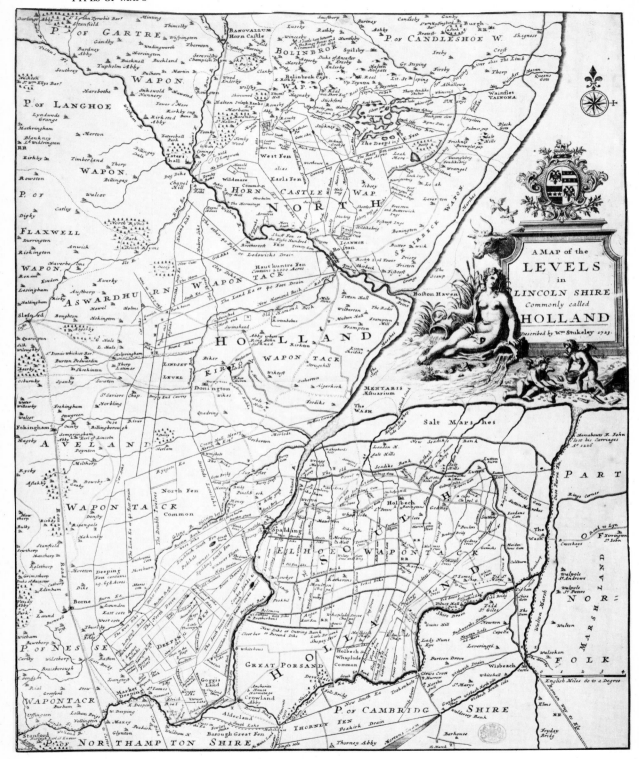

17 'A Map of the Levels in Lincoln Shire . . .' by William Stukeley, 1723. *By permission of the British Library (K.19.20)*

historians and topographers concentrated their attentions on a single county, producing detailed maps of the whole county and its divisions, generally to accompany a county history. The earliest such history was that of Warwickshire by Sir William Dugdale, published in 1656, with maps of the individual hundreds, which were replaced for the second edition of 1730 by the technically advanced

maps of the local surveyor Henry Beighton (Fig. 18). Later representative histories were: Robert Plot's Natural Histories of Oxfordshire (1677) and Staffordshire (1686), with their magnificent maps by Michael Burghers and Joseph Browne respectively; the Hertfordshire histories by Sir Henry Chauncy of 1700 and Robert Clutterbuck of 1815; the histories of Kent by John Harris of 1719 with its large map, finely decorated with heraldry, engraved by Samuel Parker, and by Edward Hasted between 1778 and 1799 with its fine detailed maps of the hundreds

18 'A Map of Hemlingford Hund.' by Henry Beighton, 1729. *By permission of the British Library (2067.d.)*

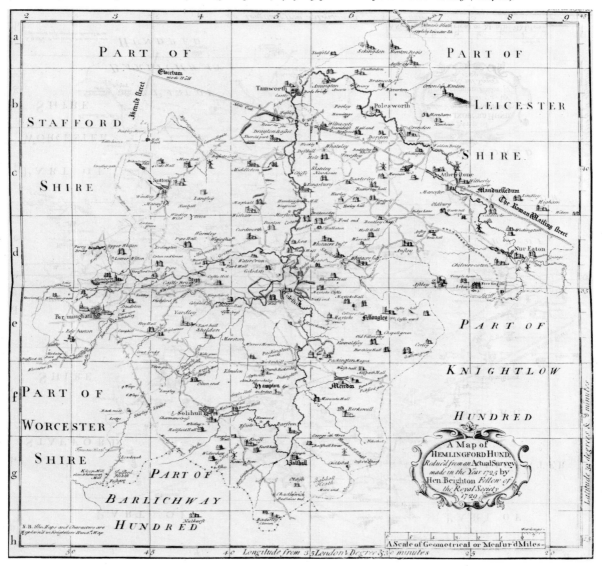

19 'A Map of the Hundreds of Barstable, Rochford & Dengy' engraved by Thomas Bowen, 1762–68. *By permission of the British Library (2064.f.)*

(Fig. 20); the *History and Antiquities of the County of Essex* by the Rev. Philip Morant with its detailed maps of the hundreds by Thomas Bowen (Fig. 19); the history of Dorset by John Hutchins of 1773 with its maps, plans and general county map by Bayly; and so the list goes on. It is both surprising and unfortunate that most county histories included only a general map of the county rather than the detailed maps of the hundreds or other local divisions, for the latter provide an exciting addition to the range of local maps available. Maps from county histories, whether of the whole county or of an area within it, are highly prized and tend to be much in demand.

Select Bibliography

BAGLEY, J. J.: 'County Maps and Town Plans.' (in *Historical Interpretation 2: Sources of English History 1540 to the Present Day*; 1971)

FORDHAM, SIR H. G.: *Notes on the cartography of the counties of England and Wales.* (1908; reprinted in *Studies in Carto-Bibliography*; 1914 and 1969)

LEE, R. J.: *English County Maps: the Identification, Cataloguing and Physical Care of a Collection.* (Library Assoc. Pamphlet; 1955)

BEDFORDSHIRE:

BEDFORD COUNTY RECORDS COMMITTEE: *A Catalogue of the Maps in the Bedfordshire County Muniments, etc.* (1930)

BEDFORD COUNTY RECORDS COMMITTEE: *Catalogue of Enclosure Awards, Supplementary Catalogue of Maps and List of Awards upon Tithe, in the Bedfordshire County Muniments.* (1939)

BERKSHIRE:

(F) LAXTON, P.: Introduction to *A topographical survey of the County of Berks, by John Rocque . . . 1761.* (1973)

NATIONAL REGISTER OF ARCHIVES (in conjunction with Berkshire County Council): *Catalogue of Exhibition. Art Gallery, Town Hall, Reading.* (1951)

20 'A Map of the Hundred of Little and Lesnes, and the Hundred of Dartford and Wilmington' published by Edward Hasted, c.1780. *Photograph: Mills-Wight Studio*

WALNE, P.: *A Catalogue of Inclosure Maps in the Berkshire Record Office.* (1954)

BUCKINGHAMSHIRE:
BUCKINGHAMSHIRE RECORD SOCIETY: *Handlist of Buckinghamshire Estate Maps.* (1963)

BUCKINGHAMSHIRE RECORD SOCIETY: *Buckinghamshire Estate Maps.* (1964)

PRICE, U.: 'The maps of Buckinghamshire 1574–1800'. (*Records of Buckinghamshire*, 15; 1947–51)

WYATT, G. (ED. C. BIRCH AND J. NUTTALL): *Maps of Bucks.* (1978)

CAMBRIDGESHIRE:
FORDHAM, SIR H. G.: *Cambridgeshire Maps: A Descriptive Catalogue of the Maps of the County and of the Great Level of the Fens 1579–1900.* (1908)

CHESHIRE:
HARLEY, J. B.: 'Ogilby and Collins: Cheshire by Road and Sea'. (*Cheshire Round*, Vol 1, No. 7; 1967)

(F) HARLEY, J. B. AND LAXTON, P.: Introduction to *A Survey of the County Palatine of Chester 1777.* (Historic Soc. of Lancashire and Cheshire; 1974). [i.e. P. P. Burdett's 1 inch to 1 mile map.]

HARRISON, W.: 'Early Maps of Cheshire'. (*Trans. of the Lancashire and Cheshire Antiquarian Soc.*, 26; 1908)

MOORE, C.: *Old Maps of Cheshire* (Published by the author; 1981)

WHITAKER, H.: *A Descriptive List of the Printed Maps of Cheshire, 1577–1900.* (Chetham Soc., 106; 1942)

CORNWALL:
(F) NORDEN, J.: *John Norden's Manuscript Maps of Cornwall and its nine hundreds.* Introduction by W.L.D. Ravenhill. (1972)

QUIXLEY, R. C. E.: *Antique Maps of Cornwall and the Isles of Scilly.* (Published by the author; 1966)

RAVENHILL, W.: 'Mapping the Lizard.' (*MC*, 13; Dec. 1980)

CUMBERLAND:
CURWEN, J. F.: 'The chorography, or a descriptive catalogue of the printed maps of Cumberland and Westmorland'. (*Trans. of the Cumberland and Westmorland Antiquarian and Arch. Soc.*, 18; 1918)

DERBYSHIRE:
NICHOLS, H.: *Local Maps of Derbyshire to 1770.* (Derbyshire Library Service; 1980)

DORSET:
HOADE, W.: 'Antique Dorset Maps'. (*Dorset. The county mag.*, 77; 1979)

SUMNER, H.: 'Old Maps of Hampshire, Dorset and Wilts'. (*Proc. of the Bournemouth Nat. Hist. Soc.*, 11; 1918–19)

DURHAM:
NEWCASTLE UNIVERSITY LIBRARY: *A Catalogue of an Exhibition of Old Maps of North-East England, 1600–1865.* (Library Pub. Extra Series 8; 1967)

TURNER, R. M.: *Maps of Durham 1576–1872 in the University Library, Durham.* (1954)

ESSEX:
EMMISON, F. G.: *Catalogue of Maps in the Essex Record Office, 1566–1855.* (Essex Record Office Pub., 3; 1947). *Supplements*: I: 1952; II: 1964; III: 1968.

EMMISON, F. G.: *County Maps of Essex 1576–1852. A Handlist.* (1955)

(F) EMMISON, F. G.: Introduction to *Essex. Chapman and André. 1777.*

ESSEX COUNTY COUNCIL: *The Art of the Map-maker in Essex 1566–1860.* (1947)

HUCK, T. W.: 'Some Early Essex Maps and their Makers'. (*Essex Review*, 18; 1909)

GLOUCESTERSHIRE:
AUSTIN, R.: *Additions to, and Notes on the 'Descriptive Catalogue of Printed Maps of Gloucestershire 1577–1911' by T. Chubb.* (Trans. of the Bristol and Gloucestershire Arch. Soc.; 1917)

CHUBB, T.: *A Descriptive Catalogue of the Printed Maps of Gloucestershire, 1577–1911.* (Trans. of the Bristol and Gloucestershire Arch. Soc., 35; 1913)

HAMPSHIRE:

BOX, E. G.: 'Hampshire in early maps and road books'. (*Hampshire Field Club, Papers and Proceedings*, 12; 1931)

(*F*) LAXTON, P.: Introduction to *250 Years of Mapmaking in the County of Hampshire*. (1976)

SUMNER, H.: op. cit. (Dorset).

HERTFORDSHIRE:

HODSON, D.: *The Printed Maps of Hertfordshire, 1577–1900*. (1974)

WALNE, P.: *A Catalogue of Manuscript Maps in Hertfordshire Record Office*. (Hertfordshire County Council; 1969)

HUNTINGDON:

DICKINSON, P. G. M.: *Maps in the County Record Office, Huntingdon*. (1968)

KENT:

BOX, E. G.: 'Kent in early road-books of the seventeenth century'. (*ACa.*, 44; 1932)

BOX, E. G.: 'Notes on some West Kent Roads on Early Maps and Road Books'. (*ACa.*, 43; 1931)

HEAWOOD, E.: 'The earliest known maps of Kent'. (*GJ*; 1938)

KENT COUNTY COUNCIL: *Catalogue of Estate Maps 1590–1840 in the Kent County Archives Office*. (1973).

LIVETT, G. M.: 'Early Kent Maps (Sixteenth Century)'. (*ACa.*, 49; 1937)

LIVETT, G. M.: 'Supplementary Notes on Early Kent Maps'. (*ACa.*, 1; 1938)

LANCASHIRE:

HARRISON, W.: 'Early Maps of Lancashire and their Makers'. (*Trans of the Lancashire and Cheshire Antiquarian Soc.*, 25; 1907)

WHITAKER, H.: *A Descriptive List of the Printed Maps of Lancashire, 1577–1900*. (Chetham Soc., 101; 1938)

LEICESTERSHIRE:

GIMSON, B. L. AND RUSSELL, P.: *Leicestershire maps: a brief Survey*. (1947)

LINCOLNSHIRE:

GOSHAWK, E.: 'Old Lincolnshire Maps'. (*Lincolnshire Historian*, 3; 1948)

MIDDLESEX:

MIDDLESEX STANDING JOINT COMMITTEE: *Middlesex in Maps and Survey*. (1957)

NORFOLK:

CHUBB, T. AND STEPHEN, G. H.: *A Descriptive List of the Printed Maps of Norfolk, 1574–1916: Descriptive List of Norwich Plans, 1541–1914*. (1928)

NORTHAMPTONSHIRE:

WHITAKER, H.: *A Descriptive List of the Printed Maps of Northamptonshire 1576–1900*. (Northamptonshire Record Soc., Pub. 14; 1948)

NORTHUMBERLAND:

NEWCASTLE UNIVERSITY LIBRARY: op. cit. (Durham).

WHITAKER, H.: *A Descriptive List of the Maps of Northumberland, 1576–1900*. (Newcastle-upon-Tyne Soc. of Antiquaries; 1949)

NOTTINGHAMSHIRE:

WADSWORTH, F. A.: 'Nottinghamshire Maps of the 16th, 17th and 18th centuries: their makers and engravers'. (*Trans. of the Thoroton Soc.*, 34; 1930)

SHROPSHIRE:

COWLING, G. C.: *A Descriptive List of the Printed Maps of Shropshire A.D. 1577–1900*. (1959)

SOMERSET:

CHUBB, T.: *A Descriptive List of the Printed Maps of Somersetshire 1575–1914*. (Somerset Arch. and Nat. Hist. Soc.; 1914)

STAFFORDSHIRE:

BURNE, S. A. H.: 'Early Staffordshire Maps'. (*Trans. of the North Staffordshire Field Club*, 54; 1920)

SUFFOLK:

ROYAL INSTITUTION OF CHARTERED SURVEYORS: *Seven Centuries of Surveying in Suffolk*. (1954)

SANFORD, W. G.: *The Suffolk Scene in Books and Maps*. (1951)

SURREY:

HOOPER, W.: 'Rocque's Map of Surrey'. (*Surrey Arch. Collection*, 40; 1932)

(*F*) RAVENHILL, W.: Introduction to *Surrey. 250 Years of Mapmaking in the County of Surrey: 1575–1825*.

ROYAL INSTITUTION OF CHARTERED SURVEYORS: *The Story of Surrey in Maps*. (1956)

SHARP, H. A.: *An Historical Catalogue of Surrey Maps*. (1929)

SUSSEX:

GERARD, E.: 'Notes on some early printed Maps of Sussex and their Makers'. (*The Library*, 3rd Series, 6; 1915)

GERARD, E.: 'Early Sussex Maps'. (*Sussex County Mag.*; 1928)

HASTINGS MUSEUM: *Catalogue of Maps and Plans in the Exhibition of Local Maps*. (1936)

SANFORD, W. G.: *The Sussex Scene in Books and Maps*. (1951)

(F) SKELTON, R. A.: Introduction to *Sussex. 250 Years of Mapmaking in the County of Sussex. 1575–1825.* (1970)

STEER, F. W.: *A Catalogue of Sussex Estate Maps and Tithe Award Maps.* (Sussex Record Soc., 61; 1962)

STEER, F. W.: *A Catalogue of Sussex Estate Maps, West Sussex Inclosure Maps, West Sussex Deposited Plans, Miscellaneous and Printed Sussex Maps.* (Sussex Record Soc., 66; 1968)

WARWICKSHIRE:

HARVEY, P. D. A. AND THORPE, H.: *The Printed Maps of Warwickshire, 1576–1900.* (1959)

WESTMORLAND:

CURWEN, J. F.: op. cit. (Cumberland).

WILTSHIRE:

CHUBB, T.: 'A Descriptive Catalogue of the Printed Maps of Wiltshire from 1576 to the publication of the 25 in. Ordnance Survey, 1855'. (*Wiltshire Arch. and Nat. Hist. Mag.*, 37, 116; 1911)

SUMNER, H.: op. cit. (Dorset).

WORCESTERSHIRE:

SMITH, B. S.: 'The Dougharty Family of Worcester, Estate Surveyors and Mapmakers, 1700–60. Catalogue of Maps and Plans by the Dougharty Family'. (*Worcestershire Historical Soc., Miscellany 11*, New Series 5; 1967)

YORKSHIRE:

RAISTRICK, A.: *Yorkshire Maps and Map-Makers.* (1969)

RAWNSLEY, J. E.: *Antique Maps of Yorkshire and Their Makers.* (Published by the author; 1970; special edition, 1971)

ROYAL INSTITUTION OF CHARTERED SURVEYORS AND LEEDS CITY LIBRARIES: *Surveyors and Map Makers. Catalogue of an exhibition . . .* (1955)

SHEPPARD, T.: 'East Yorkshire History in Plan and Chart'. (*Trans. of the East Riding Antiquarian Soc.*, 19; 1912)

WHITAKER, H.: *A Descriptive List of the Printed Maps of Yorkshire and its Ridings, 1577–1900.* (Yorkshire Arch. Soc. Record Series, 86; 1933)

ISLE OF MAN:

CUBBON, A. M.: 'The Isle of Man on Maps of the Sixteenth Century'. (*Proc. of the Isle of Man Nat. Hist and Antiquarian Soc.*, Vol. 5, No. 4; 1955)

CUBBON, A. M.: *Early Maps of the Isle of Man: A Guide to the Collection in the Manx Museum.* (Manx Museum and National Trust; 1967)

ISLES OF SCILLY:

PALMER, M.: *Maps of the Isles of Scilly.* (MCC, 3; 1963).

QUIXLEY, R. C. E.; op. cit. (Cornwall).

ISLE OF WIGHT:

TURLEY, R. V.: 'Printed County Maps of the Isle of Wight, 1590–1870: A Check-List and Guide for students (and collectors)'. (*Proc. of the Hampshire Field Club and Arch. Soc.*, Vol 31 for 1974; 1976)

GUERNSEY:

WARREN, J. P.: *Evolution of the Map of Guernsey.* (La Société Guernesiaise)

JERSEY:

(F) DUMARESQ, P.: *Map of Jersey, 1734.* (Royal Geog. Soc.)

CARDIGAN:

LEWIS, M. G.: 'The Printed Maps of Cardiganshire, 1578–1900, in the National Library of Wales'. (*Jour. of the Cardiganshire Antiquarian Soc.*, Vol. 2, No. 4; 1955)

MERIONETH:

LEWIS, M. G.: 'The Printed Maps of Merioneth, 1578–1900, in the National Library of Wales'. (*Jour. of the Merioneth Historical and Record Soc.*, Vol. 1, Part 3; 1951)

RADNOR:

LEWIS, M. G.: *The Printed Maps of Radnorshire 1578–1900.* (1977)

CAITHNESS:

MOWAT, J.: 'Old Caithness Maps and Mapmakers'. (*John o'Groats Jour.*; 1938)

DUMFRIES:

STONE, J. C.: 'The Early Printed Maps of Dumfriesshire and Galloway'. (*Trans. of the Dumfriesshire and Galloway Nat. Hist. Soc.*, 44; 1967)

WIGTOWN:

STONE, J. C.: op. cit. (Dumfries).

ANTRIM:

MORTON, D.: 'Some early maps of Co. Antrim'. (*Bull. Ulster Place-name Soc.*, 2; 1954)

DUBLIN:

(F) ROCQUE, J.: *Dublin County 1760.* Introduction by J. Andrews. (1977)

LARGE-SCALE MAPS

The most exciting development in British cartography in the eighteenth century was the growth of large-scale map production in response to the demands of a rapidly changing environment. Large-scale map production was rare in the seventeenth century and it was only from 1700 with the publication of Joel Gascoyne's map of Cornwall that it became more general. Surveyors began to produce maps at scales of 1 inch to 1 mile and greater, covering several sheets; and the end result was a virtual re-mapping of Britain between 1700 and 1850. The 1720's saw the publication of Williams's Denbigh and Flint (c.1720), Budgen's Sussex (1724), Beighton's Warwickshire (1725) and Senex's Surrey (1729), and more large-scale maps were published in the following decades. However, production received its biggest boost in the middle of the century as a result of the Royal Society of Arts' interest in large-scale surveys. The Society for the Encouragement of Arts, Manufactures and Commerce (known from 1847 as the Royal Society of Arts) had a practical interest in transport, and the need for reliable information stimulated its encouragement of the surveying of coasts and roads by the offer of premiums for large-scale maps. In 1759, it offered 'a Sum not exceeding 100L as a Gratuity to any Person or Persons who shall make an accurate actual Survey of any County ...'. The offer stipulated a scale of 1 inch to 1 mile and was repeated at intervals until 1809. The new award was viewed by most map-makers as highly desirable for the prestige it would bestow rather than the financial benefits, for the £100 was merely a token which nowhere near covered production costs; Yeakell & Gardner, for example, estimated that the planned six-year preparation of their map of Sussex would cost £2,400! The period 1759–1809 produced new surveys of virtually all English and many Welsh, Scottish and Irish counties, published at scales of 1 inch to 1 mile or greater. The first map submitted for the award was Isaac Taylor's Dorset which was rejected because its place-names were often inaccurate; and so the first prizewinner was the Bideford mathematics teacher, Benjamin Donn, for his 12-sheet map of Devon of 1765. Although Beighton's Warwickshire had been the first map based on a trigonometrical survey, Donn's map set new standards of accuracy with its application of scientific surveying techniques and its $5\frac{1}{2}$-year measurement of over 6000 miles of roads and rivers. In all, the Society awarded £460 throughout the period of the offer, plus four gold and three silver medals, and a silver palette; winners included Armstrong and Cary, but many more hopeful applicants had maps rejected as being below the required standard.

The turn of the century marked a transition to greater accuracy in large-scale map-making as private cartographers became influenced by the exacting standards set by the new Ordnance Survey and eventually started to draw material from its detailed survey work, (however, not before some of the Survey's early work had been recognised as defective and of poor quality and had generated considerable public disquiet by the early 1820s, leading to the commencement of rival large-scale projects!). The Ordnance Survey deliberately encouraged the private use of its trigonometrical data to produce 'more correct maps of the counties over which triangles have been carried' and increasingly large-scale county maps were founded on this official material rather than the piecemeal private triangulation of the past.

The most systematic exploitation of official data was by the Greenwood brothers who were the dominating figures in large-scale mapping in the 1820s and 30s with their attempt to cover the whole of England beginning in 1814. They never reached their target of complete coverage but, nevertheless, produced magnificent maps of all but six counties. Their great rival was Andrew Bryant who produced similar style maps, generally on the slightly larger scale of $1\frac{1}{2}$ inches to the mile, but he managed to map only 13 counties.

Standards of accuracy and depth of treatment varied considerably. The finest maps, such as John Rocque's superb maps of Berkshire, Middlesex, Shropshire and Surrey, and Chapman & André's 25-sheet map of Essex, offer a detailed picture of land use at a time of rapid change, but some are merely enlargements of the simplest county maps. The practice of preparing maps partly from local estate surveys produced by independent triangulation, and, indeed, from any other local maps available, inevitably produced errors which were not always corrected when the maps were submitted for revision to the scrutiny of local experts. These large-scale maps generally shared certain common features: they were drawn on the meridian of Greenwich, although some maps also added a meridian through the county town; since they were drawn at the large-scale of 1 or 2 inches to the mile, they covered several sheets; and everything was represented in plan, except churches and country houses, which were shown pictorially.

It was not enough that these large-scale maps should be accurate, they also needed to be attractively presented in order to grace the libraries of the gentry. Most maps were given an elaborate title cartouche, often depicting local industries and crafts: Armstrong's map of Durham, for instance, showed a windmill, a coal mine, a well, and a coastal scene, and Chapman & André's Essex had a vignette of a fulling-mill and cloth beaters. Most maps added inset plans of major towns: Donn's map of Devon included plans of Exeter and Plymouth and Chapman & André's Essex had an inset of Colchester. Vignettes of important places or antiquities were sometimes added as extra decoration. The need to raise local support and patronage made the dedication and the coat-of-arms another important decorative feature of large-scale maps. Some early maps incorporated the arms of the local gentry into an ornamental border, but the trend towards a more scientific approach saw this practice superseded by the marking of latitude and longitude.

Large-scale maps were produced in a number of forms: on large sheets, which were particularly susceptible to severe damage; bound in large folio volumes; mounted on canvas and rollers as a wall map; and, increasingly as they were prepared for practical use in the nineteenth century, dissected into small sections and folding into a slip case or box. The average size of an edition was about 300 copies, mainly going to subscribers, and the loose maps cost from $1\frac{1}{2}$ to $2\frac{1}{2}$ guineas, with hand colouring and special presentation at extra cost. Due to the small initial issues and the high mortality rate, large-scale maps are in short supply and this scarcity is naturally reflected in their price.

Select Bibliography

HARLEY, J. B.: 'The Society of Arts and the Surveys of English Counties, 1759–1809'. (*Jour. of the Royal Soc. of Arts*, 112; 1963–4)

HARLEY, J. B.: 'English County Map-Making in the Early Years of the Ordnance Survey: The Map of Surrey by Joseph Lindley and William Crosley.' (*GJ*, 132; 1966)

LAXTON, P.: 'The Geodetic and Topographical Evaluation of English County Maps 1740–1840.' (*CJ*, 13; 1976)

RODGER, E. M.: *The Large-Scale County Maps of the British Isles, 1596–1850: A Union List.* (2nd ed.: 1972)

TOOLEY, R. V.: 'Large Scale English County Maps and Plans of Cities not printed in Atlases'. (*MC*: in parts from 1978)

WALTERS, G.: 'Themes in the Large-Scale Mapping of Wales in the Eighteenth Century'. (*CJ*, 5; 1968)

N.B. Harry Margary (Lympne Castle, Kent) publishes facsimiles of some important large-scale maps.

ORDNANCE SURVEY

The origins of the Ordnance Survey lie in the military disasters of the Jacobite rebellion when 'Bonnie Prince Charlie', the Young Pretender, marched his highland army as far south as Derby before retreating, and being defeated at Culloden in 1746. The Duke of Cumberland's subsequent pacification campaign highlighted the unreliability of available maps and, in an effort both to map the Highlands satisfactorily and to improve accessibility by building military roads which would make rapid troop movement possible, the Military Survey of Scotland was initiated. The start of survey work in 1747 marks the birth of the Ordnance Survey and its subsequent development owes much to the enthusiasm and energy of William Roy. The Survey ended in 1755 and Roy turned his attention to campaigning for a national survey; his first recorded proposal 'to make a general survey of the whole island at the public cost' was in 1763, and this was expanded in greater detail in 1766 in 'Considerations on the Propriety of making a General Military Map of England'.[17] Roy was given military rank in 1756, made 'Surveyor General of Coasts and Engineer for making and directing Military Surveys under the Board of Ordnance' in 1765, and by 1781 had reached the rank of major-general. Despite interest in his proposals, the American War of Independence of 1776 to 1783 diverted attention and monopolized available manpower, leaving the next initiative to the French astronomer Cassini de Thury, the director of the Paris Observatory, who proposed, in 1783, a precise triangulation to connect the Paris and Greenwich Observatories, through Calais and Dover, in order to determine exactly the difference in longitude between the two, and, thus, link their scientific observations. Watched by George III, that great collector of maps, and his guests (provided with 'the most hospitable supply of every necessary, and even elegant refreshment'), Roy measured the base line for the triangulation on Hounslow Heath in 1784; the connection was eventually completed in 1788, two years before his death. The proposals for the national survey were put into effect in 1791 with the formal establishment of the Trigonometrical Survey under the auspices of the Board of Ordnance, at its headquarters at the Tower of London, by the Duke of Richmond, Master of the Ordnance, who had continued the triangulation after Roy's death. Initially, the Survey was to set out an exact trigonometrical framework for the whole country and to produce a fairly standard series of maps at the traditional scale of 1 inch to 1 mile.

Fortunately, the Survey was, from its first work, able to achieve a higher degree of accuracy than ever before due to its use of the most technically advanced equipment. The theodolite, the basic surveying instrument, was perfected by English craftsmen, in particular by the Yorkshireman Jesse Ramsden who built the massive three-feet diameter theodolites for the surveys of Roy and the Board of Ordnance. (Other contemporary advances included the improvement of the quadrant by John Hadley and the development of the chronometer by John Harrison.)

The initial military concern of the Trigonometrical Survey concentrated its early work along the southern English coast which was potentially threatened by Napoleon's invasion armies. The first series of maps produced, known as the First Edition or Old Series, superbly engraved on copper by Thomas Foot (from 1801 to 1804) and Benjamin Baker (from 1804) and their assistants, were the most accurate and detailed maps available, and clearly placed Britain ahead of France and Holland in cartographic development. Surveying started in the south-east of England and the first four sheets covering Kent were published by Faden on 1 January 1801. Although these four sheets followed the traditional representation of a single county, and, indeed, sheets were issued under county titles until the 1820s, the Survey adopted the policy of consecutive numbering of maps for England and Wales, dating from its coverage of Essex in 1805. Henceforward, all sheets continued map detail to the edge instead of stopping at the county boundary and matched up to form a continuous coverage of the country (although early issues could still be mounted as county maps since borders were not engraved where they would divide the county). The whole of the south coast, including four new sheets covering Kent and parts of East Sussex, and the London area had been mapped by 1820 (Fig. 21); England and Wales below the Hull–Preston line by 1840; and the 110 sheets were completed for the whole country by 1873. The early stages of the survey were directed by Lieutenant William Mudge who was succeeded by the equally talented and original Captain Thomas Colby who introduced a lighter, more delicate style. The expansion of the survey was not, however, always received with enthusiasm by civilian surveyors and map publishers; James Wyld, for example, fiercely resisted the Survey's mapping of London.

The 1 inch to 1 mile scale of the early Survey maps was quite inadequate for detailed delineation, particularly of urban areas; and later in the century it

21 Ordnance Survey Sheet No. I. Brentwood, c.1835. Reproduced from the 1 inch Ordnance Survey Map. *Photograph: Mills-Wight Studio*

came to be realised that a larger scale survey was needed to meet the requirements of urban, industrial, and transport development. Accordingly, the 6 inch and the 25 inch scales were both adopted by the Survey later in the century, particularly for its early work in Scotland and Ireland.

The Survey's triangulation had been extended to Scotland in 1809 but progress was hindered by a series of work suspensions culminating in 1824 with the transfer of most of the surveying force to more urgent work in Ireland. The detailed survey of Ayr and Wigtown, which had been started in 1819, was, however, continued until 1827. When work was resumed in 1843 the 1 inch to 1 mile scale was supplanted by the 6 inch scale for the counties of Edinburgh, Fife, Haddington, Kinross, Kirkcudbright and Wigtown. Following further controversy over scale in 1852, the 25 inch scale was adopted for urban and cultivated areas and the 6 inch scale retained for the remaining, mainly moorland, areas.

Problems of disputed property and local taxation forced the Survey to Ireland in 1824. Here the concern was not with small-scale military maps, but rather with the establishment of an accurate triangulation and the first detailed systematic mapping of the country since Sir William Petty's 'Down Survey' of the mid-seventeenth century. The sensible decision to survey at 6 inches to the mile was taken and the end result, produced by over 2,000 people at a cost of £820,000, was some 1,900 beautiful engravings at a larger scale than ever previously used in the British Isles, supplemented by town plans at an even larger scale for official use only. From the 1850s the Survey branched out to publish maps and plans of Ireland at a variety of scales, with the 1 inch series being published in 1860. The success of the 6 inch scale persuaded the Survey to adopt this larger scale for a similar map of Great Britain started in 1846 when men and money were made available to it.

Dating the printings of the Old Series is complex since the plates were constantly revised and imprints added or altered. (For a fuller discussion of the dating problem and of the factors enabling the dating of maps from the Old Series, see: Mumford, I., 'Engraved Ordnance Survey One-Inch Maps— The Problem of Dating', *CJ*, 5, 1968; Mumford, I., and Clark, P. K., 'Engraved Ordnance Survey One-Inch Maps—The Methodology of Dating', *CJ*, 5,

1968; and Clarke, R. V., 'The Use of Watermarks in Dating Old Series One-Inch Ordnance Survey Maps', *CJ*, 6, 1969. For 'A Note on the Dating of Irish Ordnance Survey Maps.', see: Andrews, J. H.: *A Paper Landscape: The Ordnance Survey in Nineteenth-Century Ireland*. (1975). Appendix F.) However:

(i) from c.1840, some sheets added the number of the adjoining 1 inch map within or outside some borders.

(ii) from c.1847, copies began to appear with the inscription 'Printed from an Electrotype'. Many maps added the date of electrotype printing from 1855.

(iii) from c.1856, degrees and minutes of latitude and longitude were marked within the borders.

The Old Series was replaced by the New Series or 'Second Edition' based on new survey work carried out between 1842 and 1893.

The growing importance of the Ordnance Survey as the national survey organisation sounded the death knell for the golden age of private enterprise in British cartography, although it did survive for some years side-by-side with the Survey, becoming progressively more dependant on it. Private cartography could not compete with either the financial or human resources of the Survey, which bought the finest equipment and built the best engraving, printing and selling organizations in the land. Maps increasingly became parts of a national survey rather than studies of individual counties with all their built-in appeal to local pride; and increased production brought down prices, making them available to a wider market.

However, private map-making did survive alongside the Survey by catering for the need for maps of larger areas at smaller scales, which was particularly stimulated by transport developments creating a demand for touring and excursion maps, firstly, for railways, then bicycles, then motor cars. Independent publishers increasingly based their specialized maps on the Survey's accurate surveys and, henceforth, private map-makers worked from a common base map.

Select Bibliography

ANDREWS, J. H.: *History in the Ordnance Maps. An Introduction for Irish Readers*. (1974)

ANDREWS, J. H.: *A Paper Landscape: The Ordnance Survey in Nineteenth-Century Ireland*. (1975)

CLOSE, SIR C.: *The Early Years of the Ordnance Survey*. (1926. New edition, 1969, containing an introduction by J. B. Harley.)

(*F*) HARLEY, J. B. AND O'DONOGHUE, Y.; *The Old-Series Ordnance Survey Maps of England and Wales*. (1976—to be produced in 10 vols.)

O'DONOGHUE, Y.: *William Roy 1726–1790: Pioneer of the Ordnance Survey*. (British Museum Pub.; 1977)

SEYMOUR, W. A. (ED.): *A History of the Ordnance Survey*. (1981)

SKELTON, R. A.: 'The Ordnance Survey, 1791–1825'. (*British Museum Quarterly*, 21; 1958)

SKELTON, R. A.: 'The Origins of the Ordnance Survey of Great Britain'. (*GJ*, 128; 1962)

N.B. David & Charles publish reprints of the first edition of the 1-inch Ordnance Survey of England and Wales with notes by Dr J. B. Harley.

LOCAL MAPS

Local maps may be readily available or they may be extremely difficult to find, for some were mass produced, some printed in limited numbers only, and some prepared only in a few copies. Town plans and environs' maps, where published, are generally available, but maps of hundreds, parishes and wards are less common for they were generally prepared for the small-circulation county and local histories. Large-scale detailed plans of estates, enclosures and tithe arrangements were drafted in manuscript for official purposes and have generally been appropriated by official archives. However, surveyors often made extra copies for office use, which were not deposited with authorities, and these sometimes appear on the market; and plans of estates were sometimes printed in larger numbers for sales or auctions (Fig. 22).

Select Bibliography

DOUCH, R.: 'Geography and the Local Historian'. (*Amateur Historian*, Vol 3, No. 7; 1958)

HARLEY, J. B.: *Maps for the local historian. A guide to the British sources*. (1972)

LAMBERT, A.: 'Early Maps and Local Studies'. (*Geography*, 61; 1956)

LOBEL, M. D.: 'The value of early maps as evidence for the topography of English Towns'. (*IM*, 22; 1968)

SKELTON, R. A.: 'Maps and the Local Historian'. (*Middlesex Local Hist. Council, Bulletin* 2)

SKELTON, R. A. AND HARVEY, P. D. A.: 'Local Maps and Plans before 1500'. (*Jour. of the Soc. of Archivists*, 3; 1969)

SKELTON, R. A. AND HARVEY, P. D. A.: *Local maps and plans from medieval England*. (forthcoming).

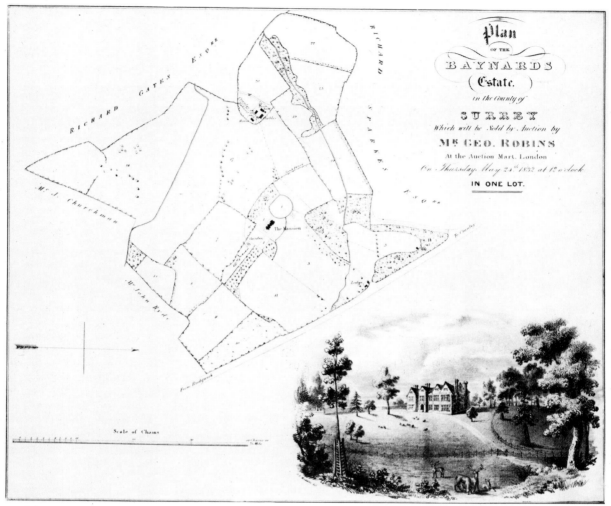

22 'Plan of the Baynards Estate in the County of Surrey' lithographed by G. E. Mudeley, 1832. *Photograph: Mills-Wight Studio*

ESTATE PLANS

The growth of an acquisitive class of landed gentry, nourished by the dissolution of the monasteries, the land redistributions of the Civil War and the Restoration, technical improvement and the enclosure of common lands, and the landowning pretensions of wealthy industrialists, created economic pressures demanding an accurate delineation of boundaries, acreages and land tenure. Surveys of farms and estates were clearly essential for efficient management and, consequently, the profession of estate surveyor developed and grew, providing a training ground for many important map-makers, such as Saxton, Norden, Symonson, Rocque, and Greenwood. From the sixteenth century, the traditional written descriptions of landed property were supplemented by large-scale, generally manuscript, plans giving details of field names, acreages, land holdings and use, buildings, rural industry, and communications. These finely detailed plans were often highly decorated, for the landowner expected a work of art as well as a practical plan, with an elegant title cartouche, border, scale, compass rose, a dedication to the patron with his coat-of-arms, a vignette of the owner's home, or simply motifs of the local countryside and contemporary life.

71

Estate plans, usually at the large-scale of about 3 to 6 chains to the inch, delineated the property of one landowner which might range from a single farm to a whole parish or parts of several parishes. Although most plans were of agricultural estates, some were produced of urban estates and some of rural industrial areas, even individual industrial works.

Estate plans were produced in numbers from the mid-sixteenth century as a result of progress in surveying techniques, but uniformity developed only in the seventeenth century as the varying local 'customary' miles were gradually replaced from about 1624 by Edmund Gunter's chain of 22 yards. The great period of estate plan production lasted from 1700 to about 1850 when the traditional manuscript plans were superseded by the large-scale work of the Ordnance Survey. Demand for plans was swelled by the increasing pace of both rural and urban change and the developing skills of the professional land surveyor produced ever more accurate, sophisticated and decorative maps.

Early estate surveys were naturally densest in lowland England since it was the most economically advanced area and the only region of concentrated land utilisation. However, as the agrarian revolution extended and marginal land was brought into cultivation, the mapping of estates spread into the English highlands, Wales and Scotland, and many plans exist for these areas from about 1750. Irish estates were mapped from the seventeenth century but the plans show little detail, possibly due to the state of underdevelopment of the land itself. Later Irish plans show disappointingly little extra information, but are notable for the ornate blank panels supplied for hand-written notes; and it was only the mid-eighteenth century influence of John Rocque and Bernard Scalé that persuaded Irish estate surveyors to pay greater attention to landscape detail and elegant decoration.

Select Bibliography
BAKER, A. R. H.: 'Local History and Early Estate Maps'. (*Amateur Historian*, 5; 1962)

EMMISON, F. G.: 'Estate Maps and Surveys'. (*History*, 48; 1963)

THIRD, B. M. W.: 'The Significance of Scottish Estate Plans and Associated Documents'. (*Scottish Studies*, 1; 1959)

THOMAS, C.: 'Estate Surveys as Sources in Historical Geography'. (*National Library of Wales Jour.*, 14; 1966)

ENCLOSURE MAPS

Common land was largely enclosed from the seventeenth century, but the pace of enclosure quickened as the agrarian revolution stimulated both private agreements and private Acts of Parliament, with the resulting maps being mainly found from about 1750. The private act would authorize a survey of the land in question by appointed commissioners who, in deciding their award, prepared a large-scale map. Generally, one copy of the map remained with the local parish and another was deposited with the Clerk of the Peace, but other copies were sometimes made and these infrequently appear on the market.

Enclosure maps show considerable variation in scale and style but the most detailed show a careful study of land ownership, types of tenure, field boundaries, land use and wasteland, footpaths, tracks and roads, settlements, and rural industry.

Early enclosure maps show transfers of land in the traditional agricultural areas of central England, but as the population growth of the nineteenth century forced up food prices and made farming more profitable, landowners progressively enclosed the common waste lands of marginally productive areas. Such maps of wasteland enclosure tend to be very sketchy for there was little detail to be represented. Parishes which had been gradually enclosed by private agreements often lack enclosure maps; and, similarly, since tithes were usually commuted at the time of enclosure, it was unnecessary for the Tithe Commissioners, following the Tithe Commutation Act of 1836, to carry out the full tithe survey and, consequently, areas well covered by enclosure maps are generally poorly covered by tithe surveys.

The enclosure movement followed a similar course in Scotland and Ireland, generating equivalent large-scale plans but prepared for individual landlords rather than Parliamentary requirements.

Select Bibliography
Several counties have published detailed information on their enclosure maps (see the detailed county listings). Consult the County Records Office for information. General background information is given by:

BEDFORD, F. T.: 'Enclosures in the 19th Century'. (*Amateur Historian*, Vol 1, No. 6; 1953)

CHALONER, W. H.: 'Bibliography of Recent Work on Enclosure, the Open Fields and related topics'. (*Agricultural History Review*, 2; 1954)

PARKER, R. A. C.: *Enclosures in the Eighteenth Century*. (Historical Assoc.; 1960)

TITHE SURVEYS

Tithes were annual taxes paid in kind to the rector of the parish. The Tithe Commutation Act of 1836 substituted a money rent based on average corn prices over the preceding seven years for this obsolete system and, in order to commute the local tithes, a large-scale survey was produced. Almost 12,000 parishes had tithes commuted; the main areas where tithe surveys were scarce were those, like the midland counties, where widespread earlier enclosure had generated tithe commutation. The Tithe Commissioners surveyed about 71% of England and Wales (Scotland and Ireland were not covered by the legislation) between 1836 and 1845, and a further 8% in the following ten years. This was the earliest attempt at large-scale mapping of the country and it provides a detailed picture of the rural landscape at the end of the agrarian revolution and before the great Victorian urban expansion.

Three sets of plans and written apportionments were prepared for the Tithe Redemption Commission, the Diocesan records, and the local parish respectively. The plan sizes varied with the parish size and ranged from 1 square foot to over 100 square feet. Various scales were used, ranging from 13 inches to 26 inches to the mile, but the plans themselves gave little information on their own; the apportionment was required in order to reconstruct land use and ownership. Each individual titheable plot was numbered on the plan and information on ownership, occupation, tithes payable, and use was contained in the accompanying documents. Since the tithe surveys were organised by the parishes and counties themselves, there was considerable variation in accuracy and presentation of material depending on the skill of the local surveyors. Although the surveys mainly covered rural areas, some did provide details of built-up areas, often giving larger-scale town plans as insets; others, however, left urban areas blank. These large tithe plans are now mainly found in official archives, but copies, produced unofficially for reference by surveyors, do very occasionally appear on the market.

Select Bibliography

Copies of tithe award maps are sometimes found in the local parish church, and copies and originals can be viewed at the County Record Office. Consult the guide to the county archives or the Public Record Office for information. General background information and guidance are given by:

KAIN, R. J. P.: 'The tithe commutation surveys'. (*ACa.*, 89; 1974)

KAIN, R. J. P.: 'Tithe Surveys and Landownership'. (*Hist. Geog.*, 1; 1975)

MUNBY, L. M.: 'Tithe apportionments and Maps'. (*History*, 54; 1969)

PRINCE, H. C.: 'The Tithe Surveys of the Mid-Nineteenth Century'. (*Agricultural Hist. Review*, 7; 1959)

PARISH AND WARD PLANS

Parish and ward plans were designed to satisfy the need for detailed local maps and also to tap the considerable market created by local interest and pride. Support and sometimes subscriptions were generated by dedications to local landowners, aldermen, and others of wealth and note in the small administrative unit. Plans generally concentrated on details of land and property ownership within the boundary of the parish or ward and were often decorated with dedication cartouches and vignettes of local buildings. However, the plans were usually unoriginal, being copied from earlier surveys. Unfortunately, these interesting local maps are difficult to find with only London ward plans being readily available.

LONDON WARD PLANS

1720: The first series of London ward plans was issued in John Strype's magnificent two-volume edition of John Stow's *Survey of London*. Some of the plans engraved by Richard Blome for Strype appear to be copies of sections from Ogilby & Morgan's large-scale plan of London and Westminster.

1738: William Maitland's *History & Survey of London* contained inaccurate ward plans mainly copied from Strype's edition of Stow by Benjamin Cole (Fig. 23). The vignettes of churches were taken from *Perspective views of all the ancient churches* ... (1736) by R. West and W. H. Toms. The plans, without revision, were reissued in the edition of 1760, in John Entick's versions of 1772 and 1775, and in *English architecture or the publick buildings of London and Westminster* in 1760.

1766: A series of ward plans, all probably prepared by Thomas Bowen, were published in the *London Magazine* and, after revision, in John Northouck's *A new history of London including Westminster and Southwark* in 1773.

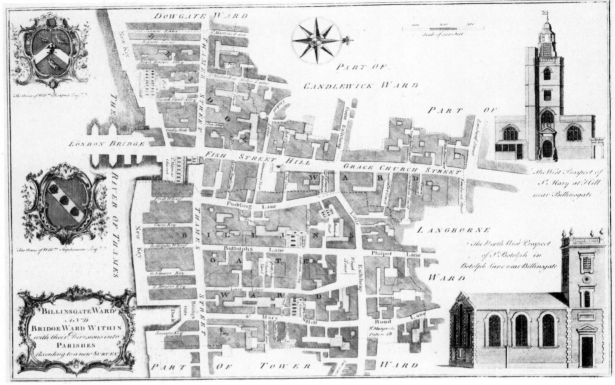

23 'Billinsgate Ward and Bridge Ward' by Benjamin Cole, 1760. *Photograph: Mills-Wight Studio*

1784: A series of ward plans appeared in William Thornton's *The new, complete and universal history . . . of London and Westminster* in 1784 and Richard Skinner's *A new and complete history and description of . . . London, Westminster . . . of c.*1796.

Although the above are the most commonly found plans, numerous other publications of the eighteenth and nineteenth centuries included ward plans of London copied from earlier works, particularly from large-scale plans.

Select Bibliography
HYDE, R.: *Ward Maps of the City of London.* (MCC, 38; 1967)

TOWN PLANS
There has always been a direct relationship between the importance of a town and the number of plans of it published. Many of today's major towns were mapped only when they grew to prominence in the nineteenth-century spread of industrialisation, while some important towns of the seventeenth and

eighteenth centuries, which were often mapped then, are of lesser note now, having been by-passed by subsequent development. Obviously London, as the major city of the British Isles, has been most frequently mapped (excluding variants, 394 printed plans are recorded between 1572 and 1845, and a further 132 in the short period from 1846 to 1865), but other regional centres such as Bristol, Cambridge, Norwich, Edinburgh and Dublin also have a long history of plans.

The early pictorial representations in medieval manuscripts evolved into the Tudor bird's-eye views which presented three-dimensional representations of buildings and other features usually on a flat ground plan. Most of these plans were prepared only in manuscript but some were engraved and printed such as Richard Lyne's plan of Cambridge of 1574 and Ralph Agas's large plan of Oxford of 1578–88. The greatest of the Tudor works was the *Civitates Orbis Terrarum*, produced in five volumes from 1573, with a sixth volume added in 1618, by George Braun & Franz Hogenberg which included bird's-eye views of Bristol, Cambridge, Canterbury,

24 'Nordovicum' by Braun & Hogenberg, c.1590

Chester, Dublin (with Cork, Limerick and Galway), Edinburgh, Exeter, London, Norwich (Fig. 24), Oxford (with Windsor), and York (with Shrewsbury, Lancaster and Richmond) taken from British plan-makers such as William Smith and William Cunningham. This monumental work is particularly interesting since it not only records the extent of town development but also offers an insight into the life of the period by decorating the plans with figures in costume and perspective views of famous buildings. A few similiar, miniature (approx. size: 95 × 150 mm; 3.75 × 5.9 in.) bird's-eye plans of towns in England, Scotland and Ireland, usually with figures or wildlife in the foreground and German and Latin text, by Daniel Meisner, were published in *Politica-Politica*, c.1700.

Throughout the seventeenth century town plans were part plan, part view and part elevation, with unfilled space around the town decorated with figures, animals and rural scenes.

The first systematic coverage of English and Welsh towns came in the 73 town plans incorporated as insets on his county maps by John Speed. Where possible, Speed took his material from earlier sources, such as the manuscript plans of William Smith, but, since many towns were being mapped for the first time, he had to conduct his own surveys and 45 plans have Speed's own 'Scale of Pases'. His plans represent an intermediate stage of development in the town plan with the modern two-dimensional plan evolving from the bird's-eye view; but his lead was not followed, probably because of lack of demand and the difficulties of actually surveying the towns, and his plans continued to be copied, without revision, for the next 150 years, notably by Rutger Hermannides in 1661, by Pierre van der Aa[18] in the *Galérie Agréable du Monde* in 1729, by J.C. Beer in *Das Neu = Geharnischte Gross = Britannien . . .* in 1690, and by Philip Lea in 1694 as insets in his edition of Saxton's *The Shires of England and Wales . . . .*

The first true plan appeared in 1676 when William Morgan published the large-scale plan of London prepared by himself and John Ogilby following the Great Fire of 1666. For the first time, buildings were shown in ground plan only, and, although Ogilby's projected volume of city plans never appeared, his great road-book *Britannia* adopted a similar two-dimensional approach to the representation of towns. Henceforward, pictorial views and building elevations would mainly appear only in blank areas beyond the town boundary, or in the plan border, or on additional sheets that were sold with the plan; and few publishers inserted building engravings on the map face. However, interestingly, copies of early plans were sometimes included in later town histories and other works and it is possible to find Tudor style plans engraved and printed in the eighteenth and nineteenth centuries (Fig. 25).

The urban expansion of the eighteenth century created interest in the mapping of towns and many new plans were produced (Fig. 26), often at unprecedented scales. Despite the disappearance of pictorial representations, there was little improvement in accuracy, and publishers often up-dated their plans simply by engraving town expansion around the outskirts where there was available blank space. However, the fine large-scale plans of such national figures as John Rocque (and the reduced versions of these by Andrew Dury) and such local land surveyors as William Fairbank and William Green gradually raised standards of accuracy. Increasingly, town plans were incorporated as insets on the large-scale county maps competing for the Royal Society of Arts' award; e.g., Benjamin Donn's prize-winning map of Devon of 1765 had inset plans of Exeter, Plymouth and Plymouth dock, and Captain Andrew Armstrong's 1775 map of 'Ayr Shire' had an inset plan of the county town.

The nineteenth century was the age of the town plan. Rapid town growth, stimulated by transport

25 Kingston upon Hull engraved by Isaac Taylor, from Hollar's plan of 1640, for the Rev. John Tickell's *The history of the town and county of Kingston upon Hull*, 1796. *Photograph: Mills-Wight Studio*

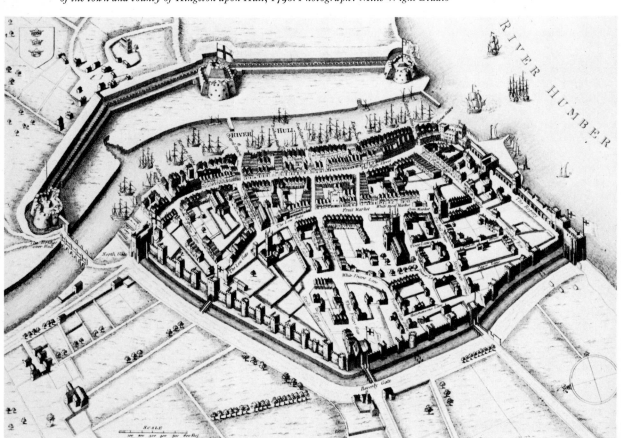

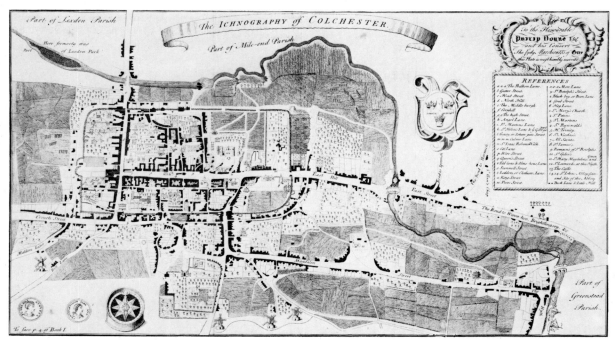

26 Colchester from Morant's *Essex*, c.1768. *By courtesy of Stanley Gibbons Antiquarian*

developments and, in particular, the coming of the railways, created increasing interest and civic pride. Town plans were published not only in atlases, geographical grammars and reference works, but also in a massive variety of gazetteers, street directories, urban histories, periodicals, and street plans and guide books for tourists. With the expansion of the railway system, the increasing

27 32: Colchester by Cole & Roper, 1805. *By courtesy of Ivan R. Deverall*

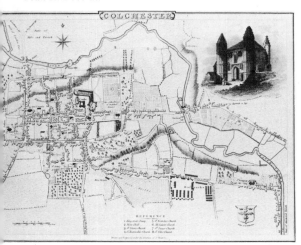

availability of relatively cheap and fast journeys and the growth of the travel habit, there was a staggering increase in the number of visitors to major towns. Costly folding maps in slip cases gave way to cheaper pocket versions concentrating on street names and transport facilities, and illustrating the 'sights' by engraved views of the principal buildings, bridges and parks. Any new developments thought to be of interest to the public were included and many of these nineteenth-century plans offer a fascinating picture of urban development by constantly devising symbols to represent new features such as public baths, police courts, water works, board schools, railway stations and gasometers (Fig. 28).

Several fine series of plans were published in the early and mid-nineteenth century. Thomas Moule included a few plans with his county maps; the Society for the Diffusion of Useful Knowledge published some in its two-volume atlas; and John Tallis published a series of beautifully engraved, decorative plans in the 1850s. However, the most generally available are the 21 attractive plans by Cole & Roper and the two series of plans, based on the Ordnance Survey, prepared by Lieutenant R. K. Dawson in connection with the re-organisation of municipal government resulting from the First Reform Act of 1832.

77

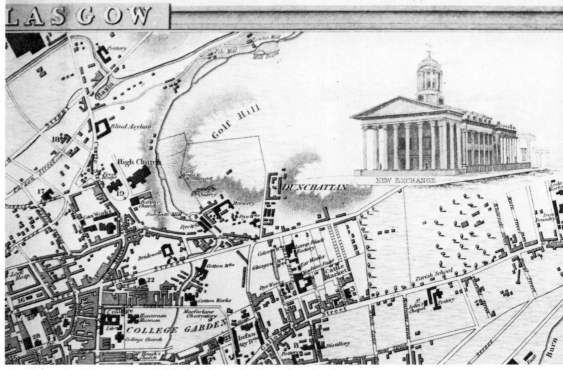

28 Glasgow by John Dower, published by Orr & Smith, c.1830 (detail)

Dawson's plans were unusual in giving wide coverage to the towns of Scotland and Ireland, which, with the obvious exceptions of Edinburgh and Dublin which had been covered in most major series of European and world cities, were poorly provided for. Few plans of either Scottish or Irish towns were published before the middle of the eighteenth century, but from the 1770s in Scotland engravers, such as James & Robert Kirkwood, and professional land surveyors, such as Charles Ross, were producing plans of some major towns. The most impressive series of Scottish town plans was that produced by John Wood in his atlas of 1818–30. There were even fewer early town plans of Ireland, the coverage being mainly limited to the large-scale surveys of John Rocque, and Richards & Scalé (Fig. 29). However, during the nineteenth century, Scotland and Ireland experienced an increase in town plan production in the same way (but at a slower rate) and for the same reasons as England and Wales had earlier.

The increasing commerce of Britain generated the production of commercial directories to aid businessmen, many of which contained town plans often taken from earlier, out-dated sources. Particularly worthy of mention were the reliable, finely engraved plans contained in Edward Baines's *History, Directory & Gazetteer of the County of York* (1822–23) and its companion volume for Lancashire (1824–25) (Fig. 30).

By the mid-nineteenth century commercial map publishers were able to base their town plans on the official large-scale plans of the tithe surveys and the Ordnance Survey, and although many plans were produced after this period, few were the result of private surveys.

Plans were also produced of sections of towns to illustrate particular features and schemes. Property and landholding plans are known from the sixteenth century, but most detailed sectional plans date from the late eighteenth and nineteenth centuries with their explosion of: public utility schemes for water supplies, lighting, sewerage and drainage, paving, etc.; housing schemes; transport schemes; and numerous other proposed local improvements and developments. Vast numbers of very large-scale plans, usually at 4 inches to the mile, but sometimes up to 25 inches to the mile, were prepared by local

29 Waterford by William Richards & Bernard Scalé, 1764. *By permission of the British Library (Maps 13760(1))*

30 'Manchester and its environs' by Edward Baines, 1824. *By permission of the British Library (Maps 1.c.10.)*

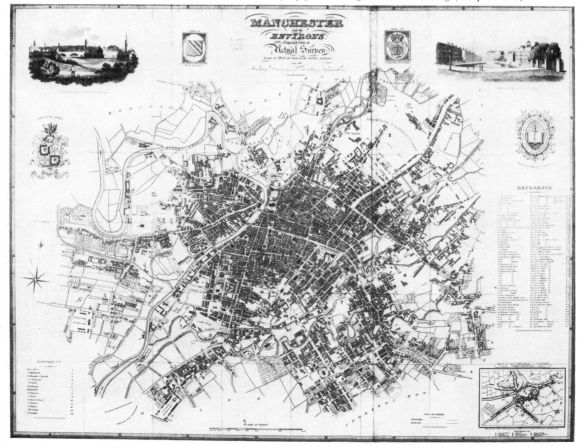

contractors and companies, and later, from the 1830s, by the local authorities themselves. Evolving political and social legislation generated large-scale plans showing changes in administrative arrangements and public health provision, and many unique plans resulted from sociological and medical studies. However, most of these large-scale specialised plans have, by now, been acquired by official archives and, although they are sometimes available, most collectors must content themselves with the smaller-scale plans of towns.

It is often very difficult to trace the origin of a plan when it has been removed from its source publication and, all too often, dates are assigned to such plans on flimsy evidence or by guesswork.

Select Bibliography
BAGLEY, J. J.: 'County Maps and Town Plans'. (*Historical Interpretation No. 2: Sources of English History 1540 to the Present Day*; 1971)

(*F*) BRAUN, G. AND HOGENBERG, F.: *Civitates Orbis Terrarum 1572–1618*. 3 vols. Preface by R. V. Tooley. Introduction by R. A. Skelton. (1965)

(*F*) COLE, G. AND ROPER, J.: *Plans of English Towns . . . 1810*. (1970)

FORDHAM, A.: *Town plans of the British Isles*. (MCC, 22; 1965)

KEUNING, J.: 'The "Civitates" of Braun and Hogenberg'. (*IM*, 7; 1963)

SKELTON, R. A.: 'Tudor Town Plans in John Speed's Theatre'. (*Arch. Jour.*, 108; 1952)

BELFAST:
EWART, L. M.: 'Belfast maps'. (*Ulster Jour. Arch.*, 1; 1894–5)

BRISTOL:
(*F*) BRISTOL AND GLOUCESTERSHIRE ARCH. SOC.: *A Gloucestershire and Bristol Atlas*. (1961)

PRITCHARD, J. E.: 'Old Plans and Views of Bristol'. (*Trans. of the Bristol and Gloucestershire Arch. Soc.*, 48; 1928)

WILLIAMS, A. F.: 'Bristol Port Plans and Improvement Schemes of the 18th Century'. (*Trans. of the Bristol and Gloucestershire Arch. Soc.*, 81; 1962)

CAMBRIDGE:
CLARK, J. W.: 'John Hamond's Plan of Cambridge, 1592. (*Proc. of the Cambridge Antiquarian Soc.*, 7; 1888)

CLARK, J. W. AND GRAY, A.: *Old plans of Cambridge, 1574–1798*. 2 parts. (1921)

CARICKFERGUS:
SWANTON, W. M.: 'Maps of Carickfergus'. (*Ulster Jour. Arch.*, 2; 1895–6)

CHICHESTER:
BUTLER, D. J.: *The Town Plans of Chichester 1595–1898*. (1972)

CORK:
CARBERRY, E.: 'The Development of Cork City (as shown by the maps of the City prior to the Ordnance Survey map of 1841–2).' (*Jour. of Cork Historical and Arch. Soc.*, 48; 1943)

DUBLIN:
MCCROSSAN, J. L.: 'Notes on some Dublin city maps'. (*Irish Booklover*, 26; 1938)

(*F*) ROCQUE, JOHN: *Dublin City, 1756*, Introduction by J. Andrews. (1977)

EDINBURGH:
COWAN, W.: *The Maps of Edinburgh, 1544–1929*. (Edinburgh Public Libraries; 1932)

ROYAL SCOTTISH GEOGRAPHICAL SOCIETY: *The Early Views and Maps of Edinburgh, 1544–1852*. (1919)

EXETER:
CONSTABLE, K. M.: 'The Early Printed Plans of Exeter, 1587–1724'. (Reprinted from the *Trans. of the Devonshire Assoc.*; 1932)

HASTINGS:
HASTINGS MUSEUM: *Catalogue of maps and plans in the exhibition of local maps*. (1936)

KINGSTON UPON HULL:
SHEPPARD, T.: *The Evolution of Kingston upon Hull as shown by its Plans*. (1911)

LEEDS:
BONSER, K. G. AND NICHOLS, H.: *Printed maps and plans of Leeds, 1711–1900*. (Thoresby Soc.; 1960)

LONDON:
The Guildhall Library, the London Topographical Society, and Harry Margary (Lympne Castle, Kent) publish facsimile early plans of London.

BAPTIST, SISTER M.: 'Eighteenth-Century Maps and Estate Plans of Bromley, Beckenham and Penge'. (*ACa.*, 81; 1967)

DARLINGTON, I: 'Edwin Chadwick and the first large-scale Ordnance Survey of London'. (*Trans. of the London and Middlesex Arch. Soc.*, 22; 1969)

DARLINGTON, I. AND HOWGEGO, J.: *The Printed Maps of London, c.1553–1850.* (1964; reprinted 1978 with revisions).

GLANVILLE, P.: *London in Maps.* (1972)

HYDE, R.: *Printed Maps of Victorian London, 1851–1900.* (1975)

HYDE, R.: 'Maps that made cabmen honest'. (*MC*; Dec 1979)

LONDONDERRY:
COLBY, T.: *Ordnance survey of the county of Londonderry: memoir of city and N.W. liberties.* (1837)

MANCHESTER:
LEE, J.: *Maps and Plans of Manchester and Salford 1650–1843.* (1957)

(*F*) MANCHESTER PUBLIC LIBRARIES: *Maps of Manchester, 1650–1848.* (Manchester Public Libraries Committee; 1969)

NORWICH:
CHUBB, T. AND STEPHEN, G. H.: *A Descriptive List of the Printed Maps of Norfolk, 1574–1916: Descriptive List of Norwich Plans, 1541–1914.* (1928)

STEPHEN, G.: *A Descriptive list of Norwich Plans and the Principal Early Views, 1514–1914.* (1928)

OXFORD:
AGAS, HOLLAR AND LOGGAN: 'Old Plans of Oxford'. (*Oxford Historical Soc.*, 38; 1898)

PORTSMOUTH:
HODSON, D.: *Maps of Portsmouth before 1801.* (Portsmouth Record Series; 1978)

SHREWSBURY:
FIELD STUDIES COUNCIL: *Old Maps of Shrewsbury.*

SOUTHAMPTON:
(*F*) SOUTHAMPTON CORPORATION: *Southampton Maps from Elizabethan Times.* (1964)

WELCH, E: 'The Earliest Maps of Southampton'. (*CJ*, 2; 1965)

WATERFORD:
DOWNEY, E.: *The Story of Waterford.* (1914)

N.B. Whitehall Press Ltd., Maidstone, Kent, publishes reproductions of town plans from the atlases of John Tallis, the Society for the Diffusion of Useful Knowledge and *The Weekly Dispatch*.

MAPS OF ENVIRONS

Although the county was the accepted unit for most early maps, it was inappropriate for showing the zones of commercial influence, the outlying residential areas, and the satellite villages of major towns. There was a clear demand for maps of surrounding areas; John Rocque defined the potential market for his map of the country ten miles round London as 'all Directors of Insurance Offices, and Commissioners of Turnpikes, ... all Church-Wardens and Overseers, ... all Persons who have occasion to travel round this Metropolis for business, health, or pleasure; and lastly ... curious persons at home and abroad'. Even in the late seventeenth century, the wealthy retreated from the congestion and 'hubbub' of the town to the quiet of the surrounding country, and there was, consequently, a considerable, potentially lucrative, market offered by this early, prosperous, 'stock-broker belt'. Robert Morden's 1686 map of 20 miles round London tried to tap this market by emphasising 'Gentlemens' Houses' and over a century later John Cary was equally ingratiating in his concentration on the presentation of country houses and estates.

Interest in areas surrounding towns was boosted in the second half of the eighteenth century by the formation of the turnpike trusts and the resulting improvement in roads and increase in traffic. Travel by private carriage and public coach stimulated demand for environs' maps and this was magnified by the subsequent rapid development of, firstly, the canals and, secondly, the railways (Fig. 31). The Georgian and early Victorian periods witnessed the publication of maps of the environs of many British towns which are of particular interest since they often show today's heavily populated suburban belts as rural areas with local economies built on the supply of perishable foodstuffs to the then small urban population.

The improvement in transport facilities, combined with greater affluence and leisure, stimulated the production of excursion maps to satisfy the demands of the day-trip into the countryside. Excursion maps were published showing public transport connections to places of interest in neighbouring areas, and later in the century, maps of accessible areas were produced specifically for the new pastimes of cycling and motoring.

POCKET MAPS

Pocket maps were usually folded, or sometimes dissected and mounted on linen, so that they were easily portable for the traveller. They became

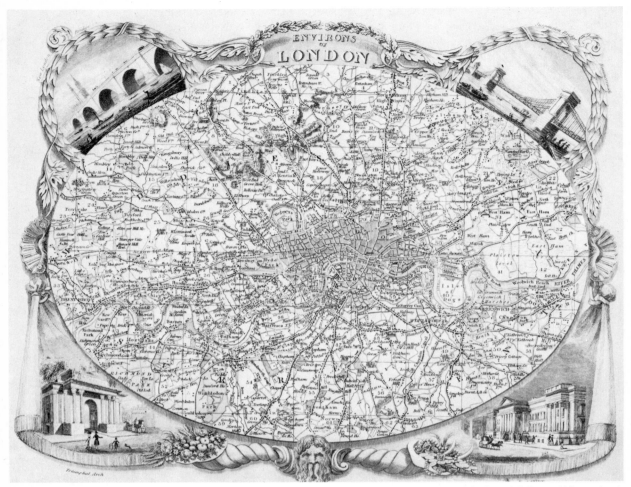

31 82(i): 'Environs of London' engraved by W. Schmollinger, 1837. *By permission of the British Library (Maps 5.b.4.)*

fashionable in the eighteenth century and by the beginning of the nineteenth century were being sold in large numbers in their attractive slip-cases. There was much competition between map-makers in this field and the cases themselves often bore elaborate titles set on marbled paper to catch the eye of potential purchasers (Fig. 32). However, the slip case had its obvious drawbacks for it was a difficult process to consult the map quickly in the open, particularly on a breezy day. Early experiments to develop alternative forms, such as George Cruchley's 1830 'New Plan of London in Miniature' which was published as a small book with 'decided advantages over all other methods by avoiding the unpleasant necessity of unfolding the whole in the street',[19] proved unpopular.

The growth of the travel habit and the increasing stream of sight-seeing day-trippers to the larger towns generated demand for cheaper, more easily handled pocket excursion maps showing omnibus and railway routes, stations and timetables, and coach and cab fares. Some maps catered for the tourist; Edward Mogg, for example, published guides 'For Viewing London in eight days'.[19] Rival publishers competed fiercely for a share of this lucrative market by introducing novelties and claiming to cover the latest urban developments, usually without justification for they paid little attention to accuracy or change. A significant improvement was the replacement of the slip case by covers attached to the map itself so that it could be folded between the protection of the two covers.

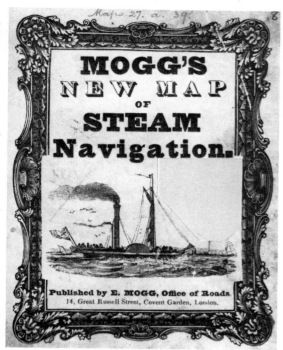

32 The slipcase cover of 'Mogg's New Map of Steam Navigation', 1837. *By permission of the British Library (Maps 27.a.39.)*

This innovation not only made the map easier to consult but also reduced its cost, thus extending the market even further.

TRANSPORT AND COMMUNICATIONS

The early concentration of detailed land survey work on the requirements of the rural estate owner and his agricultural improvements was diversified in the late eighteenth and nineteenth centuries by the promotional requirements of the great transport engineering projects stimulated by industrial and commercial development. Maps showing the general proposals for a scheme were produced to create interest and raise the necessary finance; but the necessity of gaining Parliamentary approval by private Act for the construction or improvement of a road, river, canal or railway created a demand also for accurate surveys. From 1792 promoters were required to submit a detailed plan indicating land ownership affected by a proposed route, and from 1807 these were at scales of at least 4 inches to the mile. The proposed route and the adjacent land were usually represented by a large plan showing landholdings and strongly emphasising engineering features, often with additional information supplied by cross-sections showing gradients and heights.

Such large-scale plans are in short supply, but the promotional maps which were either engraved, or, in the mid-nineteenth century, lithographed, to satisfy the appetite of a communication-minded public are more generally available.

With the rapid development of transport facilities, commercial pressures forced publishers to update continually their general maps, often with the claim that the maps were the most modern available, despite the fact that only transport representation had been revised. These revisions frequently provide a means of dating editions, particularly of nineteenth-century maps lacking a clear chronological identity.

ROADS

Roads were generally added to British county maps only from the last years of the seventeenth century, but this was, in fact, pre-dated by two types of specialised road coverage: the road book and the road map.

Road books were basically tables of distances along roads, with details of the route and descriptive notes; if they had maps at all, they would be only small index maps of the roads covered. They had a long history: originating in pilgrim and merchant guides of the Middle Ages, they were developed by Tudor topographers and became essential aids for travellers until they all but disappeared in the mid-nineteenth century when the railways superseded the roads as passenger carriers. Many map-makers, including John Cary, Daniel Paterson, John Rocque, and John Ogilby & William Morgan, produced these itineraries in addition to their maps. John Norden was particularly inventive for he not only developed the triangular distance table in his 1625 *England: An Intended Guyde for English Travailers* and thus established a format which is still in use today; but also actually marked some roads on his few county surveys (as did the herald William Smith, following Norden's lead, on some of his so-called 'Anonymous' maps of 1602–3, and other Norden imitators, such as John Bill in 1626).

The first graphic delineation of roads was John Ogilby's influential *Britannia* of 1675 which established the practice of representing the road on a continuous unfolding strip (Fig. 33). These magnificent maps, with their fine cartouches, established the use of the statute mile of 1760 yards and were the

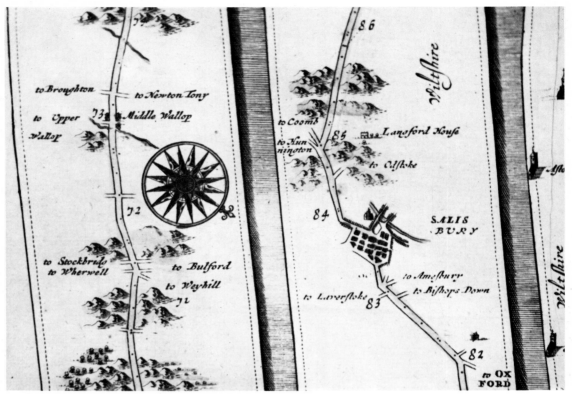

33 85(i): Andover—'Crookhorn' by John Ogilby, 1675 (detail)

34 19: 'Crookhorn'—Weymouth by Emanuel Bowen & John Owen, 1720. *Photograph: Mills-Wight Studio*

first measured maps of the major roads of England and Wales. However, Ogilby's volume was too cumbersome and heavy to be of practical value to the traveller, and publishers gradually recognised a growing demand for a smaller, portable version of the strip road maps. This realisation created a highly competitive situation in the early eighteenth century with Bowen & Owen's *Britannia Depicta* eventually dominating the market over the rival publications of John Senex and Thomas Gardner.

The smaller scales of these reduced versions necessarily diminished both decoration and detail, but they were, nevertheless, immensely popular and the plates and pirated versions continued to be published for most of the century not only by the original publishers but also by others, such as Jefferys, Desnos, Kitchin, and Bowles. Despite this proliferation of road maps, the period was actually one of serious road deterioration. Parochial road maintenance was half-hearted and unskilled, and this neglect had created dangerous conditions: in 1749 John Wesley described an Essex road as having 'ruts . . . so deep and uneven that the horses could scarce stand' and in 1770 Arthur Young reported that a Preston road had 'ruts which I actually measured four feet deep and floating in mud'.[20]

Industrial and commercial progress stimulated road improvement by the turnpike trusts. The intensified improvement following the General Turnpike Act of 1773 and the spread of coach services generated a further crop of road strips and traveller's atlases which concentrated on roads. These road maps of the late eighteenth and early nineteenth century are among the most beautifully engraved work of the period and fine series were published by John Cary, Charles Cooke and George Carrington Gray, Laurie & Whittle, Edward Mogg, Daniel Paterson, and Charles Smith. And, at last, the roads of England and Wales had been re-measured: Ogilby's measurements of 1675 were supplanted by Cary's measurement of 10,000 miles of roads for the Post Office.

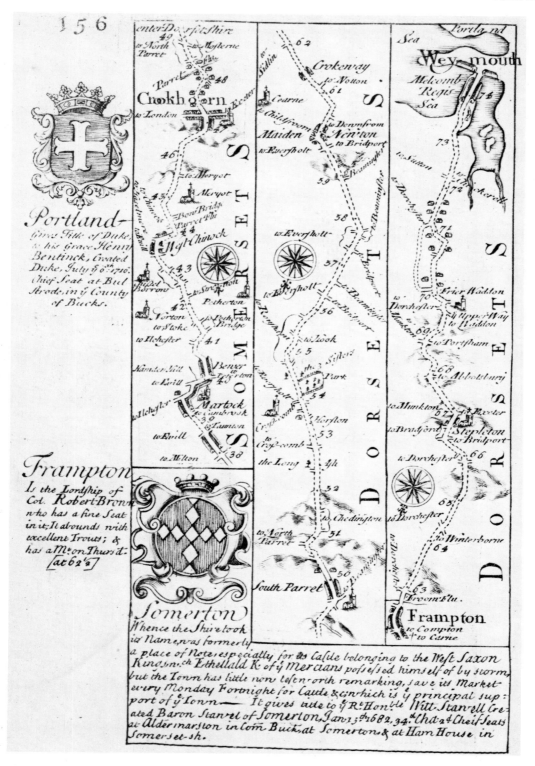

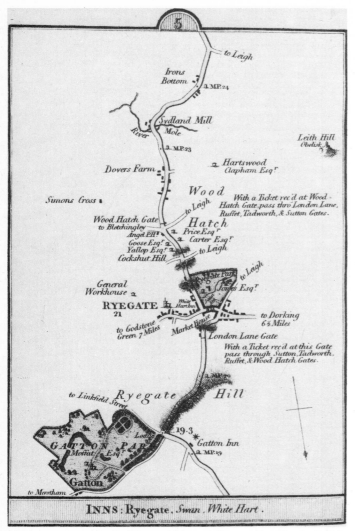

Map labels:
to Leigh · Irons Bottom · MP.24 · Sydland Mill · Mole · River · Leith Hill Obelisk · M.P.23 · Dovers Farm · Hartswood Clapham Esqʳ · Wood · Simons Cross · With a Ticket rec'd at Wood Hatch Gate, pass thro' London Lane, Ruffet, Tadworth, & Sutton Gates. · to Leigh · Hatch · Wood Hatch Gate · to Bletchingley · Price Esqʳ · Angel P.H. · Goose Esqʳ · Carter Esqʳ · Yallop Esqʳ · to Leigh · Cockshut Hill · to Leigh · Jones Esqʳ · General Workhouse · White Hart Inn · RYEGATE 21 · to Godstone Green 7 Miles · to Dorking 6½ Miles · Market House · London Lane Gate · With a Ticket rec'd at this Gate pass through Sutton, Tadworth, Ruffet, & Wood Hatch Gates. · Ryegate Hill · to Linkfield Street · GATTON PARK · Lodge · Moffat Esqʳ · 19.3 · Gatton Inn · M.P.19 · Gatton · to Merstham · INNS: Ryegate, Swan, White Hart.

35 101(i): The road 'through Ryegate' by Charles Smith, 1800. *By permission of the British Library (Maps C.27.e.16.)*

The turnpike trusts were a unique influence on road development until they were inexorably driven out of business by the railways. Their short period of influence is fascinatingly recorded on strip and road maps which often gave details of toll charges, overlapping trusts, through tickets and best value. The trusts also produced large-scale plans of proposals and improvements, showing the areas immediately adjacent to the road, for deposit with the authorities.

Since Ogilby had covered the roads of only England and Wales, his imitators accepted the same limited parameters and Scotland and Ireland received scant coverage on road maps or in itineraries. No road strip maps of either country were published until the fine works of George Taylor & Andrew Skinner in the late 1770s, and generally both countries lack the range of specialised road maps produced for England in the early nineteenth century, although some map-makers did condescend to extend their road maps north to Edinburgh and later Glasgow.

Ogilby's work of 1675 was not only influential in generating strip and road maps, but was all-pervasive in persuading map-makers to include roads on their maps. Roads were shown by John Seller and others from 1676, and Robert Morden produced the first series of county maps showing roads in 1695; by the early years of the eighteenth century, roads were a uniform feature on maps. They continued to be a pronounced feature throughout the eighteenth and nineteenth centuries, and were, in fact, given added significance by the inventions of the bicycle, the pneumatic tyre, and the motor car which inspired cycling and motoring maps in large numbers. Such was the level of demand that remarkably old plates were re-used after suitable modification; Cary's plates, for instance, were issued as touring maps until the 1920s.

Select Bibliography

DUCKHAM, B. F.: 'Turnpike Records'. (*History*, 53; 1968)

FORDHAM, SIR H. G.: *Notes on British and Irish itineraries and road books.* (1912; reprinted in *Studies in Carto-Bibliography*, 1914 and 1969)

FORDHAM, SIR H. G.: *Studies in Carto-Bibliography British and French and in the Bibliography of Itineraries and Road-Books.* (1914; reprinted 1969)

FORDHAM, SIR H. G.: 'Roads and Travel before Railways in Hertfordshire and elsewhere'. (*Trans. of the Hertfordshire Nat. Hist. Soc.*; 1915)

FORDHAM, SIR H. G.: 'Road-Books and Itineraries bibliographically considered. [With a Catalogue of the Road-Books and Itineraries of Great Britain and Ireland to the year 1850]'. (*The Library*, 13; 1916)

FORDHAM, SIR H. G.: *Road-books and itineraries of Ireland 1647–1850.* (1923)

FORDHAM, SIR H. G.: *Road-books and itineraries of Great Britain 1570–1850.* (1924)

FORDHAM, SIR H. G.: *Roads on English and French maps at the end of 17th century.* (1926)

FORDHAM, SIR H. G.: 'The Road Books of Wales with a Catalogue 1775–1850'. (*ACs*, 82; 1927)

FORDHAM, SIR H. G.:: 'The Earliest Tables of the Highways of England and Wales, 1541–1561'. (*The Library*, New Series, Vol. 8; 1927)

FRENCH, E. C. W.: 'Turnpike Trusts'. (*Amateur Historian*, Vol. 2, No. 1; 1954)

SPRENT, F. P.: 'The Beginnings of the Road Map in Europe'. (*Roadmaker*, 5; 1926)

WATERWAYS

Rivers were widened, deepened and straightened from the sixteenth century to improve navigation, but it was the canals that were the most important advance in inland water transport, and, indeed, the most commercially significant transport development before the coming of the railways. Between the 1760s and the 1830s the country was covered with a network of canals whose expansion was halted only by railway development. Not only were plans produced for canals actually built, but they were also prepared to promote schemes which never progressed beyond the drawing-board. Many ambitious schemes were scrapped due to lack of finance, choice of alternative route, or railway competition; but map-makers, anticipating construction, sometimes added these non-existent canals to their maps. Since it was common practice to up-date maps by marking canals only proposed or under-construction as completed, care should be taken in using canal evidence to date maps, although generally it tends to be more reliable than railway evidence due to the smaller number of canals projected and constructed.

A few plans of river improvements have survived, and large-scale canal plans showing landholdings, lock sites, wharves, navigation obstructions, and water-powered industry occasionally appear on the market; but it is the 'prospectus' plans, produced as propaganda to satisfy public interest and generate capital and support, that are generally available. (Figs. 36, 37). The leading map-producers, such as Cary and Stockdale, published plans of the proposals and undertakings of Brindley, Smeaton, Whitworth and other canal engineers for promoters and shareholders; and public curiosity was satisfied by coverage in such popular periodicals as the *Gentleman's Magazine*. Many general maps showing the canal network on a regional or national basis were published by such major London map-producers as Andrews and Faden; and George Bradshaw is worthy of special mention for his fine series of regional maps 'of the greatest importance to those who are interested in the union or extension of the present Canals, Railways or Turnpike Roads'.

Select Bibliography

HADFIELD, C.: Several books on the canals of England and Wales.

LINDSAY, J.: *The Canals of Scotland*. (1968)

WILLAN, T. S.: *River Navigation in England 1600–1750*. (1936)

36 'A Plan of the River Tees, and of the intended Navigable Canal from Stockton by Darlington to Winston . . .', engraved by Thomas Kitchin, 1768. *By permission of the British Library (K.6.31.)*

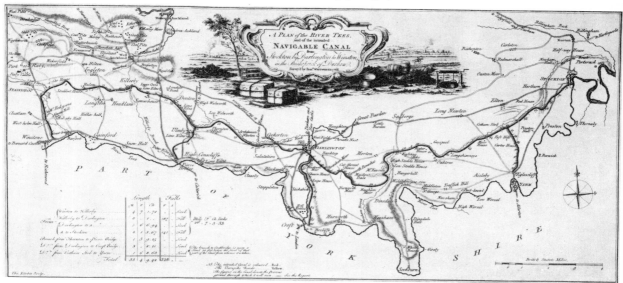

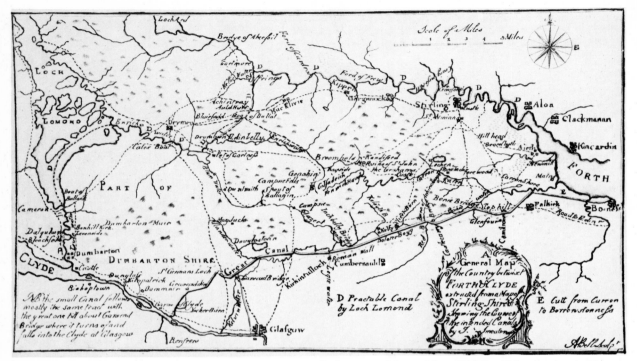

37 'A General Map of the Country betwixt Forth & Clyde extracted from a Map of Stirling Shire showing the Course of the intended Canals by J. Smeaton' engraved by Andrew Bell, 1768, *Photograph: Mills-Wight Studio*

RAILWAYS

In many ways the production of railway plans parallels that of canal plans. Large-scale plans were prepared for official deposition, but it is the smaller plans designed to interest potential shareholders that are generally available. Like the canals, many railways were projected, plans drawn up, and maps published, but the lines themselves were never constructed despite the addition of these proposed lines to their maps as fact by some cartographers. Line openings were often anticipated well in advance of the event and since, frequently, there was no indication of the 'proposed' or unopened state of the railway, dating maps by the extent of railway development should be cautious.

The most reliable railway maps were: those of Zachary Macauley, a clerk at the Railway Clearing House; the large maps and sections by George Bradshaw; and the periodic revisions of the Old Series Ordnance Survey maps. However, the enormous interest in railway development stimulated the production of maps and plans to satisfy public demand. Travellers began to be supplied with detailed railway route guides and timetable maps,

and the railway companies themselves produced promotional material advertising their facilities and services (Fig. 38). As the railway network spread from its London centre, commercial map publishers grew increasingly conscious of the competition to offer the most up-to-date information. Unfortunately, existing engraved plates could be added to relatively easily, and, as development advanced swiftly from year-to-year, publishers often simply added line extensions to existing maps, either by engraving, hand colouring, or, more frequently, lithography, without up-dating any other information, and issued them with altered titles. Most publishers offered general and regional maps emphasising railways (Fig. 39), but George Frederick Cruchley was particularly prominent with his re-issues of Cary's maps with railways and stations added.

Select Bibliography

GARNETT, D.: 'The Railway Maps of Zachary Macauley and John Airey'. (*Railway and Canal Historical Soc. Journ.*; 1959–71)

SIMMONDS, J.: *The Railways of Britain; An Historical Introduction.* (1961) (contains a full bibliography)

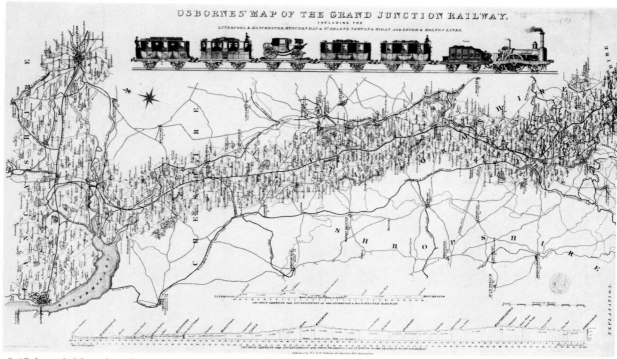

38 'Osborne's Map of the Grand Junction Railway', c.1837. *By permission of the British Library (Maps 1223(15))*

39 'Tallis's Railway Map of Great Britain' by John Rapkin, from *The Illustrated Atlas of Modern History of the World*, c.1851 (detail). *Photograph: Mills-Wight Studio*

THEMATIC MAPS

By the nineteenth century a reliable foundation of topographical information had been laid and map-makers were able to turn their attention to the representation of data previously unrecorded or overshadowed by the abundance of other detail. Distributional maps were built on a skeleton base to express a wealth of themes and were devised to represent every aspect of life that could be classified. Although thematic maps have a long history, their heyday was the nineteenth century with its passion for social reform and improvement. Innumerable commissions published reports, packed with surveys, on town improvement in the first half of the century. Transport proposals statutorily required detailed plans, as did enclosures and tithe commutations; and there were also fledgling sociological and public-health surveys.

A common theme was historical; many map-makers added maps of ancient Britain to their county or regional series. Saxon and Roman Britain showed the ancient kingdoms and major provinces respectively and were often decorated with vignettes of rulers, assassinations, coronations, and so on. The maps of the Saxon Heptarchy by Speed, Blaeu (Fig. 40) and Jansson are particularly magnificent. Maps

40 The Saxon Heptarchy by Joan Blaeu, 1645 (detail). *By courtesy of Ivan R. Deverall*

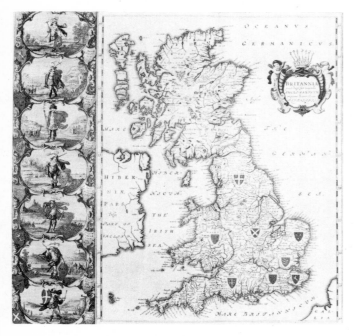

of the 'Invasions' marked all major battle sites with dates and other details.

The application of new scientific techniques to the study of the earth's surface, not only produced geological maps, but also stimulated the preparation of detailed and ingenious soil and land utilization maps.

The new scientific awareness of correlations inspired the production of public-health maps showing the incidence of disease. The terrible cholera epidemics of the 1830s, 40s and 50s inspired the mapping of outbreaks by Robert Baker in Leeds, by Thomas Shapter in Exeter, and by John Snow in London. These medical maps clearly established the relationship between cholera outbreaks, open sewers, and inadequate water supply. The consequent growth of public-health consciousness led to the regular mapping of the commoner infectious diseases such as diphtheria and scarlet fever, and to numerous public utility schemes for improved sanitation, sewerage, water supply, etc., which required the preparation of large-scale plans.

The awakening social conscience led also to the study of the distribution of wealth and poverty. The Commissioners for the Irish Census of 1841 published a plan of Dublin which categorised social conditions by differentiating population densities, literacy, and types of accommodation. The outstanding study of poverty, however, appeared later in the century when Charles Booth published his *Life and Labour of the People of London* showing the depths of deprivation of the urban poor.

The Victorians even managed to map their prejudices and obsessions. The temperance movement occasionally retreated from its 'tub-thumping' approach to attempt a serious, systematic study of the demon drink to establish the relationship between alcohol and poverty. Anti-drink maps not only covered the obvious major industrial centres but also such lesser centres as Norwich and Great Yarmouth. Since the site of every public house was marked, these temperance maps must surely have been an indispensable aid to the excursioning inebriate. Political maps marked areas voting Whig or Tory, religious and racial maps were produced to record relevant distributions, and geographical games were designed for the edification of the young (Fig. 41).

The spread of communications and the increased potential of travel was another Victorian obsession. In addition to the large-scale plans required for transport proposals, innumerable travelling maps,

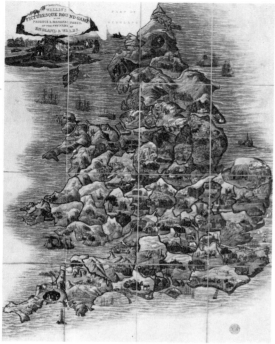

41 'Wallis's Picturesque Round Game of the Produce & Manufactures of the Counties of England & Wales', c.1795. *By permission of the British Library (Maps C.24.b.16.)*

street guides and excursion maps were produced for the insatiable hunger of the newly mobile populace. Communications' maps were produced for businesses extending their spheres of activity; for example, details of telegraphic lines and stations were supplied by Henry George Collins and George Frederick Cruchley; and Kelly & Co. produced a series of postal maps in their Post Office Directories, and later, 'corrected to the present time, December 1860', in the *Post Office Directory Atlas of England and Wales.*

The thematic map had by 1850 become a vital tool for both physical and social scientists, for businessmen, for town planners, for health authorities, and, indeed, for the general public. Any relationship that could be expressed geographically could be expressed on a thematic map, and increasingly information was presented in terms of distributions.

Select Bibliography
GILBERT, E. W.: 'Pioneer Maps of Health and Disease in England'. (*GJ*, 124; 1958)

THROWER, N. J. W.: 'Edmond Halley and Thematic Geo-cartography', in *The Compleat Plattmaker*; (1978).

GEOLOGICAL MAPS
Geological maps were produced by many commercial map-makers such as Johnston, Lizars, Reynolds, Stanford, J. & C. Walker (Fig. 118), and Wyld, in the mid-nineteenth century, following the pioneering work of William Smith, 'Mineral Surveyor', with his great correlation of rocks and fossils. Smith's 'A Delineation of the Strata of England and Wales with part of Scotland' at 5 miles to the inch, published in 15 sheets in 1815, greatly surpassed the efforts of the pioneering eighteenth-century French cartographers to represent geological and mineralogical information, and was the first modern geological map. Considering the importance of geology to engineering and land development, it is surprising that satisfactory geological maps appeared so relatively late; but the science developed only slowly with the Geological Society founded in 1807 and the official Geological Survey (Fig. 42) founded only in 1835 (however, the publication of the first 1 inch to 1 mile geological maps, prepared by the Survey's first Director, Henry Thomas De La Beche, dated from 1832).

Geological divisions were always boldly coloured by hand, or, later, by the new colour printing process of chromolithography; and the traditional county format was often adopted to display geological formations and strata.

Select Bibliography
BOUD, R. C.: 'The early development of British Geological Maps'. (*IM*, 27; 1975)

NORTH, F. J.: *Geological maps, their history and development, with special reference to Wales.* (1928)

READING UNIVERSITY: *The history and development of geological cartography: catalogue of the exhibition of geological maps in the university library . . .* (1967).

SHEPPARD, T.: *The evolution of topographical and geological maps.* (1920)

PLAYING CARDS
Some packs of playing cards were produced bearing county maps, since the 52 counties of England and Wales were an ideal number for a set of cards. Playing card maps are rare; those of 1590 by William Bowes (Fig. 43) and of 1717 by John Lenthall are extremely rare, but those by William Redmayne from the 1676 *Recreative Pastime by Card-play* and Robert Morden's from *The 52 Countries of England and Wales, described in a Pack of Cards* are sometimes found.

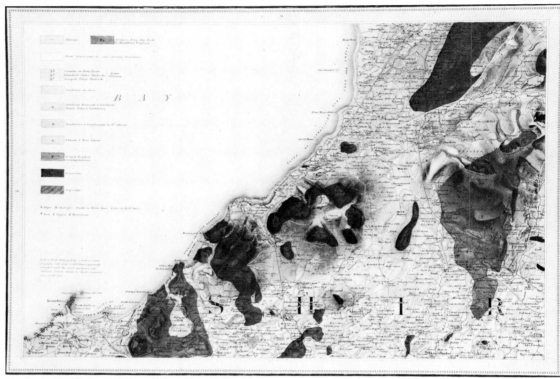

42 Geological Survey of Great Britain. No. LXXV.N.W. (Harlech), 1841. Reprinted from the 1 inch Geological Survey Map. *Photograph: Mills-Wight Studio. By courtesy of Jason Musgrave*

N.B. (a) Morden's playing card maps were issued with minor revisions in 1676 (three issues) and 1680 (?) (two issues); and in 1773 (?) in the atlas *A Brief Description of England and Wales ... published by H. Turpin.*

(b) Redmayne's playing card maps were issued with minor revisions in 1676, 1677 and, with a decorated border, in about 1711.

Select Bibliography

MANN, S. AND KINGSLEY, D.: *Playing Cards depicting maps of the British Isles and of English and Welsh Counties.* (MCC, 87; 1972)

WADSWORTH, F. A.: 'County maps as playing cards'. (*Trans. of the Thoroton Soc. of Nottinghamshire*, 45; 1942)

MILITARY MAPS AND PLANS:

Military needs have often pushed map-making techniques forward; in particular, the requirements of troop movements and artillery demanded an accurate representation of roads and topography respectively, especially in remote, little-known areas. The development of military surveying eventually led to the establishment of the Ordnance Survey, but for centuries military maps and plans were drawn to illustrate details of defences, trench placements, garrison sites, forts, access control, and patrols (Fig. 44). Often troop and artillery dispositions were superimposed on commercially printed maps. Unfortunately, the British Isles, unlike some other countries, produced few specifically military maps; rather, surveys, such as the Military Survey of Scotland which followed the Jacobite rising of 1745, and maps, such as those published by Thomas Jenner for the Parliamentary armies in the Civil War, were produced for the use of military forces. The few specifically military maps that are available are generally maps of defence positions and installations in garrison towns and ports produced by military engineers.

43 Playing cards by William Bowes: the Welsh counties, 1590. *By permission of the British Library (Schrieber Collection 1938—7-9-57 (35–47))*

FLINTE the 1 of the West hath Miles
In Quantitie superficiall 110 In Circuite 53
In Lengthe from Shropshyre to the sea 33
In Breedth from Denby to Cheshire 8

FLINTE full of plesaunt hills & fertile
And hath great plentie of barley
Cheshire & Shrop:East Denb: & the sea West
The Irishe sea North Denb: & Shrop: South

ANGLESEY the 2 of the West hath Miles
In Quantitie superficiall 220 In Circuite 71
In Lengthe from y sea to Presthoime har 22
In Breadth from the river Menai to the sea 18

ANGLESEY hath great store of cattell & mills
And an earth whereof late they make Allum & Copris
Hauinge the soundmouth East & Irish sea West
The Irishe sea North & Carnarvan South

RADNOR the 3 of the West hath Miles
In Quantitie superficiall 300 In Circuite 80
In Length from Cardiga to Herefordsher 25
In Breeth from Montgomry to Brecknock 22

RADNOR indifferent for Corne & pasture
And hath many woods, Rivers, pooles & mills
Hauinge Herefordshire East Cardigan West
Montgomery North and Brecknock South

MONMOVTH the 4 of y West hath Miles
In Quantitie superficiall 360 In Circuite 84
In Length from Heref to Glamorganshire 26
In Breedth from Seuarne to Brecknocksher 22

MONMOVTH plentfull of Corne gras & wood
And all other necessarye prouision of victualls
Hauinge Glocest: East Glamor: & Breck: West
Heref: & Breck: North & y river Seuar: South

DENBIGHE the 5 of y West hath Miles
In Quantitie superficiall 375 In Circuite 118
In Lengthe from Shropshire to the sea 36
In Breedthe from Cheshire to Menmoth 24

DENBIGHE but thinly Inhabited to y sea
Some pts hylly & barren, other som very fertile
Hauinge Chesher & Flint East Carnaruan West
The sea & Flint North Meriu: & Mogome: South

CARNARVAN the 6 of the West hath Miles
In Quantitie superficiall 420 In Circuite 115
In Length from the North sea to Wensea 48
In Breedth from Denbighsher to the sea 24

CARNARVAN a verye fertile soile
And well replenished withe townes
Hauinge Denbigh East & Irish sea West
The sea & Angle: North & y sea & Mer: South

PENBROKE the 7 of the West hath Miles
In Quantitie superficiall 410 In Circuite 125
In Lengthe from Cardygshire to the sea 35
In Breedth from Carmarthen to the sea 28

PENBROKE a very plesaunt & fertile ayre
Hauinge plentye of wheat beef, fish & wine to sell
And hath Carmarth: East the Irish sea West
The sea and Cardiga: North & the sea South

CARDIGAN the 8 of y West hath Miles
In Quantitie superficiall 460 In Circuite 109
In Length from Montgomery to Penbroke 40
In Breedth from Carmarden to Merionethsher 25

CARDIGAN champion towards the sea
Els full of fruitfull mountaines and many waters
Hauinge Radnor & Montge: East & y sea West
Merionethsher North and Carmarden South

MONTGOMERYE the 9 of y West hath Miles
In Quantitie superficiall 460 In Circuite 98
In Length from Shropsher to Merionith 33
In Breedth from Radnor to Denbighsher 30

MONTGOMERY full of mountains & hilles
Store of pasture, corne, and some half y best beef
Hauinge Shropsher East & Montmoth & Cardiga West
Denbigh & Meriou: North & y Radnor South

GLAMORGA the 10 of y West hath Miles
In Quantitie superficiall 460 In Circuite 126
In Lengthe from Brecknockshire to the sea 22
In Breedth from Breckenoshire to the sea 22

GLAMORGA is on North full of Moutaine
The other pyes lesse Moutaine & better soile
Hauinge Monouth East Carmar: & y sea West
Brecknock North & y Seuarne South

BRECKNOCKE the 11 of the West hath Miles
In Quantitie superficiall 500 In Circuite 109
In Length from Heref to Glamorganshire 35
In Breedthe from Cardigan to Monmouthsher 35

BRECKNOCKE a pleasa Country of woods
full of cattell for vaile & and watery full of fishes
Hauinge Hereford East Carmarthin West
Radnorshier North Monm: & Glamor South

MERIONETHE the 12 of y West hath Miles
In Quantitie superficiall 530 In Circuite 111
In Lengthe from Denbighshire to the sea 30
In Breedth from Montgomery to Cardigan 25

MERIONETH most Motaine of all Wales
and very cragge clift es full of sheep & cattell
Montgomery & Deby East the sea West
Dby: & Carnaru North & y Cardiga South

CARMARDE the 13 of the West hath Miles
In Quantitie superficiall 560 In Circuite 106
In Lengthe from Penbroke to Brecknocshier 38
In Breedth from Glamor: to Cardigashire 26

CARMARDE indifferent for all sids of fruit
Full of sheepe, & in some places abundance of coale
Hauinge Brecknock East Prebrokshire West
Cardiga North Glamorgan, and the sea South

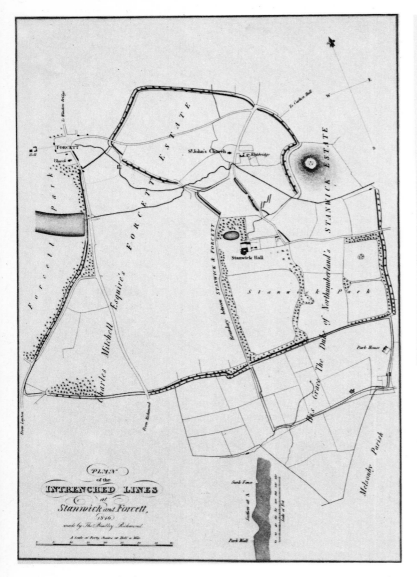

44 'Plan of the Intrenched Lines at Stanwick and Forcett, 1816, made by Thos. Bradley, Richmond'. Engraved by Sidney Hall. *Photograph: Mills-Wight Studio*

45 4(i): 'An Actual Survey of the Great Post-Roads between London and Edinburgh' by Mostyn John Armstrong, 1776. (Frontispiece). *Photograph: Mills-Wight Studio*

Select Bibliography

CLARK, P. K. AND O'DONOGHUE, Y.: *The activities of British Military map-makers in the Peninsular War.* (Paper presented at the VIIth. International Cartographic Assoc. Conference; 1974)

SKELTON, R. A.: 'The Military Surveyor's Contribution to British Cartography in the 16th Century'. (*IM*, 24; 1970)

FRONTISPIECES

An alternative, and comparatively cheaper, theme for a collection is the frontispiece and atlas title-page. These were fine productions by skilled craftsmen which often presented the extended, discursive titles in fine decorative lettering and enticed the reader with delicate vignettes of surveyors at work, coaching scenes, and portraits (Fig. 45).

VII The Map-makers

The analysis of a cartographer's work must take account of general influences. The early map-maker naturally reflected the age he lived in and his maps were inevitably influenced by the economic and social environment of the day. Different cartographers emphasised different aspects of the environment according to their perceptions, and all were biased to some extent. Furthermore, a competitive market situation forced map-makers to make claims on their maps or in their prospectuses which were often misleading, if not downright fraudulent, and such claims must be mistrusted.

A map-maker's reputation and significance in his own time can be judged from contemporary views of his work. It is fortunate that Richard Gough, in his *British Topography* of 1768 and 1780, recorded many such early opinions, in addition to his own pithy criticisms for 'there is scarce a single one that does not abound in faults.'

This chapter examines in detail the work of the major producers of British maps under the headings normally adopted for identification by dealers. The numbered descriptions and analyses of issues should enable most of the available maps of Britain to be identified and dated. Research on issues and plate changes is still in its youth and will be so for many years to come. Previously unrecorded atlas issues and plate variations do sometimes come to light and therefore the issues and variations noted here are not necessarily definitive. Inevitably, there will be gaps and errors in the detailed map bibliographies, caused by lack of knowledge or mistaken interpretation; and only time will reveal these. Conclusions must be based, all too often, on the inadequate evidence of just a few known copies; or, worse still, a single example; or at worst, an unverified report. In truth, of course, a map-maker's workshop, particularly in the late eighteenth and nineteenth centuries, was not usually solely concerned with the production of a single atlas, but, rather, was engaged in the production of several, if not many, concurrently, as well as many individual maps, and, indeed, other non-cartographic engraving and printing work.

Thus, plates were amended in random fashion as new information came to hand, as engraving time became available, as machines became free, and as new issues were projected. Whilst these changes were taking place, often over a period of years, publishers responded to customers' orders and booksellers' requests for new supplies by making up atlases from existing stocks. Consequently, atlases could be issued long after the date stated on the title-page and might contain any number of variations of map states. It is, perhaps, misleading to try to bring some order to such a minefield, for, whenever an issue is defined, that definition will be rendered inadequate by the discovery of variant examples. It is also, perhaps, unrealistic to distinguish issues which were, in reality, merely stages within an erratic continuum of atlas marketing. Nevertheless, despite misgivings, production history can only be clarified by detailed analysis and any collector may have the opportunity of adding to the stock of knowledge on the subject and any information would be greatly appreciated by the author. Generally, issues authoritatively recorded elsewhere are given the benefit of the doubt when it has proved impossible to verify them, and are noted here.

An indication of availability is given under the heading 'Supply'. Descriptions conform to the following standard format, and use, where appropriate, the abbreviations noted. Any information omitted does not appear on the map and any quoted text is worded as originally printed.

Abbreviations

Position: Outside border (*ob*); below (*b*); above (*a*); right (*r*); left (*l*); centre (*c*). The map face (*mf*). For example: *obbc*: outside border, below centre; *obar*: outside border, above right.

Ornamentation: Scrolling decoration (*sd*). Ornate script (*os*); ornate capital letters (*oc*); plain script (*ps*); plain capital letters (*pc*); varying lettering styles (*vl*). A single line (*sl*); a double line (*dl*); a triple line (*tl*).

Orientation: The map reads from bottom to top (*bt*);

the strips read from bottom to top (*bts*); the map reads from bottom left to top right (*bltr*).

Imprints and signatures: Publisher's imprint (*pi*); engraver's signature (*es*); draughtsman's signature (*ds*).

Variants: Variations in wording or design (*V*).

Map descriptions

Description: The state (*st*) of the maps described is designated. This is usually the earliest state generally available. Illustrations are noted and each map series has a reference number.

Average size: Usually of the engraved or lithographed surface including titles, imprints, decoration, border, etc.; given in both millimetres (mm) and inches (in.), always with the shorter dimension first. Average sizes are given since sizings vary between counties and, indeed, between impressions because paper can shrink or expand. Significant size variations (*V*); considerable size variations (*Vc*). The full dimensions of the engraved or lithographed surface should provide evidence of any cropping.

Features: Noteworthy features aiding identification. Reference is not normally made to printed text backing the map.

Scale: Scales are sometimes uniform (*U*) but usually vary (*V*), often considerably so (*Vc*), between maps in an atlas; therefore, the average scale is given as a general guide only (it is, of course, not even a general guide to index maps). The average scale (*av*) is expressed as 1 inch to so many miles (1:—*m*). The scale heading given on the map is noted, and variations in the wording are generally indicated (*Vw*). Scale bar (*sb*) or scale line (*sl*) with the measurement units into which it is divided: miles (*m*); furlongs (*f*). No scale given on the map (*n*).

Border: Descriptions are designed to distinguish between decorative and plain borders, and to specify those graduated into latitude and longitude (*ll*). Outer borderline(s) (*OB*) and inner borderline(s) (*IB*) are described: a thick and a thin line (*Tt*); a thick line between two thin lines (*tTt*); a thick line and three thin lines (*tTtt*); map detail sometimes breaks into or through the border (*bb*). Information is not usually given on inscriptions relating to latitude and longitude.

North Point: A description of the compass indication used on the map face: cruciform (*c*); star (*s*); quartered circle (*q*); compass rose (*r*); fleur-de-lys pointer indicating north (*f*); plain pointer indicating north (*p*); ornate pointer indicating north (*op*); a cross indicating east (*e*); cardinal points indicated by letters (*l*); cardinal points named at the edge of the map or within the borderlines (*ce*); no indication of orientation (*n*). Unless stated otherwise, north is towards the top of the maps. However, orientation frequently varies so that north is not necessarily directly to the top (*V*).

Key: The heading of any guide to the symbols used on the map. No key (*n*).

Decoration: Any decoration, such as heraldic devices or vignette views, not referred to under any other heading. No decoration (*n*).

Title: The commonest wording of the title, with a description of its lettering style and any surrounding decoration. County name only (*c*); variations in the wording of the title (*V*). Unless stated otherwise, the titlepiece appears on the map face.

Engraver: Where known. Sometimes atlases were engraved by a number of different engravers.

Issues: These are usually detailed in chronological order of appearance and the date given is the date of issue (since old title-pages were often used in later atlases, this date does not always correspond with the publication date given on the title-page). Normally, only atlas issues are recorded in detail since individual maps tended to be sold as loose sheets and folding maps continuously throughout the issue period. A question mark set in brackets following a date or title, etc., i.e. (?), indicates that some doubt exists about that dating or title, etc. Where two or more dates are given, e.g. '1818; 1819:', the atlas was issued without change apart from the date of issue. Rare issues, which are unlikely to be found, are noted without extensive description or omitted where appropriate. Maps were often sold as loose sheets as soon as they were prepared and throughout their lives; maps were changed somewhat randomly from year to year; atlas contents were sometimes varied to suit a particular bookseller's or customer's requirements; and old sheets could be mixed with new sheets in an effort to use up outdated stock when making up an atlas—examples of the use of old stock are legion! Consequently, the recording of map states and atlas contents is particularly prone to misinterpretation and this area of analysis should be treated with some slight suspicion since it is in a continuing state of revision.

Atlas: The title usually follows the wording and punctuation of the title page of the work in which the maps appear; dashes indicate omissions; later issues note only changes in the title wording and minor changes are sometimes not noted. It is not unusual to find copies of an atlas edition which contain different map editions; known cases are noted. In order to clarify atlas titles, capital letters (other than those of proper nouns and at the beginning of sentences) are eliminated and punctuation is sometimes slightly adapted to improve the sense of the wording.

Maps: An analysis of areas covered in an atlas, specifying general and regional maps, counties, islands, towns, etc.

N.B. (i) since Yorkshire is often either omitted or, because of its size, treated as individual Ridings, it is considered separately.

(ii) Monmouthshire is included under English counties.

(iii) Anglesey is considered as a Welsh county, not an island.

Where a county is noted as 'with' another county (or counties), they appear together on one map.

State: The exact state of a map can only be clearly identified by tracing the history of that individual block, plate or stone. It is not possible in a work of this nature to specify clearly the state of each map for each issue. However, it is possible to give a general guide to clearly identifiable states and to specify the broad state(s) of most maps in an issue, and thus simplify the complex task of relating maps to issues. Minor variations within a broad state category (such as minor retouching or revisions, or imprint year alterations), which do not justify consideration as a separate state in this work, are indicated (*v*). Where two states are noted, e.g. 'Second or third', an issue combines maps in different states. 'Various' describes issues which are too complex to specify because they were made up of stock originating from different years and because plates were revised haphazardly from year to year without pattern.

Imprints: That is, imprints, signatures, plate-numbers, inscriptions, etc.: the signatures of cartographer, draughtsman and/or engraver, and the imprint of the publisher or printer are normally given in full with their positions relative to the map correctly oriented described from the observer's viewpoint. Variations in signatures, imprints, dates and plate-numbers are noted where appropriate; however, minor variants, unworthy of note, are sometimes ignored.

Publisher: The publisher's name and, sometimes, address are given (as on the atlas title page, where appropriate, sometimes with adapted punctuation for clarity).

Subsequent issues are noted under the date of publication. Only changes in the publication are noted, and each issue refers to a previous issue entry which provides the basis for noting changes. Unless otherwise stated, the main features of the map previously recorded exist on subsequent issues. Only major changes to map content are detailed. Unless an issue is stated to be by lithographic transfer, or other production process, it was printed by the intaglio process.

The description of any series of maps is inevitably a compromise and there will always be variations. There are often surprising differences between the details and decoration of maps from the same series, and while many variations are noted, it is not always feasible to specify all variants. These descriptions can never be a perfect match for all maps in an issue for there are many variations not noted here; they are a general guide only to the identification of maps, and are not designed to be slavishly followed.

Select Bibliography

BANDINEL, B.: *A Catalogue of the Books relating to British Topography, and Saxon and Northern Literature, bequeathed to the Bodleian Library in the Year MDCCXCIX.* (1814). (i.e. Richard Gough's collection).

GOUGH, R.: *British Topography, or, an historical account of what has been done for illustrating the topographical antiquities of Great Britain and Ireland.* 2 vols. (1780).

WALTERS, G.: 'Richard Gough's Map Collecting for the British Topography, 1780'. (*MC*, 2; 1978).

ADAIR, John

fl. 1681–1722d. Mathematician, surveyor and cartographer

Adair began to survey Scotland in 1681, intending to replace Timothy Pont's outdated surveys. This grand project was frustrated, firstly by the financial collapse of his sponsor, Moses Pitt, and secondly, by the subsequent irregular funding from the Scottish Privy Council. Consequently only a few county maps, mainly of the Lothians, were published, mostly after his death. In the 1680's Adair compiled charts of the east coast from Sutherland Point to Aberdeen which were published in 1703 as *The Description of the Sea Coasts and Islands of Scotland.* Although intended to be issued in parts, this first part was the only one published. D.N.B. Vol. I, pp. 70–72.

ADLARD, Alfred[21]

fl. c.1840–1850. Engraver

Alfred Adlard engraved a series of plain maps (1) of grouped Irish counties for *Ireland: its scenery,* character, etc. The most notable feature is the odd grouping of counties from different provinces and, indeed, the grouping of non-contiguous counties. Presumably the maps were produced especially to match the sequence of the book's chapters, although they do not always do this. The work was initially issued in monthly parts each with 'an engraved Map of a County or District—carefully revised, according to the latest surveys, and, as far as possible, collated with the maps issued by the Ordnance ...'.

(1) **Description:** *st*: First. (Fig. 46). **Supply:** Moderate. **Average size:** 136 × 202 mm (5.4 × 8 in.). **Features:** Details of county populations and acreages noted. **Scale:** *U*/1:12.5 *m*/2 *sbm*/ 'English Miles' and 'Irish Miles'. **Border:** *OB:Tt/ IB:ll/bb*. **North Point:** *c*/north indicated by a decorative star. **Title:** *c/oc*. **Engraver:** A. Adlard.

Issues: (i) 1841–43: *Atlas: Ireland: its scenery, character ... by Mr and Mrs S.C. Hall .... Maps (18):* (a) Ireland. (b) 16 maps of Irish counties. (Six maps combine two counties each; five combine three each). (c) Lakes of Killarney. **State:** First.

Imprints: (i) *obbr:es:* 'A. Adlard, Doctors Commons'. ('Doctors Commons'—a college for the study of civil law—was Adlard's address in the St Paul's area of London). (ii) *obbc:pi:* 'London: Published by How & Parsons, 132 Fleet Street'. (except: six imprints omit the Fleet Street address; and Donegal, Mayo and Galway give the publisher as 'Jeremiah How'). Cork is dated 'Nov. 1840' and Armagh '1842'. **Publishers:** How & Parsons. (ii) **State:** Second. The maps were later issued by lithographic transfer without the *pi*.

AIKIN, John
fl. 1790. Cartographer

Aikin produced *England Delineated* (2) in 1790, as a school atlas: 'It is the principal object of this work to make my young countrymen better acquainted than they are usually found to be with their native land. ...' It contained plain, simple outline maps of little interest.

(2) **Description:** *st*: First (*v*). (Fig. 47). **Supply:** Moderate. **Average size:** 100 × 150 mm

46 1(ii): Limerick and Clare by Alfred Adlard, c.1843. *Photograph: Mills-Wight Studio*

47 2(i): Lancashire by John Aikin, 1790. *Photograph: Mills-Wight Studio*

(4.5 × 7.25 in.), [this is the average size of the page since the maps are unframed]. **Scale:** *n//V/av:* 1:12 *m*. **Title:** *c/pc*.

Issues: (i) 1790: *Atlas: England delineated; or, a geographical description of every county in England and Wales .... Maps (43):* (a) England. (b) 39 English counties. (c) Yorkshire. (d) North; South Wales. **State:** First (*v*). **Imprint:** *obar:* plate-number: this is almost invariably lost in binding. **Publisher:** Joseph Johnson, St Paul's Church-Yard. (ii) 1795; 1800; 1803; 1809: as (i) 1790, except: **State:** First (*v*). Minor retouching in 1803. N.B. The first edition of *England delineated ...* of 1788 and the enlarged edition of 1818 did not contain maps.

AINSLIE, John
fl. 1772–1813. Surveyor and engraver

After a six-year surveying apprenticeship under Thomas Jefferys, Ainslie became a prolific producer of atlases, charts, maps and plans, particularly of Scotland.

Select Bibliography
ADAMS, I. H.: *John Ainslie, Map-maker.* (Scottish Record Office; 1971).

ANDREWS, John
fl. 1766–1809. Geographer, surveyor, engraver and map-seller

Andrews produced large-scale county maps of Hertfordshire, Kent and Wiltshire with Andrew Dury and others; maps of the environs of London, Richmond and Windsor; and town plans, including 42 plans in the *Collection of plans of the capital cities of Europe and some remarkable cities in Asia, Africa and America* (1771 and 1772).

ARCHER, Joshua
fl. 1841–1865. Engraver

Archer produced 17 ecclesiastical maps for *The British Magazine* in 1841, but is best known for the county maps (3) issued in the *Curiosities of Great Britain* by Thomas Dugdale. These maps, which were finely engraved on steel, characterised the austere, functional approach adopted by most Victorian cartographers who rejected the decoration of earlier generations of map-makers.

(3) **Descriptions:** *st*: First. **Supply:** Plentiful. **Average size:** 180 × 230 mm (7.2 × 9.2 in.). **Features:** A numbered reference key to administrative divisions: e.g. 'HUNDREDS'. **Scale:** *V/av:*1:6*m*/ *sbm*/'SCALE'. **Border:** *OB:tTt/IB:ll*. **Key:** 'EXPLANATION'. **Title:** *c/oc*. **Engraver:** J. Archer.

Issues: Railway information was up-dated for most editions. Issues before c.1843 often mixed Archer's maps with those by Cole & Roper (31). (i) 1835–41 (?): *Atlas: Curiosities of Great Britain. England & Wales delineated historical, entertaining & commercial. Alphabetically arranged. By Thomas Dugdale, antiquarian. Assisted by William Burnett, civil engineer .... Maps (58):* (a) Two general maps of England and Wales. (b) 39 English counties. (c) North; Part of the North; West; Part of the East and West Ridings. (d) Isle of Wight. (e) 12 Welsh counties. **State:** First. **Imprints:** (i) *obar:* plate-number. (ii) *obbr:es/ds:* 'Drawn and Engraved, by J. Archer, Pentonville, London'. (*V*). (iii) *obbc:* 'Engraved for Dugdales England and Wales Delineated'. (*V*). This inscription seems to have been erased progressively from the series between c.1843 and c.1846. **Publishers:** Vol. 1: 'Tallis &

Co., Green Arbour Court, Old Bailey'. Vol. 2: 'John Tallis, 15, St John's Lane, Smithfield'. Vol. 3: 'L. Tallis, 3, Jewin Street, City'.

N.B. The work was also issued in different numbers of volumes c.1842–43 by John Tallis and L. Tallis.

(ii) 1846 (?): as (i) 1835–41 (?), except: *Atlas: The universal English dictionary ... By the Rev. James Barclay .... Maps (57):* as above, less a general map. *State:* First. *Publishers:* J. & F. Tallis. (iii) 1846 (?): as (i) 1835–41 (?), except: *State:* Second (*v*). *Imprint:* (iii) *obbc:* inscription erased from all maps by about this date. *Publishers:* J. & F. Tallis. (iv) 1846 (?); 1847 (?): as (iii) 1846 (?), except: *State:* Second (*v*). Minor revisions and additions. (*v*) 1848 (?): as (iv) 1846 (?); 1847 (?), except: *State:* Second (*v*). Minor revisions and additions. *Publisher:* L. Tallis. (vi) 1848 (?): as (ii) 1846 (?), except: *State:* Second (*v*). Plate revisions as (v) 1848 (?). *Imprint:* (iii) *obbc:* inscription erased. *Publishers:* John Tallis & Co. (vii) 1858–1860 (?): as (vi) 1848 (?), except: *Atlas: Dugdale's England and Wales delineated. Edited by E. L. Blanchard.* Issued in 50 parts and subsequently bound together c.1860. *State:* Second (*v*). Minor revisions and additions. *Publisher:* 'L. Tallis, 21, Warwick Square, Paternoster Row'. (viii) 1860 (?): as (vii) 1860 (?), except: *Atlas: The topographical dictionary of England & Wales. Edited by E. L. Blanchard. State:* Second (*v*). Minor revisions and additions. (ix) 1860 (?): as (vii) 1860 (?), except: *Atlas: Tallis's topographical dictionary of England & Wales. With a road & railway county atlas. State:* Second (*v*).

ARMSTRONG:

Captain Andrew, fl. 1768–1781, and Mostyn John, fl. 1771–1791. Map-makers and publishers

Andrew Armstrong retired from the army on half pay in 1763 and set up a map publishing business, which his son, Mostyn, later joined. The Armstrongs are best known for their large-scale county maps of both England and Scotland, many of which were published on a subscription basis. The map of Northumberland of 1769 won a 50 guinea award from the Royal Society of Arts.

However, it is the smaller maps of Mostyn Armstrong that are more readily available. Apparently Mostyn intended to publish a series of road books using the same scale and format for all the major roads of England. However, only the fine volumes for *London to Edinburgh* (4) and *London to*

Dover (5) were published. Mostyn also produced a useful atlas of small Scottish county maps (6) which were well engraved and attractive, despite Richard Gough's criticism that 'Armstrong has attended to his own and the engraver's profit more than that of the public or their information'.

Select Bibliography
CHAMBERS, B.: 'M. J. Armstrong in Norfolk: the Progress of an Eighteenth Century County Survey'. (*GJ*, 130; 1964).

(4) Description: *st:* Second. **Supply:** Moderate. **Average size:** 75 × 145 mm (3.0 × 5.8 in.). **Features:** Roman roads are represented by dashed lines; county boundaries are not marked. **Scale:** *n//*scale is: 1:2 *m*. **Border:** *sl/*surrounded by a decorative border of twining foliage/*bt*. **North Point:** *c/p/V*. **Title:** *ps/obac:* the name of the principal town(s).

N.B. There was an otherwise identical issue without titles in June 1776.

Engravers: Chiefly Pyle and I. Page, but also: J. Barber, Bayly, T. Conder, Harrison, D. Lizars, J. Lodge, Luffman, Prokter, and Terry & Co.

Issues: (i) 1776: two issues: (June and August): *Atlas: An actual survey of the great post-roads between London and Edinburgh. With the country three miles, on each side, drawn on a scale of half-an-inch to a mile ... by Mostyn John Armstrong, geographer .... Maps:* (a) Index map. (b) 44 maps showing the main route from London to Edinburgh, plus alternative routes between Ferrybridge and Northallerton (via either Wetherby or York) and between Morpeth and Edinburgh (via either Berwick, Kelso or Coldstream). *State:* First (without title); second (with title). *Imprints:* (i) *obar:* plate-number: 'Plate ...' or 'Pl ..'. (ii) between plain-ruled and foliated borders: *br* (a few are *bl*, or across the full width): most maps have an *es:* e.g. 'Pyle, sculp!' or 'Pyle scu^t. Ag^l. Co. Snow Hill'. *Publisher:* Mostyn John Armstrong. (ii) 1777; 1783: as (i) 1776: *State:* Second.

(5) Description: There is a close similarity between the maps of the roads from London to Edinburgh and those from London to Dover. Therefore, the description is as (4) but with the following differences: **Supply:** Scarce. **Title:** *ps/*principal town shown, named within a curved, ruffled panel incorporated into the border.

Issues: (i) 1777: *Atlas: Armstrong's actual survey of the great post-road between London and Dover with the country three miles on each side. Drawn on a scale of*

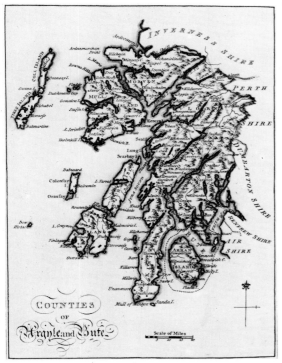

48 6(i): Argyle and Bute by Mostyn John Armstrong,
1777. *By permission of the British Library (Maps
C.24.c.12.)*

half-an-hour to a mile. . . . **Maps: (6). State:** First.
Imprints: (i) *obar:* plate-number in roman
numerals. (ii) between plain-ruled and foliated
borders: *bl:es:* 'Page sculp.'.

(6) Description: *st:* First. (Fig. 48). **Supply:**
Moderate. **Average size:** 140 × 190 mm
(5.6 × 7.5 in.). **Scale:** *Vc/av:*1:10 *m/sbm* (except:
'County of Orkney')/'Scale of Miles'. **Border:** *dl.*
North Point: *c/p/e.* **Title:** *oc/sd/*'COUNTY of . . .'.
Engraver: 'Beautifully Engraved . . . by H: Ashby'.

Issues: (i) 1777: *Atlas: A Scotch atlas; or
description of the kingdom of Scotland: divided into
counties, with the subdivisions of sherifdoms; shewing
their respective boundaries and extent, soil, produce,
mines, minerals, metals, their trade and manufactures,
also their cities, chief towns, seaports, mountains,
rivers, forests, lochs etc. with the principal great and
bye roads, passes, forts, and other particulars. The
whole taken from topographical surveys, regulated by
astronomical observations . . .'.* **Maps (30):** (a) Two
general maps. (b) 26 Scottish county maps (five
maps combine two counties each). (c) Orkney. (d)
Environs of Edinburgh (*obbl:* 'M.I.A. del. 1776').

State: First. **Imprints:** (i) *ob:* top right of page:
page number in brackets. (ii) Edinburgh environs
and Peebles have: *obbr:es:* 'Ashby Sculp!'. (iii)
obbc:pi: 'Publish'd as the Act directs by Rob!. Sayer
& Jn°. Bennett 1!st Nov! 1777' (*V*). **Publishers:**
Robert Sayer & John Bennett, 'N° 53, Fleet Street'.
(ii) 1787: as (i) 1777, except: **State:** First.
Publisher: Robert Sayer. (iii) 1794: as (i) 1777,
except: **State:** Second. No 'North Britain' or
Edinburgh Environs. **Imprint:** (iii) *obbc:pi:* erased.
Publishers: 'Laurie & Whittle, 53, Fleet Street'.

BADESLADE, Thomas
fl. 1719–1745. Engineer and surveyor

Badeslade was basically an engineer interested in the
development of waterways and he produced several
important works on the subject, particularly
concerning land reclamation in the Fens. However,
he also drew a set of small county maps (7) for
Chorographia Britanniae which was compiled for a
tour by the King: 'This Collection (conveying a
more comprehensive Idea of South Britain than any
thing hitherto publish'd) was first Drawn, and
compiled into a Pocket Book, by Order and for the
Use of his late Majesty KING GEORGE I'; it was
sold bound and coloured at a price of 12 shillings.

(7) Description: *st:* First. (Fig. 49). **Supply:**
Moderate. **Average size:** Map only: 98 × 138 mm
(3.85 × 5.5 in.). Overall: 145 × 150 mm
(5.7 × 6.0 in.) **Features:** All areas outside the
county are shaded by stippling, reinforced by
horizontal hatching to produce a band of heavier
shading along the county boundary; a panel gives a
listing of major towns with details of parliamentary
representation, and market and fair days. **Scale:** *V/
av:*1:10 *m/sbm* 'English Miles'. **Border:** *dl* or *Tt*.
North Point: *r/f/l/V.* **Title:** *pc* and *ps/c/*or: 'A Map
of . . . from London'/*V/obac.* **Engraver:** William
Henry Toms.

Issues: Old map stocks were used in later issues and
evidence suggests that some of the plate alterations
were made during the course of an issue. (i) 1742:
*Atlas: Chorographia Britanniae. Or a set of maps of
all the counties in England and Wales: . . . With the
particular map of each county, is an account of all the
cities, boroughs, market towns . . . .* **Maps (46):** (a)
Four general maps. (b) 39 English counties. (c)
Yorkshire. (d) North; South Wales. **State:** First.
Imprints: (i) *obar:* plate-number. (ii) *obbc:pi:*
'Publish'd by the Proprietors T. Badeslade & W H
Toms Sept!. 29!th 1741.' (*V*) (iii) *obbl:ds:* 'T.
Badeslade delin.'. (iv) *obbr:es:* 'W.H Toms Sculpt.'

A Map of SUFFOLK. 73 ½ from London.

49 7(iii): Suffolk by Badeslade & Toms, 1742.
Photograph: Mills–Wight Studio

(*V*). *Publisher:* 'W H Toms Engraver, in Union Court, near Hatton Garden, Holbourn'. (ii) 1742: as (i) 1742, except: *State:* Second. The county maps show additional roads and villages. (iii) 1742: as (ii) 1742, except: *State:* Third. *Imprint:* (ii) *obbc :pi* altered: 'Publish'd by the Proprietor W. H. Toms Sept. 29. 1742.' (*V*). (iv) 1743 (?): as (iii) 1742, except: *Atlas: Chorographia Britanniae. Or a new set of maps of all the counties in England and Wales .... State:* Third. *Publishers:* 'J. Clark Bookseller, at yᵉ Golden Ball, in Sᵗ Paul's Church Yard, C. Hitch Bookseller in Pater-Noster-Row, and W. H. Toms Engraver in Union Court Holbourn'. (v) 1745: as (iv) 1743 (?), except: *Atlas: Chorographia Britanniae. Or a new set of .... States:* Second and third. (This issue is particularly notable for the use of old map stock). *Publishers:* 'C. Hitch in Paternoster Row, and W. H Toms, Engraver in Union Court Holbourn'. (vi) 1749 (?)): as (v) 1745, except: *State:* Third. (Maps in the first state are also known in this issue). *Publishers:* 'C. Hitch Bookseller in Paternoster Row, W. Johnston Bookseller at the Golden Ball in Sᵗ Pauls Church Yard, and by W. H. Toms Engraver & Printseller at yᵉ Golden head over against Surgeons Hall near Ludgate Hill'.

BAKER, Benjamin
fl. 1780–1824. Engraver and publisher

Of the many maps and atlases produced by Baker from his premises in Islington, the most interesting and available is the series of county maps (8) which were issued in the *Universal Magazine*. These clearly engraved maps were essentially copies of Cary's maps from the *New and Correct English Atlas* (24) and were later issued in revised form by Laurie & Whittle (66). Baker became engraver to the Board of Ordnance at the Tower of London where he engraved sheets for the first edition of the one inch Ordnance Survey maps.

(8) Description: *st*: First. **Supply:** Scarce. **Average size:** 175 × 220 mm (7 × 8.75 in.). **Scale:** *V*/*av*:1 :7 m/*sbm*/'Scale of Miles'. **Border:** *OB :Tt*/ *IB :ll*/*bb*. **Title:** *c*/*pc*/set within a vertically hatched oval panel/inscription below the panel: 'Engraved by B. Baker Islington' (*V*). **Engraver:** Benjamin Baker.

Issues: (i) 1791–1797: *Atlas: The universal magazine of knowledge and pleasure ....* This was the second series of county maps to be published in *The universal magazine.* (The first series had been published between 1747 and 1766 by John Hinton). *Maps (45):* (a) 39 English counties. (b) North; East; Part of the West (Southern part); Part of the West (Northern part) Ridings. (c) North; South Wales. *State:* First. *Publisher:* 'W. Bent, at the King's Arms, Pater-Noster Row'. (ii) 1804: as (i) 1791–1797, except: *Atlas: Maps of the several counties and shires in England .... State:* First. *Publishers:* Darton & Harvey.
N.B. These plates were adapted for Laurie & Whittle's *New and improved English atlas ...* (see (66)).

BICKHAM, George
fl. 1702–1758. Engraver and writing-master

Bickham was a noted penman and expert on the art of lettering on copper plates. He produced a series of 'curiosities' (9) representing the counties, which were initially published in parts from 1743 to 1754 and complete as *The British Monarchy* in 1754. These and the maps (39) engraved by William Hole for Michael Drayton's *Poly-Olbion* are the only major exceptions to orthodox style in county maps.[22] They are finely engraved as idealized, picturesque, perspective views of the counties from a high vantage point. There is no attempt at accuracy

50 British Isles by Aristide Michel Perrot, 1803. *By courtesy of Ivan R. Deverall*

and often towns are moved in order to accommodate the fine lettering. The extensive foreground is occupied by local figures set in a rural scene and the maps offer '... a pleasing landscape ... with a variety of Rustic Figures, Ruins, etc. and the names of the Principal Towns and Villages, interspersed according to their apparent situation'.[23]

Bickham also engraved orthodox maps of the countries which bear his signature: 'G. Bickham Fecit'. D.N.B.: Vol. 2, p. 470.

Select Bibliography

(*F*) BICKHAM, G.: *The British Monarchy* .... (1967).

LYON, D. R.: 'A Bird's-eye view of the Bickhams'. (*MC*; March 1978).

SCHRIVE, D.: *Bickham's Birds Eye County Views and the British Monarchy.* (MCC, 27; 1966).

(9) Supply: Scarce. (Fig. 51). Average size: 145 × 228 mm (5.75 × 9 in.).

Issues: The maps were issued in parts as they were engraved from 1750. (i) 1754 (?): earlier issues of 1743, 1748 and 1749 did not contain the panoramic views. *Atlas: The British monarchy: or, a new chorographical description of all the dominions subject to the King of Great Britain .... The whole illustrated with suitable maps and tables ... and engrav'd by George Bickham ....* Maps (48): (a) Dominions in Europe, Africa and America. (b) British Isles; Ireland; Scotland; England and Wales. (c) 39 English counties. (d) Yorkshire. (e) North; South Wales. (f) A chart of the sea coast. *State:* First. Imprints: (i) *obac:* map title: 'A Map of ...' with a dedication/*os* and *oc.* (ii) *obbr:pi:* 'According

51 9(i): Cambridgeshire by George Bickham, c.1754. *By permission of the British Library (800.cc.17.)*

to Act of Parliament by G. Bickham 175–' (*V*), dated between 1750 and 1754. (iii) *obb:* distances between towns noted. (iv) *obar:* some maps have a page reference: 'before p. ––'; 'after page ––'; etc. *Publisher:* George Bickham junr. (ii) 1796: as (i) 1754 (?), except: *Atlas: A curious antique collection of birds-eye views of the several countries in England & Wales; exhibiting a pleasing landscape of each county ....* The plates have been reduced in length by between ½ and 1 inch and the title has been altered. Maps: As (c), (d), (e) above. *State:* Second. Imprints: (i) *obac:* map title altered: county name only/*pc.* (ii) *obbr:* inscription deleted. (iii) *obb:* inscription deleted. (iv) *obar:* page reference erased: plate-number added. *Publishers:* Robert Laurie & James Whittle.

BILL, John
fl. 1626. Bookseller and publisher

Bill published books in London from 1604, and in 1626 produced a set of county maps (10) in *The abridgment of Camden's Britañnia* which was a miniature copy of Saxton's maps produced on the same format as van den Keere's maps of c.1605 (57). These were the first individual county maps to show graduations of latitude and longitude; the longitude being measured from the prime meridian of the Azores.

(10) Description: *st*: First. (Fig. 52). **Supply:** Very rare. **Average size:** 85 × 120 mm (3.4 × 4.8 in.). **Features:** The sea is shaded as 'watered silk'. **Scale:** *V*/*av*:1:10*m*/'A Scale of Miles'/*sbm*: set within a panel with a fretwork frame or surmounted by dividers/*Vw*. **Border:** *dl*/the left borderlines are graduated into latitude, and the lower borderlines into longitude measured from the prime meridian of the Azores. The figures are printed outside the border *IV*. **North Point:** *n*//or: *ce*. **Decoration:** Where space allows, lettering is performed in large swash characters. **Title:** *c*/*pc*/ set within a panel with a fretwork frame.

Issues: (i) 1626: *Atlas: The abridgment of Camden's Britañnia with the maps of the seuerall shires of England and Wales ....* **Maps (52):** (a) England. (b) 39 English counties. (c) Yorkshire. (d) 11 Welsh counties (no Anglesey). **State:** First. **Imprints:** *obb*: some maps have a printer's reference signature printed from type. **Publisher:** 'John Bill Printer to the Kings most excellent Maiestie'.

BLACKWOOD, William
fl. 1839–1853. Bookseller and publisher

Blackwood published a set of plain, attractive Scottish county maps (11), finely engraved on steel plates by William Home Lizars, in his *Atlas of Scotland*. D.N.B.: Vol. 2, pp. 615–616.

(11) Description: *st*: First. **Supply:** Moderate.

52 10(i): Durham by John Bill, 1626. *Photograph: Mills-Wight Studio*

Average size: 189 × 240 mm (7.5 × 9.6 in.). **Scale:** *Vc/av*:1:5 *m/sbm/*'British Miles'. **Border:** *OB:tTt/ IB:ll/bb.* **North Point:** Usually: *c/f.* **Title:** *c/oc.* **Engraver:** William Home Lizars.

N.B. W. H. Lizars also engraved the index map and the 53 sectional maps (102 × 133 mm; 4 × 5.25 in.), for the *Travelling map of Scotland, with the distances on the great roads* published c.1820 by Peter Hill & Co. and by Oliver & Boyd c.1825, and the 17 maps (Ireland, + road maps—two with plain backs and 14 printed back-to-back) for *Road maps for tourists in Ireland* published in 1844 by William Curry Jnr. in Dublin, and Longman, Brown & Co. in London. Fourteen road plates (95 × 165 mm; 3.7 × 6.5 in.) were divided into strips of varying width (Fig. 53). Each map has the title in plain capital letters above the upper border and:

53 'Dublin to Belfast' engraved by William Home Lizars, published by William Curry, 1844. *By permission of the British Library (Maps 30.a.38.)*

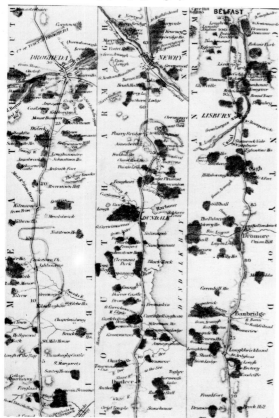

(i) *obbc:pi*: 'Dublin, Published by W. Curry J.ʳ & Co.' (V). (ii) *obbr: es*: 'Eng.ᵈ by W. H. Lizars'.

Issues: (i) 1838; 1839; 1847; 1848: *Atlas: Blackwood's atlas of Scotland: containing thirty-one separate maps of the counties and islands ....* **Maps (32):** (a) Scotland. (b) 27 Scottish county maps (Elgin with Nairn; Fife with Kinross; Perth with Clackmannan). (c) Buteshire; Orkney Islands; Shetland Islands; Western Islands. *State:* First (*v*). *Imprint: obbr:es:* 'Eng.ᵈ on steel by W. H. Lizars'. *Publishers:* William Blackwood & Sons. (ii) 1845: as (i) 1838; etc., except: *Atlas: The new statistical account of Scotland ...*, issued in parts and completed in 1845. *State:* First (*v*).

N.B. The maps were also issued as folding maps at this time.

(iii) 1853: as (i) 1838; etc., except: *Atlas: Blackwood's atlas of Scotland containing twenty-eight separate maps of the counties together with the Orkney, the Shetland, and the Western Islands ....* *State:* First (*v*). The maps were folded in this smaller volume.

Most of the above maps were reproduced, slightly enlarged, lithographically for the *Ordnance Gazetteer of Scotland ....* published by Thomas C. Jack in 1885.

BLOME, Richard

fl. 1660–1705d. Cartographer and publisher

Poor Richard Blome has been scorned and criticised from his own day to this. In his early days as a heraldic painter, his contemporary Anthony à Wood remarked: 'This person Bloome is esteemed by the chiefest heralds a most impudent person.' His great *Britannia* was accused in 1696 by Bishop William Nicholson, the antiquary, of stealing its text from William Camden and its maps from John Speed—'a most entire piece of theft out of Camden and Speed'—and Wood dismissed it as 'scribbled and transcribed from Cambden's Britannia and Speed's Maps.' Later critics have been no kinder; writing in 1780, Richard Gough described *Britannia* as 'a most notorious piece of plagiarism' and modern writers continue to condemn both the quality of Blome's maps and his business methods. Yet Blome himself claimed to be only the publisher of *Britannia*: 'I do not own myself the Author, but the Undertaker of this Work'; and he readily acknowledged that his maps were 'the epitome of John Speed' and that he had received help from 'some hundreds of experienced persons'.

Blome produced two sets of decorative county maps which were frequently carelessly engraved. However, the bold style and poor lettering do not detract from their charm, and those engraved by Wenceslaus Hollar, the 'King's Iconographer', are particularly handsome. Both sets of maps are decorated with ornate cartouches and the coats-of-arms of subscribers. Blome was mainly concerned with raising adequate funds for his projects and financed them from advance subscriptions obtained by selling the dedication of each map for £4 to the Lord Lieutenant of the county, or a local nobleman or royal officer. There were plenty of willing patrons and subscribers, and dedications often changed between issues; examples are even known with new dedications and arms simply pasted over the originals.

The smaller maps (13), first published in 1681 in *Speed's Maps Epitomiz'd*, proved to be more popular than those published in *Britannia* (12); being re-issued at later dates by the London booksellers Thomas Taylor and Thomas Bakewell. Blome produced several other cartographical works, including plans of the wards and parishes of London. D.N.B.: Vol. 2, pp. 687–688.

(12) Description: *st*: First (*v*). **Supply:** Scarce. **Average size:** 275 × 325 mm (11 × 13 in.). **Features:** 15 maps have a lettered/numbered reference key to administrative divisions: e.g. 'A Table of the Divisions and Hundreds in ...' set within a plain panel. **Scale:** *V*/*av*:1:3 *m*/'A Scale of Miles'/*sbm*: sometimes set within the title cartouche or within a separate plain or decorative panel. **Border:** *sl* or *dl*. **North Point:** *n*//or: *ce*/or: *q* with *f* and sometimes *e*/or: *r* with *f*/*V*/. **Key:** Chester has a 'DISTINCTION OF PLACES'. **Decoration:** Dedication and patron's coat-of-arms set within a crudely engraved, decorative cartouche. Some dedications are altered between some issues. Ships and sea monsters. **Title:** *pc*/'A MAPP OF ... WITH ITS HUNDREDS. BY RIC: BLOME BY HIS MA^TYS COMAND'./*V*/set within an ornamental cartouche of scrollwork, plasterwork, or foliage. **Engravers:** Some maps are signed thus: Great Britain: 'Francis Lamb sculp.'; Berkshire: 'W. Hollar fec:'; London: 'W. Hollar fecit.'; Scotland and Ireland: 'R. Palmer sculp.'.

Issues: (i) 1673: *Atlas: Britannia: or, a geographical description of the kingdoms of England, Scotland, and Ireland, with the isles and territories thereto belonging ... Illustrated with a map of each county of England, besides several general ones. The like never before published ....* **Maps: (51):** (a) 'Isles of Great Brittaine'; Scotland; Ireland. (b) 39 English counties. (c) Yorkshire; North Riding; 'Richmond Shire'; 'Y^e East Rideing of Yorkshire'; 'West Ridinge of Yorke Shire'. (d) 'Isles of Wight, Jarsey, Garnsey, Sarke, Man, Orcades and Shetland'. (e) London. (f) North; South Wales. **State:** First (*v*). **Imprint:** A few maps have: *pi*: *mf*: e.g. 'London Printed for Richard Blome'. Some maps bear dates between 1669 and 1672. **Publisher:** Richard Blome.
N.B. Some maps were slightly revised while this issue was on sale.

(ii) 1677: as (i) 1673, except: **State:** First (*v*). **Publisher:** 'John Wright at the Crown on Ludgate-Hill'.

(13) Description: *st*. Second. (Fig. 54). **Supply:** Scarce. **Average size:** 175 × 225 mm (7 × 9 in.)/*Vc*/sizes vary between: 138 × 210 mm (5.5 × 8.4 in.) [Sussex] and 185 × 258 mm (7.4 × 10.3 in) [Yorkshire]. **Features:** Some maps have a lettered/numbered reference key to administrative divisions: e.g. 'The Names of the Rapes wherewith this County is divided' set within a crudely engraved frame. (This was sometimes added at a later date.) **Scale:** *V*/*av*:1:5 *m*/*sbm*/'A Scale of Miles'. **Border:** *sl*/or: *tTt*/or: *Tt*. **North Point:** *r* with *op*/or: *ce*/or: *q* with *f* and *e*/*V*. **Decoration:** Dedication to a patron with his coat-of-arms, usually set on a decorative drape. Ships and sea monsters. **Title:** 'A Mapp of the County of ... with its divisions'/*V*/*pc* and *ps*/within a decorative cartouche of scrollwork, drapery, etc. Only 'Darbie', Middlesex and Somerset name Blome in the title but many plates show traces of his imperfectly erased name. Essex, Gloucester and Suffolk lack titles. **Engravers:** Nine maps are signed by Wenceslaus Hollar: 'W. Hollar fecit'. (*V*). (England and Middlesex add the date 1667, and Norfolk 1670). Seven are signed by Richard Palmer: 'R.P. sculp.' or 'R. Palmer sculp.'.

Issues: (i) 1681: (the first state, probably published as loose sheets between 1667 and 1671, with Blome named as author in the title, is extremely rare). *Atlas: Speed's maps epitomiz'd: or the maps of the counties of England, alphabetically placed ....* **Maps (39):** (a) 'A Mapp of y^e Kingdome of England'. (b) 37 English county maps (no Rutland; Cumberland with Westmorland). (c) 'A Generall Mapp of Yorkshire'. **State:** Second (*v*). The maps appear to have been progressively revised from the beginning

54 13(iv): Sussex by Richard Blome, engraved by Wenceslaus Hollar, 1715. *Photograph: Mills-Wight Studio*

of the 1681 issue with 14 altered during the course of the issue. *Imprint:* 'Barkshire', 'Glocester', 'Lyncolne', 'Midlesex', Shropshire, Stafford, and Surrey have: *pi:* 'London printed for Ric Blome 1671' (*V*). Surrey is dated 1667; and 'Midlesex' 1662 (i.e. 1667!). The imprint appears on *mf*, except: 'Lyncolne' and Surrey: within the hundred's reference panel; and 'Midlesex': within the title panel. *Publisher:* Richard Blome. (ii) 1685: as (i) 1681, except: *States:* Various. 16 county maps now have changed dedications and coats-of-arms. *Publisher:* 'Printed and Sold by Sam Lownes over against Exeter Exchange in the Strand'. (iii) 1693: as (ii) 1685, except: *Atlas: Cosmography and geography, in two parts: the first ... being a translation from that eminent and much esteemed geographer, Varenius ... The second part, being a geographical description of all the world ... The third impression, illustrated with maps. To which is added the county-maps of England, drawn from those of Speed ....* *Maps (39):* (a) 'A Generall Mapp of the Isles of Great Brittaine' (as published in Blome's *Britannia* of 1673 but with the date erased). (b, c): The county maps as above. *States:* Various. Northampton and Stafford retain the 1681 dedications and arms.

Suffolk retains the 1685 dedication and arms. Essex, Gloucester, Norfolk, Somerset, Surrey and Yorkshire change the 1681 dedications and arms. Cornwall, Lincoln, Middlesex, Shropshire, Sussex, Wiltshire change the 1685 dedications and arms. Cornwall has the title cartouche erased and replaced by a vignette of a country house. Shropshire has the title cartouche erased and replaced by a shield and crown with leopard supporters. All other maps have the dedications and arms erased sometimes leaving blank cartouches or panels. Variant copies of the atlas are known with Buckingham, Cambridge, Kent, Huntingdon and Oxford having new dedications and arms. These were clearly added during the course of the issue. (iv) 1715(?): as (iii) 1693, except: *Atlas: England exactly described or a guide to travellers in a compleat sett of mapps of all the county's of England being a map; for each county where every town & village in each county is perticulerly expressed with the names and limits of every hundred etc. Very usefull for all gentlemen & travellers being made fitt for the pockett ... Maps (41):* (a) 'A Mapp of ye Kingdom of England'; Scotland. (b, c) the county maps as above, plus Rutland (without decoration, often omitted, and apparently not by Blome).

107

States: Various: Buckingham, Cambridge, Hereford, Huntingdon, Kent and Oxford have the new dedications and coats-of-arms of 1693; other dedications and arms are as 1693. Minor revisions and additions to map detail. *Publisher:* Thomas Taylor 'at ye Golden Lyon in Fleetstreet where are Sold all Sorts of Mapps and fine French Dutch and Italian Prints'.

The atlas was re-issued with the maps in these states in 1718(?), sometimes also containing Thomas Taylor's maps of Wales (109) which were published separately, again in 1718, in *The principality of Wales exactly described.*

(v) 1715(?): as (iv) 1715(?), except: *States:* Various. *Imprint: mf:* top right and/or left: plate-number added (except: Scotland). (vi) 1716(?): as (v) 1715(?), except: *Atlas: England exactly described or a guide to travellers in a compleat sett of maps of all the counties of England; being a map for each county, wherein every towne and village is particularly express'd with the names and limits of every hundred, and the roads and distances in measured miles according to Mr Ogilby's survey ....* *Maps (42):* (a) 'A New Mapp of Ireland' is added (without plate-number). *States:* Various. Double-line roads with circled distances between main towns are added. *Imprint:* (i) Blome's imprint is poorly erased on Berkshire, Gloucester, Shropshire, Stafford and Surrey, and is replaced by the imprint: 'London. Printed and Sold by Tho. Taylor at ye Golden Lyon in Fleet Street' (*V*). Blome's imprint is retained on Lincoln and sometimes on Surrey. (ii) the imprint is erased from Middlesex. (vii) 1718(?): as (vi) 1716(?), except: *States:* Various.

N.B. This work was also re-issued with Taylor's *Principality of Wales ....*

(viii) 1750(?): Two issues with slightly varying atlas titles: as (vi) 1716(?), except: *States:* Various. Minor revisions and additions to some maps. *Imprint:* (i) Berkshire, Gloucester, Stafford and Surrey: new *pi:* 'Printed & Sold by Tho: Bakewell, next ye Horn Taver^n in Fleet Street' (*V*). Shropshire retains the Taylor imprint and Lincoln the Blome imprint. *Publisher:* Thomas Bakewell 'next ye Horn Tavern in Fleet Street'.

N.B. Copies of Cornwall are known with a plan of St Michael's Mount replacing the country house vignette.

BOWEN, Emanuel
fl. 1720–1767. Engraver and print-seller

Emanuel Bowen engraved maps from 1714, becom-ing one of the most prolific and important map producers of the eighteenth century and 'engraver of maps' to George II and Louis XV. In collaboration with John Owen, he engraved the maps for the half-scale reduction of Ogilby's road maps of 1675 entitled *Britannia Depicta*, published first in 1720: 'The Whole for its Compendious Variety & Exactness, preferable to all other Books of Roads hitherto Published or Proposed; And calculated not only for the direction of the Traveller [as they are] but the general use of the Gentleman and Trades-man.' This proved to be a very popular work, being re-issued many times, and was the most successful of the pocket road-books copying Ogilby's format, effectively dominating the market in the face of competition from Gardner (45) and Senex (98). The atlas was unusual in combining both county maps (18) of England and Wales and road-strip maps (19); each set of strips for a particular road following a county map. The maps were printed back-to-back in order to reduce the size of the book and make it more portable. Each charming county map is surmounted by an elaborate cartouche enclosing the title of the road strips and a distance table.

Bowen produced two small sets of attractive county maps for the *General Magazine of Arts and Sciences* (15) and John Hinton's *Universal Magazine* (52) respectively, which were boldly engraved and decorated by small rococo cartouches. However, he is best remembered for the magnificent *Large English Atlas*, produced with Thomas Kitchin, which contained the most elegant maps (14) of the eighteenth century. This atlas represented a major breakthrough in British cartography for it was the first set of maps to shed the influence of Saxton and was the most detailed, accurate and largest-scale series produced to that time. For many counties, Bowen and Kitchin were able to draw on recently conducted large-scale surveys and they also in-corporated information from the coastal charts of Greenvile Collins and the road surveys of John Ogilby. The atlas was unusual in that it was produced by more than one cartographer—all the maps being prepared by Bowen or Kitchin, except Middlesex which was produced in uncharacteristic style with the arms of the 92 City Livery Companies and of the City of London by Richard Seale. The most notable feature of the maps is that all available space is filled with fascinating notes on the history and topography of the county and its towns. This unusual feature is first found on the county maps of *Britannia Depicta* and was continued on the maps of the *Royal English Atlas* and the *Atlas Anglicanus*. Dedications to the Lord Lieutenant of the county and listings of noblemen's country houses were an attempt to stimulate interest and patronage in order to build a market for this costly production. The dominant feature of each map is the finely engraved, rococo title cartouche which was designed to educate by depicting crafts and products associated with the county. These splendid maps were often further decorated by plans and views of important towns. However, they are open to criticism for their careless spelling and placement of names, their miscalculation of longitude (which was less accurate than on Morden's maps of 1695) and the distortion of some counties along the east–west axis. The six counties of South Wales were printed as two separate maps per sheet and, since there was no space for separation, are usually found cropped, often with false margins.

The *Royal English Atlas* is often dismissed as a straightforward reduction of the *Large English Atlas*. Admittedly, it was an attempt to 'cash in' on the investment involved in the larger atlas, for reduced maps could be engraved from the same survey material. The only cost was that of engraving and this was, in fact, a traditional method of spreading overheads and increasing return. These reduced maps (16) were modified thus: (i) the title cartouches were changed or reduced but usually continued to express the same themes; (ii) the town plans and dedication cartouches were removed but views of cathedrals were added; (iii) the descriptive notes were edited to place greater emphasis on the growth of new industrial centres; (iv) there was some revision of map detail. The resulting maps were almost as splendid as the larger maps.

A final reduction of the same material was produced in the much smaller *Atlas Anglicanus* of about 1767. These maps (17) showed virtually the same details but were without the elegant decoration, having only a simple rococo title cartouche; they repeated the same errors but sometimes attempted to appear new by covering blank areas with trees and small hills. The atlas was completed by Thomas Bowen after his father's death in 1767.

Bowen's maps are sometimes found with original colouring, and it is interesting to note that originally colour was added only to the county and hundred boundaries, and not to the cartouches, views and vignettes as modern colourists tend to apply it.

Emanuel's years of hard work seem to have produced little comfort, for Richard Gough recounts that 'Mr. Bowen' was 'reduced by family extravagances, and almost blind through age', whilst also criticising his maps as 'very faulty', 'incorrect', and 'scarce two places are spelt right'.

Select Bibliography

(*F*) BOWEN, E.: *Britannia Depicta or Ogilby Improved Road Atlas of England and Wales 1731 by Emanuel Bowen. Complete Facsimile Reprint Edition*. (1979).

(*F*) BOWEN, E. AND KITCHIN, T.: *The Royal English Atlas: Eighteenth-Century County Maps of England and Wales*. Introduction by *J. B. Harley & D. Hodson*. (1971).

(14) Description: *st*: Second. (Fig. 4). **Supply:** Moderate. **Average size:** 525 × 700 mm (21 × 28 in.). **Features:** The maps have copious historical and topographical notes on the county and its towns: e.g. 'Ramsey Meer produces larger Fish and more in quantity than any of the Meers and Pools in the Fenns, which are all full of Fish and Fowl. Here Pikes of a wonderful bigness are caught and tho it is perpetually haunted by Fishers, Fowlers and Pochers, yet there's an inexhaustable store of Game left' (Huntingdon). **Scale:** *V/av*: 1 :2*m/* 'British Statute Miles 69 to a Degree'/*Vw/sbm/*some maps have *n* and some have a second scale, e.g. 'Common English Miles 60 to a Degree'. **Border:** *OB:sl/IB:ll/mf* is covered by a graticule based on the latitude and longitude graduations/the border is sometimes marked with reference letters for the graticule. **North point:** *q/*or:*r/*with *f* and *e*. **Key:** Most maps have an 'Explanation'. **Decoration:** All maps have decorative features, including magnificent title cartouches, prospects and views of important towns, town plans, decorative cartouches for the key, and dedications and arms set within decorative cartouches. The amount of decoration varies between maps. **Title:** 'An ACCURATE MAP of the COUNTY of ... Divided into its HUNDREDS, Drawn from SURVEYS and Illustrated with various additional Improvements; ALSO Historical Extracts relating its Trade, Manufactures, Natural History etc. not extant in any other Map. By Eman: Bowen Geog^r to His Majesty'/*V/vl/*set in a large cartouche of local scenery, crafts and produce. (N.B. Middlesex is by Richard Seale). **Engravers:** Emanuel Bowen, Thomas Kitchin, and J. A. Walker (Hertford).

Issues: (i) 1749–1760: The maps were issued as loose sheets when prepared. Beginning with Sussex in May 1749, there was to be 'a Map of a County publish'd once a Month, 'till the Whole is finished'. However, the series was apparently not completed until 1760 and atlases are known with incomplete sets of maps issued probably by John Tinney about 1755. The maps continued to be sold separately throughout the issue period and old map stock was frequently used in later issues. Maps issued before 1760 usually bear the publisher's imprint of John Hinton, who initiated the project and published the maps until 1752, and John Tinney, who took over publication until 1756 when he joined with Robert Sayer, Thomas Bowles, and John Bowles & Son to continue publication. *State:* First (v). *Imprints:* (i) *obbc:pi:* 'Sold by I. Hinton at the Kings Arms in St Pauls Church yard London 17 ..' (*V*) with dates from 1749 to 1752; or: 'Sold by J. Tinney at the Golden Lion in Fleet Street London 17 ..' (*V*), usually with dates from 1753 to 1755. Some maps changed from the Hinton imprint to the Tinney imprint, altering the date accordingly. (ii) 1760(?): *Atlas: The large English atlas: or, a new set of maps of all the counties in England and Wales, drawn from the several surveys which have been hitherto published ... laid down on a large scale ... By Emanuel Bowen, geographer to His Majesty, Thomas Kitchen, and others ....* **Maps (45):** (a) England and Wales. (b) 36 English county maps (Gloucester with Monmouth; Leicester with Rutland; Cumberland with Westmorland). (c) York; East; West; North Ridings. (d) North Wales. (e) Three sheets of Welsh counties (comprising six individual maps, two per sheet, of: Brecon, Cardigan, Carmarthen, Glamorgan, Pembroke and Radnor). *State:* Second (most maps). *Imprint:* (i) *obbc:pi* altered: 'Printed for Robt Sayer in Fleet Street, T. Bowles in St Pauls Church Yard, John Bowles & Son, in Cornhil & John Tinney in Fleet Street' (*V*: the names vary in order, some addresses are extended, and some imprints are dated between 1756 and 1760). *Publishers:* T. Bowles, John Bowles & Son, John Tinney, and Robert Sayer. (iii) (a) 1762(?); (b) 1763(?); (c) 1764(?): as (ii) 1760, except: **Maps (47):** Scotland and Ireland are added c.1763. *State:* Third (most maps). *Imprints:* (i) *obbc:pi* altered: John Tinney's name and address are erased from the imprint leaving a gap in some cases. (ii) within borderlines top right or *obar*, and *obbr:* plate-number added. *Publishers:* (a) T. Bowles, John Bowles & Son, and Robert Sayer. (b) T. Bowles, John Bowles, and Robert Sayer. (c) John Bowles, Carington Bowles, and Robert Sayer. (iv) (a) 1765(?); (b) 1765(?); (c) 1767; 1780; (d) 1780(?): as (iii) 1762(?), etc., except: *State:* Fourth (most maps). *Imprints:* (i) *obbc:pi* altered during these issues: 'Printed for Robt Sayer in Fleet Street, John Bowles in Cornhil, & Carington Bowles in St Pauls Church Yard' (*V*: due to the removal of the 'Son' from John Bowles's imprint when his son Carington left the firm in 1762 to take over his uncle's business, and the omission of John Bowles's name from some imprints after his death in 1779). Some imprints give extended addresses and/or do not substitute Carington for Thomas Bowles. Imprints are known dated 1777. (ii) most plate-numbers are altered or erased. *Publishers:* (a) T. Bowles, John Bowles, and Robert Sayer (i.e. use of old title-page!) (b) John Bowles, Carington Bowles, and Robert Sayer. (c) Carington Bowles. (d) Robert Sayer. (v) 1785(?): as (iv) 1765(?), etc., except: *State:* Fifth (most maps). *Imprint:* (i) *obbc:pi* altered: Robert Wilkinson's name is incorporated into about half of the publishers' imprints: 'Printed for Robt Sayer in Fleet Street, Robt Wilkinson in Cornhil, & Carington Bowles in St Pauls Church Yard' (*V*). *Publisher:* 'Robert Wilkinson, at No. 58, in Cornhill, Successor to Mr John Bowles, deceased.' (vi) 1787: as (v) 1785(?), except: *Atlas: The large English atlas: ... The whole engraved on 50 copper plates ... By Emanuel Bowen, Thomas Kitchen, Captain Andrew Armstrong, and others ...* **Maps (50):** (a) England and Wales; Scotland; Ireland. (b) English and Welsh counties as before (except: (i) some copies of the atlas substitute a map of Warwick engraved by Jefferys; (ii) new maps of Lincoln and Northumberland taken from Armstrong are substituted; (iii) an extra map of Rutland taken from Armstrong is added). (c) 35 miles round London; plan of London, Westminster and the borough of Southwark. *State:* Fifth (most maps). *Imprint:* (i) Robert Wilkinson's name is added to a few more imprints, usually in place of John Bowles's. *Publisher:* Robert Sayer. (vii) c.1794: as (vi) 1787, except: *Atlas: The large English atlas: or, a new set of maps of all the counties in England and Wales, drawn from the several surveys which have been hitherto published ....* *State:* Sixth (most maps). *Imprint:* (i) *obbc:pi* altered on most maps during the course of the c.1794 issues: 'London. Printed for R. Wilkinson 58 Cornhill, Laurie & Whittle 53 Fleet Street, and Bowles & Carver 69 St Pauls Church Yard' (*V*). *Publisher:* Carington Bowles.

N.B.: There was another issue in this state published c.1794 by Robert Sayer with the title as (vi).

(15) Description: *st:* First. **Supply:** Scarce. **Average size:** 175 × 195 mm (7 × 7.75 in.). **Features:** A lettered reference key to administrative divisions: e.g. 'Hundreds'. **Scale:** *V/av:1:7m/*

'British Statute Miles'/*sbm*. **Border**: *OB*:*sl*/*IB*: *ll*/ *bb*. **North Point**: *q*/*f*/*e*/*V*. **Key**: 'Explanation'. **Title**: '. . . Divided into its HUNDREDS. Containing the Cities Buroughs & Market Towns with the Roads and Distances. By Eman: Bowen Geog.ʳ to His Majesty'/*V*/*vl*/set within a foliated cartouche. **Engraver**: Emanuel Bowen.

Issues: (i) 1759–63: issued until at least 1767: *Atlas: The natural history of England; or, a description of each particular county, in regard to the curious productions of nature and art. Illustrated by a map of each county ... By Benjamin Martin ....* (which formed part of *The general magazine of arts and sciences* published between 1755 and 1764). *Maps (42):* (a) England and Wales. (b) 38 English county maps (Leicester with Rutland). (c) Yorkshire. (d) North; South Wales. **State:** First.

Imprint: *obbc*:*pi*: 'Engrav'd for the General Magazine, of Arts & Sciences; for W. Owen at Temple Bar 17 ..' (*V*). Most imprints are dated between 1756 and 1762. Cornwall, Devon, Dorset and Wiltshire lack this imprint. **Publishers:** W. Owen, 'Temple-Bar', and Benjamin Martin 'at his House in Fleet-street'.

N.B.: Atlas copies were possibly made up using some of the maps originally published by John Hinton in *The universal magazine of knowledge and pleasure* (52(i)) with the inscription and imprint removed.

Close copies of these maps were published in 1770 by Pieter Meijer in *Algemeene oefenschoole van konsten en weetenschappen* .... the map and title are engraved in Dutch and Meijer's name appears in the title cartouche.

55 16(i): North Wales by Emanuel Bowen, c.1763. *By permission of the British Library (Maps C.26.e.9.)*

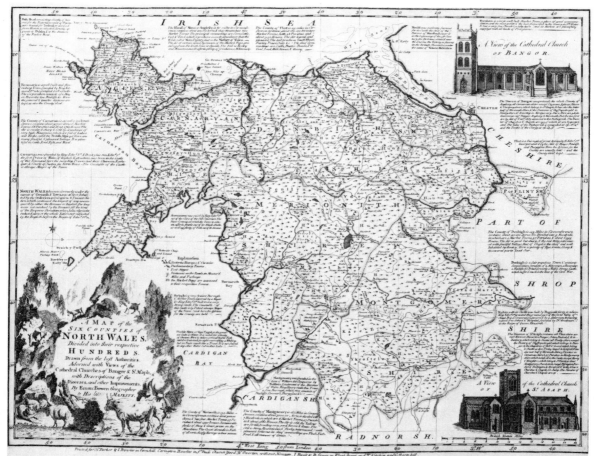

(16) **Description:** *st*: First. (Fig. 55). **Supply:** Moderately scarce. **Average size:** 388 × 500 mm (15.5 × 19.5 in.). **Features:** All available space is filled with historical and descriptive notes on the county and towns: e.g. 'Canvey I. is often over flowed by the Thames except the Hilly Part where the Sheep retire from the flood' (Essex). Some maps have listings of the nobility and of country seats. **Scale:** *V*/*av*: 1:4*m*/'British Statute Miles,' etc./*sbm*/*Vw*. **Border:** *OB:sl*/*IB*: *ll*/*bb*/*mf* has a graticule derived from the latitude and longitude graduations. **North point:** *q*/*f*/*e*. **Key:** 'Explanation' or 'Remarks'. **Decoration:** The title is set within a magnificent cartouche of local scenery, crafts and produce (except: Hampshire and South Wales which have simple foliated/scrolled cartouches). Many maps have a fine vignette view of a cathedral (Kent and North Wales show two cathedrals). **Title:** 'An Accurate MAP of the COUNTY of ..., Divided into Hundreds; Drawn from Surveys, & Illustrated wth Historical Extracts relative to its Natural Produce, Trade and Manufactures; distinguishing also the Church Livings, Charity Schools, Religious houses etc. By John Gibson. Revised, Corrected & improved by Eman. Bowen Geographer to his Majesty'/*V*/*vl*/*sd*/set within a decorative cartouche. **Engravers:** Emanuel & Thomas Bowen, John Gibson, and Thomas Kitchin.

Issues: The maps were issued as loose sheets when prepared and throughout most of the period of atlas issue. (i) 1763 (?): **Atlas:** *The royal English atlas: being a new and accurate set of maps of all the counties of south Britain, drawn from surveys ... and exhibiting all the cities, towns, villages, churches, chapels, etc. Particularly distinguishing more fully and accurately the church livings than any other maps hitherto published. Adorned with views of all the cathedrals; and a concise description of each diocese; ... By Emanuel Bowen, geographer to His late Majesty, Thomas Kitchin, geographer, and others .... **Maps (44):** (a) England and Wales. (b) 37 English county maps (Cumberland with Westmorland; Leicester with Rutland). (c) York; East; West; North Ridings. (d) North; South Wales. **State:** First. **Imprints:** (i) *obbl*: 'N.°..' (22 maps only). (ii) *obbc:pi*: the plates were engraved in two groups which bear different imprints. (a) 24 maps have: 'Printed for R. Sayer & J. Ryall in Fleetstreet, T. Bowles in S.t Pauls Church Yard, J. Bowles & Son and Mess. Bakewell & Parker in Cornhill, H. Overton without Newgate and T. Kitchin on Holborn Hill' (*V*). (b) 20 maps have: 'Printed for R. Sayer & J. Ryall in Fleet Street, T.

Kitchin on Holborn Hill, H. Overton without Newgate, Carington Bowles in S.t Paul's Church Yard, J. Bowles and H. Parker in Cornhill' (*V*). (Sussex has the imprint on *mf* at top right.) **Publishers:** See above. (ii) 1779(?): as (i) 1763(?), except: **State:** Second. **Imprint:** (ii) *obbc:pi* altered: 'London, Printed for Rob.t Sayer & John Bennett, N.° 53, Fleet Street. John Bowles, N.° 13, Cornhill. & Carington Bowles, N.° 69, S.t Pauls Church Yard, as the Act directs. 1.st of June 1777' (*V*). (Devon, Essex, Hereford, Leicester and Rutland, and Worcester: dated 1778). **Publisher:** Robert Wilkinson. (iii) 1778(?); 1781(?): as (ii) 1779(?), except: **States:** 1778(?): Second; 1781(?): first and second. **Atlas:** *The royal English atlas: being a new and accurate set of maps of all the counties in England and Wales* ....

N.B. The 1781(?) issue was made up with a mixture of all the above imprints.

Publisher: Carington Bowles. (iv) 1780(?): as (iii) 1778(?); 1781(?), except: **Atlas:** *The royal English atlas; being accurate maps of all the counties in England and Wales: from numerous surveys .... The whole comprized in fifty sheet maps. By Thomas Kitchin, geographer, and others ....* **Maps (48):** As above, plus: (a) British Isles; Scotland. (b) London and Borough of Southwark; City and Liberty of Westminster. **State:** Second (except: new maps). **Publishers:** Robert Sayer & John Bennett. (v) 1828(?): as (iv) 1780(?), except: **Atlas:** *The English atlas; or, a set of maps of all the counties in England and Wales, drawn from the best authorities ....* **Maps (43):** as c.1763: (b), (c) and (d). **States:** Various. **Imprint:** From 1794 [24] publishers' imprints were altered on Gloucester, Essex, Kent, Sussex, and South Wales to those of Bowles & Carver, Laurie & Whittle, and Robert Wilkinson for atlas issues by Bowles & Carver and Laurie & Whittle made up with old title-pages and old map stock. **Publisher:** 'R. Martin, Bookseller, No. 47, Great Queen Street, Lincoln's-Inn Fields'.

(17) **Description:** *st*: First. **Supply:** Scarce. **Average size:** 215 × 312 mm (8.6 × 12.5 in.). **Features:** All available space surrounding the map detail is used for informative notes on the county, its produce and its towns: e.g. 'East and West Cowes are two pretty Towns, the latter especially. They have each of them a castle, that at East Cowes has been neglected, but in the other a Garrison is constantly kept. This is the Rendezvous for Merchant Ships waiting for Convoy' (Isle of Wight). **Scale:** *V*/*av*: 1:6*m*/'British Statute Miles'/*sbm*/*Vw*.

Border: *OB:sl/IB:ll/*maps have a graticule based on the latitude and longitude divisions. **North Point:** *q/or: r/*with *f/*and *e*. **Key:** 'Explanation'. **Decoration:** Foliated, rococo title cartouche. **Title:** '... Divided into its HUNDREDS: Containing the City, Burough, Market Towns etc. with concise Historical Extracts relative to Trade, Manufactures & Natural Production. Describing also the Church Livings with Improvements not inserted in any other set of Half Sheet County Maps Extant by Eman: Bowen Geog.^r to His late Majesty, & Thos Bowen'/*V/vl/*set within a decorative cartouche. **Engravers:** Emanuel & Thomas Bowen.

Issues: (i) 1767(?): **Atlas:** *Atlas Anglicanus, or a complete sett of maps of the counties of south Britain; divided into their respective hundreds, wapentakes, wards, rapes, lathes etc. .... By the late Emanuel Bowen, geographer to His Majesty George II.^d and Thomas Bowen ....* **Maps (45):** (a) two general maps of England and Wales. (b) 37 English county maps (Cumberland with Westmorland; Leicester with Rutland). (c) Yorkshire; East; West; North Ridings. (d) North; South Wales. **State:** First. **Imprint:** (i) *obar*: 'N.^o ..' (*V*), (except: *obbr*: Lancashire; *obal*: Hereford, Worcester; without reference number: Berkshire, Buckingham, Cheshire, Sussex). The atlas was possibly issued in parts as the plates were prepared and the reference number may refer to the part in which the map appeared. **Publisher:** Thomas Kitchin.

N.B. Traces of an erased imprint, *obbc*, are known which suggest that there may have been an earlier issue.

(ii) 1770(?): as (i) 1767(?), except: **State:** Second. **Imprints:** (i) *obar*: reference number erased. (ii) *obbc:pi*: 'Printed for T. Kitchin N.º 59 Holborn Hill, London' (*V*).

N.B. A further issue in this state was published in 1777 by Thomas Kitchin & Andrew Dury.

(iii) 1785: as (ii) 1770(?), except: **Atlas:** *Bowles's new medium English atlas; or, complete set of maps of the counties of England and Wales: divided into their respective hundreds, wapontakes, wards, rapes, lathes, etc. .....* **Maps (44):** as (i) 1767(?) but with only one general map of England and Wales. **State:** Third. Some revisions and additions to the maps. Compass indicators are standardised as: *r/f/e*. The distances of the main towns from London are added, but the distances between towns have been erased. In particular, a new title is substituted within a plain circular or oval panel with *Tt* frame: 'BOWLES's NEW MEDIUM MAP OF .... DIVIDED into its

HUNDREDS; Exhibiting the Roads, Towns and Villages, with their Distance from London, Church Livings, Seats of the Nobility, and Historical Remarks. LONDON: printed for the Proprietor Carington Bowles, N.º 69 in St Pauls Church Yard'/*vl/V*. **Imprints:** (i) *obar* or within borderlines: new plate-number added. (ii) *obbc*: new imprint: 'Published as the Act directs, 3 Jan. 1785' (*V*). **Publisher:** 'Carington Bowles, at his Map and Print Warehouse, No. 69, in St. Paul's Church Yard'. (iv) c.1795: as (iii) 1785, except: **State:** Fourth. **Imprints:** (ii) *obbc*: publishing imprint erased. (iii) The imprint in the title panel is altered thus: '... LONDON: Printed for the Proprietors Bowles & Carver, N.º 69 in St Paul's Church Yard'. **Publishers:** Bowles & Carver.

56 18(i): Cornwall by Emanuel Bowen & John Owen, 1720. *Photograph: Mills-Wight Studio*

BOWEN, Emanuel and OWEN, John.
(18) Description: *st*: First (*v*). (Fig. 56). **Supply**: Moderate. **Average size**: Map only: 109 × 117 mm (4.3 × 4.7 in.). Overall: 117 × 183 mm (4.7 × 7.3 in.). **Features**: Administrative divisions are noted in a numbered reference key sometimes framed by a crudely engraved line. Free areas contain informative notes concerning the county: e.g. 'the Men are Strong & boisterous, great Wrestlers & Healthy' (Cornwall). Details of size, climate, industry and commerce are noted. **Scale**: *V/av*: 1:11*m*/'English Miles'/*sbm*. **Border**: A decorative, patterned frame, approximately 4 mm (0.2 in.) wide with narrow *dl IB* and *OB*. Each map has a crudely engraved page number at the top-outer corner. **Decoration**: Some maps have the arms of the principal town. **Title**: *c*/or: 'A MAP OF . . .'/ *pc*/usually within a rectangular panel with a wide decorated frame. Each map is surmounted by a large, elaborate cartouche of foliage, scrollwork, shells, grotesques, etc. containing the title of a road-strip map: 'THE ROAD FROM . . . TO . . .' above a distance table. **Engraver**: Emanuel Bowen.
Issues: (i) 1720: *Atlas*: *Britannia depicta or Ogilby improv'd; being a correct coppy of M^r: Ogilby's actual survey of all ye direct & principal cross roads in England and Wales: wherein are exactly delineated & engraven, all ye cities, towns, villages, churches, seats etc. scituate on or near the roads, with their respective distances in measured and computed miles. And to render this-work universally useful & agreeable, . . . are added . . . a full & particular description & account of all the cities, . . . & . . . by In^o. Owen of the Midd: Temple gent . . . lastly particular & correct maps- of all ye counties of south Britain; . . . by Eman: Bowen engraver . . . . Maps (273)*: printed back-to-back: (a) 39 English counties. (b) North and East Riding of 'York Shire'; West Riding of 'York Shire'. (c) 12 Welsh counties. (d) The smaller islands in the British Ocean. (e) 220 strip road maps. *State*: First (*v*). *Publishers*: Thomas Bowles 'Print & Map Seller next ye Chapter House in St Pauls Church-Yard' & Emanuel Bowen 'next ye King of Spain in S: Katherines'.
N.B. The atlas was issued, sometimes with very minor changes, as follows: (i) by Thomas Bowles & Emanuel Bowen: 1721; 1723. (ii) by Thomas & John Bowles: 1724. (iii) by Thomas Bowles: 1730; 1731; 1734; 1736; 1746(?); 1749; 1751; 1753; 1755; 1759. (iv) by Carington Bowles: 1764 (with a shorter title).
(19) Description: *st*: First (*v*). (Fig. 34). **Supply**: Moderate. **Average size**: 117 × 183 mm (4.7 × 7.3 in.). **Features**: The maps have informative notes added in any available free area: e.g. '. . . but the Town has little now left worth remarking . . .' (Somerton); '. . . here was formerly a retiring place for our Kings, from the smoaky Air of ye Town . . .' (Eltham). **Border**: The maps consist of three or four strips, each approximately 30 mm (1.2 in.) wide separated by *sl/OB:sl/bts/bltr*/the plate-number, in crude figures, is engraved at the top outer-corner of the page. **North Point**: *r/f*/since orientation varies, each strip has a north point. **Decoration**: The maps are decorated by the arms of towns or noblemen, set within decorative cartouches of scrolling, foliage, crowns, mitres, shells, etc. **Engraver**: Emanuel Bowen. **Issues**: see (18).

BOWEN, Thomas
fl. 1760–1790d. Engraver and map-seller

Thomas Bowen worked with his father, Emanuel, on the *Royal English Atlas* (16) and the *Atlas Anglicanus* (17) which he completed after his father's death in 1767. He engraved maps for Taylor & Skinner's *Survey of the Roads of North Britain* (106) and many other publications (e.g. see (53)). Thomas also produced some county maps for literary periodicals in a plainer, less ornamental style than his father's. These scarce, small maps (average size: 180 × 200 mm: 7 × 8 in.) have decorative cartouches and sometimes shields bearing coats-of-arms. Thomas died in Clerkenwell workhouse early in 1790. D.N.B.: Vol. 2, p. 956.

BOWLES FAMILY

The Bowles family were prolific and important map publishers in the eighteenth century, publishing the *Large English Atlas* (14), the *Royal English Atlas* (16), *Britannia Depicta* (18, 19), Moll's *A New Description of England and Wales* (77), and many other works. However, only Carington published atlases under the Bowles' name. His three atlases were re-issues, with altered titles, of plates previously published. *Bowles's New Medium English Atlas* adapted the plates from Bowen's *Atlas Anglicanus* (17); *Bowles's Pocket Atlas* adapted the plates from Kitchin's *Pocket Atlas* (62); and *Bowles's Post-Chaise Companion* adapted the plates from Kitchin's *New and Instructive Traveller's Companion* (63).
N.B. (a) for: 1785: *Bowles's New Medium English Atlas; or, Complete Set of Maps of the Counties of England and Wales* . . . . see (17). (b) for: 1781(?): *Bowles's Pocket Atlas of the Counties*

THOMAS BOWLES I fl.1683-c.1714
Publisher. Business premises in
St Paul's Churchyard. Acquired
the stock of Philip Lea

JOHN BOWLES fl.1720-77
Publisher. Business
premises at the Black
Horse in Cornhill

THOMAS BOWLES II fl.c.1714-c.1762
Engraver & Map-seller. In
partnership with his father
and eventually took over the
business some years before his
father's death in 1721. Since
his only son Thomas III died
in late 1762, the business
was taken over by his nephew
Carington

CARINGTON BOWLES fl.1754-93d.
Publisher. In partnership with
his father from 1753 to 1762
as 'John Bowles & Son'.
About 1762, Carington took over
his uncle's business, and his
father continued alone in
Cornhill. The business was
taken over, on John's death,
by Robert Wilkinson (fl.1779-1829)

Carington died in 1793. His
business was continued by
his son, Henry Carington
Bowles, with Samuel Carver
as 'Bowles & Carver'. The
firm purchased the map stock
of Robert Wilkinson

of South Britain or England and Wales .... see
(62). (c) for: c.1781(?): *Bowles's Post-Chaise
Companion* .... see (63).

BROWN, Thomas
fl. 1786–1820. Publisher and map-seller

Thomas Brown was an important publisher of maps
of Scotland. He produced the reduced version of
Taylor & Skinner's Scottish roads (108) in 1805(?)
and 1813(?), but is better known for his fine *Atlas of
Scotland* (20) which was sold with 'Coloured
Outlines' at £1 11s. 6d. and 'Fully Coloured' at
£1 14s. 0d. Brown also published plans of
Edinburgh and 'has always for Sale, the greatest
variety of Atlasses, Maps, Books on Geography, etc.
Drawing Materials and every description of Station-
ary Good.'

(20) **Description:** *st*: First. (Fig. 57). **Supply:**
Scarce. **Average size:** 280 × 318 mm
(11 × 12.75 in.). **Scale:** *V*/*av*: 1:5*m*/'Scale of Statute
Miles 69½ to a Degree'; or 'Scale of Miles ...'; or
simply 'Scale of Miles'/*sbmf*. **Border:** *OB:Tt*/*IB:ll*/
bb. **North Point:** *s*/*f*/*e*. **Title:** 'A New and Accurate

57 20(i): Ayrshire by Thomas Brown, 1807. *By
permission of the British Library (Maps C.27.d.28.)*

Map of ... from the latest Surveys'/*V*/*vl*/*sd*/set within a plain oval panel with a wide *dl* frame. Set within this frame, below the title, is the inscription: 'Published by Thos. Brown Bookseller Edinburgh' (*V*). Below this panel is the inscription either: 'Gavin & Son Sculp!' or 'T. Clerk Sculp!'. ('Kirkcudbright & Wigton Shires' has the inscription: 'Eng^d by T. Clerk Edin!' below the title, within the panel.) **Engravers**: Mainly Gavin & Son, but a few maps were engraved by T. Clerk.

Issues: (i) 1807(?): Issued in nine parts of four maps each from 1800: *Atlas: Atlas of Scotland being a new set of county maps from actual surveys shewing the cities, towns, & villages, principal roads, and cross roads, the rivers, canals, hills, etc. . . . . Maps (27):* (a) Index map. (b) 22 Scottish county maps. (Six maps combine two counties each; one combines three.) (c) Island of Skye; Island of Lewis; Orkney Islands; Shetland Islands. *State*: First. *Imprints*: *pi*: set within the frame of the title panel; *es*: usually appears below this panel. *Publisher*: 'Thomas Brown N° 1 North Bridge, Edinburgh'.

BRYANT, Andrew
fl. 1824–1835. Surveyor and cartographer

Bryant was the great rival of the Greenwoods in the production of large-scale county maps but his more detailed, larger-scale (1 inch to 0.66 miles) maps proved less popular and he mapped only 13 counties. The competition was so intense that both Bryant and the Greenwoods (and, in some cases, the Ordnance Survey as well) were surveying the same county at the same time.

BUTTERS, R
fl. 1803. Publisher

Butters produced an interesting series of plain maps (21) for his *Atlas of England*, which was later re-issued in William Green's *Picture of England*. These maps are often referred to as the 'upside-down' maps since only a few are engraved with north to the top of the map. Green was evidently somewhat philosophical about the commercial potential of his small atlas: 'Cheapness, elegance, and conciseness, form the leading, and perhaps the only merit of the following pages: if the work deserves public patronage, it will have it, if it has no merit, the author will not unjustly suffer for his temerity.' Butters also published John Lodge's maps (73) for *The Political Magazine*.

(21) Description: *st*: First. **Supply**: Scarce.

Average size: 90 × 120 mm (3.5 × 4.75 in.). **Features**: Very little detail shown. **Scale**: *V*/*av*: 1:10*m*/'Scale of Miles'/*Vw*/*sl*: divided into two five mile intervals. **Border**: *dl*. **North Point**: *c*/*p* or *f*/*V*: many maps have south at the top of the map, some have east or west, and a very few have north. Compass indicators on some maps point to the south. **Title**: *c*/*pc*/*obbc*. (The titles of Norfolk and Northampton are positioned below the map and consequently appear to the right of the page. These were repositioned at the bottom of the page for the 1804 issue and appear to the left of the maps.)

Issues: (i) 1803(?): *Atlas: An atlas of England* .... *Maps (41):* (a) England and Wales (as a frontispiece). (b) 39 English Counties. (c) Yorkshire. *State*: First (*v*). *Publisher*: 'R. Butters, N° 22, Fetter Lane, Fleet Street'. (ii) 1804: as (i) 1803(?), except: *Atlas: The picture of England illustrated with correct colour'd maps of the several counties ... by William Green, A.B. ... State*: First (*v*). *Publisher*: J. Hatchard.

CARY, John
fl. c.1783–1835d. Engraver, cartographer and publisher

John Cary stands as a giant amongst British cartographers. His prolific output created new standards of draughtsmanship and engraving, and determined the functional style of the nineteenth century by concentrating on content rather than decoration. Cary's maps were delicately engraved by master craftsmen and presented increasingly complex geographical information with great clarity and simplicity. They rank with the Ordnance Survey as the finest maps of the period and offer a marked contrast to the work of less skilled contemporaries. Cary allowed himself only to decorate the north point, and this lack of other ornamentation created maps of stark beauty. The wide availability of clear, clean impressions of Cary's maps, produced by the most advanced printing processes of the day, offers some of the finest maps of the nineteenth century.

Cary started as an engraver, his name first appearing as engraver on a canal plan of 1779, but from about 1800 his increasing interest in cartography and publishing forced him to delegate the engraving work to his skilled staff. He built up an extensive publications' list, including several atlases which passed through many editions, and a great variety of separate maps, charts, plans, guides, road books, celestial charts, geological maps and sections,

Brother: Francis Cary
(1756-1836)
Engraver

Brother: William Cary
(1759-1825)
Map publisher and
instrument- and globe-
maker. Collaborated
with John.

JOHN CARY
(c. 1754-1835)
c. 1783-91:
Business
premises at
the corner of
Arundel Street,
188, Strand.

Brother: George Cary
(d. 1830)

1791-1820:
Business premises
at 181, Strand;
destroyed by fire.

1820-c. 1844: Business premises at 86, St. James's
Street. John probably transferred the business to
his sons George (d. 1859) and John II (c. 1791-1852)
but remained an active partner: the firm trading as
'G. and J. Cary' and selling not only atlases but also
'Guide and Road Books, Globes, Celestial Charts,
Planetariums, Geological Maps, Optical & Mathematical
Instruments, Microscopes, Magic Lanterns, Orreries,
Air pumps & Electrical Machines'[25]

Stock-in-trade and cartographical work taken over
c. 1846 by George Frederick Cruchley of 81, Fleet Street.

Some of Cary's plates passed to Messrs. Gall & Inglis,
Edinburgh in 1877.

canal plans, and so on. The Cary firms also produced magnificent and much sought-after globes. The maps were more advanced and accurate than any comparable sets produced earlier because Cary could not only draw on his own work but also on the now numerous large-scale county surveys and the early Ordnance Survey maps.

Cary's early maps concentrated on his main interest of communication development and he produced a number of beautiful road books. He engraved the maps (22) of Aaron Arrowsmith's survey of the road from London to Falmouth and published this exquisite little series in 1784. His *Survey of the High Roads from London to Hampton Court* (27) was first issued in 1790, and, although finely engraved, was rather disappointing in that there was no indication of the quality of road surfaces—surely an important consideration at a time of such variable road maintenance. He concentrated only on high ground, heath and rivers, ignoring the Ordnance Survey's conventional symbols which were being used by some other

contemporary cartographers; but he did provide mileage, turnpike and toll information so that travellers could take advantage of the cheapest rates and achieve the maximum distance possible from their tickets. The *Survey* and other works, particularly those concerned with London, sought to guarantee their market by flattering wealthy country house owners: 'pleased with the numberless villas which so often attract his attention, his enquiry is naturally directed to whom do they belong, to explain which has been a principal object of the present publication'. Cary was engaged, in 1794, to measure the post and mail-coach roads of England and Wales for the General Post Office and these measurements were published in 1798 as his *Itinerary*. This work was re-issued many times, gradually growing in size and scope, and eventually including a few, rather plain maps (29). Cary published numerous individual and sets of maps of the environs of London (23) which were available either in sections or as miniature atlases; these remained on the market for many years.

He also issued several fine atlases of the counties of England and Wales. The smallest, the *Traveller's Companion* (which was often bound in with the *Itinerary*), proved to be so popular and went through so many editions that the plates had to be renewed twice. These charming little maps (26) were carefully prepared: 'Assisted by the report of the different Post Masters throughout the Kingdom ... of the number of Turnpike Roads leading from their respective Towns'. The *New and Correct English Atlas* of 1787 contained fine, quarto, county maps (24) which gave special emphasis to the roads by distinguishing between major and minor roads; and the *New Map of England and Wales* contained quarto sectional maps (28) which are particularly notable for the clarity of the connecting pages reference and the first general adoption of the prime longitude meridian of Greenwich instead of St. Paul's Cathedral. Cary engraved Noble's maps (25) for Richard Gough's translation of Camden's *Britannia*, showing, in particular, the hundred divisions; but his greatest works were the large county maps (30) of the *New English Atlas* which were issued many times, sometimes to display the geological discoveries of William Smith.

After the closing of the Cary firm, many of the plates passed to George Frederick Cruchley who re-issued the maps lithographically with added railway and parliamentary information, claiming that his maps were up-to-date: 'These maps' (i.e. (30) (xviii)) 'possess the following distinctive characters:

1. They are projected on the LARGEST SCALE yet adopted for any similar purpose.
2. They contain all the Latest Information of general utility or interest.
3. They have been CAREFULLY REVISED from the recent Ordnance Surveys of England and Wales.
4. The Lines of all the Railways are drawn showing the Company to which each line belongs.
5. The NAMES of all the Stations are engraved in clear and bold characters.
6. The Telegraphic Lines and Stations are especially marked on these Maps.
7. The CONTINUATION of each Railway into adjoining Counties is accurately delineated, EXHIBITING AT A GLANCE FACILITIES OF INTERCOMMUNICATION, and thus supplying an important desideratum to Commercialists'.
(*Cruchleys railway and telegraphic county atlas of England and Wales*)

Despite Cruchley's claims, the re-issued Cary maps appeared increasingly old-fashioned when compared with newer work influenced by the Ordnance Survey, and it is amazing that his plates continued to be used by publishers as a base for cycling and motoring maps until the early years of the twentieth century.

Cary's maps represent copper engraving at its best, yet his only public reward was the gold medal awarded to him by the Royal Society of Arts for the publication of Joseph Singer's large-scale map of Cardigan in 1804.

Select Bibliography
CARY:
FORDHAM, SIR H. G.: *John Cary. Engraver, Map, Chart and Print-Seller and Globe Maker 1754 to 1835.* (1925; reprinted 1976; see also: *Studies in Carto-Bibliography*, 1969 and 1974).

ARROWSMITH:
TOOLEY, R. V.: 'Aaron Arrowsmith'. (*MC*; Dec. 1979).

(22) **Description:** *st*: First. **Supply:** Rare. **Average size:** 63 × 120 mm (2.5 × 4.8 in.). **Features:** 'Every gentleman's seat, village, town, etc. within sight of the road is laid down, the principal inns on the road expressed, and the exact distances ascertained'. Most maps note inns below the lower border; some have mileage information and references to connecting plates. **Border:** *Tt/bt*. **North Point:** *p/f/V*. **Engraver:** John Cary.

Issues: (i) 1784: *Atlas: Cary's actual survey, of the great post roads between London & Falmouth, including a branch to Weymouth, as well as those from Salisbury to Axminster, either thro' Dorchester or Sherborne; those from Basingstoke to Salisbury, either thro' Popham Lane or Andover; & those from Exeter to Truro, either thro' Plymouth or Launceston ... By A. Arrowsmith land surveyor, 1782.* **Maps:** (i) Index map. (ii) 50 strip road maps. **State:** First. **Imprints:** (i) *obac*: plate-number. (ii) some maps have: *obbc:pi*: 'Published by J. Cary April 4 1784'. **Publisher:** 'J. Cary, Map, Print and Chart-seller, the Corner of Arundel Street, Strand.'

(23) **Description:** *st*: First. **Supply:** Scarce. **Average size:** 90 × 150 mm (3.6 × 6 in.). **Scale:** *n//*scale is 1:1 *m*. **Border:** *Tt*. **Engraver:** John Cary.

Issues: (i) 1786; 1800; 1811: *Atlas: Cary's actual survey of the country 15 miles round London on a scale of one inch to a mile wherein the roads, rivers, woods* and common as well as every market town, village etc. are distinguished and every seat shewn with the name of the possessor .... **Maps:** (a) Index map (double-page). (b) 50 sectional maps. **State:** First. **Imprints:** (i) *ob:* top right of page: page number. (ii) *ob:a, b,* or at the side: notes specify the pages on which the map is continued. (iii) some maps have: *obbc:pi:* 'Published by J. Cary Aug 15 1786'. **Publisher:** 'J. Cary, Engraver, Map & Print-seller No. 188 Strand.'

N.B. The index map and 28 relevant sectional maps, with altered page numbers and continuation references were issued in 1786 in *Cary's actual survey of Middlesex* ....

Cary also published in 1786: *Cary's actual survey of the country ten miles round Hampton Court & Richmond; on a scale of one inch to a mile. Wherein the roads, rivers, woods & commons, as well as every market town, village, etc. are distinguished; & every seat shewn with the name of the possessor ...:* in similar style and at the same size: index map + 18 sectional maps: plates 3, 10 and 14 only bear Cary's imprint.

(24) Description: *st:* Fourth. **Supply:** Plentiful. **Average size:** 210 × 260 mm (8.4 × 10.4 in.). **Features:** 'for the more ready application of the Turnpike Roads given in this work, it is observed, that they are connected in the Maps from one county to another by letters of reference added to those Roads at the extremity of each Map, unless adjacent places belonging to the adjoining county are given to each, so as to answer the same purpose of connecting, by affording a similar reference'. Some early issues bear the inscription: 'Note. The figures prefixed to the Towns denote their distance from London'. **Scale:** *V/av:* 1:5m/'Statute Miles 69½ to a Degree'/*Vw/sbm.* **Border:** *OB:Tt/IB:ll/bb.* **North Point:** *s/op/*positioned behind the title panel. **Title:** *c/oc/*set within a vertically hatched title panel. Beneath the panel and compass star is the curved *es:* 'By JOHN CARY Engraver'. (*V*). **Engraver:** John Cary.

Issues: Old map stocks were often used in later issues, and revisions were frequently made over periods which spanned a particular issue or several issues so that the contents of atlases could vary due to differing combinations of revised and unrevised maps. The maps were also sometimes issued in other publications. (i) 1787: **Atlas:** *Cary's new and correct English atlas: being a new set of county maps from actual surveys. Exhibiting all the direct & principal cross roads, cities, towns and most considerable villages, parks, rivers, navigable canals, etc....* **Maps (46):** (a) South Britain. (b) 39 English counties. (c) Yorkshire; Part of the West (two sheets); East; North Ridings. (d) North; South Wales. **State:** First. **Imprint:** *obbc:pi:* 'London: Published as the Act directs, Sept.ʳ 1, 1787, by J. Cary, Engraver, Map & Print-seller, the corner of Arundel Street Strand.' (*V*). **Publisher:** John Cary. The plates of some maps show evidence of constant revision throughout the issue period. Atlases with the 1787 dated title-page were made up with some plates in unrevised state and some showing various alterations and additions. This practice was continued with the issues of 1793. (ii) 1793: as (i) 1787, except: **State:** Second. **Imprint:** *obbc:pi* altered on 13 maps to a shorter form: 'London: Publish'd Sep.ʳ 1ˢᵗ 1787 by J. Cary. Engraver & Map-seller Strand' (*V*). (Durham is dated Jan 1. 1793). (iii) 1793: as (ii) 1793, except: **State:** Third. Reference letters are added to the main roads where they leave the county. (These were engraved progressively during the issues dated 1793.) **Imprint:** *obbc:pi* altered: 'London: Publish'd Jan.ʸ 1ˢᵗ 1793 by J. Cary. Engraver & Map-seller Strand.' (*V*) (Monmouth and Worcester are still dated Sep.ʳ 1ˢᵗ 1787; Leicester, Middlesex and Oxford are dated May 1ˢᵗ 1792). The imprint and date were clearly altered during the course of the 1793 dated issues since atlases with variant numbers of corrected imprints are known; maps without imprint are also known in early issues. A later issue dated 1793 but issued in 1795 corrected the imprints on the maps of Middlesex and Oxford, and altered the date to 1795 on Dorset. A further re-issue in 1795 dated all the imprints, except Dorset, 1793. The atlas was issued at various times until at least 1804, probably later, showing evidence of constant revision. (iv) 1808: as (iii) 1793, except: **States:** Various. The map plates were re-engraved from about 1808 and the 1808 and early 1809 atlas issues contain maps printed, in some cases, from original plates and, in others, from the re-engraved plates. The new plates produced a plate-mark approximately half-an-inch from the map border, whereas the mark of the earlier plates was only a quarter-of-an-inch from the border. **Imprint:** Re-engraved plates: *obbc:pi* altered: 'London. Published Jan.ʸ 1 1793 by J. Cary Engraver & Map seller Strand' (*V*), {date sometimes omitted}. (v) 1809: as (iv) 1808, except: **States:** Various. All the maps are now printed from re-engraved plates. Minor revisions

and additions. *Imprint: obbc:pi* altered: 'London: Published July 1. 1809 by J. Cary, Engraver & Map-seller Strand' (*V*). Westmorland is undated. (vi) 1812: as (v) 1809, except: *States:* Various. *Imprint: obbc:pi* altered: 'London. Published July 1.1812 by J. Cary Engraver & Map seller Strand' (*V*), (except: Rutland is still dated 1809). (vii) 1818; 1821; 1823; 1825; 1826; 1827; 1829; 1831: as (vi) 1812, except: *States:* Various. Minor revisions to map detail for many issues. *Imprint: obbc:pi*: date deleted: 'London: Published by J. Cary Engraver & Map seller Strand' (*V*).
N.B. Old map stocks were used in some copies.
(viii) 1840; 1843: as (vii) 1818, etc., except: *States:* Various. Borough boundaries are added as finely dotted lines, and railways are named and marked by thick black lines. (ix) 1863: by lithographic transfer: as (viii) 1840; 1843, except: *Atlas: Cruchley's county atlas of England & Wales shewing all the railways & stations with their names, also the turnpike roads and principal cross roads to all the cities, market and borough towns with the distance from town to town delineated on a series of 46 county maps .... Maps (46):* As above (the index map is sometimes omitted). *States:* Various. The titlepiece has been reworked so that the title panel, the compass star and the *es* are erased. The new title is: 'RAILWAY & STATION MAP OF ... WITH THE NAMES OF THE STATIONS'/*pc*. Railway information is up-dated, including the addition of stations and projected lines. Some maps are slightly increased in size and 15 maps have an 'EXPLANATION' of railway symbols added. The key to railway symbols was added to other maps before being deleted in 1868(?). Other minor revisions. *Imprints:* (i) *ob*: top right of page: plate-number added. (ii) *obbc*: new *pi*: 'LONDON. PUBLISHED BY G.F. CRUCHLEY, MAP-SELLER & GLOBE MAKER 81, FLEET STREET' (*V*). *Publisher:* George Frederick Cruchley. The maps were issued with minor changes in c.1864 and in 1864 (states: various). (x) 1868(?): by lithographic transfer: as (ix) 1863, except: *States:* Various. Minor revisions were made during this issue. Railway information is up-dated and the title is erased leaving only the county name (this name is sometimes moved causing the movement of non-topographical features). *Imprint:* (i) a few plate numbers are altered. (ii) *obbc*: there is no *pi*, (except: England). The maps were issued with minor changes in c.1872 in the four parts of *Cruchley's new pocket companion, or, handmaid to Bradshaw and all other railway time-tables for England & Wales.* (xi) 1875; 1876: by lithographic transfer: as (x) 1868(?), except: *States:* Various. Railway information is up-dated and two lines now appear below the title. *Imprints: obbc:pi*: 'LONDON. PUBLISHED BY G.F. CRUCHLEY, MAP-SELLER & GLOBE MAKER, 81, FLEET STREET' (*V*).

(25) Description: *st*: First. (Fig. 58). **Supply:** Moderate. **Average size:** *V*/420 × 490 mm (16.75 × 19.6 in.). **Features:** A lettered/numbered reference key to administrative divisions: e.g. 'REFERENCE TO THE HUNDREDS'. **Scale:** *V*/*av*: 1:3*m*/'Scale of Miles 69½ to a Degree of Latitude'/*Vw/sbm*//The maps of the West Riding of Yorkshire have *n*. **Border:** *OB:Tt/IB:ll*. **North Point:** *s/f*/an unusual 'cross of Lorraine' indicates east. **Title:** 'A MAP OF ... FROM THE BEST AUTHORITIES'/*V/oc/sd*. Beneath the titlepiece is the *es*: 'Engraved by J. Cary'. **Engraver:** John Cary.

Issues: The maps were also sometimes issued in other publications. (i) 1789: *Atlas: Britannia: or, a chorographical description of the flourishing kingdoms of England, Scotland, and Ireland ... By William Camden. Translated from the edition published by the author in MDCVII ... by Richard Gough, F.A. & R.S.S. .... Maps (60):* (a) Great Britain and Ireland; England and Wales; South part of Scotland; North part of Scotland; Ireland. (b) 39 English counties. (c) North part of the West; South part of the West; East; North (two sheets) Ridings. (d) North; South Wales. (e) Jersey; 'The Isles of Zetland'. (f) Eight maps and plans of ancient monuments, etc. **State:** First. **Imprint:** Some

58 25(i): Dorset engraved by John Cary, 1789.
Photograph: Mills-Wight Studio

maps have: *mf*: usually bottom right or left: 'E. Noble delin! et curavit.' (*V*). **Publishers:** T. Payne & Son, and G. G. J. & J, Robinson. (ii) 1805; 1809: as (i) 1789, except: *Atlas: New British atlas, being a complete set of county maps, on which are delineated all the roads, cities, towns, villages, rivers & canals; ....* *Maps (49):* as (a, b, c, d) above (excluding: Great Britain and Ireland). **State:** Second. Map detail is extensively revised and, in particular, canals are added. *Imprint: pi* added, usually below the titlepiece: 'Published by John Stockdale Piccadilly 26ᵗʰ March 1805' (*v*). England and Wales re-dated to 1809 appropriately. **Publisher:** John Stockdale. (iii) 1806: as (i) 1789, except: *Maps (51):* As above, plus maps of Roman Britain and Saxon England. **State:** Second (except: new maps). Plate changes as 1805. *Imprint: pi* added, usually below the titlepiece: 'Published by John Stockdale Piccadilly 26ᵗʰ March 1805' (*V*). **Publisher:** John Stockdale. N.B. Close copies of the home counties' maps from this series, engraved by S. Neele, were published by Stockdale (plus maps of the London area and the River Thames) in parts from 1796; e.g. *pi*: 'Published March 1ˢᵗ 1797 by J. Stockdale Piccadilly' (Essex).

(26) Description: *st*: First. **Supply:** Plentiful. **Average size:** 94 × 150 mm (3.7 × 5.8 in.). Yorkshire is a large folding map of 300 × 357 mm (12 × 14.3 in.). **Features:** 'the main Road to London from any place can be immediately traced by a reference to the Roads; where that Rout is always described by the words London Road or Road to London: the greatest care having been taken in selecting the Roads leading to the Metropolis, the traveller may place a reliance that none, but such as are described in that Direction will answer that purpose.' Set in a plain panel: 'at the bottom of each Map is prefixed the distance of the principal places in the County from the Metropolis'. **Scale:** *V/av:* 1:12*m*/'Scale of Statute Miles', or: 'Statute Miles', or: 'Scale of Miles'/*sbm*. **Border:** *Tt*/incorporated into the border, and projecting above it, at the top centre of the page, is a vertically hatched panel containing the title. On the left side of this panel is the inscription: 'By J. Cary', and on the right: 'Engraver'. **North Point:** *s/l*/half concealed behind the title panel at the top of the page/*V*/any of the four cardinal points may be directed to the top of the page. **Title:** *c/oc*/set within the vertically hatched panel at the top of the page.

Issues: (i) 1790: *Atlas: Cary's traveller's companion, or, a delineation of the turnpike roads of England and Wales; shewing the immediate rout to every market and borough town throughout the kingdom. Laid down from the best authorities, on a new set of county maps ....* *Maps (43):* (a) England and Wales. (b) 39 English counties. (c) 'The Turnpike Roads of Yorkshire'. (d) North; South Wales. **State:** First. *Imprint: obbc:pi:* 'London Published Sep! 1. 1789 by J. Cary Engraver Nº 188 Strand' (*V*). **Publisher:** 'John Cary, Engraver, Map & Printseller, Strand'. N.B. There were at least three issues in 1790. The first issue, with maps printed back-to-back, was slightly revised for the two later issues, one only with maps printed back-to-back. (ii) 1791: there were at least four issues with the titlepage dated 1791 with minor revisions and additions between some issues. In particular, communication information was up-dated with the addition of canals and the revision of mailcoach and turnpike routes. Some plates were re-engraved sometimes introducing alterations. Three of the issues were printed with the maps back-to-back. The maps were issued in this state until at least 1801: as (i) 1790, except: **State:** Second (*v*). *Imprint: obbc:pi* altered: 'London Published Sep! 1. 1792 by J. Cary Engraver Nº 181 Strand' (*V*), (except: Yorkshire retains the original imprint). (iii) 1806: as (ii) 1791, except: **State:** Third (*v*). The maps have been re-engraved and considerably revised, particularly in respect of communications. *Imprint: obbc:pi* altered: 'London. Published July 1. 1806 by J. Cary Engraver Nº 181 Strand' (*V*). N.B. The maps were issued in this state, with appropriate re-dating of the *pi* usually to: '... May 1. 18..' in 1810; 1812; and 1814; and to: '... Jan. 1.18..' in 1817; 1819; and 1821. (iv) 1822: as (iii) 1806, except: The maps have been re-engraved, with map detail up-dated and the *es* omitted. Some maps have a plate-number added about 20 mm (0.75 in.) below the lower border. Some maps are re-orientated. Maps with east or west to the top of the page have been re-engraved so that their lettering is read when the map is turned and viewed with north to the top. Old map stocks were used in some copies. **State:** Fourth (*v*). *Imprint: obbc:pi* altered: 'London. Published by G. & J. Cary, Nº 86 S! James's Str.' (*V*). **Publishers:** George & John Cary. N.B. The maps in this state were issued with minor up-dating revisions, particularly the addition of railway information, in 1824, 1826, 1828 and 1835, and possibly c.1840.

(v) 1862(?); by lithographic transfer: as (iv) 1822, except: *Atlas: Cruchley's railroad companion to England & Wales shewing all the railways & stations with their names, also the turnpike roads to all the market and borough towns with the distance from town to town delineated on a series of 42, county maps ....* **Maps:** The maps are considerably revised and printed back-to-back. Erasures: title; compass star; plate-number on some maps; note of towns and distances; *pi.* Additions: new title; new plate-number; new *pi*; new border at top and bottom; names of towns with stations are underlined. *State:* Fifth. *Imprint: obbc:*new *pi*: 'London, Published by G. F. Cruchley, Map Seller & Globe Maker 81, Fleet Street' (*V*). **Publisher:** George Frederick Cruchley.

(27) Description: *st*: First. **Supply:** Scarce. **Average size:** 129 × 189 mm (5.2 × 7.5 in.). **Features:** Country houses are represented pictorially with the names of the owners noted, sometimes in a numbered reference key; 'lines which shew the point of sight from whence the Houses are seen' are drawn; open and enclosed roads; 'the turnpikes also; a subject so often complained of from the incivility as well as imposition of the Toll-gatherers, are here regulated by distinctly marking the connection of the trust which one Gate has with another, whereby the traveller is informed of those which are separate and those which are connected and in receipt of anothers ticket, which it is presumed will be the means of preventing unpleasant altercation'; some maps note local inns: 'INNS'; within a plain oval panel set within a vertically hatched rectangular panel across the full width of a strip; 'The public Inns on each route are ... noticed with a view to utility, as it enables a party to form a meeting with certainty, and gives them a choice of pursuing their pleasures to a greater extent than they otherwise would do'. **Scale:** *n//*scale is: 1:1*m*. **Border:** *Tt/*each map consists of two strips, 55 mm (2.2 in.) wide, divided by *tTt/*titles are set in vertically hatched panels incorporated into the strips at the start of each route/*ob*: above each strip: map number/'Houses seen from the road & beyond the limits of the scale are placed between the partition ...', i.e. within the borderlines/*bts/bltr.* **North Point:** *c/p/*since orientation varies, each strip has a north point. **Title:** 'LONDON to ...', sometimes 'continued to ...'/*oc* and *os/*set within an oval panel within a horizontally hatched rectangular panel, or simply within a vertically hatched rectangular panel,

across the full width of the strip. Since the title appears at the start of a route, some maps have no titles and some have two. **Engraver:** John Cary.

Issues: (i) 1790; 1799; 1801; 1810: *Atlas: Cary's survey of the high roads from London to Hampton Court, Bagshot, Oakingham, Binfield, Windsor, Maidenhead, High Wycombe, Amersham, Rickmansworth, Tring, St. Albans, Welwyn, Hertford, Ware, Bishops Stortford, Chipping Ongar, Chelmsford, Gravesend, Rochester, Maidstone, Tunbridge Wells, East Grinsted, Ryegate, Dorking, Guildford, Richmond ....* **Maps:** (a) folding general map; plan of turnpike trusts. (b) 40 strip road maps. **State:** First (*v*). Revisions to some names of houses and owners in 1801 and 1810. *Imprint: obbc:pi:* 'Published by J. Cary, July 1st 1790'. The year was usually changed appropriately in the imprints of subsequent issues. **Publisher:** 'J. Cary, Engraver & Map Seller, the corner of Arundel Street, Strand.'

(28) Description: *st*: First. **Supply:** Moderate. **Average size:** 205 × 260 mm (8.25 × 10.4 in.). **Features:** 'the turnpike Roads to and from London, are distinguished by the letters LR, which will be a sufficient guide for uniting those Roads, and the junctions of all the turnpike Roads are shown by figures of reference'; 'several of the Canals laid down on this Map are not yet completed, but their courses are delineated according to the plans prescribed by the acts of parliament relating to each such canal. They were inserted at the request of many gentlemen who are interested in those canals, and with a hope, that an accurate delineation of them might gratify the curious as well as be useful to the publick.' **Scale:** *n//*except Plate 63/scale is: 1:5*m*. **Border:** *tTtt/*at top centre is a plan indicating connecting plates: 'The figures in the plan at the top of each page shew the manner in which the plates are to be united. The middle figure denotes the number of the plate and the figures at the top and bottom explain its connection North and South, and those at the sides, East and West.' **Engraver:** John Cary.

Issues: (i) 1794; 1808 (?); (First issued in 1792 as a wall map): *Atlas: Cary's new map of England and Wales with part of Scotland on which are carefully laid down all the direct and principal cross roads, the course of the rivers and navigable canals, cities, market and borough towns, parishes, and most considerable hamlets, parks, forests etc. etc. Delineated from actual surveys; and materially assisted from authentic documents liberally supplied by the right honourable the*

Post Masters General .... **Maps:** (a) Index map. (b) 81 sectional maps from the complete map of England and Wales extending to just north of the Clyde Valley and the central lowlands of Scotland.

N.B. 14 of these maps are blank and 15 virtually blank, e.g. Plate 69 contains only the compass star and a tiny stretch of coast from Blyth to South Shields; Plate 6 contains only the southernmost tip of the Isle of Wight; and Plate 63 contains only the scale: 'British Statute Miles $69\frac{1}{2}$ to a Degree'.

State: First (*v*). The plates were revised for the second issue. **Imprint:** most maps have: *obbc:pi*: 'Publish'd by J. Cary, June 1st 1794' (*V*). **Publisher:** 'J. Cary, Engraver & Map-seller No. 181 Strand'. (ii) (a) 1816; (b) 1822; 1824; 1828; 1830; 1832; (c) 1834: as (i) 1794; 1808(?), except: State: Second (*v*). The plates were 'Corrected to' 1822, 1828, 1830 and 1832. Re-engraved in 1830. '... an entire new Set of Plates, with material Alterations & Improvements ...'; without *pi* (except: Plate 5 in 1816–28 and 1834). **Publishers:** (a) John Cary; (b) 'G. & J. Cary, Engraver & Map-seller, N.º 86 S.ͭ James's Street'; (c) although the publisher is given as J. Cary, it was undoubtedly as (b). G. & J. Cary published a similar sectional map: *Cary's improved map of England & Wales, with a considerable portion of Scotland, planned upon a scale of two statute miles to one inch, drawn from the most authentic surveys & parliamentary documents* ... in 1832 on 65 sheets (plus an index map) each bearing the Carys' imprint: 'LONDON: PUBLISHED BY G. & J. CARY, 86 S.ͭ JAMES'S STREET, ...' (except: plates 38 and 39) usually dated in 1832. The sectional maps (505 × 640 mm; 20.2 × 25.6 in.) were issued in parts from 1820 and appeared as a complete atlas in 1832 with the imprints re-dated to 1832. G. F. Cruchley reprinted the atlas c.1852 with railways and stations added and some minor alterations as *Cruchley's complete railway & station map of England & Wales, with part of Scotland* with the altered *pi*: 'London. Published by G. F. Cruchley, Map-seller & Globe Maker, 81, Fleet Street'.

(29) Description: *st*: First (1810). **Supply:** Plentiful. **Average size:** 168 × 208 mm (6.4 × 8.2 in.). **Features:** Map detail extends to the frame. **Scale:** Some maps have a 'SCALE', sometimes set within a plain panel/*V*/*av*: 1:3*m*/*sbm*. **Border:** *tTt*/'The Environs of Brighton' plate has a second map of 'Little Hampton, Bognor, Worthing,

Arundel, etc.' separated by *tTt*. **Title:** *pc*/*obac* or sometimes on *mf*. **Engraver:** John Cary.

Issues: (i) 1798; etc.: *Atlas: Cary's new itinerary or an accurate delineation of the great roads both direct and cross throughout England and Wales with many of the principal roads in Scotland from an actual admeasurement made by command of his Majesty's Postmaster General for official purposes under the direction and inspection of Thomas Hasker Esq.ͬ surveyor and Superintendant of the Mail Coaches By John Cary; Surveyor of the Roads to the General Post Office* .... **Maps:** 1798: First edition: general map only. 1802: Second edition: two new general maps. 1803: Second edition: general map only. 1806: Third edition: general map only. 1810: Fourth edition: general map; maps of the environs of: London, Bath, Brighton, and Margate and Ramsgate. 1812: Fifth editon: general map; maps of the environs of: London, Bath, Brighton, Cheltenham, and Margate and Ramsgate; Isle of Wight. 1815: Sixth edition: as 1812. 1817: Seventh edition: as 1812. 1819: Eighth edition: as 1812. 1821; 1822: Ninth edition: general map; maps of the environs of: London, Bath, Brighton, Cheltenham, and the Lakes; Isle of Wight; mail road from London to Dublin. 1826: Tenth edition: general map; maps of the environs of: London, Bath, Brighton, Cheltenham, and the Lakes; Isle of Wight. 1828: Eleventh edition: as 1826. **Imprints:** (i) many maps have: *obbc:pi* of J. Cary or G. & J. Cary, sometimes dated, e.g. 'Published by J. Cary Jan.ʸ 2.ⁿᵈ 1810' (Fourth edition). (ii) *obar*: from 1810, most editions have 'For Cary's New Itinerary' on most maps. (iii) *obal*: from 1815, most maps have: '... EDITION'. **Publishers:** John Cary, or G. & J. Cary.

(30) Description: *st*: First (*v*). **Supply:** Moderate. **Average size:** 483 × 546 mm (19.3 × 21.8 in.). **Features:** Some maps have a numbered reference key to administrative divisions: e.g. 'REFERENCE to the HUNDREDS'; some issues of some maps are geologically adapted. **Scale:** *V*/*av*: 1:3*m*/'SCALE'/ *sbm* within a vertically hatched panel. **Border:** *OB*: *tTt*/*IB*:*ll*/*bb*. **North Point:** *s*/*f*. **Key:** *n*/from 1834 a key to parliamentary information was added: 'EXPLANATION'. **Decoration:** *n*/the 1834 issue only, has vignettes on Cumberland, Durham and Northumberland; and Westmorland bears a vignette when issued with the title date 1829 (other maps were possibly issued separately with vignettes at this time). **Title:** 'A NEW MAP OF ...,

DIVIDED INTO HUNDREDS, EXHIBITING Its Roads, Rivers, Parks etc. By JOHN CARY Engraver; 18..'/*V*/dates vary/set within a plain oval panel/*ps* and *pc*. **Engraver**: John Cary.

Issues: Throughout their life, the maps were also issued as folding maps, often with an imprinted issue date not found in atlas issues. (i) 1809: (The maps were issued in parts from 1801 and were first issued together only in 1809; evidence suggests a possible first issue in 1807): *Atlas: Cary's new English atlas; being a complete set of county maps, from actual surveys, corresponding in size with his general atlas; on which are particularly delineated those roads which were measured by order of the Right Honourable the Postmaster-General, By John Cary, as well as all others, both direct and cross; rivers, navigable canals, parks, heaths, commons, etc. etc. exhibiting also the whole of the market and borough towns, parishes and hamlets, as well as places of inferior note . . . . Maps (42):* (a) England. (b) 39 English counties. (c) Yorkshire (on four sheets). (d) 'The Principality of Wales' (on two sheets). *State:* First (*v*). *Imprint: obbc:pi:* 'London. Published by J. Cary Engraver & Map-seller N⁰ 181 Strand . . .' (*V*). Dated between 28 September 1801 and 1 June 1809. (If there was an 1807 atlas edition, either a few imprints have been re-dated, some of the maps have been re-engraved, or it did not contain the full set of maps. There are no traces of erased dates.) *Publisher:* 'J. Cary . . . N⁰ 181, near Norfok Street, Strand.'
N.B. The maps were issued with minor revisions and additions again in 1809 and in 1811.
(ii) 1811: as (i) 1809, except: *State:* First (*v*). During 1811 the dates in the titles and imprints were corrected to 1811. Copies of the atlas published during the course of the year have varying combinations of original, partially corrected, and corrected maps. Eventually atlases were issued with all the dates corrected to 1811. (iii) 1818: as (ii) 1811, except: *State:* Second. Minor revisions and additions to map detail. Dates in the title and the *pi* are corrected to 1818. Some atlases were issued containing some earlier, uncorrected stock. This issue only, substituted a larger map of England and Wales without title date or *pi*, in some copies. (iv) 1821: as (iii) 1818, except: *States:* Various. Dates in the title and the *pi* of most maps are corrected to 1820 or 1821. However, 18 maps are uncorrected and Wiltshire is undated in some copies. Some later imprints give Cary's address as 'N⁰ 86 S⁺ James's Street' without a publication date. Issues are also

known with both the title and the St James's Street imprint dated 1823; and the atlas was probably issued again in 1824 with dates altered accordingly. (v) 1828: as (iv) 1821, except: *States:* Various. Minor revisions and additions to map detail. Two maps are dated 1824 in the title, four dated 1825; one dated 1826; 12 dated 1827; the remainder are dated 1828. (These dates appear to have been revised periodically on some maps between 1823 and 1828.) *Imprint: obbc:pi* altered: 'London. Published by J. Cary Engraver & Map-seller N⁰ 86 S⁺ James's Street . . .' (*V*). Most imprints are undated but 19 sheets bear dates between 1 March 1824 and 1 April 1828.
N.B. The maps were subsequently issued with the dates altered to 1828.
(vi) 1834: as (v) 1828, except: *States:* Various. Parliamentary information is added (polling places; place of county election; boundaries of parliamentary boroughs; parliamentary representation; and a key to parliamentary information). Other minor revisions and additions; and the correction of the title date to 1831 (except: Cheshire, Lancashire, Middlesex, Northampton, Stafford, Surrey, Warwick: dated 1833). The date is erased from the *pi* (except: Berkshire, Buckingham, Devon, Dorset, Kent, Norfolk, Sussex, and the second sheet of Wales).
N.B. Maps were issued individually by Cary with altered title dates and railways added between 1834 and c.1846.
(vii) from c.1846 the maps were issued by lithographic transfer by G. F. Cruchley with a concentration on added railway and communication information. They were issued in many variant states, which were sold over overlapping periods and remained available after they had been replaced by up-dated versions, both as individual folding maps and in *Cruchley's railway and telegraphic county atlas of England and Wales* . . . . The maps were issued by Cruchley until c.1877 and from then by Gall & Inglis of Edinburgh.

N.B. Maps of some counties were designed also to be geological maps with panels for geological colour coding positioned around the county boundary and with notes on strata and number references. These maps have: *obbc*, the note: 'Note, The numbers attached to the description of each Stratum, refer to the Geological Table of British Organized Fossils, which may be had of the Publisher, Price 1ˢ 6ᵈ.' Some maps have additional geological

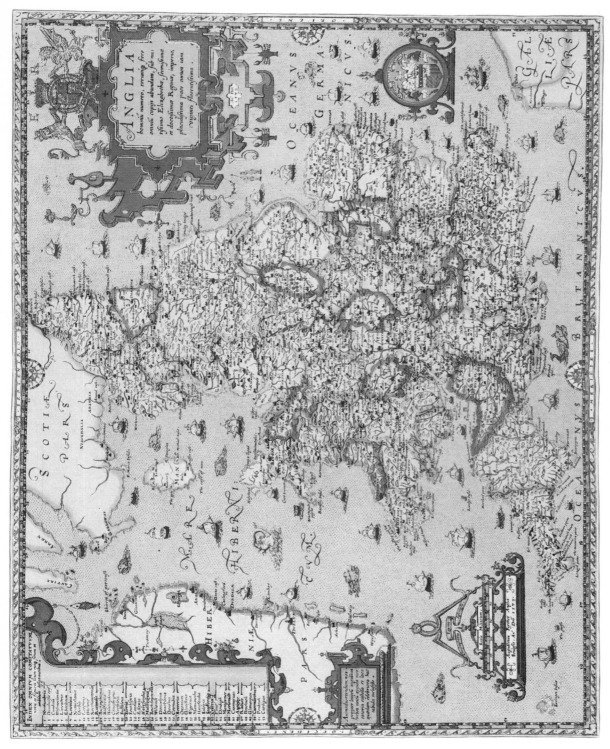

A 'Anglia' by Christopher Saxton, 1579. *By permission of the British Library* [*Maps C.7.c.1.*]

B 'The Kingdome of Scotland' by John Speed, 1610. *By permission of the British Library* [*Maps C.7.c.20.(2).*]

reference notes below the lower border. Geologically designed maps issued by G. F. Cruchley added: 'This map may be had geologically coloured price 3/6 in sheet' to the title. However, they do not appear to have been issued in that form. Geologically adapted maps were usually introduced into *Cary's new English atlas* thus: 1821: Bedford, Berkshire, Essex, Gloucester, Huntingdon, Kent, Lincoln, Norfolk, Northampton, Nottingham, Suffolk, Surrey, Sussex, Wiltshire. 1828: Buckingham, Cumberland, Leicester, Northumberland, Oxford, Rutland, Westmorland, Yorkshire. 1834: Durham. The maps were issued by William Smith with the title 'GEOLOGICAL MAP of ... by W. Smith, Mineral Surveyor' above the upper border in the parts of *A new geological atlas of England and Wales* .... Smith's issues did not, however, correspond with the appearance of the adapted maps in Cary's atlas. 1819: Part I: Norfolk, Kent, Wiltshire, Sussex. 1819: Part II: Gloucester, Berkshire, Surrey, Suffolk. 1820: Part III: Oxford, Buckingham, Bedford, Essex. 1821: Part IV: Yorkshire. 1822: Part V: Nottingham, Leicester, Huntingdon, Rutland. 1824: Part VI: Cumberland, Durham, Northumberland, Westmorland.

Cary also engraved and published: (a) 1792: *The road from the new port of Milford ; to the new passage of the Severn, & Gloucester ; survey'd in the year 1790 by C. Hassall of Eastwood, Pembrok-shire, & J. Williams of Margam, Glamorgan-shire, by order of the South Wales Association for the improvement of roads.* (b) 1795–1808: *Inland navigation ; or select plans of the several navigable canals, throughout Great Britain* ... (16 plans, dated between 1 November 1795 and 2 May 1808). (c) and many other individual maps, atlases, road books, geological sections, canal and drainage plans, etc.

COLE, G. and ROPER, J
fl. 1810 Cartographer and engraver respectively

Cole & Roper produced a finely engraved series of county maps and town plans (31, 32) which were initially issued in parts, and then together as *The British Atlas* in 1810. These accurate, detailed maps, based on those of John Cary and Charles Smith,

emphasize the mail-coach routes and are significant as one of the last series published before the dawn of the railway age. The town plans are particularly attractive with delicately engraved vignettes of famous buildings and the heraldic arms of the cities. The maps only were re-issued in Joseph Nightingale's *English Topography*: 'in some instances the reader will find reference made to certain Plans of Principal Towns, and to their accompanying Descriptions, though in the present work no such Descriptions appear. It was originally intended to add to the County Maps, Plans of the Chief Towns,—a very desirable accompaniment: but the Proprietors, on more mature consideration, anxious to present the work in as cheap a form as possible, have thought it best to omit this part of their plan, reserving its execution to a future opportunity, when they purpose to publish a distinct volume of the Principal Cities, Towns and Boroughs of England and Wales.' As the 'distinct volume' was never published, the town plans are much scarcer than the maps, which were again issued in Thomas Dugdale's *Curiosities of Great Britain* between about 1838 and 1843, when they were replaced by maps by Archer (3). Some copies of the *Curiosities*, issued during the changeover period, are known with a mixture of the two sets of maps. Subsequently, very poor lithographic reproductions were issued by Henry George Collins and Darton & Co.

(31) **Description:** Maps: *st*: First. **Supply:** Plentiful. **Average size:** 175 × 235 mm (7 × 9 in.). **Features:** A numbered reference key to administrative divisions: e.g. 'HUNDREDS'. **Scale:** *V*/*av*:1:7m/'SCALE'/*sbm*; and *f* on some maps/ /except: (i) the general maps of England and Wales have scales of 'English statute miles'. (ii) Cambridgeshire has no scale. (iii) Caermarthenshire has an untitled bar with undefined divisions. (iv) Caernarvonshire has a scale divided into chains. **Border:** *OB*:*tTt*/*IB*:*ll*/*bb*/a panel containing the title is incorporated into the border above the map; and *obb* or within the lower borderlines, most maps have the inscription: 'Drawn and Engraved, under the Direction of ...' (*V*) naming J. Britton and/or E. W. Brayley. **North Point:** *n*//or: *s*/*op*/*l*/some maps have variant designs. **Key:** 'EXPLANATION'. **Title:** *c*/*oc*/set within a horizontally shaded, slightly ornate panel, incorporated into the border above the map. **Engraver:** J. Roper (except: Cheshire: engraved by W. Maestay; Caernarvon has no *es*).

Issues: (i) 1804–1810: *Atlas:* The maps and town plans were issued in parts between 1804 and 1810 and, although designed to accompany *The beauties of England and Wales* by J. Britton, E. W. Brayley, etc. were rarely incorporated in that work. The first complete issue of all the maps and towns plans was: 1810: *The British atlas; comprising a complete set of county maps, of England and Wales; with a general map of navigable rivers and canals; and plans of cities and principal towns* . . . . Maps were also published in other works. *Maps (58):* (a) Two general maps of England and Wales. (b) 39 English counties. (c) North; Part of the North; West; Part of the East and West Ridings. (d) Isle of Wight (inset: town plan of Newport). (e) 12 Welsh counties. *State:* First. *Imprints:* (i) *obbl:es:* maps (a, b, c, d): 'Engraved by J. Roper, from a Drawing by G. Cole' (*V*), (except: Cheshire); maps (e): either as above, or 'Engraved by J. Roper', or '. . . from a Drawing by J. Britton', or '. . . from a Drawing by J. R. Thompson'; or: no *es/ds*. (ii) *obbr:* 'to accompany the Beauties of England & Wales'. (iii) *obbc:pi:* 'London; Published for the Proprietors, by Vernor, Hood & Sharpe, Poultry, . . .' (*V*). (Sharpe is omitted from 17 imprints)/The publisher's imprint is dated between 'Oct.ʳ 1ˢᵗ, 1804' and 'Jan.ʸ 1ˢᵗ, 1810' [except: Nottinghamshire is undated]. (iv) maps (e): Welsh counties: *obal:* either 'NORTH WALES' or 'SOUTH WALES'. (v) maps (e): Welsh counties: *obar:* plate-number: 'No . . .', in roman numerals. *Publishers:* 'Vernor, Hood and Sharpe; Longman, Hurst, Rees, and Orme; J. Harris; J. Cuthell; J. Cundee; W. Faden; J. and A. Arch; Crosby and Co.; J. Richardson; and J. M. Richardson'. (ii) 1816: as (i) 1804–1810, except: *Atlas: English topography: or, a series of historical and statistical descriptions of the several counties of England and Wales* . . . . (By Joseph Nightingale). *Maps (58):* (a) One general map of England and Wales (without *pi*, date or *es*). (b) Canals and rivers of England. (c) 56 county maps, etc., as above. *State:* First. *Publishers:* 'Baldwin, Cradock, and Joy, Paternoster Row'. (iii) 1816: as (ii) 1816, except: *State:* Second. *Imprints:* (i) *obbl:es* erased. (ii) *obbr:* inscription erased. (iii) *obbc: pi* erased. (iv) within border, bottom centre: inscription erased from some maps (erased from other maps in later issues). (v) *obar:* plate-number added (original plate-numbers on Welsh counties are erased and new ones substituted).

N.B. The atlas was re-issued c.1818 sometimes containing old map stock.

(iv) 1827(?): as (iii) 1816, except: *Atlas: English topography; or, geographical, historical, and statistical descriptions of the several counties of England and Wales. Accompanied by an accurate map of each county, from actual survey. By the Rev. J. Nightingale* . . . . *State:* Second. *Publishers:* James Goodwin & Thomas McLean.

N.B. Evidence suggests an issue c.1830 under the title: *A county atlas through England and Wales.*

(v) 1835–41(?): as (iv) 1827(?), except: *Atlas: Curiosities of Great Britain. England & Wales delineated historical, entertaining & commercial* . . . . *By Thomas Dugdale antiquarian. Assisted by William Burnett, civil engineer* . . . . *State:* Third (*v*). Railways are added by a double-line with cross hatching and most subsequent issues up-date railway information. Polling places are added and the new symbol is explained in the key. Other parliamentary information is added. The use of old stock sometimes delayed the appearance of these changes. Many subsequent issues show minor retouching. *Publishers:* Tallis & Co., John Tallis, and L. Tallis.

N.B. The maps were issued in this state, with minor up-dating, in the same work, as follows: (a) 1842(?): by L. Tallis. (b) 1842(?): in parts, by John Tallis.

(vi) 1843(?): as (v) 1835–41(?), except: *State:* Fourth. The horizontal shading in the title panel is erased leaving the title in a plain panel. *Publisher:* John Tallis. (vii) 1843(?): as (vi) 1843(?), except: *State:* Fifth. Minor retouching. *Imprint:* (i) *obbc:* 'Drawn & Engraved for Dugdales England & Wales Delineated' (*V*). (viii) 1854(?): by lithographic transfer: as (vii) 1843(?), except: *Atlas: Collins' railway & pedestrian atlas of England . . .* (?). *Maps (45):* (a) two general maps of England and Wales. (b) 39 English counties. (c) North; Part of North, etc.; West; Parts of the East and West Ridings. *State:* Sixth. Railways are now marked by thick black lines; the explanation of this symbol is added to the key; the explanation of the symbol for polling places is deleted from the key; the title is redrawn/*oc*/the inscriptions are removed; other minor retouching. *Imprints:* (i) *obbc:* new *pi:* 'Pub. by Henry George Collins, Paternoster Row'. (ii) *obar:* plate-number, in large black figures, sometimes altered. *Publisher:* H. G. Collins (?). (ix) 1858(?): by lithographic transfer: as (viii) 1854(?), except: *State:* Seventh. Minor retouching. *Imprint: obb:* no inscriptions or imprints *Publishers:* Darton & Co.

N.B. The Welsh maps from the series were published lithographically in variants of the sixth and seventh states above c.1858 in *Collins' railway and pedestrian atlas of Wales with all its railways and roads accurately laid down* by H. G. Collins and Darton & Co. respectively, and also as loose maps by Collins at about the same date.

(32) Description: Town Plans: *st*: First. (Fig. 27). **Supply**: Moderate. **Average size**: 175 × 235 mm (7 × 9 in.). **Features**: A numbered reference key to important buildings numbered on the plan: 'REFERENCE'; sometimes also a numbered reference listing of 'CHURCHES'. **Scale**: *Vc*/ 'SCALE'/*sb* divided into either feet, yards and/or chains (except: Derby, Oxford, and Worcester have *n*). **Border**: *OB:tTt/IB:sl*/a panel containing the title is incorporated into the upper border, and within the lower border most plans have the inscription: 'Drawn and Engraved under the direction of . . .' with the names of J. Britton and/or E. W. Brayley. **North Point**: *s/op*. **Decoration**: Heraldic shields and arms. Titled vignette view with the signatures of draughtsman and engraver. **Title**: City/town name/*oc*/set within a horizontally shaded, slightly ornate panel, incorporated into the upper border. **Engraver**: J. Roper.

Issues: as Maps (i): *Plans (21):* Bedford; Cambridge; Canterbury; Carlisle; Chester; Colchester; Coventry; Derby; Durham; Exeter; Gloucester; Hereford; Liverpool; Manchester and Salford; Newcastle-upon-Tyne and Gateshead; Northampton; Norwich; Oxford; St Albans; Winchester; Worcester.
N.B. A town plan of Newport is inset on the Isle of Wight.

Imprints: As Maps, except for the *es*; most of the town plans were drawn by G. Cole but J. Hayman (Exeter), Thornton (Manchester and Salford), Thomas Sharp (Coventry) and George Young (Worcester) prepared one each. (Sharpe is omitted from eight imprints.)

COLLINS, Henry George
fl. 1850–1858. Publisher

Collins produced poor lithographic reproductions of both the large (110) and the small (111) county maps of Henry Teesdale. These reproductions are of such poor quality that it is often difficult to read some parts of the maps despite Collins's boast that he had been awarded the only medal won by England at the New York Exhibition of maps, atlases and globes.[26]

COOKE, George Alexander
fl. 1802–1810. Topographer

Cooke produced a series of small, plain but interesting, maps (33) which were published in the 25 parts of the *Modern British Traveller* between 1802 and 1810. These maps are usually mistaken either for James Wallis's *New Pocket Edition of the English Counties* (114) or John Cary's *Traveller's Companion* (26). They were subsequently reprinted in George Carrington Gray's small pocket itinerary: *Gray's New Book of Roads*: 'If what has been frequently observed of books generally be admitted, and the observation applies here with peculiar force, that a great book is a great evil, the advantages arising out of the converse proposition must be too obvious to need further notice, particularly as, in reference to a Book of Roads, the convenience of portability is so indispensable an object of consideration.'

(33) Description:*st*:First.(Fig. 59). **Supply**:Scarce.

59 33(iii): Northamptonshire by George Alexander Cooke, 1824. *Photograph: Mills-Wight Studio*

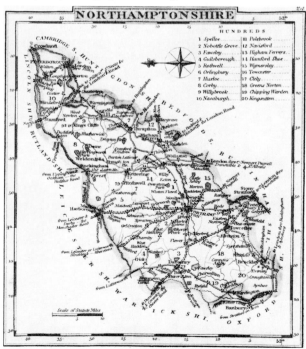

Average size: 106 × 127 mm (4.2 × 5.0 in.). **Features:** A numbered key to administrative divisions: e.g. 'HUNDREDS'. **Scale:** *V*/*av*: 1:15*m*/ 'Scale of Statute Miles'/*sbm*/*Vw*. **Border:** *OB*:*Tt*/ *IB*:*ll*/the title panel is incorporated into the border at top centre. **North Point:** *r*/*f*/*V*. **Key:** None as such; but *obbc*: 'The City & County Town, are denoted by red and the respective Hundreds of the County by different Colours which distinctions are peculiar to the superior Edition'/*V*//Somerset has no such inscription. **Title:** *c*/*oc*/within a vertically hatched panel set within the border at the top of the page.

Issues: (i) 1802–10: *Atlas: The modern British traveller: or, tourist's pocket directory. Being an accurate and comprehensive history and description of all the counties in England, Scotland, and Wales; as also the adjacent islands .... By G. A. Cooke ... Illustrated with maps of the counties, forming a complete British atlas ....*

N.B. Published in 47 undated parts between 1802 and 1810, and issued as a complete work of 25 small volumes c.1810 with the above title and, about the same year, as a complete work under the title *Topography of Great Britain: or, British traveller's directory ... Illustrated with maps of the counties, forming a complete British atlas. By George Alexander Cooke ....*

Maps (47): (a) England and Wales; Scotland (b) 39 English counties. (c) Yorkshire; West; North; East Ridings. (d) North; South Wales. **State:** First. **Imprint:** *obbc*: inscription as noted. **Publisher:** 'C. Cooke, No. 17, Paternoster Row'. (ii) 1822(?): as (i) 1802–10, except: *Atlas: Topography of Great Britain, or, British traveller's pocket directory ... Illustrated with maps of the counties, which form a complete British atlas. By G. A. Cooke, Esq. .... Also* issued in individual county sections at this time. **State:** First or second. (Maps are known with the plate-number already added.) **Publishers:** Sherwood, Neely & Jones. (iii) 1824: as (ii) 1822(?), except: *Atlas: Gray's new book of roads. The tourist and traveller's guide to the roads of England and Wales, and part of Scotland, on an entirely new plan, whereby the different lines of route leading to any required point of distance are brought under notice at one reference .... By George Carrington Gray ....*

Maps (50): (a) England and Wales (a large folding map with *pi*:*obbc*: 'London; Published by Sherwood & Cº Paternoster Row. May 1. 1824'); England and Wales. (b, c, d) as (i) 1802–10, except: (b) Derbyshire is replaced by a new folding map:

194 × 282 mm (7.75 × 11.25 in.), (*obbl*: 'J. Farey Junr. scrip!'; *obbr*: 'Neele sculp!'). (c) Scotland is replaced by a map of the south of Scotland; plus: (d) The Lakes (engraved in uncharacteristic style: *obbr*: 'Neele & Son fc. Strand'). (e) The Isle of Thanet: (folding map): 105 × 145 mm (4.2 × 5.75 in.), (published in uncharacteristic style: *pi*: 'London; Pubd for the Proprietors, by Sherwood & Cº May 1.1817'). **State:** Second (except: new maps). **Imprints:** (i) *obar*: plate-number added to most maps. (ii) the inscription is added below Somerset. **Publishers:** 'Sherwood, Jones, and Co. Paternoster Row'. (iv) 1826(?), with re-issues for a period of at least four years: as (iii) 1824, but issued in sections as *Cooke's topographical library of Great Britain: the British traveller's guide or pocket county directory for England, Wales, Scotland & Ireland. Illustrated with a map and numerous picturesque views ...* published by Sherwood, Gilbert & Piper of Paternoster Row or Sherwood, Jones & Co. at a price of 2s. or 2s. 6d. per section. **State:** Second.

COOPER, H
fl. 1806–1810. Engraver

Cooper's most important cartographic engraving work from his premises at 28, Chancery Lane, London, was the series of small, plain maps (34) for Benjamin Pitts Capper's *A Topographical Dictionary of the United Kingdom*, first published in 1808. Most maps were engraved, with separate borders, two to a plate and the sheet was cut along an engraved dividing line.

(34) Description: *st*: First. (Fig. 60). **Supply:** Moderate. **Average size:** *V*/105 × 180 mm (4.2 × 7.1 in.). **Features:** Most maps have a numbered reference key to administrative divisions, sometimes titled 'Hundreds'; and a table of statistical information concerning cities, boroughs, market towns, parishes, inhabited houses, inhabitants, acres of land, arable, pasturage, and members returned to Parliament. **Scale:** *V*/*av*: 1:8*m*/'British Miles'/*sbm*. **Border:** *Tt*/*bb*. **North Point:** *c*/*op*/*V*. **Title:** *c*/*pc*/set within a small plain panel with a narrow *dl* border. Beneath most title panels is the inscription: 'in which is laid down every Parish & Place containing upwards of 40 HOUSES' (*V*). **Engraver:** H. Cooper.

Issues: (i) 1808: *Atlas: A topographical dictionary of the United Kingdom .... Accompanied by forty-six maps, drawn purposely for this work, on an original plan. By Benjamin Pitts Capper, Esq. .... **Maps***

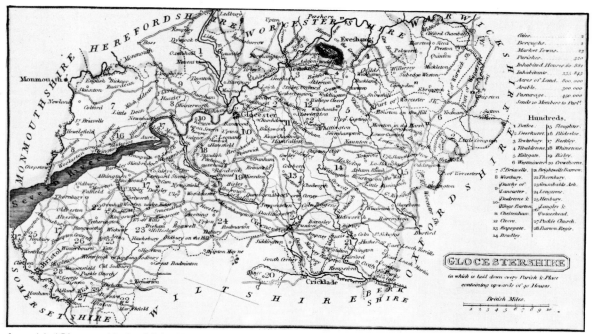

60 34(v): 'Glocestershire' published by G. & W. B. Whittaker, 1824. *Photograph: Mills-Wight Studio*

(44): (a) British Isles; Wales (large folding map); Scotland and Ireland (on two maps each). (b) 39 English counties. (c) Yorkshire.

N.B. Most of the maps were engraved two to a plate but unconnected.

State: First. *Imprints:* (i) *obar:* plate-number in roman numerals: 'Plate ...'. (ii) *obbc:pi:* 'Published Jany 1, 1808, by R. Phillips, Bridge Street, Blackfriars, London' (*V*). (iii) *obbr:es:* 'Cooper del! et sculp!' (*V*). *Publisher:* Richard Phillips, 'Bridge Street, Blackfriars, London'. (ii) 1808: as (i) 1808, except: *Atlas: A topographical dictionary ....* *Accompanied by forty-seven maps.* ... The maps were also sold separately at this time. *State:* Second. *Imprint:* (iii) *obbr:es* erased. *Publisher:* Richard Phillips. (iii) 1813: as (i) 1808, except: *Atlas: A topographical dictionary .... Accompanied by forty-seven maps, drawn purposely for this work, on an original plan, with additions and corrections, and the population tables published in 1812* .... *State:* First. *Publishers:* Longman, Hurst, Rees, Orme and Brown. (iv) 1813: as (iii) 1813, except: *State:* Second. *Imprint:* (iii) *obbr:es* erased. (v) 1825; 1826: as (iv) 1813, except: *State:* Third. Minor revisions to map detail and up-dating of statistical information. *Imprint:* (ii) *obbc:* new *pi:* 'Published by G. & W. B. Whittaker. 13. Ave Maria Lane. 1824' (*V*). *Publisher:* George B. Whittaker.

N.B. The maps were re-issued in this state in *A topographical dictionary ...* thus: (a) 1829; 1834: by Sir Richard Phillips & Co. (b) 1839: by Whittaker & Co.

COWLEY, John
fl. 1734–1744. Geographer, astronomer and writer
and DODSLEY, Robert
fl. 1744–1764d. Publisher and writer

Cowley prepared a small, attractive set of maps (35) for Dodsley's *Geography of England* published in 1744. The maps contain little detail and concentrate on the rivers as the most prominent feature.

(35) Description: *st:* First. (Fig. 61). **Supply:** Scarce. **Average size:** *V*/132 × 185 mm (5 × 7.25 in.). **Scale:** *V*/*av:*1:10m/'English Miles'/*sbm.* **Border:** *OB:sl*/*IB:ll.* **North Point:** *q*/*f*/*e*/*V.* **Key:** 'Explanation'. **Title:** 'An Improved MAP of ... containing the Borough & Market Towns with those adjoining; also, it's Principal Roads and Rivers by I. Cowley, Geographer to his MAJESTY'/*V*/*vl*/set in a cartouche of a suspended drape.

Issues: (i) (a) 1744. (b) 1745: *Atlas: The geography of England: done in the manner of Gordon's geographical grammar. ...* To each county is prefix'd a compleat mapp from the latest and best observations,

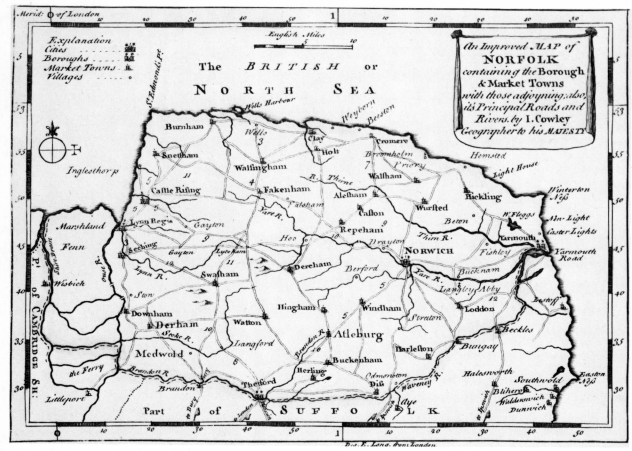

61 35(i): Norfolk by John Cowley, 1744. *Photograph: Mills-Wight Studio*

shewing the chief towns, parks, rivers and roads, both direct and across .... **Maps (55):** (a) England and Wales; correct chart of the English and St George's Channels, etc.; new and correct map of the roads of England. (b) 39 English counties. (c) Yorkshire. (d) 12 Welsh counties. **State:** First. **Publishers:** (a) 'R. Dodsley, at Tully's Head in Pall Mall'. (b) R. Dodsley & M. Cooper. This work was re-issued without maps in 1765 under the title *The geography and history of England ....* (ii) 1745: as (i) 1744, except: **Atlas:** *A new sett of pocket mapps of all the counties of England and Wales ....* **State:** First. **Publishers:** 'R. Dodsley in Pall-Mall, and M. Cooper in Pater-noster Row.'

CRUCHLEY, George Frederick
fl. 1823–1876. Map-seller, engraver and globe-maker

Cruchley's early work concentrated on the production of London maps but in 1844 he bought up the stock of George & John Cary and re-published the Cary maps (24, 26, 30) by lithographic reproduction until 1877 when the plates were purchased by the Scottish firm of Gall & Inglis, which had been set up by James Gall in Edinburgh in 1810. Cary maps were published by Gall & Inglis until the 1920s. Cruchley also purchased, over the years, the stocks of such other map publishing businesses as Bowles & Carver. His policy was to superimpose railway, postal, and other information on to the original maps or sections of them; unfortunately, the rather crudely executed additions detract from the fine engraving of the originals.

DARTON, William
fl. 1806–1834. Geographer and publisher

Darton published a number of cartographic works including the rare 1822(?) and 1825(?) re-issues of Robert Miller's tiny maps in *Darton's New Miniature Atlas ...* (94). However, he is best known for the beautifully engraved maps (36) of *A Complete Atlas of the English Counties*, prepared by Thomas Dix, a Northamptonshire schoolmaster, writer, surveyor and geographer, and published by Darton, after Dix's death, in 1822. The maps resemble the larger maps of Charles Smith, but are distinguished by the vignette views. They were also sold separately 'Coloured, on a Sheet, price 1s.; in a Case, coloured, 2s. 6d. on Canvas, Roller, and Varnished, 4s. 6d.' Although they were issued several times, these maps are surprisingly scarce today.

Select Bibliography:

SMITH, D.A.: 'An Unrecorded Edition?' (*International Map Collector's Soc.*, Vol. 1, No. 3. 1981).

(36) **Description:** *st*: Second. (Fig. 62). **Supply:** Scarce. **Average size:** V/350 × 440 mm (13.8 × 17.4 in.). **Features:** The maps were engraved by different hands; 11 being in a generally cruder style, without the notes (c) and other features: (a) 'MARKET TOWNS and MARKET DAYS'/V. (b) a numbered reference key to administrative divisions: e.g. 'REFERENCE to the HUNDREDS'. (c) 'NOTE' or 'REMARKS' (Devon is untitled): details of the county's extent, administrative divisions, houses, inhabitants, parliamentary representation, rivers, produce and manufactures. **Scale:** V/*av:* 1:4*m*/'SCALE of MILES'/ Vw/*sbm*. **Border:** OB:tTt/IB:*ll*. **North Point:** s/f/ north points do not appear on some maps in some states. **Key:** 'EXPLANATION'. **Decoration:** Titled vignette view. **Title:** '..., Divided into Hundreds, and the Parliamentary Divisions'/*vl*/ Yorkshire and North Wales have extended titles.

Issues: The maps were also published individually throughout the issue period. (i) 1822: *Atlas: A complete atlas of the English counties, divided into their respective hundreds, etc. on which are carefully marked the whole of the turnpike and parish roads, the situation*

62 36(i): Yorkshire by Thomas Dix, 1822. *By permission of the British Library (Maps I.e.19.)*

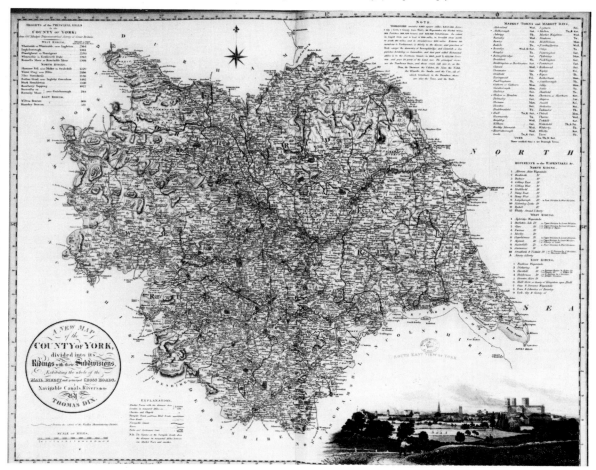

of towns, villages, parks, and gentlemen's seats, churches, chapels; navigable canals, and rivers, and every object tending to illustrate the history and antiquities of England ... to which is added, various explanatory notes ... Commenced by the late Thomas Dix, of North Walsham; carried on and completed by William Darton .... **Maps (42):** (a) 39 English Counties. (b) 'York' (two sheets). (c) North; South Wales (two sheets each). **State:** First (*v*). **Imprint:** *obbc:pi:ps* or *pc:* 19 maps bear the imprint of 'William Darton', and 23 maps the imprint of 'W. Darton, Jun!' (*V*); both with the address '58 Holborn Hill' (*V*) and a publication date between 6 July, 1816 and 21 May, 1821. **Publisher:** 'William Darton, 58 Holborn Hill'.

N.B. The maps are in their pre-description first state: Title: 'A NEW MAP of the County of ..., Divided into Hundreds, By M! Tho? DIX' (or alternatively: 'By Thomas Dix')/*V*/*vl*/*sd*/set within a circular panel with a narrow *dl* frame. The key, list of hundreds, notes and map do not yet incorporate the administrative changes resulting from the Reform Act of 1832.

(ii) 1830: as (i) 1822, except: probably issued individually: **State:** First (*v*). **Imprint:** *obbc:pi* altered to '... 1830'. (iii) As described: 1835(?): as (i) 1822, except: *Atlas: The counties of England: with general maps of north and south Wales.* **State:** Second. Original title, key, list of hundreds, list of markets, and notes have been erased and re-engraved, or altered. Some maps have the north point erased, and the scale added or altered. The maps now show symbols for representation, places of polling and places of election; boundaries of parliamentary boroughs and divisions are marked, and the divisions are named. First addition of railway information. **Imprint:** *obbc:pi* altered: *ps* and/or *pc:* e.g. 'LONDON: WILLIAM DARTON & SON HOLBORN HILL.' or '...; 58 Holborn Hill' (*V*). This state was probably re-issued c.1848 in an atlas with Kent re-engraved without vignette.

N.B. Revised maps were probably also issued c.1848 under the cover title: 'DARTON'S RAILWAY, COMMERCIAL, AND TOURIST'S MAP OF ...' with the *pi* of Darton & Co. (state: third (?)).'

(iv) 1860(?): by lithographic transfer: Hertfordshire is known issued individually as (iii) 1835(?), except: **State:** Fourth (?). Substantial addition of railway information; minor changes to the key and map detail; notes up-dated; north points were possibly added to some other maps. **Imprint:** *obbc:pi* altered: 'London: JOHN DARTON & Co.; 58 Holborn Hill' (?). **Publishers:** 'John Darton & Co., 58 Holborn Hill'.

N.B. Gloucestershire is known, produced by lithographic transfer c.1852, as above, but bearing the imprint *obbc:* 'LONDON: H. G. COLLINS, 22, PATERNOSTER ROW'. The map has the cover title: 'COLLINS' GLOUCESTERSHIRE WITH ITS RAILWAYS.' (state: fifth (?)).

(v) 1862(?): by lithographic transfer; Cornwall is known, as (iv) 1860(?). issued as a folding map by 'DARTON & HODGE, 58, HOLBORN HILL' and bearing their imprint *obbc*. The map has the cover title: 'DARTON AND HODGE'S Railway, Commercial, AND TOURIST'S MAP OF CORNWALL'. Apparently 34 English county maps were printed in the series (no Buckingham, Cambridge, Dorset, Leicester, Westmorland or Yorkshire) and sold at 'SIXPENCE' each, and the 'Lakes of Cumberland and Westmorland' retailed at 1s. **State:** Sixth (?). (vi) 1877(?): by lithographic transfer: **State:** Seventh (?). The plates were adapted for the 'Official' county map series showing railways, telegraphs, roads, rivers, canals, market towns and days, etc., published by Simpkin, Marshall & Co. The maps were very considerably changed from the state described.

DAWSON, Lieutenant Robert Kearsley
fl. 1832. Surveyor

Investigation of municipal government in the 1830s, leading to the Great Reform Act of 1832, generated a series of very plain but historically fascinating town plans, which are particularly notable in that they include very many towns not covered in other works. These plans were drawn up under the direction of Robert Dawson who was an Assistant Tithe Commissioner and was responsible for drawing up the first (unsatisfactory!) specification for the tithe survey. The first set of plans for England and Wales, which also contained county maps (37), was produced early in 1832 and several states are known reflecting the development of parliamentary representation proposals. A few months later, the volumes of Scottish and Irish town plans at a larger scale, without county maps, were published. The maps and plans of England and Wales were issued in a large two-volume atlas on the passing of the Act later in the year. A later set of plans (38) of England and Wales was published in 1837 showing ward boundaries; some are particularly interesting since they not only have the plan at a scale of 4 inches to 1 mile but also have a reference plan, covering a wider area, at a scale of 1 inch to 1 mile. D.N.B.: Vol. 5, p. 678.

(37) Description: *st*: Second. **Supply:** Plentiful. **Average size:** There is great variation in sizes of both maps and plans: sizes vary between about 180 × 212 mm (7.2 × 8.5 in.) and 460 × 570 mm (18.5 × 23 in.). *Maps:* (Fig. 63): **Features:** Concentration on parliamentary information. **Scale:** *V*/*av*: 1:5*m*/'Scale of Miles'/*slm*. **North Point:** *c*/*p*. **Key:** 'Explanations'. **Title:** *c*/*oc*. **Engravers:** Some maps are attributed to J. Gardner or R. Martin. *Plans:* **Scale:** *V*/*av*:1:0.5*m*/'Scale of 2 Inches to 1 Mile'/*Vw*/*slmf*. **North Point:** *c*/*f*. **Key:** 'Explanations'. **Title:** Town name/*pc*/with 'From the Ordnance Survey' in script below the title. **Engravers:** Some plans are attributed to J. Gardner, J^s Basire, J. Henshall, Davies and H. Waters.

Issues: (i) 1832: *Atlas:* ... *copies of instructions given by the Secretary of State for the Home Department with reference to parliamentary representation; likewise, copies of letters or reports ... in answer to such instructions* ... ten parts. **Maps and Plans:** some engraved and some lithographed: Parts I-VIII: England and Wales (*277*): (a) 39 English counties. (b) Yorkshire. (c) Isle of Wight. (d) 179 English town plans. (e) 12 Welsh counties. (f) 45

63 37(iii): Middlesex by Robert Dawson, 1832. *Photograph: Mills-Wight Studio. By courtesy of Jason Musgrave*

Welsh town plans. Part IX: Scotland: no maps; 75 plans: at an average scale of 1 inch to 0.16 mile. Part X: Ireland: no maps; 31 single plans and two plans each of Dungarvan and Mallow, at an average of 1 inch to 0.16 mile. *State:* First (*v*). **Imprints:** (i) signature in script: 'Robt. K. Dawson Lieut. R.E.' (*V*), (England and Wales only). (ii) the maps and plans sometimes carry other signatures of engraver, draughtsman, surveyor, or lithographer. (iii) some maps and plans have: *pi*: 'R. Martin, 124, High Holborn, & 51, Carey S!' (*V*). (ii) 1832: mainly by lithographic transfer: as (i) 1832, except: **States:** First or second. The maps and plans were in a process of revision from the first issue and combinations of the changes noted are found. Minor changes to the detail of maps and plans. Symbol for polling places added to the maps and explained in the key. *Imprint:* (iii) *pi* erased from some maps and plans. (iii) 1832: mainly by lithographic transfer: as (ii) 1832, except: *Atlas:* Parts I-VIII: England and Wales: were issued as a two-volume atlas in the same year: *Plans of the cities and boroughs of England and Wales: shewing their boundaries as established by the Boundaries' Act, passed 11th July 1832: together with outline maps, shewing, the divisions of the counties, the principal places of election, and the polling places, as established by the same Act.* .... **States:** First or second. **Publishers:** James & Luke G. Hansard & Sons.

(38) A similar set of 178 plans of England and Wales was produced at the larger scale of 1 inch to 0.25 mile in the *Plans of the municipal boroughs of England and Wales; showing their boundaries and divisions into wards* produced by the Municipal Corporation Boundaries Commission in 1837. The plans, average size 230 × 330 mm (9.2 × 12.2 in.), usually label the wards and add a colour coded reference key to them to the 'REFERENCE'. Large boroughs are covered by more than one plan and 95 have an index plan(s), at an average scale of 1 inch to 1 mile, of the entire borough (Fig. 64). Otherwise, the plans accord with the general style of Description (37).

Supply: Scarce.

DONN, Benjamin
fl. 1765. Cartographer, surveyor and mathematician

Donn was the first winner of the Royal Society of Arts award for a large-scale county map—for his 1765 map of Devon, engraved by Thomas Jefferys, at a scale of 1 inch to 1 mile. The map was engraved on 12 sheets (plus a single sheet index map) with

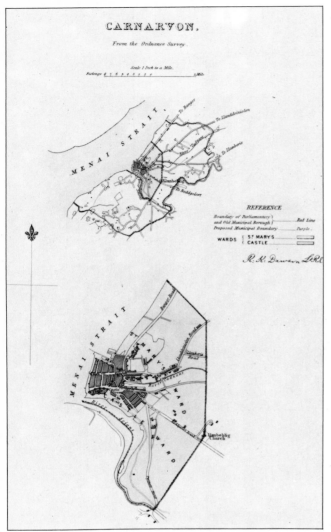

64 38: 'Carnarvon' by Robert Dawson, 1837. *By permission of the British Library (Maps 27.e.27.)*

65 'A Map of the Country Eleven Miles round the City of Bath . . .' by Benjamin Donn, 1790. *By permission of the British Library (K.37.8.)*

town plans of Plymouth and Exeter. He also produced fine maps of the environs of Bristol and Bath (Fig. 65). D.N.B.: Vol. 5, pp. 1126–7.

Select Bibliography
(F) RAVENHILL, W. L. D.: Introduction to *Benjamin Donn. A map of the county of Devon 1765* (facsimile edition. Devonshire Record Soc. and Exeter University. 1964).

DRAYTON, Michael
fl. 1612–1622. Poet

Drayton's series of poems *Poly-Olbion*, dedicated to the beauties of the British countryside, was illustrated by a series of curious maps (39) probably engraved by William Hole. Together with the perspective county views (9) of George Bickham, they are the only major exceptions to the orthodox cartographic style of county maps. The first 18 maps were issued in 1612 and 1613, and the complete set appeared in 1622. The maps are essentially allegorical representations of river basins with no title, scale or boundaries. The exaggerated rivers are attended by water-nymphs, hills by shepherds, and forests by hunters. The few towns shown are represented by standing female figures wearing the town symbols as crowns. The sea, which is sometimes engraved in an unusual style reminiscent of paw marks, is filled with ships, monsters and mythical figures. Some maps are decorated by grander scenes: for example, the area of south Buckinghamshire is covered with a profusion of figures, including musicians, attending a coronation, and in Surrey and Sussex a stag hunt crosses the Weald. These attractive maps are becoming increasingly scarce since the demand for them is wider than for most maps. D.N.B.: Vol. 6, pp. 8–13.

Select Bibliography
(F) DRAYTON, M.: *Poly-Olbion. Edited by J. William Hebel.* (1933).

(39) Supply: Scarce. (Fig. 66). **Average size:** 248 × 315 mm (9.75 × 12.5 in.).

Issues: (i) 1612(?): *Atlas: Poly-Olbion by Michaell Drayton Esqr: Ingrauē by W. Hole . . . . Maps (18):* illustrating the 18 songs by Drayton: (a) Cheshire, Gloucester, Kent, Shropshire, Stafford, and Warwick on individual sheets. (b) Cornwall with Devon; Dorset with Hampshire; Hereford with Worcester; Middlesex with Hertford; Somerset with Wiltshire; Surrey with Sussex. (c) Berkshire with Buckingham and Oxford. (d) Carmarthen with Pembroke; Carnarvon with Merioneth; Denbigh with Flint; Glamorgan with Monmouth. (e) Cardigan with Montgomery and Radnor. *State:* First. *Publishers:* M. Lownes, J. Browne, J. Helme, J. Busbie. (ii) 1613: as (i) 1612(?), except: *Atlas: Poly-Olbion. or a chorographicall description of tracts, riuers, mountaines, forests, and other parts of this renowned isle of Great Britaine . . . digested in a poem by Michael Drayton, Esq. . . . . State:* Second. *Imprint:* top right, either *ob,* or: on *mf:* page number added. *Publishers:* H. L. Mathew, J. Browne, J. Helme, and J. Busbie. (iii) 1622: as (ii) 1613, except: *Atlas: A chorographicall description of all the tracts, rivers, movntains, forests, and other parts of this renowned isle of Great Britain . . . Digested into a poem by Michael Drayton. Esquire . . . . Maps (30):* a second part was added containing the following 12 maps: (a) Cambridge, Lincoln, Northampton, Rutland, and Yorkshire on individual sheets. (b) Bedford with Huntingdon; Cumberland with Westmorland; Derby with Leicester; Essex with part of Suffolk; Lancashire with Isle of Man; Norfolk with part of Suffolk; Northumberland with Durham. *States:* New maps: First; 1612 maps:

66 39(i): Oxfordshire/Buckinghamshire/Berkshire by William Hole, 1612 (detail)

second. *Publishers:* John Marriott, John Grismand and Thomas Dewe.

N.B. A reproduction of the 1622 edition was printed for the Spenser Society in 1890.

DUNCAN, James
fl. 1833. Publisher

James Duncan re-issued William Ebden's large, finely engraved maps (40) in his *New Atlas of England and Wales* and the later *Complete Atlas of England & Wales* which sold 'Price two guineas, plain—four guineas coloured'.

(40) Description: *st:* Second (*v*). (Fig. 67). **Supply:** Scarce. **Average size:** 344 × 425 mm (13.75 × 17 in.). **Features:** A numbered reference key to administrative divisions: e.g. 'REFERENCE to the HUNDREDS'. **Scale:** *V/av:*1:4*m*/'SCALE'/ *sbm.* **Border:** *OB:tTt/IB:ll.* **North Point:** *s/f.* **Key:** 'EXPLANATION'. Inscriptions note the number of county members and the symbol for places of election. **Title:** 'New Map of the County of . . .; Divided into Hundreds Containing the District Divisions and other LOCAL ARRANGEMENTS effected by the REFORM BILL'/*vl/sd.* **Engravers:** Hoare & Reeves.

Issues: Maps from this series are also known issued in other publications. (i) The maps in a pre-description first state were published by William Cole, S. Maunder, and Hodgson & Co., all from 10, Newgate Street, between 1824 and 1828 as loose sheets. Most county maps are also known in untitled, bound volumes. They are easily recognizable since they have an expanded title attributing the map to William Ebden: 'EBDEN'S New Map of the County of . . .; Divided into Hundreds laid down from Trigonometrical Observations. By W. Ebden' (*V*). Alternatively, a few maps are entitled: 'HODGSON'S New Map . . .'. The references to Ebden, Hodgson, etc., were erased for the 1833 issue by Duncan. The second state added the parliamentary changes resulting from the Reform Act of 1832. (ii) 1833: *Atlas: A new atlas of England and Wales; consisting of a set of large county travelling maps . . . containing also the new district divisions . . . etc. agreeably to the provisions of the Reform Bill; thereby exhibiting on the map of each county both its present and former state of parliamentary representation . . . . Maps (43):* (a) England and Wales. (b) 39 English counties. (c) Yorkshire (two sheets). (d) North; South Wales. *State:* Second (*v*). *Imprints:* (i)

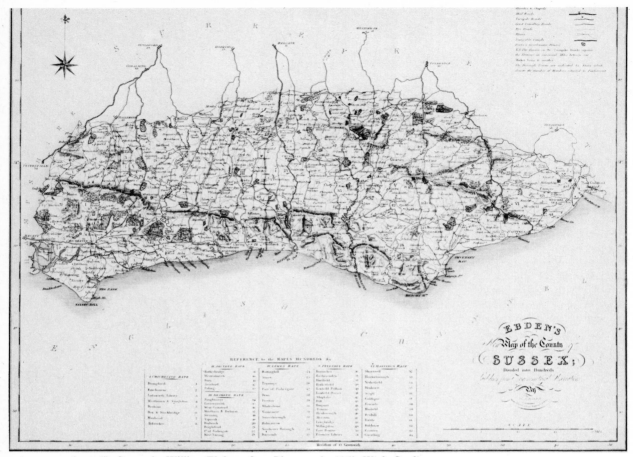

67 40(i): Sussex by William Ebden, 1825. *Photograph: Mills-Wight Studio*

obbc :pi: 'London. Published by J. Duncan. Paternoster Row' (*V*). Durham adds Coates & Farmer of Darlington. (ii) Ten maps have: *obbr :es*: 'Hoare & Reeves sc. 90, Hatton G^d', or '... Warw^k C^t Holb^n' (*V*). **Publisher:** James Duncan. (iii) 1835(?); 1837; 1838; 1840(?); 1845(?): as (i) 1833, except: *Atlas: A complete county atlas of England & Wales, containing forty four superior maps. With all the improvements—projected or completed. Divided into hundreds, with the district divisions, and other local arrangements effected by the Reform Bill ....*
N.B. The maps were also issued under a slightly different atlas title c.1845.
State: Second (*v*). From c.1840 railways were progressively added to the maps. (iv) Some maps in the series are known published by Henry George Collins about 1858 and by Edward Stanford about 1865 under the cover titles of 'COLLINS' RAILWAY & TELEGRAPH MAP OF ...' and 'COLLINS' RAILWAY MAP OF ...' respectively.

DURY, Andrew
fl. c.1770. Cartographer and publisher

In addition to his fine large-scale county maps compiled with John Andrews and others, Dury engraved a charming, decorative series of pocket-sized town plans (41), partly based on John Rocque's surveys, in *A Collection of Plans of the Principal Cities of Great Britain and Ireland ...*, 1764. These plans, which are usually found with original colouring, are often very detailed for their size because some are reduced versions of Rocque's much larger surveys. They are also unusual for the period in that they are based on contemporary survey material.

(41) Description: *st*: First (N.B. there is considerable variation between the plans). **Supply:** Scarce. **Average size:** 110 × 140 mm (4.4 × 5.6 in.). Three plans are double-page. *Maps:* **Features:** Map detail in coastal areas only. **Scale:** *n//*except Isle of Wight which has 'British Statute Miles 69 to a

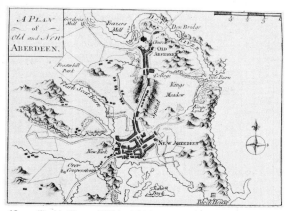

68 41(i): 'A Plan of Old and New Aberdeen' by Andrew
Dury, 1764. *By permission of the British Library (Maps
C.24.a.26.)*

Degree' with *sbm*. **Border:** *OB:sl/IB:ll/bb*. **North
Point:** *q/or:r/* with *f/* and usually *e/V*. **Plans:** (Fig.
68). **Features:** Some plans have a panel containing a
numbered/lettered reference key to buildings and
places of interest. Some others have the key outside
the border. **Scale:** *Vc/*some plans have 'Scale of
Feet' or 'Perches'/some plans have untitled scale
bars. **Border:** *sl* or *dl/bb*. **North Point:** Some plans
have *r/f/e*. **Key:** See above. **Title:** 'Plan of …'/
sometimes set within a plain panel/sometimes
obac/pc and/or *ps/*some plans have *sd*. **Engravers:**
Andrew Dury, J. Ellis, Palmer.

Issues: (i) 1764: *Atlas: A collection of plans of the
principal cities of Great Britain and Ireland with maps
of the coast of the said kingdoms; drawn from the most
accurate surveys; in particular, those taken by the late
Mr J. Rocque topographer to His Majesty …. Maps
(22):* (a) ten maps of the English coast. (b) Isle of
Wight. (c) coasts of North and South Wales. (d) five
maps of the Scottish coast and islands. (e) four maps
of the Irish coast. *Plans (18):* (a) 'A Plan of the City
of London after the great Fire in ye year 1666'
(double-page). (b) 'A Plan of the Cities of London &
Westminster & the Borough of Southwark' (double-
page). (c) 'A Plan of the Palace, Garden & Town of
Kensington.' (d) Aberdeen, Bath, Boston, Bristol,
'Bury St Edmonds', Chester, Chichester, Cork,
Dublin, 'Edinbourg' (double-page), Exeter, Lewes,
Oxford, Shrewsbury, York. *State:* First.
Imprints: (i) *obar*: some maps and plans have a
plate-number. (ii) *obbr:es*: Kent and part of Sussex:
'J. Ellis Sculp!'; Shetland Islands: 'Palmer Sc.'. (iii)
obbc:es: Leinster and Munster: 'J. Ellis Sculpt.'.
Publisher: 'A. Dury, in Dukes Court, St Martin's
Lane. Where may be had his small Universal Pocket
Atlas, to which this is designed as a Second Volume.'

ELLIS, Joseph
fl. 1760–1790. Engraver

Ellis produced a very attractive set of county maps
(42) which were published in *Ellis's English Atlas*, as
part of his very varied engraving work. These maps
were obviously copies of Thomas Kitchin's quarto
maps (59) from the *London Magazine* and contained
virtually the same geographical information. The
major difference was that Ellis replaced Kitchin's
rococo cartouche with a small scene in which the title
was usually set on a monument, building or rock
surrounded by trees and shrubs. Ellis was a skilled
engraver and the maps were finely executed.

(42) Description: *st*: First (*v*). (Fig. 69). **Supply:**
Scarce. **Average size:** 195 × 250 mm (7.5 × 9.5 in.).
Scale: *V/av*: 1:7m/'British Statute Miles 69 to a
Degree'/*sbm*. **Border:** *OB:sl/IB:ll/bb*. **North
Point:** *r/f/e*. **Key:** 'Remarks'. **Title:** 'A Modern
MAP of …', Drawn from the latest Surveys;

69 42(i): Staffordshire by Joseph Ellis, 1765.
Photograph: Mills-Wight Studio

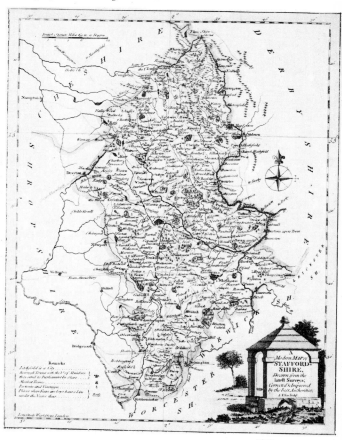

Corrected & Improved by the best Authorities
...'/V/vl/usually incorporates the engraver's name/
set within a decorative cartouche. **Engravers:** J.
Ellis, W. Palmer, W. Fowler, De la Rochette.

Issues: The maps were re-issued many times,
usually with blank backs. The only apparent change
to the plates was re-touching in 1773. (i) 1765:
*Atlas: The new English atlas; being the completest sett
of modern maps of England and Wales ... ever yet
published: accurately drawn from actual surveys ...
and engrav'd in the best manner, by J. Ellis, and others,
on fifty-four copper-plates.* **Maps:** (a) Atlas copies
were bound-up with varying combinations of
folding general maps. The enlarged atlases sometimes added the London environs. (b) 39 English
counties. (c) Yorkshire; North; East; West Ridings.
(d) Isle of Man; Isle of Wight. (e) North; South
Wales. **State:** First (v). **Imprints:** (i) *obar*:
plate-number. (ii) *obbc:pi*: 'Printed for Carington
Bowles in S! Pauls Church yard, & Rob! Sayer
in Fleet Street' (V). (The names are reversed in
some imprints.) **Publishers:** 'Robert Sayer,
at the Golden Buck, near Serjeants Inn, in Fleet
Street; and Carington Bowles, next the Chapter-
House, in St. Paul's Church-Yard.' (ii) 1766:
Two issues: as (i) 1765, except: *Atlas: Ellis's
English atlas: or, a compleat chorography of England
and Wales: in fifty maps, containing more particulars
than any other collection of the same kind. The whole
calculated for the use of travellers, academies, and of all
those who desire to improve in the knowledge of their
country. From the latest surveys of the several counties;
engraved by, and under the direction of, J. Ellis ....*
State: First (v). (iii) 1766: Three issues, two with
the county maps printed back-to-back: as (ii) 1766,
except: *Atlas: Ellis's English atlas ... in fifty-four
maps ....* **Maps:** as 1765, plus: (a) Jersey. (b)
Guernsey, Sark, Alderney and Burhou. **State:** First
(v). (iv) 1766: as (i) 1765, except: *Atlas: Atlas
britannique, ou chorographie complette de l'Angleterre
et de la principauté de Galles ....* French text. **State:**
First (v). **Publisher:** Robert Sayer. (v) 1768: Two
issues, one with maps printed back-to-back: as (iii)
1766, except: **State:** First (v). **Publisher:**
Carington Bowles. (vi) 1768: as (ii) 1766, except:
State: First (v). **Publishers:** 'Robrt Sayer, Map
and Printseller, No. 53, in Fleet-Street; Thomas
Jeffery's, Geographer to his Majesty the corner of St
Martin's-Lane, Charing-Cross; A. Dury in Duke's-
Court, St Martin's-Lane, and at the Map and Print
Shop No. 92, under the Royal-Exchange, Cornhill'.

(vii) 1773: as (ii) 1766, except: **State:** First (v).
Minor retouching of some maps. **Publisher:**
'Robert Sayer, Map and Printseller, No. 53. in
Fleet-Street; and at the Map and Print Shop No. 92,
under the Royal-Exchange, Cornhill'. (viii) 1777: as
(ii) 1766, except: **State:** First (v). **Publishers:** 'R.
Sayer and J. Bennett, Map, Chart, and Print Sellers,
No. 53, Fleet Street'. (ix) 1785(?): as (v) 1768, with
maps printed back-to-back. **State:** First (v). (x)
1786(?): as (ii) 1766, except: **State:** First (v).
Publisher: Carington Bowles. (xi) 1796: as (ii)
1766, except: *Atlas: Ellis's English atlas: being
accurate maps of all the counties in England and Wales,
according to the latest surveys ... engraved by, and
under the direction of J. Ellis: in fifty maps.* **State:**
First (v). England and Wales bears Laurie &
Whittle's imprint dated 12 May 1796. **Publishers:**
Robert Sayer (issued by Laurie & Whittle).

FADEN, William
fl. 1771–1823. Cartographer, engraver and publisher

Faden was a prolific producer of maps, mainly
colonial, and became Geographer to George III and
to the Prince of Wales. He succeeded to the business
of Thomas Jefferys on his death in 1771 and his fine
work led to a brief appointment as official engraver
and publisher of the earliest 1 inch to the mile
Ordnance Survey maps from 1801 until the Board
set up its own printing operation in the Tower of
London. Faden is particularly notable for his
publication of many large-scale county maps.

FULLARTON, Archibald
fl. 1833–1870. Cartographer and publisher

Fullarton printed and published several cartographical works including the *Parliamentary Gazetteer of
England and Wales* which contained finely engraved,
surprisingly detailed, county maps (43). These maps
are very similar to those produced by Sidney Hall
but most are decorated with a small, attractive
vignette of an important place in the county, such as
a cathedral, abbey or castle, or a panoramic view of a
major town. The preface to the *Gazetteer* includes
an interesting comment on the *modus operandi*
of mid-nineteenth century map-makers: 'the
Publisher will not impose on public confidence by
representing it as founded upon "actual survey"—a
mode of procedure which, however, desirable, and
indeed necessary to absolute correctness in a Work
of this class—would it is evident, require at once the
authority and funds of Government to execute with

any degree of accuracy and correctness; but every means in the power of private parties has been adopted to render this part of their Work satisfactory to the reader, the best Topographical authorities, and in particular, the Ordnance maps of the great trigonometrical survey of England and Wales, have been studiously consulted, . . . and local information has been obtained, when necessary, from competent sources'. Incidentally, he also neatly undermined competitive works, particularly Samuel Lewis's *Topographical Dictionary*, by describing them as 'in great part obsolete and more or less unfit.'

The collector may also find maps and plans from some of Fullarton's less well-known publications, including the small series of decorative Scottish county maps (44) from the *Imperial Gazetteer* which was 'illustrated with a beautifully-coloured Map of the country; various chorographical maps of its more important sections, plans of its principal Cities,

Ports, Harbours, and Havens, and an Atlas of County Maps, all similarly coloured'; and some small but detailed charts of important ports and estuaries, some printed several to a page, showing soundings, tide statistics, sandbanks, buoys and lights. Some of these ports, such as Whitby and Dartmouth, have been rather by-passed by subsequent economic development.

(43) Description: *st*: Second (*v*). (Fig. 70). **Supply:** Plentiful. **Average size:** *Vc*/190 × 240 mm (7.6 × 9.6 in.). Some counties are printed on larger sheets which fold into the atlas. **Features:** A numbered reference key to administrative divisions e.g. 'REFERENCE TO THE HUNDREDS'. **Scale:** *V*/*av*: 1:7*m*/'English Miles'/*sbm*. **Border:** *OB*:*tTt*/*IB*:*ll*/*bb*. **North Point:** *s*/*op*. **Key:** Only the inscription: 'The Figures prefixed to the Towns denote the distance from London.' **Decoration:**

70 43(iii): Devonshire published by Archibald Fullarton, 1842. *Photograph: Mills-Wight Studio*

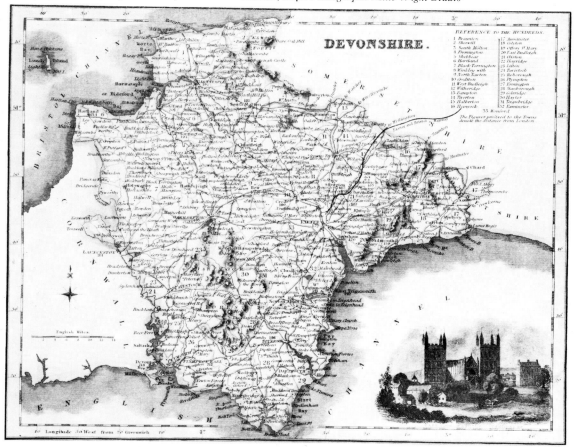

Titled vignette views on 30 maps. **Title:** *c/oc.*
Engravers: 27 maps by R. Scott; 15 by Gray & Son;
and three by James Neele & Co.

Issues: Old map stock was sometimes used in later
issues and alterations were occasionally made during
an issue. (i) 1833–1834; 1836; 1837: *Atlas: A new
and comprehensive gazetteer of England and Wales . . .
By James Bell . . . .* **Maps** *(45):* (a) England and
Wales. (b) 39 English counties. (c) 'East Riding and
Ainsty of Yorkshire'; West; North Ridings. (d)
North; South Wales. **State:** First. **Imprints:** (i)
obbc:pi: 'Published by Arch.d Fullarton & C.o
Glasgow'. (ii) *es:* in a variety of forms either *obbr* or
obbl; or below the title; or by the vignette.
Publishers: 'A. Fullarton & Co., Glasgow'. (ii)
1840: as (i) 1833–34, etc., except: *Atlas: The
parliamentary gazetteer of England and Wales . . .
illustrated by a series of maps forming a complete
county-atlas of England . . . .* **Maps:** some maps are
replaced as follows: (a) England and Wales: by J. &
C. Walker. (d) North; South Wales: by J. & C.
Walker, on two sheets each. The railways are added
to some maps, and subsequent editions of the
Gazetteer up-date railway information. **State:**
Mainly second (*v*). **Imprint:** (i) *es:* erased on
Berkshire, Lancashire, Nottingham, Oxford,
Somerset, Suffolk, Sussex, Westmorland, Wiltshire,
Warwick. Others were gradually erased for sub-
sequent issues. (iii) 1842; 1843; 1844; 1850: as (ii)
1840. **State:** Second (*v*). (iv) 1845; 1846; 1848;
1849: as (ii) 1840, except: **State:** Third. **Imprint:**
(ii) *obbc:pi* altered: 'Published by Arch.d Fullarton &
C.o' (*V*).

(44) Description: *st:* First. (The description applies to the county maps only.) (Fig. 7). **Supply:**
Moderate. **Average size:** 115 × 170 mm
(4.6 × 6.75 in.). **Features:** A numbered reference
key to administrative divisions: 'INDEX TO
PARISHES'. **Scale:** *Vc/av:* 1:8*m*/'British Miles'/
slm. **Border:** *OB:tTt/IB:sl/*the 7 mm (0.3 in.) space
between *IB* and *OB* is decorated with foliage and
decorative patterns. The border patterns were
frequently altered. **North Point:** *c/op/V.* **Key:**
*n//*or: 'Railways' identified as 'Lines in operation' or
'Passed and in progress'. **Title:** *pc/*town plans have
oc/ an inscription below, attributes the plans to G. H.
Swanston. **Engravers:** The only maps bearing an *es*
are attributed to G. H. Swanston of Edinburgh.

Issues: (i) 1854–56(?): 'The Imperial Gazetteer will
be published in Monthly Parts at Two Shillings . . . .
It will also be issued in Parts at One Shilling and

Four Shillings each, and in Half Volumes at Eleven
Shillings and Sixpence in elegant Boards . . . . It will
be completed in Twenty such Parts at Two
Shillings, and will form when complete Two
handsome Volumes . . .': by lithographic transfer:
*Atlas: The imperial gazetteer of Scotland or
dictionary of Scottish topography compiled from the
most recent authorities and forming a complete body of
Scottish geography physical, statistical and historical.
Edited by the Rev. John Marius Wilson . . . .* **Maps**
(39): (a) Scotland. (b) 27 Scottish county maps.
(Three maps combine two counties each.) (c)
Western Islands; Orkney Islands; Shetland Islands;
Buteshire. (d) Ports and harbours on the North-East
Coast (two maps). Ports and harbours on the West
Coast (two maps). (e) Edinburgh and Leith;
Glasgow. (f) Estuary of the Clyde. **State:** First.
Imprints: (i) *obbc:pi:* 'A. Fullarton & C.o London
& Edinburgh' (*V*). (ii) *obbr:es:* the maps of the ports
and harbours have: 'G. H. Swanston, Edin.r' (*V*).
Edinburgh and Leith has: 'Eng.d by G. H. Swanston
Edin.r' **Publishers:** 'Archibald Fullarton and Co.,
Stead's Place, Edinburgh; 106 Newgate Street,
London; and 196 Great Brunswick Street, Dublin'.
(ii) 1857(?): by lithographic transfer: as (i)
1854–56(?), except: *Atlas: The county atlas of
Scotland, in a series of thirty-two maps, accurately
engraved on steel, from recent surveys, and exhibiting
all the lines of road, rail and canal communication.*
Maps *(32):* (a) 'Map distinguishing particularly the
districts or countries of Scotland inhabited by the
Highland Clans'. (b) 27 Scottish county maps.
(Three maps combine two counties each.) (c)
Western Islands; Orkney Islands; Shetland Islands;
Buteshire. **States:** First or second. Some border
patterns are altered. **Publishers:** 'Archibald Fullarton & Co., Stead's Place, Edinburgh; 106
Newgate Street, London'. (iii) (a) 1859(?); (b)
1861(?): by lithographic transfer: as (i) 1854–56(?),
except: (The maps were also issued in parts between these dates.): **States:** Various. Some borders
are slightly altered with crowns either added to
or removed from each corner, and other minor
modifications. Railway information is up-dated.
Publishers: 'A. Fullarton & Co., Stead's Place,
Leith Walk, Edinburgh; and: (a) 73 Newgate Street,
London'. (b) 115 Newgate Street, London'. (iv)
1868(?): by lithographic transfer: as (iii) 1859(?);
1861(?), except: **States:** Various. The borders have
been simplified. They now consist of a hatched band
4 mm (0.15 in.) wide sometimes with a shield at each
corner bearing the lion of Scotland. **Publishers:** 'A.

Fullarton & Co., London and Edinburgh. Fullarton, Macnab & Co., New York'. N.B. Fullarton also published the following: (a) 1862: *The royal illustrated atlas, of modern geography ... containing:* (a) Scotland. (b) West coast ports and harbours. (c) Estuary of the Clyde; Firth of Forth. (d) Glasgow; Edinburgh and Leith; Dundee; Peterhead. (b) 1850–56(?): *A gazetteer of the world ... containing:* (a) West coast ports and harbours (two maps). (b) North-east coast ports and harbours (two maps). (c) Edinburgh and Leith; Glasgow.

GARDNER, Thomas
fl. 1719. Engraver

Gardner's *A Pocket Guide to the English Traveller* was one of the first smaller format copies (45) of the Ogilby road maps of 1675: 'The Method of the original Undertaker on the Whole Sheet Maps (which is esteem'd, as the first, so the best of the kind), is strictly observ'd in the following smaller ones, and which 'tis hop'd, on Comparison, will appear to be so in the most minute Circumstances, none of which are omitted.' These attractive strip maps are scarce since there was only one edition of the atlas. Gardner rather miscalculated the size

suitable for the pocket, and the market was taken by the handier sized copies by Senex in his finely engraved *Survey of all the Principal Roads of England and Wales* (98) of 1719 and by Bowen & Owen in their immensely popular *Britannia Depicta* (18) of 1720. D.N.B. Vol. 7, p. 872.

(45) Description: *st:* First. (Fig. 71). **Supply:** Scarce. **Average size:** 180 × 270 mm (6.5 × 10.25 in.). **Features:** Relief shown by exaggerated molehills which are reversed to show depressions. **Border:** The map is engraved on an imitation scroll/*bts/bltr.* **North Point:** *r/f*/since orientation varies, each strip has a north point. **Title:** 'The Road from ... to ...'/*vl*/contains a note of towns included, with mileages between them and from other important towns/also contains a dedication to owners of houses close to the route (sometimes found below the title panel)/set within a plain panel at top centre 'By THOS. GARDNER, ...'/*V*.

Issues: (i) 1719: *Atlas: A pocket-guide to the English traveller: being a compleat survey and admeasurement of all the principal roads and most considerable cross-roads in England and Wales .... Maps:* 100 strip maps of roads in England and Wales. *State:* First.

71 45(i): 'The Road from Shrewsbury and Chester to Holywell' by Thomas Gardner, 1719. *Photograph: Mills-Wight Studio*

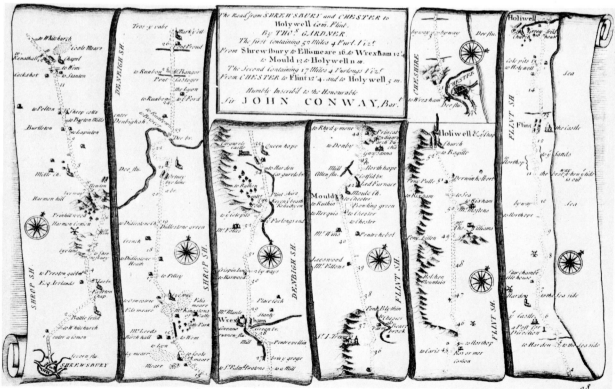

Imprint: bottom right, below scroll: plate-number.
Publishers: 'J. Tonson at Shakespear's Head over-against Katherine-Street in the Strand, and J. Watts at the Printing-Office in Wild-Court near Lincoln's-Inn Fields'.

GIBSON, John
fl. 1750–1787. Engraver

Gibson was a prolific engraver of maps, including the rare *Maps of the Chief Roads in England, showing the various Routes from London*, 1765. His best known work is the *New and Accurate Maps of the Counties of England and Wales* (46). These small, decorative, rococo-style maps each carry a short description of the county; for example, Gibson describes Pembroke as '... fruitful in Corn, rich Pastures & has Plenty of Marl to manure the Ground, with many Coal-Pits & the Sea-Coasts abound in Fish. The Air is pleasant & good & the Hills & Mountains produce Grass sufficient for Cattle Sheep & Goats.' The atlas was sold at 'Price 4s, bound in Calf, 5s 6d with maps color'd.'

(46) Description: *st:* First. (Fig. 72). **Supply:** Scarce. **Average size:** 65 × 110 mm (2.5 × 4.25 in.). **Features:** A description of the county notes numbers of houses, inhabitants, parishes, market towns, members of Parliament, and details of main produce, manufactures and cities. **Scale:** *V/av:* 1:15*m*/'English Miles'/*sbm.* **Border:** *OB:sl/IB:ll.* **North Point:** *c/op/*an *op* also indicates east. **Title:** *c/os/*set within a small rococo cartouche.

Issues: (i) 1759(?): *Atlas: New and accurate maps, of the counties of England and Wales drawn from the*

72 46(i): Pembrokeshire by John Gibson, 1759. *By courtesy of Ivan R. Deverall*

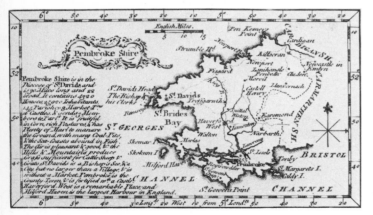

latest surveys by J. Gibson .... **Maps (53):** (a) England and Wales. (b) 39 English counties. (c) Yorkshire. (d) 12 Welsh counties. **State:** First. *Imprint: obar:* plate-number. **Publishers:** 'J. Newbery at the Bible and Sun in St. Paul's Church-Yard.' (ii) 1770(?): as (i) 1759(?), except: **State:** First. *Publisher:* 'T. Carnan, in St. Paul's Church Yard'.

N.B. Gibson also produced the *Maps of the chief roads in England showing the various routes from London*, 1765, containing maps similar in style, but on a smaller format, to the road maps (53) published in *The universal magazine*; and a few county maps for *The universal museum*, ... published by 'J. Payne of the Feathers in Paternoster Row' between 1765 and 1769. (average size: 165 × 204 mm: 6.5 × 8 in.).

GREENWOOD, Christopher and John
fl. 1817–1834. Cartographers and surveyors

Christopher Greenwood, born at Gisburn in Yorkshire in 1786, practised as a surveyor in Wakefield before moving to London in 1818 and setting up business in Leicester Square. He was elected a Fellow of the Royal Society of Arts and in 1820 entered into partnership with the two George Pringles, senior and junior. His younger brother John became a partner in 1821. However, after 1828 the business experienced increasing difficulties, possibly due to heavy engraving costs; George Pringle, junior, resigned in 1828 and John Greenwood had returned to surveying in Gisburn by 1838. Despite schemes to salvage the firm's fortunes, it failed, and Christopher eventually died in Hackney in 1855.

Christopher's grand design was to map the country at the large-scale of 1 inch to 1 mile and he published the first map of the series, of his home county of Yorkshire, in 1817 and 1818. The maps were usually on four or six sheets and most sold at 3 guineas each; the complete set being advertised at an advance subscription rate of £125. A prospectus of May 1824 announced that 15 maps had already been issued and that the survey would be finished in about six years, but unfortunately it never was. No large-scale maps were published of Buckingham, Cambridge, Hereford, Hertford, Norfolk and Oxford. The maps are extremely detailed, giving an intricate picture of land-use as the enclosure movement finally slowed down, and marking the boundaries of townships and parishes for the first time in areas not previously covered by estate or enclosure maps. 'With a view to render the County maps as ornamental as useful, the Proprietors will use every means to join superior elegance with minutest accuracy. Vignettes from the pencils of distinguished artists will be added to the Maps of such Counties as furnish appropriate subjects.'[27] Thus, the maps were decorated with delicate vignettes of buildings and landscape scenes, and also by titles of elaborate lettering and scrollwork. The Greenwoods' large-scale maps represented serious competition to the Ordnance Survey, which surveyed the country at a slower rate, but the non-completion of their scheme was indicative of the decline of private cartography.

The *Atlas of England and Wales* was a scheme to revive the flagging fortunes of the firm by producing a series of county maps (47) at a scale of about 3 miles to 1 inch. The maps were essentially reductions of the large-scale surveys and, although they failed to save the firm, the result was the most visually striking of all the county maps. The plates were superbly engraved by the top craftsmen of the day and beautifully composed and balanced, placing the map between the vignette and the elaborate calligraphic title. These maps are usually found in surprisingly good condition for such large maps but can suffer from offsetting, particularly of the title and the vignette.

Select Bibliography

HARLEY, J. B.: *Christopher Greenwood County Map-Maker, and his Worcestershire map of 1822.* (1962)

(47) Description: *st*: First (*v*). (Fig. 73). **Supply:** Moderate. **Average size:** 580 × 700 mm (22 × 27.5 in.). **Features:** Numbered reference keys to hundreds, wards, divisions, liberties, boroughs, places of election, etc. **Scale:** *U*/1: approx. 3*m*/'Scale of miles'/*sbmf*/a note below gives the area of the county in square statute miles/*vl*/*Vw*. **Border:** Wide, 'keyboard' style, hatched border with latitude and longitude figures within diamond-shaped panels set into the hatched panels/*bb*. **North Point:** *s*/*op*. **Key:** 'Explanation'. **Decoration:** Titled vignette view(s). **Title:** 'MAP of the County of . . ., from an Actual Survey made in the Years . . ., BY C. & J. GREENWOOD. Published by the Proprietors GREENWOOD & Cº . . .'/*V*/ten maps give the initials as C. & I.; Monmouth gives them as C. & H.; and the East Riding is attributed to C. only/large titlepiece in elaborate calligraphic

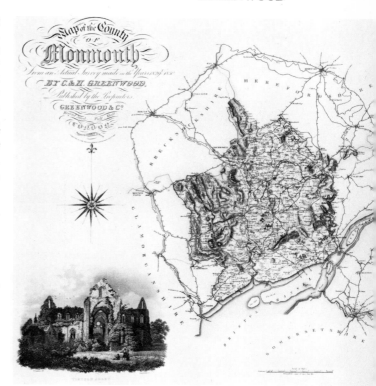

73 47(iii): Monmouth by Greenwood & Co., 1834 (detail). *By permission of the British Library (M.T.6.c.1.)*

style/*vl*/*sd*/most other titlepieces on the maps have *os* and *oc*/the date of survey and details of the engraver are noted in the titlepiece (except: Somerset). **Engravers:** J. & C. Walker (26 maps), J. & J. Neele (ten), J. Dower (four), H. Frost (two).

Issues: (i) 1829–34: The atlas was originally issued in four parts, in 1829, 1830, 1831 and 1834. Consequently only the maps in Part 4 (Cambridge; Hertford; Buckingham; Oxford; Hereford; Norfolk; East Riding; West Riding; North Riding; Cardigan, Pembroke and Caermarthen; Flint, Denbigh and Montgomery; Anglesey, Caernarvon and Merioneth) show the parliamentary representation resulting from the Reform Act of 1832. *Atlas: Greenwood & Comp*ys *atlas of England and Wales.* ***Maps (46):*** (a) 39 English counties. (b) North; East; West 'Riding of the County of York'. (c) Four maps of Welsh counties, grouping three counties on each map. *State:* First (*v*). *Imprint: es:* in or below the titlepiece, except Somerset which has it: *obbr.* ***Publishers:*** 'Greenwood & Co. Burleigh Street, Strand, London'. (ii) 1834: as (i) 1829–34, except: *Atlas: Atlas of the counties of England, from actual* *surveys made from the years, 1817 to 1833, by C. & J. Greenwood.* **State:** First (*v*). During the course of this 1834 issue some maps were slightly revised and added to. (iii) 1834: as (ii) 1834, except: **State:** Part 4: First; Parts 1–3: second.

All maps show the administrative changes introduced by the Reform Act of 1832. Numbers of members returned to Parliament by each borough are indicated and new parliamentary county divisions, boroughs and other parliamentary information are added.

GRIERSON, George and John
fl. 1822–1826. Publishers

The *New and Correct Irish Atlas* is little known and only a few maps (48) from it have reached the collectors' market. The maps are particularly noted for finely engraved, romantic style, title cartouches. Those that are signed were drawn either by W. Beauford, an Irish schoolmaster, antiquarian and estate surveyor, or J. Taylor, a well-known Dublin map-engraver. Known atlases seem to have been prepared during two periods, one in c.1818 and one in the early and middle 1820s.

(48) Description: *st*: First. (Fig. 74). **Supply:** Very rare. **Average size:** 210 × 261 mm (8.4 × 10.4 in.). **Features:** (i) Provinces: 'Post and great roads; garrison towns and barracks; boroughs; bishops sees; post towns.' (ii) Counties: 'Public roads and

74 48(i): 'County of Donegal' published by G. & J. Grierson, c.1818. *By permission of the British Library* (*Maps c24 aa6*)

milestones; private and cross roads; turnpikes; churches; ruins of churches; ruins of castles; ruins of monasteries; bridges; demains and improvements; baths; tumuli; druidic monuments; round towers.' Monaghan, Tyrone and Wicklow have a panel containing a lettered 'Reference to Baronies'. **Scale:** (i) Provinces: 2 *sbm*/'Irish Miles': $V:av:1:13m/$ and 'English Miles': $V:av:1:16m.$ (ii) Counties: 2 *sbm*/'Irish Miles': $V:av:1:4.5m/$ and 'English Miles': $V:av:1:5.25m.$ **Border:** $OB:Tt/$ $IB:ll/$longitude is measured from Dublin and the maps of the provinces have additional graduations, in roman numerals, for 'Minuets of Time West of Dublin'. **North Point:** Most maps have a very decorative north point. A pointer indicating north emerges from a motif of flowers, shells, sheaves of corn, agricultural implements, barrels, sacks, fish, brushes and palette, etc. **Title:** (i) *c*, or (ii) province title/*pc*/set on (i) a shield or rock set in a rural scene with accompanying figures and/or animals, (ii) a large urn with an accompanying figure. **Engravers:** Two maps are attributed to J. Taylor and two to Neele.

Issues: (i) 1818 (?); 1825 (?): *Atlas: New and correct Irish atlas being a complete set of provincial and county maps divided into baronies; containing the principal cross-roads, cities, towns, rivers, canals etc. . . . .* **Maps (37):** (a) folding index map of Ireland. (b) Four Irish provinces. (c) 32 Irish counties. **State:** First. **Imprints:** (i) *obbl:ds:* Antrim, Ulster: 'W. Beaufort delin.'. (ii) *obbl:ds:* Cavan, Down, Galway, Limerick, Sligo, Waterford: 'W. Beauford delin.'. (iii) *obbr:es:* Antrim, Down: 'Neele sc. Strand.' Down adds 'London' to the imprint and this longer signature also appears below the title cartouche of Waterford. (iv) *obbr:ds/es:* Monaghan, Tyrone, Wicklow: 'Drawn & Engraved by J. Taylor 8 Upp.ʳ Bagot S.ᵗ Dublin'. **Publishers:** George & John Grierson, and Martin Keene, 'His Majesty's Printers', (1825 issue; apparently they acquired the atlas from an earlier publisher.)

HALL, Sidney
fl. 1818–1860. Engraver and cartographer

Hall was a prolific engraver who produced maps for many atlases and publishers. In particular, he engraved a set of plain, interesting county maps (49) which were issued under several atlas titles. These maps went through many editions and show a series of revisions; it is common, for example, to find railway information up-dated by hand.

(49) Description: *st*: Fourth (*v*). **Supply:** Plentiful. **Average size:** 190 × 245 mm (7.6 × 9.75 in.). **Features:** A numbered reference key to administrative divisions: e.g. 'Reference to the Hundreds'. **Scale:** *V*/*av*:1:5 *m*/'English Miles'/*sbm*. **Border:** *OB*:*tTt*/*IB*:*ll*/*bb*. **North Point:** *c*/*p*. **Key:** 'The Figures prefixed to the Towns denote the distances from London'. Symbol for 'Railway Stations' added to later issues. **Title:** *c*/*oc*/set within a rectangular panel with a wide *tl* frame/inscription: 'ENGRAVED BY S. HALL' or 'ENGRAVED BY SID^Y HALL' below the title panel (Hampshire and Isle of Man, etc. have this *obbr*). **Engraver:** Sidney Hall.

Issues: These maps were issued over a period of 54 years in atlases and as folding maps; most issues updated railway and other information. They were also published in other works. Old stock was frequently used. (i) 1831–33: *Atlas: A topographical dictionary of Great Britain and Ireland, compiled from local information, and the most recent and official authorities. By John Gorton. . . . With fifty-two quarto maps, drawn and engraved by Sidney Hall. . . . Maps (47):* (a) Wales; Ireland; Scotland: (each folding on two sheets); England. (b) 39 English counties. (c) Yorkshire (folding on two sheets). (d) Isle of Man, Guernsey, Jersey; Isle of Wight. (e) Inland communication (four sheets). *State:* First (*v*). *Imprint: obbc:pi:* 'London. Published by Chapman & Hall, N.º 186 Strand, . . .' (*V*).

N.B. Bedford, Berkshire and Middlesex bear the address 'Arundel St! Strand' and Devon, Dorset, Hereford, Hertfordshire and Lancashire give the number as '168'. The imprint on the Yorkshire sheets is divided between the two, and is often partially obscured by overlapping. *pi*: dated between 1830 and 1832 [except: Northumberland has no imprint or date]. Yorkshire tends to lose this imprint in binding.

Publishers: Chapman & Hall. (ii) 1833: as (i) 1831–33, except: *Atlas: A topographical dictionary of Great Britain and Ireland . . . with fifty-four quarto maps . . . . State:* First (*v*). Some imprint dates were altered and some maps were revised during the course of the issue. (iii) 1833; 1834: as (ii) 1833, except: *Atlas: A new British atlas; comprising a series of 54 maps, constructed from the most recent surveys and engraved by Sidney Hall . . . . State:* Second. *Imprint: obbc:pi* altered: 'London, Published by Chapman & Hall, N.º 186 Strand, 1833' (*V*). (Northumberland now has the imprint;

Hereford and Lancashire still note the address as 'N.º 168 Strand'; Bedford retains the Arundel Street imprint).

N.B. From 1833, the maps were revised to incorporate the results of the Reform Act of 1832. A broken line (usually) was added to mark the boundaries of the new parliamentary divisions. Atlases were sometimes made up containing both revised and unchanged states of the maps.

(iv) 1835 (?): as (iii) 1833; 1834, except: *Atlas: A topographical dictionary of Great Britain and Ireland . . . . State:* Third (*v*). *Imprint: obbc:pi* altered: date erased (progressively from 1834) and imprints corrected: 'London, Published by Chapman & Hall, N.º 186 Strand', (*V*) (except: (e) Inland communication). The imprint is erased from the map of the islands. The maps were issued in this state, or with minor revisions and additions of railway and parliamentary information, in: (a) 1835(?): *Sidney Hall's British atlas . . . .* (b) 1836: *A new British atlas . . . .* (c) 1842: *A travelling county atlas . . . .* (v) 1842; 1843; 1845; 1846; 1847; 1848; 1850 (?): as (iv) 1835 (?), except: *Atlas: A travelling county atlas: with all the coach and rail roads accurately laid down and coloured, and carefully corrected to the present time . . . . (V). Maps (46):* (a) Wales; Ireland; Scotland: (each folding on two sheets); England. (b) 39 English counties. (c) Yorkshire (folding on two sheets). (d) Isle of Wight; Isle of Man, Guernsey, Jersey. *State:* Fourth (*v*). Railway stations are added and the symbol is explained: 'Railway Stations marked thus . . . .' The maps were issued in this state, or with minor revisions and additions of railway information, in: 1847: *A new county atlas: with all the coach and rail roads accurately laid down and coloured. Carefully corrected to the end of the session of M.DCCC.XLVI. . . . .* (vi) 1852 (?); 1853 (?); 1854 (?); as (v) 1842, etc., except: *State:* Fifth (*v*). *Imprints:* (i) *obbc:pi* altered: 'London, Published by Chapman & Hall, 193 Piccadilly' (*V*). (ii) top right, within border: plate-number added. The marking of the railways is usually altered to a thick black line and the explanatory symbol is revised accordingly. Projected railways that were engraved on the map but never actually constructed are left as originally printed, i.e. as two fine lines shaded with cross-hatching. The maps were issued in this state, or with minor revisions and additions of railway information, in: 1855 (?); 1857 (?): *Sidney Hall's travelling atlas of the English counties with all the railroads accurately laid down, and the boundaries*

coloured .... (vii) 1859 (?); 1860 (?); 1862 (?); 1864 (?); 1866 (?): by lithographic transfer: as (vi) 1852 (?), etc., except: *Atlas: A travelling atlas of the English counties. By Sidney Hall. With all the railroads accurately laid down, and the boundaries coloured .... State:* Sixth (*v*). The maps were issued in this state, or with minor revisions and additions of railway information, sometimes without *pi*, in an enlarged lithographic reproduction of approximately 296 × 370 mm (11.25 × 14.75 in.), at an average scale of 1 inch to 3 miles, in: 1860 (?); 1862 (?): *The English counties. By Sidney Hall. With all the railroads accurately laid down, and the boundaries coloured ... (V).*
N.B. England was replaced by 'Great Britain & Ireland'.
(viii) 1868 (?); 1869 (?); 1871 (?); 1873 (?); 1874 (?); 1875: by lithographic transfer: as (vii) 1859 (?), etc., except: **State:** Seventh. *Imprints:* (ii) within border, top right: plate-number deleted from most maps (some are known both with and without the original plate-number). (iii) *ob:* top right or bottom left of page: all maps have a plate-number added: 'N°. ...'. (ix) 1875: by lithographic transfer: as (viii) 1868 (?), etc., except: *State:* Eighth (*v*). *Imprints:* (ii) within border, top right: plate-number, and (iii) *ob*, top right or bottom left of page: plate number: 'N°. ...'. (x) 1885 (?); by lithographic transfer: as (ix) 1875, except: *State:* Eighth (*v*) or ninth. Some maps have simply an updating of railway information and others have railways no longer labelled. *Imprint:* (i) *obbc:pi* deleted from some maps.

HARRISON, John
fl. 1791. Publisher

Harrison published a set of large, plain maps (50), prepared by John Heywood, in his folio *Maps of the English Counties* of 1791. The maps were finely engraved in an austere style. Evidence suggests that an unusual issue pre-dated the 1791 atlas: '... an advertisement in *The Morning Herald*, 2 May 1787 may refer to this series of maps: 'This day are published, by J. Harrison, No. 115, Newgate street, Specimens of Maps of the Counties of England and Wales, printed on white sattin, with crimson ink, and the Hundreds, etc. beautifully coloured, at 10s. each. Few of those prints, with which our rooms are usually decorated, will appear so beautiful as a fine impression of a map on white sattin, the softness of which relieves the eye, while the interesting nature of the subject at once attracts and fixes attention; our

leisure moment may then be agreeably filled up; and the occasional inspection of an elegant piece of furniture, will save the trouble of many hours study'.[28]

(50) Description: *st:* Second. **Supply:** Scarce. **Average size:** 312 × 438 mm (12.5 × 17.5 in.). **Features:** A numbered reference key to administrative divisions e.g. 'Reference to the Hundreds'. **Scale:** *V/av:*1:4*m*/'British Statute Miles 69½ to a Degree' or 'English ...'/*Vw/sbm*. **Border:** *OB:Tt/IB:ll/mf* is divided into reference squares/*bb*. **North Point:** *s/f*. **Title:** 'A MAP OF ... ENGRAVED FROM AN ACTUAL SURVEY; with Improvements'/*V/vl*/set within a panel with *dl* frame. **Engravers:** 28 maps are signed by Sudlow and one by G. S. Allen of 'N° 4, Sadlers Wells Row'.

Issues: (i) 1791: (evidence suggests that at least some of the maps were issued before 1791): *Atlas: Maps of the English counties, with the subdivisions of hundreds, wapontakes, lathes, wards, divisions etc. .....*
Maps (38): (a) 36 English county maps (Leicester with Rutland; Cumberland with Westmorland; 'Glocester' with Monmouth). (b) Yorkshire. (c) North and South Wales. *State:* First. *Imprints:* (i) *obbl* or *obbr:es:* 'Sudlow sculp.' (*V*). Wales is signed by G. S. Allen. Nine maps have no *es*. (ii) 32 maps have: *obbl* or *obbr:ds:* 'Haywood del.' or 'Heywood del.' (*V*). (iii) *obbc:pi:* 'London, Engraved for J. Harrison, 115, Newgate Street, as the Act directs, ...' (*V*). Variously dated between 1 September 1787 and 26 February 1791. *Publisher:* John Harrison. (ii) 1792: as (i) 1791, except: *Atlas: Maps of the English counties; with the subdivisions of the hundreds, wappintakes, wards etc. etc. which are curious and valuable. Drawn upon the most approved scales, exhibiting everything interesting, clear & distinct ....* *State:* Second. Minor revisions; particularly the addition of hills. (iii) 1815 (?): as (ii) 1792, except: *Atlas: General and county atlas .... States:* Second or third. *Imprint:* (iii) *obbc:pi:* the date is imperfectly erased from almost all imprints.

HERMANNIDES, Rutger
fl. 1661. Topographer

Hermannides produced a set of early town plans (51) of the British Isles, excluding Wales, in his *Britannia Magna* of 1661. These small attractive plans vary considerably in their design; they are based almost exclusively on the town plans of John Speed's maps (except Dover which did not appear on Speed's map of Kent).

(51) Description: *st*: First. (Fig. 75). **Supply:** Very scarce. **Average size:** 120 × 150 mm (4.8 × 6 in.). N.B. Edinburgh is a bird's-eye view, not a plan. **Features:** Surrounding areas are shaded and decorated with: figures, animals, plough teams, etc.; and, on water: ships, boats and oarsmen. **Border:** *sl*. **North Point:** Some plans have *q*. **Decoration:** Some plans have the heraldic arms of the town. **Title:** Town name/*ps*/in English and/or Latin. Set within either a plain *dl* framed panel or a simple scrollwork cartouche.
Issues: (i) 1661: *Atlas: Britannia Magna sive Angliae, Scotiae, Hiberniae & adjacentium insularum. Geographico – historica descriptio.* **Map:** Index map of the British Isles: 'Magnae BRITANNIAE et HIBERNIAE nova Descriptio'. **Plans (31):** (a) Berwick, Buckingham, 'Bristow', Cambridge, Canterbury, 'Cester', Colchester, 'Douer', Durham, Ely, 'Excester', 'Glocester', Hull, Ipswich, Lancaster, Leicester, London, 'Newe Castle', Newport, Norwich, Oxford, 'Redding', Rochester, Salisbury, Stafford, 'Yorke'. (b) 'Edenborrow'. (c) 'Corcke', Dublin, Galway, 'Limrick'. **State:** First. **Publisher:** 'Jansonii Valckenier'. (ii) 1666: as (i) 1661, except: *Atlas: Historische landbeschryringe van Groot-Brittanjen.* **State:** First. **Publisher:** 'Wilhelmus Goeree'.
N.B. Most of the above plans were also copied, at the same size, from Speed by Pierre van der Aa

75 51(i): Dublin by Rutger Hermannides, 1661. *By permission of the British Library (796.a.5.)*

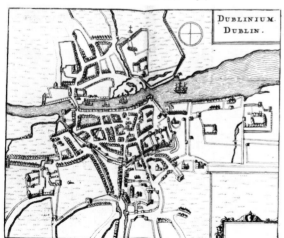

for his 1729 *La Galérie Agréable du Monde . . .* which usually added some decoration and a numbered key to buildings outside the borderlines and presented them individually or with engraved views two, three or four to a plate. Twenty-three of the above plans, copied from Speed probably via Hermariedes also appeared in Johann Christoph Beer's *Das Neu-Geharnischte Gross-Britannien* of 1690. These very rare plans measure approx. 130 × 161 mm (5.1 × 6.3 in); are framed by a narrow *dl*; and bear the title in English and, usually, Latin upon a ribbon supporting the arms of the town decorated with foliage. The plans have no scale, but are decorated with coats-of-arms, vignettes, figures, animals and ships.

HINTON, John
fl. 1745–1781. Publisher and bookseller

Hinton published some of the large maps by Bowen and Kitchen which were issued separately between 1749 and 1751, prior to the publication of the *Large English Atlas*. He also published volumes 1–68 of *The Universal Magazine of Knowledge & Pleasure* which contained two interesting sets of maps. The attractive, rococo style, county maps (52), engraved by Emanuel Bowen, Thomas Kitchin and Richard Seale, are decorated by ornate cartouches and coats-of-arms which compensate for the lack of detail. The rarer, large strip road maps (53), issued under the title *The Roads of England*, although following the style of Ogilby's strip maps of 1675 (but lacking their decorative embellishments), seem to take their detail mainly from the road maps (98) of John Senex.

(52) Description: *st*: First. (N.B. Derbyshire differs significantly from this description since it was copied from Samuel Simpson—who, in turn, had plagiarised Rocque and Moll). (Fig. 76). **Supply:** Moderate. **Average size:** 185 × 202 mm (7.25 × 8.00 in.). **Scale:** *V/av*:1:8 *m*/'English Statute Miles', or 'English Miles', etc./*sbm*. **Border:** *OB:sl/IB:ll/bb*. **North Point:** *q/f* usually *e*. **Key:** *n* //or: 'Explanation'. **Decoration:** Most maps have the arms of the county town set within a cartouche of foliage and flowers. Derbyshire also has views of 'The Devils Arse' and 'Pooles Hole'. **Title:** 'An Accurate Map of . . . Drawn from late SURVEYS with Improvements'/*V/vl/sd*/set within a cartouche of foliage and flowers. **Engravers:** Four county maps are attributed to Thomas Kitchin, 16 to

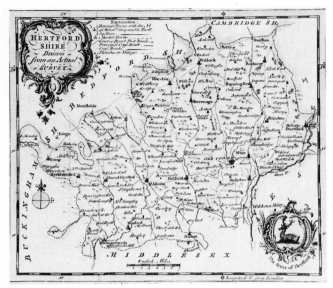

76 52(i): Hertfordshire published by John Hinton, 1751.
Photograph: Mills-Wight Studio

Emanuel Bowen, and nine to R. W. Seale. The remainder are unattributed but are apparently by the same engravers.

Issues: (i) 1747–1766: *Atlas: The universal magazine of knowledge and pleasure ... Published monthly according to Act of Parliament, for John Hinton* .... **Maps (52):** (a) England, Scotland, and Ireland; Post Roads of England and Wales. (b) 39 English counties. (c) North; East; West Ridings. (d) Isle of Man. (e) North Wales. (f) Six Welsh counties ('Brecknock', Cardigan, Carmarthen, Glamorgan, Pembroke, Radnor). **State:** First. **Imprints:** Either: (a) Maps by Bowen and Kitchin: (i) *obbc:pi:* 'Printed for I. Hinton at the Kings Arms in S.t Pauls Church Yard' or '... in Newgate Street London' (*V*). The imprint is usually dated. (N.B. John Hinton moved premises from St Paul's Church Yard to Newgate Street in 1752). (ii) *obac:* 'Engrav'd for the Universal Magazine' (*V*). or: (b) Maps by Seale: within the cartouche, below the title: 'Univers. Mag. J. Hinton, Newgate Str.' **Publisher:** John Hinton.

N.B. Two states of some maps are known: one without plate-numbers; and the other with 'Plate ...' at top left and 'page ...' at top right. Some of the maps, without inscription or imprint, were possibly issued in Benjamin Martin's *The natural history of England* (15 (i)).

(53) Description: *st*: First. **Supply:** Scarce. **Average size:** 302 × 400 mm (12.1 × 16 in.). **Features:** Notes are given concerning connecting maps and other general information: e.g. 'S.t Davids a Town of Pembroke Shire in S. Wales, with a Bishops See. It was once a considerable Place & had walls which are now demolished, but it is small at present, and thinly Inhabited, however, the Cathedral is a pretty good Structure. From the Cape near this Place, there is a prospect into Ireland'. The notes appear in blank sections of strips or in the title panel. **Border:** *OB:dl*/maps consist of eight strips, averaging 45 mm (1.75 in.) wide, separated by *sl/bts/bltr*. **North Point:** *c/f/e*/each strip has a north point/orientation varies. **Key:** Some maps have an 'Explanation' below the border, across the width of the map: including: 'The Flower de Lis every where points to the North'; 'the little openings on the Roads shew the Turnings'. **Decoration:** Ships occasionally decorate sea areas. **Title:** e.g. 'The ROAD from LONDON to ABERISTWITH on the Sea Coast of CARDIGAN SHIRE, wherein are Included the Roads both to Oxford and Worcester, from an actual Survey'/*vl*/set within *dl* framed panel at the top centre of the strips, or, where there are several titles on the map, at the top of the relevant strips. The title panel usually includes a distance table and sometimes references to connecting plates. Roads are measured from 'the head of Cornhill in London' or 'the Standard in Cornhill'.

Issues: (i) Aug. 1765 (Vol. 37) – Dec. 1773 (Vol. 53): Issued in *The universal magazine of knowledge and pleasure* .... **Maps:** (a) England and Wales. (b) 39 strip road maps of England and Wales. **State:** First. **Imprint:** *obar*:plate-number: 'Plate ...' in roman numerals. **Publisher:** 'John Hinton, at the King's-Arms in St. Paul's Churchyard, London'.

N.B. Reduced maps in similar style by Thomas Bowen are known for some roads; engraved usually on ten strips, 28 mm (1.1 in.) wide, with an overall map measurement of 170 × 285 mm (6.2 × 11.25 in.) and the *es:* 'Tho.s Bowen sculp.t Fleet street.'

HOBSON, William Colling
fl. 1850. Cartographer

Hobson's Fox-Hunting Atlas contained lithographic reproductions of the maps (113) from the *British Atlas* of J. & C. Walker. These maps have the names and areas of the hunts superimposed on the original detail and the hunt boundaries are usually brightly coloured.

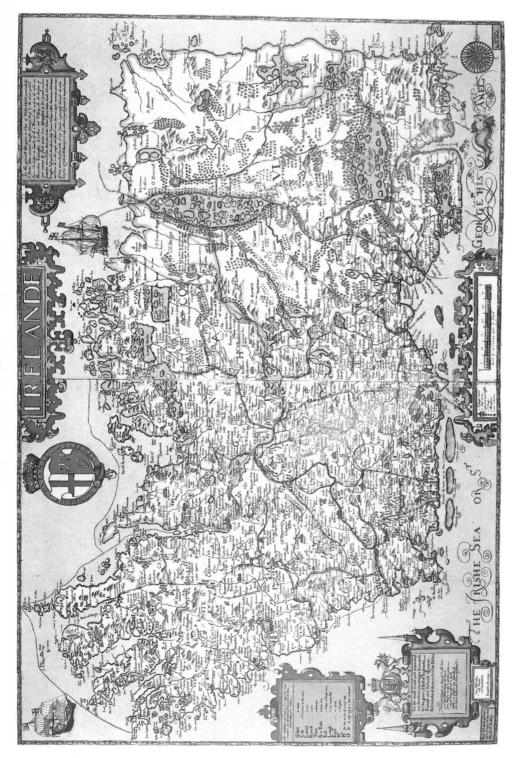

C 'Irelande' by Baptista Boazio, 1599. *By permission of the British Library* [*Maps C.2.cc.1.(1).*]

D 'Cambriae Typus Auctore Humfredo Lhuydo' published by Abraham Ortelius, 1573-1580. *By permission of the British Library* [*Maps C.2.d.1.*]

Supply: Moderate. (Fig. 77)

HODGSON, Orlando
fl. 1820. Publisher

Orlando Hodgson re-issued J. Thomson's charming, tiny maps (54) in his *Pocket Tourist & English Atlas.*

(54) Description: *st*: First. Supply: Very scarce. Average size: 58 × 85 mm (2.3 × 3.4 in.). Scale: *V/ av*:1:20 *m*/'Scale of Miles'/*slm*. Border: Decorative 3 mm (0.1 in.) wide border with the pattern set upon a hatched background. The border incorporates a title panel at the top, and, at the bottom, a larger panel containing statistical details of acreage, parishes, market towns, inhabitants and members of Parliament. North Point: *c*/*f*/*V*/the lettering is engraved so that it reads without turning the map to place north at the top. Title: *c*/*pc*/set within a plain panel incorporated into the upper border.

Issues: (i) 1823: Atlas: *The new English atlas, being a complete set of county maps, neatly coloured; exhibiting the whole of the turnpike roads, cities, market towns, great rivers, with the distances from London; also, the number of acres & inhabitants, members of Parliament, ... Maps (43):* (a) England and Wales. (b) 39 English counties. (c) Yorkshire. (d) North; South Wales. State: First. Publisher: 'Printed for the proprietor, J. Thomson, and sold by all booksellers'. (ii) 1827 (?): as (i) 1823, except: Atlas: *The pocket tourist & English atlas, being a new and complete set of county maps, exhibiting the whole of the turnpike roads, cities, market towns, great rivers and navigable canals with the distances from London* .... State: First. Publisher: 'O. Hodgson, Maiden Lane, Wood St.'

HOLE, William
fl. 1607–1646. Engraver

Little is known of William Hole except that he engraved portraits, maps, book-illustrations and title-pages in London from about 1600 to 1646. He engraved maps (39) for Michael Drayton's *Poly-Olbion* (probably) and for the 1607 edition of Camden's *Britannia* (58). 'On 29 May 1618 he received a grant for life of the office of head-sculptor of the iron for money in the Tower and elsewhere.' D.N.B: Vol. 9, p. 1022.

JEFFERYS, Thomas
fl. 1732–1771d. Engraver, geographer and publisher

77 113(iv): Lincolnshire by J. & C. Walker, from *Hobson's Fox-Hunting Atlas*, c.1849. *Photograph: Mills-Wight Studio*

Jefferys was one of the most important map publishers in London in the second half of the eighteenth century and became 'Geographer of Maps and Charts' to the Prince of Wales (later George III). His particular speciality was North America, but he also produced many maps of the British Isles, and, indeed, engraved many non-cartographical works. An early work was the *Small English Atlas*, published with Thomas Kitchin, containing small, attractive, but derivative, county maps (55): 'we thought it necessary to compile a correct sett of portable pocket Maps of all the Counties in England and Wales ... being prompted thereto by the inaccuracy of some lately published wherein upwards of 50 Boroughs are omitted or not distinguish'd and Towns without number plac'd in wrong counties . . . .'

Jefferys also published large-scale town plans, few of which have survived, and from the 1740s was very much involved in the large-scale mapping of the counties encouraged by the Royal Society of Arts. He engraved Benjamin Donn's prize-winning map of Devon of 1765 and produced his own large-scale maps of Stafford (1747), Bedford (1765), Oxford (1767), Huntingdon (1768), Buckingham (1770), Westmorland (1770), Northampton (with T. Eyre, 1779), and the fine 20 sheet map of Yorkshire (1771–2). However, none of his maps won the Society of Arts' award and his commitment to winning the prize was probably the reason for his bankruptcy in 1766. Nevertheless, the following year, Jefferys 'found some Friends who have been compassionate enough to re-instate me in my Shop' and business was resumed at his Charing Cross premises. In 1775, Jefferys produced the little-known, plain, strip road maps (56) of *Jefferys's Itinerary* using the plates of Monsieur Desnos (98) which he reworked. Jefferys died on 20 November 1771 and his business was taken over by Willian Faden. D.N.B: Vol. 10, p. 706.

Select Bibliography

HARLEY, J. B.: 'The Bankruptcy of Thomas Jefferys: An Episode in the Economic History of Eighteenth Century Map-making'. (*IM*, 20; 1966).

(F) HARLEY, J. B. AND HARVEY, J. C.: Introduction to *A survey of the County of Yorkshire by Thomas Jefferys*, 1775. (1974)

KISS, G.: 'Correspondence of continental mapmakers of the 1770s and 80s with a London Firm'. (i.e. with Thomas Jefferys and William Faden; *IM*, 4; 1948).

(55) Description: *st*: First (*v*). (Fig. 78). **Supply**: Scarce. **Average size**: *V*/Map only: 128 × 132 mm (5.2 × 5.3 in.). Overall: 132 × 170 mm (5.3 × 6.75 in.). **Features**: Below most maps, in three columns across the full page, is information on: parliamentary representation, and market and fair days. Yorkshire and the Islands of Man, Scilly, Jersey and Guernsey have general notes only. **Scale**: *V*/*av*:1:12 *m*/'English Miles'/*sbm*. **Border**: *OB:sl*/ *IB:ll/bb*. **North Point**: *q/op/e*//Durham has *r*; and South Wales and the two general maps have *n*. **Title**: 'A Map of . . .'/*pc* and *ps/obac*.

Issues: (i) 1748–49: The maps were apparently first published in 12 parts in 1748–49 for a variety of London publishers. They were first published

78 55(ii): Cheshire by Thomas Jefferys & Thomas Kitchin, 1749. *By permission of the British Library (Maps C.24.aa.6.)*

together in 1749 by Kitchin & Jefferys. **Atlas**: *The small English atlas being a new and accurate sett of maps. of all the counties in England and Wales . . . .* **Maps (49)**: (a) Two general maps of England and Wales. (b) 39 English counties. (c) East; North; West Ridings. (d) Jersey, Guernsey, etc.; Isle of Man; Isles of Scilly. (e) North; South Wales. **State**: First (*v*). **Publishers**: 'Mess.[rs] Kitchin & Jefferys'. (ii) 1749; 1751: as (i) 1748–49, except: **State**: First (*v*). Minor additions and revisions. (iii) 1751: as (ii) 1749; 1751, except: **State**: Second (most maps). **Imprint**: *obar*:plate-number added to most maps (N.B. Evidence suggests that the sheets had a reference number, 'N.º . . .', at either the top or bottom left. This was normally cut off in binding). (iv) 1775 (?): as (iii) 1751, except: **State**: Third (most maps). Boundaries of the hundreds are added as dotted lines. Revisions and additions to roads and place-names. Re-engraving of the columns of information below the map so that the towns are listed in alphabetical order, with a new heading detailing cities, boroughs and market towns in the county. Some copies of this issue have alterations to the plate-number on some maps. All maps now have a plate-number. *Publishers:* Robert Sayer & John Bennett, John Bowles, and Carington Bowles. Most maps were issued in this state thus: (a) 1785 (?): *The small English atlas ... by Robert Sayer.* Issued again by Bowles & Carver c. 1795. (b) 1787: *An English atlas or a concise view of England and Wales ... by Robert Sayer.* (c) 1794: *An English atlas ... by Laurie & Whittle.*

(56) Description: *st:* Second (Desnos). **Supply:** Rare. **Average size:** 157 × 205 mm (6.25 × 8.25 in.). **Features:** Some maps incorporate panels containing explanatory notes about the routes. Below the border, across the full width of some maps, are further notes concerning route continuations and alternatives on other sheets. **Border:** *sl/*the six or seven strips of varying width are each enclosed within *sl* frame/*bts*/*bltr*. **North Point:** *c/op/*each strip has a north point and orientation varies. **Title:** 'From ... to ...'/*oc* and *os*/below the map title is a distance table. The whole is set within *sl* framed panel positioned at the top centre of the map. Only the first sheet of any route is titled; subsequent sheets of a route have no title.

Issues: (i) 1775: *Atlas: Jefferys's itinerary; or travellers companion, through England, Wales, and part of Scotland, containing all the direct and principal cross roads; with the addition of every new road, carefully collected from all the actual surveys hitherto published. Improved with many thousand names of places more than are in any similar publication ....* *Maps:* (a) Index map. (b) 104 strip road maps, printed back-to-back, including the road from Berwick to Edinburgh. *State:* First (Jefferys); second (Desnos) *Imprints:* (i) *obar* and *obal:* plate-number. (ii) most plates have: *obac* or *obbc:pi:* 'Publish'd as the Act directs by R. Sayer & I. Bennett 16 Jan.ry 1775'. *Publishers:* Robert Sayer & John Bennett.

JENNER, Thomas
fl. 1622–1673d. Engraver and bookseller

Jenner acquired the plates (99), engraved by Jacob van Langeren, which had been published by Mathew Simons in 1635. He erased the original skeleton maps and engraved new ones at double the scale. The names of the towns, apparently chosen at random, were now given in full. The Puritan Jenner was a keen supporter of the Parliamentary cause and rush-released his new maps for the use of the Parliamentary armies in the Civil War. 'Emergency' issues of his *A Direction for the English Traviller* are known made up of both newly engraved plates and the original van Langeren maps. After re-issues by Jenner, the plates passed to John Garrett who succeeded to Jenner's shop and business in 1673 and re-issued the plates until 1677.

Jenner also contributed what is known as the 'Quartermaster's Map' to the Civil War effort. This was a reduced (though still large-) scale copy of Saxton's large wall map of England and Wales which had been published in 1583. It was engraved by Wenceslaus Hollar and published by Jenner in 1644: 'The Kingdome of England, & Principality of Wales Exactly Described with every Sheere, & the small townes in every one of them, in Six Mappes, Portable for every Mans Pocket.' As the title suggests, despite being printed on six sheets (measuring: 400 × 525 mm; 16 × 21 in.), it was cleverly designed to fold small enough for the military pocket. The 'Quartermaster's Map' is an interesting example of a map produced for military purposes, but the fact that the early issues omitted the roads must seriously have reduced its effective use. D.N.B: Vol. 10, p. 762.

Select Bibliography
FORDHAM, SIR H. G.: 'A note on the "Quarter-master's Map" 1644'. (GJ, 70; 1927)

KEERE, Pieter van den
fl. 1599–c. 1646. Engraver and bookseller

Pieter van den Keere came to England in 1584, as a Protestant refugee from his home town of Ghent, with his sister, Colette, who married another refugee, Jodocus Hondius, in 1587. It was probably from the skilled Hondius that Keere learned the craft of engraving. Both engravers left London in 1593 to settle in Amsterdam.

Keere began to engrave a series of miniature map plates in 1599 in preparation for a small atlas of the British Isles. The maps (57), which are very rare in their first state, with only proof copies known, were taken from Saxton's maps of England and Wales and the Ortelius and Boazio maps of Scotland and Ireland respectively. The plates were first published by Willem Blaeu in 1617 with page numbers and Latin text added. They then passed to George Humble, who decided to cash in on the popularity of his editions of Speed's folio atlas, by publishing in c. 1619 a pocket-sized atlas 'Abridged from A farr larger vollume: By John Speed.' Humble had the plates reworked, substituting English titles for the original Latin; the groups of counties copied from Saxton were separated and each county was covered individually; and some new maps, based on Speed, were added. Evidently the new plates were not engraved by Keere. They were issued again in 1627 with some additional maps, and, for the first time, Speed's text was reprinted verbatim on the back of each map. The connection with Speed has resulted in these maps sometimes being misleadingly referred to as 'miniature Speeds', but in truth the only connection was Speed's text, the new maps taken from Speed, and Humble's business acumen! In fact, the original Keere plates had been engraved earlier than the Speed plates they were supposed to imitate! From 1627 to 1676 the miniature atlas was re-issued, usually to coincide with new editions of Speed's *Theatre*, by Humble and the later publishers of the *Theatre*. Since it proved to be very popular, the post-1627 state of these small, attractive maps, although scarce, is in good supply for an early map.

Select Bibliography

KEERE:

KEUNING, J.: 'Pieter van den Keere (Petrus Kaerius), 1571–1646 (?)'. (*IM*, 15; 1960).

SKELTON, R. A.: 'Pieter van den Keere'. (*The Library*, 5th Series, 5; 1950).

(F) TAYLER, E. G. R.: *John Speed's Atlas of England & Wales* (1951).

(F) VAN DEN KEERE, P.: *Atlas of the British Isles. Facsimile of the 1605 miniature Atlas.* Introduction by Helen Wallis. (1972).

HONDIUS:

HEAWOOD, E.: 'Hondius and his newly-found map of 1608'. (*GJ*, 54; 1919).

KEUNING, J.: 'Jodocus Hondius, Jr.'. (*IM*, 5; 1948).

(57) **Description:** *st*: Fourth (*v*). **Supply:** Scarce. **Average size:** 83 × 120 mm (3.25 × 4.75 in.). **Features:** Some maps have the sea shaded as 'watered silk'. **Scale:** *V*/*av*: 1:12 *m*/'Scala Milliarium' or 'Milliaria Anglicana'/*Vw*/*sbm*/set within the title cartouche or within a separate panel, sometimes with fretwork decoration/county maps added in 1619 usually have a double row, 'chessboard' style, scale with mileage numbers positioned diagonally opposite to each other. **Border:** *dl*. **North Point:** *n*//or: labelling of the map sides

'Occidens' and 'Oriens', and sometimes also 'Septentrio' and 'Meridies'/or: *r* with *f*, *e* and rhumb lines/or: *q* with *l*/*V*. **Decoration:** Where space allows, lettering is performed in large swash characters. Isle of Man has a decorative ship. **Title:** *c*/*pc*/in Latin before the 1619 (?) issue, and, thereafter, in English/usually set within a panel with a fretwork frame. **Engraver:** 21 maps are signed by Pieter van den Keere.

Issues: (i) c. 1605: *Atlas:* Title unknown. *Maps (44):* (a) 27 maps of English counties: (grouped thus: (i) Oxford, Buckingham and Berkshire. (ii) Warwick and Leicester. (iii) Kent, Hampshire, Surrey and Middlesex. (iv) Northampton, Bedford, Cambridge, Huntingdon and Rutland. (v) Lincoln and Nottingham. (vi) Westmorland and Cumberland). (b) Six maps of Welsh counties: (grouped thus: (i) Radnor, Brecon, Cardigan and Carmarthen. (ii) Montgomery and Merioneth. (iii) Anglesey and Caernarvon. (iv) Denbigh and Flint). (c) Four regional maps of Scotland. (d) West coast of Scotland and Hebrides; North East Scotland and Orkneys. (e) Five regional maps of Ireland, (Connaught; North Leinster; South Leinster; Munster; Ulster). *State:* First. *Imprint:* (i) 21 maps bear the *es*: either set within the title or scale cartouche, or at bottom right or left of *mf*: e.g. 'Petrus Kaerius caelavit.' (*V*). Three maps are dated 1599 ((i) Warwick and Leicester, (ii) Radnor, etc., (iii) North West Scotland and Skye). (ii) 1617: as (i) c. 1605, except: *Atlas: Guilielmi Camdeni, viri clarissimi Britannia, sive florentissimorum regnorum Anglia, Scotiae, Hiberniae, & insularum adjacentium … descriptio …* *Maps (46):* (a) British Isles (double size folding map). (b) Yorkshire (double size folding map). (This map is known issued in a copy of the 1605 (?) atlas): added to the 44 maps of c. 1605. *State:* Second (except: new maps). *Imprint:* (ii) *ob*, various positions: page number and, in some cases, the printer's reference; printed from type, not engraved (except: new maps). *Publisher:* Willem Jansz Blaeu.

N.B. The Latin text of this edition was reprinted by Blaeu's successors in 1639 with 19 maps from Petrus Bertius's miniature world atlas *Petri Bertii tabularum geographicarum contractarum libri septem* of 1616. The maps (average size: 95 × 138 mm; 3.75 × 5.5 in.) were reductions from the Mercator-Hondius *Atlas* and included England, Scotland, and Ireland (all with the *es* of Salomon Rogiers), Britain, regional maps of Britain, and a map combining Anglesey, Jersey, Guernsey and the Isle of Wight. The miniature world atlas was reprinted in Latin, German and French editions in 1617, 1618, 1620, c. 1640, and 1650; and this Regner Vitellius abridgement of Camden's *Britannia* was published in 1639.

(iii) 1619 (?): as (ii) 1617, except: *Atlas: England, Wales, and Ireland: the seuerall counties. Abridged from.a.farr.larger.vollume: By.John, Speed* .... *Maps (57):* (a) General map. (b) 38 English county maps. (Westmorland with Cumberland). (c) Yorkshire. (d) Six Welsh county maps. (e) Four regional maps of Scotland. (f) Hebrides; Orkneys; (as above). (g) Five regional maps of Ireland. *States:* First, second or third. The titles of the maps are now in English. The new maps and four of the original maps (Dorset; North-West Scotland; Orkneys; Ulster) have the scale inscription in English: e.g. 'The Scale of Miles'. Other original maps retain the Latin scale inscription. *Imprint:* (ii) Usually lower right corner of *mf*: a new plate-number, crudely engraved in large figures, replaces the earlier page number and printer's reference. *Publisher:* 'George Humble in pops head alley'. (iv) 1627; 1632; 1646: as (iii) 1619 (?), except: *Atlas: England Wales Scotland and Ireland described and abridged with y*ᵉ *historie relation of things worthy memory from a farr larger voulume done by John Speed* ....

N.B. The maps were also published in 1646 by William Humble in *A prospect of the most famous parts of the world* ....

Maps (63): (a) England, Scotland and Ireland; Kingdom of England; Wales; Kingdom of Scotland; Kingdom of Ireland. (b) 38 English county maps. (Westmorland with Cumberland; (Fig. 79)). (c) Yorkshire. (d) Wight Island; Isle of Man (Fig. 80); Holy Island, 'Garnsey', Farne and 'Jarsey'. (e) Six Welsh county maps. (f) Four regional maps of Scotland. (g) Hebrides; Orkneys. (h) Four Irish provinces. *States:* First, second, third or fourth (v). The maps now have Speed's text verso (except: Great Britain and Ireland; Yorkshire.) *Imprint:* (ii) The plate-numbers are altered, sometimes leaving traces of the erased earlier plate-number. *Publisher:* 'Georg Humble at y*ᵉ* Whithorse in popeshead Alley'. (George Humble actually died in 1640 and the 1646 edition was almost certainly published by William Humble).

N.B. From 1627 some plates display progressive damage due to the development of cracks, sometimes necessitating repair; and some

79 57(iv): Westmorland and Cumberland by Pieter van den Keere, 1627. *By courtesy of Ivan R. Deverall*

80 57(iv): The Isle of Man published by George Humble, 1627. *Photograph: Mills-Wight Studio*

even fractured completely and had to be replaced by newly engraved plates.

(v) 1662 (two issues bound and issued with *A prospect of the most famous parts of the world*): as (iv) 1627, etc., except: *Atlas: England Wales Scotland Ireland described* .... *States:* First, second, third or fourth (v). *Publishers:* 'Roger Rea the Elder & younger at y*ᵉ* Golden Crosse in Cornhill against y*ᵉ* Exchange'. The maps were issued again in 1666 as *England Wales* ..., and also by Rea in 1665 with *A prospect of the most famous parts of the world* .... The maps were issued, with *A prospect* ..., with minor retouching as follows: (a) 1668: by Roger Rea in *England Wales* .... (b) 1676: by Thomas Bassett & Richard Chiswell in *England Wales* ....

N.B. Since the text was re-set for every issue from 1627 (except those of 1662), issues may be identified by the typesetting of the text backing the maps. From 1662 the maps were probably issued in the same years separately under the title *England Wales ...* as well as being bound in with *A prospect ....*

KIP, William
fl. 1598–1635. Engraver

The first edition of *Britannia*, with text in Latin, by William Camden, the historian and antiquarian, was published in 1586 containing only a general map. However, from 1589 Camden was thinking of incorporating county maps and he engaged William Kip and William Hole to engrave reduced copies of the great Elizabethan cartographers Saxton, Norden and Smith. The sixth and last Latin edition of 1607, the last to be published during Camden's lifetime, contained these reductions plus general maps of England and Wales, Scotland and Ireland taken from Mercator's maps of 1595. This atlas pre-dated Speed's folio atlas and, with the exception of the very rare playing card maps of 1590, contained the first separate delineation of many counties, since in Saxton's atlas they had been grouped together. Saxton is quoted as the source on 41 maps; Norden on six; and the map of Pembroke is attributed to George Owen, sometime Deputy Vice-Admiral of Pembroke and Cardigan and a noted local historian. Since most maps quote the source, they are sometimes mistaken for the originals and it should be noted that they are confusingly referred to as

Saxton/Norden//Kip/Hole depending on the combination of source and engraver. These superb maps (58) display the fine calligraphy, decoration, layout and appearance of the Elizabethan originals, but the thin paper of the 1607 edition does tend to allow the text on the reverse of the map to show through. The maps were re-issued with blank backs in 1610 in the first English translation of the *Britannia*, the text being separately engraved; and again in 1637.

Kip engraved many other works, including the map of Hertfordshire in Norden's *Speculi Britanniae pars: The Description of Hertfordshire*, 1598, and the small, circular map of England and Wales in Mathew Simons's *A Direction for the English Traviller*, 1635.

(58) Description: *st*: First. (Fig. 81). **Supply:** Scarce. **Average size:** *Vc*/280 × 355 mm (11.2 × 14.2 in.). **Features:** Some maps have a numbered reference key to administrative divisions set within a panel with a decorative strapwork frame: e.g. 'The names of the hundreds of this mappe'. **Scale:** *V*/*av*: 1:3 *m*/'Scala Miliarium'/*sbm*/usually set within a panel with a decorative strapwork frame, sometimes surmounted by a semi-circular compass rose or dividers. **Border:** *sl* or *dl*. **North Point:** Most maps have: *r* with *f* and *e*/some compasses have *l*/*V*//26 maps have no compass indicator, just *ce*. **Key:** Some maps have a key: e.g. 'Caracters distinguishing the difference of places'. **Decoration:** Titles, scales, *es*, source attribution, and key

81 58(iv): Warwickshire by William Kip, 1637 (detail). *By Courtesy of Ivan R. Deverall*

are set within decorative strapwork cartouches sometimes embellished with putti, birds, scrolling, garlands, etc. Some maps have the royal arms. Abundant swash lettering. Some maps are decorated with ships, monsters, Neptune, vignettes, etc. **Title:** Lengthy Latin title/*vl*/usually beginning '... comitatus ...'/set within a decorative cartouche. **Engravers:** William Kip (34 maps), William Hole (21); Middlesex and Anglesey are unsigned.
N.B. 41 maps attribute Christopher Saxton as source: e.g. 'Auctore Christophoro Saxton'; six attribute John Norden: e.g. 'Johannes Norden descripsit'; and Pembroke quotes George Owen as source. Nine maps are unattributed.

Issues: (i) 1607: *Atlas: Britannia, sive florentissimorum regnorum Angliae, Scotiae, Hiberniae ... chorographica descriptio ... chartis chorographicis illustrata. Guilielmo Camdeno authore ....* **Maps (57):** backed with Latin text (except: England, Rutland and Anglesey). (a) England; Scotland; Ireland. (b) 39 English counties. (c) West; East; North Ridings. (d) 12 Welsh counties. **State:** First. **Imprint:** 55 maps have the *es*: usually set within one of the cartouches: e.g. 'Wilhelmus Kip Sculpsit' (*V*) or 'Gulielmus Hole sculpsit' (*V*). **Publishers:** George Bishop & John Norton. (ii) 1610: as (i) 1607, except: *Atlas: Britain, or a chorographicall description of the most flourishing kingdomes, England, Scotland, and Ireland, and the ilands adioyning, out of the depth of antiquitie: beautified with mappes of the severall shires of England: written first in Latine by William Camden ... Translated newly into English by Philémon Holland ....* **Maps:** 57 maps, without text verso. **States:** First or second. Some maps are slightly revised during this issue and appear in either the first state (but without the backing text) or the second state in copies of this atlas: ten have a compass rose added (Cornwall, Leicester, Lincoln, Middlesex, Norfolk, Northampton, Rutland, Suffolk, Sussex, Warwick) and Wiltshire has its cruciform indicator placed within a circle. (iii) 1610: as (ii) 1610, except: **States:** Second or third. **Imprint:** A plate-number, in crude figures, is added on *mf* in the bottom left corner (except: (a) Scotland; Ireland: (b) Buckingham; Cheshire; Huntingdon; Shropshire; (c) East; North Ridings; (d) Brecon; Denbigh; Flint; Merioneth; Pembroke; Radnor.) (iv) 1637: as (iii) 1610, except: **States:** Second or third. The plates are worn (in some cases so badly that substitute maps were bound into some atlases). Brecon is printed from a new plate engraved

by Robert Vaughan. Some others have been retouched. **Publishers:** William Aspley; Andrew Crooke; Andrew Heb; George Latham; Joyce Norton & Richard Whitaker.
N.B. Some of the maps were possibly also issued in the late seventeenth or early eighteenth century, probably by Christopher Browne.

KITCHIN, Thomas
fl. 1738–1776. Engraver and publisher

Kitchin was a major map producer in the middle years of the eighteenth century and his massive output of maps, plans and charts earned him the title of 'Hydrographer to the King.' Generally his maps are characterised by an attractive rococo style with decorative cartouches and coats-of-arms; the larger county maps have magnificent cartouches depicting local scenes and crafts, dedication cartouches, vignettes of cathedrals, and informative notes. Kitchin collaborated with Thomas Jefferys to produce the *Small English Atlas* (56) and with Emanuel Bowen to produce the much sought after *Royal English Atlas* (16) and *Large English Atlas* (14). Some of his earlier work was produced for the *London Magazine* (59) and the *Universal Magazine* (52) and these small attractive maps are often confused with those (61) first published c. 1764 in *England Illustrated*: 'in all the accounts that have been hitherto published of England and Wales, the geographical and topographical description, natural history, antiquities, memorable events and other particulars, have been thrown together with such unaccountable disorder and confusion, that they can neither be read with pleasure, nor consulted occasionally with advantage: the present work was undertaken chiefly to regulate this chaos ...'. Kitchin also produced the very rare *Pocket Atlas* with maps (62) drawn to one uniform scale; the only other sets of county maps to be produced on this format were the playing cards of 1590, *A Direction for the English Traviller*, etc., 1635 (99), Thomas Taylor's atlas of Wales (109) of 1718, the Greenwoods' county atlas (47) of 1834, and Alfred Adlard's Irish maps (1) of 1841. A charming and fairly scarce series of Scottish county maps (60), based on John Elphinstone's map of Scotland, were published in 1749 in *Geographiae Scotiae*. Kitchin also ventured into the field of road maps with his *Ogilby's Survey Improv'd* (63), which was re-issued by Carington Bowles under the title *Bowles's Post-Chaise Companion*; and his pirated copy of John

Senex's road maps: *Kitchin's Post-Chaise Companion.*

Kitchin engraved many other cartographical works, including the Society of Arts' award-winning large-scale map of Northumberland by Andrew Armstrong, and died at St Albans in June 1784.

Select Bibliography

(*F*) KITCHIN, T.: *County Map 1761–7 in 3 sheets.* (Derbyshire Archaeological and Natural History Soc.; 1958); (i.e. the 1 inch to 1 mile map surveyed by P. P. Burdett and engraved by Kitchin). Introduction by J. B. Harley, D. V. Fowkes, and J. C. Harvey.

(59) Description: *st*: First. (N.B.: 'The Islands of Scilly' differs from this description in several respects, (Fig. 82)). **Supply**: Moderate. **Average size**: *Vc*/162 × 212 mm (6.5 × 8.5 in.). **Scale**: *V*/*av*: 1:8 *m*/'British Statute Miles 69 to a Deg'/*Vw*/*sbm*.

Border: *OB*:*sl*/*IB*:*ll*/*bb*. **North Point**: *q*/or: *r*/with *f* and *e*. **Key**: 'Explanation'. **Decoration**: 31 maps have the arms of the county town set within a small rococo cartouche. **Title**: 'An Accurate Map of ... Drawn from the best Maps Charts etc & Regulated by Astron! Observ.ns By T. Kitchin Geog.r'/*V*/*vl*/set in an attractive cartouche of fanciful scenery, figures, cherubs, local produce, agricultural implements, etc.

Issues: (i) 1747–60: *Atlas: The London magazine: or, gentleman's monthly intelligencer . . . . Maps (61)*: (a) 39 English counties. (b) Yorkshire; East; West; North Ridings. (c) Isles of Jersey, Guernsey, Alderney, etc.; Isle of Man; Islands of Scilly; Isle of Wight. (d) 12 Welsh counties. (e) Haddingtonshire; Edinburghshire. (Yorkshire is attributed to Thomas Conder.) *State*: First (*v*). **Imprints**: (i) Some maps have: *obbc*:*pi*: 'Printed for R. Baldwin

82 59(i): The Islands of Scilly by Thomas Kitchin, 1753. *Photograph: Mills-Wight Studio*

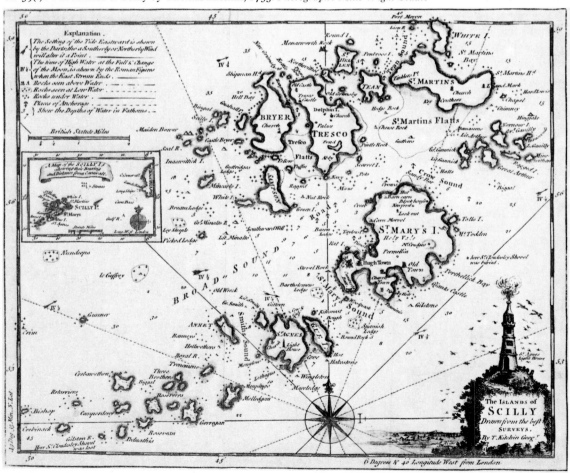

Jun.ʳ at the Rose in Pater Noster Row.' (*V*) Some of the maps were issued in the Dublin edition of the *London magazine* with the *pi* of S. and I. Exall or without imprint. (ii) *obac*, or *obbc* replacing the *pi*: 'For the Lond. Mag.' (*V*; sometimes with the volume date). **Publishers:** 'R. Baldwin, jun., at the Rose in Pater-Noster-Row' in London, or S. and I. Exall in Dublin. (ii) 1786 (?): as (i) 1747–60, except: *Atlas: Historical descriptions of new and elegant picturesque views of the antiquities of England and Wales: being a grand copper-plate repository of elegance, taste, and entertainment .... Published under the inspection of Henry Boswell, Esq. F.A.R.S. assisted by Robert Hamilton ... and other ingenious gentlemen .... Maps (52):* (a) 39 English counties. (b) Yorkshire. (c) North; South Wales. (d) Southern part of Scotland; Middle part of Scotland; and combining two maps with adjoining borderlines on each plate: Argyle, Bute, and Dumbarton, and the Western Isles; Orkney, 'Cathness', Sutherland, Ross and Cromarty, and the Shetland Isles and the Orkney Isles. (e) Four Irish Provinces.

N.B. Yorkshire, the Scottish maps, North Wales, South Wales, Munster, Connaught and Ulster were engraved by T. Conder; and Leinster by Terry.

States: First (*v*) or second. **Imprint:** the *pi* and all references to the *London magazine* are erased. The maps engraved by Conder and Terry bear the *pi*: 'Published by Alex.ʳ Hogg, at the King's Arms, N.º 16 Paternoster Row'. **Publisher:** Alexander Hogg: 'at the King's-Arms, No. 16, Paternoster-Row, and Sold by all Booksellers, Printsellers, and News-Carriers, in Towns and Country'.

N.B. Cheshire, Cornwall, Devon, Dorset, Oxford, Somerset, Wiltshire, Yorkshire, Cardigan, and Carnarvon were also published in *England displayed ... in* 1769 in the above state, (see (95) (vi)).

(iii) 1790 (?): as (ii) 1786 (?), except: *Atlas: Complete historical descriptions of a new and elegant collection of picturesque views and representations of the antiquities of England and Wales .... State:* Mostly second. (iv) 1795: as (iii) 1790 (?), except: *Atlas: The antiquities of England and Wales displayed ... By Henry Boswell, Esq. F.A.S. ...* Gloucester, Hereford, Kent, Lancashire, Munster, and all the Scottish maps except Argyle, etc. were apparently not issued. **State:** Mostly second. (v) 1798: as (iv) 1795, except: *Atlas: A new and complete abridgment or selection of the most interesting and important subjects in the antiquities of England and Wales ... By Francis*

Grose, Esq. F.A.S. *To which will be added ... a complete set of county maps, by the best artists ....* **State:** Mostly second. Some minor retouching. **Maps:** as (ii) 1786 (?): (a), (b) only. **Publishers:** H. D Symonds & Alexander Hogg.

(60) Description: *st*: First. (Fig. 83). **Supply:** Scarce. **Average size:** 142 × 168 mm (5.7 × 6.7 in.). **Scale:** *V*/*av*: 1:8 *m*/'English Miles'/*sbm*. **Border:** *OB*:*sl*/*IB*:*ll*/longitude is based on the meridian of Edinburgh/*bb*. **North Point:** *q*/*f*. **Key:** Only the map of Berwick has: 'Remarks'. **Title:** 'A Map of the SHIRES of ... & ... Drawn from the best Authorities by Thos. Kitchin'/*V*/*vl*/set within a cartouche of varying styles: either a plain *dl* frame panel, or a panel with a carved wood style frame, or an arrangement of flowers, shells, etc., or a small rural scene. All but five maps are attributed to Thomas Kitchin. Haddington is attributed to 'Mr Adair' and Edinburgh and Linlithgow have been 'survey'd by Mr Adair'. **Engraver:** Thomas Kitchin.

Issues: This atlas was sometimes issued bound with Thomas Osborne's *Geographia Magnae Britanniae.* (i) 1749: (evidence suggests that the fourth edition of the atlas was published in 1746, but no earlier copies have so far been traced). *Atlas: Geographia Scotiae:*

83 60(i): 'A Map of Dumbrittonshire' by Thomas Kitchin, 1746. *By permission of the British Library (Maps C.24.a.34.)*

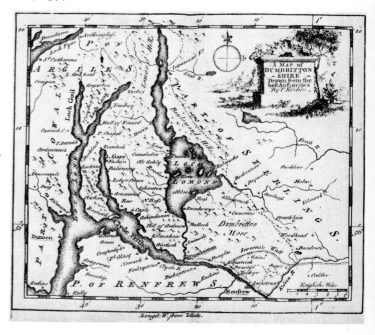

being new and correct maps of all the counties and islands in the kingdom of Scotland. Containing the universities, cities, presbytery, and market-towns, rivers, locks, roads, etc. .... *Maps (33):* (a) Index map. (b) 25 maps of Scottish counties. (six maps combine two counties or areas each). (c) Bute; Orkney Shire; Western Islands; Isles of Illay, Jura, etc.; Isles of Mull, Coll ... etc.; Isles of Shetland; Isle of Sky. *State:* First. *Imprints:* (i) *obal* or *obar:* plate-number: 'N^o ...' (ii) *obb:* 'Long^d W. from Edinb:'. *Publishers:* S. Birt, D. Browne, T. Osborne, J. Hodges, J. Osborne, A. Millar, and J. Robinson. (ii) 1756: as (i) 1749, except: *State:* First. *Publishers:* D. Browne, T. Osborne, J. Hodges, J. Osborne, A. Millar, J. Robinson, W. Johnston, and P. Davey and B. Law.

(61) Description: *st:* First. **Supply:** Moderate. **Average size:** *V*/195 × 253 mm (7.75 × 8.1 in.). **Scale:** *V*/*av:* 1:6 *m*/'British Statute Miles 69 to a Degree'/*sbm.* **Border:** *OB:sl*/*IB:ll*/*bb.* **North Point:** *r*/*f*/*e* designs vary. **Key:** 'Remarks'. **Title:** 'A New MAP of ... Drawn from the best Authorities. By Thos, Kitchin Geog^r, Engraver to H.R.H. the Duke of York'/*vl*/set within a rococo cartouche of flowers, twining foliage and scenery /*V.* **Engraver:** Thomas Kitchin.
Issues: (i) 1763 (?); 1764–65 (issued in 12 monthly parts): *Atlas: England illustrated, or, a compendium of the natural history, geography, topography, and antiquities ecclesiastical and civil, of England and Wales. With maps of the several counties .... *Maps (54):* (a) Two general maps. (b) 39 English counties. (c) Yorkshire; West; East; North Ridings. (d) Isle of Wight; Isle of Man. (e) North Wales. (f) Six southern Welsh counties. *State:* First. *Publishers:* 'R. and J. Dodsley, in Pall-mall'. (ii) 1765 (?): as (i) 1764 (?), except: *Atlas: Kitchen's English atlas: or, a compleat set of maps of all the counties of England and Wales ... The whole engraved ... from drawings after actual surveys .... *State:* First. *Publisher:* J. Dodsley, variously in association with 'T. Kitchen', J. Wilkie and H. Parker.

(62) Description: *st:* First. **Supply:** Rare. **Average size:** map sizes vary from 86 × 110 mm (3.4 × 4.4 in.) [Rutland] to 290 × 296 mm (11.6 × 11.75 in.) [West Riding]. **Scale:** *U*/1:7 *m*/'A Scale of British statute Miles' or 'British Statute Miles'/*sbm*/*Vw.* **Border:** *OB:sl*/*IB:ll.* **North Point:** *r*/*f*/*e.* **Key:** 'Remarks'.
Issues: (i) 1769: *Atlas: Kitchin's pocket atlass, of the counties of south Britain or England and Wales, drawn to one scale: by which the true proportion they severally bear to each other may be easily ascertained, with the measured distances from London by the nearest roads annexed, to all the cities, borough & market towns in the kingdom. Being the first set of counties, ever published on this plan .... *Maps (57):* (a) England and Wales (*pi:* 'Printed for T. Kitchin in Holborn & J. Gapper in New Bond Street London'). (b) 39 English counties. (c) East; North; West Ridings. (d) 12 Welsh counties. (e) Isle of Man; Isles of Scilly. Nine pages have two separate county maps each, printed from different plates. *State:* First. *Publishers:* 'T. Kitchin Engraver, Map & Printseller, N^o, 59 Holborn Hill; & J. Gapper, Map & Printseller, No^o, 56 New Bond Street'. (ii) 1781 (?): as (i) 1769, except: *Atlas: Bowles's pocket atlas of the counties of south Britain or England and Wales, drawn to one scale: by which the true proportion they severally bear to each other may be easily ascertained, with the measured distances from London by the nearest roads annexed, to all the cities, borough and market towns in the kingdom. Being the only set of counties, ever published on this plan .... *State:* Second. A new title: 'BOWLES's REDUCED MAP OF ...' is added/*pc*/set within a narrow, slightly ornate panel, positioned: *obac.* *Imprint:* *obar:* plate-number added. *Publisher:* 'Carington Bowles, No. 69 in St. Pauls Church Yard'.

(63) Description: *st:* First. (Fig. 84). **Supply:** Scarce. **Average size:** 125 × 150 mm (5 × 6 in.). **Features:** Some maps have notes concerning the route and connecting pages: *obbc,* or: in blank sections of the strips. **Border:** *sl*/the maps are divided into six strips, usually 25 mm (1 in.) wide separated by *sl*/*bts*/*bltr*/a change of route is separated by a line. **Title:** Title in *pc* and *ps*/*V*/outside upper border, across the width of the map. Some maps have two titles relating to the routes covered.

Issues: (i) 1771: *Atlas: Ogilby's survey improv'd: or Kitchin's new and instructive traveller's companion for the roads of England and Wales. Laid down in a plain intelligible manner, with all the towns, villages, etc. thereon and the distances in single miles on each road .... *Maps:* (a) Index map. (b) 95 strip road maps printed back-to-back. *State:* First. *Imprint:* *obar:* plate-number. *Publisher:* 'T. Kitchin, at N° 59 Holborn Hill, London'. (ii) 1781 (?) as (i) 1771, except: *Atlas: Bowles's post-chaise companion; or, travellers directory through England & Wales; being an actual survey of all the principal, direct, & cross

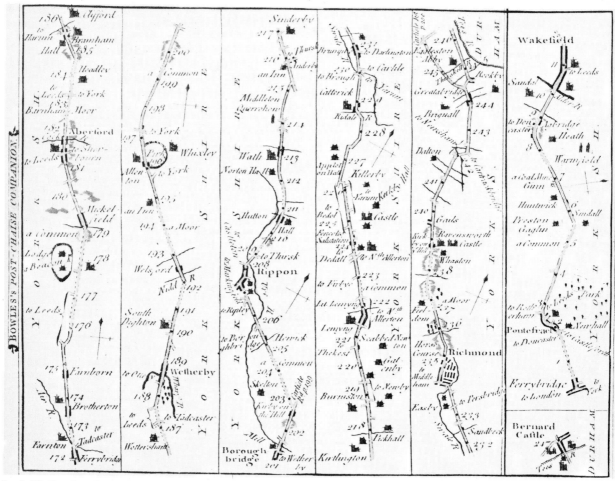

84 63(ii): London–Barnard Castle published by Carington Bowles, c.1781. *Photograph: Mills-Wight Studio*

roads, both ancient & modern; with the distances expressed in single miles according to measurement: exhibiting the several towns, villages, post-stages, etc, on or near the roads . . . . **Maps:** (a) Index map (b) 100 strip road maps extending north to Berwick directly and via Carlisle, Castleton, Jedburgh and Kelso; and from Berwick to Edinburgh. Pages 185–186 are partially re-engraved reversing the route from Manchester to Derby. Five maps are added covering the routes from London to: 'Brighthelmston' (by Cuckfield), Bath (by Devizes), Bath (by Sandy Lane), Bedford, Exeter (by Dorchester), Gosport, Falmouth, Carlisle (by Boroughbridge); and from Canterbury to Margate. **State:** Second (except: new maps). The following changes are made: (i) some mileage figures are altered and mileages are marked by larger dots in the road. Traces of the erased mileage figures are evident on some plates. (ii) north points are added. Sometimes sections of road have been re-engraved to accommodate the north point/c/p/e/Since orientation varies, each strip has a north point. (iii) title altered. In a panel, across the full-width of the maps above the strips: '. . . to . . .'/ vl/followed by a distance table noting the distances from the starting point of the first strip of the map. (iv) in a scroll-type panel along the left borderline: 'BOWLES's POST-CHAISE COMPANION'. (v) in a panel across the full-width of the map, below the strips: (a) at centre: page references for other sections of the route. Some notes below the maps are erased, others altered, and others added. (b) at left: 'VOL. . . .'. (vi) average overall size is now 136 × 158 mm (5.4 × 6.2 in.). (vii) some plates have place-names and roads added; some have place-names erased. *Imprints:* (i) *obal*: page number added. (ii) *obar*: following page number added. *Publisher:* 'Carington Bowles, at his Map and Print Warehouse, No. 69, St. Paul's Church Yard'. (iii) 1782: as (ii) 1781(?), except: *Atlas: Bowles's post-chaise companion . . . the direct and principal cross roads with the mile-stones expressed as they stand out at present . . . . States:* Second or third. *Imprint:* along the right borderline: publishing imprint added: 'London: Published 2 Jan.ʸ 1782'.

N.B. Thomas Kitchin also produced:

> (i) 1747–1766: maps for *The universal magazine . . .*, see (52). (ii) 1760(?): maps for *The large English atlas . . .*, see (14). (iii) 1763(?): maps for *The royal English atlas . . .*, see (16). (iv) 1767: *Kitchin's post-chaise companion . . .*, see (98) (iv).

LAMB, Francis
fl. 1667–1701. Engraver and publisher

Lamb was a prolific engraver who worked for most of the great Restoration map-publishers including Blome and Ogilby. *A Geographicall Description of yᵉ Kingdom of Ireland* was apparently a private venture on his part, designed as a pocket version of Sir William Petty's *Hiberniae Delineatio*. The maps (64) contain little new information but are attractive with interesting, small title cartouches on most maps. Despite the publication of several editions, the maps are now difficult to find, probably due to small original printings and careless treatment.

(64) Description: *st*: First. (Fig. 85). **Supply:** Rare. **Average size:** 112 × 150 mm (4.5 × 6 in.). **Scale:** *V*/counties: *av*:1:7 *m*; provinces: *av*:1:25 *m*/ 'English Miles' and 'Irish Miles'/2 *slm*. **Border:** *OB:sl/IB*: latitude only/the plate-number is given in brackets within the borderlines at the top right corner of the county maps only/*bb*. **North Point:** *ce* within the borderlines. **Decoration:** Small ships and sea monsters. **Title:** '. . . COUNTY' or '. . . PROVINCE'/*V*/*pc*/set within a small rococo cartouche (counties) or within the borderlines, top centre (provinces). **Engraver:** 'Engraven & Published for yᵉ benefit of yᵉ Publique by Fra: Lamb'.

Issues: (i) 1689(?): *Atlas: A geographicall description of yᵉ kingdom of Ireland. Collected from yᵉ actual survey made by Sᵗ. William Petty. Corrected & amended, by the advice, & assistance, of severall able artists, late inhabitants of that kingdom . . . Being very usefull for all gentlemen and military officers, as well for*

85 64(ii): 'Mayo County' by Francis Lamb, 1720. *By permission of the British Library (Maps C.7.a.11.)*

sea, as land service . . . . Maps (38): (a) Great Britain and Ireland; Ireland (signed by Francis Lamb). (b) Four Irish provinces. (c) 32 Irish counties. *State:* First. *Publisher:* Francis Lamb: 'Sold at his House in Newgate streete, next door but one to yᵉ White Swan, toward yᵉ Gate', in partnership with Robert Morden and William Berry.

N.B. The atlas was re-issued, as above or with minor revisions, again c.1689 and in about 1690 by Francis Lamb, Robert Morden, William Berry, and 'John Seller Ju.'

(ii) 1720: as (i) 1689(?), except: *Atlas: A geographical description of the kingdom of Ireland, newly corrected & improv'd by actual observations. . . . With the addition of several market towns and other places of note omitted in former maps, together with all the principal roads, and the distances in comon reputed miles. . . . The whole being laid down from the best maps viz: Sᵗ. Wᵐ. Petty's Mr. Pratt's etc . . . . Maps (37):* (a) Great Britain and Ireland is omitted; the general map of Ireland is replaced. *State:* Mostly second. Roads are added to the counties and 14 maps have been re-engraved with new title cartouches and without brackets around the plate-number (Ulster, Leinster; Dublin, Antrim, Downe, Londonderry, Donegal, Tyrone, Fermanagh, Monaghan, Armagh, Roscommon, Clare and Tipperary). *Publisher:* Thomas Bowles: 'Print & Map Seller near the Chapter House in St. Paul's Church Yard, London'.

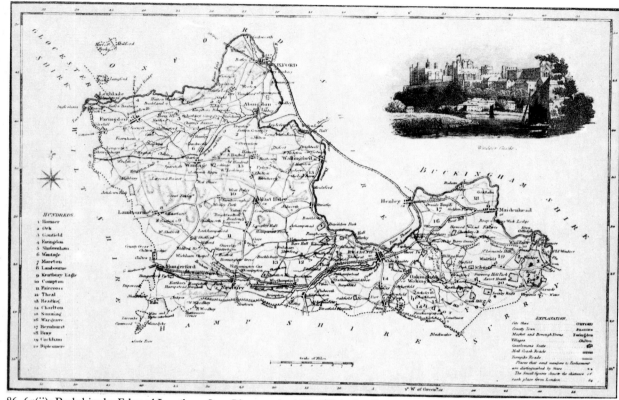

86 65(ii): Berkshire by Edward Langley, 1820. *Photograph: Mills-Wight Studio*

(iii) 1728; 1732: as (ii) 1720, except: **State:** Mostly second. **Maps (37):** (a) The general map of Ireland is replaced again. **Publisher:** John Bowles: 'at Mercers Hall in Cheapside, London'.

LANGLEY, Edward

fl. 1804–1835. Engraver, printer, bookseller and publisher

Langley produced a fine series of county maps (65) in his *New County Atlas* of 1818. These scarce, attractive maps are well engraved and decorated with a vignette of an important town or building. The atlas was re-issued in 1820 by the bookseller and publisher Joseph Phelps. Some vignettes were changed during the period of issue of the maps.

(65) Description: *st*: First (*v*). (Fig. 86). **Supply:** Very scarce. **Average size:** 170 × 260 mm (7 × 10 in.). **Features:** A numbered reference key to administrative divisions: e.g. 'Hundreds'. **Scale:** *V/ av*:1:6 *m*/'Scale of Miles'/*sbm*. **Border:** *OB:sl/ IB:ll*. **North Point:** *s/f/l*. **Key:** 'Explanation'. **Decoration:** Titled vignette view (Kent and Sussex

have two vignettes). **Title:** 'LANGLEY'S new MAP of ...'/*ps* and *oc/obac*.

Issues: The maps were also issued separately as folding maps and are known without imprint. (i) 1818(?): **Atlas:** *Langley's new county atlas of England and Wales, embellished with a beautiful vignette to each map exhibiting all the mail coach, turnpike & principal cross roads, with the cities, towns, villages, parks, rivers, & navigable canals, peculiar to each county ....* **Maps (53):** (a) England and Wales. (b) 39 English counties. (c) Yorkshire. (d) 12 Welsh counties. **State:** First (*v*). **Imprint:** *obbc:pi*: 'Printed and Published by Langley & Belch, No. 173, High Street, Borough, London ....' (*V*), with dates in 1817 and 1818. (Some maps are known without this date). **Publishers:** Langley & Belch. (ii) 1820(?): as (i) 1818(?), except: **State:** First (*v*). Minor revisions. England and Wales dated 1820. **Publisher:** Joseph Phelps. (iii) 1820(?): as (ii) 1820(?), except: **State:** Second (*v*). Old stock in the first state was also used in the issue. **Imprint:** *obbc*: new *pi*: 'Printed & Published by J. Phelps, No. 27, Paternoster Row, London. 1820.' (*V*).

LAURIE, Robert & WHITTLE, James
fl. 1794–1812. Engravers and publishers

The partnership of Laurie & Whittle took over the business of Robert Sayer in 1794 and published many important works, including new editions of several famous atlases. Laurie retired in 1812 and his son, Richard Holmes Laurie, became Whittle's partner. Laurie died in 1836, and Whittle in 1818.

They published a series of plain county maps (66) in their *New and Improved English Atlas* which was a re-issue of the maps engraved by Benjamin Baker for the *Universal Magazine* from 1791–97. Even in 1807, Laurie & Whittle were expressing concern in their atlas at the run-down of natural resources and the lack of conservation planning: 'this country was formerly plentifully provided with timber and particularly with large oaks fit for ship-building; but for want of planting in time, we are obliged to be supplied with great quantities from abroad.' They also published the interesting and unusual road maps (67) by Nathaniel Coltman in *Laurie and Whittle's New Traveller's Companion*. These are unusual as the roads are shown as straight lines between the towns and several routes may be shown on a single map because map detail extends to the borderlines. D.N.B.: Robert Laurie: Vol. 11, p. 652.

(66) Description: Laurie & Whittle adapted the plates engraved by Benjamin Baker for the *Universal magazine* to produce their *New and improved atlas* ... (The description is as (8) with the noted additions and changes). **Supply**: Moderate. **Features**: 'Cities with their distance from London; County and Market Towns with distance from London; Number of Members each place returns to Parliament; Turnpikes and principal travelling roads, cross and bye roads; rivers, navigable canals and Iron Railways ("placed with great care on the respective maps"); Parks, Gentlemens Seats and Houses; Hills or Mountains; The connection of the Turnpike Roads from one county to another are shown by Reference Letters a, b, c, etc.' Many additions and revisions: e.g. ports, castles, beacons, etc. **Border**: Longitude measurements from Greenwich are substituted for those from London on some maps. **North Point**: A partially visible compass star is added behind the title panel/*p*.

Issues: (i) 1807: *Atlas: Laurie and Whittle's new and improved English atlas, divided into counties: shewing their respective situations, boundaries, and extent ... with the turnpike and principal roads, accurately laid down from the most recent surveys and* authorities .... ***Maps (48):*** (a) England and Wales. (b) 39 English Counties. (c) Yorkshire; North; East; West (Southern Part); West (Northern part) Ridings. (d) Isle of Wight. (e) North; South Wales. **State:** Second (*v*). Some maps revised during this issue. **Imprint:** *obbc:pi:* 'Published, October 13th 1806, by LAURIE & WHITTLE, N.° 53 Fleet Street London' (*V*), (dates vary on some maps). **Publishers:** Robert Laurie & James Whittle. (ii) 1816: as (i) 1807, except: *Atlas: A new and improved English atlas, divided into counties ...* **State:** Second (*v*). **Publishers:** James Whittle & Richard Holmes Laurie.

N.B. Laurie & Whittle also published the rare 1805 *Laurie and Whittle's Welsh Atlas* by Nathaniel Coltman with maps (av. size: 175 × 216 mm; 7 × 8.5 in.) bearing their *pi*. It was re-issued c.1807.

(67) Description: *st*: First (*v*). (Fig. 87). **Supply:** Scarce. **Average size:** 245 × 300 mm (9.75 × 12 in.). **Features:** 'the rivers, and the whole of the navigable canals, (for which acts of parliament have passed,) intersecting the roads, are inserted to gratify the curiosity of the traveller; but, as it is impossible

87 67(i): 'Completion of the Roads to Holyhead ...' published by Laurie & Whittle, 1806. *By permission of the British Library (Maps 16.b.32.)*

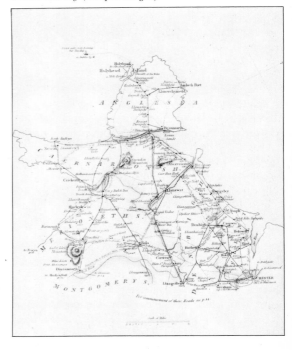

to obtain an accurate knowledge of the intended course of such as are not yet completed, any information from gentlemen tourists, or surveyors concerned in such works, will oblige the publishers.' Cross roads which 'may be travelled with safety at any season of the year' and 'indifferent cross roads'. **Scale:** *V*/*av*:1:10 *m*/'Scale of Miles'/*shmf*. **Border:** *OB*:*Tt*/*IB*:*dl*/within the border, below centre, is a plain panel containing the measurement explanation, and within the border above, information on route coverage extends across the full width of the map/*bt*. **North Point:** *c*/*op*/*V*/'It has ... a great advantage over a general Map of England, from the names of the places reading parallel to the sight, whereas all the southern and south-western roads in the general maps read upside down'. **Title:** (i) set within the border, across the full width, above the map/*vl*/details of the roads covered by the map: e.g. 'Roads to . . .'; or, 'Commencement of the Road to . . .'; or, 'Continuation of . . .'; or, 'Completion of . . .', etc. The plate-number is noted within a circle at the centre of this information. (ii) set within the border, below centre: a panel containing the inscription: 'ROADS MEASURED FROM . . .'. The roads are measured from London Bridge; Westminster Bridge; Hyde Park Corner; Tyburn Turnpike; Hicks' Hall; Tyburn Turnpike and Hicks' Hall; Shoreditch Church; Whitechapel Church. **Engravers:** J. Bye, B. Smith, E. Jones, W. West.

Issues: (i) 1806: *Atlas: Laurie and Whittle's new traveller's companion exhibiting a complete and correct survey of all the direct and principal cross roads in England, Wales, and Scotland, as far north as Edinburgh, and Glasgow: by Nath! Coltman . . . . Maps:* double-page: (a) Index map of England and Wales. (b) 24 road maps including: (i) roads to Milford Haven, Aberystwyth, and Holyhead, and (ii) roads 'as far North as Edinburgh and Glasgow': 'together with The Roads to Perth and Aberdeen, Greenock, Irvine, Ayr, Port-Patrick, Wigton, etc.'. (c) 'Roads in the Isle of Wight'. (See Imprints below, for qualification on the number of maps.) **State:** First (*v*). **Imprints:** (i) *obbc*:*pi*: 'Published 12.th Feb.y 1806, by LAURIE & WHITTLE, N.o 53 Fleet Street, London' (except: (a) index map of England and Wales: dated 1st January 1808'. (b) plate 25: 'Completion of the Roads to Greenock, Irvine, and Ayr . . .': dated Jan.y 12th, 1809'. These maps were added appropriately to the later issues of the *Traveller's companion*.) (ii) Some maps have: *obbl*:*es*: '. . . sculp.' (*V*). **Publishers:** Robert Laurie

& James Whittle. (ii) The *Traveller's companion* was issued with minor changes and up-dating, and the map additions noted above, thus: 1807(?); 1808(?); 1809; 1810(?); 1810; 1811; 1812; 1813; 1814; 1817; 1818; 1824; 1828; 1830; 1834; 1836; 1846: as (i) 1806, except: *Imprints:* (i) from 1814 (7th edition): *obbc*: added below existing imprint: 'A New Edition, 1815' (second state). (ii) from 1824 (9th edition): *obbc*:*pi* altered: 'London: Published by R.H. LAURIE, N.o 53 Fleet Street' (third state). **Publishers:** (i) 1810–1818: Laurie & Whittle; (ii) 1824–1846: R. H. Laurie.

LEIGH, Samuel

fl. 1820–1842. Publisher

Leigh published a small, plain set of county maps (68) of England and Wales which proved to be very popular and were issued several times. The maps were generally bound in with his *New Pocket Road Book of England and Wales*, but note that only general maps are found in his *New Pocket* road books of Scotland (general map and 'Panorama of remarkable objects in Edinburgh') and Ireland (general map, 'Panorama of remarkable objects in Dublin', and, in some editions, a plan of Dublin and a map of the Lakes of Killarney). Incidentally, in his 'Table of the Price of Posting showing the Charges usually made for a Pair of Horses', Leigh notes that 'It is usual to pay the Postillion at the rate of 3.d per mile'.

(68) Description: *st*: First. (Fig. 88). **Supply:** Plentiful. **Average size:** 70 × 120 mm (2.75 × 4.5 in.). **Scale:** *V*/*av*:1:15 *m*/'English Miles'/*shm*. **Border:** *Tt*/an inset rectangular panel at the top of the page contains the title. For counties shown sideways, this title panel is at the right-hand side of the map when oriented correctly. **North Point:** *s*/*f*. **Title:** *c*/*pc*/set within a rectangular panel incorporated into the border. **Engraver:** Sidney Hall.

Issues: Many issues up-date canal and railway information. (i) 1820: *Atlas: Leigh's new pocket atlas, of England and Wales, consisting of fifty-five maps of the counties . . . . Maps (56):* (a) England and Wales. (b) 39 English counties. (c) North; East; West Ridings. (d) Isle of Wight. (e) 12 Welsh counties. **State:** First. **Imprints:** (i) *ob*: top right of page: plate-number. (ii) *obbl*:*pi*: 'Pub. by S. Leigh, 18 Strand' (*V*). (iii) *obbr*:*es*: 'Sid.y Hall sculp.t'. **Publisher:** 'Samuel Leigh, 18, Strand'. (ii) 1820: as (i) 1820, except: *Atlas: Leigh's new picture of*

88 68(iii): East Riding of Yorkshire published by M. A. Leigh, 1833. *Photograph: Mills-Wight Studio. By courtesy of Jason Musgrave*

England and Wales .... **State:** First. (iii) 1825; 1826; 1831; as (ii) 1820, except: *Atlas: Leigh's new atlas of England & Wales.* Issued bound in with *Leigh's new pocket road-book of England and Wales* .... (*V*). (Published by Samuel Leigh.) **State:** First (iv) 1831; 1833; 1835: as (iii) 1825, etc., except: **State:** Second (*v*). Minor revisions to parliamentary representation information on some maps in 1833. **Imprint:** (ii) *obbl: pi* altered: 'Pub. by M. A. Leigh 421 Strand' (*V*). **Publisher:** M. A. Leigh. (The pocket road-books were published by: 1831: Samuel Leigh; 1833: M. A. Leigh; 1835: Leigh & Son.) (v) 1834: as 1833; 1835, except: *Atlas: Leigh's new pocket atlas of England and Wales ... Corrected since the passing of the Reform Bill.* **State:** Second (*v*). (vi) 1837; 1839: as 1833; 1835, except: **State:** Third (*v*). **Imprint:** (iii) *obbr: es* erased (except: Flintshire). **Publisher:** M. A. Leigh. (The pocket road-books were published by Leigh & Son). (vii) 1840; (a) 1842; (b) 1842; 1843: as (vi) 1837; 1839, except: **State:** Third (*v*). **Publisher:** Leigh & Son. (The pocket road-books were published by: 1840: Leigh & Co.; (a) 1842: G. Biggs; (b) 1842; 1843: G. Biggs & Orlando Hodgson. In 1842, the maps also appeared under the title *Leigh's new pocket atlas of England and Wales ...*, published by 'G. Biggs. Successor to Leigh & Son, 421, Strand, (Removed from No. 18)'.

LEWIS, Samuel
fl. 1831. Cartographer and publisher

Samuel Lewis produced a series of austerely elegant atlases to accompany his Topographical Dictionaries of England, Wales and Ireland (69, 70, 72). 'The MAPS accompanying the work are engraved on steel plates, from drawings made from the best authorities, and corrected to the present time'. The maps were issued sometimes in separate atlases and sometimes interleaved within the Dictionaries. A scarcer atlas—the *View of the Representative History of England*—was issued to cover the changes brought about by the Reform Act of 1832. It contained maps and plans (71) showing the electoral divisions of the counties and the former and present boundaries of the boroughs. D.N.B.: Vol. 11, p. 1074.

(69) **Description:** *st:* Fourth. **Supply:** Plentiful. **Average size:** *Vc* since many maps are folded into the atlas/sizes range from 180 × 230 mm (7.2 × 9.2 in.) to 240 × 305 mm (9.6 × 12.2 in.). **Features:** A numbered reference key to poor-law unions: 'Reference to the Unions' (from 1840). **Scale:** *V/av*:1:6 *m*/'Scale of Miles'/*sbm/Vw*. **Border:** *OB:tTt/IB:ll/bb.* **North Point:** *s/f.* **Title:** *c/pc* shaded by diagonal hatching. **Engravers:** 30 maps by J. & C. Walker; 13 by T. Starling.

Issues: Old map stock was sometimes used in later issues. (i) 1831; 1835: *Atlas: A topographical dictionary of England, comprising the several counties, cities, boroughs ... illustrated by maps of the different counties and islands ... By Samuel Lewis ....* **Maps** *(43):* (a) England and Wales. (b) 39 English counties. (c) Yorkshire. (d) Isle of Man. (e) A plan of London and its environs. *State:* First. *Imprints:* (i) *obbc:* 'ENGRAVED FOR LEWIS' TOPOGRAPHICAL DICTIONARY' (*V*), or 'DRAWN AND ENGRAVED ...' (*V*). (ii) *obbl:ds:* 'Drawn by R. Creighton'. (iii) most maps have: *obbr:es:* 'J. & C. Walker Sculp!' or 'T. Starling scul! Wilmington Square, London' (*V*). *Publishers:* 'S. Lewis & Co., 87, Aldersgate-Street'. All subsequent editions show minor changes, particularly the up-dating of railway information. (ii) 1833; 1835: as (i) 1831; 1835, except: *State:* Second. Notes on election and polling places are added: *obac;* parliamentary divisions are marked and named. (iii) 1837(?): as (ii) 1833; 1835, except: *State:* Third. Notes on election and polling places are erased. (iv) 1840: as (iii) 1837(?), except: *State:* Fourth (*v*). The poor-law unions are added with reference numbers to the new 'Reference to the Unions' key, (somet-imes necessitating the movement of non-topographical features). (v) 1842: as (iv) 1840, except: *Atlas: An atlas, comprising maps of the several counties, divided into unions, and of the islands of Guernsey, Jersey, and Man; with a map of England and Wales, and a plan of London and its environs ....* *Maps (45):* as before, plus (a) Guernsey and its dependent isles. (b) Jersey. both signed: 'Engraved by J. & C. Walker'. *State:* Mostly fourth (*v*). *Publishers:* 'S. Lewis and Co., 87, Hatton Garden'. (vi) 1844; 1845; 1848; 1849: as (v) 1842, except: *State:* Mostly fourth (*v*). Minor revisions in 1845 and 1848. *Atlas: Atlas to the topographical dictionaries of England and Wales ....* (vii) 1845; 1848: as (vi) 1844, etc., except: *State:* Mostly fourth (*v*). *Atlas: Atlas to the topographical dictionary of England ....*

(70) Description: as (69): *st:* Second.

Issues: (i) 1833: *Atlas: A topographical dictionary of Wales ... illustrated by maps of the different counties ... By Samuel Lewis ....* *Maps (13):* (a) Wales (without imprints, but with the information incorporated in a splendid calligraphic titlepiece). (b) 12 Welsh counties. *State:* First. *Imprints:* (i) *obbc:* 'DRAWN AND ENGRAVED FOR LEWIS' TOPOGRAPHICAL DICTIONARY'. (ii) *obbl:ds:* 'Drawn by R. Creighton'. (iii) *obbr:es:* 'Engraved by J. & C. Walker'. *Publishers:* S. Lewis and Co., 87, Aldersgate-Street'. (ii) 1838; 1840; 1844; 1845; 1850: as (i) 1833, except: *State:* Second. The poor-law unions are added with reference numbers to the new 'Reference to the

Unions' key. The maps were issued bound with those of England in 1840. (iii) 1842: as (ii) 1838, etc.: except: *Atlas: An atlas, comprising maps of the several counties, divided into unions ....* *State:* Second. (iv) 1844; 1845; 1848; 1849: as (iii) 1842, except: *Atlas Atlas to the topographical dictionaries of England and Wales ....* *Maps (57):* (a) England and Wales. (b) 39 English counties. (c) Yorkshire. (d) Guernsey; Jersey; Isle of Man. (e) 12 Welsh counties. (f) Plan of London. *State:* Second.

(71) Description: *st:* First. (Fig. 89). **Supply:** Moderate. **Average size:** 180 × 230 mm (7.2 × 9.2 in.). **Features:** Concentration on parliamentary information. **Scale:** (i) Maps: *V/av:*1:7 *m/* 'Scale of Miles'/*sbm.* (ii) Plans: *V/av:*1:0.75 *m/*'Scale of ... Mile(s)'/*sbm.* **Border:** *OB:sl/IB:dl/* decorative twist pattern between borderlines/each corner has a tiny flower-style decoration within a square incorporated into the border. Plans are separated by a simple *tl* division. **North Point:** (i) Maps: *s/f.* (ii) Plans: *s/op.* **Key:** (i) Maps: 'Explanation'. (ii) Plans: *obbc:* 'Explanation'. **Title:** *c,* or town name/*pc.* **Engravers:** J. & C. Walker.

Issues: (i) 1835; 1837: by lithographic transfer: *Atlas: A topographical dictionary of England ... with historical and statistical descriptions; illustrated by maps of the different counties and islands ... Third edition. With a supplementary volume, comprising a representative history of England with plans describing the electoral divisions of the several counties ... By Samuel Lewis ....* *Maps (42):* (a) 39 English counties. (b) North; East; West Ridings. *Plans:* 74 sheets of plans: towns within a county are often grouped together on one sheet, ranging from one to four towns per sheet. *State:* First. *Imprints:* (i) *ob:* top right of page: plate-number in roman numerals. (ii) *obbl:ds:* 'Drawn by R. Creighton'. (iii) *obbr:es:* 'Engraved by J. & C. Walker'. *Publishers:* S. Lewis & Co.
N.B. The maps were also issued with the 4th edition of the *Topographical Dictionary* in 1840.
(ii) 1835; 1840: by lithographic transfer: as (i) 1835; 1837, except: *Atlas: View of the representative history of England, with engraved plans, shewing the electoral divisions of the several counties ... By Samuel Lewis ....* *State:* First.

(72) Description: *st:* First. **Supply:** Plentiful. **Average size:** 190 × 245 mm (7.5 × 9.5 in.). **Scale:** *V/av:*1:4 *m/*'Scale of Irish Miles' and 'Scale of English Miles'/2 *sb* divided into Irish and English miles respectively. **Border:** *OB:tTt/IB:ll/bb.*

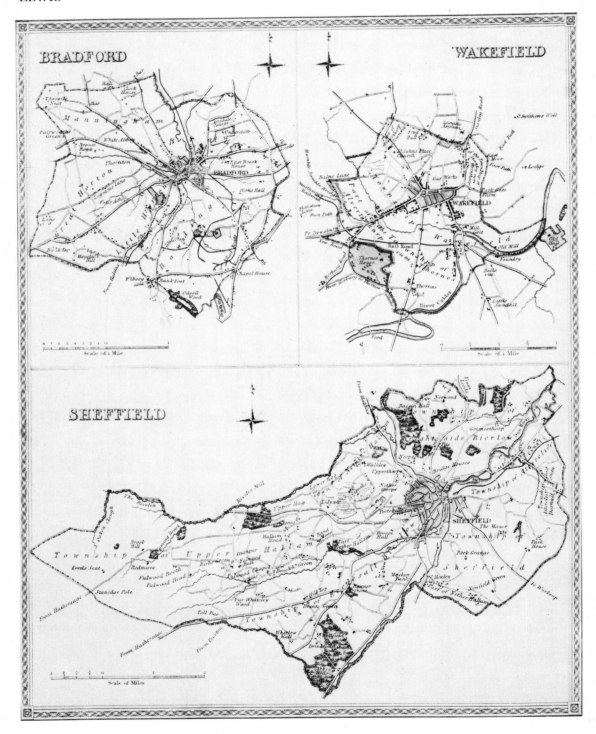

89 71(i): Bradford, Sheffield and Wakefield published by Samuel Lewis, 1835. *Photograph: Mills-Wight Studio*

North Point: *s/f.* **Title:** *c/pc.* **Engraver:** John Dower.
Issues: (i) 1837; 1840: *Atlas: Lewis's atlas comprising the counties of Ireland and a general map of the kingdom . . . . Maps (33):* (a) Ireland divided into Provinces and Counties (*obbc:pi*: 'Published by S. Lewis & Co. . . . London, June 27ᵗʰ, 1837' [1837 issue only]). (b) 32 Irish counties. *State:* First. *Imprints:* (i) *obbc:* 'DRAWN AND ENGRAVED FOR LEWIS'S TOPOGRAPHICAL DICTIONARY'. (ii) *obbl:ds:* 'Drawn by R. Creighton'. (iii) *obbr:es:* 'Engraved by J. Dower, Pentonville, London'. *Publishers:* 'S. Lewis & Co. 87, Aldersgate Street'. (ii) 1846; 1849; 1850: as (i) 1837; 1840, except: *State:* First (except: Ireland . . .). *Imprint:* (i) *obbc:pi:* erased from Ireland . . . . *Publishers:* 'S. Lewis & Co, 13, Finsbury Place South'.

LEWIS, William
fl. 1819–1836. Publisher

William Lewis published a re-print of the miniature James Wallis maps (114) in 1819(?) under the title *Lewis's, New Traveller's Guide . . . .* These revised maps are scarcer than those from the original Wallis issues.

LODGE, John
fl. 1754–1794. Geographer and engraver

Lodge engraved a series of large, plain maps (73) for the *Political Magazine* issued between 1782 and 1790, which were re-issued in atlas form in 1795. These maps closely resemble those of Joseph Ellis and Emanuel Bowen in detail, but are without their attractive decoration. The engraving is disappointingly crude in comparison with other contemporary work. Lodge also engraved a series of canal maps for the *Gentleman's Magazine* between 1754 and 1772.
(73) Description: *st:* Second. **Supply:** Scarce. **Average size:** 264 × 323 mm (10.5 × 13 in.). **Scale:** *V/av*:1:5 *m*/'British Statute Miles 69 to a Degree'/ *sbm.* **Border:** *OB:sl/IB:ll.* **North Point:** *r/f.* **Key:** 'Remarks'. **Title:** 'A NEW MAP of . . . , FROM THE LATEST AUTHORITIES'/*pc/V.* **Engraver:** John Lodge.
Issues: (i) 1782–1790: *Atlas: The political magazine, and parliamentary, naval, military and literary journal . . . . Maps (45):* (a) folding general maps of: England and Wales; Scotland; Ireland. (b) 39 English counties. (c) Yorkshire. (d) Isle of Wight; Isle of Man. *State:* First. *Imprints:* (i) *obbr:es:* 'J.

Lodge sc.' (*V*). (ii) most maps have: *obbc: pi* of either J. Murray, R. Butters, or J. Bew: e.g. 'London. Published as the Act directs Augˢᵗ 31ˢᵗ by R. Butters, Nº 79, Fleet Street' (*V*). Dated between 30 April 1782 and 31 December 1790. (iii) *obac:* some maps bear the dated inscription: 'Political Mag. . . .'. *Publishers:* J. Murray, No. 32, Fleet Street; R. Butters, No. 79, Fleet Street; J. Bew, Pater Noster Row. (ii) 1795(?): as (i) 1782–1790, except: *Atlas: Atlas of Great Britain and Ireland . . . (?).* *State:* Second. *Imprints:* (i) *obbr:es* erased. (ii) *obbc:pi* erased. (iii) *obac:* reference to the *Political magazine* erased.

LOTHIAN, John
fl. 1825–1835. Geographer, bookseller and publisher

Lothian produced several cartographic works, including a plan of Edinburgh and vicinity, but is best known for his finely engraved *County Atlas of Scotland* (74) of 1827, which was apparently sold at an attractive price: 'In the view of a considerably extended circulation, the price of the Atlas has been fixed at a rate considerably less than that of similarly detailed maps of individual countries; while an examination will shew that the cost, such as it is, has likewise been distributed among the various maps in the way most advantageous and useful for the purchaser—each county being presented on a scale proportioned rather to its relative interest and statistical importance, than to its actual geographical magnitude'. A separate *Historical Atlas of Scotland*, containing seven maps on five sheets, was produced in 1829 showing Scotland in Roman times plus a map of 'Modern Scotland', and this was available either separately or as an appendix to the county atlas. Three county maps have delicately drawn vignettes but the other maps are without decoration. Despite their plainness, the maps are beautifully composed: 'the names are inserted in a methodical and parallel style—embracing much in small compass with distinctness;—what is really useful being neither buried in a random crowd of confused lettering, nor cloaked and concealed in a surtout of overwrought hill-work'.

(74) Description: *st:* Second. (Fig. 90). **Supply:** Moderate. **Average size:** 183 × 242 mm (7.25 × 9.6 in.). **Features:** 'the district divisions—constantly met with in history, and currently named though indifferently known, except in their respective vicinities, are properly exhibited'; '. . . the page at which any bordering county may be found is

90 74(iii): 'Edinburgh' by John Lothian, 1838. *By permission of the British Library (Maps 18.a.15.)*

shown by a number inclosed in a circle, and placed in juxtaposition with the name.' Most maps have short descriptive notes: 'the leading features of past geography and altered boundary are shortly sketched in the title to each plate'. **Scale:** *Vc/ av:1:6 m/*'Scale of Miles'*/sbm.* **Border:** *OB:tTt/ IB:sl* with the left and bottom lines divided by dots into *ll*, and the right and top lines divided into letter referenced divisions corresponding to 10 minutes of latitude or longitude/a graticule covers *mf/*latitude and longitude were added for the 1835 issue which also incorporated the above revisions and additions/*bb.* **North Point:** *c/f/V.* **Decoration:** Argyle and Bute, Edinburgh, and Roxburgh have titled vignettes; and Lanark has an inset plan of Glasgow. **Title:** *c/oc/*with historical notes above, and notes of divisions below.

Issues: The maps were also sold separately. (i) 1827 (?); 1829 (?): *Atlas: Lothian's county atlas of Scotland.* **Maps (34):** (a) Scotland. (b) 26 Scottish county maps (five sheets combine two counties each; and Argyll and Bute, Perth, and Inverness appear on two sheets each). (c) Orkney Islands; Shetland Islands; Western Islands—North portion; Western Islands—South portion. **State:** First. **Imprint:** *obbc:* the maps bear the imprint of John Lothian. The accompanying dates were altered several times during the period of issue for both atlas and individual issues; consequently most copies of the atlas have varying dates throughout. **Publisher:** 'John Lothian, Geographer, Edinburgh'. (ii) 1830

(?): as (i) 1827 (?); 1829 (?), except: **Maps:** seven additional historical maps of Scotland in Roman times on five sheets, and a map of 'Modern Scotland', are added as an appendix. (iii) 1835 (original title); 1838: as (i) 1827 (?); 1829 (?), except: (the maps were issued separately and as a set folded in three or four boxes in 1834–35): **Atlas:** *Atlas of modern Scotland containing maps of all the counties in their district divisions, earldoms & lordships. With the roads, railways, canals, country seats, villages, towns, lighthouse & harbour lights, fishing streams, rivers & lakes, places of historical & legendary note, memoranda of battles and former boundaries ....* **Maps:** I have here revised the whole, and introduced improvements collected from perhaps every available source—historical and geographical. The longitude and latitude are reduced to modern observation—brought to one bearing throughout the counties, and divided to every minute of a degree. The meridians and parallels introduced are at the same time sufficiently numerous to form useful leading lines from one map to another .... Memoranda are inserted of the different battles— their dates, combatants, and victors ... the light-houses briefly described—and the sandbanks, and many lines of road and railway supplied .... It first appeared in the midst of much competition for public favour, and the easy preference it obtained has naturally led to a great extension and improvement of those characteristics which at first established its popularity, and to a restless exertion to work out such a general and marked superiority in the present edition as might admit of being recognised on a slight and even superficial inspection'. **State:** Second. **Imprints:** (i) 16 county maps and the Orkney Islands: *obbc:pi:* 'Lothians Maps of Scotland Published by John Sutherland 12. Calton St. Edinburgh 10th Sep. 1838.' (*V*). These maps bore the following imprint before 1838, in the issues of 1834–35. (ii) All other maps: *obbc:pi:* 'Published by J. Lothian, Edinburgh, ...' with various publication dates c.1835. (iii) *obar* or *obbr:* most maps have a circled plate-number (except: (a) Argyll and Bute: the plate-number is not set within a circle; (b) 'Modern Scotland' has the number in white upon a black circle, within the borderlines top right). **Publishers:** 1835: John Lothian; 1838: John Sutherland. (iv) 1848: as (iii) 1838, except: **Atlas:** *Black's county atlas of Scotland, with the parochial divisions, including seven historical maps, topographical descriptions, ...* **Maps (39):** (a) North; South Scotland. (b) Seven historical maps (on five sheets). (c) 26 maps of Scottish counties (five maps combine two counties each; Argyll and Bute, Perth, and Inverness are 'double' maps, i.e. they have the two separate sheets pasted together and folding). (d) Orkney Islands; Shetland Islands; Western Islands (two maps). **State:** Third. The north point and/or the scale are sometimes moved to accommodate an 'Index to Parishes' with numbered references within *sl* framed panel. Reference numbers and dotted parish boundaries are added. Titles and scales are erased from the 'North portion' of Argyle and Bute, the 'Western portion' of Inverness, and the 'South portion' of Perth (north point also erased). Railway information is up-dated. *Imprints:* (i) *obbc : pi:* 'Edinburgh. Published by A. & C. Black, 27, North Bridge, 1st May, 1847'. (ii) *obar* or *obbr:* plate-numbers altered; enclosing circle erased (except: (a) Edinburgh and Roxburgh retain their circled plate-numbers; (b) the historical maps and Argyle and Bute have no plate-numbers; (c) Two maps of Scotland have the number: *obal*). *Publishers:* 'Adam and Charles Black, North Bridge, Booksellers and publishers to her Majesty'. (v) c.1852; c.1877: by lithographic transfer: as (iv) 1848, except: *Atlas: Black's tourist's and sportsman's companion to the counties of Scotland. A series of thirty-six maps shewing all the roads, railways, villages ...parish divisions, earldoms and lordships .... Maps (35):* (a) Scotland. (b) Highlands of Scotland (unnumbered). (c) 33 counties and islands as (i) 1827 (?). **State:** Fourth. *Imprints:* (i) *obbc : pi:* 'Edinburgh. Published by A. & C. Black, 6 North Bridge'. (ii) Edinburgh and Roxburgh have uncircled plate-numbers; Argyle and Bute (southern portion) has a plate-number. (iii) *obbr : es:* (a) Scotland: 'W. Hughes'. (b) Berwick: 'J. Bower Sct Edinr'. (iv) *obbc* or *obbl:* 'Schenck and McFarlane, Lithrs Edinburgh' (Lanark, Linlithgow, Stirling).

LUFFMAN, John

fl. 1776–1820. Engraver, geographer and publisher

Luffman produced a large number of maps, plans and books including some of the plates for Taylor & Skinner's *Roads of North Britain* (106), Mostyn Armstrong's *Great Post-Roads between London and Edinburgh* (4) and Andrew Armstrong's large-scale map of 'Rutland'. However, Luffman is best known for his children's textbook, *A New Pocket Atlas and Geography of England and Wales* produced in 1803, which contained tiny, attractive maps (75) set in an unusual circular frame. 'With a view to this Part of Juvenile Education, I have been induced to offer to the Public the following Sheets, elucidated by Maps, that will at once make the Pupil acquainted, not only with the Form and Situation, but with every Particular relative to each County.' Beneath each map are type-printed notes describing the county; for example, the notes on Lancashire clearly place the county at the heart of the Industrial Revolution: 'The air is in general healthy, but it is one of those counties which are the least favored as to natural advantages .... As a manufacturing county, Lancashire is distinguished before most others in the kingdom. Silks, linens and cottons, flannel, hats, sail-cloth, plate-glass, etc, are manufactured in different parts; and the commerce of Liverpool is only surpassed by that of London ...'. The notes give details of size; number of towns, parishes, houses and population; climate; topography; industry; and products.

(75) Description: *st:* First. (Fig. 91). **Supply:** Very scarce. **Average size:** 82 × 133 mm (3.25 × 5.25 in.) including the text below the map. **Scale:** *V/ av:1:40 m/*'Scale of ... miles'/curved *sbm/*set within a slightly ornate, curved panel within the map border at bottom centre. **Border:** Circular: inner diameter is 43 mm (1.7 in.); width of border is: 8 mm (0.35 in.); overall diameter is 59 mm (2.35 in.)/ *OB :tTt/IB :tTt/*within the border are the title, the scale and (a) at left centre, within a slightly ornate,

91 75(i): Huntingdon by John Luffman, 1803. *By permission of the British Library (Maps 24.aa.17.)*

curved panel: 'Sends ... Members to Parliament' (*V*), and (b) at right centre, within a slightly ornate, curved panel: '... Town ... miles from London'. **North Point:** *c/op/*an arrow-flight indicates south. **Title:** *c/pc/*set within a slightly ornate curved panel, at top centre, within the border. **Engraver:** John Luffman.

Issues: (i) 1803: *Atlas: A new pocket atlas and geography of England and Wales, illustrated with fifty-five copper plates. Shewing all the great post roads with the towns & villages situated thereon: also, a description of the air, soil, productions and manufactures as well as the number of hundreds, cities, boroughs, market-towns, parishes, houses & inhabitants* .... **Maps (55):** (a) Index map. (b) 39 English counties. (c) North; East; West Ridings. (d) 12 Welsh counties. **State:** First. **Imprints:** (i) *obac*: plate-number: positioned between 6 and 10 mm (0.25 and 0.4 in.) above the outer-borderline. (ii) *obbc:pi*: following the curve of the border: 'Sold by Luffman, 28, Little Bell Alley, Coleman Street, London' (*V*). **Publisher:** John Luffman. (ii) 1803: as (i) 1803, except: **State:** Second. **Imprint:** (i) *obac*: the plate-number has been erased and re-engraved much closer to the map border. It is now approximately 1 mm (0.03 in.) above the outer-borderline.
N.B. There was possibly also an issue c.1805.
(iii) 1806: as (ii) 1803, except: **State:** Second (except: index map). **Imprint:** (ii) imprint added to index map only: 'Publish'd Oct.1.1803 by J. Luffman, № 28, Little Bell Alley, Coleman Street, London'. **Publishers:** 'Lackington, Allen and Co., Temple of the Muses, Finsbury Square.'

MILLER, Robert
fl. 1810–1821. Publisher

Miller published a series of very small county maps (94) in his *New Miniature Atlas* of about 1821. These were re-issued in *Darton's New Miniature Atlas* with colourful descriptions of the counties; for example: 'The aspect of Merionethshire is extremely wild and mountainous, and the county every where abounds with the most romantic and sublime scenery'; and were later used for the children's maps of 'Reuben Ramble'. The maps in their pre-Ramble state are scarce.

MOGG, Edward
fl. 1808–1826. Cartographer and publisher

In addition to the later editions of *Paterson's Roads* (88), Mogg published two beautifully engraved sets of road maps. The parts of *A Survey of the High Roads of England and Wales* ... (76) were issued from c.1814: 'the gratification derived from an excursion of pleasure does not always terminate with its performance, but is often produced by reflections which naturally arise on a subsequent review of past occurrences or remarkable objects, and which the peculiar construction of this work is eminently calculated to assist.' Despite re-issues in c.1815, 1817 and 1828 only Part I covering the southern counties of England was ever issued. In the same style, Mogg published his *Survey of the Roads from London to Brighton* in 1808 on which he had 'not hesitated to bestow such care and attention in its execution ...'.

(76) Description: *st*: First. **Supply:** Rare. **Average size:** 137 × 200 mm (5.5 × 8.0 in.). **Features:** Some strips incorporate notes giving information on mileages, connecting pages, etc. **Scale:** *n//*scale is 1:1 *m*. **Border:** The maps consist of two strips 59 mm (2.3 in.) wide/*bts/bltr/OB:sl/IB*: a hatched section between black bands/incorporated into the border above the strips is a panel 5 mm (0.2 in.) wide containing the title, and incorporated below the strips on some maps is a panel, in some cases a panel for each strip, containing the inscription 'measured from ...'. The roads are measured from Hyde Park Corner, London Bridge, 'the Standard in Cornhill', and Westminster Bridge, and, in the case of the road from Bath to Brighton, from the Market House, Bath/*bb*. **North Point:** *c/p/ V/*each strip has a north point. **Title:** 'London to ...'/*V/ps/*set within a panel incorporated into the border above the strips.

Issues: (i) c.1814: 'to be continued Monthly till the whole is completed. The First Part, comprising the Southern division, will be completed in Fourteen Numbers ...'. The first 162 strips were issued bound together c.1815. (ii) 1817: as (i) c.1814, but issued as a complete atlas: *Atlas: A survey of the high roads of England and Wales planned on a scale of one inch to a mile, including the seats of the nobility and gentry and every object worthy of remark, whether situated on, or contiguous to the road. Part I— comprising the counties of Kent, Surrey, Sussex, Hants, Wilts, Dorset, Somerset, Devon and Cornwall with part of Buckingham and Middlesex* .... **Maps:** (a) England and Wales (double-page), [dated 'May 1st 1817' and issued only after that date]. (b) 112 maps containing 223 road strips. (Plate 163: London to Exeter is not divided into strips.) *State:* First. *Imprints:* (i) *ob*: above each strip is the strip number. (ii) *obbc*: some maps have notes concerning connecting pages. (iii) *obbc:pi*: strips 1–84: 'Published by E. Mogg ... 1ˢᵗ 1814' with months from June to November; strips 85–98: no imprint; strips 99–130: 'Published ... by E. Mogg Nº 51 Charing Cross' dated either 1 December 1814 or 18 February 1815; strips 131–223: no imprint. *Publisher:* 'Edward Mogg, Nº 51 Charing Cross'. (iii) 1828: as (ii) 1817, except: *State:* Second. *Imprint:* (iii) publisher's imprints erased. *Publisher:* 'E. Mogg 14, Great Russell Street, Covent Garden'.

N.B. In 1808, Mogg also issued: *A survey of the roads from London to Brighton, Southampton, Portsmouth, Hastings, Tunbridge Wells, Margate & Dover, laid down on a scale of one inch to a mile ... in the same style as the above.* It contained 24 maps ('surveyd in the first instance at my own expence,') noting 'the Inns annexed to the Market Towns are those only which supply Post Horses.'

MOLL, Herman
fl. 1688–1732d. Engraver and publisher

Moll was possibly born in Holland, but more likely Germany; later, he came to England, and was first recorded as working with Moses Pitt in 1678 in London. After working for other publishers, he established his own business and eventually dominated the map trade in the early decades of the eighteenth century. He produced many maps and atlases including county atlases of England and Wales, Scotland and Ireland. His county maps were all boldly engraved in a characteristically heavy style and were unoriginal, being based on the earlier work of Norden, Ogilby, Speed and others—despite his claim that he 'omitted no pains to have them very correctly done, according to the Newest Observations and latest discoveries.' The county maps (77) of England and Wales are particularly attractive since the early issues were decorated with small vignette views or engravings of antiquities excavated in the county. The exception was Shropshire—'For want of Antiquities etc. in this County we have Inserted some out of yᵉ Neighbouring County of Stafford Shire'. Moll's scarcer maps of Scotland (78) were the first Scottish county maps to be published since Blaeu's volume, and his maps of Ireland (79)

are particularly scarce: 'that nothing might be wanting, these Maps of Ireland have been sent to Dublin single as they were finish'd, for the perusal of the Curious there, and were returned to England again improved'. Moll died in St Clement Danes church on 22 September, 1732. D.N.B.: Vol. 13, pp. 575–577.

Select Bibliography
BAKER, J. N. L.: 'The Earliest Maps of H. Moll'. (*IM*; 1937).

(77) Description: *st*: First. (Fig. 92). **Supply:** Moderate. **Average size:** 188 × 312 mm (7.5 × 12.5 in.) including the marginal decoration. **Features:** Some maps have the appropriate administrative divisions marked with large reference letters and bounded by dotted lines. The maps have a lettered reference key: e.g. 'Names of Divisions'. **Scale:** *V/av*:1:5 *m*/'English Miles'/*Vw/sbm//* Denbigh and Flint has two scales of measured and computed miles. **Border:** *OB:sl/IB:ll/bb*. **North Point:** Many maps have: *q/f/e*. **Decoration:** *ob*: engravings of antiquities excavated in the county; e.g. coins, fossils, statues, etc., and sometimes views of monuments, palaces, etc. **Title:** *c/pc*/'By H. Moll Geographer' or 'By Herman Moll Geographer'/set within a plain rectangular panel with a narrow frame. **Engraver:** Herman Moll.

Issues: (i) 1724: *Atlas: A new description of England and Wales, with the adjacent islands. Wherein are contained, diverse useful observations and discoveries in respect to natural history, antiquities, customs, honours, privileges etc. ... To which is added, a new*

92 77(i): 'Midlesex' by Herman Moll, 1724. *Photograph: Mills-Wight Studio*

and correct set of maps of each county, their roads and distances; and, to render 'em the more acceptable to the curious, their margins are adorn'd with great variety of very remarkable antiquities, etc. ... **Maps (50):** (a) Two general maps. (b) 39 English counties. (c) Yorkshire; West; East; North Ridings. (d) Isle of Wight; Isles of Man, 'Garnsey', Jersey and Alderney. (e) North; South Wales. (f) Denbigh and Flintshire. **State:** First. **Publishers:** 'H. Moll over-against Devereux-Court in the Strand, T. Bowles Printseller near the Chapter-House, and C. Rivington Bookseller at the Bible and Crown, in St. Paul's Church-yard, and J. Bowles Printseller over-against Stocks-Market.' (ii) 1724: (this atlas was possibly first issued in 1723): as (i) 1724, except: *Atlas: A set of fifty new and correct maps of England and Wales, etc. with the great roads and principal cross-roads, etc. Shewing the computed miles from town to town. A work long wanted, and very useful for all gentlemen that travel to any part of England ....* **State:** First. **Publishers:** H. Moll, Thomas Bowles, and J. Bowles. (iii) 1724; 1728: as (i) 1724, except: *Atlas: A new description of England and Wales ....* **State:** Second. A plate-number in brackets is added within the borderlines top left. The maps in this state were issued in: (a) 1724: *A set of fifty new and correct maps ....* (b) 1733: *A new description of England and Wales ....* (c) 1739: *A set of fifty new and correct maps ...* published respectively by: (a) H. Moll, Thomas Bowles, and J. Bowles. (b) J. Wilford, T. Bowles, C. Rivington, and J. Bowles. (c) Thomas Bowles & J. Bowles. (iv) 1747: as (iii) 1724; 1728, except: *Atlas: The geography of England and Wales; or, a set of maps of all the counties in England and Wales ....* **State:** Third. The plate-numbers are altered since the maps now appear in alphabetical order. **Publishers:** Thomas Bowles & J. Bowles. (v) 1753: as (iv) 1747, except: *Atlas: H. Moll's British atlas: or, pocket maps of all the counties in England and Wales .... Composed and engraved by Herman Moll, geographer; and lately revised and improved, with the addition of many hundred places, by Emanuel Bowen, geographer to His Majesty ....* **State:** Fourth. Some revisions and additions. The engravings of antiquities, etc., outside the map border have been cut from the plates and no longer appear. Average size is now: 188 × 248 mm (7.5 × 9.9 in.). **Publishers:** Thomas Bowles, and J. Bowles & Son.

N.B. Examples are known of a later issue with a second plate-number, in bolder figures, also in brackets, within the borderlines at top right. (state: fifth).

(78) Description: *st:* First (*v*). **Supply:** Very scarce. **Average size:** 189 × 263 mm (7.5 × 10.5 in.). **Features:** The Islands of Shetland and the Western Islands have informative notes added to *mf:* e.g. 'The Violence of the Tides and Tempestuous Seas deprives the Inhabitans of all foreign Correspondance from October till April and often till May'. **Scale:** *Vc*/*av*:1:7 *m*/'Miles of Great Britain'/*sbm*. **Border:** *OB:sl*/*IB:ll*/within the border at top right and left are plate-numbers in brackets/*bb*. **North Point:** *n*//except: Orkneyshire, the Western Islands and the Isle of Ila have: *q* with *f* and *e*. **Title:** 'The Shires of ... By H. Moll Geographer'/*V*/*pc* and *ps*/set within a rectangular panel with a plain imitation wooden frame.

Issues: (i) 1725: *Atlas: A set of thirty six new and correct maps of Scotland divided into shires, etc. A work long wanted, and very useful for all gentlemen that travel to any part of that kingdom. All, except two, composed and done by Herman Moll, geographer ....* **Maps (36):** (a) Scotland; 'Scotia Antiqua' by Robert Gordon. (b) 27 maps of the counties or areas of Scotland: '... to make the Geographical Part more plain and useful, we have been obliged to divide Five of the large Shires into several parts, to avoid too great a contraction of the scale, and have taken a special care to lay down all the hills of note etc.' (c) 'shire of Bute'; 'Orkney Shire'; Islands of Shetland; Western Islands; Isles of Mull; Isle of Jura; Isle of Ila. **State:** First (*v*). **Publisher:** 'H. Moll over against Devereux-Court, between Temple-Bar and St. Clements-Church in the Strand.'; Thomas Bowles; and John Bowles. (ii) 1745: as (i) 1725, except: **State:** First (*v*). Minor revisions. Altered atlas title. **Publishers:** 'Thomas Bowles, Print and Map-Seller near the Chapter-House in St. Paul's Church-Yard, and John Bowles, Print and Map-Seller at the Black-Horse, Cornhill'. N.B. In 1896, R. S. Shearer & Son of Stirling reprinted the first edition of 1725.

(79) Description: *st:* First. **Supply:** Rare. **Average size:** 204 × 272 mm (8.2 × 10.8 in.). **Scale:** *V*/provinces: *av:* 1:15*m*; counties: *av:* 1:7*m*/ 'English Miles' [two scales are 'English Miles 60 to one Degree' and the scale of Dublin and Louth is 'Irish Miles 48 to one Degree. According to S.r William Petty']/*sbm*. **Border:** *OB:sl*/*IB:ll*/the plate-number, in brackets, is noted within the borderlines, top right/*bb*. **Title**: 'The Province of . . . Divided into its Counties and ye Counties into their severall Barronies etc with the Great Roads 1727 By H. Moll Geographer' or 'The Counties of . . . By H. Moll Geographer'/*ps* and *pc*/*V*/set within a plain rectangular panel with a *dl* or *tl* frame. **Engraver**: Herman Moll—'all the maps are done and colour'd according to his Direction'.

Issues: (i) 1728: *Atlas: A set of twenty new and correct maps of Ireland, with the great roads and principal cross-roads, shewing the computed miles from town to town; very useful for all gentlemen that travel to any part of that kingdom. All composed and done by Herman Moll, geographer . . . . Maps (19): (a)* British Isles; Ireland. (b) Four Irish provinces. (c) 13 maps of Irish counties (one map combining four counties; six combining three each; four combining two each; and two of one each). *State*: First. *Publisher*: 'H. Moll, over-against Devereux-Court between Temple-Bar and St. Clement's Church in the Strand where may be had his set of fifty new and correct Maps of England and Wales, etc, with the Great-Roads and principal Cross-Roads, shewing the computed Miles from Town to Town. His Set of thirty-two new and correct Maps of Scotland, with Roads, divided into its Shires, never done before . . .'. (ii) A second edition, revised and improved by Emanuel Bowen, was printed by John Bowles under the title *The Atlas of Ireland* with the Grand Canal or the projected canal marked on appropriate maps, extra information included on the maps of the provinces, and some titles altered.

N.B. Moll also produced extremely rare, road strip maps—'Made Useful for the Pocket'—bearing his signature. Known copies were probably only proofs.

MORDEN, Robert
fl. 1669–1703d. Cartographer, publisher and bookseller

In 1695, Dr Edmund Gibson, later Bishop of Lincoln (1716–20) and of London (1720–48), produced a new translation of William Camden's *Britannia* to supersede Philémon Holland's first English translation of 1610. He engaged Robert Morden to prepare a new set of county maps for this edition, to replace the outdated maps of William Kip and William Hole. Morden prepared a set which Gibson rejected as too small and it is probable that these were actually issued by Morden in 1701 (81). He then produced a new set on double the scale,

usually by sending the most up-to-date survey data available to 'the most knowing Gentlemen in each County, with a request to supply the defects, rectifie the position, and correct the false spellings.' Thus, Morden based his maps on manuscript sources, plus the county surveys of Ogilby & Morgan, Seller, and Oliver & Palmer, plus the coastal charts of Captain Greenvile Collins. However, for many counties there were no such surveys available, and he was forced to fall back on the same source maps of Saxton, Norden, and Smith as used by Hole, Kip and Speed about 80 years earlier. The resulting maps (80) were attractive, with pleasant cartouches, despite the coarse engraving and lack of geographical originality. They were significant in being the first set of county maps to include roads (surprisingly, showing little agreement with Ogilby's roads of 1675) and in following John Seller's lead in measuring longitude from the prime meridian of St Paul's in London. Morden also marked minutes of time from London in the upper borderlines in an effort to clarify the local times that were taken from the sun, for there was no national standardized time. He also tried to clarify the confusion caused by the lack of standardized linear measurement—'. . . the difference of miles in the several parts of the Kingdom perplex the whole . . .'—by providing three scales representing (roughly) great (2,430 yards), middle (2,200 yards), and small (1,830 yards) miles on most maps (however, the proportions between the scale measures varied between counties), to cover the various 'customary' miles used in different parts of the country (but his scales bore no fixed relationship to customary miles). Morden took great pains to revise place names—'. . . the various Spellings of Places; wherein it will be impossible to please all, till men are agreed which is right'—and many modern name-forms date from these maps. A few maps name the engravers as Sutton Nicholls and John Sturt, but the similarity of style and engraving technique suggests that all were engraved by them. Morden's maps represent a transitional stage of development between the elegant, decorative but unreliable cartography of earlier times and the more accurate and functional maps of the eighteenth century. Despite Gibson's claim that 'Upon the whole, we need not scruple to affirm, that they are by much the fairest and most correct of any that have yet appear'd', the maps were severely criticised at the time, and, writing later in 1780, Richard Gough commented that 'the maps in the bishop's first edition, engraved by Morden, were very faulty; and no notice was taken of the hints for their amendment . . . .'

Loose copies of Morden's larger maps are difficult to date. The first edition of 1695 was generally printed on thin, good quality paper and is often found with trimmed margins; the 1715 and 1722 editions were printed on thicker, coarser paper and the latter edition often has the watermark of a horse within a circle; later editions were also printed on thicker paper but with a rather smoother surface. Morden's plates were retouched for and during each edition so that impressions are usually dark and strong and there is, generally, little progressive wearing of the plates to indicate age.

Morden produced a set of small county maps (81) in 1701 which, unlike the larger maps of 1695, included maps of individual Welsh counties. 'Several weighty Reasons have persuaded the Undertakers to be at the Expence of this necessary Work, for the conveniency of the Publick. The Bulk and Largness of other Volumes that treat of these Matters, becoming too chargeable for the Purses of many, and too tedious for the Perusal of Men of Business; the Mistakes and Errors of other Maps, that misplace divers considerable Towns and neglect the mentioning of others of note, are some of the Reasons that have incourag'd them to this Abbreviation'. These attractive smaller maps, which may have been originally prepared for Gibson's translation before 1693, are far scarcer than the larger maps actually used in it.

Morden produced many other maps, charts and globes including the rare set of playing card maps of 1676 which were re-issued with the suits removed, as a miniature atlas, by Turpin in about 1773. D.N.B. Vol. 13, pp. 857–58.

Select Bibliography
(F) MORDEN, R. *The County Maps from William Camden's Britannia, 1695.* A facsimile with an introduction by J. B. Harley. (1972).

(80) Descriptions: *st*: First (*v*). (Fig. 93). **Supply**: Moderate. **Average size**: 360 × 420 mm (10.4 × 16.8 in.)/*Vc*/Kent and Norfolk measure 350 × 625 mm (10 × 25 in.). **Features**: 39 maps bear the *pi* on *mf*: 'Sold by Abel Swale, Awnsham & Iohn Churchil' (*V*). Cornwall has a numbered reference table of administrative divisions. **Scale**: *V*/*av*: 1:2.5*m*/'Scale of Miles'/*Vw*//38 maps have a three-fold scale of great, middle and small miles//Durham, Hampshire, Rutland, and North and South Wales

have double scales of undefined miles//Shropshire has scales of measured and computed miles//the Smaller Islands and Buckingham have *n*//*sb*(s) or *sl*(s) in *m*/sometimes set within a panel with a plain-ruled frame. **Border**: *OB*:*sl*/*IB*: graduated into latitude at the sides, longitude at the bottom, and 'Minuits of Time' (*V*) at the top/*bb*. **Key**: *n*//or: Cornwall and Rutland have an explanation of settlement symbols; Rutland's appears within a small decorative cartouche. **Title**: *c*/*V*/*pc*/most maps are 'By Rob! Morden' (*V*)/set within a decorative cartouche of swags of fruit, shells, leaf motifs, scrolls, drapery, volutes, cornucopia, grotesques, plinths, etc. **Engravers**: 'Bark Shire', Buckingham, Essex, Cambridge, and Stafford are signed by Sutton Nicholls, and 'Britannia Saxonica' and Norfolk by John Sturt. The *es* appears in either the bottom left or right corner of the map.

Issues: (i) 1695: *Atlas: Camden's Britannia, newly translated into English: with large additions and improvements. Publish'd by Edmund Gibson . . . . Maps (50):* (a) England; Scotland*; Ireland; two historical maps of Britain. (b) 39 English counties. (c) West; East; North Ridings. (d) The smaller islands in the British Ocean. (e) North*; South Wales. *State:* First (*v*). **Publishers**: 'A. Swalle, at the Unicorn at the West-end of St. Paul's Church-yard; and A. & J. Churchil, at the Black Swan in Pater-noster-Row'. The maps were issued, with minor revisions, again in 1695, and probably at various times until at least c.1715, by A. Swalle and 'A. & J. Churchil'; and by 'Awnsham Churchill' alone in 1722 in *Britannia: or a chorographical description of Great Britain and Ireland . . . by William Camden . . . translated into English, with additions and improvements . . . by Edmund Gibson, D.D.* (New maps of North Wales and Scotland were substituted for the originals.) Further issues, with more minor revisions, were made as follows: (a) 1730(?): by James & John Knapton and ten others. (b) 1753: by R. Ware and 12 others. (c) 1772: by W. Bowyer and 26 others.
*Replaced in 1722.

(81) Description: *st*: First. **Supply**: Scarce. **Average size**: 160 × 200 mm (6.4 × 8 in.). **Features**: Detached parts of counties have a reference letter and, where appropriate, maps have a lettered reference key naming the areas. Many maps have a lettered reference table of administrative divisions, often set within a plain panel, and another lettered reference key to buildings, etc. marked on the map,

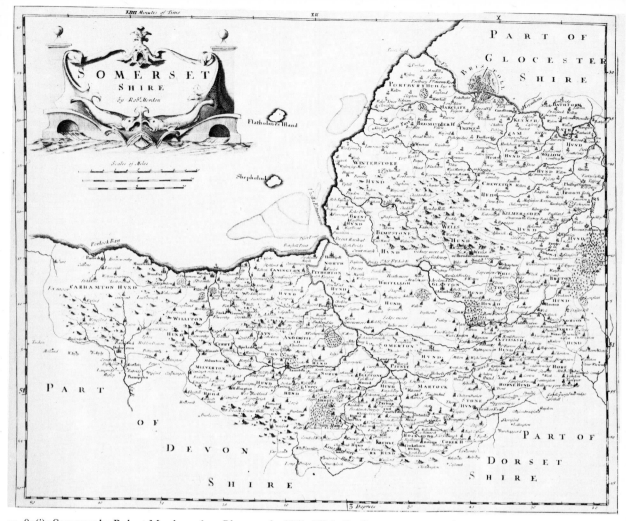

93 80(i): Somerset by Robert Morden, 1695. *Photograph: Mills-Wight Studio*

also often within a plain panel. **Scale:** *V/av:* 1:5*m*/ 'English Miles' or 'A Scale of Miles'/*Vw*/26 maps have a threefold scale of small, 'midle' (*V*) and great miles//Shropshire has a twofold scale of computed and measured miles//Rutland has a double scale of undefined units//Lancashire and Wiltshire have *n*//*sb*(s) or *sl*(s) in *m.* **Border:** *OB: sl/IB:* graduated into latitude at the sides, longitude at the bottom, and 'Minutes of Time' or 'Hours from London' at the top. The borders of the Welsh county maps are ungraduated/*bb.* **North Point:** Buckingham, Hereford, Middlesex, Northampton, Sussex, Suffolk, West Riding, and the North and East Ridings have some or all of the cardinal points named either *ob,* within the borderlines or at the edge of *mf*/*V*// In 1708, Herman Moll added: *q* with *f* and *e.* **Title:** *c/pc/*'By Rob. Morden'/*V*/set in a panel or cartouche of foliage, drapes, etc. **Engrav-**

ers: Leicester, Lincoln and Wiltshire are signed by R. Spofforth; Buckingham and Gloucester by J. Harris; and Hampshire by Sutton Nicholls. **Issues:** (i) 1701: *Atlas: The new description and state of England, containing the mapps of the counties of England and Wales, in fifty three copper-plates, newly design'd, exactly drawn and engraven by the best artists* .... *Maps (55):* (a) England. (b) 39 English counties. (c) West; North and East Ridings. (d) The smaller islands in the British Ocean. (e) 12 Welsh counties. *State:* First. *Publishers:* 'Robert Morden, in Cornhill; Thomas Cockerill, at the Three Leggs and Bible against Grocers-Hall in the Poultry; and Ralph Smith, at the Bible under the Piazza of the Royal Exchange'. This was re-issued in 1704 by 'S. and J. Sprint, J. Nicholson, and S. Burroughs in Little Britain, A. Bell, and R. Smith in Cornhill' with a slightly altered title. (ii) 1704: as (i)

1701, except: *Atlas: The new description and state of England ... exactly drawn and engraven by Mr. Hermann Moll and the best artists ....* **State:** First. **Publisher:** 'Ralph Smith, at the Bible under the Piazza of the Royal Exchange. Cornhill'. (iii) 1708: as (ii) 1704, except: *Atlas: Fifty six new and acurate maps of Great Britain, Ireland and Wales ... Begun by Mr. Morden: perfected, corrected and enlarg'd by Mr. Moll ...* **Maps (56):** (a) England and Wales, Scotland, and Ireland: by Herman Moll. (b) 39 English counties. (c) Yorkshire. (d) Isles of Wight, Jersey, Guernsey, Scilly, Sark, Alderney, Man, etc. (e) 12 Welsh counties. **State:** Second. Some revisions, and additions; particularly of: roads with destinations noted; boundaries between adjoining counties; and asterisks representing the number of members returned to Parliament. Compass indicators have been engraved. **Publishers:** 'John Nicholson at the King's-Arms, and John Sprint at the Bell in Little-Britain; Andrew Bell at the Cross-Keys and Bible in Cornhill, and Ralph Smith under the Piazza of the Royal-Exchange'. (iv) 1720–31: as (iii) 1708, except: *Atlas: Magna Britannia et Hibernia, antiqua & nova. Or, a new survey of Great Britain, wherein to the topographical account given by Mr. Cambden, and the late editors of his Britannia, is added a more large history ....* 6 vols. **Maps (47):** (i) Great Britain and Ireland: by Moll. (ii) Britannia Romana; Britannia Saxonica. (iii) East; West Thames (separately on one plate), English rivers and coasts; Great Level of the Fens (after Moore) sometimes added. (iv) 38 English counties (no Monmouth). (v) North and East; West Ridings. (vi) Smaller islands in the British Ocean. **State:** Second. **Publishers:** 'M. Nutt in Exeter-Exchange in the Strand, and J. Morphew near Stationers-Hall' (Vols. 1–2) and Thomas Cox 'at the Corner of Swithin's Alley, Cornhill' (Vol. 3) and 'at the Lamb under the Royal Exchange, Cornhill' (Vols. 4–6). This work was issued in parts and the maps also sold separately. They were again published in the second edition of the work in 1738, entitled *Magna Britannia antiqua & nova: or, a new, exact, and comprehensive survey of the ancient and present state of Great-Britain .... And illustrated not only with general mapps, but also particular ones of each county ...,* by Caesar Ward & Richard Chandler which was also issued in parts. Later issues of some maps are known.

MOULE, Thomas
fl. 1822–1842. Topographer, writer, bookseller and publisher

Moule was a scholar and writer on heraldry who worked as a bookseller before becoming inspector of 'blind' letters at the General Post Office in 1823 responsible for deciphering illegibly addressed letters. He was also Chamber-keeper in the Lord Chamberlain's Department for some years, dying in January 1851 at his official residence in St James's Palace. Moule produced a set of deservedly popular maps (82), in parts from 1830 and as a complete work from 1837, based mainly on his own observations: 'Without assuming any extraordinary pretensions to topographical information, the Editor may mention that he has, with 'expensive diligence' personally visited every county in England, excepting only Devonshire and Cornwall ...'. The county maps, town plans and environs' maps were finely engraved on steel and mostly richly decorated in flamboyant style with armorials and crests, secular and clerical figures, vignettes of local scenes and buildings, and architectural embellishments. This was the last series of decorative county maps produced and was an unusual product in a period when map-makers were rejecting ornamentation in favour of an austere, functional style. The maps were issued over a long period and display some interesting plate changes; railway information was added and regularly revised, vignettes were reworked and in some cases completely altered, and, most intriguingly, the names of the engravers on some of the maps were changed; for example, Warwickshire was attributed to Schmollinger before 1838 and to Bingley after 1838. The early issues of the maps, which were generally printed on better quality paper than later issues, were often coloured either in outline or with colour washes on the hundreds, but the decorative features were not coloured as they tend to be by modern colourists. Later issues are more frequently found close cropped than earlier issues, with little or no margins, since the format of *Barclays Universal English Dictionary* was slightly smaller than the original *English Counties Delineated* and the sheets had to be trimmed during binding. D.N.B. Vol. 13, pp. 1096–97.

(82) Description: *st:* Second. (Fig. 94). **Supply:** Plentiful. **Average size:** 210 × 270 mm (8.4 × 10.75 in.). **Features:** A numbered reference key to administrative divisions: e.g. 'REFERENCE TO THE HUNDREDS', sometimes set within a plain or decorative panel. **Scale:** V/av: 1:7m/most maps have: 'Scale of Miles' or 'Scale of English miles'/sbm//the plan of Boston has a 'Scale of

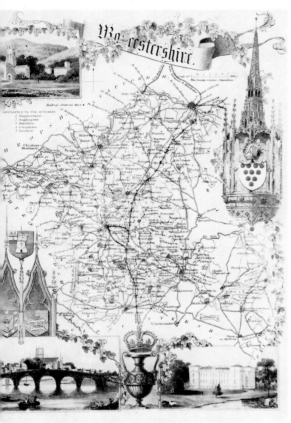

94 82(vi): Worcestershire engraved by J. Bingley,
c.1844. *Photograph: Mills-Wight Studio. By courtesy of
Ben Hardisty*

Chains', and Northamptonshire has 'A Scale of
Feet'! (added in 1838 and corrected c.1844 to '. . . of
Miles'). **Border:** Very decorative. Gothic architecture with incorporated figures, coats-of-arms,
vignettes, foliage, etc./*bb*. **North Point:** Some maps
have *c/p*. These were added to some maps in later
issues. **Decoration:** *n//*or titled vignettes of local
scenes, buildings and monuments. Coats-of-arms of
the gentry and bishoprics, and the seals of the cities.
Much other engraved decoration: e.g. animals,
angels, dragons, Neptune, Britannia, eagles, secular
and clerical figures, beacons, etc. **Title:** *c/oc/*set
within a decorative cartouche of varying style.
Engravers: the first edition of *The English counties
delineated* . . . attributed 24 maps to W. Schmollinger, nine maps and plans to John Dower, and 16
maps and plans to James Bingley.

Issues: The maps were also sometimes issued in
other publications. (i) 1837; 1838: The maps were

issued in parts from 1830 to 1836 by G. Virtue,
Simpkin & Marshall, and Jennings & Chaplin as
Moule's English counties. The often quoted first atlas
edition of 1836 was, in fact, published in 1837
despite the engraved titlepage being dated 1836.
Page XV of the 'Introduction' gives the date of
opening of the London and Greenwich Rail-road as
14th December, 1836, and, therefore, the edition
must have been published after that date. *Atlas:
The English counties delineated; or, a topographical
description of England. Illustrated by a map of London,
and a complete series of county maps. By Thomas
Moule* . . . . **Maps (57):** (a) England and Wales;
Inland navigation. (b) 39 English counties. (c) East;
West; North Ridings. (d) Isle of Thanet. (e) Isle of
Wight; Isle of Man. (f) New plan of London,
Metropolitan Boroughs (both without decoration);
Environs of London. (g) Cambridge; Environs of
Plymouth and Devonport; Environs of Portsmouth;
City of Bath; Environs of Bath and Bristol; City and
University of Oxford; Plan of Boston (environs have
no decoration). **State:** First (*v*). **Imprints:** (i) most
copies of the maps have: *obbc:es*: 'Engraved for
MOULES' ENGLISH COUNTIES, by . . .' (*V*)
with the name, and sometimes address, of Bingley,
Dower or Schmollinger. (ii) *obbc*: Berkshire,
Gloucester, Oxfordshire, Oxford, London, Isle of
Man, Hereford, Staffordshire and Shropshire have
the *pi* (usually dated) of G. Virtue: e.g. 'London. G.
Virtue, 26 Ivy Lane May 1, 1830' (Berkshire) (*V*).
(iii) Metropolitan Boroughs has no imprint.

N.B. Maps without *es* and/or *pi* were also issued at
this date and subsequently. Other maps lost
the imprints due to close cropping during
binding.

Publisher: 'George Virtue, 26, Ivy Lane Paternoster Row'. (ii) 1838: as (i) 1837; 1838, except:
Maps: 'Inland Navigation' omitted. **State:** First
(*v*). Minor revisions and additions. (iii) 1839: as (ii)
1838, except: **State:** Second (*v*). During the period
1837–39 the plates were revised to change the
engravers' signatures and sometimes erase the
publisher's imprint; and to incorporate railways and
parliamentary information, including the marking of
parliamentary boroughs and their boundaries and
the addition of a note giving the number of members
returned to Parliament. In some cases both revised
and unrevised maps were issued in the same years.
Railway information was up-dated for subsequent
issues. The maps were also sold separately as
'Moule's Pocket County Maps'. (iv) 1842(?): as (iii)
1839, except: *Atlas: A complete and universal*

English dictionary, by the Rev. James Barclay, illustrated by numerous engravings & maps. Revised by Henry W. Dewhurst, Esq, F.E.S.L. .... **Maps (49):** The combinations of maps bound into the different issues of *Barclay's dictionary* varied. However, the usual contents was: (a) England and Wales (without decoration; *obbc:pi:* 'LONDON. GEO VIRTUE, IVY LANE'; *obbl:es:* 'Engraved by the Omnigraph. F. P. Becker & Cº Patentees'). (b) 39 English counties. (c) North; East; West Ridings. (d) Isle of Thanet. (e) Isle of Wight; Isle of Man. (f) Environs of London (new map without vignettes); Oxford; Environs of Portsmouth. Variant copies are known which exclude: (a)/(d)/(e)/(f)/and include: Scotland (as (a)), Ireland (*es:* as (a) or of W. Hughes), Bath, Boston, Cambridge, Environs of Bath and Bristol, Environs of Plymouth and Devonport. *State:* Third.

N.B. Maps of some counties are known without any decorative embellishments, enclosed by a plain frame.

Imprints: (i) *obbc:* imprints erased and replaced by a plate-number on most maps. However, at a later date, other maps had the number added; and some had it erased. There is no clear pattern of additions and erasures. (ii) Isle of Man (now dated 1843) and sometimes the Environs of London bear the *pi* of G. Virtue. (iii) Environs of London bears the *es* of W. Hughes.

N.B. Maps are frequently found close cropped from binding, thus losing the imprints and plate-numbers.

Publisher: George Virtue. (v) 1842(?): as (iv) 1842(?), except: *Atlas: Barclay's universal English dictionary, newly revised by Henry W. Dewhurst, Esq: F.E.S.L.* .... *State:* Third. (vi) 1844(?): as (iv) 1842(?), except: *State:* Fourth (*v*). Railways are now marked by three (instead of two) lines with cross-hatching, and stations are indicated. An explanation of the station symbol is added, i.e. 'Railway Stations thus'. Minor revisions and additions. Scales are added to some maps. (vii) 1845(?): as (vi) 1844(?), except: *State:* Fourth (*v*). Minor revisions and additions. (viii) 1848(?); 1850(?): as (vii) 1845(?), except: *Atlas: A complete and universal dictionary of the English language ... By the Rev. James Barclay. A new edition ... by B. B. Woodward, B.A.* .... *State:* Fourth (*v*). Minor revisions and additions. (ix) 1852(?): as (viii) 1848(?), 1850(?), except: *State:* Fourth (*v*). Minor revisions and additions. *Publisher:* James S. Virtue.

N.B. Most of the counties (about 30 maps—

numbers vary) were also issued in some editions of *The history of England by Hume and Smollett* ... published, in varying numbers of volumes, by George Virtue.

MURRAY, T. L.

fl. 1830–1834. Surveyor and cartographer

Murray's *Atlas of the English Counties* ... contained large, clearly engraved maps (83) without decoration.

(83) Description: *st:* First (*v*). **Supply:** Scarce. **Average size:** 356 × 455 mm (14.25 × 18.2 in.). **Features:** A numbered reference key to administrative divisions: e.g. 'REFERENCE to the HUNDREDS'. **Scale:** *V/av:* 1:3m/'SCALE'/*sbm.* **Border:** *OB:tTt/IB:ll.* **North Point:** *s/f.* **Key:** 'EXPLANATION'. **Title:** *c/oc.* **Engravers:** Hoare & Reeves.

Issues: (i) 1830(?): *Atlas: An atlas of the English counties divided into hundreds, etc., containing the rivers, roads, parks, parishes, etc. in each, exhibiting the whole of the inland navigation, rail roads, etc. ... on the basis of the Trigonometrical Survey by order of the Honᵇˡᵉ the Board of Ordnance. Under the superintendance of T. L. Murray* .... (Plate changes suggest a possible earlier issue.) **Maps (44):** (a) England; Wales; Scotland; Ireland. (b) 39 English counties. (c) Yorkshire. *State:* First (*v*). *Imprints:* (i) *obbl:* 'Drawn under the Superintendance of T. L. Murray' (*V*). (ii) *obbr:es:* 'Hoare & Reeves sc.' (*V*). (iii) *obbc:pi:* 'London. Published May, 1ˢᵗ 1830, by T. L. Murray, 19, Adam Street, Adelphi (*V*). *Publisher:* T. L. Murray.

N.B. Another issue c.1830 up-dated railway information in Durham and Lancashire.

(ii) 1831(?): as (i) 1830(?), except: *State:* First (*v*). *Imprint:* (iii) *obbc:pi:* date altered: 'London. Published May, 1ˢᵗ 1831, by T. L. Murray, 19, Adam Street, Adelphi' (*V*). (iii) 1832(?): as (ii) 1831(?), except: *State:* Second. New parliamentary information has been added to the maps; parliamentary divisions and polling places are marked and appropriate changes have been made to the key. *Imprint:* (iii) *obbc:pi:* date altered: 'London. Published May, 1ˢᵗ 1832, by T. L. Murray, 19, Adam Street, Adelphi' (*V*).

N.B. There may possibly have been a further issue c.1834.

(iv) Some maps were issued c.1838–40 with several revisions and additions, in particular the addition of railways and the poor law unions, by William Robson & Co. as folding maps and in commercial directories. The *es, obbr*, and the inscription, *obbl*, were both erased and the maps bore the new *pi*: 'William Robson & C?. Directory Office London' (state: third).

NEELE, Samuel John
fl. 1795–1824d. Engraver

Samuel John Neele and his son Josiah were prolific early nineteenth-century engravers who produced maps for many atlases and topographical works, including town plans and county soil maps. They are best known for the elegant series of county maps (85) published in parts by John Wilkes and others in the *Encyclopaedia Londinensis* and the plain maps (84) first published in *The New British Traveller*: 'as a whole, THE NEW BRITISH TRAVELLER will, it is confidently presumed, be found to answer the most sanguine expectations of enlightened readers;—and will be regarded as a noble monument of the greatness of the nation to which its records are devoted.' Josiah Neele also worked with the engravers George and James Neele.

(84) Description: *st*: First. **Supply:** Scarce. **Average size:** 195 × 240 mm (7.5 × 9.75 in.). **Scale:** *V/av*: 1:5*m*/'British Miles'/*sbm*/*Vw*. **Border:** *OB:tTt/IB:ll/bb*. **North Point:** *s/f*. **Title:** *c/pc*/set within a horizontally hatched panel with a narrow *dl* frame. **Engraver:** Samuel John Neele.

Issues: (i) 1819: *Atlas: Robins's atlas of England and Wales, accurately engraved by Neele, from the latest surveys*. Evidence suggests that the atlas was issued in parts from 1812 onwards since the maps are variously dated and some appear to have had the publisher and date corrected. Presumably the series was published by James Cundee 1812–14, J. & J. Cundee 1814–15, and completed by J. Robins & Co. It was certainly issued in nine parts by Robins. *Maps (45):* (a) England and Wales. (b) 39 English counties. (c) North; East; West Ridings. (d) North; South Wales. *State:* First. *Imprints:* (i) *obbr:es*: 'Neele sculp! Strand' (*V*). (ii) *obbc:pi*: 'Published by J. Robins, & Co. Albion Press, London, January 1 ...' (*V*) [except Norfolk and Northampton, which bear the *pi* of James Cundee]. The maps are dated 1818, except the general map (1819) and Northampton, Norfolk, Nottingham and Stafford (1812). *Publishers:* 'J. Robins & Co., Albion Press, Ivy Lane, Paternoster Row'. (ii) 1820(?): as (i) 1819,

except: *Atlas: The new British traveller; or, modern panorama of England and Wales ... By James Dugdale, LL.D. Illustrated by a complete set of correct maps, views of public buildings, antiquities. ... States:* First or second. *Imprint:* There were two issues of this atlas c.1820 with the *pi* on some maps in different states. Some maps bear the Robins' imprint as in (i) 1819 and some have alternative imprints of J. Robins & Co. dated 1820; or James Cundee 1812–1814; or J. & J. Cundee, 1814–1815; e.g. 'Published by J. & J. Cundee, Albion Press', ... [or Ivy Lane] ... 'London, January 1, 1815' (dates vary), (except: Cheshire has no imprint and other maps tend to lose the imprint during binding), [the Cundee imprinted maps were old stock unused in the original parts' issue]. *Publishers:* 'J. Robins & Co.' or John Cundee (given on the engraved and printed title-pages respectively).

N.B. County maps were also issued in the publication of individual county sections from E. W. Brayley's *The beauties of England and Wales ... c.1820*. They were also sometimes published without imprint in other works.

(85) Description: *st*: First. (Fig. 95). **Supply:** Scarce. **Average size:** 195 × 240 mm (7.5 × 9.75 in.). **Scale:** *n//* or: 'Statute Miles 69½ to a Degree'; 'Scale of Miles'; 'British miles'; 'Statute miles'; 'British statute miles'; 'Scale'/*V/av*: 1:5*m*/ *sbm*. **Border:** *OB:tTt/IB:ll/bb*. **North Point:** *s/p* or *f/V*. **Decoration:** Heraldic arms on the maps of Norfolk, Northampton, Northumberland and Oxford only. **Title:** *c/oc/obbc*. **Engravers:** Samuel Neele, Josiah Neele, J. Pass. (Maps by Pass vary slightly in style from those of the Neeles).

Issues: (i) 1810–1829(?): *Atlas: Encyclopaedia Londinensis; or, universal dictionary of arts, sciences, and literature ... Embellished by a most magnificent set of copper-plate engravings ... Compiled, digested, and arranged, by John Wilkes ... assisted by eminent scholars ... Published in parts from c. 1810. Maps (45):* (a) United Kingdom of Great Britain and Ireland; England; Scotland; Ireland. (b) 39 English counties. (c) Yorkshire. (d) London. *State:* First. *Imprints:* (i) *obbr:es* of either: Neele, Neele & Son, or J. Pass: e.g. 'Neele & Son 352 Strand'. (ii) *obbc:pi*: in a variety of forms and variously dated. e.g. 'London. Pub^d as the Act directs, Decr 1st 1803, by J. Wilkes' (Essex); 'London Published as the Act directs May 21st 1806, by J. Wilkes' (Hertfordshire); 'Engraved for the Encyclopaedia Londinensis, 1820' (Oxfordshire); 'Published August 7th 1811, by

95 85(i): Oxfordshire by Samuel Neele, 1820.
Photograph: Mills-Wight Studio

Adlard & Jones Ave Maria Lane' (Kent).
Publishers: J. Wilkes; Adlard & Co; Adlard &
Jones; G. Jones.

OGILBY, John
fl. 1666–1676d. Geographer, historian, translator
and publisher

Before embarking on map production, the multi-
talented Ogilby enjoyed a varied and eventful career.
His winnings in a Virginian plantation lottery
purchased him a dancing apprenticeship, but his
successful career as a dancing teacher was ended by a
leg injury. He was appointed Deputy Master of the
Revels in Ireland and opened a theatre in Dublin
which he subsequently lost with all his possessions at
the start of the Civil War in 1641. Sailing back to
England, Ogilby was shipwrecked and arriving back
penniless, was forced to take work translating the
classics. In 1662 he returned to Ireland now as
Master of the Revels and built another theatre in

Dublin which was quickly closed by a dispute. He
then returned to London, opening a publishing
business which was duly destroyed in the Great Fire
of London in 1666. Despite the loss of his entire
stock-in-trade and all his printing equipment,
valued at £3,000, Ogilby turned the situation to his
advantage by being appointed as one of four 'sworn
viewers', or surveyors, by the Lord Mayor, to plot
the sites of disputed properties and to mark out the
ground of the devastated area. Also appointed were
his wife's grandson William Morgan, and John
Oliver and Thomas Mills. The 'sworn viewers'
prepared the magnificent 20-sheet plan of London at
a scale of 100 feet to the inch which was published by
Morgan in 1677 a year after Ogilby's death.

Ogilby then turned his attention to county
mapping, producing fine, rare, large maps of Kent
and Middlesex published in 1672–3, and Essex in
1678. The survey of Surrey undertaken in 1673 was
never completed. Essex and Middlesex were issued
c. 1689 by Philip Lea, and Middlesex was again
issued in 1720 by George Willdey. These maps show
the influence of Dutch style with elaborate cartouches and embellishments, and it is a great pity
that Ogilby was unable to cover other counties.

Ogilby's greatest work was his *Britannia*, first
published in 1675 as the first of three projected
volumes; the second was to consist of descriptions
and plans of 25 cities, and the third, of a
topographical description of the country. However,
only this first volume was produced. Ogilby was
granted the title of 'King's Cosmographer and
Geographic Printer', the first cartographer since
Saxton to receive full royal approval, and Charles II
ordered that he should have free access to local
records and information. The resulting beautifully
engraved strip road maps (86) had a profound effect
on the development of cartography. The continuous
strip format was imitated in many reduced pocket
atlases and is, indeed, still used today. *Britannia*,
produced 'with many Years Travel, and the Expence
of 7,000 l.', was the first set of road maps produced in
this country, and, henceforward, roads would be an
important feature of British maps. 'Ogilby, from
introducing roads into maps, made maps of little else
but roads' (Gough). Ogilby possibly took the idea
for his road atlas from the printed road books that
had been in use in France for over a century, for
there was no earlier English equivalent. For the first
time English travellers had a pictorial representation
of a route showing all the intermediate points,
although the size and weight of the volume must

have made it difficult to handle and it was not without its critics (Henry Beighton, for example, thought the road maps 'might have been more useful to Travellers had they not proved so erroneous, irreconcileable to truth, and one another'). Since Ogilby was 69 when the work was proposed, it is unlikely that he actually carried out the practical measurement himself; the roads would have been measured by assistants using a way-wiser and surveying probably by compass traverse, and these measurements were used in 1740 for positioning milestones along the main roads. Ogilby's use of the statute mile of 1,760 yards, which had been established by Parliament in 1593, contributed to the general acceptance of this measurement in place of the local or 'customary' miles which had varied between about 1,600 and 2,700 yards. Each map covers about 70 miles and the longer routes extend over several sheets. They each have an attractive central cartouche giving details of the route and incorporating varied designs or scenes of surveying, farming, hunting, and so on. Map titles are sometimes confusing since they name the overall route rather than the section actually covered by the map. Unfortunately only the roads of England and Wales were mapped by Ogilby; Scotland and Ireland had to wait a century for their first road maps to be produced by Taylor & Skinner. D.N.B.: Vol. 14, pp. 908–11.

Select Bibliography

VAN EERDE, K. S.: *John Ogilby and the Taste of His Times.* (1975)

FORDHAM, SIR H. G.: 'John Ogilby (1600–1676). His Britannia and the British Itineraries of the eighteenth century'. (*The Library*, 4th Series, Vol. 6; 1925)

HYDE, R.: 'John Ogilby's Eleventh Hour'. (*MC*, 11; June 1980)

(*F*) OGILBY, J.: *Britannia. A coloured facsimile.* (1939)

(*F*) OGILBY, J.: *Britannia, Volume the First: or, an Illustration of the Kingdom of England and Dominion of Wales .. 1675.* Bibliographical Note by J. B. Harley. (1970)

(*F*) OGILBY, J.: *Ogilby's road maps of England and Wales from Ogilby's Britannia, 1675.* Introduction by Roger Cleeve. (1971)

(86) Description: *st*: First. (Fig. 96). **Supply**:

96 86(i): London–Rye by John Ogilby, 1675. *Photograph: Mills-Wight Studio*

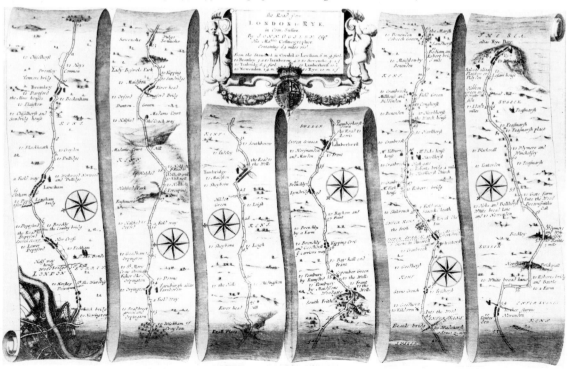

Scarce. **Average size**: 325 × 450 mm (13 × 18 in.).
Features: Some land use designated: e.g.: 'arrable', 'heath on both sides', 'sheep farms', etc. Mileages from the Standard in Cornhill, London, noted. Informative notes are sometimes added: e.g. 'ye worst way …'. **Scale**: *n//* scale is 1:1*m*. **Border**: The strips are engraved on six or seven imitation lengths of scroll each approximately 65 mm (2.5 in.) wide/*bts*/*bltr*/two maps (Plate 25: London to Andover, and Plate 28: Andover to Crewkerne) have reference letters above each strip running from A to F and F to M. respectively. The continuation of the route from Crewkerne to 'Plimouth' does not have reference letters/the scrolls are framed by *sl* or *dl*.
North Point: Since orientation varies, each strip has a north point and some have two with the strip divided by a line/*r*/*f*/generally, the compass design is the same for each strip on a map, but Plates 23–28 (the four maps of the London to Lands End route) have a very ornate compass in the first strip and plain, quartered circles in the rest. **Decoration**: The title is set within a very decorative cartouche at the top centre of the scrolls. Designs vary and sometimes show subtle variations on a common theme. 68 cartouches are fairly plain, showing fruit, foliage, shells, grotesques, garlands, scrollwork, etc. The remaining 32 are more spectacular, showing: rural scenes of cattle, sheep, cowherds and milk-maids; hunting scenes; Neptune and Aphrodite emerging from the waves; surveyors taking road measurements with a way-wiser; and so on. Many cartouches incorporate the royal arms set within the garter and surmounted by a crown. **Title**: 'The Road from LONDON to … By JOHN OGILBY Esqr His Maj^ties Cosmographer'/*V*/*vl*/followed by an extensive distance table/set within the decorative cartouche. **Engravers**: Only two plates are signed—by Joseph Moxon and Wenceslaus Hollar. Gregory King claimed to have engraved some and others were probably by Richard Shortgrave.

Issues: (i) 1675: *Atlas: Britannia, volume the first: or, an illustration of the kingdom of England and dominion of Wales: by a geographical and historical description of the principal roads thereof. actually admeasured and delineated in a century of whole-sheet copper-sculps. Accomodated with the ichnography of the several cities and capital towns; and compleated by an accurate account of the more remarkable passages of antiquity, together with a novel discourse of the present state. By John Ogilby Esq; His Majesty's Cosmographer, and Master of His Majesty's Revels in the kingdom of Ireland …. Maps:* 100 strip road maps of England and Wales. (There was also an index map and the title page was handsomely engraved by Wenceslaus Hollar). **State**: First (*v*). Minor alterations were made to some plates. **Imprint**: The first issues of 1675 have no plate-numbers. These were added for the 1675 issue of the *Itinerarium Angliae* … and appear on all later issues: outside scrolls, inside outer-frame, bottom right (second state). **Publisher**: John Ogilby, 'at his House in White-Fryers'. The *Britannia* was issued with minor changes throughout 1675 and again in 1676, and the maps also appeared, with plate-numbers added but without most of the accompanying text, in 1675 under the title of *Itinerarium Angliae: or, a book of roads, wherein are contain'd the principal road-ways of His Majesty's kingdom of England and dominion of Wales …*. The maps were also sold individually in 1676. In (possibly) 1677(?) and 1698 the maps were re-issued without change in *Britannia: or, the kingdom of England and dominion of Wales, actually survey'd with a geographical and historical description of the principal roads … by 'Abel Swall, at the Unicorn in Pater-noster-rows, and Robert Morden, at the Atlas in Corn-hill'. Some copies of the maps are found on large, thick paper with the maps framed by red, ruled lines.

N.B. Ogilby also produced, with his step-grandson William Morgan: *The traveller's pocket-book; or, Ogilby and Morgan's book of the roads, improved and amended, in a method never before attempted … in 1676. This pocket book was very popular and there were 24 editions terminating in 1794. It contained only a general map: 'A New Map of England with a table readily to find the Townes' in early editions and 'A new and correct map of all the Direct and Principal Cross Roads in England & Wales to which is added a view of the roads in Scotland from the late survey' in later editions.

OSBORNE, Thomas
fl. 1748. Publisher

Osborne's *Geographia Magnae Britanniae* contained charming, small decorative maps (87) in an early style. D.N.B.: Vol. 14, pp. 1197–1199.

(87) Description: *st*: First. (Fig. 97). **Supply**: Moderately scarce. **Average size**: *V*/145 × 170 mm (5.75 × 6.5 in.). **Scale**: *V*/*av*: 1:8*m*/'Miles'/*sd*/*sbm*. **Border**: *OB*:*sl*/*IB*: graduated thus: vertical borders

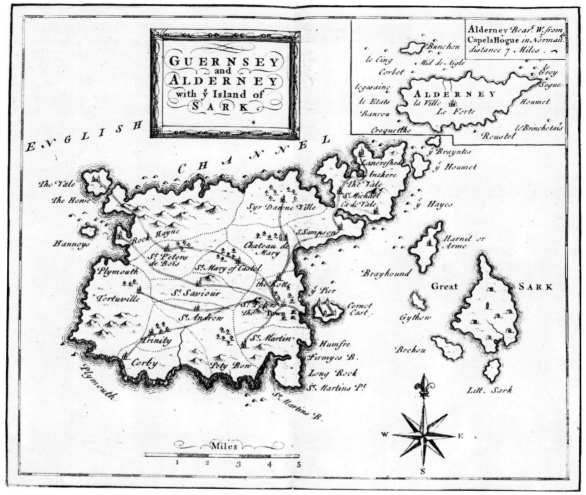

97 87(i): 'Guernsey and Alderney with ye Island of Sark' published by Thomas Osborne, 1748. *By permission of the British Library (Maps C.24.aa.29.)*

graduated into degrees of latitude; horizontal borders graduated into degrees of longitude but the upper border is sometimes graduated in 'minutes of time' instead/*bb*. **North Point**: Style varies/usually *s* or *r*/*f*/*l*/*V*. **Title**: 'A Correct Map of . . .'/*V*/*vl*/*sd*/set within a panel usually having a decorative frame resembling carved wood. **Engraver**: 'A New Map of England and Wales', and 'A New and Correct Map of Glocester-Shire' are both signed by Thomas Hutchinson. Although all the other maps are unsigned, similarity of style suggests that they were all engraved by Hutchinson.

Issues: This atlas was sometimes issued bound with Thomas Kitchin's *Geographia Scotiae*. (i) 1748: *Atlas*: *Geographia Magnae Britanniae. Or, correct*

maps of all the counties in England, Scotland, and Wales; with general ones of both kingdoms, and of the several adjacent islands: each map expressing the cities, boroughs, market and presbytery towns, villages, roads and rivers . . . . **Maps (61)**: (a) England and Wales. (b) 39 English counties. (c) Yorkshire; North; East; West Ridings. (d) 12 Welsh counties. (e) Isle of Wight; Isle of Man; Guernsey and Alderney; Island of Jersey; Islands of Scilly. **State**: First. **Imprint**: *obar*: plate-number. **Publishers**: S. Birt, T. Osborne, D. Browne, I. Hodges, I. Osborne, A. Millar, and I. Robinson. (ii) 1756(?): as (i) 1748, except: **State**: First. **Publishers**: 'T. Osborne, D. Browne, J. Hodges, A. Miller, J. Robinson, W. Johnston, P. Davey & B. Law'.

PATERSON, Daniel

fl. 1770–1811. Cartographer, soldier and administrator

Paterson was, for many years, an assistant to the Quartermaster-General of His Majesty's forces; was promoted to captain in 1783; and retired as a lieutenant colonel. In 1771 he produced *A New and Accurate Description of all the Direct and Principal Cross Roads in Great Britain* which contained only a general map but went through many editions, not least because it was used to calculate the distance of military marches and thus the charge to the public accounts. This work—commonly known simply as *Paterson's Roads*—was published from 1822 by Edward Mogg with ten maps (88). From 1799, the work was increased in size by the addition of material taken from *Cary's New Itinerary*, and this forced Cary to sue successfully the publishers of Paterson's work. Lord Kenyon, passing judgment, thought 'the twelfth edition of Paterson was a most impudent plagiarism.'

Of greater interest is the set of small road strip maps (89) published in 1785 and 1803. These informative maps show the countryside in the neighbourhood of the main road and were among the first road maps to cover any part of Scotland. D.N.B.: Vol. 15, pp. 461–2.

Select Bibliography
FORDHAM, SIR H. G.: 'Paterson's Roads. Daniel Paterson, His Maps and Itineraries. 1738–1825'. (*The Library*, 4th Series, Vol. 5; 1925)

(88) Description: *st*: First. (1826). **Supply**: Moderate. **Average size**: 175 × 218 mm (7 × 8.75 in.). **Scale**: *V*/*av*: 1:2.5*m*/'English Miles'/*sbm*/where two maps appear on one plate, the scale is set within a plain panel incorporated into the dividing line. **Border**: *tTt*. **North Point**: *c*/*p*/*V*. **Title**: *pc*/either *mf*; or: *obac*; or: *obbc*/except: 'The Lakes ...' has a decorative calligraphic titlepiece. **Imprint**: *obar*: 'Plate ...'; where two maps appear on the same plate, there is a second plate-number, *obbr*; (except: 'The Lakes ...' has no plate-number).

Issues: (a) By Daniel Paterson: 1771; 1772; 1773; 1776; 1778; 1781; 1784; 1786; 1789; 1792; 1794; 1796; 1799; 1803; 1808; 1811. (b) By Edward Mogg: 'the whole remodelled, augmented and improved, by the addition of numerous new roads and new admeasurements': 1822; 1824; 1826; c.1829; c.1832. *Atlas*: (a) *A new and accurate description of all the direct and principal cross roads in Great Britain ... the whole on a plan far preferable to any work of the kind extant ....* (b) *Mogg's improved edition of Paterson's roads ....* **Maps**: (a) (i) 1771–1796: general map of England and Wales. (ii) 1799: 'A general view of the Roads of Scotland' was added for this edition and in some copies of the 13th edition, 1808. (iii) 1808: a new, large fold-out map of England and Wales and part of Scotland was substituted for the general map. (b) from 1822: ten maps: (i) general map. (ii) Holyhead road. (iii) the Lakes of Cumberland, Westmorland, and Lancashire. (iv) seven maps covering the south coast from the Isle of Thanet to the Isle of Wight. (Some of the maps are printed two to a sheet).

N.B. Copies are known with an extra, unindexed map of the 'Banks of the River Wye'.

(89) Description: *st*: First. (Fig. 98). **Supply**: Scarce. **Average size**: 85 × 160 mm (3.4 × 6.4 in). **Border**: The maps consist of two strips of 42 mm (1.7 in.) width separated and framed by *sl*/*bts*/*bltr*/ above the strips: mileage information is contained in a panel, across the full width of the strips, with octagonal end-pieces containing the strip number. Below the strips is a similar panel with a letter reference key to country houses and their owners. **North Point**: *c*/*p*/*e*/the orientation of each strip varies and each has a north point. **Title**: Each route has a title at its starting point only and, consequently, most maps have no title. 'LONDON to ...' measured from London Bridge'/*V*/*vl*/set within a semi-circular panel at the start of the strip. Measurements are taken from: London Bridge; Westminster Bridge, 'the Stones-end (near the King's Bench) in the Borough of Southwark'; Hyde-Park Corner; Tyburn Turnpike; 'from Cornhill, top of Gracechurch-street'; Shoreditch Church; 'Holborn Bars, near Gray's-Inn Lane'; West Smithfield; Whitechapel Church; and 'the Scite of Hicks's Hall, end of St. John's-Lane, in St. John's Street.'

Issues: (i) 1785: *Atlas*: *Paterson's British itinerary being a new and accurate delineation and description of the direct and principal cross roads in Great Britain ... By Capt.ⁿ Daniel Paterson ....* **Maps**: (a) Index map. (b) 358 road strips, printed back-to-back, including the roads from London to Edinburgh via: Berwick; Coldstream; Carlisle; and Carlisle and Moffat. **State**: First. **Imprints**: (i) *obbc*:*pi*: 'Printed for the Proprietor CARINGTON BOWLES, London, 3 Jan. 1785'. (ii) *obac*: front

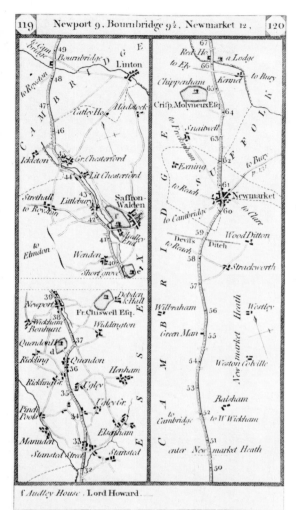

98 89(i): Saffron Walden–Newmarket by Daniel
Paterson, 1785. *Photograph: Mills-Wight Studio*

side: 'PATERSON'S (VOL. ..) ITINERARY'.
reverse side: 'DIRECT (VOL. ..) ROADS'.
Publisher: 'Carington Bowles at his Map and Print
Warehouse No. 69, St. Pauls Church Yard'. (ii)
1796: as (i) 1785, except: ***Maps:*** (a) Index map. (b)
386 road strips on 193 maps printed back-to-back
(strips 89 and 113/114 are altered; strips 187–198
and 434–449 are added). ***State:*** Second (except:
new maps). ***Imprint:*** (i) *obbc:pi* altered: 'Printed
for the Proprietors BOWLES & CARVER,
London, 6 Jan 1796'. ***Publishers:*** 'Bowles & Carver
at their Map & Print-Warehouse No 69 St. Paul's
Church Yard'. (iii) 1803; 1807: as (ii) 1796, except:
State: Second or third. ***Imprint:*** (i) *obbc:pi*

altered: 'Printed for the Proprietors BOWLES &
CARVER, London'.

PETTY, Sir William
1623–1687. Mathematician, statistician, physician
and cartographer
Petty was born on 26 May, 1623, at Romsey in
Hampshire and, after studying in Amsterdan, Caen,
Leyden, Oxford and Utrecht, eventually became
Physician-General to the army in Ireland.

Cromwell put down the Irish rebellion between
1649 and 1652 and, as a result, the Commonwealth
Parliament passed the Act of Satisfaction in 1653
which confiscated Irish land in order to settle arrears
of pay for the army and to repay the London
merchants who had provided funds for Cromwell.
Petty was appointed to survey the estates of the Irish
landowners. The 'Down Survey', as it was called,
was a mammoth task, carried out by over 1000 men,
and completed in 1657. Fortunately, Petty always
saw his task as something more than the surveying of
separate parcels of land and set out to produce a
topographical and hydrographic survey of the whole
country. He produced his *Hiberniae Delineatio* from
the 'Down Survey' and, thus, the 'modern' map of
Ireland was born.

The first printed atlas of Ireland was issued in
1685 containing maps (90) of both provinces and
counties of uneven size and shape; in fact, these were
often printed on irregularly shaped sheets made up
of smaller sheets pasted together. Since Petty's
survey had been concerned only with the delineation
and classification of forfeited lands, much basic
topographical information did not appear on the
maps and areas not covered by the 'Down Survey'
were only superficially represented. The maps were
crudely engraved with the conventional decorative
features of the period and some carelessness—many
names being mis-spelt or mis-placed. Some appear
to be unfinished having blank shields, panels and
geographical areas. Yet, despite their inadequacies,
these maps remained the basis for the mapping of
Ireland, being widely copied, for over a century.

Petty was appointed to supervise the redistribu-
tion of the forfeited lands and was awarded estates
near Limerick for himself. He also produced large-
scale maps of the 214 baronies, from his survey
material, in the late 1650s; but these were never
published since one of the only two sets was
captured by French pirates 'en route' from Dublin
to London (where it was possibly to be engraved) in
1707, and the other set was dispersed.

Sir William died on 16 December 1687 in London and was buried in Romsey Abbey. D.N.B.: Vol. 15, pp. 999–1005.

Select Bibliography

FITZMAURICE, LORD E.: *Life of Sir William Petty, 1623–1687.* (1895)

STRAUSS, E.: *Sir William Petty: portrait of a genius.* (1954)

(90) Description: *st*: First. (Fig. 99). **Supply**: Scarce. **Average size**: *Vc*/375 × 475 mm (15 × 19 in.). **Features**: Administrative divisions named in crude lettering and bounded by solid or dashed lines. **Scale**: *V*/provinces: *av*: 1:6*m*; counties: *av*: 1:2.5*m*/'Scala Miliarum Hibernicorum' and 'Scala Miliarum Anglicorum'/*Vw*/2 *sbm*, sometimes set within a plain or decorative cartouche with dividers, armillary spheres, figures, etc. **Border**: *sl*, *dl*, or *tl*/*bb*. **North Point**:*n*//or: 22

county maps have the cardinal points named in Latin at the edge of the map or within the borderlines. The general map, the provinces and seven counties have north points of varying design: *q* with *f* and *e*; *r* with *p*; *s*. **Decoration**: 11 maps have empty shields or what appear to be empty panels without coats-of-arms, inscriptions, etc. Large decorative ships, sea monsters, etc. **Title**: 'THE PROVINCE OF . . .' or 'THE COUNTY OF . . .'/ *pc*/set within a simple cartouche usually resembling plaster-work.

Issues: (i) 1685: **Atlas**: *Hiberniae delineatio quoàd hactenus licuit perfectissima. Studio Guilielmi Petty Eq^{lis} aurati.* **Maps (36)**: (a) 'A Generall Mapp of Ireland'. (b) Four Irish provinces. (c) 31 maps of Irish counties. Louth and Dublin are printed from one plate; Donegal, Kerry, Mayo and Tipperary from two plates each; Galway from three plates and Cork from four plates: the additional plates have the

99 90(i): Ulster by Sir William Petty, 1685. *By courtesy of Richard Nicholson of Chester*

county name engraved at the edge of the plate in issues from c.1732. The additional engraved county names appear to have been engraved during the course of the 1732 issue probably in preparation for the printing of each plate on a separate sheet. *State:* First. *Publisher:* Sir William Petty(?).

N.B. Individual impressions of the maps and copies of the atlas were produced in succeeding years. (ii) 1690(?): as (i) 1685, except: *Maps:* New general and provincial maps with the imprint of William Berry were substituted in some copies. *State:* First. (iii) 1732(?): as (ii) 1690(?), except: *State:* First (except: Donegal has been re-engraved). A cruder general map of Ireland is substituted in this issue only. *Publisher:* George Grierson. (iv) 1850–75(?): as (iii) 1732(?), except: *State:* First (except: Donegal). *Publisher:* the fourth Marquess of Landsowne (probably printed privately).

PIGOT, James
fl. 1825–1846. Topographer and engraver

Pigot & Son produced a very finely engraved series of oblong county maps (91) for their various National Commercial Directories, and these were issued collectively as *Pigot & Co's British Atlas* in 1831. These maps are detailed and attractive, showing the country at the height of the canal age, and each is decorated with a fine vignette of the principal cathedral or church in the county. The maps are usually found with brilliant original outline colouring. From c.1843–44, they were published by Isaac Slater and since early impressions tend to have very dark vignettes, these later issues produce a clearer, more attractive vignette due to the wearing of the plate. Less well known are the smaller maps (92) issued in *A Pocket Topography*: 'The Maps are engraved from the very latest and best surveys, & exhibit, distinctly & faithfully, every Town, Travelled Road, Canal & Railway Line, that is laid down upon more costly and larger maps.' The format of the *Pocket Topography* placed the maps opposite a distance table and a view of a church or cathedral and consequently it is common to find the maps with the impression of the vignette offset from the opposite page.

(91) Description: *st*: Second (*v*). (Fig. 100). **Supply:** Moderate. **Average size:** 220 × 360 mm (8.6 × 14 in.). **Features:** A numbered reference key to administrative divisions with a curved title/sometimes with *sd*/: e.g. 'REFERENCE to the HUNDREDS', and the note: 'The Larger Figures

100 91(ii): 'Leicestershire & Rutlandshire' by Pigot & Co., c.1830. *By permission of the British Library (Maps 3.d.40.)*

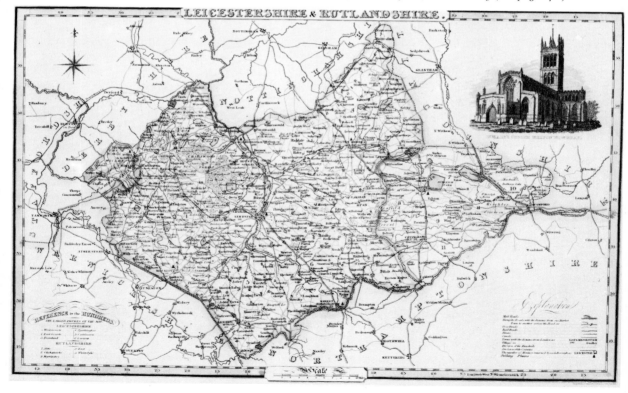

on the Map'. **Scale:** $V/av: 1:5m/$ 'Scale'/*os*/*sd*/*sbm*/set within a plain panel incorporated into the border below the map. **Border:** $OB:tTt/IB:ll/$incorporates plain panels containing the scale below the map and the title above the map/*bb*. **North Point:** *s*/*op*. **Key:** 'Explanation'/*os*. **Decoration:** Titled vignette view of a cathedral or church. **Title:** *c*/*oc*/set within a plain panel incorporated into the border above the map.

Issues: The maps were issued regularly over a period of about 30 years and most issues were revised and up-dated, particularly in respect of transport developments. The maps were also issued as an 'appendage' to the volumes 'of their National and Commercial Directories' and as folding maps. Larger folding maps of the nations were also published separately and in the commercial directories. (i) c.1826: *State:* First (*v*): Some examples of an early state without the distances from London engraved and without the inscription 'Longitude West from Greenwich' (or just 'Longitude West') within the lower border are known. Another early state of c.1826 has the distances from London engraved and from c.1826–1829, examples are known with the 'longitude' inscription also added. All the above states bear the imprints: (i) *obbc:pi*: 'Published by Pigot & Co 24 Basing Lane London & Fountain St. Manchester' (*V*) or '... & 18 Fountain ...'. (ii) *obbr:es*: 'Engraved on Steel by Pigot & Son Manchester,' (*V*). (ii) 1828–30 (?): as (i) c.1826, except: *Atlas: Pigot & Co.'s British atlas. of the counties of England ... the whole engraved on steel plates, and embellished with a correct graphic series of vignettes of the cathedrals and some of the handsomest churches in England ....* **States:** First (*v*) and second (*v*). This three-part edition appears to be the first edition of the complete set of county maps. The maps in Parts 1 and 2 were published from 24, Basing Lane, London, and 18, Fountain Street, Manchester; and most of the maps in Part 3 are imprinted with the address 17, Basing Lane, etc. The maps were again issued c.1830 with some maps revised during the course of the issue. (iii) 1831: as (ii) 1828–30 (?): except: *States:* First (*v*) and second (*v*). (iv) 1832: as (iii) 1831, except: *Atlas: Pigot & Co.'s British atlas, ...* **Maps (41):** (a) England and Wales with part of Scotland (Imprint: 'Pigot & Co., London & Fountain St., Manchester 1830'). (b) 38 English county maps (Leicestershire with 'Rutlandshire'). (c) Yorkshire. (d) 'Pigot's new map of the environs of London' (*pi*: dated 1832). **States:**

Various. Additions and revisions to map detail. *Imprints:* (i) *obbr:es*: 'Engraved on Steel by Pigot & Son Manchester' (*V*). (ii) *obbc:pi*: 'Published by Pigot & Co .....' at: either: '24 Basing Lane & Fountain St Manchester' or '... 18 Fountain ...'. (16 maps) or: '17 Basing Lane & 18 Fountain St Manchester' (17 maps) or: '1 Basing Lane London & Fountain St. Manchester' (7 maps), (*V*). *Publishers:* 'Pigot & Co'.

N.B. A further issue was made c.1833 with some maps revised to show the new parliamentary divisions and polling places, and some more imprints altered to 1, Basing Lane, etc.

(v) 1839 (?): as (iv) 1832, except: *Atlas: Pigot & Co.'s British atlas, comprising the counties of England ... with separate large sheet maps of England and Wales, Ireland, and Scotland .... Maps (43):* as above, plus: (a) Pigot and Co's New Map of Scotland (Imprint: 'Published by Pigot & Co., 59, Fleet Street London and Manchester, 1837'). (b) Pigot and Co's New Map of Ireland (Imprint: 'Published by Pigot & Co. Basing Lane, London & Fountain St., Manchester, 1834'). *States:* Various. Polling places are marked on more maps and the symbol for them is added to the key. *Imprints:* (ii) *obbc:pi* altered: 'Published by Pigot & Co. 59 Fleet Street, London, & Fountain St. Manchester' (*V*), or '... & 18 Fountain ...'. (iii) England and Wales: *pi*:date altered to 1838. (iv) Environs of London: *pi*:date altered to 1839. (vi) 1840 (?); 1841 (?); 1842 (?): as (v) 1839 (?), except: *States:* Various. More parliamentary information added. *Imprints:* (i) *obbr:es* altered c.1839–41: 'Engraved on Steel by Pigot & Co. Manchester'. (ii) some imprints are slightly altered. (iii) England and Wales; Scotland; Ireland: *pi*: date altered to 1840. (vii) 1843 (?): as (vi) 1840 (?), etc., except: *States:* Various. *Publishers:* J. Pigot & J. Slater.

N.B. A further issue was published c.1844 by Slater alone.

(viii) 1846 (?); 1847 (?); 1848 (?); 1857 (?): as (vii) 1843 (?), except: *Atlas: I. Slater's new British atlas, comprising the counties of England, (upon which are laid down all railways completed and in progress) ... Published by Isaac Slater (late Pigot & Slater) ....* **States:** Various. **Imprints:** (i) *obbr:es* altered: 'Engraved on Steel by I. Slater, Manch.' (*V*). (ii) *obbc:pi* altered: 'Published by I. Slater, Fleet Street, London, & Fountain St. Manchester' (*V*). (iii) 1846 (?); 1847 (?); 1848 (?): England and Wales: *pi*: dated 1846, 1847 and 1848 respectively. From 1857 (?): (iii) England and Wales; Scotland:*pi*:dates altered to 1854. (iv) Ireland:*pi*:date altered to 1853. (v)

Environs of London:*pi*:date erased. **Publisher:** 'Isaac Slater, Fleet Street, London; Fountain Street, and Portland Street, Manchester.' (ix) Some counties were later issued, sometimes lithographically, with alterations, in commercial directories by Isaac Slater from Portland Street, Manchester.

(92) Description: *st*: First. **Supply:** Scarce. **Average size:** 105 × 160 mm (4.25 × 6.4 in.). Yorkshire is a larger map measuring 300 × 350 mm (12 × 14 in.). **Features:** Many roads are continued to the map border. **Scale:** *V/av*:1:10*m*/'Scale of Miles'/*sbm*/set within a panel incorporated into the lower map border. **Border:** *OB:tTt/IB:ll*/a plain panel containing the scale is incorporated into the border below the map and another plain panel containing the title is set within the upper border/*bb*. **North Point:** *c/op/V*//Dorset and Somerset have *n*. **Key:** 'Explanation'. **Title:** *c/oc*/set within a plain panel incorporated into the border above the map. **Engravers:** Pigot & Slater.
Issues: The county maps were issued separately lithographically in individual county sections from c.1835, with the first 25 parts subsequently bound together. (i) 1841 (?); 1850 (?): by lithographic transfer: *Atlas: A pocket topography and gazetteer of England: with historical and statistical descriptions ... By Pigot & Co ... in two volumes ....* **Maps (40):** (a) England and Wales (large folding map without *es*). (b) 38 English county maps. (Leicestershire with 'Rutlandshire'). (c) Yorkshire. **State:** First (*v*). **Imprints:** (i) *obbr:es*: 'Pigot & Slater Engravers Manch!' (24 maps) or 'Pigot & Son, Engravers. Manch!' (12) or 'Pigot & C? Engravers. Manch!' (2), (*V*); Yorkshire has: 'Engraved on Steel by Pigot & C? Manchester'. Some signatures were altered, naming Slater alone, c.1850.' (ii) *obbc:pi*: 'PUBLISHED BY PIGOT & C? LONDON, AND MANCHESTER'. Yorkshire has 'Published by Pigot & C? 59 Fleet Street, London & Fountain St. Manchester' (altered to Slater's imprint c.1850).
N.B. Copies of some maps are known without *es* or *pi*.
Publishers: 'Pigot & Co. Fleet-Street; Longman & Co. and Sherwood & Co. Paternoster-Row, and Simpkin and Marshall, Stationer's-Court; and Pigot and Slater, Fountain-Street, Manchester'.

PINNOCK, William
fl. 1833. Editor and publisher

Pinnock edited the periodical *The Guide to Knowledge* which contained poor woodcut county maps

and town plans (93) mainly by Joshua Archer, but also by Sidney Hall. The maps are unusual in that they are printed in white on a black background. These were later issued by lithographic transfer in Thomas Johnson's railway atlas. D.N.B.: Vol. 15, pp. 1207–8.

(93) Description: *st*: First. (Fig. 101). **Supply:** Scarce. **Average size:** 160 × 224 mm (6.4 × 9 in.). **Features:** The features, etc., appear in white on a black background. **Scale:** *V/av*:1:5*m*/'English Miles'/*sbm*//Northamptonshire has *n*. **Border:** *OB:tTt/IB:ll/bb*. **North Point:** *n*//or: some maps have: *c/p*. **Decoration:** Most maps have the arms of the county town or a local nobleman. **Title:** *c/pc*/set within a slightly ornate panel. **Engravers:** Joshua Archer and Sidney Hall.

Issues: (i) 1833–6: relief printed: *Atlas: The guide to knowledge. Edited by W. Pinnock ....* **Maps and Plans (60):** (a) England; Scotland; Ireland; Wales. (b) 39 English counties. (c) Yorkshire. (d) Isle of Wight. (e) London in Roman Times; London in Elizabethan Times; London in 1833 (later: 'in 1837'); Environs of London. (f) Birmingham; Brighton; Dublin; Edinburgh; Glasgow; Leeds; Liverpool; Manchester; Norwich; Oxford; Sheffield. **State:** First. **Imprints:** (i) usually beneath the title panel, but also in various positions at the bottom of *mf*: most maps have: *pi*: usually of W. Edwards: e.g. 'London Published for the Proprietors by W. Edwards 12 Ave Maria Lane', but some have the imprint of James Gilbert: e.g. 'Pub^d by J. Gilbert, Regent Str!'. (ii) on *mf*, usually positioned at bottom right or left: most maps have: *es*: usually of J. Archer: e.g. 'J. Archer sc. 100 Drummond Str. Euston Sq.', but some have the signature of Sidney Hall: e.g. 'Eng^d by S. Hall, Bury Street, Bloomsbury'. Some maps have, printed from type: (iii) *ob*; top centre of page: 'GUIDE TO KNOWLEDGE'. (iv) *ob*; top left of page: 'No. ....' in roman numerals. (v) *ob*; top right of page: 'PRICE ONE PENNY'. **Publishers:** J. Gilbert & W. Edwards.
N.B. Later series of *The guide to knowledge* did not contain county maps.
(ii) 1847: by lithographic transfer: as (i) 1833–6, except: *Atlas: Johnson's atlas of England; with all the railways containing forty two separate maps of the counties and islands.* **Maps (41):** (a) 39 English counties. (b) Yorkshire (on two sheets). (c) Isle of Wight. **State:** Second. The features, etc., now appear in black on a white background. The area between the *IB* and *OB* now has a 'piano-key' style

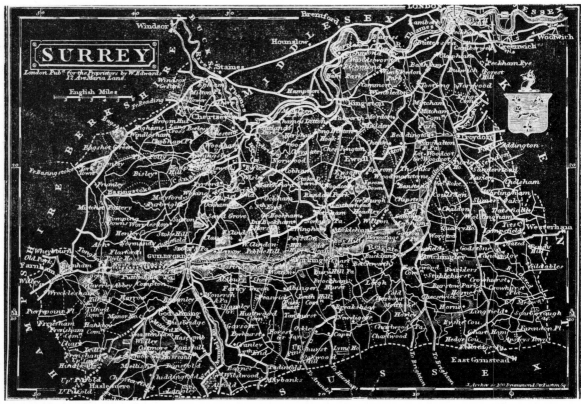

101 93(i): Surrey engraved by Joshua Archer, for William Pinnock's *The Guide to Knowledge*, 1833–6. *Photograph: Mills-Wight Studio*

pattern with the latitude and longitude figures set in small circles or panels. Some roads are extended to the map border. Stations are marked and the inscription: 'Railway stations marked thus ...' is added to most maps. Other minor revisions. **Imprints:** (i) below title panel: *pi* deleted. (ii) inside border, below right or left: *es* deleted (except: Dorset: 'J' Archer, Sc. 100 Drummond St., Euston Sq.'). **Publisher:** Thomas Johnson.

N.B. Some maps of this series, as above but printed directly from the wood block, also illustrated the *Descriptive county atlas of England and Wales* ... published in parts from 1844 by R. Groombridge, and Shepherd & Sutton. However, no complete copy is extant.

'RAMBLE, Reuben'.
fl. 1845. Topographer

The charming miniature maps (94) of 'Reuben Ramble' were lithographic reproductions of those published by Robert Miller, with the addition of small vignettes around the border, showing local rural scenes and places of interest and importance. The issue was designed for children and it is, therefore, unusual to find the maps in good condition, and particularly without some juvenile additions! The maps were initially issued in a series of booklets: 'Foolscap Quarto, secured in neat Wrappers, Each containing eight large coloured Plates with the letter press in a bold type. Price one shilling each.' The accompanying text is full of intriguing early nineteenth-century images: e.g. in Suffolk 'steam engines are sometimes used here for ploughing & other purposes'; Brighton 'is a large and fashionable place, where there is a very noble pier, constructed chiefly of iron bars and chains'; and Northampton 'is a pretty town'; while Cambridge 'is a disagreeable town'.

(94) Description: *st*: Third. **Supply:** Very scarce. **Average size:** Map alone: 70 × 105 mm

(2.4 × 3.8 in.). Overall: 145 × 185 mm (6.0 × 7.5 in.). **Scale:** *V*/*av*:1:12*m*/'Scale of Miles'/*sbm*. **Border:** *OB*:*tTt*/*IB*:*ll*/the map border is surrounded by a wide pictorial border of small vignettes of rural scenes and places of interest in the county/*bb*. **North Point:** *p*/or:*c* with *f*. **Key:** On most maps: 'Railways': represented by a finely dotted line, usually located just below the title. Westmorland, Dorset, Bedford, Shropshire, Huntingdon, Lincolnshire and Rutland have no railways marked. **Decoration:** Pictorial surround which frequently obscures the plate-number. **Title:** *c*/*pc*.

Issues: Pre-description states: without pictorial border or railways; the title is: *c*/*pc*/set within a narrow, vertically hatched panel with *dl* frame. (i) 1821 (?): **Atlas:** *Miller's. New miniature atlas containing a complete set of county maps, in which are carefully delineated all the principal direct & cross roads, cities, towns, villages, parks, seats, rivers, & navigable canals, with a general map of England & Wales ....* **Maps (56):** (a) England and Wales; Scotland; Ireland. (b) 39 English counties. (c) Yorkshire. (d) London, Westminster and Southwark. (e) 12 Welsh counties. **State:** First. **Imprints:** (i) *ob*: top right of page: page number. (ii) *obbc*:*pi*: 'London. Published by R. Miller, 24, Old Fish Street' (*V*). (Scotland has: 'London. Published by R. Miller, 24, Old Fish S! Doctors Commons'). **Publisher:** 'R. Miller, 24, Old Fish Street, St. Pauls'. (ii) 1822 (?); 1825 (?): as (i) 1821 (?), except: **State:** Second. (Fig. 102). **Atlas:** *Darton's new miniature atlas containing a complete set of county maps ....* **Imprint:** (ii) *obbc*: new *pi*: 'London: William Darton; 58, Holborn Hill' (*V*). **Publisher:** 'William Darton; 58, Holborn Hill'.

102 94(ii): Merioneth by Robert Miller, 1822.
Photograph: Mills-Wight Studio

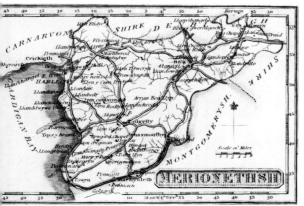

(iii) 1845 (?): by lithographic transfer: as (i) 1821 (?), except: As described: with the pictorial surround added; the title panel erased and the new, simpler titlepiece substituted in the same position; and the railways added to most maps: **Atlas:** Five booklets in the *Pictorial instruction for young children* series: 1. *Reuben Ramble's travels in the northern counties of England.* 2. *... eastern counties ....* 3. *... southern counties ....* 4. *... midland counties ....* 5. *... western counties ....* **Maps (40):** Each booklet contains eight maps. (a) 39 English counties. (b) Yorkshire. **State:** Third. (Fig. 103). **Imprint:** (ii) *obbc*:*pi* deleted. **Publishers:** 'Darton and Clark, 58 Holborn Hill, Print and Map publishers'. (iv) 1845 (?): by lithographic transfer: as (iii) 1845 (?), except: **Atlas:** *Reuben Ramble's travels through the counties of England. With maps and historical vignettes.* **Maps (41):** general map of England and Wales added. **State:** Third. The atlas was re-issued c.1850 by Darton & Co.

ROCQUE, John
fl. 1734–1762d. Engraver, surveyor and publisher

Rocque was a Huguenot who left his native France to settle in London about 1734, probably as a result of the loss of religious freedom following the revocation of the Edict of Nantes in 1685. For the next 28 years he was a prolific producer of maps and plans, and an important influence on cartographic development in the British Isles through his introduction of Continental techniques and conventions. His careful differentiation and representation of land use on his large-scale maps originated in European techniques and was developed during his years as a 'dessinateur de jardins'. Until about 1750, Rocque surveyed the estates of the nobility and the wealthy and prepared plans and views of the parks and gardens being landscaped by Lancelot 'Capability' Brown and other fashionable garden architects. From this background developed a careful and effective designation of land use into arable, pasture, marsh, rough grazing, heath, orchard, garden, and so on. This approach was used to great effect on the large-scale plans which Rocque prepared from 1737 when he started work on his magnificent survey of London, engraved on 24 sheets (measuring 6.5 × 12.75 feet) by Pine and published in 1746. He also produced other large-scale town plans and accurate and original large-scale county maps of Shropshire (1752), Middlesex (1754), Berkshire (1761) and Surrey (published in

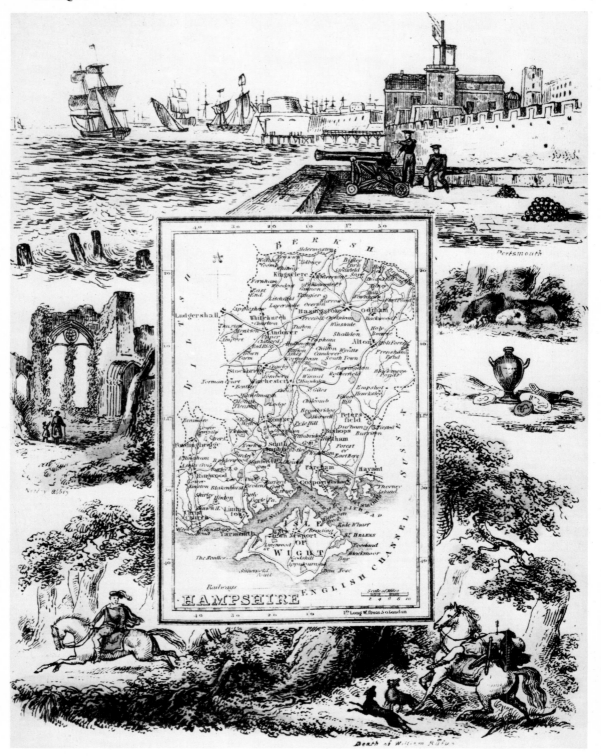

103 94(iii): Hampshire by 'Reuben Ramble', c.1845. *By permission of the British Library (1302.g.2.)*

1765, after his death, by his widow Mary Anne who continued his business) incorporating much detail previously found only on manuscript plans of estates. However, Rocque's application to the Royal Society of Arts for an award for his map of Berkshire was rejected because the survey had been started ten years before the date of publication, and Richard Gough rated him only fourth among the contemporary large-scale county cartographers.

From 1754 to 1760 Rocque worked in Dublin producing a very detailed large-scale plan of that city in 1756, plans of other towns, and large-scale county maps of Dublin (1760) and Armagh (1760), based largely on Petty's surveys.

Unfortunately the maps by Rocque that are generally available do not live up to the high standards of his large-scale work. A miniature atlas of town plans (41) was engraved by Andrew Dury partly from Rocque's survey material and *The English Traveller* of 1746 contained a carelessly executed set of small, plain county maps (95).

Select Bibliography

HOOPER, W.: 'Rocque's Map of Surrey'. (*Surrey Archaeological Collection*, 40; 1932)

(*F*) LAXTON, P.: Intoductory notes to *A topographical survey of the county of Berks, by John Rocque 1761.* (1973)

PHILLIPS, H.: 'John Rocque's career'. (*London Topographical Record*, 20; 1952)

VARLEY, J.: 'John Rocque. Engraver, Surveyor, Cartographer and Map-Seller'. (*IM*, 5; 1948)

(95) Description: *st*: First. (Fig. 104). **Supply:**

104 95(i): 'Hereford Shire' by John Rocque, 1746. *Photograph: Mills-Wight Studio*

Moderate. **Average size:** 155 × 200 mm (6.25 × 8.0 in.). **Features:** County boundary marked by a dotted line with heavy hatching on the outer-side. The similarity to the shading along the coastline gives each county the appearance of being surrounded by water. **Scale:** *V*/*av*:1:8m/'English Miles'; 'Measured Miles'; 'English Miles Measured'; etc./*sbm*. **Border:** *sl*. **North Point:** *r*/*f*. **Decoration:** Titled vignette views on Devon, Kent, Oxfordshire, and West Riding. Heraldic arms on Hereford and Isle of Man. **Title:** *c*/*pc*/*obac*.

Issues: (i) 1746: *Atlas: The English traveller: giving a description of those parts of Great-Britain called England and Wales. Containing ... a map of every county, from the best and latest observations ... after the designs of Herman Moll .... Maps (54):* (a) Two general maps of England and Wales. (b) 39 English counties. (c) East; North; West Ridings. (d) Islands of Guernsey and Jersey; Isle of Wight; Isle of Man. (e) Seven Welsh county maps (Pembroke, Radnor, and five maps combining pairs of counties). *State:* First. *Publisher:* Thomas Read, 'in Dogwell-Court, White-Fryars, Fleet-street'. (ii) 1746 (?): as (i) 1746, except: *State:* Second. Minor changes to some scales. *Imprint: obar*:plate-number added. (iii) 1753: two issues: as (ii) 1746 (?), except: *Atlas: The small British atlas: being a new set of maps of all the counties of England and Wales ... Published according to Act of Parliament 1753 .... State:* Third. Minor revisions. *Imprint: obar*: plate-number erased. (however, traces sometimes remain). *Publishers:* (i) John Rocque, (ii) 'John Rocque, Chorographer. to his Royal Highness the Prince of Wales, near Old Round Court in the Strand, and Robert Sayer, Map and Printseller, at the Golden Buck, opposite Fetter-Lane, Fleet-Street'. (iv) 1762: as (iii) 1753, except: *State:* Fourth. *Imprint: obar*: plate-number added. *Publisher:* John Rocque. (v) 1764: as (iv) 1762, except: *States:* Fourth or fifth. *Imprint: obar*: some plate-numbers altered. (vi) 1769: as (v) 1764, except: *Atlas: England displayed. Being a new, complete, and accurate survey and description of the kingdom of England, and principality of Wales ... By a society of gentlemen: each of whom has undertaken that part for which his study and inclination has more immediately qualified him. The particulars respecting England, revised, corrected, and improved, by P. Russell, Esq; and those relating to Wales, by Mr. Owen Price ....* (a) Issued in weekly parts from April 1769 and (b) as a complete work in two volumes in 1771. *Maps (53):* (a) Great Britain. (b) 39 English county maps: 30 from *The small British atlas* by John Rocque; Bedford, Berkshire and Buckinghamshire by G. Rollos; and Cheshire, Cornwall, Devon, Dorset, Oxford, Somerset and Wiltshire from the *London magazine* by Thomas Kitchin. (c) Yorkshire by Thomas Kitchin from the *London magazine*. (d) Nine maps of Welsh counties: Denbigh with 'Flintshire'; 'Merioneth Shire' with 'Montgomery Shire'; 'Radnor Shire'; 'Pembroke Shire'; 'Carmarthen Shire' with 'Glamorgan Shire': from *The small British atlas* by John Rocque; Anglesey, and 'Brecknock Shire' by G. Rollos; and Cardiganshire, and 'Carnarvanshire' by Thomas Kitchin from the *London magazine*. (e) Isle of Wight; Isle of Man; by John Rocque. (f) Country 20 miles round London by Thomas Bowen. ***States:*** Various. The maps are printed in the middle of large pages with very wide blank margins. ***Imprint:*** *obar*: plate-number erased. ***Publishers:*** (a) S. Bladon, T. Evans, J. Coote, W. Domville and F. Blythe. (b) J. Cooke.

ROLLOS, G.

fl. 1766–1779. Engraver, geographer, map- and print-seller

Rollos's main business was selling prints and paintings from his shop in Long Acre, London, but he also engraved maps. His most commonly-found maps are the five attractive, rococo style, county maps (95 (vi)) which he contributed to Russell & Price's *England Displayed* of 1769. (Fig. 105).

Supply: (95, vi): Scarce. 1769: *England displayed* ...: see (95) (vi).

SCALÉ, Bernard

fl. 1760–1787. Surveyor and geographer

Scalé's main work was in estate surveying but he is renowned for producing the fine *Hibernian Atlas*, one of the few Irish atlases of the eighteenth century. 'In an Age of Dissipation and Pleasure, when the Instructive Faculties are loosened by Inattention, and the Minds of the People, in a great Measure, too much attached to trifling Novelties, nothing but a Work of extraordinary Merit can reclaim the Attention of the Publick to a Subject of real Utility, wherein Novelty is blended with Instruction; which, at the same Time, amuses the Imagination and gratifies the judgement'. These attractive maps (96) are particularly notable for their complex, artistic north points which combine a fascinating variety of themes. Scalé also produced some plans of

105 95(vi): Bedfordshire by G. Rollos, 1769.
Photograph: Mills-Wight Studio

Irish towns and harbours, notably of Dublin and Waterford.

(96) Description: *st*: First. (Fig. 106). **Supply:** Scarce. **Average size:** 140 × 189 mm (5.6 × 7.5 in.). **Features:** Surrounding counties named: 'COUNTY OF ....'; boundary lines between surrounding counties are marked by a characteristic small cluster of dots and angled lines; no detail is shown beyond the county boundary. **Scale:** *V*/ provinces: *av*:1:21*m*; counties: *av*:1:6*m*/'A Scale of Miles'/*sbm*. Border: *dl*/Leinster has the vertical borders graduated into latitude, and the general map is graduated into both latitude and longitude. **North Point:** Very large and decorative/*f*/pointers mark the other cardinal points/at the centre are elaborate

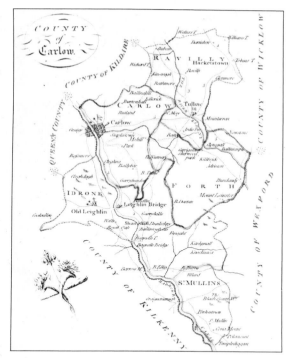

106 96(i): 'County of Carlow' by Bernard Scalé, 1776.
By permission of the British Library (Maps C.24.d.10.)

designs of: agricultural implements, bundles of corn, farm carts, beehives, woolcombs and sacks, spinning wheels, barrels, urns, flowers, foliage, flying birds, masks, hats, cherubs, antiquities, flags, etc./*V.* Title: 'COUNTY of . . . .'/*V*/*vl*/*sd*. **Engravers**: '. . . beautifully engraved . . . by Messʳˢ Ellis and Palmer'.

Issues: (i) 1775(?); 1776: *Atlas: An Hibernian atlas; or general description of the kingdom of Ireland: divided into provinces; with its sub-divisions of counties, baronies, etc. Shewing their boundaries, extent, soil, produce, contents, measure, members of Parliament, and number of inhabitants; also the cities, boroughs, villages, mountains, bogs, lakes, rivers and natural curiosities together with the great and bye post roads. The whole taken from actual surveys and observations . . . .* **Maps (37)**: (a) Ireland. (b) Four Irish provinces. (c) 32 Irish counties. **State: First. Imprints**: (i) *obbc:pi*: 'Published as the Act directs, by Robᵗ Sayer & John Bennett, 1. Feb. 1776'. (ii) *obac*: map number in brackets. **Publishers**: 'Robert Sayer, and John Bennet, Map and Printsellers, Noº 53 in Fleet Street'. (ii) 1788: as (i) 1775(?); 1776, except: **State**: First (except: County of Longford:

second) *Imprint:* (i) as before, except: 'County of Longford' has a new *pi*: 'Published as the Act directs by Robᵗ Sayer, 53, Fleet Street'. **Publisher**: Robert Sayer. (iii) 1798: as (ii) 1788, except: **State**: Second. *Imprint:* (i) *obbc:pi* altered: 'Published as the Act directs, by Robᵗ Sayer, 53, Fleet Street' (except: Provinces of Leinster and Munster: 'Published 12ᵗʰ May 1798 by LAURIE & WHITTLE, 53, Fleet Street, London'). **Publishers**: 'Robtᵗ Laurie & Jas. Whittle, Noº 53, Fleet Street, London. Successors to the late Mr. Robᵗ Sayer'. (iv) 1809: as (iii) 1798, except: **State**: Third (except: Leinster and Munster: second). *Imprint:* (i) *obbc*: all imprints are now: 'Published 12ᵗʰ May 1798 by LAURIE & WHITTLE, 63, Fleet Street, London'.
N.B. The maps were possibly again issued in 1824 by Laurie & Whittle.

SEALE, Richard William
fl. 1732–1775. Engraver and cartographer

Seale engraved maps (52) in the decorative rococo style of Bowen and Kitchin for the *Universal Magazine*, sea and river charts, town and harbour plans, and the map of Middlesex in the *Large English Atlas*. He also engraved a set of nine maps of southern England (Cornwall, Devon, Dorset, Hampshire, Isle of Wight, Somerset, Surrey, Sussex, Wiltshire) which were published by Overton & Hoole. Presumably, it was intended to produce maps of all the counties, but only these nine were published. These very rare maps are crude copies of Moll's maps with the coats-of-arms of the main cities replacing his antiquities. The larger counties (Devon, Dorset and Sussex) were printed on separate sheets pasted together. The maps were re-issued by Sayer & Bennett c.1775. Seale also engraved ward plans for Stow's London *Survey*.

SELLER, John
fl. 1660–1697. Hydrographer, cartographer, instrument-maker, and map-seller

Seller's principal interest was the compilation and publication of maritime works and his best known work is probably the unoriginal *English Pilot*, the first volume of which was published in 1671. He was appointed 'Hydrographer' to Charles II (and later to James II and William III) and although granted a 30-year monopoly of the material in his 'maps, plans and charts', had to abandon his projected sea atlas. His efforts to produce the folio county atlas *Atlas Anglicanus* also had to be abandoned. Buckingham,

Hertford, Kent, Middlesex, Oxford and Surrey were surveyed between 1676 and 1690, but only these six maps were published and the plates had been sold to Philip Lea by 1693.

Fortunately, Seller also published an attractive, small series of county maps (97) in his *Anglia Contracta* in about 1694. These charming, crudely engraved maps were essentially reductions of Speed's maps, decorated with small title and scale cartouches. They were often carelessly executed with places wrongly sited and names mis-spelt. The maps were re-printed in the editions of *The History of England* and in *Camden's Britannia Abridg'd* which was produced because the full version of the *Britannia* was 'a very large Volume, and, upon account of its Maps and other Sculptures, unavoidably high in its price'. Over 80 years later, the plates were used for Francis Grose's *The Antiquities of England and Wales* with altered titles and some reworking. The maps appeared with text describing the county below the map and on the reverse of the page and are most commonly found in this format.

Seller published many other cartographical works and is particularly noted for being the first cartographer to show longitude measured from the prime meridian of London (from 1676). D.N.B.: John Seller: Vol. 17, pp. 1165–66. Francis Grose: Vol. 13, pp. 715–6.

Select Bibliography
VERNOR, C.: 'John Seller and the chart trade in seventeenth century England', in Thrower, N. J. W. (ed): *The Complete Plattmaker . . .* (1978)

(97) Description: *st*: First. (Fig. 107). **Supply:** Moderate. **Average size:** *V*/120 × 155 mm (4.8 × 6.2 in.). **Features:** Nine maps have a lettered reference key to administrative divisions, sometimes set within a panel with a plain-ruled frame or isolated by a dashed line. **Scale:** Most maps have a scale/*V*/*av*:1:10*m*/'English Miles'; 'Miles'; 'A Scale of Miles'/*slm* or *sbm* sometimes set within a panel with a plain-ruled frame. **Border:** *OB*:*sl* or graduated line/*IB*:vary:*sl*; *dl*; sometimes graduated into miles with inscriptions either inside, within, or outside the border giving details of the mileage graduations, e.g. 'Note that the side of each Square is three miles.' 12 county maps and the islands (except Man) have a graticule based on mileage divisions (four measuring mileages from London). Most county maps have the cardinal points noted within the borderlines. General maps have graduations of

107 97(vi): 'Brecknock Shire' by John Seller, c.1780.
Photograph: Mills-Wight Studio

ll, sometimes with a graticule/*bb*. **North Point:** Some maps have: *q* or *r*/*f*/*e*// most have *ce*//Isle of Man has *n*/*V*. **Title:** Most maps have: *c*/*pc*/some signed: 'By John Seller'/*V*/set within a decorative cartouche, decorated panel or plain panel.

Issues:
N.B. The number of general maps in copies of each atlas can vary.
(i) 1694 (?): *Atlas: Anglia contracta. or a description of the kingdom of England & principality of Wales. in several new mapps of all the countyes therein contained by John Seller hydrographer to the king . . . . Maps (67):* (a) Great Britain and Ireland; two general maps of England; Wales; five other general and historical maps. (b) 39 English counties. (c) Yorkshire. (d) 'Island of Man'; 'Island of Wight'; 'Island of Garnsey'; 'Island of Jarsey'; 'Holy-Iland'; 'Island of Farne'. (e) 12 Welsh counties. *State:* First. (ii) 1696: originally issued in sheets at 'a Penny a sheet': as (i) 1694 (?), except: *Atlas: The history of England . . . with exact maps of each county, by John Seller . . . Maps (44):* (a) England and Wales; Wales; two general and historical maps. (b) 39 English counties. (c) Yorkshire. *State:* First. *Publisher:* 'John Gwillim against Crosby-Square, in Bishopsgate-street'. (iii) 1697: as (ii) 1696, except: *Atlas: The history of England . . . together with a particular description of the rarities in the several counties of England and Wales. By John Seller . . . State:* First. *Publisher:* 'H. Newman, at the Grass-hopper in the Poultrey'. (iv) 1701: as (iii) 1697, except: *Atlas: Camden's Britannia abridg'd; with improvements, and continuations, to this present*

time . . . The whole carefully perform'd, and illustrated with above sixty maps exactly engraven . . . . **Maps (60):** (a) England and Wales; Wales; Scotland; Ireland; 'Insulae Albion et Hibernia . . .'. (b) 39 English counties. (c) Yorkshire. (d) 'Island of Man'; 'Island of Wight'; 'Island of Garnsey'. (e) 12 Welsh counties. **State:** First. **Publisher:** 'Joseph Wild, at the Elephant at Charing-Cross'. (v) 1703: as (i) 1694 (?), except: **Atlas:** *The history of England . . . With the maps of all the counties and islands belonging to England . . . By John Seller . . . .* **Maps (68):** (a) A map of Ireland is added. Minor retouching of some plates. **State:** First. **Publisher:** 'J. Marshall, at the Bible in Grace-Church-street'. (vi) 1783–1787: as (v) 1703, except: **Atlas:** *The antiquities of England and Wales by Francis Grose Esq. F.A.S. . . . . (V).* **Maps (56):** (a) 39 English counties. (b) Yorkshire. (c) Islands of: Guernsey; Jersey; Man; Wight. (d) 12 Welsh counties. **State:** Second. Some minor revisions and alterations, notably to some scales. The title has been re-engraved and now usually appears in a simpler, plain panel with a narrow *dl* frame. Titles no longer refer to John Seller. Informative notes concerning each county are printed below the map and verso, and the map and text together measure approximately 120 × 225 mm (4.8 × 9 in.). **Publishers:** 'S. Hooper, № 25 Ludgate-Hill' or 'No. 212, High Holborn', or Hooper & Wigstead.

SENEX, John

fl. 1702–1740d. Cartographer, engraver, globe-maker, publisher and bookseller

Senex produced a number of cartographical works, but is best known for his set of plain strip road maps (98) which were one of the first reduced copies of Ogilby's maps of 1675. *An Actual Survey of all the Principal Roads of England and Wales* contained 'the addition of some roads newly drawn, which were omitted by Mr. Ogilby, and several necessary Corrections made in others: Together with a great number of explanatory references, by which this Edition of the Roads is rendered of more general Use for Travellers.' The history of Senex's map plates illustrates the complex dealings of the map trade and the difficulties of tracing issues. The plates were first published by Senex in 1719 and were re-issued by his widow, after his death, in 1742. They were then re-engraved and published by Bowles between 1757 and 1762 under two different atlas titles and with one issue in French in 1759. In 1767 the maps were copied in French and issued by Monsieur Desnos;

and the plates were then reworked into English for the two issues of 1775, one entitled *Jefferys's Itinerary*. To complicate the picture, Thomas Kitchin also copied the Senex plates and issued his copies under the title *Kitchin's Post-Chaise Companion* in 1767 and c.1770. D.N.B.: Vol. 17, p. 1182.

(98) Description: *st*: First (Senex). (Fig. 108). **Supply:** Moderate. **Average size:** 159 × 214 mm (6.3 × 8.5 in.). **Features:** 'the plan of each Road is laid down in such a distinct manner, that the Traveller before he begins his stage, may have the satisfaction of seeing in what places his journey leads over a plain; where he is to pass over hills; what rivers he must cross; how far his rout is through one county, and where he enters into another'; computed miles and direct horizontal distances noted at the end of each road 'by which the curious will see how many miles the Road winds in travelling to that place, and how much nearer it lies upon a straight line, without the ups and downs of hills in the way'; 'a great number of useful references are now engrav'd, by which the Traveller is directed to the pages, where the Roads either branch from, or intersect each other. These references will assist him in forming circuits round the Country, and are so necessary in a work of this kind, that it is astonishing the first edition of Mr Ogilby, and all the subsequent ones till now, should have appeared without them'. **Border:** The maps consist of six strips, usually approximately 33 mm (1.3 in.) wide, engraved as an imitation scroll/*bts/bltr*. **North Point:** *c/op/e/*since orientation varies, each strip has a north point. **Decoration:** Some ships decorate issues from 1757. **Title:** 'The ROAD from . . . to . . . .'/*pc* and *ps*/ beneath is a double column distance table/set within a panel with a *tTt* frame, positioned at top centre of the imitation scroll/only the first plate of a route has a titlepiece. **Engraver:** A few maps bear the *es* of John Senex, e.g. 'I. Senex Sculp!' These signatures were omitted from the later copies by Desnos and Kitchin.

Issues: (i) 1719: **Atlas:** *An actual survey of all the principal roads of England and Wales; described by one hundred maps from copper plates. On which are delineated all the cities, towns, villages, churches, houses, and places of note throughout each road. As also directions to the curious traveller what is worth observing throughout his journey: the whole described in the most easy and intelligible manner. First perform'd and publish'd by John Ogilby, Esq; and now*

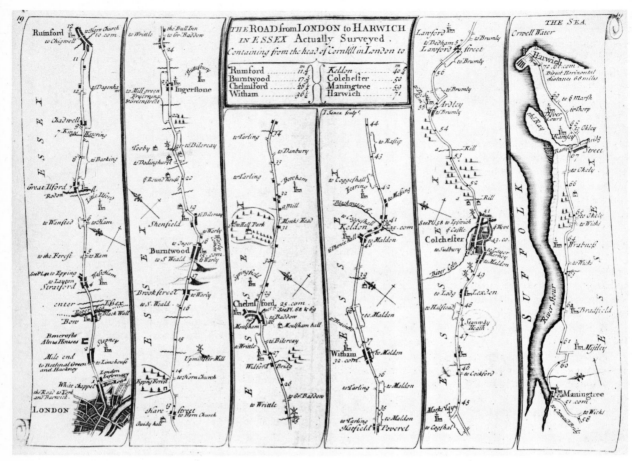

108 98(iii): The road from London to Harwich by John Senex, 1757. *Photograph: Mills-Wight Studio*

improved, very much corrected, and made portable by John Senex .... **Maps:** 100 strip road maps of England and Wales with plain backs: (a) 58 routes on single plates. (b) Eight on two. (c) Three on three. (d) Three on four. (e) 'London to Barwick' on five. **State:** First (Senex). **Imprint:** outside scroll, bottom right: plate-number. **Publisher:** 'J. Senex at the Globe in Salisbury-Court, Fleetstreet'. (ii) 1742: (two issues): as (i) 1719, except: **State:** First (Senex). **Publisher:** 'M. Senex, at the Globe ag^st St. Dunstans Church Fleetstreet'.

N.B. John Senex died on 30 December 1740, but his widow continued his business.

(iii) 1757; 1757 (with original title); 1759 (with original title); 1759 (issued in French); 1762; 1762 (with original title): **Atlas:** *The roads through England delineated or, Ogilby's survey, revised, improved, and reduced to a size portable for the pocket.*

By John Senex F.R.S. Being an actual survey of all the principal roads of England and Wales .... **Maps:** the plates have been re-engraved fractionally smaller: 155×204 mm (6.15×8.2 in.); and are now printed back-to-back. (a) Index map. (b) 101 strip maps: a new map (plate 42) is added showing, in seven strips, the roads from London to Epping, Northampton and Nottingham. Many maps have notes giving references to plates with connecting or cross routes added below the scroll or inserted in previously blank strip sections. Some decoration and notes are added to *mf.* **State:** Second (Senex). **Imprints:** (i) outside scroll, bottom right: plate-number erased. (ii) outside scroll, above right and left: plate-number added. **Publisher:** 'John Bowles and Son at the Black Horse in Cornhill London'. (iv) 1767: as (iii) 1757, etc., except: **Atlas:** *Kitchin's post-chaise companion, through England and Wales;*

*containing all the ancient and new additional roads, with every topographical detail relating thereto. By Thomas Kitchin .... **Maps:** A pirated edition at the smaller size: 157 × 206 mm (6.25 × 8.25 in.) with some additions and revisions of notes and detail, in a generally cruder style of engraving. Most maps are still divided into six strips despite changes of format. (a) the index map is replaced by a new map extending to Edinburgh in the north. (b) 103 strip maps: five new road maps are added, including 'The Road from London to Edinburgh' but 'London to St. Neots' is omitted and the routes from London to Holyhead and London to Lands End are each reduced from four to three sheets. **State:** First (Kitchin). **Imprint:** in most cases the plate-numbers are altered. **Publishers:** 'John Bowles ... in Cornhill; Carington Bowles at No. 69 in St. Paul's Church-Yard; and Robert Sayer, at No. 53 in Fleet-street'.

N.B. c. 1770: a reprint of the above was published by Carington Bowles alone.

(v) 1767: as (iii) 1757, etc., except: **Atlas:** *Nouvel atlas d'Angleterre ... The roads through England or Ogilby's survey revised, improved and reduced by Senex distinctly laid down ... with the addition of some roads newly drawn, and general corrections of more general use to travellers ... For Desnos, geographer, at the Globe St. James Street.* **Maps:** The plates from (iii) 1757, etc. were copied in a cruder style and substantially revised. (a) Index map. (b) 101 strip maps: as (iii) 1757, with titles, route directions, notes and map detail in French and the maps printed with plain backs. The titles now have only the towns named in script lettering without the distance tables. The strips no longer appear on the imitation scroll but are set in plain rectangular frames separated by single plain-ruled lines. A plate-number now appears above the border at either the top left or the top right corner. **State:** First (Desnos). **Publisher:** 'Desnos ... at the Globe St. James Street'.

The above plates were acquired and re-engraved into English by Thomas Jefferys and issued in 1775 by Robert Sayer & John Bennett as Jeffery's Itinerary (56). Sayer & Bennett also issued the maps, without change, in the same year as *The roads of England delineated*, and, at about the same time, re-issued *Kitchin's Post-chaise companion!*.

SIMONS, Mathew
fl. 1635–1654d. Cartographer and publisher

Jacob van Langeren engraved a set of triangular distance tables which were published by Mathew Simons in 1635. The distance tables were reduced copies of those by John Norden, published in *England, an Intended Guyde, for English Travailers* in 1625. The bottom right-hand corner of each plate contained a tiny, skeleton county map (99), known as a 'thumb-nail' map due to its small scale. These rare maps were first published in *A Direction for the English Traviller* which was the earliest English road book to contain maps. The plates were then acquired by Thomas Jenner.

Select Bibliography
KEUNING, J.: 'The Van Langren Family'. (*IM*, 13; 1956)

(99) Description: *st*: First. (Fig. 109). **Supply:** Rare. **Average size:** 100 × 100 mm (4 × 4 in.). The maps on average occupy an area of 37 × 37 mm (1.5 × 1.5 in.). **Features:** Major towns are marked by initial letters. **Scale:** *U*/approximately: 1:40*m*/*sbm*/usually surmounted by dividers. **Border:** *sl*/the top left, upper diagonal half of the plate contains a distance table for the major towns of the county. **North Point:** The cardinal points are marked by their initial letters and eight lines radiate from the county border to the main compass points. **Titles:** *c*/*ps*/*V*/set in the square in the top-left corner formed by the distance table: e.g. 'Shropshire Wth some confining Town^s.' **Engraver:** Jacob van Langeren.

Issues: (i) 1635: **Atlas:** *A direction for the English traviller by which he shal be inabled to coast about all England and Wales. And also to know how farre any market or noteable towne in any shire lyeth one from other, and whether the same be east, west, north, or south from ye shire towne as also the distance betweene London and any other shire or great towne: with the scituation thereof east, west, north, or south from London. By the help also of this worke one may know (in what parish, village, or mansion house soeuer he be in) what shires, he is to passe thorough & which way he is to trauell, till he come to his journies end ....* **Maps (38):** (a) England and Wales (circular frontispiece). (b) 37 English county maps. (Leicester with Rutland; no Monmouth). **State:** First. **Imprint:** *mfbc*: plate-number. **Publisher:** 'Mathew Simons at the golden Lion in Ducke laine'. (This appears to replace the imprint of an earlier unknown publisher). (ii) 1636: as (i) 1635, except: **State:** First. **Maps (40):** (a) a folding map of England and Wales with distance table but without plate-number is added: 215 × 240 mm

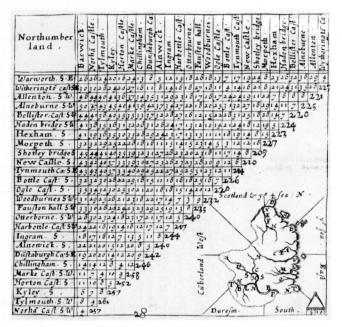

109 99(i): Northumberland by Mathew Simons, 1635.
Photograph: Mills-Wight Studio

(8.6 × 9.6 in.). (b) a folding map of Yorkshire with distance table but without plate-number is added: 198 × 200 mm (7.9 × 8 in.). (iii) 1636: as (ii) 1636, except: *State:* Second (except: Essex and Middlesex). The mileage of each town from London is given by an extra line of distance figures engraved along the distance table diagonal (except: Essex and Middlesex). (iv) 1643: the plates passed into the hands of Thomas Jenner who erased the maps and engraved entirely new ones: *Features:* The sea is sometimes shaded as watered silk; towns are fully named. *Scale: U*/approximately: 1:20m/*sbm* usually surmounted by dividers. *Border: sl*/since the maps are now double size, the map detail frequently breaks through the border and also into the distance table. In some cases parts of the border and distance table are erased to accommodate the new map. *North Point:* Some maps retain some of the initial letters of the cardinal points. Since the maps are now larger, many have to be re-oriented to fit the available space/*V*/the maps are engraved to be read with north uppermost. *Engraver:* Thomas Jenner. *Atlas: A direction for the English traviller ....* **Maps (40):** (a) England (a new map). The circular frontispiece is omitted. (b) 37 English county maps. (c) Yorkshire. (d) Wales, with distance table but without plate-number: 218 × 237 mm

(8.75 × 9.5 in.). *State:* Mainly third. (Fig. 110). *Imprint:* The plate-number is erased on some plates to accommodate the new, larger maps, and is sometimes so faint on others that it is virtually illegible. *Publisher:* 'Thomas Jenner at the South entrance of the Exchange'.

N.B. Wales and the county maps (possibly excluding Yorkshire) were issued in this form by Jenner in 1644 (?) in *A booke of the names of all the hundreds contained in the shires of the kingdom of England together with the number of the towns parishes villages and places of every hundred: if you desire to know the names of places contained in any hundred look into the book of the shire mapps of England, and near or about the town which the hundred is named by lyeth the parishes, villages, & places that are in the hundred. Usefull for quartermasters, brief-gatherers, and all such as have to doe the shires of England ....*

(v) 1657; 1662: as (iv) 1643, except: *Atlas: A book of the names of all parishes, market towns, villages, hamlets, and smallest places, in England and Wales ... A work very necessary for traveilers, quartermasters, gatherers of breefs, strangers, carriers, and messengers with letters, and all others that know the name of the place, but can neither tell where it is, nor how to goe unto it ....* *State:* Mainly fourth (v). The maps are now printed at the top of the page with a three-column list of the hundreds type-printed below and on the reverse of the map. The county name and page number are type-printed: *obac* (except: England, Wales and Yorkshire have no type-printing. In the 1657 issue: Berkshire has no page number and its title is below the map, and Stafford and Wiltshire have the title and page number printed inside the border, top centre, across the list of towns in the distance table). Some mileage figures are corrected in the 1662 issue and some plates are progressively reworked during 1662. (vi) 1668: as 1662, except: *States:* Various. Some more plates are reworked. (a) Berkshire again has no page number and its title below the map. (b) Buckingham, Devon, Gloucester, Nottingham, Oxford, Stafford have misprinted titles. (Variant copies are recorded/ known with Nottingham spelt correctly and Lincoln mis-spelt). (c) Dorset has the type-printed title upside down. (d) Lancashire is entitled Kent. (e) several page numbers are incorrect. (vii) 1668: as (vi) 1668, except: *States:* Various. (c) and some (e) are corrected. The plates have now all been reworked, particularly the mileage tables which had been

110 99(iv): Shropshire by Thomas Jenner, 1643. *Photograph: Mills-Wight Studio*

showing considerable wear. (viii) 1668: as (vii) 1668, except: **Atlas**: *A direction for the English traviller* .... **States:** Various. The plates are reprinted without the type-printing, i.e. without type-printed titles, page numbers, etc. (ix) 1677(?); 1680(?): as (viii) 1668, except: **States:** Various. **Publisher:** 'John Garrett at the south Entrance of ye Royall Exchange in Corn-hill, where you may have a most exact Mapp of England with the small Townes described in six large Sheets, also other large Mapps of ye World or any other part thereof'. (x) 1677: as (vii) 1668, except: **States:** Various. **Publisher:**

'John Garret, at his Shop as you go up the Stairs of the Royal Exchange in Cornhill'.

SIMPSON, Samuel
fl. 1746. Geographer
Simpson produced a set of rare, small county maps (100), 'after the Designs of Herman Moll, and others', each decorated with one, sometimes two, coats-of-arms, in *The Agreeable Historian, or the Compleat English Traveller* of 1746. These are often confused with the maps (95) from *The English Traveller* by John Rocque.

DERBY SHIRE

111 100(i): Derbyshire by Samuel Simpson, 1746. *By permission of the British Library (1034.b.20.)*

(100) Description: *st*: First. (Fig. 111). **Supply:** Rare. **Average size:** *Vc*/150 × 200 mm (6 × 8 in.). **Features:** County boundary by a dotted line with heavy horizontal shading on the outer-side. **Scale:** *n*//or: *V*/*av*: 1:7*m*/'English Miles'/*sbm*. **Border:** *sl*/ *bb*. **North Point:** Most maps have a north point/*r* or *q*/*op*/*V*. **Decoration:** The maps (except Somerset) are decorated by heraldic arms, usually of the county town. Some also have a second coat-of-arms of the county's principal nobleman or another town. Buckingham has a vignette of Windsor Castle; Cumberland has an inset of the Isle of Man; Derbyshire has vignettes of 'The Devil's Arse' and 'Pooles Hole'; Devon has two vignettes of the 'Edystone light house'; Oxford has vignettes of Blenheim House and Blenheim Bridge. **Title:** *c*/*pc*/ *obac*. **Engraver:** Huntingdon has the *es*: 'H. Burgh Sculpt'/*obbr*.

Issues: (i) 1746: *Atlas: The agreeable historian, or the compleat English traveller: giving a geographical description of every county in that part of Great-*

Britain, call'd England ... With a map of every county prefix'd to each, from the best and latest observations, after the designs of Herman Moll, and others ... Compiled from Camden, Leland, Dugdale, Ogilby, Morgan, and other authors, by Samuel Simpson, gent'. **Maps (42):** (a) 39 English counties. (b) West; East; North Ridings. **State:** First. **Publisher:** 'Printed by R. Walker, in Fleet Lane'. (ii) At least some of the maps were issued again between c. 1749 and c. 1757.

SMITH, Charles
fl. 1800–1852. Engraver and publisher

Charles Smith was the great rival to John Cary in the early nineteenth century and produced work of equal distinction. His *New English Atlas* of 1804 contained large, handsome and detailed county maps (102) which included much up-to-date information and were, in fact, the model for the maps (30) in Cary's *New English Atlas* of 1809. Smith's large maps have the distinction of being the first county maps showing longitudes based on the meridian of Greenwich Observatory. Less well-known are the reduced versions (103) of his folio maps which were first published in 1822, appearing to adopt the format of Cary's quarto county maps (24). It is not generally recognised that Smith was also a producer of road maps. He produced two rare, finely engraved, sets of road maps (101, 104) which are both interesting and attractive. These were, apparently, an effort to produce an alternative to the many road books offering purely written route descriptions: 'In all Modern Works of this nature, the Roads are invariably described in Letter-press; while in this they are clearly laid down and delineated by actual MAPPING, and by ENGRAVING THE PRINCIPAL DIRECT ROADS, ON COPPER'. Charles Smith issued many other works including some town plans and canal maps.

(101) Description: *st*: First. (Fig. 35). **Supply:** Rare. **Average size:** 88 × 140 mm (3.5 × 5.5 in.). **Features:** Public houses marked 'P.H.'; 'when an Asterisk is annexed to the word Inn, the traveller may depend on being well accomodated, tho' not with Post Horses & Carriages'; the maps give references to connecting plates. Notes on inns supplying post horses and carriages are given at the bottom of each page. **Scale:** *n*//scale is 1:1*m*. **Border:** *dl*/incorporated within the border at top-centre is a semi-circular, vertically hatched panel containing the map number. Within the border below is a vertically hatched panel across the full width of the map containing either the title or other information/*bt*. **North Point:** *c*/*p*/*V*. **Title:** 'London to ...'/*ps*/set within the panel below the map on the first sheet of each route. Since routes cover several sheets, other panels contain information on the locations of post chaises and horses, or inns, or are blank. **Engravers:** Jones and Smith.

Issues: (i) 1800: *Atlas: Smith's actual survey of the roads from London to Brighthelmstone, through Ryegate, Crawley & Cuckfield, with a branch to Worthing. Also from London to Worthing, through Dorking, Horsham & Steyning, with a branch from Steyning to Brighthelmstone. Exhibiting all the noblemens & gentlemens seats and every remarkable object on, or within view of the road ....* **Maps:** 27 road maps. **State:** First. **Imprint:** *obbc :es*: the first sheet of each route (Plates 1, 12, 15, 25) has: 'Jones & Smith sculp! Pentonville' (*V*). **Publisher:** 'C. Smith, Mapseller, No. 172, Strand'.

(102) Description: *st*: First (*v*). **Supply:** Moderate. **Average size:** 450 × 502 mm (18 × 20.1 in.). **Features:** 'The roads to the different Counties which are connected may be traced by Alphabetical Letters placed at the extremities of each Map for that purpose'. A numbered reference key to administrative divisions: e.g. 'REFERENCE to the HUNDREDS'. **Scale:** *V*/*av*: 1:3*m*/'Scale'/ *sbmf*. **Border:** *OB :tTt*/*IB :ll*/*bb*. **North Point:** *s*/*f*/ beneath the star is the curved *es*: e.g. 'Jones & Smith sculp.' (*V*) sometimes with the address '14, Beaufort Buildings, Strand', (or '24 ...'), or simply 'Pentonville' (*V*). **Key:** 'EXPLANATION'. **Title:** 'A NEW MAP of the COUNTY of .... Divided into Hundreds. LONDON Printed for C. SMITH, No 172, Strand, January 6th 1801'/*V*/*vl*/set on *mf*/Wales is dated 1804. **Engravers:** Jones, Smith and Bye.

Issues: Throughout their life, the maps were issued separately as folding maps; sometimes with publication dates in the imprints not found in atlas issues. They were also issued in other publications. (i) 1804: issued initially in parts: *Atlas: Smith's new English atlas being a complete set of county maps, divided into hundreds on which are delineated all the direct and cross roads part of which are from actual measurement cities, towns, and most considerable villages, parks, gentlemen's seats, rivers, and navigable canals: ....* *Maps (42):* (a) England and Wales. (b) 39 English counties. (c) Yorkshire (on four sheets). (d) Wales (on two sheets). **State:** First (*v*). **Imprints:** (i)

below titlepiece: *pi*: see 'Title'. (ii) below north point: *es*: see 'North Point', (except: Cheshire and Lancashire). (iii) *obbc :pi*: Yorkshire sheets 2 and 3: 'Published by C. Smith, 172. Strand, Jan.y 6th 1801'; Yorkshire sheet 4: 'Published by C. Smith, 172 Strand, Jan.y 6th 1804' (*V*). **Publisher:** 'C. Smith, Mapseller, No. 172 (Corner of Surrey Street,) Strand'.

N.B. There were at least three other issues in (i) 1804 with minor revisions and additions to the maps.

(ii) 1804: as (i) 1804, except: **State:** Second (*v*). Minor revisions and additions. **Imprints:** (i) below titlepiece: *pi*: date altered to 'January 6th 1804'. (ii) *es*: added to Cheshire and Lancashire.

N.B. There was a further issue in this form with minor revisions and additions.

(iii) 1808: as (ii) 1804, except: **State:** Third. Minor revisions and additions. **Imprints:** (i) below titlepiece: added below the *pi*: '2.nd Edition Corrected to 1808' (*V*). (ii) *obbc :pi* altered: sheets 2, 3 and 4 of Yorkshire have '2nd Edition Corrected to 1808' added to the imprint. (iv) 1818; 1820: as (iii) 1808, except: **State:** Fourth. Minor revisions and additions. **Imprints:** (i) below titlepiece: the note added below the imprint is altered to: '3rd Edition Corrected to 1818' (*V*). (ii) *obbc :pi* altered: '3rd Edition Corrected to 1818' substituted into the imprint on sheets 2, 3 and 4 of Yorkshire. (v) 1821: as (iv) 1818; 1820, except: **State:** Fifth. **Imprint:** (i) below titlepiece: the date and note are erased from the imprint: 'Corrected to 1821' is substituted. (vi) 1827: as (v) 1821, except: **State:** Sixth. The maps were issued separately as folding maps, but were also sometimes bound into later atlas issues. Minor revisions and additions. **Imprints:** (i) below titlepiece: the note below the imprint is altered to 'Corrected to 1827'. (ii) *obbc :pi* altered: South West and South East Yorkshire: '3rd Edition Corrected to 1827'. (iii) *es*: erased. (vii) 1830: as (vi) 1827, except: **State:** Seventh. Minor revisions and additions. **Imprint:** (i) below titlepiece: the note below the imprint is altered to 'Corrected to 1829', or ' ... to 1830'. (viii) 1832: as (vii) 1830, except: **State:** Eighth (*v*). New parliamentary information is added to the maps and key (parliamentary boroughs, polling places, election places, etc.) The wording of the title is altered to: 'A NEW MAP of the COUNTY of .... Divided into Hundreds and the Parliamentary Divisions'. **Imprint:** (i) below titlepiece: the note below the imprint is altered to 'Corrected to 1832'. (ix) 1835: as (viii) 1832, except:

States: Eighth (*v*) or ninth. Minor revisions and additions, including railway information. *Maps (43):* (c) a 'New Map of Yorkshire' is added to some copies. *Imprints:* (i) below titlepiece: the note below the imprint is altered to 'Corrected to 1834'; or '. . . to 1835'; or remains unchanged, dated 1832. (ii) *obbc:pi:* the 'New Map of Yorkshire' has 'Printed for C. Smith, N⁰ 172 Strand, 1834. J. Smith Delin! Pickett Sculp!' Some copies of this issue were made up with pre-1808 sheets of Yorkshire. *Publisher:* 'C. Smith, Mapseller extraordinary to His Majesty'. (x) 1839 (?): as (ix) 1835, except: *States:* Ninth or tenth. Minor revisions and additions. *Imprint:* (i) below titlepiece: the note below the imprint is altered to 'Corrected to 1837' or 1838 or 1839.

N.B. The maps were later sold separately 'Corrected to 1846'.

(xi) The maps were re-issued c.1864, by lithographic transfer, as folding maps, with altered titles: 'MAP OF .... SHEWING ALL THE RAILWAYS & STATIONS and the Parliamentary Divisions LONDON. SMITH & SON, 63 CHARING CROSS' (*V*) as 'Smith & Son's new series of county maps' (Tenth or eleventh state).

(103) Description: *st:* First. **Supply:** Scarce. **Average size:** 210 × 230 mm (8.4 × 9.2 in.). *Features:* 'For the purpose of facilitating the connexion of the respective Maps the surrounding Counties are filled in, and the distance given from the last Market Town on the Map to the nearest market Town in the County adjoining'. **Scale:** *V/av:* 1:6*m*/'Scale of Miles'/*sbm* incorporated into the outer borderlines at bottom centre. **Border:** *OB:tTt/IB:ll/bb* incorporated into the border at top centre is the title panel and at bottom centre the scale bar. **North Point:** *s* half concealed behind the title panel with three visible cardinal points/*l*//Devon and Cornwall have an ornate *s* with *f* and *l*. **Title:** *c/pc/*set within a vertically hatched panel set into the outer borderlines at top centre. **Engravers:** Gardner (26 maps) and Pickett (17).

Issues: (i) 1822; 1825: *Atlas: Smith's new English atlas, being a reduction of his large folio atlas containing a complete set of county maps on which are delineated all the direct & principal cross roads, cities, towns & most considerable villages, parks, rivers and navigable canals ... The whole carefully arranged according to the stations & intersections of the trigonometrical survey of England ...* **Maps (43):** (a) England and Wales. (b) 39 English counties. (c) Yorkshire (large folding map). (d) North; South

Wales. **State:** First. *Imprints:* (i) *obbc:pi:* 'Printed for C. SMITH, N⁰ 172 Strand 1822' (*V*). (ii) *obbr:es:* 'Pickett sc.' or 'Gardner, sculp!' (*V*). **Publisher:** 'C. Smith, Mapseller extraordinary to his Majesty'. (ii) 1829; 1830: as (i) 1822; 1825, except: **State:** Second. *Imprint:* (i) *obbc:pi:* date erased: 'Printed for C. SMITH, N⁰ 172 Strand' (*V*), [except: Yorkshire dated 1829 and 1830 respectively].

N.B. The maps in this state were issued, in atlas form in 1844 and as folding maps, with railway information and parliamentary divisions added to some maps. These additions were possibly made progressively from 1832 since maps of Shropshire and Yorkshire with the imprint dated 1832 are known with parliamentary divisions added and other alterations and additions, and there may have been an atlas issue at this date. The series was possibly also issued by James Wyld, senior, c. 1832.

(104) Description: *st:* First. **Supply:** Rare. **Average size:** 95 × 160 mm (3.75 × 6.4 in.). **Features:** The maps give references to connecting plates. Some note the origin of the road measurements: *obbc:* e.g. 'From Hyde Park Corner.' The road measurements are given from Hick's Hall, Hyde Park Corner, Shoreditch Church, Tyburn Turnpike, and Whitechapel Church. **Border:** Each page consists of three strips, each 30 mm (1.2 in.) wide, separated and framed by a border of *tTt*. Titles of the routes are given in plain panels across the full width of the strip at the point where the route starts/ *bts/bltr.* **North Point:** *op/V/*each strip has a north point and some have an extra one where a new route starts. **Title:** 'To ....'/sometimes with details of intermediate towns/*ps*/set within a plain panel across the width of the strip at the point where the route starts/above each strip, outside the border, the town of route destination is noted in plain lettering, and above that is the strip number. **Engravers:** Pickett or Gardner.

Issues: (i) 1826; 1827; 1830: *Atlas: Smith's new pocket companion to the roads of England & Wales & parts of Scotland. Engraved on forty-three copper plates. Comprehending the routes from London to every considerable town in England & Wales & the principal cross roads ....* **Maps:** (a) Index map. (b) 42 strip road maps including roads to Edinburgh, Glasgow and Port Patrick. (c) Isle of Wight. **State:** First. *Imprint: obbr:es:* right-hand page maps have:

'Pickett sc.' or 'Gardner sc.' **Publishers:** 'Charles Smith & Son, 172 Strand'.

SMITH, William
fl. 1815–1839. Geologist and engineer

William Smith was the pioneer of geological mapping; his great work *A Delineation of the Strata of England and Wales with part of Scotland* published in 1815 on 15 large sheets at a scale of 5 miles to the inch with the strata colour keyed is now very rare. However, Smith also issued separate geological maps for some counties in his unsuccessful attempt to produce a geological atlas of England. These scarce maps, from Cary's *New English Atlas* (30), were hand-coloured to show geological formations. D.N.B.: Vol. 18, pp. 559–561.

Select Bibliography
DAVIS, A. G.: 'William Smith's Geological Atlas'. (*Jour. of the Soc. for the Bibliography of Nat. Hist.*; 1952)

EYLES, J. M.: 'William Smith (1769–1839): A Bibliography of his Published Writings, Maps and Geological Sections, Printed and Lithographed'. (*Jour. of the Soc. for the Bibliography of Nat. Hist.*; 1969)

FENTON, C, L, AND M. A.: *Giants of Geology.* (rev. ed.; 1952)

PICKFORD, R. F.: *William Smith. Father of English Geology.* (Bath Municipal Libraries; 1969)

SHEPPARD, T.: *William Smith, his maps and memoirs.* (1920)

SOCIETY FOR THE DIFFUSION OF USEFUL KNOWLEDGE
fl. 1827–1856

The S.D.U.K., founded by Henry Brougham in 1827, produced the two-volume atlas *Maps of the Society for the Diffusion of Useful Knowledge* in 1833. This atlas contained a number of rather dull maps of the regions of Britain, finely engraved by J. & C. Walker and clearly imprinted 'Published under the Superintendence of the Society for the Diffusion of Useful Knowledge'. However, of greater interest are the very detailed and superbly engraved plans of Birmingham, Dublin, Edinburgh, Liverpool and London (average size: 325 × 375 mm; 13 × 15 in.). These are characterised by views of parts of the city and by miniature elevations of the principal buildings; and clearly show the ancient city nucleus surrounded by industrial revolution growth and development. The Society began issuing these maps and plans in parts from 1829 and publication was

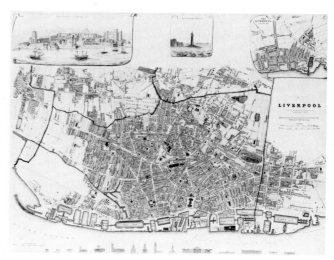

112 Liverpool published by the Society for the Diffusion of Useful Knowledge, 1833. *Photograph: Mills-Wight Studio*

continued until about 1876 by Baldwin & Cradock (later Charles Cradock & Co.), Chapman & Hall, Charles Knight, Edward Stanford, and Thomas Letts & Co.

Supply: Moderate. (Fig. 112).

STOCKDALE, John
fl. 1781–1814d. Bookseller and publisher

Stockdale was a Cumbrian who worked as a blacksmith, a valet and a book-porter before opening his own bookselling and publishing business in Piccadilly. He published numerous cartographical works but is particularly noted for his *New British Atlas* of 1805 which contained the maps (25), drawn by E. Noble and engraved by John Cary, originally published in Gough's 1789 edition of Camden's *Britannia*. Stockdale also published some town plans and environs' maps, and an example of a quarto county map with his imprint is known. D.N.B.: Vol. 18, pp. 1276–77.

TALLIS, John
fl. 1850. Publisher

Tallis published an extremely attractive series of town plans (105), delicately engraved on steel by John Rapkin and others. Each plan has a number of fine vignettes of scenes and buildings (taken from Dugdale's *Curiosities*) and an ornate border, and is very detailed. The composition of the series was significant since it included the new industrial towns

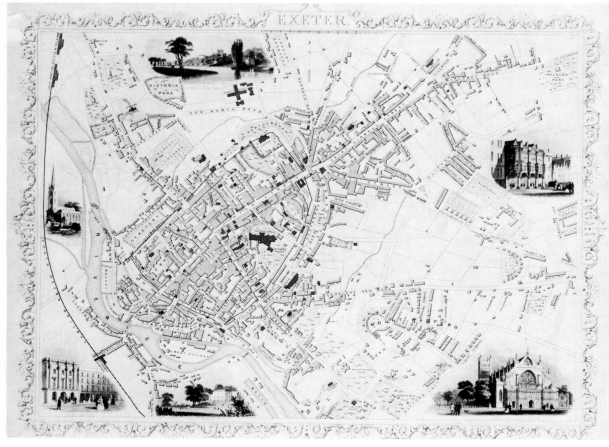

113 105(i): Exeter published by John Tallis, c.1851. *Photograph: Mills-Wight Studio*

of the North and Midlands which were growing rapidly in the mid-nineteenth century. Although Tallis never produced a series of county maps, his maps of the British Isles and the individual countries are worthy of special mention since they are particularly fine and are unusually decorative for the period.

Select Bibliography
LEE, R.: *Antique maps published by John Tallis.* (published privately in Bermuda, c.1973)

(105) Description: *st*: First. (Fig. 113). **Supply:** Moderate. **Average size:** Vc/245 × 325 mm (9.5 × 13 in.)/ some plans are considerably larger, e.g. Birmingham: 345 × 490 mm (13.75 × 19.7 in.). **Scale:** V/'Scale of Feet' with *sb* divided into feet; or: 'Scale of $\frac{1}{4}$ of a mile' or ' ... half a mile' with *sb* divided into furlongs/sometimes set within the title

panel. **Border:** Decorative border of fretwork, scrolling, vine leaves, etc., with the title incorporated at top centre/*bb*. **North Point:** c/p/an arrow-flight indicates south. **Decoration:** Usually four to six small, titled vignette scenes. **Title:** Town name/*pc*/ set within the plan border, top centre. **Engravers:** H. Bibby, D. Pound, J. Rapkin, H. Winkles.
Issues: (i) c.1850–60: the plans were published in some issues of *The illustrated atlas and modern history of the world. Geographical, political, commercial & statistical. Edited by R. Montgomery Martin ....* They were usually added at the end of the atlas and were not recorded in the contents; plans included vary between copies. The large plans were often carelessly folded into the atlas. *Plans (23):* (a) Bath; Birmingham; Bradford; Brighton; Clifton and Bristol; Exeter; Leeds; London and its environs; Liverpool; Manchester and its environs; Newcastle-on-Tyne; Plymouth, Devonport and Stonehouse;

Preston; Sheffield; Southampton; York. (b) Aberdeen; Edinburgh; Glasgow; Perth. (c) Belfast; Cork; Dublin. *State:* First. *Imprints:* (i) *obbc:pi:* 'JOHN TALLIS & COMPANY, LONDON & NEW YORK'. (ii) *obbl:ds/es:* 'The Illustrations Drawn & Engraved by ...'. (iii) *obbr:ds/es:* 'The Plan, Drawn & Engraved by ...'. *Publishers:* J. & F. Tallis, and later 'The London Printing and Publishing Co.'

TAYLOR, George, and SKINNER, Andrew
fl. 1775–1777. Surveyors

Taylor & Skinner produced the only strip road maps of Scotland and Ireland generally available. Their maps were well engraved and included a wealth of detail. The large, unwieldy, oblong *Survey and Maps of the Roads of North Britain* (106), published in 1776 and covering over 3000 miles of road, offers an optimistic insight into the state of Scottish road development in the third quarter of the eighteenth century: 'the Military Roads are kept in the best Repair, and so much has been done of late Years to the other Roads, by the attention of the Nobility and Gentry, that Travelling is made thereby incredibly easy, expeditious and commodious; and such a Spirit of Improvement prevails throughout Scotland, that we may venture to say, a few Years will complete all the public Roads in that part of the United Kingdom'. However, the project was not a financial success: 'The survey cost £306, engraving and binding 3000 copies £487, paper, expenses of distribution and allowances to booksellers £640, a total of £1433. The subscriptions at 10s 6d did not amount to 2000, a possible revenue of less than £1050 ...'[29] This shortfall had to be covered by a series of grants from the Commissioners for the Forfeited Estates. A reduced version (108) of the survey was produced c.1805 by Thomas Brown in a smaller, more convenient, format. Taylor & Skinner published a map of Louth in 1777 and also issued proposals and accepted subscriptions for a map of Perthshire, but, according to Gough, 'The surveyors neglected the scheme for a more lucrative employ of publishing the roads of Ireland: since that was finished they have gained office in the army in America and have quitted that project.' Their *Maps of the Roads of Ireland* (107) was published in 1778 at a price of £1 4s.

Select Bibliography
ADAM, I. H.: 'George Taylor, a Surveyor o' Pairts.' (*IM*, 27; 1975)

FAIRCLOUGH, R. H.: "Sketches of the Roads in Scotland, 1785'; The Manuscript Roadbook of George Taylor.' (*IM*, 27; 1975)

(106) Description: *st:* First. (Fig. 114). **Supply:** Moderate. **Average size:** 187 × 455 mm (7.5 × 18.2 in.). **Features:** The maps give references to connecting plates and occasional informative notes: e.g. 'The Road by the Boat at Hamilton which breaks off at the New Inn is 1 Mile 6 Furlongs shorter than by Bothwell Bridge, but as the River Clyde is sometimes impassable at the Boat, the Miles are Numbered by the Bridge forward to Ayr'. **Scale:** *n//*scale is: 1:1*m*. **Border:** Each map consists of

114 106(i): 'The Road from Edinburgh to Carlisle' by Taylor & Skinner, 1775. *By permission of the British Library (Maps 143.c.2.)*

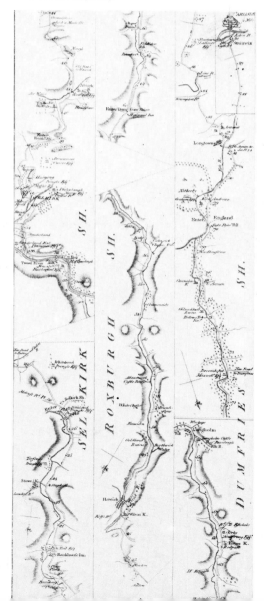

three strips, averaging 58 mm (2.3 in.) wide, separated by *sl*/*OB*:*dl*/*bb*/*bts*/*bltr*. **North Point:** *c*/*f*/*V* most strips have a north point but some share. **Title:** 'ROADS FROM . . . to . . . & . . . by . . . & also by . . . . Miles measured from . . .'/*V*/*pc* and *ps*/set within a plain panel at the start of the route. The roads are measured from the 'Nether Bow Edin^r.', 'Cowgate Port Edin^r.', 'the Chapel of Ease distant from ye Cross ¾ Mile', 'West Port', and 'the Chapel of Ease, Edinburgh on the Peebles R^d.', or from the 'Cross of Stirling in Glasgow'. Other maps have 'The Road from . . . to . . . Continued' across the width of the map either above or below the top border and some strips have individual headings. **Engravers:** Barber, Thomas Bowen, Flynn, J. Luffman, J. Prockter, S. Pyle, Jn. Roberts, I. Taylor, G. Terry. **Issues:** (i) 1776: *Atlas: Taylor and Skinner's survey and maps of the roads of north Britain, or Scotland. To his Grace John Duke of Argyll, Commander-in-Chief of His Majestys Forces in north Britain etc. . . . . Maps:*(a) Index map. (b) 61 strip road maps printed back-to-back. *State:* First. *Imprints:* (i) *obbc*:*pi*: 'Published according to Act of Parliament . . .'. Dated between June 1775 and March 1776. (ii) most maps have: *obbr*, or *obbl* and *obbr*:*es*. (iii) *obar*: 'Pl . . .'. *Publishers:* George Taylor & Andrew Skinner.

(107) Description: *st*: First. **Supply:** Scarce. **Average size:** 102 × 205 mm (4.5 × 8.25 in.). **Features:** 'The roads leading from Dublin are measured from His Majesty's Castle Gate, to the Market House of every Town'; some maps have short explanatory notes concerning distances or local features: e.g. 'This Road to Castle-Martyr, tho' not the best or most travelled is 4 Miles 7 Furlongs shorter, than by Kilworth and Castle Lyons'. **Scale:** *n*// scale is: 'Irish Miles 54½ & 34 Poles to a Degree'; ('Eleven Irish Miles are equal to Fourteen British'). **Border:** *dl*/broken at top centre by the map number/some maps are full page but most are of two strips, 55 mm (2.25 in.) wide, separated by *dl*/*bts*/*bltr*. **North Point:** *c*/*f*. **Title:** 'Road from . . . to . . .'/*V*/*ps*/usually set in a plain panel separated from the map by a dashed line/some title panels contain a distance table. **Engraver:** 'G. Terry No. 54 Paternoster Row, Cheapside, London'. **Issues:** (i) 1778: *Atlas: Taylor and Skinner's maps of the roads of Ireland, surveyed 1777 . . . . Maps:* (a) Index map. (b) 89 full page road maps printed back-to-back. (c) 199 strip road maps printed back-to-back. *Imprints:* (i) some maps have: *obbc*:*es*: either 'Terry Sculp.' or 'Terry Sculp., Pater noster Row'. (ii) some maps have: *obbc* or *obbr*:*pi*: 'Published as the Act directs, . . .'. Dated between 29 July 1778 and

3 November 1778. (iii) Plates 147 and 159 have no imprints or signatures. *State:* First. *Publishers:* George Taylor & Andrew Skinner. (ii) 1783: as (i) 1778, except: *Atlas: Taylor and Skinner's maps of the roads of Ireland, surveyed in 1777 and corrected down to 1783. The second edition. Originally published for the authors as the Act directs 14 Novr. 1778 . . . Maps:* (a, b): as (i) 1778. (c) 200 strip road maps printed back-to-back (the extra map is: 'Road from Mount Charles to Shallagan-Bridge' and 'Dublin to Black Rock, Dunleary, Bullock, Dalkey & Bray'). *State:* First. *Publishers:* 'Sold by T. Longman, Paternoster Row, London. W. Wilson, N° 6, & W. Allen, N° 88, Dame Street Dublin'.

(108) Description: *st*: First. **Supply:** Scarce. **Average size:** 79 × 164 mm (3.1 × 6.5 in.). **Features:** Mileages are usually measured from Nether Bow, Edinburgh. **Scale:** *n*//scale is: 1:1.7m. **Border:** *dl*/the maps consist of two strips divided by *sl*/*bts*/*bltr*. **North Point:** *c*/*f*/most strips have one north point, but some share, and some have two/ orientation of the strips varies. **Title:** 'ROAD FROM . . . to . . . by . . .'/*oc* and *os*/*oba* across the full width of the map/some maps have titles for each strip/a narrow panel across a strip sometimes gives a subsidiary title at the start of a route. **Engravers:** Daniel Lizars and Paton. **Issues:** (i) 1805(?); 1813(?): *Atlas: Taylor & Skinner's survey of the roads of Scotland on an improved plan to which is prefixed an accurate map of Scotland with the new roads etc. etc. since the survey was taken . . . Maps:* (a) Index map. (b) 178 strip road maps printed back-to-back. The map of the road from Inverness to Fort Augustus and Fort William, backed by 'A Plan of the Cross Roads in the Shires of Ross & Cromartie', is a large fold-out map measuring 150 × 389 mm (6 × 15.5 in.). *State:*First. *Imprint: obar:* 'Page . . .'. The fold-out map has: top left 'Page . . .' and top right 'PLATE . . .'. *Publisher:*Thomas Brown, Edinburgh.

N.B. Taylor & Skinner also produced:

(i) 1776: *The traveller's pocket book, or an abstract of Taylor & Skinner's survey of the roads of Scotland.* A tiny abstract of the large survey of 1776 containing only a general map of the roads of Scotland. (ii) 1776: *Taylor & Skinner's survey of the great post roads, between London, Bath & Bristol. London. Printed for the authors, and sold by J: Murray, N° 32 Fleet Street. Published as the Act direct Oct^{br} 21st 1776. Price 2^s 6^d.* This work contained an index map (*obbc*:*pi*: 'Engrav'd by S. Pyle N° 6 Angel Court, Snow Hill') and 20 small maps (57 × 123 mm; 2.25 × 4.9 in.) of the road, and neighbouring country, from London to Bath and Bristol, including three plates showing the alternative route through Calne and Chippenham. Each road map has: (i) *obbc:es*: 'Pyle sculp'. (ii) *obac*: plate-number.

TAYLOR, Thomas

fl. c.1712–1724. Publisher and map-, print- and bookseller

In addition to his publications of Richard Blome's maps (13), Taylor produced the first published atlas relating entirely to Wales, containing ten crudely engraved maps. (109)

Select Bibliography
LEWIS, M.G.: 'Thomas Taylor's Maps of Wales 1718'. (*Jour. of the Welsh Bibliographical Soc.*, 7; 1953)

(109) Description: *st*: First. (Fig. 115). **Supply:** Rare. **Average size:** 176 × 250 mm (6.9 × 9.9 in.). **Features:** A numbered reference key to 'Hundreds in . . .' set within a plain panel with *dl* frame (except: Denbigh and Flint, and Caernarvon). **Scale:** *U*/ 1:6.66m/'Scale of Miles'/*sbm*. **Border:** *dl*. **North Point:** *r*/*f*/sometimes also an east marker. **Decora-**

tion: Decorative title cartouches of plasterwork, grotesques, foliage, cherubs, etc. Pembroke has the title within a plain panel with *dl* frame but has a decorative cartouche containing a dedication to Sir John Phillips. Merioneth has the title within a plain panel only. **Title:** 'A New Mapp of . . . with its Hundreds by Tho. Taylor 1718'/*V*/*vl*/usually set within a decorative cartouche.

Issues: (i) 1718: *Atlas: The principality of Wales exactly described in a compleat sett of maps of all its county's wherein are express'd the chief roads and distances in each county with the names and limits of every hundred; being very usefull for gentlemen and travellers . . . .* **Maps (10):** Ten Welsh county maps. ('Brecknockshire' with Radnor; Denbigh with Flint). **State:** First. **Imprint:** at the bottom of *mf*: 'Sold by Tho: Taylor at the Golden Lyon in Fleetstreet'. (*V*). **Publisher:** 'Tho: Taylor Map and Printseller at the Golden Lyon Over against Serjants Inn in Fleetstreet, Where are Sold all Sorts of the best Maps and French Dutch and Italian Prints at Reasonable Rates'.

N.B. The maps also appeared in Taylor's 1718(?) issues of Richard Blome's *England exactly described* . . . .

115 109(i): Glamorgan by Thomas Taylor, 1718

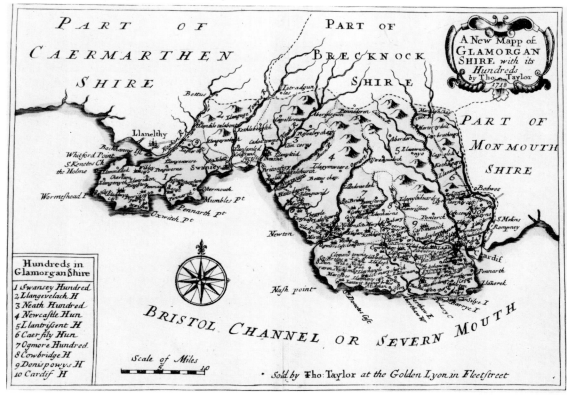

TEESDALE, Henry
fl. 1828–1857. Publisher

Henry Teesdale & Co. were prolific publishers of maps and atlases in the early nineteenth century, including large-scale county maps of Yorkshire (1828), Cheshire (1830), Lancashire (1830) and Stafford (1832). However, Teesdale is best known for his many re-issues of the finely engraved, large, detailed and interesting maps (110) of Robert Rowe. These maps, which are usually found with original wash colouring, were later published from c.1848 by Henry George Collins.

Teesdale also produced a plain set of small maps (111) in his *A New Travelling Atlas* in 1830. Although rarely found with the original Teesdale imprint, they are in plentiful supply with the later imprints of Collins and Orr.

(110) Description: *st*: Second (*v*). (Fig. 116). **Supply:** Moderate. **Average size:** 340 × 410 mm (13.25 × 16.25 in.). **Features:** A numbered reference key to administrative divisions: e.g.

116 110(vii): Nottinghamshire published by Henry George Collins, 1852 (detail). *Photograph: Mills-Wight Studio*

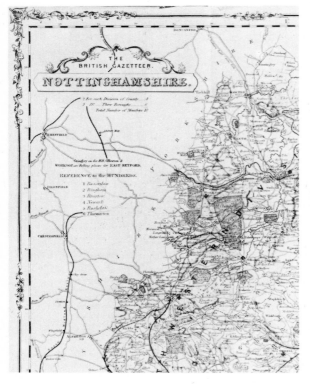

'REFERENCE to the HUNDREDS'. **Scale:** *V/av*: 1:4*m*/'Scale'/*sbm*. **Border:** *OB:tTt/IB:ll.* **North Point:** *s/f.* **Key:** 'EXPLANATION'. **Title:** *c/oc.*

Issues: Although the maps were issued many times by Henry Teesdale, and later by Henry Collins, they were, in fact, first issued by Robert Rowe initially individually and together, in 1816: (i) 1816: Pre-description state: *Atlas: The English atlas; being a new & complete set of county maps, divided into hundreds, exhibiting the direct and cross roads, cities, towns, villages, parks, rivers and navigable canals, with the distances marked between the towns and from London . . . . Maps (43):* (a) England and Wales. (b) 39 English counties. (c) Yorkshire (four sheets). (d) North; South Wales. *State:* First. The titlepiece on each map consists of an oval panel containing the wording 'A NEW MAP of the COUNTY of . . . Divided into Hundreds. By R. Rowe.' In the panel border, below the title, is the dated *pi*: 'London: Printed for R. Rowe, Nº 19, Bedford Street, Bedford Row, . . .'. (ii) 1829: as (i) 1816, except: As described above: with the original title erased and the new, simpler title engraved, and minor additions and corrections. The maps were issued several times during the next 35 years, and most issues up-dated communication information, particularly concerning railways, and included other minor revisions and additions. The plates appear to have been in a continuing state of revision concerning parliamentary representation information between 1829 and 1832 when the results of the First Reform Act were added. Asterisks representing the number of members returned to Parliament were added to some maps and noted in the keys of 23 maps as 'The Stars prefixed to the Towns denote the number of Members return'd to Parliament'. *Atlas: New British atlas, containing a complete set of county maps, on which are delineated all the principal cross roads, cities, towns, & most considerable villages, parks, rivers, navigable canals & railways . . . . Maps (45):* as above plus: Ireland; Scotland. *State:* Second (*v*). *Imprint: obbc:pi:* 'London, Published by Henry Teesdale & Cº 302, Holborn. (*V*), (except: Cambridge and Durham have the address as '302, High Holborn'; and Bedfordshire and Warwickshire lack the address). *Publishers:* Henry Teesdale & Co.

N.B. This state, sometimes with minor revisions and additions, was issued in the 1830 edition of the atlas. Some parks are added as stipple shaded areas.

(iii) 1831: as (ii) 1829, except: *State:* Third. Minor

revisions and additions. Commons are now symbolised by rough horizontal hatching and many parks are added often without the trees and the paling fences usually originally symbolised. (iv) 1832: as (iii) 1831, except: *Atlas: Improved edition of the new British atlas ... corrected to the year, 1832 ... State:* Fourth. Parliamentary representation information is added to the maps. Appropriate changes are made to the key on some maps and population statistics for 1831 and tax information for 1830 are added. A second issue in 1832 added notes, beneath the title, on representation, giving details of numbers of members returned to Parliament by the boroughs, and of county divisions. The atlas was reissued in 1833. (v) 1835: as (iv) 1832, except: *State:* Fifth (*v*). Minor revisions and additions were made during the issue. *Imprint: ob*: top right of page: plate-number added during the issue.

N.B. This state, with minor revisions and additions, was published twice in 1842.

(vi) 1848(?): by lithographic transfer: issued in parts: as (v) 1835, except: *Atlas: New British atlas, containing a complete set of county maps ... The whole carefully revised & corrected ...* The maps were also probably issued individually from about this date under the cover title: 'ENGLAND DEPICTED IN A SERIES OF SPLENDIDLY FULL-COLOURED MAPS ....'. *State:* Sixth. The population and tax information is erased; destinations of roads leaving the county are erased; railways are now marked by a heavy black line, and this and the new symbol for stations are represented in the key; other minor changes. The map title is now enclosed in a slightly ornate panel with *sl* border. The *OB* is decorated at the corners and along sections by twining foliage. *Imprints:* (i) *ob*: top right of page: plate-number deleted. (ii) *obbc*: new *pi*: 'London, Published for the Proprietors by H.G. Collins 22, Paternoster Row'. (*V*). *Publisher:* Henry George Collins. (vii) 1852: probably issued initially in monthly parts: by lithographic transfer: as (vi) 1848(?), except: *Atlas: The British gazetteer ... illustrated by a full set of county maps, with all the railways accurately laid down; forming at once an iron road-book and county atlas. By B. Clarke .... Maps (48):* (a) England and Wales*; British railroads*. (b) 39 English counties. (c) Yorkshire (four sheets). (d) Liverpool*; London* (*pi*: 'London. Henry G. Collins, 22, Paternoster Row and George Philip, 51, South Castle Street, Liverpool'); 15 miles round London*. (e) Isle of Wight*. (f) North; South* Wales. *State:*

Seventh. More information is added in areas beyond the county boundary; major roads are extended to the map border and destinations are noted. A curved panel, with foliated border, is added above most title panels and contains the wording 'THE BRITISH GAZETTEER'/*pc*/* these maps, plus Northumberland, Rutland, Stafford, and Worcester omit the wording and usually simply enclose the title with decorative scrolling. The 'EXPLANATION' is expanded. Other minor revisions and additions. (viii) c.1852–1864: The maps were issued, as folding maps and separate sheets, in variant states of the above lithographic transfers, with minor revisions and additions, by various publishers, and are, sometimes, found with the wording 'THE BRITISH GAZETTEER' in the titlepiece covered by a triangular label of foliated decoration.

(III) **Description:** *st*: Second (*v*). **Supply:** Moderate. **Average size:** 143 × 183 mm (6.2 × 7.3 in.). **Scale:** *V*/*av*: 1:10*m*/'Scale of Miles'/*sbm*. **Border:** 1830: a thick *OB* and a 4 mm (0.15 in.) inner hatched panel resembling piano keys. 1848(?): *tTt*. **North Point:** *s*/*f*. **Title:** 1830: *c*/*ps*/set within a slightly ornate panel which is set within a larger, vertically hatched, rectangular panel. 1848(?): *c*/*ps*/set within the slightly ornate panel only.

Issues: (i) 1830: *Atlas: A new travelling atlas, containing a complete set of county maps, on which are delineated all the mail & turnpike roads, the cities, towns, parks & gentlemens seats ... The whole carefully revised and corrected to the year 1830 .... Maps (45):* (a) England and Wales. (b) 39 English counties. (c) North; East; West Ridings. (d) North; South Wales. *State:* First (*v*). *Imprint: obbc:pi*: 'London, Published Sept. 1830, by Henry Teesdale, & Co. 302, Holborn', (*V*). **Publishers:** Henry Teesdale & Co.

N.B. Maps of some counties are known with the above *pi* erased, railways added, and a plate-number added at top right; issued c.1842–46.

(ii) 1848(?): by lithographic transfer: as (i) 1830, except: *Atlas: The travelling atlas, of England & Wales, with all the railways & coach roads, the cities, towns, parks & gentlemens seats ... The whole carefully revised and corrected to the present time .... State:* Second (*v*).

N.B. This atlas was probably also issued c.1848 with maps in the first state.

The alterations, noted above, are made to the border and title panel. Railways are named and marked by thick black lines. No distinction is made between constructed and projected lines. *Imprints:* (i) *obbc*: new *pi*: 'London. Published for the Proprietors by H. G. Collins, 22, Paternoster Row'. (*V*). (ii) there is . no plate-number. *Publisher:* Henry George Collins.

N.B. The maps in this state were issued again c.1850 with up-dated railway information.

(iii) 1852(?): Two issues under slightly different titles, one initially in parts: by lithographic transfer: as (ii) 1848(?), except: *State:* Third. Minor revisions and up-dating of railway information. Only constructed railway lines are shown. *Imprint:* (i) *obbc*: new *pi*: 'London: (Published for the Proprietors) by W. S. Orr & Co, 2, Amen Corner, Paternoster Row.' (*V*). *Publishers:* William S. Orr & Co. (iv) 1856(?); 1858(?): by lithographic transfer: as (iii) 1852(?), except: *State:* Fourth. Minor revisions. *Imprint:* (i) *obbc*: new *pi*: 'Printed and Published by John Heywood, 170, Deansgate, Manchester'. (*V*). *Publisher:* John Heywood. (v) The series was issued lithographically by John Heywood with some maps replaced and others with up-dated information in: 1860(?); 1868(?); 1870(?); 1875(?): *The travelling atlas of England & Wales ....* (*V*); 1865(?): *The tourist's atlas of England and Wales ....*; 1882(?): *John Heywood's country atlas of England and Wales ....* The maps are much altered, resembling the earlier Teesdale issue, and most exhibit changes and revisions for most issues. The maps were issued both with and without Heywood's imprint and plate numbers.

THOMSON, John
fl. 1814–c.1835. Bookseller and publisher

The most detailed maps of Scotland produced before those of the Ordnance Survey were the exceptional, finely engraved county maps (112) published in Thomson's *Atlas of Scotland.* Where possible, existing county maps were used as the base for the new maps; they were corrected and revised by surveyors and local persons and the names of these attestors to the new maps' accuracy are given on the map face. However, adequate county maps did not always exist and Thomson was forced to produce new surveys for some counties. Some maps have attractive vignettes and others have town plans taken from John Wood's *Town Atlas* (119).

The maps were issued to subscribers and sold loose from 1820 as they were engraved and printed, but the full atlas was issued only in 1831.

Thomson was less than enamoured with the

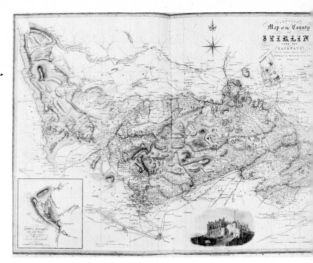

117 112(ii): Stirling by W. & A. K. Johnston, c.1855. *By permission of the British Library (Maps 11.e.11.)*

project: '... since that period, the work has been continually in progress, but the great difficulty of finding assistants, materials, and making the necessary surveys, have retarded the completion much longer than anticipated. The Publisher will now take leave of the ATLAS OF SCOTLAND—a Work which he never would have undertaken, had he known the difficulties to be encountered, the great number of people to be employed, the advance of capital, and the time necessary to carry through such an arduous undertaking, which required at least one surveyor to each county to correct the drawings, and find respectable names to guarantee their accuracy.' In fact, Thomson was forced to petition successfully for bankruptcy both in 1830 and 1835.

(112) **Description:** *st:* First. (Fig. 117). **Supply:** Scarce. **Average size:** 500 × 663 mm (20 × 26.5 in.). **Features:** Since the maps were engraved by different engravers, the style of the relief hachuring varies; some maps have heavily emphasised relief features, whilst others have minimal faint hachuring only. Ten counties have inset town plans (after John Wood's *Town atlas*) set within *dl* frame or on an imitation parchment. **Scale:** *V/av:* 1:2*m*/'SCALE OF BRITISH MILES' or 'ENGLISH MILES'/ *sbmf*/sometimes set within a plain rectangular panel with a narrow border. The inscription giving the names of the draughtsmen and engravers is positioned below the scale on some maps. **Border:** A thick black line between two wide blank strips with a central hatched panel, 8 mm (0.3 in.) wide, containing circled reference letters. The map is divided into a corresponding reference grid. Latitude and

longitude are given outside *OB/bb*. **North Point:** *s/ f/V*. **Decoration:** seven counties have titled vignette views.

N.B. Kirkcudbrightshire, Lanarkshire, Stirlingshire, and Dumbartonshire have both vignette views and town plans.

Title: *c*, or area covered/*pc*/set within a horizontally hatched panel. Most titlepieces incorporate details of surveyors, testators, compilation, etc. within and/ or below the title panel. (Multi-sheet counties have the title on one sheet only.) **Engravers:** E. Butterworth, T. Clerk, W. Dassauville, Sidney Hall, N. R. Hewitt, J. & G. Menzies, J. Moffatt, and S. I. Neele & Son.

Issues: (i) 1820–1831: The maps were initially issued to subscribers as they were completed (starting with Berwick, Edinburgh, Kircudbright, Linlithgow, Peebles and Stirling) and were first issued together in 1831 (under an early version of the atlas title); 1831; 1832: *Atlas: The atlas of Scotland, containing maps of each county, on a scale so large as to exhibit the features of the country, and places of importance; the boundaries of the shires, attested with respectable names to verify their accuracy, laid down from actual survey ....* **Maps (35):** (a) Index map. (b) 29 Scottish counties. (12 counties are one sheet each; Nairn with Elgin; six counties on two sheets each; Fife with Kinross on two sheets; four counties on four sheets each; Aberdeen with Banff on four sheets; Inverness-Shire is divided into Northern and Southern Parts on two sheets each).
N.B. Clackmannan is not individually specified.
(c) Buteshire; Skye Island, etc.; Orkney Islands; Shetland Islands: on one sheet each; Western Isles: on three sheets. **State:** First. **Imprint:** (i) most maps have an *es*/various positions: e.g. *mf*; or: *obbr*; or: *obbl*; or: under the title panel or the scale; etc. Wordings vary according to engraver and/or draughtsman: e.g. 'Engraved by S. I. Neele & Son, 352, Strand.' (ii) *obbc:pi*: 'Published by John Thomson & Co., Edinburgh...' dated between 1820 and 1830. (iii) *obar*: plate-number: 'N⁰ ... Part ...' (*V*). **Publishers:** 'John Thomson & Co. Edinburgh: Baldwin & Cradock, London; and John Cumming, Dublin'. (ii) 1855(?): as (i) 1820–31, except: **State:** Second. The names of the testators, surveyors, engravers, etc. have been erased. The titlepieces have been re-engraved in fine calligraphic style: e.g. 'JOHNSTON'S Map of the County of .... WITH THE RAILWAYS W. & A.K. Johnston Engravers Edin!'/*V*/*oc* and *os/sd*. The

original map of 'Roxburgh-Shire' has been replaced by a new 'Map of the County of Roxburgh', surveyed by N. Tennant and engraved by W. & A. K. Johnston. Clackmannan is now included in the title of the map of Perth. Communication information has been up-dated; in particular, railways have been added. A key to: 'Railways in Operation or in Progress' and 'Dº Projected' is added. **Imprints:** (i) *es* erased. (ii) *obbc:pi*: imprint erased. **Publishers:** W. & A. K. Johnston, William Blackwood & Sons, Cowan & Co., and J. Lunsden & Son.

WALKER, John and Charles
fl. 1830. Engravers and cartographers

The Walker brothers were prolific engravers, producing maps for the Greenwoods and many others. They issued a series of beautifully engraved, folding county maps (113) which were collected together as *The British Atlas* in 1837. These plain but very detailed maps were deservedly popular and the atlas ran through many issues. An interesting feature is that the maps were usually issued with all railways built marked in red by hand. Often these red railways are more extensive than lines actually engraved on the maps since old stock could be used up whilst still claiming that the maps contained the latest information.

(113) Description: *st*: First. **Supply:** Plentiful. **Average size:** *V*/320 × 390 mm (13 × 15.5 in.). **Features:** A numbered reference key to administrative divisions, sometimes untitled: e.g. 'REFERENCE TO THE HUNDREDS'.. Also listings of: 'BOROUGHS'; 'Places of Election'; and 'Polling Places'. Statistical information on the county is given below the titlepiece. **Scale:** *V*/av: 1:4*m*/'English Miles 69.1 = 1 Degree'/*sbmf/Vw*. **Border:** *OB:tTt/IB:ll/bb*. **North Point:** *s/f*. **Key:** 'The Figures to the Towns show the distance from London in Miles ... along the roads ... from Town to Town.' Later editions also have: 'Railways'. **Title:** *c/oc*/set within a plain panel with a frame of two or three very fine lines/signed: 'BY J. & C. WALKER' beneath the title panel. **Engravers:** John & Charles Walker.

Issues: Issued individually from 1835 and as boxed sets from c.1837. Old map stock was frequently issued in later atlases. The maps were also issued in other works. (i) 1837: *Atlas: To their Royal Highnesses the Duchess of Kent & the Princess Victoria, this British atlas, comprising separate maps of every county in England each Riding in Yorkshire*

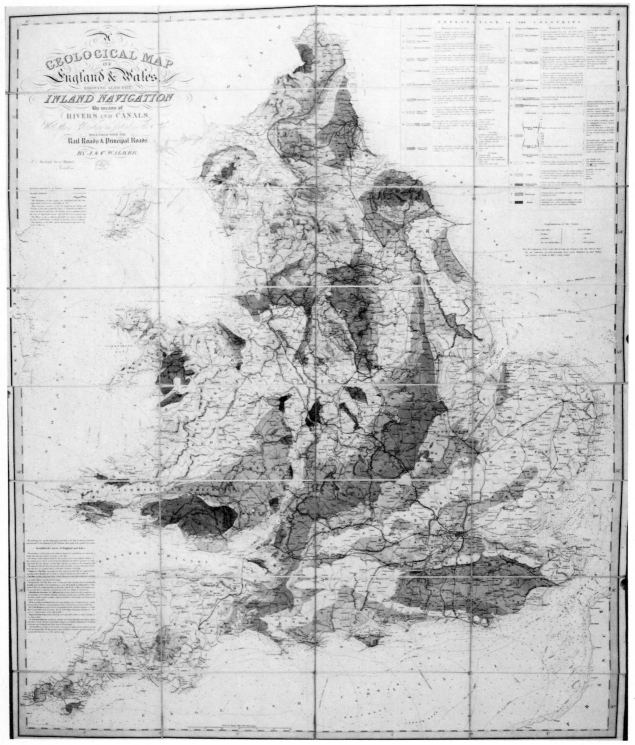

118 'A Geological Map of England & Wales showing also the Inland Navigation by means of Rivers and Canals . . .' by J. & C. Walker, 1835. *By permission of the British Library (Maps 3.b.21.)*

214

and North and South Wales showing the roads, railways, canals, parks, boundaries of boroughs, etc. compiled from the maps of the Board of Ordnance and other trigonometrical surveys .... *Maps (45):* (a) England and Wales; (Scotland and Ireland were added from c.1845). (b) 39 English counties. (c) East; West; North Ridings. (d) North; South Wales (two plates each). *State:* First (v). *Imprint: obbc:pi:* all maps have the imprint in various forms:

'Published by ...': usually:
'Longman,   Paternoster Row, London ...'
Rees, Orme,
Brown & C?,
but also:
'Longman, Orme,   Pater Noster   ....',
  Rees & C?,   Row
'Longman, Rees,
  Orme & C?',   '
'Longman, Hurst,
  Rees, Orme & C?',   '
       in varying combinations:

dated between 1 April 1835 and 1 March 1837. (*V*). *Publishers:* 'Longman, Rees & C? Paternoster Row, and J. & C. Walker, 3, Burleigh Street, Strand'. (ii) 1837: as (i) 1837, except: *Atlas: To Her most excellent Majesty Queen Victoria, and to Her Royal Highness the Duchess of Kent, this British atlas* .... *State:* First (v). (iii) 1839; 1840; 1841; 1842; 1843; 1844; 1845; 1846; 1849; 1851; 1852; 1854; 1856; 1860; 1861; 1862; 1864; 1865; 1869; 1870; 1872; 1873; 1877; 1879: (copies of the atlas probably continued to be sold until the early 1890's): as (ii) 1837, except: There were many editions of the atlas over a long period and, consequently, the maps were in a continual state of modification. The major changes were the constant up-dating of railway information; the up-dating of statistical information; and the addition of place-names, particularly the addition of the hunt meeting-places in preparation for the use of the maps for *Hobson's fox-hunting atlas.* The date in the *pi* was altered periodically until 1849 when it was erased (dates were sometimes added again later). Some imprints were altered in later issues, some were erased and some were changed to that of 'J. & C. Walker, ...'. The maps were also issued individually as 'Walker's County Maps' until the late 1880s. *States:* Various. By lithographic transfer using current editions of the *British atlas:* (iv) 1849(?): *Atlas: Hobson's fox-. hunting atlas; containing separate maps of every*

county in England, and the three Ridings of Yorkshire; comprising forty-two maps, showing the roads, railways, canals, parks, etc., etc. Compiled from the maps of the Board of Ordnance and other surveys .... *Maps (42):* (a) 39 English counties. (b) East; West; North Ridings. The maps are as in the *British atlas,* with the following additions: (i) hunt boundaries are marked by dotted lines and coloured. (ii) hunt meeting places are marked by a black dot and the underlining of the place-name. (iii) 'PLACES OF THE MEETING OF FOXHOUNDS' explains the added symbol. (iv) the hunts are named/*pc*/in some cases with references to the maps of adjacent areas (the c.1849 issue has the hunts named by lithographed hollow outline letters, presumably for hand colouring; later issues had the names overprinted). The map references were omitted from c.1850.

N.B. Lancashire and Westmorland have no hunts marked.

States: Various. *Imprints:* (i) *obar,* and *obbr* (to be read sideways): plate-number: 'N? ...'. (ii) *obbc:pi:* date deleted. Some imprints were altered, deleted, or changed to that of 'J. & C. Walker, ...', in later issues. *Publishers:* 'J. and C. Walker, 9, Castle Street, Holborn'. (v) 1850(?); 1851(?); 1852(?); 1855(?); 1860(?); 1866(?); 1868(?); 1869(?); 1871(?); 1875(?); 1878(?); and as *Walker's fox-hunting atlas* ...: 1880(?); 1882(?); 1886(?); 1892; 1894; 1895: as (iv) 1849(?), except: The atlas was published over many years by J. & C. Walker from their premises at: (a) 9, Castle Street, Holborn (until c.1869) [however, this address was still in use as late as c.1885]. (b) 37, Castle Street, Holborn (c.1870–1892). (c) 37, Furnival Street, Holborn (from 1894). Consequently, the maps are found in many states since they were modified not only for the editions of the *British atlas* but also had their hunting information modified and up-dated for the editions of the *Fox-hunting atlas.* *States:* Various.

N.B. The maps later appeared in *Lett's popular county atlas* in 1884 and 1887 in a much changed state.

WALLIS, James
fl. 1810–1820. Engraver and publisher

Wallis produced three sets of county maps that are generally available. The largest set, issued in *Wallis's New British Atlas* (115) were close copies of those issued by Cole & Roper (31), in a similar plain style, but apparently engraved in 'a superior manner'. The maps (114) in the *New Pocket Edition of the English Counties* were similarly copies of Cary's *Traveller's Companion* (26). The most attractive and scarcest of Wallis's maps (116) are the tiny, charming copies of Miller's maps (94) published in *The Panorama*, partly in the hope that it would be adopted as a school atlas: 'The utility of such a work, so brief, yet comprehensive, cannot but be acknowledged, as it condenses in its pages all necessary information which would be acquired by the perusal of an immensity of volumes. To all classes of persons, the merchant, the trader, the farmer, but especially the traveller, from its portable size, will be found of infinite service. In schools and seminaries it would be an elementary book of British Topography, which we wish was made a subject of juvenile instruction conjointly with English History'.

(114) Description: *st*: First. **Supply:** Plentiful. **Average size:** 95 × 130 mm (3.75 × 5.25 in.). Isle of Wight measures 55 × 84 mm (2.2 × 3.3 in.). The map of the 'Isle of Wight' differs from this description in many respects. **Scale:** *V/av*: 1 :12*m*/'Scale of Miles'/*sbm*. **Border:** *OB:dl/IB:ll*/the title, within a panel, is incorporated into the border at the top of the page and a full-width panel containing the 'Explanation' is set within the border at the bottom of the page. **North Point:** *s/f/ V*. **Key:** 'Explanation'. **Title:** *c/pc*/within a vertically hatched panel incorporated into the map border. **Engraver:** James Wallis.

Issues: (i) 1812(?): *Atlas: Wallis's new pocket edition of the English counties or travellers companion in which are carefully laid down all the direct & cross roads, cities, townes, villages, parks, seats, and rivers .... Maps (44):* (a) England and Wales. (b) 39 English counties. (c) Yorkshire. (d) Isle of Wight. (e) North; South Wales. *State:* First. *Imprint: obbc:pi:* 'London, Publish'd by J. Wallis, Engraver, 77, Berwick Str. Soho'. (*V*). *Publisher:* 'J. Wallis, Engraver, Berwick St., Soho, and sold by Davies & Eldridge, Exeter'. (ii) 1814(?): as (i) 1812(?), except: *State:* Second (except: Yorkshire). *Imprint: obar:* plate-number added (except: Yorkshire), {these appear to have been engraved from c.1812 in some cases}. (iii) 1818; 1819: as (ii) 1814(?), except: *Atlas: Martin's sportman's almanack, kalendar, and travellers' guide, ...; containing ... a series of maps for every county in England .... State:* Third (except: Yorkshire: second). Many plates are altered or retouched, and some are re-engraved; in particular: relief hachuring and sea shading are erased.

Imprint: obbc: new *pi*: 'London, Publish'd by P. Martin No 198 Oxford Street'. (*V*). **Publishers:** Simpkin & Marshall. (iv) 1819(?): as (iii) 1818, 1819, except: *Atlas: Lewis's, new traveller's guide, or a pocket edition of the English counties, containing all the direct & cross roads in England & Wales. With the distance of each principal place from London .... Maps:* (d) Isle of Wight omitted. *State:* Fourth (except: Yorkshire: third).

N.B. This atlas was issued with some maps still in their third state and some in their fifth.

Imprint: obbc:pi erased. *Publisher:* 'W. Lewis, No 21 Finch Lane, Cornhill'. (v) 1819(?): as (iv) 1819(?), except: *State:* Fifth (except: Yorkshire: fourth). *Imprint: obbc:* new *pi*: 'London Publish'd by W. Lewis, Finch Lane'. (*V*). (vi) 1835; 1836: as (v) 1819(?), except: *Atlas: Lewis's new traveller's guide, and panorama of England and Wales, containing forty-four superior maps .... State:* Fifth (except: Yorkshire: fourth). (vii) c.1840: There may possibly have been a further issue of these maps since Cheshire is known with the imprint of J. & F. Harwood, 26, Fenchurch St.

(115) Description: *st*: First (v). (Fig. 119). **Supply:** Moderate. **Average size:** 180 × 265 mm (6.5 × 9.75 in.). **Features:** Relief is represented by heavy hachures but some copies are known without relief marked. A numbered reference key to administrative divisions: e.g. 'WAPENTAKES'. **Scale:** *V/av*: 1 :8*m*/'Scale of Miles'/*sbm*//Lancashire and Nottingham have *n*. **Border:** *OB:tTt/IB:ll/bb*. **North Point:** *s/f/*the title panel crosses the centre of the north point. **Key:** 'EXPLANATION'. **Title:** *c/ oc*/set within a vertically hatched panel positioned across the north point/curved signature below the title: 'Engrav'd by J. Wallis'. (*V*). **Engraver:** James Wallis.

Issues: (i) 1813: *Atlas: A new and improved county atlas. Wallis's new British atlas containing a complete set of county maps divided into hundreds in which are carefully delineated all the direct and cross roads, cities, towns, villages, parks, seats, rivers and navigable canals, ... The whole engraved in the most accurate manner from the latest actual surveys .... Maps (43):* (a) England and Wales (imprint: 'Published by S. A. Oddy, Pickett Street, Strand'). (b) 39 English counties. (c) Parts of the East and West: West; North Ridings. *State:* First (v). *Imprint: obbc:pi:* 'London Published by S. A. Oddy, 1812'. (*V*), except: (a) general map. (b) 'Glocestershire': 'Publish'd by S. A. Oddy, 1813'. (c) Essex, Nor-

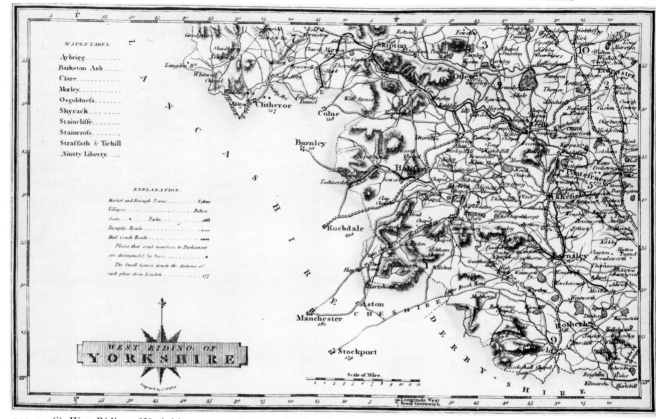

119 115(i): West Riding of Yorkshire engraved by James Wallis, 1813. *Photograph: Mills-Wight Studio*

thamptonshire, Wiltshire, three Yorkshire maps: date in imprint is 1813. (d) Lancashire, Oxfordshire, Shropshire: no imprint or date. **Publisher:** J. Wallis. (ii) 1813: as (i) 1813, except: *Atlas: Wallis's new British atlas containing a complete set of county maps . . . .* **States:** First (v) or second (v). **Imprint:** *obbc:pi:* Oxfordshire: 'Publish'd by S. A. Oddy, 1812'; Shropshire: 'London, Published by S. A. Oddy, 1813'. **Publisher:** S. A. Oddy.

N.B. There was a further issue in 1813 with very slight modifications to some plates.

(iii) 1814(?); 1816(?): as (ii) 1813, except: *Atlas: Wallis's second & superior British atlas, containing a complete set of county maps, divided into hundreds . . . .* **Maps (45):** as above, plus (d) North; South Wales. **States:** various. **Imprints:** all maps carry the *pi* as before, except: (i) general map: 'London. Published by J. Wallis Berwick Street Soho'. (ii) Cornwall, Cheshire, Hampshire, Sussex, South Wales: 'London Publish'd by J. Wallis 1814'. (*V*). (iv) North Wales: 'London Publish'd by S. A. Oddy 1813'. Cambridge and North Wales are re-dated

1816 appropriately. (v) Leicester and Lancashire: no imprint.

N.B. Shropshire is also known without imprint.

(vi) Cornwall bears the inscription: *obac:* 'Second Edition, with Considerable Improvements & Additions, by G. Hebert, Geographer'. This inscription was added to other maps during these and the c.1819 issues (sometimes giving the name as 'L. Hebert'). **Publisher:** James Wallis.

N.B. There was a further issue in 1816(?) with the modifications made to the plates for the second issue of (ii) 1813 above.

(iv) 1819(?): as (iii) 1814(?); 1816(?), except: *Atlas: Ellis's new and correct atlas of England and Wales, being an entire new set of county maps . . . accompanied by letter press descriptions of each county . . . .* **States:** Various. A scale bar: 'SCALE', is added to Lancashire. **Imprints:** most maps have the *pi* erased. Lancashire now has: *obbc:pi:* 'London. Published by J. Wallis 1814'. **Publisher:** G. Ellis. (v) the maps were re-issued at a later date, by lithographic transfer, in a much changed state with:

many revisions and alterations to the detail and key; the removal of the *es* below the title; and the addition of railways, and statistical and explanatory notes.

(116) **Description:** *st*: First. **Supply:** Scarce. **Average size:** 70 × 105 mm (2.5 × 3.75 in.). **Scale:** *V*/*av*: 1:15*m*/'Scale of Miles'/*sbm*. **Border:** *OB:Tt*/ *IB:ll*/*bb*. **North Point:** *c*/*p*. **Key:** 'Mail Coach Roads thus ...'. **Title:** *c*/*pc*/set within a vertically hatched panel with a narrow *dl* frame.

Issues: (i) 1820(?): *Atlas: The panorama: or, traveller's instructive guide; through England and Wales: exhibiting all the direct & principal cross roads, cities, towns, villages, parks, canals etc., accompanied by a description of each county, with the cities & principal towns: likewise a list of fairs, London & county bankers, members of Parliament, the route of the mail coaches, & the portage of letters, with a variety of other useful information .... Maps (53):* (a) England and Wales. (b) 39 English counties. (c) Yorkshire. (d) 12 'Welch' counties. *State:* First. *Imprints:* (i) (a) *obbc:pi*: general map: 'London, Published by J. Wallis 77 Berwick Str. Soho; & C. Hinton 1 Ivy La. Paternoster Row' (publishers are reversed in some of the following imprints, *V*). (b) 18 English counties have the above imprint. (c) Yorkshire has the above imprint. (ii) *obar* or *obal*: seven maps have a plate-number.
N.B. There was a further issue in 1820(?) with the imprint erased. (states: first or second).
Publisher: 'W.H. Reid, Charing Cross'. (ii) 1825(?): as (i) 1820(?), except: *Atlas: The panorama of England and Wales.* **States:** Second or third. *Imprint: obbc*: new *pi*: 'Published by Hodgson & Co. 10, Newgate Street' (*V*). **Publishers:** Hodgson & Co./William Cole.

WALPOOLE, George Augustus
fl. 1784. Topographer

Walpoole issued a series of small, attractive, rococo style county maps (117) in his *New British Traveller* of 1784. 'Besides the elegant and numerous Set of other Copper Plates, will be given a complete Set of County Maps, for England, Scotland and Ireland (from actual Surveys) which was never hitherto attempted (though absolutely necessary) in any Undertaking of the Kind, and will alone be worth Double the Price of the whole Work'.

Combinations of two, three or four county maps are found on 17 of the plates but it is usual for the counties to be separated. Since there was no space

allowed for such separation, the maps are usually found closely cropped and often require false margins.

(117) **Description:** *st*: First. (Fig. 120). **Supply:** Scarce. **Average size:** *Vc* since varying numbers of maps were engraved on plates measuring approximately 210 × 325 mm (8.5 × 13 in.). However, average size: 155 × 200 mm (6.2 × 7.75 in.). **Scale:** *V*/*av*: 1:8*m*/'British Statute Miles'/*sbm*. **Border:** *OB:sl*/*IB:ll*/*bb*/foliated decoration outside the plain-ruled border adorns 14 maps. **North Point:** *q*/ some circles are divided into eight segments/*f*/*e*. **Key:** 'Remarks'. **Decoration:** Decorative title cartouche. Heraldic shields with the arms of the counties covered or the county towns. Some maps have an ornamental foliated decoration outside the border. **Title:** 'A New MAP of .... Drawn from the Latest Authorities'/*V*/*vl*/within a decorative cartouche/Berkshire and Somerset are attributed to 'Thos Bowen, Geogr.', and England and Wales, Scotland, and Ireland to 'T. Kitchin'. **Engraver:** 1784: only the maps of North and South Wales are attributed to Thomas Conder. Later issues attribute all the maps to Conder except Cornwall and Devon which are attributed to Hatchett, and Berkshire and Somerset which have no *es*.

Issues: (i) 1784: *Atlas: The new British traveller; or, a complete modern universal display of Great-Britain and Ireland ... being really the result of an actual and late general survey, accurately made by a society of gentlemen ... including a valuable collection of landscapes, views, county-maps, etc .... The whole published under the immediate inspection of George Augustus Walpoole, Esq. assisted ... by David Wynne Evans .. Alexander Burnet .. and ... Robert Conway .... Maps:* 23 plates: 46 maps: (a) Two general maps of England and Wales; Scotland; Ireland. (b) 16 plates of English counties. (i) 12 plates with two county maps each (including Cumberland with Westmorland). (ii) One plate with three county maps (including Leicester with Rutland). (iii) Three plates with four county maps each (including one plate with maps of the Isle of Man and the Isles of Guernsey, Jersey, etc.). (c) Yorkshire (measuring 180 × 300 mm {7.1 × 11.8 in.}; alone on one plate). (d) North; South Wales. *State:* First. *Imprints:* (i) *obac*: i.e. across the width of all the maps on the plate: 'Engraved for WALPOOLE's New & Complete BRITISH TRAVELLER'. (ii) *obbc*: i.e. across the width of all the maps on the plate: *pi*: 'Published by ALEX^R HOGG at the Kings Arms.

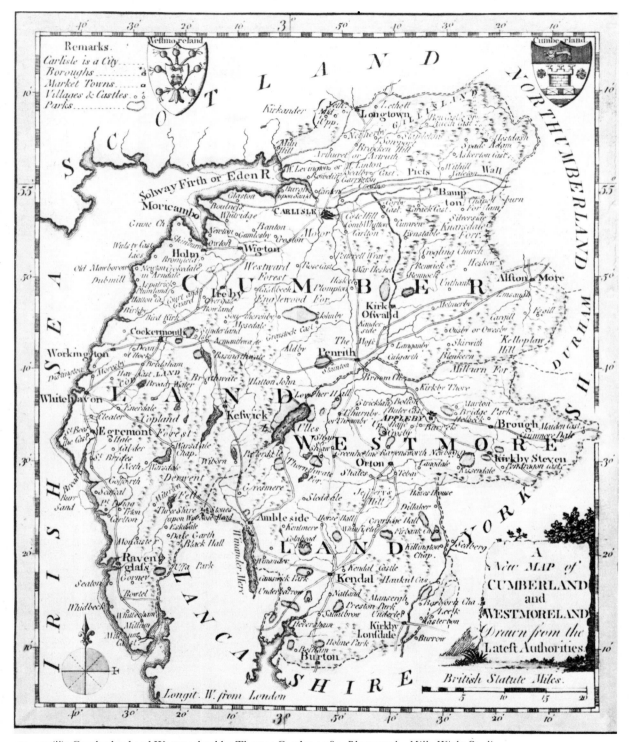

120 117(ii): Cumberland and Westmorland by Thomas Conder, 1784. *Photograph: Mills-Wight Studio*

No 16, PATERNOSTER ROW'. (*V*). **Publisher:** 'Alex. Hogg'. (ii) 1784; 1790(?): as (i) 1784, except: The ornamental foliated decoration outside the border has been erased leaving only the plain-ruled border. **State:** Second. Old stock in the first state was sometimes used in later issues. **Imprints:** (i) *obac*: inscription erased. (ii) *obbc :es*: at right of plate: 'T. Conder Sculp!' (*V*), (except: Berkshire and Somerset lack the signature; Devon and Cornwall have 'Hatchett sculpt.').

N.B. Where maps from a plate have been separated the signature will appear only on the map located at the bottom right of the plate since it was the plate that was signed and not each individual map.

(iii) 1794(?): as (ii) 1784, etc., except: *Atlas: The new and complete English traveller: or, a new historical survey and modern description of England and Wales. A work calculated equally to please the polite—entertain the curious—instruct the uninformed—and direct the traveller ... Written ... by a society of gentlemen ... Revised, corrected, and improved, by William Hugh Dalton, Esq ....* **State:** Second. **Publisher:** 'Alex. Hogg, No. 16, Paternoster-Row; and Sold by the Booksellers of Bath, Bristol ... and by all other Booksellers and Newsmen in England, Wales, Scotland, and Ireland'.

WHITTAKER, G. and W. B.
fl. c. 1823. Publishers

The Whittakers published the fairly common 1825 and 1826 editions of Capper's *A Topographical Dictionary of the United Kingdom* (118); and the less well-known 1821, 1823 and 1825 editions of *The Travellers Pocket Atlas ...* and *Pinnock's County Histories ...* (*V*), which contained the same small, plain maps. D.N.B.: Vol. 21, p. 144.

(118) **Description:** *st*: Second. **Supply:** Moderate. **Average size:** 135 × 160 mm (5.4 × 6.4 in.). **Features:** Distances between towns are noted along the roads and the distance from London is given in ovals. **Scale:** *V/av*: 1:10*m*/'Scale of Statute Miles' or 'Statute Miles'/*sbm*. **Border:** *tTt*. **North Point:** *s/op*. **Key:** 'Explanation'. **Title:** *c/pc*/set within a vertically hatched panel with a narrow *dl* frame. **Engravers:** Neele & Son.

Issues: (i) 1820(?): *Atlas: The travellers pocket atlas consisting of a complete set of county maps, for England & Wales, on an original & improved plan. The roads leading to the nearest towns in the adjoining counties* being delineated on each map ....*Maps (44):* (a) England. (b) 39 English counties. (c) Yorkshire. (d) North; South Wales. (e) Environs of London (dated 1 Feb. 1820). **State:** First. **Imprint:** (i) *obbr:es*: 'Neele & Son, sc. 352, Strand' (*V*), (except: England and Berkshire; Warwickshire is mis-spelt 'Nelee'!). **Publishers:** Pinnock & Maunder.

N.B. The maps were also published in *Pinnock's county histories* at this time.

(ii) 1822(?); 1823: as (i) 1820(?), except: *Maps (43):* as (i) without London environs. **State:** Second. Minor revisions and additions. **Imprint:** (ii) *obbc:pi* added: most maps have: 'Published by G. & W. B. Whittaker, Ave-Maria Lane, 1821' but Derby, Hereford and Oxford bear the imprint: 'Published by Pinnock & Maunder, and G. & W. B. Whittaker, Ave-Maria Lane, 1821', (*V*). Oxford is undated and Dorset is dated 1822. Most imprints were corrected to 1822 during the issue. **Publishers:** G. & W. B. Whittaker, and Pinnock & Maunder.

N.B. The maps were published c.1823 in this state, and between 1823 and 1825 again usually without a *pi*, in *Pinnock's county histories*.

The Whittakers also published: 1825: *A topographical dictionary of the United Kingdom ...*, see (34) (v).

WOOD, John
fl. 1818–1826. Surveyor

John Wood, the Permanent Director of the Land Surveyors' Society, carried out his extensive surveys of Scottish towns between 1818 and 1826. The resulting plans (119) which were finely engraved and very large and detailed, were issued as they were completed, and in atlas form in 1828.

(119) **Description:** *st*: First. (Fig. 121). **Supply:** Scarce. **Average size:** *Vc*/500 × 650 mm (20 × 26 in.). **Features:** Some plans incorporate a panel giving area and population figures for parishes. Some plans have a reference key to important buildings and places of interest. **Scale:** *Vc*/'Scale of Scotch Chains each 74 feet $1\frac{1}{4}$ inch' or 'Scale of Chains each 66 ft'/*Vw/sb* divided into chains and links. **Border:** *tTt/bb*. **North Point:** *s/f/V*. **Decoration:** Arbroath has a small vignette of Arbroath Abbey. **Title:** *V*/e.g. 'PLAN OF THE CITY OF ST. ANDREWS SURVEYED BY JOHN WOOD EDINBURGH 1820 ENG^D BY N. DOUGLAS'/*vl*/dates and engravers vary/*sd*.

121 119(i): Glasgow published by John Wood, 1822. *By permission of the British Library (Maps C.21.e.4.)*

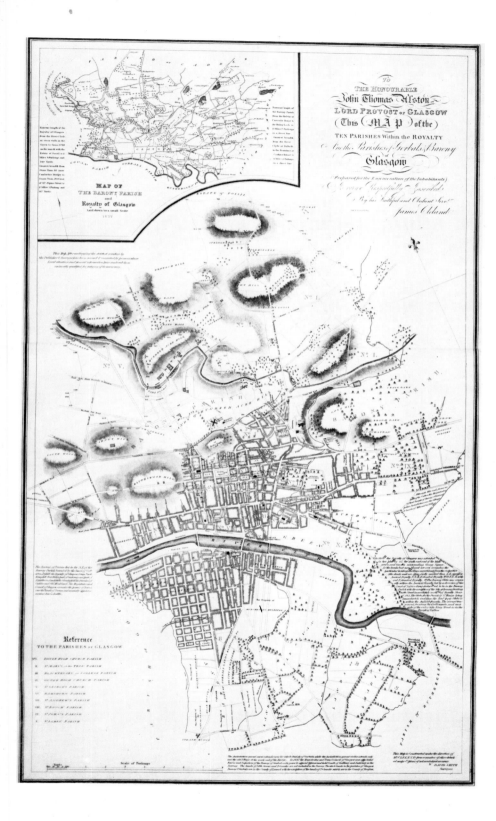

Engravers: The plans were mainly engraved by T. Clerk. Other engravers were W. Murphy (2), Kirkwood & Son (3), N. Douglas (2), W. & A. K. Johnston (2), Chas. Thomson, and Geo. Bartholomew/*es* appears either in the titlepiece, below it, or *obb*.

Issues: (i) 1828: *Atlas: Wood's town atlas ....* *Plans (48):* (a) Berwick upon Tweed. (b) 46 mainland Scottish towns. (c) Stornaway, Island of Lewis (inset: plan of the town and harbour with the bay). Early issues were made up lacking plans; later issues added plans of Alloa, Burntisland, Dunse, Galashiels, and Melrose and Gattonside. *State:* First. *Imprint:* inside border, *bc*, or *obbc:pi*: (i) Nine plans have: 'Published by the Proprietor Canaan Wm Swinton 60 Princes S.^t & J. Ritchie High St Edin.^r' (*V*). (ii) 18 plans have an appropriate variation of: 'Published as the Act directs Sold at ... and at N.º 1 North Bridge Edin.^r'. (iii) Jedburgh and Selkirk have: 'Published by the Proprietor Canaan Edinburgh'. (iv) Five plans have: Published by the Proprietor Canaan & Wm Swinton 60 Princes St Edin.^r'. (v) Leith has: 'Published by J. Lothian 41 St Andrew Square Edinburgh'. *Publishers:* Canaan & William Swinton, J. Ritchie and J. Lothian.

ZATTA, Antonio
fl. 1757–1797. Cartographer and publisher

Although Zatta did not produce any British county atlases, he did include maps of the regions of Scotland and Ireland, and of Essex, Kent, Middlesex and Surrey in his four volume *Atlante Novissimo* published in Venice between 1779 and 1785. These scarce maps are instantly recognizable by Zatta's signature in the title cartouche which is usually a pastoral scene with trees and foliage. The maps are generally found with original colour to the boundaries, cartouche and border only.

Glossary

Armillary sphere: a skeleton globe of metal rings representing the equator, tropics, etc.

Armorial: a device, usually a shield, bearing a heraldic coat-of-arms.

Aquatint: a method of engraving on copper using nitric acid to cut the design into a plate prepared with a resin solution. The resulting print has a finely grained, transparent appearance.

Atlas factice: an atlas made up by a mapseller from his own stock and/or from the stocks of other publishers; the maps not necessarily being in the latest state.

Bailiwick: an area under the jurisdiction of a bailiff.

Barony: the Irish equivalent of the English hundred. Baronies were originally small kingdoms which later became divisions of counties.

Baroque: a style of art which evolved in Italy about 1600 out of that of the Renaissance. It was adopted throughout Europe, particularly by Catholic countries, and lasted well into the eighteenth century. The style was one of massive and complex design blending illusionism, movement, light and colour, and was intended to overwhelm by emotional appeal.

Bird's-eye view: the representation of an area as seen by a bird flying over it and viewing features from an angle of 60°–70°. The advantage of such representation is that it shows both the site and façade, and, consequently, it was used to depict churches, country houses and some settlements until the nineteenth century.

Borough: a town with corporation and privileges granted by royal charter or defined by statute.

Burin: an engraving tool with a fine cutting edge.

Cadastral survey: a survey showing the extent, value and ownership of land for taxation purposes.

Calligraphy: the art of beautiful handwriting using various lettering styles.

Cardinal points: the four chief points of the compass; i.e. Septentrio, (North): the seven stars of the Great Bear; Oriens, (East): the rising sun; Meridio, (South): the midday sun; Occidens, (West): the setting sun.

Cartographer: the preparer of a draft map for the engraver.

Cartouche: an ornamental device of scrolling, strap-work, figures, fruit, flowers, artefacts, etc. used to present a map's title, scale, dedication, etc.

Chain: a land surveyor's 66 ft. measuring device of connected metal links.

Chalcography: the art of engraving on metal plates.

Chart: a map of sea areas designed as a navigation aid.

Chorography: the description of districts.

Chromolithography: a technique of colour-printing from stone.

Chronometer: an accurate time-measuring instrument used particularly for the fixing of longitude at sea.

Circumferentor: a surveying compass provided with sights for taking horizontal angles.

Classical: the restrained art style of the ancient Greeks and Romans.

Colophon: an inscription at the end of a book with name, date, etc.; a publisher's imprint or device.

Colour wash: a thin coating of watery colour.

Compass: a device for the determination of direction.

Compass rose: the representation of a compass card on a map. A circle of the principal directions.

Compass traverse: a series of connected straight lines whose lengths are measured by a chain and directions by a compass.

Contour: a line joining points of equal height above sea level on a map.

Cornucopia: a horn of plenty: a goat's horn overflowing with fruit, flowers, etc.

Cosmographer: a map-maker.

County: a regional division introduced by the Normans which eventually replaced the old English 'shire'.

Cropping: the cutting of the map's margin close or into the engraved surface.

Cross-hatching: an engraving style producing a grid of lines at right angles to each other.

Cruciform: cross-shaped.

Cursive: a flowing style of writing with the letters joined together.

Degree: a unit of measure for arcs: one 360th part of the circumference of a circle.

Distance table: a triangular device allowing the distance between any two towns given in the table to be read easily.

Dividers: an instrument for the measuring or marking of distances.

Draft: a sketch of work to be executed.

Draughtsman: a skilled producer of drawings and plans.

Dry-point: an engraving technique using a sharp, fine needle-type tool to produce very fine lines, fine shading, and stipple dots.

Edition: all issues and re-issues printed from one state of a block, plate or stone.

Electrotype: a printing plate made by electrolytically depositing copper on to a mould of wax or lead.

Elevation: a flat drawing of one side of a building.

Engrave: cut a design into a metal plate or wood block.

Etching: the use of acid to incise a design into a metal plate.

Fleur-de-lys: the Iris flower, much used in heraldry, particularly as the royal arms of France.

Foliate: leaf-like.

Form lines: lines running parallel to the shore to represent water; resembling a receding tide.

Foxing: brown stains, usually in spots, caused by damp or chemicals in the paper.

Gauffered, goffered: describes the embossed edges of books.

Geodesy: a branch of mathematics dealing with the figure and area of the earth.

Graticule: a network of lines of latitude and longitude on a map; or a grid system of reference or distance squares based on mileage divisions.

Graver: a tool used for engraving a metal plate.

Grotesque: a comically distorted figure or design.

Guard: a protective strip of paper pasted behind the centre-fold which allows the map to be sewn into the atlas binding without damage to the engraved surface and without obscuring detail along the centre-fold.

Hachures: short lines of shading following the direction of maximum slope to represent relief; usually indicating slope by the closeness and thickness of the shading.

Hatching: a series of engraved or drawn lines producing the effect of shading.

Hundred: a division of a county particularly important in Saxon and Norman times but continuing in use as a unit of local administration intermediate between parish and shire until the Local Government Act of 1894 replaced it with the district council. There are several theories as to the origin of the hundred; possibly it consisted of 100 families or the settlements of 100 invading warriors.

Hydrographer: a maker of marine charts.

Iconographer: an illustrator of a subject.

Illumineur: a map colourist.

Impression: a single print taken from an engraved metal plate, wood block or lithographic stone.

Imprint: name of printer or publisher, and date and place of printing or publication.

Index map: a map of the overall area covered by the larger-scaled sectional (i.e. county, regional, road, etc.) maps in an atlas.

Intaglio: a design cut into a metal plate creating an incised mirror image.

Issue: the total number of impressions taken from an engraved plate, woodblock or lithographic stone at one time.

Laid down: the map has been pasted to a backing card or other suitable material.

Lathe; Laithe: an administrative division in Kent, equivalent to the hundred in other counties. Confusingly, each lathe was itself divided into hundreds. In Norman times there were six lathes, but this was later reduced to five.

Latitude: a place's angular distance on its meridian, north or south of the equator, measured from the earth's centre.

Leet: the East Anglian equivalent of the hundred.

Legend: an inscription or motto. An explanation of the symbols and conventions used on a map.

Letterpress: matter printed from type, as distinguished from that printed from metal plates, etc.

Liberty: (i) an area situated outside a borough where freemen had certain rights of pasture, etc.; (ii) a group of manors, the lord of which was granted privileges by the Crown; (iii) in the Isle of Wight, it was used as another name for a hundred.

Ligature: (i) a cord or band used in tying; (ii) two or more letters joined together in one character.

Linear scale: a scale of measurement in one dimension.

Line engraving: a hand method of cutting into a metal plate a design which is to be printed.

Lithograph: a print produced from a stone block bearing the design applied by greasy crayon.

Longitude: the angular distance, along the equator east or west, from a standard meridian to the meridian of any place.

Lozenge: a panel designed as a tablet.

Manor: the land held by a lord. The manor could be a subdivision of a parish or it could extend over two or more parishes.

Manuscript: a map drawn by hand, not printed.

Meridian: a great circle passing through the poles and any point on the earth's surface, i.e. a line of longitude. The prime meridian is the line of longitude given the value 0° from which all other longitudes are measured.

Mile: British unit of linear measure; one minute of longitude measured on the equator.

Minute: one sixtieth of a degree of an arc.

Moiré: having a watered, or wavy, pattern.

Molehill: a small hummock symbol used to represent relief before the development of hachures; sometimes also referred to as a 'sugar-loaf'.

Municipality: a town or district having a local self-government.

North Point: a design indicating the direction of north on a map.

Off-setting: the transfer of ink from a printed sheet to another which has been in contact with it for a considerable time, producing a faint mirror image. This occurs particularly on folded maps; for example, the large titles and vignettes of the Greenwood county maps are frequently transferred faintly to the opposite side of the map.

Orient; Orientate: to determine exactly the position with regard to the points of the compass.

Pagination: the numbering and arrangement of pages.

Palatinate: an area administered by an earl or a bishop.

Paper-mark: a watermark: a device incorporated into the paper at the time of manufacture.

Parish: originally the area served by the parson from the parish church. Acts of Parliament, particularly in the sixteenth and seventeenth centuries, established the parish as an adminstration unit to supersede the manorial courts which fell into decay. The parishes did not necessarily correspond with either manor or county boundaries. The importance of the parish as a unit of local administration was ended by nineteenth-century reforms creating municipal and county boroughs, and rural councils.

Patronage: support given by a wealthy patron to finance survey work and map production.

Perambulator: a way-wiser: a device which records distance by the revolutions of a wheel measuring 8.25 ft. in circumference, i.e. half a pole in circumference.

Plane-table: a surveying instrument used for measuring angles in mapping.

Plate: a sheet of smooth metal on which a design was engraved.

Plate-mark: the impression made in the paper when the plate was pressed into it. The outer edges of the plate formed a ridge around the printed area.

Pontuseaux: the impression in paper of the wire grid which supported the pulp in the tray during the paper-making process.

Profile: a representation of the side view of a feature.

Proof: a print taken before engraving is completed to check that progress is satisfactory.

Prospect: a view.

Pull: the process of printing an impression from a metal plate, woodblock or stone.

Quadrant: a graduated instrument for taking angular measurement.

Rape: the Sussex equivalent of a hundred. The six rapes, each possessing a castle and a harbour, were the units of local government.

Re-issue: another issue printed from an unchanged metal plate, woodblock or stone at a later date.

Relief process: a woodblock is carved so that the design stands in relief with surrounding areas cut away.

Re-print: a subsequent impression taken from a plate, block or stone after the original issue.

Reproduction: a modern copy of a map.

Re-strike: a modern impression taken from an old printing plate.

Re-touching: the reworking of a worn plate by deepening worn lines and faint areas so that the plate is restored to its original condition.

Rhumb-lines: lines drawn on maps to indicate direction. From the earliest times, direction at sea in the Mediterranean had been identified by the prevailing winds from eight equally spaced directions around the horizon. These 'rhumbs' allowed navigators to steer crude courses. Although the use of rhumb lines was superseded by the development of Mercator's projection, map-makers continued to use them for decorative purposes.

Riding: a third of a shire. Yorkshire was divided into ridings, each with its town courts, by the Danes.

Road map: a medium- or small-scale map of the road network designed for route finding and planning.

Rococo: a style of art prevalent in Europe c.1730–80, characterised by elaborate ornamentation. It developed in reaction to the baroque splendours of Louis XIV and was based on the use of scrolls and curves. It was basically a gay and pretty style of interior decoration.

Romantic: a free expression of the passions characterised by a love of the exotic, occasionally becoming absurd. This art movement reached its heights about 1830 in Britain, France and Germany.

Sextant: an instrument including a graduated arc equal to a sixth of a circle for taking angular measurements.

Soke: a right of local jurisdiction which probably originated from the settlement of townships by Danish soldiers who owed personal allegiance to a lord and a court. The soke was the lord's private jurisdiction even though it came within the jurisdication of one or more manors.

Spot height: a figure on a map showing the altitude of a certain point.

State: the state of a plate refers to the condition of the printing plate. The plate in its first engraved condition is in its first state. The first change to the engraved design is referred to as the second state. Subsequent changes to the plate produce corresponding states.

Stippling: a method of engraving by using dots.

Strapwork: the imitation of cut, fashioned leather; the design originated from interwoven and interlaced strips of leather with curling ends.

Strip map: a type of road map depicting individual routes and not attempting overall topographic coverage.

Stucco: the fine plasterwork of cornices, mouldings, ceilings, etc.

Sugarloaf: a molehill: a hill in the shape of a conical moulded mass of hard refined sugar.

Supporters: the pair of figures shown standing by or holding a shield with armorial bearings.

Surface process: i.e. lithography: the design to be printed is drawn directly on to a specially prepared surface.

Swag: an ornamental festoon of flowers, fruit, etc.

Swash lettering: lettering having flourished strokes at top and bottom.

Theodolite: an instrument for the measurement of angles in surveying by means of a rotating telescope.

Tithes: taxes paid in kind to the local church on the basis of one-tenth of production. Under the Tithe Commutation Act of 1836, tithes could be commuted to a rent-charge based on the prevailing price of corn.

Triangulation: mapping by the measurement of the sides and angles of a series of triangles on determined base-lines.

Triton: a sea-god.

Vellum: skin dressed and prepared for writing and drawing (strictly calfskin).

Verdigris: a green or greenish-blue poisonous compound prepared by treating copper with acetic acid.

Verso: the left-hand page or back of a sheet.

Vignette: a small illustration or decoration.

Volute: a spiral formation.

Wapontake: a county subdivision, corresponding to a hundred, in some eastern and midland counties covered by the Danelaw.

Ward: administrative division of a borough or a city; or an administrative division, corresponding to a hundred, in Cumberland, Durham, Northumberland, Westmorland, and some Scottish counties.

Wash colouring: a thin coating of watery colour.

Watermark: a papermark: a device incorporated into paper at the time of manufacture.

Way-wiser: a perambulator: a device which records distance by the revolutions of a wheel measuring 8.25 ft. in circumference, i.e. half a pole in circumference.

Woodblock: a block of wood carved in relief for printing.

Woodcut: an illustration printed from a block of wood on which a design has been cut.

Select Bibliography

Elementary texts
Booth, J., *Looking at old maps*, (1979)
Hodgkiss, A. G., *Discovering Antique Maps*, (2nd ed.; 1975)

General texts
Baynton-Williams, R., *Investing in Maps*, (1969)
Lister, R., *Antique Maps and their Cartographers*, (1970)

Detailed and reference texts
Bagrow, L., *History of Cartography*. Revised and enlarged by R. A. Skelton, (1964)
Bricker, C., *Landmarks of Mapmaking: An illustrated survey of maps and mapmakers*. Maps chosen and displayed by R. V. Tooley, text by C. Bricker, preface by G. R. Crone, (1976)
British Museum, *The British Museum Catalogue of Printed Maps, Charts and Plans*, 15 vols., (1967)
British Library, *The British Library Catalogue of Printed Maps, Charts and Plans. Ten-Year Supplement 1965–1974*, (1978)
Harvey, P. D. A., *The history of topographical maps*, (1980)
Koeman, C., *Atlantes Neerlandici*. Bibliography of terrestrial, maritime and celestial atlases and pilot books, published in the Netherlands up to 1880, 5 vols., (1967–71)
Lister, R., *How to Identify Old Maps and Globes*, (1965). Contains: *The use of watermarks in dating old maps and documents* by Edward Heawood. (Reprinted as *Collecting Old Maps and Globes*, 1979)
National Maritime Museum, *Catalogue of the Library. Vol. 3. 2 pt: Atlases and Cartography.* (1971)
Phillips, P. L., and LeGear, C. E., *A List of Geographical Atlases in the Library of Congress*, (8 vols.; 1909–74)
Ristow, W. W., *Guide to the History of Cartography*. An annotated list of references on the history of maps and mapmaking, (1973)
Skelton, R. A., *Decorative Printed Maps of the 15th to 18th Centuries*, (Revised edition of *Old Decorative Maps and Charts* by A. L. Humphreys, 1926; new text, 1952; reprinted 1965)
Skelton, R. A., *Maps. A Historical Survey of Their Study and Collecting*, (2nd ed.; 1975)
Tooley, R. V., *Maps and Map-Makers*, (1949; 6th ed., 1978)
Tooley, R. V., *A Dictionary of Mapmakers*, (1979)

APPENDIX I COLLECTIONS

The main early map collections in the British Isles are housed at the following libraries and institutions:

LONDON

(i) *The British Library*: admission by pass only, for serious research and reference.

(ii) *Guildhall Library*: public admission: concentration on maps of London.

(iii) *National Maritime Museum, Greenwich*: admission by pass only: concentration on sea charts and nautical atlases.

(iv) *Public Record Office, Kew*: admission by reader's ticket: maps and plans largely transferred for permanent preservation by Government departments and Courts of Law and certain other official bodies.

(v) *Royal Geographical Society*: the Map Room is open to the public but the Library and Archives are normally restricted to Fellows and Members.

ENGLAND

(i) *Cambridge University Library*: no general public access but admission to carry out research may be granted.

(ii) *Bodleian Library, Oxford*: open to non-members of the University upon recomendation: the Library is endowed with the map collection of Richard Gough.

Special collections:

(i) *G. E. H. Allen collection in the Lancashire Record Office, Preston*: access by appointment.

(ii) *E. G. Box collection in the Fellows' Library, Winchester College*: no general public access but admission to carry out research may be granted.

(iii) *Lewis Evans collection in the City Museum, St Albans*: public admission, preferably by appointment.

(iv) *Eric Gardner collection in the Surrey Archaeological Society, Guildford*: non-members may be admitted for research purposes.

(v) *Harold Whitaker collection in the Brotherton Library, University of Leeds*: access is normally restricted to members of the University and local scholars.

WALES

(i) *National Library of Wales, Aberystwyth*: admission by reader's ticket.

SCOTLAND

(i) *National Library of Scotland, Edinburgh*: admission for research and reference not readily available elsewhere.

(ii) *Royal Scottish Geographical Society, Edinburgh*: open to the public.

IRELAND

(i) *Linen Hall Library, Belfast*: access open to any member of the public engaged on research.

(ii) *National Library of Ireland, Dublin*: admission by reader's ticket.

(iii) *Royal Irish Academy, Dublin*: admission by arrangement.

N.B.: Most reference libraries have a map collection; some are surprisingly comprehensive, but most concentrate on items of local interest. County Record Offices house map collections relating to the particular county, including manuscript as well as printed maps.

APPENDIX II ANTIQUE MAP DEALERS

It is always wise to telephone dealers before visiting them, to make sure that they are still in business at the same premises, that they will be open (many dealers are notorious for their unusual business hours!), and that they have the maps you seek in stock.

Key
Sh: Shop premises; *Pr*: Private premises, appointment necessary; *Pb*: Postal business; *sm*: Small stock only; *sp*: Specialities; *C*: Catalogue; *s*: Search service; *v*: Valuations; *f*: Framing; *m*: Mount cutting; *r*: Restoration; *c*: Colouring; *a*: Investment advice.

Where dealers do not offer particular facilities, they will usually be able to advise on their availability.

LONDON

ALAN BRETT: *Sh*: 24, Cecil Court, Charing Cross Road, W.C.2., Tel. 01-836 8222; *sp*: continental maps.

ANTIPODEAN BOOKS, MAPS AND PRINTS; *Pr*: 79, Grosvenor Road, Muswell Hill, N.10., Tel. 01-444 6483; *sp*: Australia, South Pacific; *s*; *sm*.

AVRIL NOBLE; *Sh*: Sat: Panton Gallery, 159, Portobello Road, W.11., Tel. 01-328 2377/01-624 0826 Mon.-Fri.: Grays Antique Arcade, Davies Street; *C*; *s*.

BAYNTON-WILLIAMS; *Sh*: 18, Lowndes Street, S.W.1., Tel. 01-235 6595.

CLIVE A. BURDEN; *Sh*: 13, Cecil Court, Charing Cross Road, W.C.2., Tel. 01-836 2177; *Pb*: 36, High Street, Rickmansworth, Herts; *sp*: British Isles and county maps; *v*.

COLLECTORS TREASURES; *Sh*: Harrods, Knightsbridge; *m*; *f*.

DAWSON RARE BOOKS; *Sh*: 16, Pall Mall, S.W.1., Tel. 01-930 2515; *Pb*; *C*; *sm*.

EDNA WHITESON; *Sh*: 343, Bowes Road, N.11., Tel. 01-361 1105; *Pb*: 66, Belmont Avenue, Cockfosters, Herts; *C*.

J. A. L. FRANKS; *Sh*: 180, Fleet Street, E.C.4., Tel. 01-405 0274; *Pb*; *sp*: early miniatures; *C*.

HENRY SOTHERAN; *Sh*: 2, Sackville Street, W.1., Tel. 01-734 1150; *C*; *m*;*f*; *sm*.

JON ASH (RARE BOOKS); *Sh*: 25, Royal Exchange, E.C.3., Tel. 01-626 2665; *Pb*; *C*; *m*;*f*; *s*.

JONATHAN POTTER; *Sh*: 1, Grafton Street, W.1., Tel. 01-491 3520; *Pb*; *C*; *s*; *r*; *c*; *v*.

LEYCESTER MAP GALLERIES; *Sh*: Grays in the Mews, Davies Mews, W.1., Tel. 01-493 7861; *s*; *c*.

MAPPAMUNDI; *Pb*: 5, Albemarle Street, W.1., Tel. 01-493 9836; *sp*: Holy Land, Asia; *a*.

MAP HOUSE; *Sh*: 54, Beauchamp Place, S.W.3., Tel. 01-589 4325; *Pb*; *C*; *m*;*f*; *v*; *s*.

MAPSELLERS LTD; *Sh*: 37, Southampton Street, W.C.2., Tel. 01-836 8444; *Pb*: 391, Strand, W.C.2.; *C*; *v*; *s*; *c*.

PARKER GALLERY; *Sh*: 2, Albemarle Street, W.1., Tel. 01-499 5906; *Pb*; *C*; *sm*.

RAYMOND O'SHEA GALLERY; *Sh*: 6, Ellis Street, off Sloane Street, S.W.1., Tel. 01-730 0081; *Pb*; *C*; *sp*: cartographic curiosities; *r*;*f*.

ROBERT DOUWMA PRINTS AND MAPS; *Sh*: 93, Great Russell Street, W.C.1., Tel. 01-636 4895; *Pb*; *C*.

SARUM (ERICSSON & CHRISTOPH); *Pr*: 10, Chapel Street, S.W.1., Tel. 01-235 6744; *Pb*; *C*.

STANLEY CROWE; *Sh*: 5, Bloomsbury Street, W.C.1., Tel. 01-580 3976; *Pb*; *C*; *sp*: large-scale county maps and town plans of the British Isles.

TOOLEY'S; *Sh*: 33, Museum Street, W.C.1., Tel. 01-637 9724; *Pb*; *C*.

WARWICK LEADLAY GALLERY; *Sh*: 5, Nelson Road, Greenwich, Tel. 01-858 0317; *Pb*; *sp*: South-East London and Kent; *r*; *c*; *m*;*f*.

ENGLAND

ALCESTER, WARWICKS: April Antiques; *Pr*: April Cottage, Coughton Lane, Coughton, Tel. Alcester 762661; *sp*: Midland counties; *C*.

ALRESFORD, HANTS: Laurence Oxley; *Sh*: The Studio Bookshop, 17, Broad Street, Tel. Alresford 2188;*f*; *m*.

ARNESBY, LEICS: Leycester Map Galleries; *Pb*: Well House, Tel. Peatling Magna 462; *s*; *c*.

AMERSHAM, BUCKS: Collectors Treasures; *Sh*: 91, High Street, Tel. Amersham 7213; *C*;*f*; *m*.

BARNSTAPLE, DEVON: Minerva Gallery; *Sh*: 123, Boutport Street, Tel. Barnstaple 71025; *Pb*; *m*;*f*.

BATH, AVON: George Gregory; *Sh*: 8, Green Street, Tel. Bath 66055; *Pb*; *sm*.
: Lantern Gallery; *Sh*: 9, George Street, Tel. Bath 63727; *Pb*; *sp*: South-West counties; *v*; *s*; *r*;*f*; *m*.

BIDEFORD, DEVON: Minerva Gallery; *Sh*: 20, Buttgarden Street, Tel. Bideford 6483; *Pb*; *m*;*f*.

CAMBRIDGE, CAMBS: Charles Wood; *Pr*: 9, Rutherford Road, Tel. Cambridge 840346; *Pb*; *sp*: Saxton.

CANTERBURY, KENT: Fitchett's; *Sh*: 26, Palace Street, Tel. Canterbury 62729; *Pb*; *m*;*f*.

CHELTENHAM, GLOS: Regent Gallery; *Sh*: 10, Montpellier Arcade, Tel. Cheltenham 512826; *Pb*; *C*;*f*; *m*; *r*.

CHESTER, CHESHIRE: J. Alan Hulme; *Sh*: The Gallery, 54, Lower Bridge Street, Tel. Chester 44006; *Pb*: 52, Mount Way, Waverton, Chester; *sp*: British Isles; *C*; *s*; *v*.
: Richard Nicholson of Chester; *Sh*: 25, Watergate Street, Tel. Chester 26818; *Pb*: Stoneydale, Christleton, Chester CH3 7AG, Tel. Chester 36004; *C*;*f*; *m*; postal auctions.

CIRENCESTER, GLOS: Walsh & Powell; *Sh*: 47, Dyer Street, Tel. Cirencester 3174; *Pb*; *C*.

CLEVEDON, AVON: Clevedon Fine Arts Ltd; *Sh*: The Gallery, Cinema Buildings, Old Church Road, Tel. Clevedon 875862; *Pb*; *sp*: English counties; *C*; *m*; *c*.

CROYDON, SURREY: H. Crossley; *Pb*: 20, Goston Gardens, Thornton Heath, Tel. 01-684 9448.
: J. F. LeButt-Musgrave; *Pr*: 3, Montpelier Road, Purley, Tel. 01-660 7966; *sp*: English county maps; *c*;*f*; *m*; *v*; *s*.

EAST LOOE, CORNWALL: Chapel Court Bookshop; *Sh*: Shutta Road, East Looe, Tel. Looe 3700; *sp*: Cornwall; *C*; *v*; *s*;*f*; *r*.

FERRIN, W. SUSSEX: Apstanley Maps and Prints; *Pr*: 41, Sea Lane, Tel. Worthing 43570; *Pb*; *C*.

FOLKSTONE, KENT: G. & D. I. Marrin & Sons; *Sh*: 149 Sandgate Road, Tel. Folkestone 53016; *Pb*; *sp*: Kent, English counties, English Channel; *C*; *s*;*f*.

HASLEMERE, SURREY: Mrs Julia Holmes; *Pr*: Muirfield Place, Tel. Haslemere 2153; *Pb*; *sp*: county maps of the British Isles; *C*; *s*; *v*;*f*; *c*.

LIVERPOOL, MERSEYSIDE: Paul Breen; *Sh*: The Lyver Gallery, 8, Hackins Hey, Tel. Liverpool 236 7524; *C*; *v*; *r*;*f*.

NEW BARNET, HERTS: Andrew Leverton; *Pr*: 12, Walton Court, Lyonsdown Road, Tel. 01-886 6038; *Pb*; *sp*: Middle East, British counties.

NEWPORT, ISLE OF WIGHT: Holyrood Galleries; *Sh*: 1, Holyrood Street, Tel. Newport 522467; *Pb*; *sp*: Isle of Wight; *r*; *f*; *m*.

OXFORD, OXON: Magna Gallery; *Sh*: 41, High Street, Tel. Oxford 45805; *sp*: early English county maps, particularly by Speed, and Oxford plans; *C*.
: Roger Mason; *Pb*: 86A, Banbury Road, Tel. Oxford 59380; *Pr*; *C*; *s*.
: Sanders of Oxford; *Sh*: 104, High Street, Tel. Oxford 42590; *Pb*.

PRESTON, LANCS: Ingol Maps and Prints; *Pr*: Cantsfield House, 206, Tag Lane, Ingol, Tel. Preston 724769; *Pb*; *C*; *sp*: British county maps.

READING, BERKS: Waterloo Investments; *Pr*: The Penthouse, Calcot Grange, Mill Lane, Calcot, Tel. Reading 586876; *Pb*; *sp*: West Indies, South America; *C*.

RICKMANSWORTH, HERTS: Eiddon Morgan; *Pr*: Laburnums, Heronsgate, Tel. Chorleywood 2786; *Pb*; *r*; *c*.

: Northwood Maps; *Pr*: 71, Nightingale Road, Tel. Rickmansworth 72258; *Pb*; *sp*; British maps, road atlases, small atlases; *C*; *a*.

SALISBURY, WILTS: D. M. Beach; *Sh*: 52, High Street, Tel. Salisbury 3801; *Pb*; *s*.

SEVENOAKS, KENT: John Speed (Maps); *Pr*: Bretaneby Hall, Seal High Street, Tel. Sevenoaks 62772; *Pb*; *sp*: John Speed maps.

SOUTHAMPTON, HANTS: Ben Hardisty; *Sh*: 34, Northam Road, Tel. Southampton 38916; *Pb*; *sp*: British Isles; *C*; *m*; *c*; *Pr*: 65, Bury Road, Gosport, Tel. Gosport 82125.

STAMFORD, LINCS: Antique maps and Prints; *Sh*: 10, St Mary's Hill, Tel. Stamford 52330; *Pb*; *sp*: English counties; *C*.

UCKFIELD, SUSSEX: Ivan R. Deverall; *Pb*: Duval House, The Glen, Cambridge Way, Uckfield, Tel. Uckfield 2474; *C*; *s*; *c*.
: P. J. Radford; *Sh*: Gallery, Sheffield Park, Nr. Uckfield, Tel. Dane Hill 790531; *Pb*; *C*.

WENDOVER. BUCKS: Collectors Treasures; *Sh*: Hogarth House, High Street, Tel. Wendover 624402; *Pb*; *C*; *f*; *m*; Map Collectors Club.

WEYBRIDGE, SURREY: Mrs D. M. Green; *Pr*: 7, Tower Grove, Tel. Walton-on-Thames 41105; *Pb*; *sp*: county maps of England and Wales; *s*; *v*.

WIGAN, LANCS: Clifton Books; *Sh*: 5a, Dicconson Street, Tel. Wigan 36716; *Pb*; *sp*: Lancashire; *C*.

WIMBORNE MINSTER, DORSET: Wimborne Bookshop; *Sh*: 26, West Street, Tel. Wimborne 887320; *sp*: Dorset; *C*; *sm*.

WINCHESTER, HANTS: Printed Page; *Sh*: 2, Bridge Street, Tel. Winchester 4072; *Pb*; *sp*: English counties, particularly Hampshire; *C*; *f*; *m*; *c*; *v*; *r*; *s*.

YORK, YORKS: McDowell & Sterne; *Sh*: 56, Petergate, Tel. York 22000; *sp*: Yorkshire; *sm*.

WALES

ABERGAVENNY, GWENT: Books & Arts; *Sh*: The Town Hall, Tel. Abergavenny 5149; *Pb*; *sp*: Wales and Welsh counties; *s*.

CARDIFF, SOUTH GLAMORGAN: Albany Books; *Sh*: 113, Albany Road, Tel. Cardiff 498802; *Pb*; *sp*: Welsh maps; *C*; *s*.
: W. A. Beynon; *Sh*: Cardiff Antique Fayre, Mill Lane; *Pb*: 28, Cwm Nofydd, Cardiff CF4 6JX, Tel. Cardiff 612077; *sp*: Welsh maps.

MONMOUTH, GWENT: Brian Stevens; *Sh*: 3, Church Street, Tel. Monmouth 3701; *Pb*; *sp*: Monmouthshire; *sm*.

SCOTLAND

AYR: Bruce Marshall; *Sh*: 24, River Street, Tel. Ayr 84505; *Pb*; *sp*: early atlases, world maps, travel books.

EDINBURGH: John Grant; *Sh*: 9, Dundas Street, Edinburgh 3, Tel. 031-556 9698; *sp*: early Scottish maps.
: Scotia Maps; *Sh*: 173, Canongate, The Royal Mile, Tel. 031-556 4710; *Pb*; *C*; *s*; *v*; *a*.

IRELAND

BELFAST: The Bell Gallery; *Sh*: 2, Malone Road, Belfast B.9, Tel. Belfast 662998; *sp*: Irish maps.

DUBLIN: Patrick Brown; *Pb*; 15, South William Street, Dublin 2, Tel. Dublin 719013; *sp*: early maps, mainly of Ireland; *C*; *s*; *a*.
: Cathair Books; *Sh*: 26, South King Street, Dublin 2, Tel. Dublin 753194; *Pb*; *sp*: Irish maps; *f*.
: The Neptune Gallery; *Sh*: 42, South William Street, Dublin, 2, Tel. Dublin 715021; *Pb*; *sp*: Irish maps; *s*.

GALWAY: Kennys Bookshops & Art Galleries Ltd; *Sh*: High Street, Tel. Galway 62739; *sp*: Irish maps.

CHANNEL ISLANDS

ST PETER PORT, GUERNSEY: Channel Island Galleries; *Sh*: Island Craft Centre, Trinity Square, St Peter Port, Tel. Guernsey 23247; *Pb*; *sp*: Channel Islands; *s*; *f*.
: Stevens Cox; *Pr*: Birling, Mt Durand, St Peter Port; *sm*.

APPENDIX III PRICE

The price of an antique map is determined by several variables: popularity, scarcity, condition, age, and aesthetic appeal. The rise in map prices can only be described as phenomenal and has consistently run ahead of the inflation rate. In the last 20 years prices have risen by about 2,500% and, at the present time, rare maps can increase by 50–100% a year, popular maps by 30–40%, and even common maps in little demand by 15–30%. The densely populated counties of industrial England and South Wales, for instance, experience faster rising prices than the remote rural counties of mid-Wales, Scotland and Ireland. Certainly there are not, at present, enough high quality antique maps available to meet demand, and, as supply must inevitably diminish, prices will continue their steep rise for as long as antique maps remain popular.

However, antique maps have been and continue to be underpriced in comparison with other antiques. C. V. A. Duggleby, writing in the *National Westminster Bank Quarterly Review*, commented that: '... despite rise in prices and popularity, it still seems to be a relatively underpriced market in many respects.'[30] This situation is bound to disappear eventually but there are few other fields of antique collecting where 200- and 300-year -old items can be purchased so relatively cheaply. Tony Levene, writing in the *Financial Weekly*[31] noted that 'Prices of antique maps . . . have trebled and quadrupled in five years' but also counselled: 'Avoid anything after the mid-1800's, when maps became etched on steel. The older copper and woodblock engravings are far more valuable'; and Ray Maughan, in an article in the *Financial Times*[32] on 'maps as an investment medium' quoted the Head of Sotheby's map department as estimating 'that maps by John Speed and the Blaeus have appreciated by three, four and even five times in some cases over the past five or six years'. Despite price increases, good quality, scarce antique maps are a sound financial investment.

Prices quoted by dealers usually show considerable variation, and careful study of catalogues and auction records will build up a picture of the current price structure and level, and may reveal unrealistically priced items. The days of '2 de Wits worlde on cloth £1:4s:od, 100 of Speeds County Mapps 18s:od, 100 of Mr. Jenners mapps devised 8s:od'[33] are, alas, long vanished, but many maps are still to be found at bargain prices. Diligent sifting through dealers' stocks is often rewarded, more so than searching the back-street book stores and junk shops which have, by now, been largely picked clean by collectors and dealers.

APPENDIX IV DATING

Generally, an unidentified map can be assigned to a particular period by its style and decoration. The nature of the paper and its watermark also provide evidence of the map's age, but it must be remembered that this dates the paper rather than the engraving of the map, which may not originate from the same years.

Fixing a precise date for a map is sometimes difficult, particularly for maps which bear no date of publication.

Even dated maps may be misleading, for it was common for map plates to remain in use, often for many years, without having their imprint dates altered. However, changes in publishers' imprints (giving details of dates, addresses, source publications, etc.) can provide clues to dates of issue; and for maps issued with text on the reverse, changes in language and typesetting can identify editions. Since copper plates gradually lost detail and definition with prolonged use, a study of the state of wear of a plate can indicate the amount of usage since the first printing. Wear should be assessed on such features as the map border or the scale which are less likely to have been re-engraved at any time. The further the date of printing was from the date of the first issue, the more worn the impression is likely to be.

Intense competition in the map trade forced publishers to revise printing plates in order to incorporate the latest information and thus allow them to acclaim their maps as the most up-to-date available. However, such plate revisions were expensive and changes were often kept to a minimum with the result that issue dates appearing on the map or in the imprint were sometimes not changed to correspond with topographical revisions, or were changed only intermittently. Conversely, imprint dates were often changed without any revision of map detail.

There may well be a difference between the date of the information shown on the map and the actual date of issue. It was common practice among early map-makers to utilise the results of earlier survey work, often without acknowledgment, and the collector should beware of identifying the state of topographical development shown with either the date of publication or any other quoted date. Most seventeenth-century maps, including those of John Speed, were based on the earlier surveys of Saxton and Norden and such regional pioneers as Timothy Pont. Sir William Petty's important *Hiberniae Delineatio* of 1685 was produced from his famous 'Down Survey' of 1655-56 plus material from surveys of 1636–40 and 1656–59. Inevitably, much of the information shown was out-of-date. Even some of the important large-scale surveys of the eighteenth and nineteenth centuries were based on out-of-date surveys; William Yates's 1786 map of Lancashire, for example, was drawn from material approximately ten years old.

Maps sometimes quote the dates of the surveys from which they were drawn; but these dates can be misleading, since surveys often continued for many years and survey information for one section of a map might be of considerably later origin than for another. John Strachey's survey of Somerset for his 1736 map lasted a remarkable 25 years; William Day & C. Harcourt Masters took seven years to survey the same county for their 1782 map; Thomas Jefferys worked on his 20 sheet map of Yorkshire from 1767 to 1770; and Yeakell & Gardner estimated that the surveying, drawing and engraving of their four-sheet map of Sussex (actually published between 1778 and 1783) would take them a period of six years. Therefore always judge the dates on maps critically and do not blindly accept the state of topographical development shown as being the state at the date quoted.

Nevertheless, a study of topographical detail can lead to a more accurate identification of a map's issue date; for example, nineteenth-century maps can frequently be dated fairly exactly by reference to the extent of development of the canal and railway systems. But even here market pressures often forced cartographers to include canals and railways only proposed or under construction, particularly during the canal manias of the 1790s and the railway manias of the 1840s. Detailed regional, county or local histories can provide useful information for dating topographical changes, and there is a wide range of other evidence available that can also aid accurate map dating from topographical detail.

APPENDIX V SOCIETIES

The main societies in the British Isles interested in the study and collecting of early maps are:

British Cartographic Society
(Partick E. Sorrell, Honorary Secretary), Department of Land Surveying, North East London Polytechnic, Forest Road, London E17 4JB.

Geographical Society of Ireland
(Dennis Pringle, Secretary), St Patrick's College, Maynooth, Co Kildare, Ireland.

International Map Collector's Society
Woodstock, Flyford Flavell, Worcs. WR7 4BS.

Map Collector's Club
Hogarth House, High Street, Wendover, Bucks. HP22 6DU.

Royal Geographical Society
Kensington Gore, London SW7 2AR.

Royal Scottish Geographical Society
10, Randolph Crescent, Edinburgh EH3 7TU.

The International Society for the History of Cartography (Harry Margary, Honorary Treasurer), Lympne Castle, Kent.

APPENDIX VI HOW TO IDENTIFY AND DATE A MAP

The identification and dating of an antique map is a complex process requiring care and patience. However, the process may be made a little easier and more certain by following a set procedure:

1 Most maps name the engraver, draughtsman or publisher and if the series is dealt with in this work, the name(s) will appear in the index.

2 If there are no identifiable names, there may be other information on the map which can aid identification—for example, the source publication may be named and will be listed in the index.

3 If a date is given on the map, consult the 'Chronology of cartographers, engravers and publishers' for the names of map-makers active at that period. This listing will also prove useful when only a rough dating can be assigned from the style and decoration of the map.

4 Compare the map with the illustrations in order to locate similarities of style, design and decoration.

5 These steps should lead to an identification, but in some cases there will still be several similar possibilities. A check of the average dimensions of the maps should eliminate further options.

6 Finally, the map can be positively identified through a comparison of its features with the detailed descriptions in Chapter VII. However, remember that these descriptions are inevitably compromises which cannot cover all variations and there are bound to be slight differences between map and description.

7 If the map has not been identified by this process, it is unlikely that it was published as one of a series in an atlas. It will probably be one of the vast number of maps which illustrated guide books, gazetteers, directories etc., and as such is very difficult to identify.

8 Having identified the map, it is now possible to date its issue. Starting with the first issue, compare the state of the loose map with the features and changes designated for each issue. Eventually the two will match, thus identifying the date of issue. However, continue the comparison through later issues, since maps were frequently issued in the same state over a considerable period. Remember, again, that the noted changes are generalisations and that the analysis may be complicated by random alterations or the issue of remaindered stock.

If the date of issue is not clear or the designated map state appeared over a period of issues, then reference must be made to the more detailed carto-bibliographies which specify each individual state of a map, for minor revisions of detail on individual maps cannot possibly be specified in this work. The county bibliographies available are noted in Chapter VI, pages 62–5. County maps published before 1703 are individually specified in R. A. Skelton's *County Atlases of the British Isles* and Thomas Chubb's *The Printed Maps in the Atlases of Great Britain and Ireland 1579–1880* details the contents of many atlases of the British Isles. However, Chubb has not been revised since it was first published in 1927 and many of the county bibliographies date from the same period—consequently, they do not incorporate the results of a vast amount of recent research work and may often serve to confuse rather than clarify.

10 Hopefully, by the end of this process, not only has the map been identified, but also its date of issue has been determined as closely as possible. If not, in many cases, you have arrived at the boundary of current knowledge and may be able to make a contribution to the subject, for you are on the threshold of research.

Notes

PREFACE

1　Perhaps surprisingly, scarce county maps and atlases of the early nineteenth century (such as those by William Cobbett from his *Geographical dictionary of England and Wales* of 1832 and 1854; by Samuel Tymms from his *Family topographer* of c. 1831–34 and *Camden's Britannia epitomized* of c. 1842; or the children's geography tests by Mary Martha Rodwell from *The geography of the British Isles* of 1834) appear in dealers' lists even less frequently than rare maps of earlier centuries — probably because they are in short supply due to limited printings in the face of competition from firmly established atlases and more ambitious projects, and because they usually go unrecognized or are discounted for their plain design.

INTRODUCTION

2　Saxton's map of Wiltshire marked the village by a village symbol without naming it.

CHAPTER II MAP PRODUCTION

3　Reprinted from *Five Centuries of Map Printing*, edited by David Woodward, by permission of The University of Chicago Press, p.65. © 1975 by The University of Chicago.

4　Thorpe, H.: *Introduction* to *The Printed Maps of Warwickshire 1576–1900*, p.41.

5　Harley, J. B. and Hodson, D.: *Introduction* to the facsimile of *The Royal English Atlas*, p.10.

6　Cited by R. V. Tooley in *Collecting Antique Maps*, p.7.

7　*London Gazette*, 1–4 Feb 1675.

CHAPTER III CONVENTIONAL SYMBOLS

8　See: Lynam, E.: *The Mapmaker's Art*, p.45.

9　Close, Sir Charles: 'The Old English Mile'.

10　Harvey, P. D. A. and Thorpe, H.: *The Printed Maps of Warwickshire, 1576–1900*.

11　Seebohm, F.: *Customary acres and their historical importance, being a series of unfinished essays.* (1914).

12　For a detailed analysis of customary mile lengths in all parts of the country, see J. B. Harley's Figure 2: 'Lengths of the customary or old English miles between stages along Ogilby's roads; derived from data in the text of *Britannia*' (p.xxi of the facsimile *Britannia* {1970}).

CHAPTER V THE MAP TRADE

13　*London Gazette*, 18–21 May 1668.

CHAPTER VI TYPES OF MAPS

14　*The London Catalogue of Books published in Great Britain from 1814–1846* reported an English county atlas published by 'Jas Wyld' in 1842. Several county maps are known, similar in style to Cary's quarto maps (24), bearing Wyld's imprint, but no copy of the atlas is extant.

15　These maps, or variants of them, plus additional maps added at various dates were issued until 1636 and reduced 'pocket' versions of them were published between 1607 and 1673.

16　Fordham, Sir H. G.: 'Descriptive List of the Maps of the Great Level of the Fens, 1604–1900'. (in *Studies in Carto-Bibliography*; 1914 and 1969) see also: Lynam, E. W.: 'Early Maps of the Fen District'. (*GJ*, 84; 1934) : Lynam, E.W.: 'Maps of the Fenlands'. (in *Victoria History of the Counties of England: Huntingdonshire*; 1936)

17　Harley, J. B. and O'Donoghue, Y.: *The Old Series Ordnance Survey Maps of England and Wales*, pp.xi–xv. Vol. I.

18　Van der Aa also adapted the pocket (av. size: 140 × 200 mm; 5.5 × 7.9 in.) county and regional maps of the British Isles, published by Jansson in 1651 in his *Atlas minor Gerardi Mercatoris à I. Hondio . . .*, and published them in 1712 in his *L'Atlas Soulagé . . . .* The original ornate Latin title cartouches were replaced by French titles in simpler decorative cartouches. For the *Galérie Agréable . . .* of 1729 the maps were surrounded by a wide frame resembling carved wood bearing the *pi* below the map: 'A Leide, Chez Pierre vander Aa, Avec Privilege'.

Van der Aa also produced very decorative general maps of the British Isles which usually name him in the title cartouche.

19　Cited by Phillipa Glanville in *London in Maps*.

20　Cited by John West in *Village Records*, p.158.

CHAPTER VII THE MAP MAKERS

21　I am indebted to Dr John Andrews for information on Adlard.

22　Also included in this category could be the strange county and regional maps by the French geographer Aristide Michel Perrot, engraved by Mme Migneret and published in the six-volume work *L'Angleterre, ou Description Historique et Topographique du Royaume uni de la Grande-Bretagne . . .* in 1823, 1828 and 1835. These tiny maps show very little detail and are dwarfed by their surrounding vignettes.

23　Cited from Bickham by A. Hodgkiss in *Discovering Antique Maps*.

24　For a detailed analysis of the publishing history and imprints of these maps see the Introduction by J. B. Harley and Donald Hodson to the facsimile of the *Royal English Atlas*.

25　Cited by R. V. Tooley in *Maps and Map-Makers*, p.57.

26　Cited by Ralph Hyde in *Printed Maps of Victorian London 1851–1900*, p.2.

27　Cited from a Greenwood prospectus by A. Hodgkiss in *Discovering Antique Maps*.

28 Cited by Donald Hodson in *Printed Maps of Hertfordshire 1577–1900*, p.68.

29 Royal Scottish Geographical Society: *The Early Maps of Scotland*, Vol. 1, p.122.

APPENDIX III PRICE

30 Duggleby, C. V. A.: 'The Lure of Collecting' in *National Westminster Bank Quarterly Review*, May 1978.

31 Levene, Tony: 'Alternative Investments' in *Financial Weekly*, 8 February, 1980.

32 Maughan, Ray: 'Contours of Cartography' in *Financial Times*, 9 November, 1979.

33 'On 27 Jan 1673/4 an inventory of Jenner's house and property was taken by John Garrett and John Overton for probate.' This listing is taken from the itemization of his shop goods. Cited by Sarah Tyacke in *London Map-sellers 1660–1720*, p.118.

Abbreviations

1 Used on maps:

For the cartographer or draughtsman: i.e. author, drawn by, etc.:
auctore, auct., auct^d; delineavit, delin., delt., del.; descripsit; invenit; composuit.
Copied from: autographum.

For the engraver: i.e. engraved by, etc.:
sculpsit, sculp., sc.; fecit, fec., fc.; caelavit; incidit, incidente, incidebat.

For the printer or publisher: i.e. after, etc.:
apud.; excudit, excudebat, excud., exc.; ex officina; formis; sumptibus; typis; impensis; pub., pubd.

For the lithographer:
lith.

With permission of:
cum privilegio (i.e. a copyright privilege had been granted to the owner of an engraved plate).

More commonly: vulgo.

Initiated the engraving or printing of the plate:
fieri curabat; procurante.

2 Used in reference literature:

Born: b.
Died: d.
Circa: c. (i.e. about)
Flourished: fl. (i.e. floruit: the most productive period)
Edition: edn.; ed.
D.N.B.: *Dictionary of National Biography*

3 Notes to the select bibliography:

(*F*): Facsimile

A comprehensive bibliography of the subject would be too lengthy for this work for there are innumerable studies of every aspect of antique maps in a wide variety of books and journals. The sources offered will lead to many more not recorded here; hopefully, enough are noted for at least some to be locally available to collectors.

Imago Mundi (*IM*) is a periodical devoted to the history of early cartography which has been published annually since 1935.

The Map Collectors' Circle published 110 highly specialised illustrated monographs (MCC) between 1963 and 1975 to assist serious collectors and librarians by providing biographical, bibliographical and other detailed studies on cartographic history. The series is now discontinued.

The Map Collector (*MC*) has been published quarterly since December 1977. It is 'the leading medium of communication between collectors, investors and dealers throughout the world'.

Other journals:

Archaeologia Cambrensis (*ACs*); *Archaeologia Cantiana* (*ACa*); *Cartographical Journal* (*CJ*); *Geographical Journal* (*GJ*); *Geographical Magazine* (*GM*); *Scottish Geographical Magazine* (*SGM*).

Index

Subjects

Individual map titles are generally not indexed, nor are place-names, canals, railways, etc. mentioned in atlas titles or in the detailed analyses of chapter VII

Addresses, Premises and Imprints
An imprint or address may be the only clue available to the identity of a damaged map or atlas

Paranormal
GLASGOW

Geoff Holder

The
History
Press

In memory of Dominique Dupuy, a cantankerous, bloody-minded and battle-hearted individual. *Avec appreciation.*

First published 2011

The History Press
The Mill, Brimscombe Port
Stroud, Gloucestershire, GL5 2QG
www.thehistorypress.co.uk

British Library Cataloguing in Publication Data.
A catalogue record for this book is available from the British Library.

ISBN 978 0 7524 5420 7
Typesetting and origination by The History Press
Printed in Great Britain

CONTENTS

ACKNOWLEDGEMENTS

My thanks go out to: Janet Bord of the Fortean Picture Library; Winnie Tyrrell, Photo Library Co-ordinator at Glasgow Life/Glasgow Museums; the team at Inchinnan parish church; the indefatigable staff of the A.K. Bell Library, Perth; the good people at the Mitchell Library and the National Library of Scotland; Jane Gallagher, Special Collections Assistant at the Templeman Library, University of Kent; Derek Green of The Ghost Club; and, *bien sûr,* to Ségolène Dupuy, photo-paragon of this parish.

INTRODUCTION

The medium who channelled the autobiography of one of Jesus' companions. The children who hunted Spring-Heeled Jack. The other children who claimed they were tormented by invisible witches. The upper-class men who burned the witches. The ordinary people who glimpsed panthers and pumas. The ministers who saw the future. The mother who 'knew' her son had just died many miles away. The rake who was dragged to Hell. Vampires. Demons. Martians. The spirits of the dead. Doppelgangers. Poltergeists. Welcome to *Paranormal Glasgow*. Prepare to have your mind boggled and your preconceptions shattered. For strangeness of all stripes lurks within.

Chapter one explores episodes from the ghostly and psychic worlds, with emphasis on inexplicable experiences recorded by the Society for Psychical Research, and the utterly far-out story of the medium David Duguid. Chapter two rounds up the many sightings of

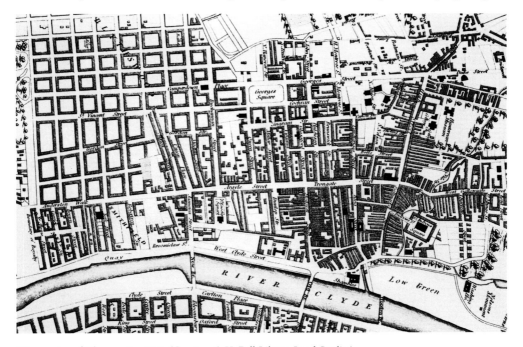

The centre of Glasgow in 1822. *(Courtesy A.K. Bell Library, Local Studies)*

A view of the small town of Glasgow around 1680, by John Slezar. *(Courtesy A.K. Bell Library, Local Studies)*

Jamaica Street, in the heart of the industrial city, early twentieth century. *(Author's Collection)*

'alien big cats' and other out-of-place animals in the Glasgow area, from the Paisley Panther to the Parkhead Fox. Chapter three is almost the freakiest of the lot, with tales of one Glasgow man who allegedly lived without food for months, and a second who developed the bleeding wounds of Christ. Chapters four and five bring together, in documented detail, the horrors and sheer 'otherness' of the witch-hunting era, with episodes of folk-magic, Caledonian 'voodoo dolls', levitation, demonic possession, second-sight, and some truly horrible children. Chapter six unearths some long-forgotten corners of folklore and anthropology in its search for the Fearless Vampire Hunters of Old Gorbals Town. Look out for the Ogre of Glasgow Green and the Hobgoblins of Cowcaddens. And Chapter seven rummages through both the daily ordinariness and the outer fringes of the world of belief, from the Knights Templar and miracle-working saints to kissing trees and cholera denial.

In many ways, all the chapters in this book grapple in some way with the issue of *belief*. Belief in the divine. Belief in the Devil. Belief in the afterlife. Belief in psychic powers. Belief in monsters. Some of these beliefs are directed by ideological or religious motives, while others fall into the category of what might be termed superstitions. Superstition is a word often used as a weapon – what *we* believe is of course right and proper, but what *those people over there* believe is superstitious nonsense. Such implicit judgements can sometimes justify the dismissal (or even the suppression) of divergent beliefs. On the other hand, on a small, personal scale, 'superstition' is a useful, meaningful word, while some of the beliefs aired in this book are truly bizarre.

What many of these cases demonstrate is the way people employ 'magical thinking'. Magical thinking is the thought process you engage in order to perform 'magic', that is, when you artificially link two events that have no causal connection. Using the birthdates of your loved ones on a lottery ticket is a prime example of magical thinking; the numbers will be no more likely to win than a randomly-chosen selection, but through magical thinking you are

The River Clyde, early twentieth century. *(Courtesy A.K. Bell Library, Local Studies)*

The River Clyde, a hundred years later. *(Photograph by Geoff Holder)*

persuaded they are somehow charged with special significance and will therefore be 'luckier' for you.

How many of the stories in *Paranormal Glasgow* are merely the result of magical thinking, and how many are authentic intrusions of the supernatural into our lives? It is impossible to tell. However, you shouldn't take my word for it. References are given for all the stories, so if you wish you can delve further, evaluating the original sources against my interpretations – and thus make up your own mind.

Welcome to *Paranormal Glasgow.* And let's be careful out there.

CHAPTER ONE

SPECTRES, PSYCHICS AND SPOOKY EVENTS

We start with what is probably the most frequently-reported aspect of the paranormal – experiences that have a *personal* dimension, such as ghosts and psychic episodes. This area encompasses a wide range of phenomena, and there is often no clear boundary between the various elements. The overlapping elements include: *apparitions* (visible ghosts); *hauntings* (repeated phenomena in one location); *poltergeists* (literally, 'noisy ghosts', renowned for physical annoyances); *clairvoyance* (receiving knowledge or impressions from a distance by unknown means); *time-slips* (experiencing a vivid sense of being immersed in the past); *precognition* (receiving information about future events, which then come to pass in real life); and *crisis visitations* (being visited in spirit by a friend or relative at the moment of their death or other severe crisis). To these can be added the collective effusions of *mediumship*, in which discarnate spirits or entities communicate through the voice or body of the medium.

THE NIGHT SIDE OF NATURE

The Victorian period was when many tales of these phenomena started to become systematically collected, and one of the best works of the period was *The Night Side of Nature,* written by Catherine Crowe in 1848, its popularity so great that it went through three editions in five years. Crowe (1790-1872) was an English novelist who lived in Edinburgh in the 1830s and '40s, during which period she cultivated middle-class Scottish informants and collected many personal experiences which otherwise would have been lost (this also means that many witnesses are only named by their initials, so as to throw a veil of discretion over their identities). Crowe was keen on phrenology, spiritualism and contemporary Continental thinking on ghosts, and her book has the distinction of introducing the German word 'poltergeist' into the English language.

Night Side features many episodes involving prophetic or telepathic dreams and visions. Mr W., a student at Glasgow College, dreamed that his aunt in Russia had just died. On awakening he scribbled down the date of his dream on the bedroom window-shutter. When the news of her death duly arrived, the two dates did not match; but then it was realised

A typically spookified cover for an edition of Catherine Crowe's *The Night Side of Nature*. *(Author's Collection)*

that Russia still kept to the old style Julian calendar, long since abandoned in the West. Once the difference was calculated, there was an exact match between the date of the dream and the time of the lady's death. A Glasgow businessman dreamed of a coffin inscribed with the name of a friend and the date of the man's death. This was curious, as the friend was in full health at the time. Shortly afterwards he died, and at the funeral the businessman saw the plate on the coffin, inscribed exactly as he had seen it in his dream. Dr W. of Glasgow dreamed he was called to attend a patient at a remote spot across a moor, where a bull attacked him. The following morning he was summoned to the very patient. Getting lost on the moor, he was indeed pursued by a bull, and took refuge in a safe spot he had seen in his dream. It took several hours for the local people to set him free from the bull's attentions. 'Dr W. declares, that but for the dream, he should not have known in what direction to run for safety.' The night before visiting Glasgow on business, Mr H. dreamed a close friend of his was dead. So vivid was the dream that he delayed his journey so as to check on his friend, who was as hale and hearty as ever. After three days in Glasgow, Mr H. returned to find that his friend had had a sudden fatal seizure.

Mrs Crowe also recorded apparitions, although the following extraordinary case actually concerned a doppelganger (literally, a 'double walker'), the double of a living person. In the 1750s or 1760s a servant girl suddenly disappeared; it was known she had been the lover of a surgeon's assistant, and it was assumed she had retired to her country village when her pregnancy became too obvious. No foul play was suspected. At the time, the observance of the Sabbath was strictly enforced, and busybodies called 'compurgators' patrolled open areas such as Glasgow Green during church services, ensuring no one had defaulted from the pleasures of hearing the lengthy sermons. One Sunday morning, the religious enforcers found the surgeon's assistant — who was well known to them — lying on the grass in the Green. As they took his name, he stood up and said, 'I am a miserable man; look in the water!' Following this he walked off along the path leading east along the river to the Rutherglen road.

To their horror, the compurgators found a female corpse floating in the Clyde. They recovered the body and carried it westwards into the town, their arrival coinciding with the end of divine service. As the congregation emptied from one of the principal churches, among their number was seen the surgeon's assistant.

Old Glasgow College on High Street, now demolished. *(Author's Collection)*

The corpse was identified as the pregnant girl, and the murder weapon, a surgeon's knife, was found entangled in her clothes. The young man was arrested, and the Baillies testified to his 'confession' on Glasgow Green. But the assistant had a cast-iron alibi: he had been in church all morning, and there were dozens of witnesses to this. As the rest of the evidence linking him to the murder was merely circumstantial, he was acquitted. Catherine Crowe finished the story with a suitable air of mystery:

> The public were left in the greatest perplexity, to account as they could for this extraordinary discrepancy. The young man was well known to the inspectors, and it was in broad daylight

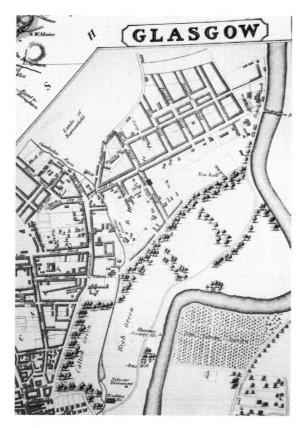

Glasgow Green and area in 1822. North
is to the left. *(Courtesy A.K. Bell Library,
Local Studies)*

Glasgow, the River Clyde and the Green from Polmadie in 1843. From Hugh MacDonald's *Rambles
Around Glasgow.*

Looking through the McLennan Arch to Glasgow Green. (*Photograph by Geoff Holder*)

that they had met him and placed his name in their books. Neither, it must be remembered, were they seeking for him, nor thinking of him, nor of the woman, about whom there existed neither curiosity nor suspicion. Least of all, would they have sought her where she was, but for the hint given to them. The interest excited, at the time, was very great; but no natural explanation of the mystery has ever been suggested.

The story was fictionalised to powerful effect by the horror writer Marjorie Bowen (the pseudonym of the prolific Gabrielle Margaret Vere Campbell Long); her short story 'The Avenging of Ann Leete' first appeared in *The New Magazine* in December 1923, and was reprinted in Bowen's collection *The Bishop of Hell and Other Stories* (1949).

THE METHODIST'S DREAM

The year 1871 saw the publication of another book on the supernatural featuring a precognitive dream based in Glasgow. *Strange Footsteps; Or, Thoughts on the Providence of God* was a joint publication by a pair of English vicars, Charles and Henry Kendall. One of their correspondents was the Revd Moses Lupton, a minister in the Methodist church. Back in 1833 Revd Lupton was based in Lincoln, and was expecting a new posting to Malton, close to his Yorkshire roots. Then he had a dream with detailed images of architecture and domestic furnishings, which he related in full to his wife the following morning:

We shall not go to Malton, as we expect, but to some large town: I do not know its name, but it is a very large town. The house we shall occupy is up a flight of stairs, three stories high.

We shall have three rooms on one level: the first – the kitchen – will have a closed bed in the right corner, a large wooden box in another corner, and the window will look down upon a small grass plot. The room adjoining will be the best room: it will have a dark carpet, with six hair-seated mahogany chairs. The other will be a small bedroom.

In the dream, the reverend gentleman was further granted a sighting of his professional life:

We shall not worship in a chapel, but in a large hall, which will be formed like a gallery. There will be a pulpit in it, and a large circular table before it. The entrance to it will be by a flight of stairs, like those in a church tower. After we have ascended so far, the stairs will divide – one way leading up to the left, to the top of the place. This will be the principal entrance, and it leads to the top of the gallery, which is entered by a door covered with green baize fastened with brass nails. The other stairs lead to the floor of the place; and, between the door and the hall, on the right-hand side, in a corner, is a little room or vestry: in that vestry there will be three men accustomed to meet that will cause us much trouble; but I shall know them as soon as ever I see them, and we shall ultimately overcome them, and do well.

Around a week later he received a letter giving him his posting: not Malton, but, to his disappointment, the city of Glasgow. After an arduous coach journey, the Luptons finally arrived at their designated accommodation at No. 6, Rottenrow. To their surprise its three storeys, with a triple-room arrangement on one level, and the grass plot visible from the kitchen, matched the dream. And every detail of the furnishings was also familiar from Lupton's sleeping vision. Then Lupton learned he was to preach, not in a religious building, but in the Mechanics' Institution Hall on the corner of North Hanover Street and George Street. The internal architecture of the hall, right down to the green baize and brass nails on a door, was the exact duplicate of the dreamland equivalents. And in the little room in the corner, as foreseen, Lupton encountered three gentlemen, Messrs J. McM— J. P— and J.Y— who soon proved to be thorns in Mr Lupton's flesh. 'But, by God's help,' finished the Methodist minister, 'their schemes were frustrated, and I left the station in a healthy and prosperous state.'

Of course, the Revd Lupton was writing many years after the events, and his memory may have been at fault. Sadly, Mrs Lupton was not called upon to corroborate the description of the dream. That being said, the sheer quantity and nature of the fine detail of the locations, furnishings and people, is mightily impressive.

CRISIS VISITATIONS FROM THE FILES OF THE SOCIETY FOR PSYCHICAL RESEARCH

The Society for Psychical Research, or SPR, was set up in 1882 with the express purpose of bringing principles of scientific investigation to the world of phantoms and psychics. The society is still active, and its files are a treasure trove of carefully noted incidents and investigations – and there are several examples of crisis visitations associated with the Glasgow area.

In 1830 or 1831, ten-year-old Colin Campbell McKechnie was resident at the house of John McKechnie, his grandfather, in Sneddon Street, Paisley. He was very much attached to the old man, who was an elder in the Kirk of Scotland. When John became severely ill, the young Colin stayed for a few days at his father's home, about a mile away. He described what happened next:

I was leaning in a listless sort of way against the kitchen table, looking upwards at the ceiling, and thinking of nothing in particular, when my grandfather's face appeared to grow out of the ceiling, at first dim and indistinct, but becoming more and more complete until it seemed in every respect as full and perfect as I had ever seen it. It looked down upon me, as I thought, with a wonderful expression of tenderness and affection. Then it disappeared, not suddenly, but gradually; its features fading and becoming dim and indistinct, until I saw nothing but the bare ceiling.

The boy mentioned the experience to his mother at the time, but she took no notice of it. Some minutes later, a breathless messenger boy arrived with awful news: John McKechnie had just died.

In 1870 – and again in 1889 – Colin, now the Revd C.C. McKechnie, described the vision to psychic investigators. In his 1889 letter to the SPR, he gave his thoughts on the event: 'I have never been able to persuade myself that the vision was purely subjective. I have rather been

Paisley in the late nineteenth century. *(Courtesy A.K. Bell Library, Local Studies)*

inclined to think that the explanation is to be sought in my grandfather's exceptionally strong love for me, impelling and enabling him to bring himself into connection with me, at the moment of his death.' The account appeared in the *Report on the Census of Hallucinations*, in the *Proceedings* of the SPR in 1894.

On the evening of Saturday, 14 July 1894, Edward Kerr, the fireman on Engine 1 of the Johnstone to Glasgow passenger train, fell off the engine and struck his head against Bridge No. 18 near Blackhall Farm by Paisley. As he rebounded against the train, the wheels ran over his leg. A goods train following behind stopped, and the driver and guard took the unconscious Kerr to Paisley Infirmary. The accident took place around 10.35 p.m.

Seventy-five miles away, a woman woke screaming from her sleep. Ellen Kerr had just had a vivid dream that her son Edward had been severely injured in an accident. She woke her husband, who said 'it's only a dream', and just wanted to get back to sleep. Unable to rest, Mrs Kerr got up, lit the fire, and went to the house of her neighbour, Mrs Dickson, to whom she related the dream. She also woke another woman, Mrs Mundell, asking her to send the youngest Mundell boy to fetch James Kerr, Ellen Kerr's other son, who lived a few miles away at Hardlaw Bank Farm. The message was that a serious accident had happened to his brother on the railway. Before James arrived, sometime between 1 and 2 a.m., a telegram came: Mr and Mrs Kerr were summoned to Paisley Infirmary, where their son was seriously ill. They took the first train in the morning, arriving at the hospital shortly before Edward Kerr expired; he had never regained consciousness.

The Kerrs lived at Gateside, Holywood, near Dumfries. In 1904 the case came to the attention of the local physician, Fred Hugh Clarke, who proceeded to interview all the key figures, as well as obtaining confirmation of the chronology from the Superintendent of the Line and the Secretary of the Glasgow and South Western Railway, the Medical Superintendant of the Royal Alexandra Infirmary (the successor to the Paisley Infirmary), and the Station-Master at Holywood, who accompanied the distraught Kerrs as far as Kilmarnock. Ellen Kerr and her husband James both gave sworn statements ('on soul and conscience'). Dr Clarke described Mrs Kerr as 'absolutely trustworthy' and 'the least likely woman to have had such a strange experience – a solid, matter-of-fact, practical, hard-working woman of the smaller farmer class.'

Unfortunately, the neighbour, Mrs Dickson, had died in the ten years that had elapsed since the incident, but Dr Clarke did manage to speak to the Mundells, mother and daughter, who clearly remembered Mrs Kerr describing her dream to them that night. They, however, thought the dream description came *after* the telegram arrived, while Mrs Kerr remembered that she related the dream to the Mundells *before* the arrival of the message. Everyone was in agreement, however, that Ellen Kerr had described her dream to both her husband and Mrs Dickson well before the telegram appeared. 'It is all very perplexing,' wrote Dr Clarke. 'The only thing I am quite certain of is that these people are speaking the truth, or at least what they believe to be the truth.'

Sir James Crichton-Browne, a friend of Dr Clarke, compared Mrs Kerr's dream with the real-life events, and presented the case in the SPR's *Journal* in November 1905:

> *Mrs Kerr dreamt that her son fell from the tender of the engine.*
>   He actually did so.
> *She dreamt that his head struck the masonry of a bridge.*

That is what actually took place, and she afterwards saw his hair and blood adhering to the stonework.

She dreamt that the wheels seemed 'to pass up along his body.'

The official report says he 'rebounded against the train.'

She dreamt that his head was seriously injured on the right side.

The official report shows that the skull was fractured on the right side.

She dreamt that his right arm was seriously injured, and his right leg completely severed below the knee.

The official and medical reports set forth that the right arm was seriously injured, and that there was a compound fracture of the right leg necessitating amputation at the knee.

She dreamt that the boot remained upon the foot of the severed foot.

When the amputated leg was produced to be placed in the coffin it was seen that the boot was still on the foot.

Mrs Kerr's dream ended by her clock at 10.50 p.m.

The accident, according to the official report, took place 'about 10.35.' Allowing for possible inaccuracy in the clock or in the noting and reporting of the time, the dream and the accident must have been nearly if not absolutely simultaneous.

Sir James regarded the dream as not so much precognitive as 'co-cognitive', as it took place within the same time as the real-life events. Mrs Kerr's description was uncannily precise in all its details. There was only one discrepancy, a difference that both Dr Clarke and Sir James regarded as actually *confirming* the veracity of the account. In Ellen Kerr's dream, the bridge on which her son was injured was not near Paisley, but just a few miles from her home in Dumfriesshire.

In August 1926, Glasgow resident Lawrence Nathan was on holiday in Bradford. At 2 p.m. he was overcome by an irresistible need to sleep. Fifteen minutes later he was awake again, telling his relatives of his peculiar dream:

I dreamed that I was back in Glasgow, I was walking. My desire to reach an unknown destination was very strong within me. I came to an overhead railway bridge which is in Nelson Street, Glasgow. As I was passing under the bridge a thick, black, dense smoke came rolling through the archway towards me. I was determined to reach my destination, so I pressed forward. The further I went on my way, the thicker became the smoke, until I began to cough and choke. The choking sensation became so acute that I suddenly developed panic. My desire to go on was still strong; but I had a deeper, more intense feeling to 'about-turn'. So, precipitately, I turned and ran for my life, out the way I had come. On again reaching the light of day I awoke.

At the time the dream made no sense. Some ten days later Mr Nathan returned to Glasgow, where his wife told him that during his absence their baby boy had almost choked to death when eating potatoes. Nathan interrupted her, and much to her astonishment, gave her the exact date and time of the crisis – which was when he had had the choking dream. The episode was in the SPR's *Journal* in September/October 1943.

On 29 April 1930 Mrs Jessie Finniecome, of Barskimmine, Paisley Road, Renfrew, was wakened about 11.20 p.m. by a cold kiss on her forehead. Looking up, she saw her old friend Baroness Liebieg. 'She looked as though she desired to say something, or was waiting for me to

Renfrew in the early part of the twentieth century. *(Courtesy A.K. Bell Library, Local Studies)*

speak or answer,' wrote Mrs Finniecome, 'but I was so startled, not to say, afraid, I was speechless, so after gazing at one another for a minute or two, the Baroness turned and vanished. Her expression was so sad and enquiring I cannot forget it… I only wish I knew what it was the Baroness wished to ask or tell me – for I am sure she wanted to know something. I really saw the Baroness as clearly as I see the paper I am now writing on and I was wide awake.' The following morning she described the experience to her husband, who reminded her that she had had a similar experience when his mother died, even though the two women had never met.

On 4th or 5th May, Mrs Finniecome learned from the newspapers that Baroness Liebieg had died at No. 5 Petterhofengasse, Vienna, on 29 April. No time of death was given. A contact in Austria made enquiries and found that the Baroness, who had been very sick for a long time, expired at 11.20 p.m. local time. Normally, Vienna was an hour ahead of British time. But British Summer-time was in operation as of 13 April 1930, and therefore on 29 April clock times in British and Vienna were the same. Baroness Liebieg, it appeared, had visited her old friend at the very moment of her death. The case was reported in the SPR's *Journal* in 1930.

At 10.30 a.m. on 12 November 1960, Marion Law was sitting in the kitchen of her Glasgow house when she heard the word 'Mum' repeated in her right ear. Next came a loud crashing noise as if a bundle of chains had been dropped from a height onto a hard surface. Seconds later there was a bang like the slamming of a door, and the feeling of a wind blowing powerfully through the hall next to the kitchen. At first she was convinced her son Angus was mucking about, but the fourteen-year-old was asleep in his bedroom. Trembling, Marion touched the other bed in the room, and had a strange sensation that her eldest son, Iain, was present.

At three o'clock that afternoon a telegram arrived. Iain, who was with the RAF in Singapore, had suffered a serious motorbike accident. He died the following day without regaining consciousness. Several weeks later, after the initial shock had worn off, Marion and her family talked about her experience. Iain had died at 5.30 p.m. in Singapore. Allowing for time differences, that was 10.30 a.m. in Glasgow. It appeared that Marion had somehow received the final conscious thoughts of her son, accompanied by the sounds and sensations that accompanied the crash that led to his death. Marion wrote up her experience for the SPR's magazine *The Paranormal Review* in July 1999.

APPARITIONS

Glasgow's first Theatre Royal stood on Dunlop Street from 1782 until 1805, when it was renamed the Caledonian Theatre, and became the centre of a dispute between two flamboyant theatrical impresarios. Later the reconstructed building on Dunlop Street was again named the Theatre Royal. In 1849 it became the scene of a notorious panic caused by a false cry of fire – seventy people were trampled to death trying to flee the building. A genuine fire broke out in 1863, and the theatre was completely rebuilt.

With that kind of dramatic history, it is ironic to find a ghost story that is exceptionally low-key. Ross Mackintosh, a popular matinee idol of the nineteenth century, entered the theatre one morning to find a large yellow dog sitting on the staircase. The actor threw a candied sweet to the animal, which ignored the offering and padded down the stairs towards the foyer. The next day the same thing happened, at the same time and place. Thinking it was unusual for a dog to turn its nose up at free food, Mackintosh turned round to look at the animal but it was nowhere to be seen – and in the brief moment the actor had looked away, there had not been enough time for the dog to have reached the bottom of stairs or moved elsewhere. The following day Mackintosh arrived to find the dog sitting in its usual spot. He carefully threw it a piece of aniseed fudge; once again the hound was indifferent to the sweetmeat, so the actor extended his silver-topped cane and prodded the ungrateful beast. The cane passed right through the yellow dog, which then slowly faded away before the astonished actor's eyes.

The case is in Raymond Lamont Brown's book *Phantoms of the Theatre*, which sadly does not give a date or the original source for the episode. The back-story, apparently, was that a dog matching the apparition's description had belonged to a former manager of the theatre, and had died some ten years previously. Actors are, of course, notoriously keen to tell stories about themselves that make them appear more interesting than they may actually be. Could this have been such a theatrical invention? Or did it really happen? The location, unfortunately, is no longer open to investigation. The theatre was finally demolished in 1869 to make way for the massive redevelopment around St Enoch's station. These days Dunlop Street connects Argyle Street with the St Enoch's Centre.

Other Glasgow theatres have an extensive history of hauntings, many of which are documented in my book *The Guide to Mysterious Glasgow*. One episode that has recently come to light is an investigation at the Glasgow Royal Concert Hall by The Ghost Club. The hall opened in 1990, built on the site of St Andrew's Halls, a famous venue that burned down in 1962. Staff at the GRCH have frequently reported low-level phenomena, including anomalous noises, a 'sense of presence' even though no one is visible, and numerous moving shadows.

The Ghost Club has been investigating and researching strange phenomena since 1862. The GRCH investigation, headed by Derek Green, took place on 7 March 2009. As ever, the official report is a model of caution, considering factors such as: external noises (the Concert Hall is at the junction of Sauchiehall Street and Buchanan Street, the very heart of the city's nightlife); reflective surfaces (which can create anomalous lights through reflections of torches, instruments and camera flashes); the acoustic nature of the vast and labyrinthine spaces of the hall and its facilities; the large number of machines and electromagnetic sources in the building, from soft-drinks dispensers to fridges, lights, audio systems, stage machinery, air conditioners/ heaters and other devices; and the possibility that people working late in one part of the building can create noises that resonate elsewhere. To this I would add that the various spaces of the large venue may be conducive to the accidental generation of ultrasound, sound waves below the level of human hearing that have been shown to create feelings of 'hauntedness' or a sense of being watched by invisible or barely-visible figures.

Four teams of investigators were present, moving between the various parts of the building in turn. Audio anomalies were reported from the kitchen, where the sound of bells ringing was a regular feature, along with others noises such as sighs and the sound of movement. The most consistently-reported phenomena, however, were black human-shaped figures or shadows. Members of all four groups saw these fleeting figures, which were mostly concentrated in

the main auditorium, particularly the upper level. No features could be clearly seen, although the figures were sometimes standing still, and other times in motion. The number and frequency of these sightings is the most striking figure of the report. Could they have resulted from some kind of unusual but explicable arrangement of the concert hall's internal lighting, combined with reflections and the movements of the investigators? Or were they genuinely paranormal? Interestingly, two weeks after the investigation, GRCH staff reported seeing a shadowy shape pass behind a glass-panelled office door. When the door was opened the corridor was empty, and no one else was working in the building.

FRENCH TIME SLIP

For her book *The Mask of Time* (1978), Joan Forman appealed for experiences of timeslips, precognition and hindsight. One

The statue of Donald Dewar, former Secretary of State for Scotland, stands outside the Glasgow Royal Concert Hall. (*Photograph by Geoff Holder*)

respondent was Mrs M. McGee from Glasgow, who described how she was indoors listening to Grieg's *Piano Concerto* – of which she was not particularly fond, and which she thought may have triggered the event – when she suddenly found herself in the South of France in the mid-1800s. She was sitting in an upper room with the blinds drawn to keep out the sun. Outside, she knew, was a deserted street, 'and oh, the desolation and boredom – utter complete boredom for the rest of my life, nothing changing. I was unbelievably unhappy.' The flash was very brief, but vivid and real. Mrs McGhee's sister also had 'past life' recollections of France, and when she first saw the Loire she could 'remember' going down to it to launder clothes on the riverbank.

DAVID DUGUID, THE GLASGOW PAINTING MEDIUM

Spiritualism is a belief system in which it is asserted that not only do our souls survive the death of the body, they can actually communicate meaningfully with the living from the 'other side'. To do this the spirits require a human being to channel their communications, such individuals usually being termed 'mediums'. A medium may speak with the voice of the dead, or the spirit may take over part of the medium's body, causing the medium's hand to create writings or drawings that have been transmitted directly from the shadow realm. Some mediums physically manifest spirit beings that are visible to others, while in rare cases of transfiguration, the medium's face may become transformed into the likeness of the controlling spirit.

There is a vast literature on spiritualism, dating back to 1847 when the Fox sisters in America created the entire religious system with their experiences of raps and noises allegedly produced by spirits of the dead. For its followers, this literature is proof positive for survival after death. For its detractors, the reports are merely a catalogue of human credulity and subterfuge. This latter point of view is based on the endless stream of mediums who have been caught red-handed in fraudulent activities. A good example of this took place in Glasgow in 1864, when Dr John Pattison attended a number of séances given by a London-based 'rapping' medium of some thirteen years' standing. Pattison published his experience in a pamphlet, *Spirit-Rapping in Glasgow in 1864: A true Narrative. By One of those Present.*

The medium's technique was to have the sitters write out questions while sitting opposite him, but not show him the paper or speak the questions aloud; the spirits would then produce a reply through rapping, each rap signifying a letter, or a common word such as 'Yes' or 'No'. Dr Pattison surmised the medium was studying the sitters' hands as they wrote out their questions, and was thus making good guesses at the written content. This was made easier because sitters thought they were in the presence of their dearly departed, and in such emotional circumstances, questions tend to be fairly stereotyped. Deliberately allowing the medium to see some but not all of his messages, and then writing unexpected words, Pattison received the following nonsensical replies:

Addressing a question to the spirit of his deceased father: 'Are you hungry?' 'Yes,' came the immediate answer (Pattison had gambled on the fact that the medium would guess the question as 'Are you happy?') His next question read, 'Have you seen my mother, and is she hungry?' 'I have, and she is,' came the reply. 'Are all then hungry in heaven?' he asked next. 'Yes,' was the inevitable response. Then Pattison played his trump card. His final question read: 'Is the medium a gross humbug?' To which the table rapped out an immediate 'Yes.' Oops.

Rather more complicated is the case of David Duguid (1832-1907), one of the more extraordinary mediums of the nineteenth century. A Glasgow cabinet-maker, his spiritualistic skills started in 1865 with simple raps but soon expanded into a gallimaufry of visitations from the beyond, including strange voices and lights, invisible hands, floating objects, glorious perfumes, and even, on one occasion, levitation. He was also able to perform psychometry (the ability to learn an object's history and personal associations simply by touching it), handle red-hot coals, and produce images on unexposed photographic plates. He was most famous, however, for producing drawings and paintings under the influence of the gifted dead, including the Dutch masters Jakob Ruisdael (1628–1682) and Jan Steen (1626–1679).

A typical example of his activities was given in the Glasgow *Weekly News* of 29 November 1903, towards the end of his career. On this occasion Duguid was performing in Dundee, blindfolded as usual:

> The medium entered into a state of trance, and then in the most businesslike way opened his paint-box, and set to work… Absolute silence reigned as Mr Duguid picked out a pencil, and with firm and confident touch began to draw upon the blank cardboard a little landscape. Then the palette was called into requisition. Some of the colours were already mixed, and others were squeezed from their tubes, with unfaltering hand some oil was poured into a tiny cup… Rapidly the picture grew… It was curious to note how as the work grew the blindfolded man would hold it from him at arm's length as if admiring his handiwork. One or two additional touches, and the sketch was finished – as dainty and artistic a picture as one could see, and all executed within half-an-hour.

The medium explained that the scene was Loch Fyne, and it had been painted under the direction of Jakob Ruisdael (who was noted for his landscape scenes). Duguid then went on to produce for the Dundonian spiritualists his other speciality, miniature paintings produced in darkness:

> From a leather envelope the medium drew a number of photo mounts of *carte-de-visite* size. Two of these were selected, and the corners torn off for future identification. The hands of the medium were then securely tied beyond possibility of moving them. Except for a chink of light between the closed curtains the room was in complete darkness. A verse or two of

David Duguid, from *The 'Two Worlds'* *Portrait Album of Spiritual Mediums, Workers and Celebrities*, 1897.

a hymn was sung. Suddenly in the direction of the table were seen tiny sparks, and then came a sound as of wood rapping on the ground. Up went the lights instantly, and there on the table lay the two cards, each with a complete little sketch freshly painted on it. One of these was a replica of the larger picture painted by the medium. The other was a tiny woodland scene. The cards were handed round, and the torn corners, produced from the pocket of an onlooker, were found to fit exactly.

Duguid had done this kind of thing hundreds if not thousands of times before; the enthusiastic true believers of spiritualist churches lapped it up. Other observers were less kind. In 1878 Frank Podmore, one of the luminaries of the Society for Psychical Research, attended a séance in which Duguid produced two miniature landscape paintings in exactly the same manner as described above, the colours still moist as if they had been just applied. In his book *Modern Spiritualism: A History and a Criticism,* Podmore surmised that when the medium tore off the corners, the pieces he gave to the spectators for future verification were substituted through sleight-of-hand and actually came from pre-painted cards that the medium brought to the séance ready-made. In his 1920 book *The Physical Phenomena of Spiritualism,* Hereward Carrington revealed two distinctly unspiritual techniques for the production of spirit paintings:

One method is for the medium to take an ordinary oil-painting, as fresh as possible (so long as the oil is quite dry), and over this lightly gum, around the edges, another piece of blank canvas, seeing to it that it looks neat at the edges. Now, as soon as the medium is alone in the cabinet, he carefully peels off this outside piece of canvas, secreting it about his person, and exposing the under canvas (the one upon which is the painting) to view. In order to produce the impression of the painting still being wet, he quickly rubs over the painting with poppy-oil, and there is your spirit painting!

Sneaky. As for the second method:

The oil-painting in this case is first varnished, and, after this is thoroughly dry, it is covered with a solution of water and 'zinc white.' The canvas will now have the appearance of being blank, and may be inspected. All the medium has to do, in order to restore the painting, is to wash over the canvas with a wet sponge, when the painting will appear as before.

David Duguid's larger paintings were often executed in plain sight, and so could not have been manufactured in this manner; if he was genuinely blindfolded during the operation, this may well have been a case of genuine trance-based painting. This would not necessarily have required preternatural input from a long-dead Dutchman, and could have been an aspect of the medium's own subconscious skill; a few other 'sightless' workers have been known. But even if its origins were not psychic or supernatural, the activity itself was still remarkable, a true marvel.

Alas, the same could not be said for Duguid's miniatures. In 1905 members of an audience at Manchester caught him doing something suspicious with the blank cards; he was searched, and the pre-painted cards were found hidden in his trousers. As Podmore had suspected, Duguid was using sleight-of-hand and trickery to fool the believers.

Perhaps the strangest moment in Duguid's long career, however, came in 1870. Already a producer of spirit drawings and paintings, he now added spirit writing to his portfolio. And not just any old rambling jottings from the spiritual realm, either – this was nothing less than the true story of the boyhood of Jesus Christ.

Duguid had now gained a third spirit guide. Joining the two Dutch painters – who always communicated to Duguid in English, albeit silently – was a third distinguished individual. Hafed, by his own account, was a prince of the Persian royal family in the first century BC. After fighting against an invading Arab army, Hafed had given up his wealth and his warrior ways to join the Magi, the priestly élite of Persia. Eventually he rose to become Arch Magus, and as such when a strange star appeared in the sky he was chosen to lead two other adepts across the desert – to Bethlehem.

Having delivered gifts to the infant Jesus, Hafed stayed with the young Messiah, accompanying him on his travels through Persia, India and other countries, and personally witnessing the young Galilean perform many miracles. After the Crucifixion, Hafed converted to Christianity, met St Paul in Greece, preached the new religion in Venice and Alexandria, and finally, aged 100, was martyred in the arena in Rome.

All this was dictated through Duguid over a marathon forty-six sittings, Hafed's words being taken down by an amanuensis. The completed work was published in 1876 under the snappy title *Hafed, Prince of Persia; his experiences in Earth Life, being spirit communications being recited through Mr David Duguid, the Glasgow Trance Speaking Medium, with an Appendix, containing communications from Spirit Artists Ruisdale and Steen, illustrated by Facsimiles of forty-five Drawings and Writings, the direct work of the Spirits.*

But there was a slight problem. Several of the 'forty-five Drawings and Writings, the direct work of the Spirits' turned out to be copies of illustrations in the *Cassell Family Bible*, a popular edition of the time. M'learned friends were consulted. The phrase 'breach of copyright' was uttered. The first edition of *Hafed, Prince of Persia* was withdrawn. In 1887 a sequel to *Hafed* was published, entitled *Hermes, a Disciple of Jesus: His Life and Missionary Work; also the Evangelistic Travels of Anah and Zitha, two Persian Evangelists, sent out by Hafed; together with Incidents in the Life of Jesus given by a Disciple through Hafed.* Rather wisely, it was not illustrated. The few non-spiritualists who took *Hafed* even half-seriously spotted error after error in the 'ancient history'.

Despite being a Magus and deeply learned in several languages, Hafed, it seemed, did not know Arabic. One illustration in the first book showed a doorway inscribed with a common Arabic inscription, 'There is no conqueror but God'. The image was in Cassell's Bible, but the engraver, not knowing the Arabic script, had made several errors; those mistakes were reproduced exactly in Duguid's book.

Duguid and his supporters insisted that no deliberate fraud had been intended: the spirits had taken their images not from memory, but *from the minds of the sitters*. This apparently fantastic solution neatly sidestepped the thorny issue of why, if Hafed had such total recall of his life 2,000 years ago, he couldn't do any better for illustrations than a bunch of slightly sentimental engravings from a middle-brow edition of the Good Book. It does, however, raise the possibility that something else, and something truly extraordinary, was going on.

If we give David Duguid the benefit of the doubt and accept that no deliberate fraud was intended, and if we also exclude the likelihood that Hafed was a genuine disembodied Persian who had gone rambling with Christ, we are left with another possibility. I wonder if Duguid

Three of the plagiarized illustrations that caused the first edition of *Hafed, Prince of Persia* to be withdrawn. 'Two priests of the Order of the Leopard Skin,' 'Figures representing the Consecration of an Egyptian Princess' and 'A Royal Princess'.

The originals, entitled 'Costumes of the Egyptian Priesthood', from *Cassell's Family Bible*. The damning comparisons appeared in Edward Bennett's *The Direct Phenomena of Spiritualism*, 1908.

One of the less contentious images from *Hafed*. This is supposedly the palace where Hafed was born.

Another typical illustration from *Hafed, Prince of Persia*. As with the previous image, it was transmitted to Duguid directly by the 'spirits'.

was actually a telepath. My suggestion is that perhaps he did indeed 'pick up' images from the minds of his sitters. On some occasions the medium had painted pictures that bore a distinct resemblance to paintings the sitters had at home, or were similar to places they had known in America or Australia. And during his spirit photography stage, one of his more popular projections onto photographic plate was a mystic beauty who was supposedly the priestess of a Cypriot temple. It turned out to be a copy of a German painting called *Night* that was known to one of the sitters.

If Duguid was indeed a telepath, it is possible that he was not fully aware of the exact nature of his ability. Spiritualism, if nothing else, is a structured belief system in which faith is bolstered by apparent direct evidence of survival after death. It provided a way of understanding and explaining a range of anomalous phenomena and experiences which in other contexts may have been deeply upsetting, even regarded as demonic in nature. I suggest that Duguid found in spiritualism a tool to engineer his inchoate abilities into something comprehensible and acceptable, something that could be understood within a context of a faith shared by many others. For an ordinary, pious Scot who found himself manifesting a truly extraordinary ability, spiritualism helped him make sense of it all. And it also provided him with a structured network in which he could travel, meet interesting people, be admired, and generally have a more interesting life than the average nineteenth-century Glaswegian cabinetmaker.

Of course, I cannot offer any solid evidence for this. Duguid may simply have been a clever charlatan. Or perhaps all the spirit communications were genuine. But the known facts – Duguid's attested abilities in plain sight, the case of the *Hafed* illustrations, and the other examples of paintings apparently plucked from the minds of the sitters – do suggest something was going on other than mere chicanery or the input of ascended masters from the Other Side. I also suspect Duguid perpetuated multiple ongoing frauds with his miniature paintings simply in order to appear a better 'draw' on the spiritualist circuit. His telepathic abilities may have been variable, fluid or unreliable; when push came to shove, he could always depend on creating a crowd-pleasing effect by sneaking out the miniatures hidden in his clothes. It is impossible to know now how much of his vast output of phenomena was genuine, and how much was fraudulent. If the modern entertainer Derren Brown can create fake but utterly convincing 'spiritualistic' phenomena on stage using his self-declared mix of 'magic, suggestion, psychology, misdirection and showmanship', then we have to have deep suspicions about the Victorian originals.

David Duguid was controversial in his lifetime and after. The many books that feature him include *The Veil Lifted* by John Traill Taylor (1894), *The Direct Phenomena of Spiritualism* by Edward Bennett (1908), *Photographing the Invisible* by James Coates (1911), and psychologist Nandor Fodor's *Encyclopedia of Psychic Science* (1934) and *These Mysterious People* (1936). An excellent overview of 'Spirit Painting' can be found in an article of that name by Joe Nickell in the March 2000 issue of *Skeptical Enquirer*. Spiritualists adored Duguid uncritically; but the proven frauds damaged his reputation hugely, and gave his critics sufficient cause to dismiss him outright. I suspect these simple hero/villain dichotomies do not do sufficient justice to this complex and intriguing individual.

POLTERGEISTS AND POSSESSION

Peter Underwood in *Gazetteer of Scottish Ghosts* gives the undated story of a family who fled their Glasgow council house because of the sound of knocks and bumps, and the sight of furniture and other items being moved around. An investigation team sat up all night, but experienced nothing. On the second night there were bangs and crashes, and articles moved of their own accord, including a pair of iron fire-tongs 'which behaved as if propelled by invisible hands.' For the next sitting a medium attended and spoke in what sounded like the croaking voice of an old woman. The delivery was agitated and the content confused, but eventually the team worked out that the woman was worried about a baby: there was something wrong with its throat, and it must be taken to hospital immediately or it would die. The spirit said she was a relative of the young couple who had been driven from the flat, and claimed she had caused the disturbances to attract their attention. The couple were sceptical but arranged for their six-month-old child to have an X-Ray. The same day surgeons removed a small obstruction from the baby's throat which could have caused the infant to choke to death.

The April 2001 issue of the *Psi Report*, the newsletter of the Scottish Society for Psychical Research, contains a remarkable observation by Dorothy Ross, who was sitting on a train at Glasgow when three men got on. Two of the group appeared to be carers or escorts, as the third man was blind and exhibiting extreme behaviour consistent with severe mental illness. As soon as he sat down, the man, who seemed about forty years of age, began to make bizarre noises. He barked like a dog, and then spoke with the voice of a frightened child, before reverting to the deep bass of a very old man. *None of these sounds came from his mouth.*

There was no movement of lips, throat, mouth or face. As far as Dorothy could see, the barks and voices originated from the man's chest. Anomalous voices have a long history in the paranormal literature, and a variety of observers, from awe-struck witch-hunters to serious-minded parapsychologists, have speculated that some of the voices are produced by external entities, possibly manipulating the anatomy of the subject's 'false vocal cords' in the lower larynx. Such cases are more likely to have a medical rather than a supernatural causation, but for the paranormally-minded, there seems to be a crossover between this dysphonia and the phenomena of poltergeists, particularly those that seem to temporarily possess the subject, as with the famous Enfield poltergeist (or with the case described above). Was the man on the train possessed or channelling a polt? Probably not. Were his voices strange, anomalous and a bit disconcerting, even for the most rational of observers? Most certainly.

CHAPTER TWO

BIG CATS AND OTHER STRANGE ANIMALS

Perhaps one of the most common 'weird' stories found in the press involves a sighting of a big cat. As the last big cat native to Britain was the Eurasian lynx, *Felis lynx* (a tawny-coloured animal with distinctive tufted ears), and as that species became extinct in these islands in the early Middle Ages, such reports obviously require an explanation. Either people are mistaking ordinary animals for exotic big cats, or the big cats are real, in which case the question is – how did they get here?

Perhaps there are no actual big cats in Britain. It is possible that witnesses are misidentifying creatures that are actually feral domestic cats, or the rare native Scottish wildcat, or unusually large pedigree cats, or even Kellas cats, black-furred wildcat/domestic cat hybrids. Some big cat sightings could conceivably be traced to viewings under poor lighting conditions of feral dogs, foxes or mink. It is useful to remember that most reports of big cats are mere glimpses, it is notoriously difficult to estimate the size of a moving animal, and the vast majority of

The Eurasian lynx, *Felis lynx,* once native to Scotland. (*Michael Pierrot, FreePhotoBank.org*)

The black panther (melanistic leopard), *Panthera onca*. (*Bruce McAdam / Wikipedia, licensed under the Creative Commons Attribution-Share Alike 2.0 Generic license*)

The North American puma (*Felis concolor*), also known as the cougar and mountain lion. (*AskJoanne / Flickr, licensed under the Creative Commons Attribution-Share Alike 2.0 Generic license*)

witnesses have no experience with big cats, and can easily be mistaken. This is borne out by a consistent theme found in many reports described below – time after time witnesses describe what they saw as a 'black puma'. The puma, *Felis concolor*, also known as the cougar or mountain lion, has a tawny or brown coat; it is never black. The only black big cat is the black panther, *Panthera onca*, which is a melanistic variant of the leopard, where a black coat replaces the leopard's spots. Such melanistic leopards are very rare in the wild, yet, bizarrely, they appear to be the most commonly-sighted big cats in Britain. Given that witnesses may be confused as to whether they have seen a lynx, puma or leopard, many big cat researchers now prefer the generic term 'felids' to describe the mystery animals.

Support for the 'big cats are not real' position is often found in the undeniable fact that when the police are called out, their search is almost always fruitless. But a great deal has recently been learned about big-cat behaviour, and it is clear they can remain virtually invisible in their native habitats. Even experienced hunters can pass close by and not detect their presence. And most police officers are not trained in tracking wild animals. There is also what you might call the 'bodies of evidence' – the undeniably real physical bodies of exotic animals that have been found in Scotland: a live puma turned up in Inverness-shire in 1980, while the bodies of two small leopard cats were photographed in the Scottish Borders in 1988 and 1990.

It is likely, then, that at least some sightings are of genuine big cats. Almost certainly some were released in the 1970s, after the Dangerous Wild Animals Act of 1976 required owners of exotic animals to obtain an expensive license. But big cats rarely live longer than twenty years, so more recent sightings may be of more recent releases. There is a persistent rumour that big cats are periodically released to provide 'sport' for hunters. On the other hand, some animals may have bred in the wild in Scotland; if we are already looking at third or fourth generation felids, there is the possibility that a British sub-species may be on the cards.

In *Paranormal Dundee* I reported how big cats had been seen in the built-up areas within that city. Felids in the greater Glasgow region have apparently not been quite so bold, with reports largely confined to the southern edge of the Paisley/Barrhead area, and the less urbanised locations north of the metropolis. There are also intriguing reports from parks in south Glasgow.

Anyone encountering a big cat should report the experience to the Big Cats in Scotland website (www.bigcatsinbritain.org/scottishsightings.htm), where such sightings are co-ordinated and investigated. A big cat is very unlikely to attack a human being unless it is cornered or feels threatened; it is probably more scared of you than you are of it. Even so, approaching one is not advised.

What follows is a more-or-less chronological pad through sightings of big cats, interspersed with accounts of other out-of-place animals that have become honorary, if temporary, Weegies.

THE EARLY REPORTS

The first 'big cat' incident around Glasgow took place as long ago as 5 November 1949. On that day, Sheila the Bengal tigress got out of her cage at Calderpark Zoo, and appeared to be menacing her keeper, John Duffy. There was also a party of schoolgirls on the grounds. Alex Innes, the zoo gardener and ex-policeman, attacked the 500lb animal with only a shovel, distracting it from the cowering Duffy. A short time later S.H. Benson (Director-Secretary of the Zoological Society) and Zoo Overseer John Crawford shot the tigress dead with rifles. In retrospect, Sheila, who was amiable around humans, may have just wanted to play, but the risk could not be taken. For his courageous action Alex Innes was awarded the George Cross, the highest bravery honour for civilians.

A few other animals managed to escape from the Calderpark site in the south-east of Glasgow. Shortly after the zoo opened in 1947 several Bennett's wallabies launched a bid for freedom, one of them making it as far as Mount Vernon, a mile away, where the police captured it. A few years later, some raccoons – the expert escapologists of the animal world – migrated from the zoo to Baillieston, just to the north, where they set up a breeding colony. Strange animals of a raccoon-like nature were still being reported raiding the local rubbish bins into the 1970s. Two seals took to the North Calder Water where it flowed through the zoo, never to be recaptured – perhaps they made it to the sea via the River Clyde. And one dark rainy night a large, black and bizarre animal was reported to the police as sauntering along the Baillieston Road. This turned out to be a sealion, which had broken down a fence in its desire to explore the wider world. It was recaptured safely.

In its later years the zoo went into a decline and finally closed in 2003. The stories of the escapes, along with much more of interest, can be found in an online history of the zoo at www.glasgowzoo.co.uk.

The earliest definite 'big cat on the loose' report that I can trace is from 1979. On 12 November of that year H.C. Mullin wrote to the *Herald* describing an encounter early on a Saturday morning the previous summer. The lorry driver was leaving the Honeywells Controls factory at Viewpark, Uddingston, when he saw the creature near the M74. 'The animal was grayish in colour, with white tufts of hair on its side,' he wrote. 'It walked with a peculiar padding motion on big flat feet or paws. It had a very long tail, quite smooth, which swept back in a long upward curve.' In his opinion it was a mountain lion. 'I actually stopped the lorry and ran across the road to see it going through a thick hedge. Then I realised that this was a big cat and might be partial to a bit of lorry-driver for tiffin. So I ran back to the safety of the cabin and drove off.' The next report is from 27 December 1992, when oil worker William McRoberts saw an Alsation-sized fawn-coloured cat nonchalantly padding beside the A726 perimeter road around Glasgow Airport. It was after 7.30 p.m. and dark, but Mr McRoberts had a clear view in his headlights, and watched in astonishment as the puma leapt over the airport perimeter fence. When the police arrived they told him a second driver had also seen the cat, and there had been earlier sightings in Erskine.

2002 – THE MODERN ERA OF BIG CAT SIGHTINGS BEGINS

On 3 July 2002, BBC Scotland television news and the BBC website carried the story of a tan-coloured felid seen by three members of staff in the grounds of Merchiston Hospital, in Johnstone. The animal was described as 5ft long with pointed ears and a long tail. The patients at the psychiatric hospital were kept indoors while police, including a helicopter, searched the area. Nothing was found.

At 10 p.m. there was another sighting and corresponding (and fruitless) police search. Then astronomer Robert Law saw a cat at Durrockstock Park, in the Foxbar area of Paisley. At first he thought it was an urban fox growling outside his flat in Waverley Road, but then he realised it was a big cat. 'I know what I saw and it was definitely a large lynx-like creature,' he told the *Paisley Daily Express* (6 July). 'It had a distinctive square-shaped face, big ears, long legs and a stealthy, loping walk.' Another tan-coloured animal had been spotted in Barrhead earlier in the year. Johnstone, Paisley and Barrhead all border the high ground between the Renfrewshire urban sprawl and the Ayrshire towns of Beith and Stewarton, a rural area where big cats had been reported since the 1980s.

THE 'PAISLEY PANTHER'

The big cat reports for 2003 started with a whimper and ended with a bang. Things kicked off on 18 February with a report in the *Paisley Daily Express* that 'giant paw prints' had been found in a garden in Walnut Crescent, Johnstone. After much speculation about the nature of the creature responsible, Mark Fraser of the Big Cats in Scotland Society was called in; as described on the BCIB website, an analysis of the photographs showed that the mysterious tracks had been made by... a rabbit. On 20 May the *Paisley Daily Express* reported the experience of Paisley man Andy Carlin who saw something strange near the old Poulson dam on Glenfield Road: 'It was probably the build of a good-sized male fox, and had a grey coat with black spots through it,' Andy said. 'Its tail was pure black, long and bushy. And it had black pointy ears and black markings round its eyes – a bit like Alice Cooper!' This comparison with the famously mascara'd rock star led Andy Christie, of Hessilhead Wildlife Rescue, to suggest the creature was a raccoon. Had one of the raccoon escapees from Calderpark Zoo made it over to the southwest of Glasgow? There were more reports in the newspaper on 29 May, with one local man seeing an animal in the Gleniffer Braes Country Park, just south of Paisley – it was 'grey with a black tail which curled up and was bushy at the end, and it stood slightly bigger than a fox'. Hugh Brown of Arthurlie Street in Barrhead claimed to have seen a very fast, 'steely blue' animal with a curled 3ft-long tail, some ten or fifteen times over the previous six months. 'My dog actually tried to chase but had no chance of keeping up,' he said. 'It set off at some speed, bounding like an animal jungle. It was amazing.'

One anonymous interviewee cast doubt on the big cat/raccoon theory, stating the animal was an unusual breed of collie, kept by a local person as a pet, while Laura Matthews of Paisley stated she had first seen a big cat in the area sixteen years earlier, in 1987.

There were no more reported sightings of the Renfrewshire raccoon, or whatever it was, but November brought a more frightening beast – a large black panther, with multiple reports from the village of Lochwinnoch, off the A737 south of Johnstone.

'A bit like Alice Cooper' – the North American raccoon, *Procyon lotor*. ('Darkone'/Wikipedia, licensed under the Creative Commons Attribution-Share Alike 2.5 Generic license)

On 12 November the *Paisley Daily Express* reported the animal was seen near the primary school between 7.30 a.m. and 8 a.m., running with a dead animal in its mouth. The following day the paper published a host of related sightings. Lesley Campbell from Paisley had to swerve to avoid hitting a 'huge' jet-black animal that jumped in front of her car in the early hours of the morning between Lochwinnoch and Johnstone. Around the same time George Bremner from Johnstone and his friend saw the creature on the same road: 'My pal slammed the brakes on and stopped the car. This huge monster of a beast was sitting in a field with what looked like a baby fox in its mouth. It stared straight at us before disappearing into the night.' Sarah Sweeney of Glenfield Road in Paisley saw a big back cat on two successive nights at Thornley Dam. There was an unconfirmed report that mystery scratches and bite marks had been found on cars around Lochwinnoch. As an attempt to calm what was clearly becoming something of a panic, it was comfortingly reported that, 'the creature is much larger than domestic cats, and is unlikely to come through a cat flap near you.'

On the 14th the *Daily Record* reported that the children at Lochwinnoch Primary were being confined to the school grounds, and staff were carrying out regular patrols. A police helicopter had also been called in on the hunt. On the 18th Iain Riley told the *Paisley Daily Express* that at about 7 a.m. the previous day he had encountered a black cat at least as big as his German Shepherd in Kintyre Avenue, Linwood. The next day the paper carried the account of Mary O'Connor, a cleaner at Auchenlodment Primary in Johnstone. Around 6 a.m. she was on her way to the school when she encountered a large jet-black animal near Maple Drive. 'I've never been so frightened in my entire life,' she said. 'I just bolted and tried to put as much distance between us as possible. I didn't know I could run so fast and I was in such a hurry to get away that I managed to rip my jacket.'

Warning letters were issued to parents and the school's gates and entrances were to be locked at all times. A few hours later there was a second sighting near a cycle track in the Collier Street area of Johnstone. Further accounts came in of sightings at Moss Road in Linwood (reported by Linda Brown, who could see the cat's large white teeth glinting in the dark) and at Gibson Crescent in Johnstone (reported by John Junner, who watched the cat cross the Johnstone to Paisley railway line in the early hours). Police were consistently reported as being called out to search for the animal, but, as usual, nothing was found.

Things then went quiet for a while, but on 11 December Andy and Susan McCallum were having a cup of tea in the kitchen when the rear security light came on. Looking out into their garden they saw a large black cat sitting in their garden. It had long pointed ears, broad shoulders and a large round face. After a moment the cat leapt over a low wall and melted into the darkness. The couple, from Elm Drive in Johnstone, were very frightened by their encounter: 'There is no way we are going into the back garden at night, that's out of bounds from now on,' said Mrs McCallum.

After a quiet winter, the 'Paisley Panther' appears to have returned in the summer of 2004. On 7 June the *Paisley Daily Express* was back in the saddle. There had been multiple sightings of the beast near the swing park on Johnstone's Maple Drive. Parents were stopping their children from playing on the swings. One thirty-two-year-old woman claimed the large black cat had chased her neighbour. The same witness had found the rotting corpse of a pony on the Gleniffer Braes, near to the Brandy Burn in Johnstone; she was convinced it was a big cat kill, although other scavengers could have been responsible for the removal of the stomach and lights. On 28 June the paper reported that the Scottish Big Cat Society was intending to stake out the sites at Lochwinnoch and Gleniffer Braes with infra-red cameras (in the end the project was curtailed because public interest disrupted the proceedings). Mark Fraser of BCIB mentioned further sightings earlier in the month, with big black animals seen on three separate locations – close to Barrhead, heading into Parkhill Woods on the outskirts of Clyde Muirshiel Park, and running across the A737 near Howwood. Unusual tracks had been found at Lochwinnoch, and a group of young people attending a late-night barbecue said a big black cat had been observing them from nearby fields (perhaps the smell of cooking meat had attracted the animal). The *Paisley Gazette* for 30 June reported the claims of John Dow that he had found the cat's lair somewhere near Lochwinnoch. 'There was a skinned sheep with its fleece lying next to it and the carcasses of four mutilated lambs scattered about,' said John in an interview. 'It was 1.30 in the morning and I was wearing night-vision goggles. When I approached the lair I heard this deafening scream and howling like a banshee. It was like nothing I have heard in my life before. When I put the torch on, the howling stopped; when I turned the torch off it started again. I slowly retreated and got away.'

On 7 August the *Barrhead News* reported a further sighting in the Paisley area, while the *Paisley Daily Express* for 16 August described Michael McFadden's encounter close to Gryfebank Avenue, on the outskirts of Houston. 'It stretched its body and limbs against a tree in fairly open ground and I watched it for about three minutes,' said Mr McFadden, who kept his eager dog firmly on the lead. 'It was about 50 yards away. Suddenly, the cat saw us and vanished back into the woodland, which borders houses in the Gryfebank area.' In contrast to several other witnesses, the dog-walker was not at all scared by the experience. After another quiet few months, the 'Paisley Panther' was again spotted walking across Aurs Road in Barrhead at 1.45 a.m. The report was in the *Evening Times* on 29 March 2005.

THE 'BEAST OF LINN PARK'
In March 2005 the black panther, or an entirely different felid, appears to have moved into the parkland on the south side of Glasgow. Linn Park is a green space which borders the heavily built-up areas of Muirend, Netherlee, Croftfoot and Castlemilk. With an area of 203 acres, it includes a golf course, equestrian centre, river walks and managed woodland. The *Paisley Daily Express* described a man's sleepless night after seeing a black panther close to a rubbish bin near the golf course's tenth tee. Deciding to brave the possibility of ridicule, the golfer reported the sighting to a park official the following day. Two days later a second golfer came forward with a separate sighting. Park staff were advised to be on alert when setting out flags on the greens early in the morning. The story was also published in the *Herald* on 1 April, leading some to think it was an April Fool's jape, but the earlier reports in the *Paisley Daily Express* (24 and 25 March) showed this was not the case. Mark Fraser's *Big Cats in Britain Yearbook 2006* states that the cat was seen several more times in April, and again on 4 May, when a cyclist on the path to the main car park saw a 'Labrador-sized' cat sprint across his path towards the golf course. It was carrying a pigeon in its mouth. On 7 May a cast was taken of a pawprint that was 3.5ins (8.9cm) long.

THE RETURN OF THE 'PAISLEY PANTHER'
Again, there was a dearth of reports until 2006. An article in, yet again, the *Paisley Daily Express*, gave a round-up of recent sightings as of 18 July. One woman saw a big black cat twice over

a few days as she was driving along the B790 between Houston and Renfrew on her way to work. In each case the sighting was around 5 a.m. 'It was about 3ft high and very slender and lithe,' she said. 'It just loped across the road and disappeared into the dense forests around the former Royal Ordnance Factory. It was a marvellous sight.' From the description, the cat was moving from south to north; south of the road is the River Gryfe, where anglers fishing after dark had seen a big cat on the bank. A further late-night sighting came from further east, with a motorist spotting a large black cat in woodland near Bridge of Weir. And, finally, a teenage member of Kilbarchan Athletic club was out running in the Gleniffer Braes Country Park, near Bardrain Wood, when he came across a large dark-coloured animal, which was 'bounding across a moor very gracefully.' Mark Fraser's *Big Cats in Britain Yearbook 2007* further indicates that sometime in July a group of youths camping on the outskirts of Neilston (south-west of Barrhead) heard strange noises at night. Looking out they saw a large cat-like creature circling the tent. Once the animal had left, the terrified group packed up their tent and skedaddled. On 8 August came an extraordinary report in the *Paisley Daily Express* that an adult female black panther had been seen with two cubs in woodlands between Paisley and Bishopton. If true, this means there was also a daddy cat somewhere nearby.

The *Big Cats in Britain Yearbook 2007* also throws a different cat altogether into the mix, with a report of a sighting of a sandy-coloured puma-like animal in a field on the outskirts of Nielston on 28 August. The indefatigable *Paisley Daily Express* was on the case again on 1 October 2007, with a gruesome report of three Blackface sheep being attacked over a single night on East Mitchelton Farm in Kilbarchan, between Howwood and Lochwinnoch. Based on the size of the bite marks, farmer Hugh Caldwell was convinced a big cat was responsible. 'It was the teeth marks on their necks that worried me.' The bite marks were from ear to ear, giving a span of 9ins (22.9cm) between the teeth, too large for a fox or most dogs. All three sheep survived the attacks, but two later died of infected wounds. Mr Caldwell had also come across carcasses with their heads ripped off, and had had instances when cattle stampeded for no obvious reason. In his opinion, several big cats were stalking and attacking his livestock: 'There is no doubt in my mind a panther or leopard is on the prowl in the Renfrewshire woodlands. There is possibly a family of them.'

CATS NORTH OF THE CLYDE

2007 and 2008 were quiet years for big cat sightings in Renfrewshire and south Glasgow, although there was an intriguing 2009 report of a large black cat seen sitting under the railway bridge near Pollokshaws West station, by the White Cart Water; the river links with Linn Park, and might provide a 'green corridor' for the movement of the cat. The witness saw the animal about 10 p.m. on 25 June 2009, and the sighting was reported in the *Glasgow Extra* on 17 July. In contrast to this lack of sightings among the now-traditional big-cat locations, the areas north and northwest of Glasgow appeared in the sightings logs. On 17 August 2007 the *Kirkintilloch Herald* had two reports of a big black cat close to the River Kelvin, one being at the back of Waverley Park. Over a year later, on 17 September 2008, the *Airdrie & Coatbridge Advertiser* turned up three separate accounts of undated but recent encounters with big cats east of Airdrie. A taxi driver had a lynx-like animal run across the road in front of him just outside Salsburgh. From three miles further north came the report of a dark or black animal the height of a large greyhound but more muscular, spotted by a dog walker near Hillend Reservoir, outside Caldercruix. And most dramatically, Gartness resident Lindsay Duncan found her dog cowering in a corner of her garden, the object of its fear being a black panther – which then leapt some 8ft or 9ft onto some scaffolding. 'I went closer to get a better look and it spat and hissed,' said Lindsay. 'I got the impression that it was more afraid of me than I was of it. I couldn't believe the size of it, it was huge.'

In 2010 it was the turn of Milngavie to host a big cat 'flap'. The *Milngavie & Bearsden Herald* for 4 February described how 'huge' paw prints were found in the snow near Dunglass Place. The resident who found them connected them with big cats because she had seen a big black cat in the area towards the end of 2009. It was described as about 4ft high with green eyes. Her husband and a neighbour had apparently also seen the animal. More paw prints turned up in the paper on 10 February; as with many similar paw prints photographed across Scotland during the severe winter of 2009/10, it is likely these had a more prosaic nature, being the prints of ordinary animals such as hares, magnified by partial snow-melt and refreezing.

LION!

Perhaps the most baffling and enigmatic sighting came on 22 April 2010, on Meikle Bin, a hill in the Campsies, north of Glasgow. In good visibility, Dr Bob Sharp, former leader of the Lomond mountain rescue team and a vastly experienced mountaineer who 'bagged' all the Munros as far back as 1991, was on the final slope to the 570-metre summit. What he witnessed

Was a lioness (*Panthera leo*) wandering on the Campsie hills? (*Michael Pierrot, FreePhotoBank.org*)

was reported in the *Caledonian Mercury* on 2 May: 'I saw a large animal running from left to right about 20 metres away. My brain tried to fit its shape to that of a fox but failed miserably. The animal I saw was, for all intents and purposes, a female lion… It was beige/brown in colour, had chunky, fur-covered legs, a long tail and rounded-off ears. It was large, at least 4ft to 5ft long, and it moved just like a female African lion. I followed it as it ran towards the treeline, then it was gone in about ten seconds.' Even in the strange world of big cat sightings, a lioness is a *rara avis*.

On 14 July the journalist who broke the story, Dave Hewitt, posted an online comment to his story; he had recently bumped into Bob Sharp, who told him he had returned to Meikle Bin, this time with a camera, and he had taken photographs of paw prints that he thought might have belonged to a puma or lynx. Pumas, lynx and lions all have similar coloured coats, so Dr Sharp *may* have seen a *Felis concolor* or a *Felis lynx*; or did he really encounter a *Panthera leo* less than ten miles from Glasgow?

SHARK!

Rudolph Kenna and Ian Sutherland's *They Belonged to Glasgow* notes that someone in the nineteenth century was deeply concerned about man-eating sharks in the Clyde: 'It is certainly in everyone's interests to prevent these monsters getting acclimatised in British waters,' wrote the individual to a local newspaper. The solution to the menace, obviously, was for the Clyde steamers to tow 'fully baited shark hooks' behind them.

VULTURE!

On 18 August 2010 a vulture became a threat to Scottish airspace. Gandalf, a female Ruppell's Griffon Vulture, was soaring above the World of Wings birds of prey centre in Cumbernauld when she was caught by the wind, and vanished in a northerly direction. Such vultures can fly higher than any other bird, on at least one recorded occasion reaching 36,000ft – which is well within the range used by commercial aircraft – and so an alert was issued to pilots using Glasgow and Cumbernauld airports. The vulture could have caused severe damage to any aircraft, but with a 10ft (3m) wingspan, a collision with a light aircraft or helicopter would be catastrophic. Numerous sightings were reported from a wide area, but turned out to be misidentified birds such as herons. On 21 August Gandalf was located near Falkirk. The 4ft tall bird was returned to World of Wings safe and well, but having lost weight from not eating. The reports appeared on the BBC News website on the 18th and 22nd August.

AND FINALLY… THE FANTASTIC MR FOX

On 14 November 1996 Celtic and Rangers were playing another Old Firm game at Parkhead. Eight minutes into the second half, the crowd roared its appreciation – but not at the actions of the players. For, racing around the pitch, was a fox. The animal, clearly panicked by the huge noise from the terraces, ran around two-thirds of the pitch trying to escape. The clip can be seen on YouTube and several other websites. The fox tried one exit, but that was a dead end, so it carried on, finally vanishing into a corner of the stadium area. Play resumed after a delay of forty-eight seconds. Rangers won the game 1-0. There is no information as to the fate of the vulpine visitor.

CHAPTER THREE

THE WEIRD HUMAN BODY: MIRACULOUS FASTS, STIGMATA AND SPONTANEOUS HUMAN COMBUSTION

THE GLASGOW FASTING MAN

Because eating is such a fundamental part of our daily existence, stories of people who appear to be able to survive without food for long periods always attract attention. Often such 'extreme fasting' is described within a religious context, the ability of the particular individual to apparently live without sustenance being ascribed to some form of divine favour. And one Glaswegian faster even 'proved' his abilities – with a certificate from the Pope, no less.

On 21 July 1532 Pope Clement VII signed a Papal Bull in favour of John Scott, 'Layman of the Diocese of Glasgow', granting him a license to visit the holy places of Jerusalem. The document describes Scott's recent history. A man of some wealth and property, he had been persecuted by his enemies who wished to steal his estates. As a result he was thrown into prison, where he survived without food or drink for thirty-three days. This is medically impossible, but Scott maintained he was sustained by the spiritual comfort he received from Christ, the Virgin Mary, and 'St Ninian, bishop and confessor, whose miracles in Scotland become daily more resplendent.'

Eventually Scott was released from his cell, but had to take refuge from his persecutors in the monastery of Holyrood in Edinburgh, where he again remained without food or water, this time for a credulity-stretching 106 days. During this period he only spoke twice. At Holyrood he made a vow to God that if he survived, he would undertake several pilgrimages, 'without eating flesh or fish'. His first destination after being freed was Whithorn in Galloway, where he viewed the body and relics of St Ninian, after which he travelled through England, 'where he suffered much adversity'. The next destination of his pilgrimage was the Sepulchre of Christ in Jerusalem, hence his petition to the Pope for authorised passage to the Holy Land.

Scott was stated to have insufficient means to pay for the journey, so the Pope granted him a sum of twelve crowns, and instructed that Christian institutions in the Eastern Mediterranean shelter and feed Scott during his pilgrimage. It appears that Scott spent the rest of the summer in Rome, as he is mentioned in another despatch of 30 September, where Marco Antonio Venier, the Venetian ambassador to Rome, states that Scott had volunteered to demonstrate his fasting abilities to the Pope: 'His Holiness gave him in custody to trustworthy persons, who kept him securely locked up for thirteen days without having eaten. He remained there the whole time, always in prayer, and would have staid longer had not the Pope desired him to be set at liberty, and that food should be given him.' The document notes that the official Papal decision was that Scott's abilities to survive without food was derived not from any form of deceit, but from divine grace.

The Pope had entrusted John Scott to Lucchese Silvestro Dario, the Nuncio (Papal Ambassador) to the court of James V, the King of Scotland. Dario in turn had passed Scott onto Vianesio Albergati, a member of a prominent family from Bologna. Albergati left a record of his encounter with Scott, described in detail in a document written in Latin and dated 1 September:

> Vianesio Albergati to his candid readers, greeting.
> ...John Scott, a man of probity, and of noble Scottish lineage, abstained from food and drink during three consecutive months. Lest this should appear incredible, I interrogated the said Scott, by an interpreter. As he maintained that it was perfectly true, I asked him whether he would abstain for some days from eating and drinking.

Albergati therefore decided to set up an experiment, with suitable controls:

> Having stripped him of all his apparel, lest he should secrete anything whereby to recruit his strength and deceive me, and having clad him in other raiment, I kept him for eleven consecutive days and nights in my house, in a bedchamber most carefully closed and sealed. I kept the strictest watch, lest anything could enter that could serve for food and drink, for I always kept the keys of said bedchamber in my own possession, in order that I might convince myself whether any one could live so long without eating and drinking. On the expiration of 11 days, the said John having most constantly endured so long an abstinence, and having always preserved the same complexion, vigour, and pulse, which seemed singularly marvellous to the learned physicians who came very frequently to visit him; and as he had now exceeded the number of days during which a man can live without food and drink, I let him out of the bedchamber, he neither requesting nor expecting his discharge; and I enabled him to depart.

Albergati finishes with a statement of his own bona fides:

> During the whole time that I watched him under close custody, he prayed God and the saints continually, save when he talked or slept; of which thing I call to witness God Almighty, whose Majesty may not be deceived; and if I lie, I do not deprecate His eternal wrath. Farewell, excellent readers, and as no advantage can accrue to me from so impudent a lie, in case I do lie, believe the thing itself to be most true and most certain, as it is.
> So it is with my own hand, Vianesio Albergati, Bolognese.

Note that Albergati states that Scott was without food for eleven days, while the Venetian ambassador says the duration was thirteen days, and another document in the archives of Venice gives the period as ten days. Clearly the details evolved slightly in the retelling, but the core story remains unchanged, and, given that he was the direct instigator of the experiment, Albergati's detailed description is to be preferred.

By 5 October John Scott, armed with his Papal certificate stating that he had the ability to fast for long periods by divine grace, was on his way to Venice. A letter on the remarkable Scotsman was read out in the Venetian Senate, and by the time Scott arrived in the city of canals the following day, *le tout* Venice was agog to see this mysterious visitor. A courtier named Sanuto described the Glaswegian as: 'about fifty years old; long hair, red face, rather fat; is wrapped around the body in a very sorry cloth garment; and holds in his hand a book of offices [prayers] on which his eyes are bent. He has with him a Scot, who can speak nothing but Scotch, and no one understood him.'

As a result of his time at the Vatican, Scott was well-connected. He carried with him a letter of introduction from Cardinal Pisani, which brought him to the influential Venetian Michiel Morosini, who in turn presented him to the Doge, the leader of the city-state. Scott and his travelling companion were first accommodated in the Church of San Giorgio Maggiore for ten days, and then lodged on the island of San Spirito in the Venetian Lagoons. From there they were to be transferred from friary to friary, until safe passage to Jerusalem could be procured for them. And at this point John Scott, the Glasgow Fasting Man, quietly disappears from the pages of history.

The Campanile and the Doge's Palace, Venice. John Scott, complete with his Papal certificate of fasting, was presented to the Doge here. (*Alejandro Fonesca, free distribution license via Wikipedia*)

The island Church of San Giorgio Maggiore, John Scott's lodging in Venice. (*Matthew Field, www. photography.mattfield.com, licensed under the Creative Commons Attribution-Share Alike 3.0 Unported license*)

The documents relating to Scott, translated from the original Latin and Italian, can be found in *Calendar of State Papers Relating to English Affairs in the Archives of Venice, Volume 4 – 1527-1533,* edited in 1871 by Rawdon Brown. Most of them also appeared in *Northern Notes and Queries; or, The Scottish Antiquary,* Vol. 3, published in 1889.

A rather more modern faster turned up in the early years of the twentieth century. Monsieur Victor Beautè, a professional faster, exhibited himself for money at Pickard's American Museum on Trongate, a wild 'freakshow'-type establishment owned by the flamboyant entrepreneur A.E. Pickard, Glasgow's answer to the American huckster P.T. Barnum. On 1 October 1906 Beaute, weighing in at 11st 7lb (73kg), entered an enclosed wooden cage in an attempt to fast for forty days. The 'Fasting Man' brought queues around the block, the onlookers shuffling past twenty-four hours a day as the dapper gent sat in his armchair reading a newspaper, smoking prolifically, and taking the occasional sip of water. The crowds were obsessed with the statistics of the man's weight. On the thirty-ninth day Beaute, now down

A signed postcard of Monsieur Victor Beautè, 'The Fasting Champion'. *(Author's Collection)*

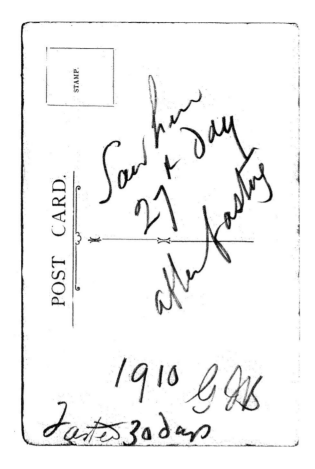

The reverse of the postcard. 'Saw him 27th day after fasting,' writes the witness. 'Fasted 30 days, 1910.' This would have been from a fast after the Glasgow episode. *(Author's Collection)*

to 8st 11lb (55kg), withdrew from the fast, amid more of Pickard's sensational publicity. Judith Bowers' book *Stan Laurel and Other Stars of the Panopticon* revealed that, after midnight when the crowds had gone, The Fasting Man secretly consumed a steak pie baked by the stage manager's wife.

STIGMATA

For his 1994 book *Stigmata*, Ted Harrison, former religious affairs correspondent with the BBC, interviewed George Hamilton, then an unemployed former steel worker living on an estate on the outskirts of Glasgow. George was a stigmatic, one of the people who display the stigmata, or the wounds of Christ on the cross. He was a devout Roman Catholic and a lay Franciscan. Just before Lent in 1986 he woke one morning to find the backs of his hands were bleeding. It may be relevant that at the time he had been reading about the Turin Shroud and St Francis of Assisi — St Francis was a famous stigmatic. Later, marks appeared on his feet but did not bleed immediately; when they did they bled on the upper side, while walking on his soles was painful. His other symptoms included: severe pain; small marks occasionally appearing on his palms (unlike most other stigmatics he did not bleed from his palms); marks of scourging on his back; a wound on the right side; and bruising on one shoulder as if he had been carrying a heavy object, such as a wooden cross. By 1992 he was unable to eat and had a tube inserted to keep him alive with liquid food. Doctors could find no organic or psychiatric cause. New bleeding occurred in Lent leading up to Holy Week, but the painful marks were still visible the rest of the year, so he kept his hands covered by mittens.

As well as the obvious problems, Hamilton's life had been negatively affected by the stigmata because people wanted to seek his touch 'for superstitious reasons' and when, for example, he refused to lay his hands on their baby, they would abuse him. He no longer attended Mass regularly since his presence disrupted the service, which was a great loss, because when he took Communion he experienced a kind of religious ecstasy in which he slipped outside the here and now. He frequently prayed to God for help in understanding his condition — 'What is it

'Vocation of Saint Francis' by father Anton Bleker S.J., Jezuïetenberg, Netherlands. The painting shows him receiving the stigmata. ('*Otter*'/*Wikipedia, licensed under the Creative Commons Attribution-Share Alike 3.0 Unported license*)

you want of me, Lord?' – and had experienced visions of Christ, when he felt as if he entered another world. On one occasion Jesus was accompanied by the Virgin Mary, who said that her son was unhappy with the way George was being treated. He believed that his marks were a sign of divine protection against a very real evil. He had been threatened by the Devil, his front door was set alight, a dead cat was exhumed from his garden, and a music tape in his cassette player gave forth a mocking voice which addressed him by name and reacted to his responses.

SPONTANEOUS HUMAN COMBUSTION (SHC)

In his 'Pig-ignorant' column in *New Scientist* (23 March 1978), Peter Laurie mentioned that he had encountered a SHC case while researching fire-fighting techniques in Glasgow. One morning a fire was reported from an old people's home. 'An old man had been sitting by the window on a hardwood chair... The nurse had seen him happily smoking in the sun; when she came back ten minutes later he was gone. There was a pile of ashes on the floor; the ceiling of the room was black with greasy smoke; there was a strong smell of roasting.' The standard prosaic explanation was suggested – the cigarette had set his dressing-gown on fire. Laurie however was dubious that the limited combustible materials to hand could have completely consumed an entire human being in such a short time.

CHAPTER FOUR

WITCHCRAFT IN GLASGOW

PART 1: A HUNDRED YEARS OF WITCH-HUNTING

THE BACKGROUND

Popularly, the witch-trials are thought of as belonging to the Middle Ages, with hordes of furious and prejudiced pitchfork-wielding peasants descending on a poor village biddy. But persecution of witches in Scotland did not really take off until after the Protestant Reformation of 1560, and it was a legalistic affair, replete with lawyers, witness statements, juries and judges. With a few exceptions, witchcraft in Scotland was not pursued by mob rule, but by the rule of law.

In 1563 the Reformed church pushed through the Witchcraft Act, which made witchcraft a capital offence for the first time. Witch-trials were part of the normal administration of justice, and, more or less, tended to follow a standard procedure. The initial investigation was usually undertaken by the Kirk Session of the local parish church, and typically involved the Minister and Elders. Sometimes the complexity of the case required the involvement of the next level of kirk hierarchy, the Presbytery, or even up as far as the Synod. In a godly society the Sessions were frontline enforcers, dealing with moral discipline, and most Session records endlessly catalogue minor infractions of moral behaviour such as non-attendance at church or, more usually, fornication. To give an indication of the tenor of the times, in 1593 the Glasgow Session required a parishioner to make public repentance for his sin of buggery; once he had done so, and thus satisfied the requirements of the Kirk for 'God's punishment', he was handed over to the civic authorities for 'man's punishment': the magistrates executed him and exhibited his severed head on a spike.

The Sessions also dealt with what they regarded as 'superstition' – such as pilgrimages to holy wells, a holdover from Catholic times – and magical practices which were usually termed 'charming'. Charmers were practitioners of folk magic, which typically involved employing small-scale rituals and incantations to heal people and animals. For these offences, those censured by the Session or Presbytery could expect to be fined or to have to make public repentance in church while wearing sackcloth. Excommunication was also wielded as a threat to those who were not penitent. If however the offence involved *malefica* – magic designed to cause serious harm to crops, animals or people – things moved up a grade. First, attempts were made to make the witch confess, sometimes involving the use of torture. In a minority of cases, brutal physical torture was sanctioned. At other times, the common torment was sleep-deprivation; this does not sound like a particularly serious process, but after several days of being imprisoned without sleep and 'watched' continually, people will say *anything* just to be allowed to close their eyes. An alternative approach taken by the men of God was to 'prick' the alleged witch with a sharp instrument designed to find the insensitive 'Devil's Mark' that Satan was supposed to give his followers (there are many places on the human body that in some cases can be insensitive to pain, from moles and blemishes to horn-like extrusions of skin). All these tortures, and more, were perfectly legal in Scotland. Witnesses were then sought, usually neighbours eager to vent their longstanding grievances against the 'witch'.

Once the religious authorities were convinced of the guilt of the accused, the witch was handed over to the state for a full legal trial. Such trials varied: sometimes the trial took place at the High Court in Edinburgh itself; at other times it was dealt with by a travelling Circuit Court, which was a group of High Court judges who made regular 'circuits' around the country. More commonly the Privy Council in Edinburgh – the supreme legal authority in Scotland – granted a Commission for the local gentry to prosecute the witch at a specially-constituted local court. This had the advantage of taking the pressure off the overburdened High Court, and keeping things local meant neither witnesses nor officials had to undertake the expensive travel to Edinburgh. On the debit side, some local Commissioners were more noted for their enthusiasm for witch-persecution than for their knowledge of the law, and they could be fatally prejudiced against the accused, whom they often knew personally.

If the 'panel', or accused person, was found guilty, he or she was usually strangled to death and then burnt at the stake. On rare occasions they were first executed by hanging, and then burned. Such was the legal situation until 1736, when the 1563 Act was repealed. During the 170 years of the persecution in Scotland, 85 per cent of those put on trial were women; around 55 per cent of these were executed (of the men accused, 52 per cent were executed), while 22 per cent of the women and 20 per cent of the men accused were actually acquitted. Somewhere above 2,000 people are known to have been executed, although the real figure was perhaps a quarter higher again.

There are of course many 'popular' or 'folk' tales of magical powers that circulate independently of the legal witchcraft prosecutions. Skye storyteller George Macpherson, in *Highland Myths and Legends,* gives a typical example. Roving sailor Iain Dhu was out of pocket in Glasgow and so went to Finnieston Quay to find a ship. One captain refused to take him because he knew his troublesome reputation as a famous 'cunning man'. Iain therefore demonstrated his powers, stating: 'I tell you now this ship will never sail without me aboard her.' And true enough, every time the hawsers were cast off, they snaked back to the quay to hold the ship fast to the bollards. Only when the skipper relented and Iain joined the crew could the voyage proceed. Macpherson claims the incident was recorded in the ship's log and the *Lloyd's Register,* but, as is typical of folktales, no checkable details (such as the name of the ship or the date) are provided.

Here, however, we are concerned with real-world events in which alleged magical powers were deployed. Reconstructing witchcraft trials depends on the quality of the initial documents. In many cases the records are incomplete, so sometimes we do not know names, or what they

Steamers at the Broomielaw; it was here Iain Dhu was said to have demonstrated his magic powers. *(Courtesy A.K. Bell Library, Local Studies)*

were specifically charged with, or what was the actual outcome of the trial. But what remains is damning enough.

A CENTURY OF WITCHCRAFT CASES

The first great witchcraft frenzy took place in the 1590s, with eruptions throughout Scotland, notably in Aberdeen. Fife woman Margaret Aitkin, 'the great witch of Balweary,' staved off torture and execution in 1597 by claiming she could identify other witches at a glance, saying 'they had a secret mark, all of that sort, in their eyes, whereby she could surely tell, how soon she looked upon any, whether they were witches or not.' (The quote and the rest of the story are in Archbishop John Spottiswoode's *The History of the Church of Scotland*.) For several months she was carried around Scotland by a specially-constituted official commission, casually identifying witches willy-nilly. Those identified were tortured to confess. In Glasgow the minister, John Cowper, was so credulous that on Aitkin's say-so he caused several innocent women to be burned. As Spottiswoode wrote, eventually her imposture was rumbled: 'In the end she was found to be a mere deceiver (for the same persons that the one day she had declared guilty, the next day being presented in another habit, she cleansed).'

Aitkin was returned to Fife, where at her subsequent trial she confessed that all her identifications of other witches had been false – and the Establishment realised they had been

Lynne McClymont of
History and Horror Tours
demonstrating the way the
punishment branks were
used. (*Ségolène Dupuy*)

'hustled' by a poor illiterate peasant. The result was the usual unedifying spectacle of political leaders denying any responsibility for their own disastrous policies. An article in a book of academic essays, *The Scottish Witch-hunt in Context*, by the volume's editor, Julian Goodare, shows how the collapse of this enterprise caused those politicians who had supported the witch-hunt to backpedal furiously, while James VI, the witch-hunting king, was damaged by association, and various Presbyterian historians were so embarrassed that they omitted the episode completely from their chronicles. In Glasgow the Presbytery threatened to place the iron punishment branks in the mouth of anyone who repeated the 'slander' that the Revd John Cowper was in any way responsible for the death of innocents.

A couple of years later the Glasgow Presbytery heard several cases of charming. Sibyl Dowe told a fellow servant that an owl's heart rubbed on a man's shoulder was a dead cert as a love charm. John Robeson of Lenzie had to make public repentance for attempting to divine the identity of a thief by the ancient art of 'turning the riddle'. The riddle or sieve was placed on a pair of tongs held by only two fingers, while names of suspects were spoken, the sieve moving round at the mention of the guilty party. On 24 March 1602, William Grinlay of Lenzie and William Baird of Balloch were found guilty of asking Annie Forsythe to ensure Baird's mill ground freely. Baird had brought a sack of grain with him; Annie put her hand in the sack and after a while simply said, 'Mill good'. The Presbytery claimed the men 'committed a capital crime replenischit with sorcerie,' but the secular authorities declined to execute and Grinlay and Baird were lucky to escape with a fine and having to make public repentance in three churches, barefoot, barelegged and bareheaded. All these cases are in Andrew Macgeorge's *Old Glasgow*.

Glasgow Cross in the late eighteenth century. The tall tower centre-right was part of the former Tolbooth, where those accused of witchcraft were held. *(Courtesy A.K. Bell Library, Local Studies)*

The remains of the Tolbooth tower today, isolated amidst traffic and modern buildings. *(Photograph by Geoff Holder)*

In 1614 the Glasgow Presbytery investigated one of their own. As noted in volume one of *The Miscellany of the Maitland Club*, published in 1833, numerous witnesses lined up to accuse the Revd George Semple of fraud, greed, corruption, slander, singing lascivious ballads, owning forbidden books of occult lore, and practicing magic and divination. The minister, from Killellan in Renfrewshire, denied accusations that he could tell in advance the date of his own death, or had preternatural knowledge of what was hidden in a locked cupboard, or that he had taken a bribe to use his powers to protect a man from leprosy. The investigation appeared to not so much be concerned with magic *per se*, but with the question of whether the Revd Semple was a fit person to be a minister; he was removed from his post. In the latter part of 1630 the former preacher was charged by the Privy Council with being a 'practizer and consulter in points of witchcraft', but nothing more is known.

In 1613 or 1614, at Glasgow Kirk Session, Archibald Glen, Minister of Carmunnock, accused Margaret Wallace of killing his brother-in-law Robert Muir by witchcraft. Glen himself then died in 1614, and his death was added to the long list of crimes with which Margaret was eventually charged in March 1622. These also included cursing Cuthbert Grey with disease and then removing the illness, and laying disease on others. The core of Margaret's misfortune seemed to be that she was a mouthy besom, always quarrelling with her husband's lower-middle-class business associates around Rutherglen; once they started to call her a witch she sought revenge on them, and they in turn were her main accusers in court. She was also an associate of Christiane Grahame, a healer who had been executed for witchcraft on 27 October 1621. Like Christiane, Margaret was tried and executed in Edinburgh, meeting her fiery end on 22 March 1622.

In many instances the information on a particular case is scant. We do not know the outcomes of the Commissions appointed to investigate Catherine Blair (3 May 1622), Margaret Spreull (1 August 1629) or Grissell Boill, Jean Miller and Janet Miller (all 3 December 1629). On 14 December 1630 Agnes Boyd of Paisley was convicted of charming, managed to avoid the death penalty, and was sent to the Bishop of Glasgow for punishment. On 15 October 1649 the Presbytery heard the case of Mauld Gauld, from Briggait in Paisley. As with the Margaret Wallace case almost thirty years earlier, it was a case of a neighbourhood dispute that had escalated to the courts. Mauld's husband was a craftsman, and Mauld had been engaged in a longstanding spat with other craftsmen and their wives. The quarrelling escalated to cursing; when several of those so cursed went on to become ill, suspicions arose. Mauld openly bragged about her ability to cause harm, and was seen with a clay model of a penis, the purpose of which was to cause impotence. It is not clear what happened to her, but on 2 November of the same year there were several unnamed witches languishing in the tolbooths of Renfrew and Paisley.

In February 1650 Margaret Finlasoune was on trial in Renfrew; there is no record of the outcome, but one of the witnesses mentioned recently attending the execution of the witch Jeane Craufurd in Glasgow. On 9 December of the same year Agnes Gourlay had to make public repentance in sackcloth for charming cattle to make good cream; the process involved casting some milk into the byre drain, and putting salt and bread into the cow's ears. P.G. Maxwell-Stuart's *An Abundance of Witches* mentions Janet Tulloch, who had been imprisoned in Renfrew for at least four years, accused of causing illness, injury and death by magic. She was pricked and the Devil's mark discovered. Her long journey from Kirk Session to Presbytery to court, all in Paisley, ended in May 1657 when she was executed in Glasgow. In

1658 Bessie Neveing of Renfrew was up in front of the Glasgow Circuit Court but no further details of her fate are known. Three years later William Sutherland, the Irvine hangman, gave a declaration that he had recently been engaged to execute a witch at Paisley; the witch is not named. In 1662 several confessing witches from the Renfrewshire village of Inverkip were probably executed, although it is not clear how many. In January 1663 Hew Montgomery of Silverwood was granted a Commission to try Jonet Patoun from the Glasgow parish of Eastwood; she was in the Paisley Tolbooth at the time. In 1667 Janet Finnie, suspected of witchcraft, died in the same Tolbooth.

By the end of the seventeenth century, intellectual scepticism as to the reality of witchcraft was reducing the number of trials drastically. The *Old Statistical Account* claims that a woman was burnt for witchcraft at Sandyford, near Old Kilpatrick, around this time, but no details are given. Devil's marks were found on Janet Widdrow or Wodrow in Inchinnan in 1696. In March she was in the Paisley Tolbooth, by May she had named several other witches in the area, and in December she was still being proceeded against. Time and again the suspicion arises that, if the case against the suspected witches was not strong enough to go to court, or if the accused were without influence, then they just remained in the Tolbooth until eventually someone noticed their plight, or the authorities ran out of money and patience. In Janet Widdrow's case we do not know the outcome of her case, nor in that of her fellow-accused, Isobel Cochrane.

A curious reversal of the usual process came before the Regality Court of Paisley on 8 April 1692, when a number of prominent citizens took an action of criminal libel to counter a rumour that they were witches. Four young men and two women from the middling rank of society (wrights, maltmen and small merchants) had spread gossip that the Devil's health had been toasted at a gathering of the upper echelon of Paisley society. Further, one of the maltmen, John Pirrie or Perhie, had stood on the Mercat Cross and proclaimed in public that the wealthy women, especially Elizabeth Parkhill, deserved 'to be marked with a burning iron upon their face.' Everyone understood that this meant Pirrie thought the women were witches. The population of Paisley at the time was less than 2,000, so it is easy to imagine how such gossip could spread quickly and damage the reputation of those accused – and possibly even lead to official suspicions of witchcraft.

Unfortunately for Pirrie and his cronies, the slander about drinking the Devil's health had encompassed not only two gentlemen, three former Bailies of the town, and four lawyers, but also William Tarbert, the Procurator-Fiscal of Paisley himself. Not surprisingly, the legal response was swift and effective. Pirrie, John White, James Hall, John Cocheran and Jannet Fyfe were each fined the enormous sum of £100 and ordered to stand at the Paisley Cross with a paper fixed to their person reading in large letters, *WE STAND HERE FOR SCANDALISING THE GOOD NAMES OF JOHN ADAM, WILLIAM HENDERSONE, WILLIAM TARBERT, ELIZABETH PARKHILL, MARGARET HOUSTON, AND MARGARET PATISON,* or variations to that effect, depending on whom they had personally slandered. Each had also to repeat the standard slanderer's phrase, 'false tongue, we lie.' Margaret Finnie also suffered the public humiliation at the cross, but appears to have escaped the fine. The details are in William Hector's *Selections from the Judicial Records of Renfrewshire.*

Unless specified, the information on the cases mentioned in this chapter has been drawn from a variety of sources including: *The Darker Superstitions of Scotland* by John Graham Dalyell; *The History of Witchcraft in Scotland* by Charles Kirkpatrick Sharpe; *A Calendar Of Cases*

Gary Knight of History and Horror Tours 'branding' a miscreant in the stocks. The sign is of the kind worn by the Paisley slanderers. The identity of the 'offender' has been obscured to preserve a degree of dignity. (*Ségolène Dupuy*)

of Witchcraft in Scotland 1510-1727, compiled by George Black; *Witchcraze* by Anne Llewellyn Barstow; Christina Larner's *Enemies of God: The Witch-Hunt in Scotland; The Scottish witch-hunt in context*, edited by Julian Goodare; and Edinburgh University's Survey of Scottish Witchcraft at www.sch.ed.ac.uk/Research/witches.

In the next chapter, we will consider in detail one of the more extraordinary – and best-recorded – cases in the history of Scottish witchcraft: the Pollok Witches.

CHAPTER FIVE

WITCHCRAFT IN GLASGOW

PART 2: THE WITCHES OF POLLOK, AND THE POSSESSED CHILDREN OF BARGARRAN AND GOVAN

THE BEGINNINGS

One of the most notorious witchcraft episodes was the case of 'the bewitched baronet'. In 1647 Sir George Maxwell of Auldhouse inherited the Pollok estate. The vast estate within the parish of Eastwood in the south of Glasgow was centred on Pollok Castle, which has now vanished, replaced by the eighteenth-century Pollok House, a fine Georgian mansion open to the public. Across the river from the castle was the humble village of Polloktoun, long since demolished. The Pollok name lives on in the area names of Pollokshields and Pollokshaws, and of course the popular Pollok Park, home of the magnificent Burrell Collection.

Sir George came from a strict Presbyterian family and was an active Covenanter during their bloody inter-Protestant conflict with the rival Episcopalian hegemony favoured by the king. As a consequence of both his social position and his religious convictions, Sir George was a keen prosecutor of witches. In January 1662 he was part of the Commission appointed to try several witches of Inverkip in Renfrewshire. In 1676 he participated in a similar trial at Gourock.

The seventeenth century was a time of religious and civil wars, leading to widespread suffering. As a result omens, prophecies and belief in supernatural

Sir George Maxwell, the bewitched baronet. The painting, by an unknown artist, is from a private collection currently hanging in Pollok House.

Pollok House, the Georgian replacement for the castle of Sir George Maxwell (*Photograph by Geoff Holder*)

Another view of Pollok House. (*Photograph by Geoff Holder*)

events were widespread as people tried to make sense of the blizzard of chaos and horror around them. George Campbell's book *Eastwood* hints at the febrile and crisis-ridden nature of the atmosphere of the time: '[In 1676] There was an apparition of a man clothed in red, on a hill above Eastwood Moor, crying "wo, wo, to this land"… it was a time of great tension and excitement, one which lent itself to all bordering on the marvellous.'

On 14 October 1676, Sir George Maxwell was inspecting his soap and candle works in Candleriggs in Glasgow. Suddenly he was attacked by a terrible pain in his right side. After seven weeks the doctors were baffled. The suggestion went up that the illness was caused by witchcraft – it was remembered that Sir George had recently participated in the witch-trial at Gourock, and the prophetic apparition of Eastwood Moor was also fresh in everyone's memory.

At this point a thirteen-year-old girl came forward. She was allegedly a vagrant, with no known history; as far as anyone could tell, she had been staying in Polloktoun for the previous month. She was apparently deaf and mute. Several months later, when the events had passed their gruesome climax, she would give her name as Janet Douglas.

The White Cart Water in Pollok Park; the hamlet of Polloktoun once stood on its banks. Here Janet Douglas discovered the Scottish equivalent of 'voodoo dolls'. (*Photograph by Geoff Holder*)

By virtue of her status as a deaf-mute, Janet Douglas became a kind of mascot for Sir George's two daughters. One day she was in a crowd at Pollok when she pointed out a particular woman. Using hand gestures she somehow conveyed the notion that this woman had made a wax image of Sir George, and had stuck it with pins. This, she intimated, was the cause of the baronet's mysterious illness. 'At first they hardly understood her,' wrote Sir George's son John some years later, 'till she went to one of the gentlewoman's closets, and bringing thence a little beeswax, she plyed it before the fire,' and showed them how wax effigies were created for witchcraft. We have already met with clay or wax effigies (some of the whole body, some merely of parts of it) in the case of Mauld Gauld (*see* chapter four); at Pollok, these Scottish equivalents of 'Voodoo dolls' played a significant role in the case.

The case attracted a considerable amount of notoriety, and it appears in a number of works by educated men who heard of the proceedings at close hand, or even participated in them. Key episodes from these contemporaries can be found in: the Revd Robert Law's *Memorials of Remarkable Things in His Time, from 1638 to 1684* (Law was minister of Easter Kilpatrick, near Bearsden); the Revd Robert Wodrow's *Analecta*, compiled around 1730 (Wodrow was minister of Eastwood parish); the notes and journals of Sir John Lauder of Fountainhall, one of the most senior figures in the Scottish justiciary (Fountainhall's manuscripts are frequently quoted by later writers); a description of the events written by Sir John Maxwell (and allegedly dictated, at least in part, by Sir John's father Sir George, the bewitched baronet himself); George Crawford's *History of Renfrewshire* (1710); and even in the famous *Diary* of Samuel Pepys.

Later works which contain significant sections on the case include *The Philosophy of Witchcraft*, published in 1839 by J. Mitchell and J.N. Dickie, which contains Sir John's account, as well as other primary sources; the anonymous *A History of the Witches of Renfrewshire* (1807/1877); *The Darker Superstitions of Scotland*, written by John Graham Dalyell in 1834; Robert Chambers' *The Domestic Annals of Scotland* (1874); *The History of Witchcraft in Scotland* by Charles Kirkpatrick Sharpe, published in 1884 but written several decades earlier; and George Campbell's 1902 book *Eastwood: Notes on the ecclesiastical antiquities of the parish*, mentioned previously, which brings together many earlier documents.

In a small number of direct quotes from these works I have modernised the spelling, so as to improve comprehension. Although these writings often contradict each other or have different details — perhaps not surprising in such a complex and fraught history such as this — by moving between the various accounts we can build up a picture of what must have been a truly extraordinary episode, with its combination of sympathetic magic, image or effigy witchcraft, animal bewitchment, second-sight and Satanic sex.

THE ARREST OF JANET MATHIE

After some persuasion, it seems one or more of Sir George's daughters came to believe that Janet Douglas was telling the truth about the wax image, and the girl was empowered to take two manservants, Andrew Martin and Laurence Pollock, and enter the cottage of the woman she had pointed out — this being Janet (or Jonet) Mathie, widow of the under-miller at the Shaw Mill. The teenager put her hand up the chimney and pulled out a wax figure stuck with three pins, the two deepest being in the right side, the very location of Sir George's most severe pains. Janet Mathie was arrested and imprisoned in Paisley. When questioned about the wax figure, she merely stated, 'It was the deed of the dumb girl.' The sheriff-depute of Renfrew had Mathie examined for 'insensible' marks, and several were found upon her skin: clearly, her master, the Devil, had marked her.

The pins were removed from the wax image, and as proof of the connection, that night the laird allegedly started to recover. At least, that was what Lawrence Pollok and Sir George's servant Andrew Martin swore happened, when they came to give their depositions at the subsequent trial. But the laird's son, John, merely noted, 'There was some abatement of Sir George's sickness, but not to any observable degree.'

With an affirmed witch in custody, speculation began to run rife as to the extent of her *malefica*, or wicked deeds. In his *Memorials* Robert Law noted that Janet Mathie was also suspected of cursing the brother-in-law of Sir George, a Mr Jamieson, the Minister at Govan: 'He himself suspected he was witched, though he knew not by whom, for he had a great pain betwixt his navel and his back, which the physician could not well understand, and continued with him a long time, and brought him very low, and at length ended his days. Surely the Lord, in the deep of his wisdom, may give up the bodies of his people to be troubled and tormented by Satan.' As far as can be ascertained, this is the only suggestion in the records implicating Janet Mathie in this alleged magical attack: it was not mentioned at the trial.

Mathie's malign influence continued to be felt beyond her prison cell, or at least that was what Robert Law in his *Memorials* claimed. Shortly after Mathie's arrest, the Earl of Dundonald, who had been instrumental in granting the warrant, was travelling in a party from Paisley, *en route* to Eglinton to attend his granddaughter's wedding. As they passed the door of the mean cottage inhabited by one of Mathie's daughters, the coach-horses refused to move a further foot, and even turned their heads homeward. Faced with the recalcitrant beasts, the riders in the party dismounted and yoked their own horses to the coach; but these animals too refused to pass by the cottage door. In the end the entire party had no choice but to turn around and head back to Paisley, all thoughts of attending the wedding forgotten.

THE ARREST OF JOHN AND ANNABIL STEWART

Sir George Maxwell's slightest of recoveries took place about 12 December 1676. On 4 January 1677 his illness became worse. Janet Douglas appears to have been absent from Pollok House for a few days, for on 7 January she sent a message to the family that John Stewart, Janet Mathie's eldest son, had been carrying on his mother's wicked work. According to Janet Douglas, John had made an effigy out of clay and roasted it before the fire with pins. When not in use it was hidden beneath the bolster among the bed-straw. This remarkably detailed description led to the discovery of the effigy and the arrest of John Stewart and his fourteen-year-old sister Annabil. Both confessed to attending witch-meetings in their houses, and socialising therein with the Devil ('the black gentleman', as Annabil called him). The pair also named three other witches who had been present at the effigy-making – Margaret Jackson, Marjory Craig and Bessie Weir. All three were promptly arrested and held in the Paisley Tolbooth.

The first witch-meeting had been in October 1676, just before Sir George was taken ill. The second took place on 4 January 1677, the day the baronet's illness took a turn for the worse. At these get-togethers Satan enthusiastically assisted in the manufacture of the effigies. Once the effigy was complete, it was passed from hand to hand by all present, and each person had to say, 'I, John Stewart [or whomever, each giving their own name] have the portraiture of Sir George Maxwell of Nether Pollock in my hand, and I consent unto his death.' Janet Mathie, according to her daughter, had suffered a few minor slights from the laird, and hence the widow's entire family detested the whole Maxwell clan, a vendetta magnified by the hatred of the very poor for the very rich. John confessed he was angry with Sir George for having arrested his mother. Indeed, all the accused seemed to have a problem with Maxwell as their landlord, so it may have been a case of collective revenge.

The Devil was described by Annabil as, 'A man with black clothes, a blue band, and white handcuffs.' He wore hoggers [footless stockings] over his cloven feet. According to Robert Law, John Stewart confessed that his mother had dedicated both himself and his sister to the Devil when they were still in the womb. But Satan clearly required what might be termed 'informed consent' from those who were to be his servants, and so he visited Janet Mathie again when her children were of an age to make a voluntary act of will. Both John and Annabil renounced their baptism and entered into a Satanic pact. As part of the pact, The Evil One give John and Annabil a painful nip as his mark, and during interrogation many 'insensible marks' were found all over John's body. Annabil described how she performed what was the standard description of the Satanic ritual in Scotland: 'She put her hand to the crown of her head, and the other to the sole of her foot, and did give herself up to the Devil.' In return she was promised a new coat. At the end of the ritual, the Devil lay with her; she found his manhood to be cold as ice.

Annabil seemed to positively revel in revealing secrets of the Satanic shenanigans. She described how the Devil renamed his followers – Annabil was 'Anippy', her mother 'Landslady', her brother 'Jonas', Bessie Weir 'Sopha', Margaret Jackson 'Locas', and Marjory Craig 'Rigeru'. The Devil, interestingly, was referred to by an unusual personal name: Ejoal (Robert Law renders this as 'J. Jewell'). A strange episode occurred during Annabil's confession – when asked about the name she used for the Devil, 'she, being about to tell, was stopped, the bed being made to shake, and her clothes under her blown up with a wind.' (This is described in Robert Chambers' account.) In the view of her interrogators, Satan was trying to dissuade his acolyte from revealing too many personal details.

Margaret Jackson, who seems to have been related to Janet Mathie, possibly even being her mother-in-law, confessed within a day or two; at eighty years of age, she was presumably unable to bear the pressure of the interrogations. Bessie Weir, Marjory Craig and Janet Mathie absolutely refused to confess. With three 'witches' confessing to their crimes, combined with the discovery of the effigies, and a consistent series of stories implicating the three 'obstinate' accused, the Privy Council had enough evidence to proceed with a trial. A local Commission was appointed, consisting of Sir Patrick Houstoun of that Ilk; James Brisbane of Bishopton; Sir John Shaw the younger of Greenock; John Anderson the younger of Dovehill; John Preston of Haltrees, advocate and former justice-depute; and George, Lord Ross. The latter two gentlemen, sent out from Edinburgh, were the only ones with any significant legal experience, although among the local gentry, Sir Patrick Houstoun and Sir John Shaw had previously been Commissioners in the notorious Inverkip witch-trial in 1662. Robert Alexander of Blackhouse, from Renfrew, filled the role of the prosecutor. The terms of the Commission specified that no torture was to be used.

THE TRIAL AND THE EXECUTIONS
The trial opened at Paisley on 27 January 1677. The first to appear was Annabil Stewart, who made another frank and fulsome confession. John Stewart then confirmed everything his sister

had stated. Margaret Jackson was next, adding a few more intriguing details: unlike Annabil, who first met the Devil in autumn 1676, and John, who had taken the pact in early January 1677, Margaret had been a servant of Satan for some forty years, having renounced her baptism and entered into his service at Pollokshaw-croft around 1637. Despite her age, the Devil was still physically interested in her to this day: 'About the third or fourth of January instant, or thereby, in the night time, when she awaked, she found a man to be in bed with her, whom she supposed to be her husband, though her husband had been dead twenty years, or thereby, and that the man immediately disappeared; and declares, that this man who disappeared was the Devil.' This detail is given in Sir John Maxwell's account.

On 17 January a third effigy had been found under Janet Mathie's bolster in her cell in Paisley. Once again, it had been discovered thanks to the young mute girl. This image, however, was different to the others, being distinctively female in shape. Robert Law's *Memorials* states the image was designed to 'kill the daughter-in-law of the said Sir George, who was an active gentlewoman in the detection of the foresaid effigies; the ground of the presumption was that she fell sick at the same time.'

The making of an occult clay effigy was not the only thing that Janet Mathie got up to in her prison cell. Sir John Maxwell's account says that at the end of the first day of the trial, 27 January, the court commanded the jailor to put her in the stocks. This apparently was not a punishment, but a precaution, because it was feared she might try to end her life. That night Janet had her feet fixed in the heavy, almost immovable stocks, with her sleeping bolster some six yards away, out of reach. The following morning the jailor found her still trapped in the stocks but now asleep on the bolster. When questioned, she stated she had crept along the floor, dragging the stocks with her. Later she said she, 'had gotten one foot free out of the hole, and with the other had drawn the stocks.' The jailor swore that it would have been impossible for her to either drag the weight of the stocks, or to take her foot out of the hole. The implication was that Janet had transported the bolster the six yards through the power of witchcraft.

Around this time Bessie Weir escaped from Paisley and fled to Carmunnock parish, where she lived under the alias of Bessie Aikin. In February the mute girl took six men to raid a house in Carmunnock belonging to an unnamed 'witch-woman', who was presumably Bessie Weir. Another clay effigy, again studded with pins, was uncovered. This was thought to represent Hugh Smith, the minister of Eastwood. 'Before this time,' wrote Robert Law, 'Mr Hugh was much afflicted with pain and sweating, to the changing of half a dozen of shirts some days, and was brought very low; and after this discovery, and the effigy gotten, and these pins taken out, he grew well again.' Law also gave an intriguing back-story for the effigy, which suggests there were more 'witches' active in the area: 'It was convoyed from another witch-woman with whom it was made, in the place where Mr Hugh lived in Eastwood, to this woman, that lived in Carmunnock, to be keeped by her, lest it should have been detected by the dumb lass at Pollok, where it was first made; yet did this dumb lass receive the knowledge of this secret afterwards.'

On 15 February the court re-convened. Several witnesses testified that Janet Mathie, Bessie Weir and Margory Craig had widespread reputations as witches. The three 'obstinate' accused women now appeared in court for the first time, and were confronted with the three 'confessing witches'. Despite her children's exhortations to confess – often accompanied by tears and vivid descriptions of the visits of the Devil to the household – Janet Mathie refused to change her plea. She, along with Bessie Weir and Marjory Craig, maintained a plea of innocence to the end.

Janet Douglas, whose actions had almost single-handedly brought about the imprisonment of the six, was not called to give evidence.

On 20 February 1677 Bessie Weir, Margaret Jackson, Marjory Craig, Janet Mathie and John Stewart were hanged on the Gallowgreen at Paisley, and their bodies burned on a collective pyre. Robert Law describes how Janet Mathie was the first to die – 'obduredly... without any confession of her guilt' – and the alleged tools of her trade destroyed with her: 'The effigies both of wax and clay being put in a napkin and dashed in pieces, were thrown in the fire with her.' He also noted that Bessie Weir had previously been condemned for witchcraft in Ireland, but had escaped through Satanic intervention: 'When the hangman there was about to cast her over the gallows, the devil takes her away from them out of their sight'. At Paisley, Bessie's death was accompanied by another supernatural visitation: 'When she was cast off the gallows, there appears a raven, and approaches the hang-man within an ell of him, and flies away again. All the people observed it and cried out at the sight of it!'

Despite her extravagant confession, Annabil Stewart was not executed, being reprieved on account of her age. She remained in prison, however, and on 4 April she was removed from Paisley to the Tolbooth in Glasgow, where she was to receive spiritual instruction from ministers keen to deflect her from the path of damnation. It is not clear whether this guidance had any effect, because the only time Annabil subsequently features in the records is in May 1688, when she was mentioned as having taught witchcraft to Catharin Mactaggart of Dunbar in East Lothian. Catharin had been first prosecuted in 1679 (she absconded) and so it is likely she and Annabil had linked up around that date.

THE AFTERMATH – JANET DOUGLAS AS CELEBRITY

At Pollok, the route from accusation to execution had taken just over two months, a period which must have been intoxicatingly exciting for the destitute teenager later to be known as Janet Douglas. Not only had she been a key player in a major drama, she had also been shown favour by a rich and powerful family. Several subsequent commentators – including Walter Scott in *Letters on Demonology and Witchcraft* – have seen Janet Douglas as a vindictive fraud who planted the effigies which she so conveniently discovered, her original purpose being some obscure revenge on the tenants of Polloktoun. Thereafter, having been supported and empowered by people of influence, she may have wanted to maintain her position by continuing to identify witches. Take a witch-haunted collective imagination, add one disturbed and manipulative teenager, and five people die on the gallows, their corpses burned to ash. (On the other hand, it is possible the Mathie/Stewart family and their associates were indeed engaged in some kind of magical malice against their landlord.)

Robert Law showed that Janet was not about to let the execution of one set of witches stall her new career as Witchfinder-Corporal. After the five executions, Sir George improved again; the mute girl immediately communicated the existence of 'another picture of him in Kilbride, and offered to discover it'. For some reason the family refused to authorise a further incursion. Then in April 1677 Sir George, 'worn to a shadow,' died of the 'sweating sickness'. Conventional wisdom suggested that the execution of the witches responsible for his illness should have allowed him to recover his health; but clearly conventional wisdom was foxed in this case. The girl now moved on to other influential individuals. Back in February, as we have seen, she had detected an effigy of Hugh Smith, minister of Eastwood. In May her effigy-radar was once again in operation, finding a second image of the minister. 'She, being assisted by his brother, Mr James, finds it in a house near to Renfrew, the said Mr Hugh at the time being very unwell, and near to death.' Shortly after, Robert Law noted: 'Mr Hugh dies of his disease.'

Janet Douglas' history at this point is confusing. Lord Fountainhall claimed that she moved on to Dumbarton, where she detected an image of Robert Hamilton of Barnes, who at the time was lying in his sick-bed. On her say-so, several local women were imprisoned, including: Margaret Wright of Ledameroch; her daughter Christian Donald of Wester Cesnok; Issobell Layng of Duntaglennie; Margaret Paterson of Milntoun of Duntocher; and Jonet Mun of Lawmuir. The Privy Council forbade the local Commission to use torture or to prevent the accused from sleeping. Nevertheless, two of the women committed suicide, while the other four were strangled and burned. In 1874 Robert Chambers stated that the mute girl had also travelled to Stirling, where she persuaded Robert Douglas of Barloch that his sons – found drowned at a river crossing – had been murdered by witchcraft. Barloch consequently had John Gray, Janet McNair, Thomas Mitchell and Mary Mitchell imprisoned in the Stirling Tolbooth, where they remained for fourteen weeks without any evidence against them other than insensible marks found by a pricker. Barloch, who had been paying for the expenses, appealed to the magistrates of Stirling to take over the cost, but the canny burghers were having none of it. After further investigation by the Privy Council, all four accused were let go without charge. There is no official mention of Janet Douglas being involved in the accusation.

What is beyond dispute is that by the early Spring of 1677 the mute girl was something of a minor celebrity. George Hickes, later a prominent Jacobite intellectual, wrote to Samuel Pepys about the effect she had in Glasgow:

> The people in great numbers ran out to meet her. As she was surrounded with the crowd, she called out to one man, a goldsmith, as I remember, and told him that of so long a time he had not thriven in his trade, though he was very diligent in it, because an image was made against him, which he might find in such a corner of his shop; and when the man went home, there he found it where she said it was; and the image was such, both as to matter and form, as she had described it, viz., a little rude image made of clay. She told another, that he and his wife, who had been a very loving couple, of late had lived in great discord, to the grief and astonishment of them both; and when the man asked the reason, she answered, as she did before, that there was an image made against them.

It will be noticed that the girl is described as talking normally. For, by now – miracle upon miracle – the deaf-mute had recovered all her senses. Truly the Lord moved in mysterious ways.

The girl's previous muteness and deafness definitely contributed to her apparent otherworldliness or mystic regard, and gave weight to her accusations against the witches. Throughout this period mutes or deaf-mutes were regarded as having special psychic powers, and such individuals frequently turn up in cases where people were charged with using divination to detect a lost item or foretell the future. Sometimes the 'dumb men' were also employed as witch-prickers or witchfinders. For a Glasgow example of how 'dumbies' were regarded as mystically gifted, we find a case in Robert Law's *Memorials*. In 1676, a few months before the Pollok case, a woman, deaf and mute from birth, visited the daughter of the Laird of Bardowie, in Baldernock parish (Bearsden area). The Laird's daughter was intending to visit her sister-in-law in Hamilton, but the mute woman tried to put her off: 'She makes many signs to her not to go, and takes her down to the yard, and cuts at the root of a tree, making signs that it would fall and kill her.' The young gentlewoman ignored the warning; at Hamilton a few days later a tree, cut through at the root, fell on her, and she died of her injuries shortly afterwards.

As well as possessing the ability to detect witches, Janet Douglas in her mute period was credited with marvellous powers, as attested in the account of the affair written by Sir John Maxwell:

> She knew what was done in distant places, and understood languages. For instance, when a chapter in the Greek New Testament was read, she made us understand by signs what the purposes were, (for at that time she was dumb, whether really or counterfeitly, it is hard to determine) and did exactly give an account to myself, what we did at two miles distant from the place where she was, without any information given to her which I knew of.

She apparently also understood Latin and French, neither of which she had learned, and could 'most wonderfully' discover secrets from the past.

All this and more made her an object of curiosity to educated men intrigued by such subjects as second-sight and its relationship with powers gifted by God or granted by Satan. As a result of the chaotic scenes and supernatural rumours that accompanied the girl's public appearances, the magistrates of Glasgow had her confined, and sent a report to the Privy Council (the gist of which was 'what do we do with this extraordinary person?'). There was also some dispute as to whether she was a seer, a witch, or possessed by an evil spirit. In Glasgow, she was allowed no visitors while the Privy Council debated the matter. Two people, however, did manage to gain access, and they each left an account of their respective interviews, which probably took place in May 1677.

The first individual was a former student of George Sinclair, the witch-fascinated Professor of Philosophy at Glasgow University, to whom he sent a letter describing his visit (it is in Mitchell and Dickie's *The Philosophy of Witchcraft*). In a short work entitled *A Brief Discourse concerning the Second Sight,* John Frazer, the minister of Coll and Tiree, identified the interviewer as a minister named Gray, whose parish was somewhere in Glasgow. In response to Gray's questions, the girl claimed she had never been actually mute, but had simply suffered from a swelling in her throat and tongue, which had now been cured by the application of *Album graecum*. This term, literally translated as 'Greek white', was one of those cures from yesteryear that raise the distaste of modern readers: it was dog dung that had turned white through exposure to air, then powdered and mixed with honey, and used as a medicine for inflammations of the throat. Although several contemporaries wrote that the girl could neither speak nor hear, Mr Gray made no mention of her deafness, which may simply have been assumed by those around her who conflated 'dumb' with 'deaf'.

Understandably, Mr Gray was interested in how she knew about the witches and their practices. She simply answered that, 'She had it only by a vision, and knew all things as well as if she had been personally present with them.' During the visions she received no communications from spirits, nor heard the voices of any supernatural being – especially not the Devil, of whom she insisted she knew nothing. She also knew – through the visions, which came in full colour with surround-sound – that witches perverted the meaning of the Lord's Prayer, subtly changing words so that they referred to the Devil and not to God. And she claimed to have the ability to identify witches simply by encountering them in person. She described how one Glasgow woman so identified, 'ran away in great confusion, being indeed a person suspected of Witchcraft, and had been sometimes imprisoned on that account.' Another woman named Campbell was accused on the basis of the Devil's mark on her arm – although this mark was in fact invisible to all but Janet Douglas (!). Campbell later confessed her crime to her neighbours and begged them to turn her in, otherwise Satan would make her kill herself; the next morning the woman, who was probably suffering from a mental illness, was found drowned in the River Clyde.

The second visitor was George Hickes, who gained access through his job as the personal chaplain to the powerful Duke of Lauderdale, the Lord High Commissioner for Scotland. Hickes took with him Mr Scott, Minister of the Church of the Abbey of Holyrood, and, twenty-three years later, described what transpired in a letter to the London diarist Samuel Pepys. Having exhaustively established that the girl was not a limb of Satan – through having her pray to God, repeat the Lord's Prayer accurately, and recall her baptism vow to renounce the Devil and all his works – Hickes moved on to his main interest, second-sight. Janet told him she had visions of the witches manufacturing the images, and that such visions always came when she was awake, and the visions were realistic in style and content. In contrast to other seers from the Highlands and Islands who had been investigated, she had no bodily warning that the visions were about to arrive, and never suffered any physical symptoms either during or after the visions. Further, she was not 'troubled' by her visions, and did not regard them as a burden – again in contrast to other seers, who often felt themselves cursed.

The question of Janet Douglas' origins also exercised these fine gentlemen. She told Mr Gray that she had no knowledge of her parents, and had run away at an early age from a poor woman who beat her. With Hickes, she refused to discuss her parentage, although he had heard from others that she had represented herself as coming from the West Highlands or the Western Isles. Hickes also thought that, far from being a destitute vagrant, she had been brought up in a family of quality – she was well-spoken, had a wide vocabulary, and had an air of self-confidence bordering on impudence – 'a bold, undaunted spirit,' as Hickes described her. Through signing, she had indicated to Sir George Maxwell that three years before she had received a vision, indicating that she should come to Glasgow. If true, this would have meant her psychic powers first manifested when she was ten or eleven years old. However, as with most things concerning Janet Douglas, her real background remains utterly obscure.

JANET DOUGLAS IN EDINBURGH – A CLIMAX OF SORTS

According to Mr Gray, Janet Douglas revealed to him that she had received a vision of her future: 'She would be carried before the great council at Edinburgh, imprisoned there, and scourged through the town.' Given that she was currently in prison and the Privy Council was debating her situation, this was hardly an astounding act of precognition. And indeed, within a short time she was conveyed to the Canongate Tolbooth in Edinburgh, and investigated by the Privy Councillors, including Lord Fountainhall, who described her effect on the city: 'The first night she came to the Canongate, C. Charteris, one of the town baillies, she told him his wife was bewitched by two old women in the Castlehill, and condescended on them, and they were imprisoned'. Janet caused the two accused to repeat the Lord's Prayer, insisting to the judicial witnesses that she could hear the witches change the words so as to implicate Satan as their Lord. Fountainhall found the display 'very incredible [unbelievable] and fallacious'. Once gain, crowds flocked to see the girl, so, as in Glasgow, she was held *incommunicado*.

A story is told of Janet Douglas in her Edinburgh jail, although this has all the hallmarks of a Presbyterian folktale. It is recorded in the *Analecta*, the Revd Robert Wodrow's miscellany of correspondence and ecclesiastical gossip, Wodrow's informant being a Mr P. Tullideph. According to this tale, James Sharp, the Episcopalian Archbishop of St Andrews, was presiding over the Privy Council and decided to interrogate the girl on charges of sorcery and witchcraft. The Archbishop threatened her with transportation to the West Indies, to which she coolly replied: 'My Lord, who was with you in your closet [study] on Saturday night last, betwixt twelve and one a-clock?' On hearing this the Archbishop turned pale, and the subject was dropped. The Duke of Rothes then spoke to Janet in private, asking her to reveal the identity of the person who was with the prelate. When he promised that in exchange she would be freed, she agreed to divulge the secret: 'My Lord, it was the meekle black Devil!' This would have played well with Wodrow's audience and correspondents, as Archbishop Sharp was hated by the Presbyterians, whom he had persecuted during the horrors of the Covenanting period. In numerous ballads and popular accounts Sharp was represented as a traitor to Scotland, and in league with the Devil to boot. He was assassinated by a group of Covenanters in 1679.

It appears Janet was released at some point during that summer of 1677. But then she committed several (unspecified) offences in Edinburgh, was arrested again, whipped, and sentenced to transportation to an overseas plantation – which sounds like an easy way of getting rid of a very inconvenient individual. But, given her magical reputation, removing her to the Americas was more easily said than done. Lord Fountainhall recorded that skippers, notoriously superstitious at the best of times, were steadfast in their opposition to having the 'possessed lass' on board: 'There is no master can yet be persuaded to take her with them, they are so feared, and some choose rather to hazard away without a pass, as to go in such bad company, as they think.' In fact, there is no record of Janet Douglas' actually leaving the country, and her fate – as with so much else – is unknown.

What opinion of Janet Douglas was formed by the educated men who met her? The Revd Gray confined himself to her answers, and did not venture an opinion of her character. In the view of Lord Fountainhall, she was possessed by a familiar spirit: 'What made her very suspect to be haunted only by a familiar, was her dissolute idle life, having nothing of austerity, and not so much as a show or semblance of piety in it, but much lightness and vanity, so that many concluded her to be a very cheat.' Charles Sharp's book includes a letter from the Revd Robert Knox written in February 1677, when the girl was still mute: 'I judge Dumby the greatest prodigy in the whole business… her age, her deafness and dumbness, make it improbable she had that charm [power] from observation and experience'. Knox thought she was not in communication with an evil spirit, but with the 'white devils' or 'aerial sprites' of the lower order of heaven, which 'have easy access to our little business here below, and are able to give their favourites clear information thereof.' The Privy Council damned her as 'an impostor, or cheat at least.' Sir George Maxwell was convinced she had extraordinary powers. George Hickes weighed his options and then agreed: 'People were divided in their opinions of her: some suspected her for an impostrix: but others, of whom I was one myself, thought that she really was what she pretended.' Later writers, such as Robert Chambers, Sir Walter Scott and the joint authors of *The Philosophy of Witchcraft*, have been less kind, universally regarding Janet Douglas as an attention-seeking, vindictive and manipulative brat. At the very least she had considerable skills of dissembling and invention. No one was ever able to test her alleged powers of second-sight.

The entire sad, sordid story was dramatised by Anne Downie as *The Witches of Pollok*, performed by the Tron Theatre Company in 1990. In 2010 the author reprised the story in a novel of the same name.

Sir George Maxwell's son, Sir John Maxwell, went on to become one of the most prestigious figures in the Scottish legal system. In 1684, seven years after the events, he wrote an account of his father's bewitchment, partly based on Sir George's own words. As far as can be determined from the language used, Sir John believed every word. He went on to sit on the Commission that tried and executed Elspeth McEwen and Mary Millar for witchcraft in Kirkudbright in 1698. He was also involved in one of the most extraordinary cases of the period – the bewitchment of Christian Shaw.

THE WITCH-HAUNTED CHILDREN OF BARGARRAN AND GOVAN

The witchcraft era in the Glasgow area came to a close with a strange spate of cases centred round accusations by children. The first was in Bargarran (now part of Erskine) in 1696-7, while the second centred on Govan and Paisley in 1699. At Bargarran the laird's ten-year-old daughter, Christian Shaw, claimed to have been tormented over several months by a 'crew'

Bargarran House, the now-demolished home of witch-possessed Christian Shaw. From *A History of the Witches of Renfrewshire*, 1877.

of invisible witches, whose attentions allegedly brought about bodily contortions, trances, levitation, vomiting of bizarre and disgusting objects, the supernatural appearance or movement of objects, and a host of other disturbing symptoms. She was the Linda Blair (the demonically-possessed girl in *The Exorcist*) of her day. Christian was not called to give testimony in court but a case featuring numerous other witnesses, bolstered by a cabal of witch-hunting ministers, saw the sensational trial proceed in Paisley in 1697.

One of the accused, seventeen-year-old Elizabeth Anderson, was positively keen to confess, naming her own father as a witch and going into great detail about night-time meetings, broomstick rides, the magical strangulation of several children and the death of a minister through witchcraft. Elizabeth was not put on trial, perhaps because even the prosecuting authorities found her story hard to swallow. Of the twenty-eight people originally denounced, some were not proceeded against; some were released for reasons of youth, pregnancy or breastfeeding; some, usually the younger people, became star witnesses for the prosecution (often against members of their own family); some were found not guilty and released; and a number were simply committed for further trial, although there is no evidence this trial ever took place. Seven, however, were executed – Agnes Naismith, Katherine Campbell, brothers John and James Lindsay, John Lindsay of Barloch, Margaret Fulton and Margaret Lang, who were all strangled and burnt at Paisley's Gallowgreen on 10 June 1697. Lang made an extraordinary speech just before her death, saying that although she was innocent of the charges, in her youth she had promised herself to the Devil after committing an unnamed sin of 'unnatural lust'.

Christian Shaw joined a specific sub-section of witchcraft accusations where the principal players were children or young people who were beset with extreme bodily torments. Other examples included Agnes Brigges and Rachel Pinder (1574, London), Marmaduke Jackson (1601, Yorkshire), Mary Glover (1602, London), Thomas Harrison (1602, Cheshire), Anne Gunther (1604, Berkshire), Katherine Malpas (1621, Essex), Helen and Elizabeth Fairfax (1621-2, Yorkshire), Elizabeth Mallory (1656, Yorkshire), the Corbett girls (1660s, Yorkshire), Richard Dugdale (1689, Lancashire), and the infamous American case at Salem, Massachusetts (1692). A number of these were later shown to be faking their symptoms. Most of them shared not only a standard, even stereotyped pattern of torments – fits and trances, speaking in strange voices, vomiting of foreign objects – but also a sociological context. The 'victims' were typically the sons or daughters of the gentry; there was often a powerful fundamentalist Protestant input, or some form of religious tension in the household or community; the 'possession' saw the young people acting outrageously, blaspheming or otherwise kicking against the constricting influence of religion or morality, and to do so without being punished; the spectacle often took place in front of many witnesses, typically gentry or ministers; and the proceedings developed over months and were often conceived of by the adults present as a theological conflict between Good and Evil, with the body and soul of the child as the battleground. All these factors were present in the Bargarran case.

Several of the cases listed above, notably the Salem trials, were sufficiently well-known through published pamphlets for them to have influenced the Bargarran case. Even if Christian herself did not know the details, some of the adults around her would have knowledge of how a case of possession should proceed. In due course Christian's case was described in a pamphlet entitled *A True Narrative of the Sufferings and Relief of a Young Girle*. It remains the core text for the case, although much of it is probably exaggerated or invented as part of wider late seventeenth–century agenda. As a new wind of scepticism, rationalism and materialism blew through the European mind in the late seventeenth-century, God was being re-imagined from the almighty creator to a mere clockmaker, and suspicions were abroad that witchcraft, magic and fairies were superstitious delusions. In 1691 the Revd Robert Kirk of Aberfoyle wrote *The Secret Commonwealth of Elves, Fauns and Fairies*, a detailed description of fairy life. His explicit purpose was to show that as God made the fairies, to disbelieve in them was to doubt the very existence of God. Similarly, the writer of *A True Narrative*, by emphasising the role of Satan, and piling on the demonic phenomena, may have wanted to convince his readers of the reality of the Devil and witchcraft, and hence of God.

THE BARGARRAN COPYCATS

Just as the Shaw case may have been influenced by Salem, so too its own behavioural fingerprints can be found all over a pair of later, but less celebrated, Glasgow demoniacs. In April 1699 two young girls, Margaret Murdoch, daughter of John Murdoch of Craigtown in Govan, and Margaret Laird of Paisley, became Christian Shaw copycats. They had convulsions, presented bitemarks and bruises from unseen assailants, showed great strength, and spat or vomited wool, stones, hair and pins. Laird was unable to eat or drink. Both publicly denounced numerous 'witches' as their invisible tormenters. These denunciations and their associated fits were witnessed by several ministers, who subsequently became the main witnesses in the cases against twenty-five local people.

The nature of those accused gives an insight into what factors probably influenced the two girls in choosing whom to denounce. A number of the accused had previous 'form'. Several

Govan in 1849. *(Courtesy A.K. Bell Library, Local Studies)*

had been implicated in the Christian Shaw trial, including John Paterson of Gills and Elspeth Wood of Over Gurroch, both in Renfrewshire (they had each been denounced but not tried in the 1697 case), Mary Morisone of Greenock, and Annabel Reid of Inchinnan. Others had a longstanding reputation for troublemaking and cursing, such as Jean Drummond of Kilbarchan, Bessie Miller of Killellan, Jannet Laing of Pennretersane in Renfrewshire (who cursed illness onto the children of a woman who had called her a witch), and Jean Woodrow of Kilmacolm, who turned blood to milk, prevented butter from churning, and damaged a mill when she was refused alms. Margaret Alexander of Paisley was a poor woman who made a habit of muttering and cursing when she was refused charity – Robert Patersone claimed his horse had lost the power of its hind legs because he had refused Margaret a shilling. (In 'Fatal Feeds?', a 1990 article in the journal *Folklore*, Sally Hickey examined many similar instances of animal paralysis allegedly caused through witchcraft, and concluded that the cases were well-known livestock illnesses caused by the consumption of, for example, aconite, ergotised grain, hemlock, oats, or radishes.)

Others of the accused were equally dodgy characters. John Dougall from Greenock was a healer of animals and people with a rap sheet stretching back to 1672. He had been investigated at Presbytery and Kirk Sessions in 1695 and escaped with public repentance. To take away someone's illness he collected their nail clippings, eyebrow hair and hairs from the crown of their head, then wrapped the collection in a cloth with a halfpenny and left it outside; whoever opened the parcel would inadvertently receive the disease from the first person (a classic case of sympathetic magic). He used a belt made from rowan tree bark to cure frigidity, taught a man how to use magic to obtain part of another man's fishing, advised John Hunter to sow sour milk amongst his corn on Beltane (1 May) to make the crop grow well, and told another man whose cattle were afflicted with the sturdie disease (scrappie) to boil a stirk (young cow), burn the bones to ashes and bury them. Isobell Houston knew how to remove her neighbour's milk by holding a leather strap as if she were milking a cow. Alexander Cochran, who was fifteen years old or less, had tried to impress other children by telling them he was a warlock who had been abducted by the Devil in the form of a black man. The other kids seemed to have ducked him in water, and he proved his warlockness by floating (they then did the test on another boy, who sank). He also happened to mention that his mother was a witch, and so Bessie Cochran, an itinerant pauper from Kilmacolm, was caught up in the frenzy. And Jean Ross, who ran a school in Paisley, was apparently a known witch of twenty years' standing. She had quarrelled with the local version of the PTA, and was under suspicion for causing child illness and associating with rats and cats, which were believed to be her demonic familiars.

In contrast to these 'usual suspects' there was a trio of respectable matrons, all wives of Glasgow merchants. Margaret Duncan, Marion Ure and Jannet Gentleman were accused of dancing round a man's bedchamber in spirit form, and transforming themselves respectively into a sow, a cat and an ape. And Anna Hill, along with her mother Janet Robertson, and Jean Gilmore, all women of good reputation from Govan, were said to have placed a frog at a threshold to curse those who passed over it. Janet was further accused of trying to persuade Margaret Murdoch to sign a piece of paper, place one hand on her head and another on her foot, and state that everything in between belonged to the Devil (a common Scottish form of the Satanic Pact). The origins of the Govan denunciations can perhaps be found in a key incident that took place just before the 'possession' began, when Janet Robertson caught someone stealing from her home: the culprit's name was Margaret Murdoch, one of the two girls who were handing out the accusations. Once this fact comes to the fore, it looks very much as if Margaret Murdoch and Margaret Laird were simply seeking revenge on people they did not like. Hell hath no fury like a thwarted adolescent thief.

In the end, the Murdoch and Laird case did not become a facsimile of the Shaw slaughter. Several of the accused were released without further ado. A trial was set for the remainder in Glasgow on 19 May 1699; it did not take place. Finally, on 12 March 1700, at the High Court, in Edinburgh, the diet was deserted, that is, all the charges against the accused were withdrawn and the cases dropped. It is not clear why the prosecutions were abandoned; perhaps Laing and Murdoch were unconvincing witnesses; perhaps there was no corroborating evidence; or perhaps, in the time since 1697, senior figures in the legal profession had simply stopped believing in the reality of witchcraft, and hence came to a view that a successful prosecution was unlikely. The Christian Shaw case therefore became, if not the last Scottish witch execution – there were several more isolated examples, with the final burning taking place in Dornoch in 1727 – at least the last large-scale prosecution that resulted in multiple deaths.

The author of *A True Narrative* clearly believed Christian was the innocent victim of supernatural evil. Nineteenth-century writers in contrast saw her as a devious impostor who manipulated those around her in pursuit of some unguessable childish malevolence. Christian's symptoms lasted some six months and never returned. In adulthood she went onto become a successful businesswoman in the textile trade, and lived a life untroubled by supernatural eruptions. An article in the *Scottish Medical Journal* in 1996 provided a retrospective diagnosis of Christian Shaw, surmising that she might have been suffering from one or more of a range of serious illnesses:

Dissociative disorder/conversion disorder. Conversion disorder was once known as 'hysteria' and describes cases where the patient exhibits neurological symptoms (such as fits) but the cause is not found in the physiological-neurological system – the brain or nerves – but in the patient's mind. It is a serious psychiatric disorder. Dissociation involves a disruption of a person's normal functioning in terms of memory, self-identity or awareness, and in children is often associated with a constellation of symptoms related to experiences of physical or psychological trauma or sexual abuse.

Trance and possession disorder. The medical term for those who consider themselves possessed by external entities. In Western psychiatry, of course, such entities are by definition non-real; in other cultural belief-systems – or in seventeenth-century Scotland – the entities are very much 'real'.

Pica of infancy and childhood. Pica is the eating of non-food items (presumably the source of the bizarre objects Christian vomited up).

Localisation-related (focal) (partial) idiopathic epilepsy. The International Classification of Epileptic Syndromes and Epilepsies published in 1989 defines localisation-related epilepsy (sometimes referred to as focal or partial epilepsy) as related a specific localised 'focus' in the brain, while 'idiopathic' means that the root cause is unknown but is probably genetic (rather than caused by damage to the brain). Idiopathic syndromes often manifest in childhood or adolescence and may disappear by adulthood.

Acute and transient psychotic disorder. ATPD is an umbrella term describing extreme symptoms that appear very quickly (within two weeks or less, rather than building up gradually over time) and typically vanish or reduce within two to three months.

To add another twist, I notice that no one has tried to map Christian's symptoms against the typical phenomena associated with poltergeists; although there is nothing like a complete correspondence, certain elements, such as the bruising she suffered, the bodily contortions, the movement of objects and the levitation, can be found in many poltergeist cases. And as a number of investigators have noticed, the poltergeist 'energy' often seems to be associated with a child on the cusp of adolescence.

If you wish to dig deeper into the Christian Shaw and related cases, go to *A History of the Witches of Renfrewshire* (two different editions in 1807 and 1877) or *The Kirk, Satan and Salem*, a 2006 compendium of these and many earlier works, edited by Hugh McLachlan. More useful background can be found in an article by Professor McLachlan and Kim Swales entitled 'The Bewitchment of Christian Shaw' (in *Twisted Sisters: Women, Crime and Deviance in Scotland Since 1400*, edited by Yvonne Galloway Brown and Rona Ferguson), and in Keith Thomas' *Religion and the Decline of Magic* and James Sharpe's *Instruments of Darkness: Witchcraft in England 1550-1750*.

Notions of malevolent witchcraft retain a popular hold to this day, specious scapegoats for life's problems. On 14 March 1999 the *News of the World*'s Ann B. Anderson ('The Psychic Detective, Ann uses her amazing gift to help solve reader's problems, no matter how big or small') published a letter from a Glasgow woman who gave her name only as 'H.O.'. The reader claimed that when she was pregnant her husband had been lured away by another woman through the use of witchcraft. Several months later, on 4 July, 'Harry' from Glasgow asked Anderson to put a spell on his ex-lover, who he claimed was making his life hell. On 9 March 2001 Joan Burnie, the *Daily Record*'s agony aunt, had a letter from a man who was worried that his pregnant girlfriend, her brother, and the rest of her family, were 'all into witchcraft' and as a result he wondered whether his lover should have an abortion. Anderson's and Burnie's responses to their respective correspondents were admirably robust.

CHAPTER *6*

HUNTING THE VAMPIRE WITH IRON TEETH

Hansard, the official record of all words spoken in the House of Commons, has an unusual, not to say bizarre, entry for 22 December 1955:

Mr John Rankine (Glasgow, Tradeston): Last September a school in the Gorbals division of Glasgow closed for the day. By some system of bush telegraph, no one knows how, and as the children poured out of school, the word went round like wildfire that there was a vampire in a nearby cemetery; that this vampire had iron teeth and had eaten two young children. With that prattle, there went talk of space ships and men from Mars, and all the time there was talk about a monster. The 'monster' had gripped the minds of the children, and so they armed themselves with sticks and stones and anything they could obtain, because they were out on a great mission – to destroy evil, to destroy the monster.

That is always a good thing, so we are told, although in Scotland, we must remember, there are good monsters and bad monsters. In the north of Scotland we have a loch called Loch Ness. It is inhabited by a monster, and anybody who said anything bad against the Loch Ness monster would find himself in great danger –

Mr Deputy-Speaker (Sir Rhys Hopkin Morris): I do not think that this Bill is directed against the Loch Ness monster.

Mr Rankine: That is the very point I am making. That is just what I am about to say, because our monster is a 'verrey parfait gentil' creature indeed. She keeps out of the way all winter and only surfaces during the tourist season. She is a very thoughtful monster. Of course, the Loch Ness monster is a lady. We like her so much that we call her 'Nessie' and no lady – not even the bearded lady – could ever be a really successful monster.

But we can see how the children from that school had their minds gripped by this idea, and how easily the idea spread and their impulses were directed to a particular end. The police found exceeding difficulty in controlling these children, which is an added reason why I hope that this Bill will receive unanimous support in the House, because its object is entirely worthy. I believe that it is an attempt to free the minds of our children from evil influences.

Police Had To Clear "Vampire" Hunters

The story that sparked it all: the headline in *The Bulletin* on 24 September 1954. *(Author's Collection)*

Genteel lady Nessies aside, the MPs were debating the Children and Young Persons (Harmful Publications) Bill, a piece of legislated censorship designed to control what were regarded as the pernicious influences of sensational horror and crime comics imported from America. The Gorbals incident referred to by the Honourable Member for Tradeston took place on 22 September 1954, when hundreds of schoolchildren invaded the Southern Necropolis off Caledonian Road, in search of a monster with iron teeth.

The best guide to the chronology of the 'Gorbals Vampire Hunt' is in an article by Sandy Hobbs and David Cornwell entitled 'Hunting the Monster with Iron Teeth'. It was published in an academic work edited by Gillian Bennett and Paul Smith in 1998, *Monsters with Iron Teeth: Perspectives on Contemporary Legend Volume III*. On the morning of Thursday 23 September, crime reporter Malcolm Nicolson did his usual telephone circuit around Glasgow's police stations in the search for stories. When he rang the station at Lawmoor Street, he heard laughter in the background and a voice saying, 'Tell him about the vampire.' Intrigued, he visited the station and interviewed PC Alex Deeprose, who had been called to deal with the crowds of children, and had even been approached by parents asking him if there was any truth in the vampire story. The next day, 24 September, Nicolson's sensational scoop, headlined 'Police had to clear "Vampire" hunters,' appeared on the front page of the now-defunct Glasgow morning paper *The Bulletin*.

Without the reporter's fortuitous call, the vampire hunt may never have reached the press, and would probably have blown over as just another transient playground fad, unknown to anyone outside the economically-deprived area of Gorbals and Hutchesontown. As it was, the vampire achieved world-wide fame, and helped to fuel both thought-vigilantes and, as we have seen, national legislation.

On the Friday evening the city's two popular tabloids – the *Evening News* and the *Evening Times* – had caught up with the story. By now, the Gorbals vampire was 'hot news', and the media interest pushed events forward. On Saturday *The Bulletin*'s follow-up story described a second hunt that had taken place on Friday – 'Vampire Hunters Out Again'. The *Scottish Daily Express*, the *Daily Record* and the *Evening News* also ran the story, as did the UK-wide tabloid the *Daily Mirror*, with the headline 'Amazing Scene as Hundreds of Children Rush Cemetery'. Coverage continued the following day in the *Scottish Sunday Express*, *Sunday Post* and *Sunday Mail*, the latter

AMAZING SCENE AS HUNDREDS OF CHILDREN RUSH CEMETERY

'DAILY MIRROR' REPORTER

A FANTASTIC story of a "vampire with iron teeth" led to amazing scenes in a city cemetery for the second day running last night.

The story of the fictitious monster spread through Glasgow's schools, say teachers and parents, after the children had been reading horror comics.

The "vampire," according to the tale that spread around, had "strangled and devoured" two little boys in the cemetery.

Hundreds of comic-reading youngsters became an easy prey to this gruesome invention—and the result has been a nightmare

They were hunting a "vampire"—part of the amazing scenes in a Glasgow cemetery last night.

The Daily Mirror, 25 September. *(Author's Collection)*

declaring, 'Vampire with Iron Teeth is "Dead"'. On Monday *The Bulletin* announced 'Vampire Doesn't Scare Any More' and stated that the kids of the Gorbals were now laughing off the hunts. It had been a veritable three-day wonder.

But if the vampire was largely forgotten, its alleged source was not. Right from the get-go, the newspapers tried hard to find a deterministic link between some outside influence and the kids' behaviour – the idea was that something external must have sparked the vampire hunt, for why else would children do such things? The first accusing fingers were poked in the direction of H-certificate films (which were soon to be renamed X-certificate), but this was a fruitless avenue, and very soon the culprit was identified as imported American horror comics such as *Tales From the Crypt* and *The Vault of Horror*. Although the very first news stories made no link with comics, within a week the connection was regarded as unassailable: Yankee Trash Is Corrupting Our Kids.

The death of the vampire: the *Sunday Mail*, 26 September. *(Author's Collection)*

VAMPIRE WITH IRON TEETH IS "DEAD"

THE vampire with iron teeth is dead. The vampire which was supposed to be running amok in Glasgow's Southern Necropolis on Thursday after devouring two little boys—started children armed with penknives, sticks, and stones on a mammoth hunt.

They swarmed over the seven-foot-high wall and started searching the cemetery. The rumours swept through the Hutchesontown district of Glasgow with amazing speed. Police were called out.

Lurid comics and a horror film are blamed with starting the scare.

But last night all was quiet at the necropolis. Youngsters who swarmed the surrounding streets guiltily laughed at the idea of a vampire.

The entire anti-comics campaign was based on assumptions rather than hard evidence. And as Martin Barker showed in his 1984 study *A Haunt of Fears*, ideological beliefs also played their part. As well as the expected Christian groups, many of those behind the crusade were actually members of the Communist Party of Great Britain, a group that aimed to limit US cultural influence in the UK. But as bishops, teachers and moral guardians (crypto-Communist and otherwise) lined up to condemn the comics, no one bothered to ask the children at the centre of the incident about their reading habits. In 2010, when BBC Radio Scotland produced a documentary on the incident, two veterans of the vampire hunt made it clear that getting hold of an American comic in the Gorbals was unlikely in the extreme: neither Tam Smith nor Ronnie Sanderson, who were eight years old at the time, had television at home or had ever seen a scary movie or read a horror comic. 'I didn't really know what a vampire was,' said Mr Sanderson. No campaigner could actually point to a comic featuring a metal-fanged vampire, although when the story was back in the news in 2009/2010 a candidate did emerge on Stephen Banes' 'The Horrors Of It All' blog. *Dark Mysteries* #15, published in America in December 1953, does indeed feature a story with the title 'The Vampire With Iron Teeth'. However, just because the comic was theoretically available does not mean it was the actual catalyst – there is no evidence that the comic was distributed in Glasgow, and it is impossible to tell whether any of the children had actually read the issue.

Hobbs and Cornwell wondered whether other elements in the media or within popular culture could have influenced the vampire hunt. The Bash Street Kids, with their hallmark of communal mischief, were a favourite in the Scottish-produced comic *The Beano*. The Glasgow newspaper *The Evening Citizen* had recently published features on the Monster of Glamis Castle and the mass-murderer Gilles de Rais, while *The Evening Times* was serialising Jack House's just-published book of historical Glasgow homicides, *Square Mile of Murder*. The *Daily Record* and *Sunday Mail* had run 'shock horror' stories on homosexuals molesting children. Cinemas had recently shown the 'attack of the giant ants' B-movie *Them!* as well as *The Bowery Boys Meet the Monsters*, a Z-grade 'comedy' bedecked with horror clichés including vampires – and the Bowery Boys themselves were a 'gang', with an emphasis on collective action. Of course, no one knew whether the fearless vampire-hunters of Glasgow had seen any of these publications or films.

John Rankine's parliamentary contribution had included mention of 'talk of space ships and men from Mars.' UFOS and aliens, 1950s-style, were a feature of the vampire panic. On 23 September the *Daily Record* received many calls about a mysterious 'thing' or a 'flying saucer' over Glasgow. This turned out to be a light aircraft on an advertising stunt. On 25 September, the Saturday after the story broke, the *Scottish Daily Express* reported some of the things the children were saying: 'A man with a green mask had landed from Mars,' and, 'A space ship crashed into the cemetery and caught fire'. *Devil Girl from Mars*, a 1954 British science fiction film, featured a Martian woman and her giant robot landing their flying saucer on the Scottish moors. It had been shown in local cinemas from 6 to 8 September; could it have been an influence on the vampire hunt? Again, who knows? What is clear, however, is that the 'vampire with iron teeth' was only one identity ascribed to the entity supposedly inhabiting the Southern Necropolis; the figure was a fluid, shifting monster whose description was transient, subject to childish whim and playground rumours. Sometimes it was a vampire, sometimes it was a Martian, and sometimes it was something else. Its one distinguishing feature was that it was monstrous, and therefore deserving of being hunted.

As for the iron teeth, Hobbs and Cornwell identified other bearers of the feature within the cultural *milieu* of 1950s Glasgow, and these not from the allegedly dangerous comics, but from approved educational sources. The Biblical Book of Daniel, for example, contains a visionary description of the following bizarre entity:

> I saw in the night visions, and behold a fourth beast, dreadful and terrible, and strong exceedingly; and it had great iron teeth; it devoured and brake in pieces, and stamped the residue with the feet of it… the fourth beast, which was diverse from all the others, exceeding dreadful, whose teeth were of iron, and his nails of brass. (Daniel 7v7 and v. 19)

In addition, in 1897 the poet Alexander Anderson composed a poem in Scots entitled 'Jenny wi' the airn teeth'; told from the point of view of a harassed mother who invites the titular monster to come and take her fractious child:

> What a plague is this o' mine,
> Winna steek his e'e,
> Though I hap him ow'r the head
> As cosie as can be.
> Sleep! an' let me to my wark,
> A' thae claes to airn;
> Jenny wi' the airn teeth,
> Come an' tak' the bairn.

By the end of the poem, the bairn — no doubt petrified by the approach of Jenny and 'the dump-dump o' her beetle feet' — has quietened down and so the monster is no longer needed. She does not leave empty-handed however, as 'wee Tam next door' – 'a crabbit, greetin' thing, the warst in a' the toon' – is dragged off to the iron-toothed cannibal's den. The poem was frequently anthologised in works such as *The Home Book of Verse* by Burton Egbert Stevenson, George Burnett's *A Book of Scottish Verse*, *A Book of Scots* by W. Robb, and Robert Ford's *Ballads of Bairnhood*. At least two of these works were widely circulated in schools, and so it is possible that the poem was taught to some of the children who were involved in the hunt for the iron-toothed vampire.

Jenny wi' the airn teeth is a variant of Jenny Greenteeth, a vicious child-devouring monster who inhabited stagnant pools and canals. In the nineteenth century she operated out of Castle Semple Loch near Lochwinnoch in Renfrewshire. In 1951 the journal *Folklore* conducted a survey of folk-beliefs and found numerous still-current references to Jenny Greenteeth in northern England. Both Jennies are examples of *bogeymen* or *bogeys*, scare-figures designed to make children behave in certain ways (Jenny Greenteeth, for example, is the bogey of 'stay away from dangerous water'). Other iron-toothed bogeys are not hard to find. In his 1851 collection *Rhymes, Reveries, and Reminiscences*, William Anderson recalls an old aunt singing him a nursery rhyme about the Marquis of Montrose (who had brutally attacked Anderson's hometown of Aberdeen). Part of the rhyme ran:

Has he seen that terrible fellow Montrose –
Wha has iron teeth wi' a nail on his nose?
An' into his wallet wee laddies he throws?

Tom or Tommy Dockin was a bogey-figure from the Sheffield area who would devour misbehaving children with his iron teeth. In Eyam, Derbyshire, parents threatened their children with an unusual bogey, the curfew bell: 'If thou doesn't get off to bed th' curfew wi' th' iron teeth will come and fetch thee.'

Even more intriguing, there had once been a real-life iron-toothed bogey in Glasgow. Hugh Macintosh's *The Origin and History of Glasgow Streets*, published in 1902, contains the following passage referring to events from the early 1800s around Glasgow Green (my emphasis):

On the boundary wall of the Green, the windows looking into the Planting, this being the local name for the pathway which runs parallel to the boundary wall of the Green eastwards from John Street to the river. At that time it was in great part a deep hollow or ravine thickly-studded with saugh trees and the lower part filled with a dense undergrowth, and towards nightfall it had rather a weird appearance, police in this locality being unknown at this period. The gamins made frequent raids from the Planting into the garden of the Allans, and occasionally defied the ladies, one of whom had rather prominent teeth, which had been operated upon by a clumsy dentist, who had left the metallic fixings quite too apparent, and in the course of her expostulations with the raiders the addition to her molars was spotted at once by the belligerents, who dubbed her *'Jenny with the iron teeth,'* and this title getting exaggerated as time went on, *the youngsters of the East End came to the belief that a veritable ogre existed on the other side of Greenhead wall*, the result being that for many years children in their peregrinations through the park, invariably avoided the Planting through fear of Jenny.

There are several other iron-toothed British examples. Loch Sguir na Geile in the Strathtay area of Perthshire was home to a monster called a 'Fury', which had eels and snakes for hair and a mouthful of iron teeth. A mermaid with iron teeth was reputed to live in a distillery dam in Banffshire. In Yorkshire, the Dragon of Wantley had forty-four iron teeth. *The Violet Fairy Book,* written by the prolific author and folklorist Andrew Lang in 1901, describes a magical river on whose banks sleep 'lions with iron teeth and claws'. In Edmund Spenser's epic Elizabethan poem *The Faerie Queene*, Sir Calidore, the patron knight of courtesy, battles the allegorical 'Blatant Beast of Slander', described as possessing a 'poison-foaming mouth, grisly grim, with its iron teeth an enormous cavern, like the vast gateway into Hades.'

Further afield, a Serbian folktale tells of a profligate peasant who buys a set of iron teeth from a mouse; at first her new teeth are a boon, as they allow her to cut down trees in seconds, but later the teeth turn her into a cannibalistic vampire. Her three brothers kill her after she has murdered and eaten her own mother. The witch-fairy Tante Arie ('Aunt Arie') of the Jura mountains in France and Switzerland has a mouth full of iron teeth. The Asanbosam or Asasabonsam of West Africa is a tree-dwelling vampire-like creature with fearful claws and teeth of iron. A legend associated with the Japanese sage Nichiren tells of a beautiful woman who shapeshifted into a giant snake with golden scales and iron teeth. The Hindu fire-god Agni is represented in the earlier Vedic literature as slaying goblins or demons with his iron teeth.

This is of course not to suggest that the vampire-hunters of the Gorbals were influenced by folk-tales from other lands or even childlore from Glasgow's own history. The list of ferrous-fanged fiends simply demonstrates that human beings from many different cultures and periods have all independently come up with the idea of a threatening monster with iron teeth. The kids in the Gorbals did not need to be influenced by a comic, or a film, or a poem, or the Bible, or anything else; all they needed to invent a vampire with iron teeth was one thing – imagination.

All of us have been children, but although as adults we can sometimes reconstruct the *emotional* realm of childhood (we can remember being sad, or hurt, or happy) we often struggle to recall the *intellectual* or *cognitive* world of the child we once were. It can be argued that young children live in a world of *magical realism*, where strange and wondrous things can intrude into the ordinary, everyday world without causing *cognitive dissonance*. For example, some adults may reject out of hand an apparently paranormal experience because it is *dissonant* with the way they think the world works. For children, however, the bizarre event can be seen as 'normal', because they have not yet learned the 'common sense' limits of normality.

With this in mind, the culture of children in overcrowded, low-income areas such as the Gorbals reveals other aspects of the vampire hunt. Jimmy Boyle, a notoriously violent criminal turned celebrated author, was born in the Gorbals in 1944. The first volume of his autobiography, *A Sense of Freedom*, describes the Southern Necropolis as the area's *de facto* playground. In the absence of any other open spaces, young Jimmy and his pals would scale the 8ft high wall of the 'gravey' and play hide-and-seek among the gravestones and the jungle-like weeds. A gang hut was erected in one of the trees, the wood cut with bayonets nicked from an open window in Lawmoor Street police station. But despite the cocky anarchy of young boyhood – 'it was all free and easy with no adult interference,' wrote Boyle – the threat of the uncanny was still a factor in the Caledonian Road graveyard. The boys would not stay after dark because they were scared of 'The Fiddler', an old man who was rumoured to play the fiddle at his wife's grave each night. The Fiddler inspired the kind of fear that suggests he was more than just an eccentric lonely widower – he was a bogeyman, a threat to any boy still playing within the gravey walls come sundown.

Other factors contributed to the atmosphere of the Southern Necropolis. Behind it was the Dixon's Blazes ironworks, whose furnaces often cast an eerie glow over the area. John Burrowes' 1984 life of Gorbals boxer Benny Lynch, *Benny*, describes how Dixon's Blazes was used as a kind of bogey – the furnace fires were the 'bad fire' (Hell, of course) to which naughty children would be sent if they misbehaved. Tam Smith, one of the vampire hunters interviewed for the BBC documentary, recalled that a furnace was operating on the evening of the hunt: 'It turned the sky flaming red right across the top end of the Gorbals and when that went up, everyone jumped. They thought that was the vampire.'

The graveyard, then, was both a playground – in fact, the sole child-only open space in the area – and a site imbued with a sense of the uncanny. The perfect location for an adventure. And it is the adventure aspect of the story that Hobbs and Cornwell put their finger on. In contrast to the notion first put forward in 1954 – and still current in some newspaper reports in 2010 – the Gorbals vampire hunt was not a case of mass hysteria. Instead, groups of children, swept up by an intoxicating and fluid wave of exciting rumours, gathered together and engaged in a communal activity to hunt down the monster. It was *enjoyable*. Some of the children turned

An artist's impression of Spring-Heeled Jack, one of the several 'monsters' hunted by children in Glasgow over the decades. (*Anthony G. Wallis/Fortean Picture Library*)

up on the hunt armed with home-made tomahawks, improvised stakes, and other monster-hunting weaponry. But they weren't playing at monster-hunting – they *were* monster-hunting. The group mentality allowed individual kids to overcome their fear and act more courageously than they would if they had been alone – 'If children go "hunting" a frightening figure, they do so because the presence of others strengthens their curiosity at the expense of their fears,' as Hobbs and Cornwell insightfully noted. The hunt was a group adventure.

The pair of folklorists also discovered that the vampire hunt was just one of a number of similar 'children's hunts' that had taken place in and around Glasgow over the years. Correspondents recalling their childhood escapades remembered the following 'hunts':

- Early 1930s, Govan: a large number of children hunting a 'banshee'. (No-one could suggest that American horror comics were to blame for this one!)
- 1934 or 1936, Linthouse: 100-150 children over two or three nights hunting a 'White Lady'.
- 1935/6? and 1938, Hutchesontown/Gorbals: hundreds of children over several nights hunting 'Spring-Heeled Jack' (Jack had been a regularly-recycled urban horror since his first appearance in London in 1837). One correspondent recalled standing with other children in Erroll Street looking up at an open window waiting for Spring-Heeled Jack to appear, while another remembered waiting in a similar sense of anticipation near Dixon's Blazes (that place again!) One correspondent said he used to scare his pals by saying 'Here comes Spring-Heeled Jake.'
- 1950s? St Francis School, Gorbals: children would gather outside the school hoping to get a glimpse of a disembodied hand that haunted the building, where it wrote on blackboards and moved statues.
- 1960? Paisley/Foxbar: around a hundred children on successive nights hunting a 'Maniac'.
- 1969/70? Paisley/Glenburn: around ten children spent an afternoon hunting a 'Miniman'.
- 1985? Kilmarnock/Dean Castle: more than 100 children over several nights hunting a ghost called the 'Grey Lady'.
- No date: an uncanny man nicknamed 'Staring Eyes' wandered round Dalmarnock; he could be made out in the darkness of unlit closes because his staring eyes shone brightly.

To this I add an 1878 report on the 'Hobgoblins of Cowcaddens' from James Grant's sceptically-minded Victorian supernatural compendium, *The Mysteries of All Nations*:

> One night it was whispered that the school at the corner of Stirling Street and Milton Street had become the abode of a horde of warlocks… It was seriously averred by dozens of persons that they had actually witnessed the hobgoblins in the enjoyment of their fiendish fun. In a brief space of time the whole neighbourhood turned out to see the terrible visitants that had come among them. Frequently as many as from four to six thousand people – the large majority of whom were children in groups of threes and fours, clinging to each other's hands, and evidently in mortal terror of being suddenly spirited away no one knew where – assembled to catch a glimpse of the mysterious cause of the commotion. To such a height did the excitement grow, that one night the authorities stationed no fewer than nine policemen round the school, for the purpose of restoring order.

Ghosts cannot be allowed to waste police time, and so serious efforts were instigated to get to the bottom of the phenomenon:

> On the following night 'the ghost,' as it was now called, still uncaught, and gliding as noiselessly and swiftly through the deserted rooms as on the first night of its appearance, frightening the souls and raising the hair of all who believed in it, and the authorities, being suspicious of mischief on the part of someone concealed on the premises, sent two detectives into the attics of the building, for the purpose of arresting the apparition should it stalk in their direction and prove to be made of flesh and blood. After waiting several hours the officers relinquished their watching, and left the school to its ghostly occupant… it turned out that a very innocent combination of circumstances had caused all the excitement. It was believed that *the reflection from a set of mirrors in the house opposite, falling upon a series of thickly-glazed maps hanging upon the school wall, had produced the appearances which served to create so great a sensation.*

No doubt there were many other similar hunts over the decades, most long forgotten. The only difference between the hunts listed above and the vampire hunt is that, through a series of chance events (the police being called and a reporter uncovering the story), the vampire hunt actually made it to the media. Had the press not picked it up, it would have been as evanescent as the other hunts. The Gorbals hunt was not a one-off; it has just had a better PR campaign.

Such children's hunts are not confined to Glasgow. On 2 July 1964 the *Liverpool Daily Post* gave the first of several reports describing how hundreds of Scouse kids – some throwing stones – were engaged in a hunt for leprechauns. It seems that, in some times and places, children collectively invent threatening, uncanny or non-human figures, and then engage in enjoyable collective adventures to hunt these figures down. I look forward to contemporary cases of hunts sparked by rumours spread by social media and mobile phones, and the inevitable reaction of moral guardians blaming modern technology.

CHAPTER SEVEN

BIZARRE BELIEFS, STRANGE SUPERSTITIONS AND MAGICAL THINKING

'Superstition brings the gods into even the smallest matters.'
Titus Livy (59 BC– AD 17)

EXAMPLES OF EVERYDAY STRANGE BELIEFS

The journal *Folklore* has recorded various Glasgow vernacular beliefs. In 1907 cheap bangles from Africa, otherwise *très ordinaire*, somehow acquired a reputation for being lucky. An actress appearing in a pantomime in Glasgow received an anonymous gift of a 'Zulu bangle', which, she wrote to a friend the same day, meant she was certain to have a 'good stroke of luck, as Zulu bangles are very lucky indeed.' That evening, she received a letter informing her of an inheritance from a forgotten relative. Thereafter, African bangles were all the range in the theatrical profession. In 1951 there was an example of the hitherto-unsuspected supernatural role of goldfish. An unnamed person in Glasgow had written to a popular newspaper citing several examples of misfortunes hitting households that had recently acquired goldfish, from the smashing of crockery to the disappearance of a husband (who came home the day after the goldfish was found floating at the top of the bowl). As *Folklore*'s correspondent, H.J. Rose, noted, 'Now that the idea has found its way into print, doubtless other coincidences of domestic troubles with the keeping of goldfish will be noticed… it would be interesting to know if the sale of these creatures falls off in Glasgow.'

The Anecdotage of Glasgow by Robert Alison has the following nineteenth-century baptism custom: 'A young unmarried woman takes the child to church, and she carries in her hand a slice of bread and cheese, wrapped up and pinned with a pin out of the child's dress, which she is bound to give to the first male person she meets, and which the said person is equally bound to receive.' One Sunday an English aristocrat, just arrived in Glasgow, was promenading when he was presented with the bread and cheese as described. His many refusals fell on deaf ears, so finally he sought to overawe the young woman with his status, and announced he was a duke of England. The determined lassie countered, 'Though you were the king on the throne, sir, *ye maun tak' that bread and cheese!*' His Grace meekly accepted the sandwich.

Hugh MacDonald's still-enjoyable walking guide of the 1850s, *Rambles Round Glasgow*, describes a 'kissing tree' at the summit of the Fereneze Braes west of Barrhead. The hawthorn was thickly studded with nails, driven through the tough bark by lads seeking to impress their sweethearts with their strength and skill. The tradition was that every nail punched in was rewarded with a kiss, while from the girl's point of view, the nails indicated that their lover would be faithful. David Pride's *A History of the Parish of Neilston* states that the original tree fell around 1860, but its replacement could still be seen in the year he was writing (1910). Sadly there is no kissing tree visible now. An enjoyably breezy walking route links Fereneze Braes with Gleniffer Braes Country Park.

In 1983 stamp-collector Mark Schumacher bid for a lot of 33,000 assorted postcards at a London auction. It turned out that almost all of them were addressed to 'Little Buddy', supposedly a young lad from Paisley or Glasgow who was dying of cancer and was determined to appear in *The Guinness Book of Records* for receiving the largest number of postcards. Researching further, Schumacher found that the appeal had originated on Scottish CB radio, had been picked up by newspapers and publicised worldwide, and between 1982 and 1987 perhaps two million postcards arrived. But there never was a 'Little Buddy'. Although the CB enthusiasts had promoted the appeal in good faith, the postcard-loving cancer victim was a figment of an unknown person's imagination. When *Fortean Times* reported on the story in September 1991, mail for the non-existent boy was still arriving. 'Buddy' was an American slang word popularised among British CB users, but people from Paisley are often called 'Buddies', which may indicate the origin of the fake appeal.

SIXPENCE NONE THE RICHER
For years Mrs M. Coyle of Glasgow had carried in her purse a lucky sixpence marked with her initials. Then in 1971, the day before she went on holiday, she accidentally spent it, and was most upset. Two days later, in a small village in Northern Ireland, she received the same coin in her change. (Source: *The Sun*, 19 August 1971.)

CHOLERA HUMBUG!
In his book *Folk Lore* James Napier listed the lamentable series of delusions demonstrated by all classes of society during the outbreak of Asiatic cholera in 1831-1832. The Church fulminated about proclaiming a national day of fasting – an archaic echo of a seventeenth-century practice when fasts were declared as a way of demonstrating to God that the Scottish people were very, very sorry for whatever sins they had committed (and so could He see His way to removing the particular pestilence, famine or war with which He in His wrath had smote the country? Please?). Religious conservatives also saw the cholera epidemic as God's judgement on the proposals for the disestablishment of religion.

The main delusions, however, were in the political arena. Agitation had been intense both for and against the Reform Bill, which would see the extension of the voting franchise (it was passed on 4 June 1832). The coincidence of the cholera outbreak occurring in the same time-frame as the debate over Reform brought the two separate issues into false alignment. Political conservatives viewed cholera as divine disapproval of the Reform Bill. Political progressives argued it was a trick of the Tories to prevent Reform and, further, that doctors were actually the origin of the disease. Large posters went up around Glasgow, proclaiming 'Cholera Humbug,' stating that medical men, as tools of the establishment, had been bribed to poison wells and streams. Many working-class people, their faith in doctors already annihilated by the Burke and Hare trial of 1828 and the continuing depredations of the bodysnatchers, took matters into their own hands. A mob in the Gorbals attacked doctors treating sufferers of the cholera. In Paisley a full-scale riot destroyed the Cholera Hospital, the van for transporting the dead, and many doctors' offices. As a result twenty-two doctors resigned *en masse* and refused to treat any further cholera victims in Paisley.

Similar 'Cholera Humbug' scenes were enacted in Liverpool and other major cities, and the phrase was a widespread marker of the belief that the disease was manufactured by the doctors, or even did not exist at all. Meanwhile, the medical authorities were often derided or ignored, and many sufferers were deprived of care. By the time the disease had run its course in the winter of 1832, it had claimed some 52,000 people across Britain.

THE SURFING SAINT AND THE KNIGHTS TEMPLAR

Some time in the sixth century, St Conval stepped onto a stone in Ireland and commanded it to carry him across the Irish Sea to Scotland. The surfing saint made landfall on the River Clyde near what is now Renfrew. The *Currus Sancti Convalli*, St Conval's Chariot, can still be seen just east of the swing bridge over the White Cart Water, where the riverside walkway passes the Normandy Hotel (the National Grid Reference is NS49476783). The saint's surfboard is the smaller of the two mossy stones within a railinged enclosure. Its neighbour is the base of a medieval free-standing cross, the missing shaft of which may be one of the carved stones in the church at Inchinnan (*see page* eighty-four). Water from the hollow in the cross-base, if drunk, would miraculously cure both humans and cattle. The stones are not in their original positions, having been moved here before 1836. The traditions are given in James MacKinlay's *Folklore of Scottish Lochs and Springs* and *The Church and Parish of Inchinnan* by Robert McClelland. Conval is supposed to have been a contemporary of Glasgow's patron saint, St Kentigern, also known as St Mungo. There were dedications to Conval at Arthurlie near Neilston, and at Eastwood (Pollok). Like most Dark Age saints, what is written of him is a conflation of later legend and speculation.

The cross-base is also known as the Argyle Stone, after Archibald Campbell, the 9th Earl of Argyle, who led a brief ill-fated rebellion against James II/VII in 1685. Frederick Mort's history of Renfrewshire describes the events: 'Dissensions and delay led to a general break-up of his troops in Dumbartonshire. The Earl crossed the Clyde and was making his way to Renfrew. He had just forded the Cart when he was attacked by two of the king's men, who concluded, in spite of his peasant's disguise, that he must be someone of position from the indifferent way in which he abandoned his horse at the river. After a struggle he was wounded and taken prisoner.' He rested on the cross-base, and the red marks on it were said to be the indelible marks of his blood. The Earl was beheaded at Edinburgh for treason.

Before the advent of industrialisation and motorways, the bleak and marshy low-lying geography west of Renfrew and north of Paisley was dominated by its network of rivers. From around the year 1100 a church dedicated to St Conval stood at the junction of the Black Cart Water and the River Gryfe. Later in the century David I granted it to the Knights Templar, who had a preceptory nearby at Northbar. The Templar connection ensured the church's independence and prevented it being swallowed up by Paisley Abbey. The Templars were a continent-spanning chivalric order that protected pilgrims to the Holy Land, virtually invented banking as we know it, and whose brutal extinction in 1314, spurred on by accusations of demonology and sexual perversion, has given rise to an endless wave of conspiracy theories, including links with the Holy Grail, the Freemasons and the 'secret history of the world'.

The Argyle Stone and St Conval's Chariot inside their railinged enclosure. *(Photograph by Geoff Holder)*

St Conval's Chariot (in the foreground) and the
Argyle Stone. Water from the hollow that once held
the upright cross is said to have miraculous healing
properties. *(Photograph by Geoff Holder)*

Left: One of the several cross-sculptured so-called 'Templars' Gravestones' at Inchinnan. *(Photograph by Geoff Holder)*

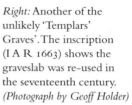

Right: Another of the unlikely 'Templars' Graves'. The inscription (I A R 1663) shows the graveslab was re-used in the seventeenth century. *(Photograph by Geoff Holder)*

The ownership of the church passed to the Order of the Knights of St John Hospitaller, who held it until the Reformation of 1560. In 1828 the decrepit medieval building was replaced with a new structure on the same footprint, the demolition revealing a floor level paved with skulls. Sadly this ossuary was never fully investigated. A later church of 1904 was built on the same site. The extension of Glasgow Airport was the death-knell for the church, and it closed in 1965, the parish being transferred to a modernistic church in the village of Inchinnan about a mile to the north. The site of the original church is still there (NS463669), with a few scattered walls of the dismantled 1904 building, and a handful of gravestones. As it falls within the boundary of the airport it can only be visited by permission and when accompanied by security staff. The utter abandonment of the ancient site contrasts with the jets taking off right above your head.

During the physical transition from the old site to the new, several intriguing carved stones were moved, and can still be viewed at Inchinnan church. Three stones lie in an enclosed alcove near the bell tower. One, decorated with a representation of Daniel in the Lions' Den, may well have formed part of a tenth-century shrine containing the bones of St Conval. Pilgrims were still visiting the shrine in search of healing miracles in the years just before the Reformation. Next to it is what is probably the shaft of the cross that originally was secured in the base now known as the Argyle Stone, which stands a mile further east. The third stone is a decorated grave-cover, probably dating from the tenth or eleventh century.

Around the back of the church is a collection of gravestones that has prompted a great deal of speculation. The ridged slabs are skilfully carved with great swords. As long as people have been writing about them, these have been known as the 'Templars' Graves'. However, the carvings on the stones are not exclusive to Templar iconography, so the swords do not define those commemorated by the stones as Templars. And there is no documentation, and the inscriptions on the stones, if they were ever present, have long since eroded away. Were the bones found beneath the old church the last remains of the Renfrewshire Templars? Again, we know nothing about the ossuary. Both the gravestones and the bones could have perfectly ordinary origins. But this does not stop Templarphiles. Just as medieval supplicants believed the relics of St Conval or the water from Argyle's Stone would cure them, so some modern adherents have an enduring faith in the Templar myth.

ARCHIBALD GOES TO HELL

Catherine Crowe's *The Night Side of Nature* (mentioned in chapter one) describes an episode from the 1750s related to what she calls the 'Glasgow Hell Club.' This group of well-heeled young men would regularly engage in activities of the debauched kind:

> Beside their nightly or weekly meetings they held one grand saturnalia, in which each one tried to excel the other in drunkenness and blasphemy; and on these occasions there was no star among them whose lurid light was more conspicuous than that of young Mr Archibald B—— who, endowed with brilliant talents, and a handsome person, had held out great promises in his boyhood, and raised hopes which had been completely frustrated by his subsequent reckless disposition.

According to the tale that then unfolded, Archibald B—— went to bed after the annual meeting of the club, and dreamed that he was pulled off his horse by a dark stranger. When the gilded youth asked his assailant, 'Where are you taking me?' the answer was straightforward: 'TO HELL'. Hell, as it turned out, did not appear too bad on first acquaintance. There was drink, and gambling, and saucy behaviour, and all manner of other attractions. But on being questioned, the inhabitants revealed that the pleasures that had preoccupied them during their lifetimes were now compulsory, 24/7, for all eternity. One denizen expressed the true horror of their situation: 'There is no rest in Hell!' The dark stranger then escorted Archibald to the surface, leaving him with the ominous remark, 'Remember in a year and a day we meet again.'

The young man woke both feverish and reflective; but after describing the dream to his fellow sots, and following several days' bed-rest, he was back to the bacchanalia. The seasons turned, and soon it was time for the annual shindig. 'Gentlemen,' began the president in his opening speech, 'this being leap year, it is a year and a day since our last anniversary.' Archibald was shocked by the phrase, but partied on regardless and rode home. 'Some hours afterwards,' Mrs Crowe writes, 'the horse was found with his saddle and bridle on, quietly grazing by the roadside, about half way between the city and Mr B——'s house. Whilst a few yards off lay the corpse of his master.'

The finger-wagging moral of the tale had an instant appeal to those who believe the way to bring people to religion is to threaten them with eternal punishment. *The Night Side of Nature* was published in 1848; within four years the tale, usually reproduced *verbatim* from the original, was being widely circulated in British and international newspapers and publications such as *The Working Man's Friend and Family Instructor*. I have also found it – usually amplified with pious exhortations and Biblical quotations – in dozens of examples of Victorian Christian literature, from works with titles as *Touching Incidents and Remarkable Answers to Prayer*, to the *African Methodist Episcopal Church Review*. It remains a favourite on American Christian websites and any Google search will turn up multiple hits. The tale is sometimes titled 'There Is No Rest In Hell'; it is almost always presented as a genuine event, often described as being 'An Authentic Narrative', being taken 'from an old tract', or 'something that took place in the 1800s'. The modern versions almost never mention *The Night Side of Nature* as the original source. The main actor in the tale is typically named Archibald Boyle, although there is nothing in the original story to suggest a surname other than that it begins with 'B'; perhaps 'Boyle' was simply chosen because it was a good Scottish name, or because someone knew the Earls of Glasgow were named Boyle, and put two and two together to get five. Sometimes the Glasgow origin of the story is dropped altogether, London being the favoured substitute; it would be uncharitable to suggest that the change has been implemented because certain geographically-challenged citizens of the USA may only recognize the name of one British city.

Was there any truth to the original version? This is how Catherine Crowe describes the episode: 'It is no fiction; the circumstances happened as here related. An account of it was published at the time, but the copies were bought up by the family. Two or three, however, were preserved, and the narrative has been reprinted.' No sign of this mysterious account has ever appeared; the Catherine Crowe Collection at the University of Kent in Canterbury, which holds the world's largest archive of documents related to the writer, has no reference to the account, or indeed any notes mentioning Archibald B——, the Glasgow Hell Club, or any of the other elements in the story.

In terms of biography, *The Night Side of Nature* merely tells us that the episode took place 'about ninety years ago' (so perhaps some time in the 1750s or 1760s), and Archibald's house was 'a country seat embowered with trees, and forming part of the city of Glasgow'. Working on the assumption that he was a toff, I searched through *Burke's Peerage*, which lists the landed gentry of Great Britain. No-one with the forename Archibald and a surname beginning with 'B' could be found. My conclusion is that if the story was indeed based on a genuine report, then Mrs Crowe invented the name Archibald B—— in order to draw a veil over the individual's identity and family name.

Assuming for the moment that young Archibald was not actually dragged to Hell, what form of scandal could have brought forth such a *cordon sanitaire*? If there is anything authentic in the tale, we know the young man joined in licentious and drunken behaviour with a group of wealthy ne'er-do-wells who met on a regular basis and held an annual convocation. This was clearly a club, and that gives us the first clue to the mystery.

Gentlemen's social clubs blossomed in the eighteenth century, and any city-dwelling man of means would have regularly met with like-minded fellows in taverns or private premises. There were intellectual, literary and artistic clubs, clubs devoted to antiquarianism, science, politics, sport, friendship or business, clubs for professionals or hobbyists, ex-army or navy clubs, debating clubs, quasi-Masonic clubs, and clubs designed primarily for social advancement. What they all had in common was that they were men-only environments, and they tended to emphasise conviviality and the consumption of good food and drink. Perhaps not surprisingly, some clubs were less respectable than others. 'The Sweating Club,' wrote the Revd Charles Rogers in *Social Life in Scotland from Early to Recent Times*, 'flourished at Edinburgh about the middle of the [eighteenth] century. In a state of intoxication, the members sallied forth at midnight, when they attacked or jostled any inoffensive citizen whom they chanced to meet.'

In a 1724 passage in his *Analecta*, Robert Wodrow mentioned an unnamed club in Glasgow which he regarded as a corrupter of youth, as its members were always proposing 'foolish and idle questions, and sometimes profane ones'. In 1726 he was ranting about 'some secret Atheisticall Clubs in or about Edinburgh.' 'Atheisticall' was a term often used at the time to deride educated people – such as university students – who wished to debate religious topics including the infallibility of the Bible: clearly, in the opinion of Wodrow and others, if Christians started to think too much, then disaster beckoned. Wodrow linked these intellectual rebels to contemporary 'Hell-fire Clubs' in England and Holland; in both London and Leiden the clubs were led by upper-class Scottish students who were keen 'to drink their own damnation, and the Devil's health'. The most famous Hell-fire Club, centred on the English estate of Medenham and set up by Sir Francis Dashwood as a temple of religious, political and personal freedom, was not flourishing until the 1750s. The term 'Hell-fire Club' had no fixed meaning, and throughout the eighteenth century was applied to a wide variety of disaffected gentlemen who ranged from serious quasi-revolutionaries to full-on hedonists. Glasgow's own version of the Hell-fire Club accidentally burned down the Tron Kirk on Trongate during a drunken prank in 1793. Previously the club's members had distinguished themselves by drinking, mocking religion, drinking, blowing 'resurrection' trumpets in graveyards to tempt the dead out of their graves, drinking, half-heartedly promulgating revolutionary ideas, and drinking.

It is clear that, for a young man of wealth and taste in eighteenth-century Glasgow, there were ample club-based opportunities for getting into mischief, whether this involved intellectual rebellion against the precepts of a strict Presbyterian religion, provocatively celebrating the Devil and his works, or just getting on with drinking and bad behaviour – or indeed all the above. So, what kind of club was Archibald B— a member of? I have a suggestion that fits the few facts we have, and the sense that the young aristocrat's sin was so great that the scandal was utterly blanked out. I think it was a sex club.

The Beggar's Benison was a curiosity among gentlemen's clubs. Although one of the main advantages of any club was the opportunity to get drunk and talk dirty in an all-male environment, the Benison took it one stage further. It was the only club specifically devoted to masturbation. Founded in the 1730s in the Fife town of Anstruther, by the 1750s it had branches in both Edinburgh and Glasgow. Records for the big city clubs are sparse, but we know that in Anstruther, ladies of negotiable affection were sometimes allowed in to provide 'inspirational displays' for the members, although, as in modern lap-dancing clubs, direct contact was discouraged. At other times, the fellows toasted each other with phallically-decorated drinking vessels, many of which still survive. These and many more details are in David Stevenson's exemplary study, *The Beggar's Benison: Sex Clubs of Enlightenment Scotland and their Rituals*.

The members of the Glasgow Beggar's Benison were not shy about publicising their existence. An advert in the *Glasgow Journal* on Thursday, 16 May 1765 desired 'the knights companion of the Beggar's Bennison, in or about Glasgow' to attend a meeting at the Black Bull Inn on Argyll Street at 5 p.m. on the following Wednesday. The Black Bull was a swanky place with rooms to hire for a price, so there must have been a goodly number of attendees with well-lined pockets. The Glasgow branch was still active in 1792, when an advert from 'Beggar's Benison Hall' announced a chapter meeting and dinner on 11 July. The highwater-mark of the Benisons was from the 1750s to the 1780s, and thus fits in well with the approximate date given for Archibald's adventure.

Sadly, the link with Archibald is all just speculation. Although I contend that membership of a sex club would provide the perfect reason for a rake's progress to be extirpated from the written record, and the dates fit, I cannot provide even the slightest of evidence to link Archibald – if he existed – with the Beggar's Benison. No record of the Glasgow membership of the club has survived; and without names, the connection falls at the first hurdle. The story of Archibald B— and his trip to Hell may forever remain just a pious fable, endlessly recycled by those ideologically committed to the apparent 'truth' of simplistic moral homilies. But perhaps that long-suppressed original account mentioned by Catherine Crowe may one day surface, and we'll know the truth…

BIBLIOGRAPHY

Anon *A History of the Witches of Renfrewshire who were burned on the Gallowgreen of Paisley* (Alexander Gardner; Paisley, 1877)

Anon 'Glasgow Fasting Man in Italy' in *Northern Notes and Queries; or, The Scottish Antiquary* Vol. III 1889

Anon *The 'Two Worlds' Portrait Album of Spiritual Mediums, Workers and Celebrities* ('Two Worlds' Publishing Co.; Manchester, 1897)

Anon 'Apparition of a Friend at the Moment of her Death' in *Journal of Society for Psychical Research* Volume 26, 1930

Anon 'Two Dreams Apparently Conveying Paranormal Impressions' in *Journal of Society for Psychical Research* Volume 33, September–October 1943

Adam, Isabel *Witch Hunt: The Great Scottish Witchcraft Trials of 1697* (MacMillan; London, 1978)

Addy, Sidney Oldall *A Glossary of Words Used in the Neighbourhood of Sheffield: A Selection of Local Names, and some Notices of Folk-Lore, Games, and Customs* (The English Dialect Society/ Trubner & Co.; London, 1888)

———— *Household Tales with other Traditional Remains Collected in the Counties of York, Lincoln, Derby, and Nottingham* (David Nutt; London / Pawson and Brailsford; Sheffield, 1895)

Alison, Robert *Anecdotage of Glasgow, Comprising Anecdotes and Anecdotal Incidents of the City of Glasgow and Glasgow Personages* (Morison; Glasgow / Simpkin, Marshall; London, 1892)

Anderson, William *Rhymes, Reveries, and Reminiscences* (John Finlayson; Aberdeen, 1851)

Barker, Martin, *A Haunt of Fears: the Strange Case of the British Horror Comics Campaign* (Pluto Press; London, 1984)

Barstow, Anne Llewellyn *Witchcraze: A New History of the European Witch Hunts* (Pandora; London, 1994)

Bennett, Edward T. *The Direct Phenomena of Spiritualism—Speaking, Writing, Drawing, Music and Painting: a Study. With Facsimile Illustrations of Direct Writing, Drawing and Painting* (Rider; London, 1908)

Black, George F. *A Calendar of Cases of Witchcraft in Scotland 1510-1727* (New York Public Library; New York, 1938)

Blair, Robert & William Row (ed. Thomas McCrie) *The Life of Mr Robert Blair, Minister of St Andrews* (The Wodrow Society; Edinburgh, 1848)

Bowen, Marjorie *The Bishop of Hell and Other Stories* (Wordsworth Editions; Ware, 2006 – first published 1949)

Bowers, Judith *Stan Laurel and Other Stars of the Panopticon: The Story of the Britannia Music Hall* (Birlinn; Edinburgh, 2007)

Boyle, Jimmy *A Sense of Freedom* (Pan Books; London, 1977)

Brown, Rawdon (ed.) *Calendar of State Papers Relating to English Affairs in the Archives of Venice, Volume 4 - 1527-1533* (Longmans, Green & Co.; London, 1871)

Brown, Raymond Lamont *Phantoms of the Theatre* (Satellite Books; London, 1978)

Burrowes, John *Benny: The Life and Times of a Fighting Legend* (Fontana Press; Glasgow, 1984)

Campbell, G.E.. *Notes on the ecclesiastical antiquities of the parish of Eastwood* (New Club; Paisley, 1902)

Carrington, Hereward *The Physical Phenomena of Spiritualism* (American Universities Publishing Co.; New York, 1920)

Chambers, Robert *Domestic Annals of Scotland from the Reformation to the Revolution* 3 Vols (W. & R. Chambers; Edinburgh and London, 1859)

Clark, Sylvia *Paisley: A History* (Mainstream; Edinburgh, 1988)

Coates, James *Photographing the Invisible. Practical Studies in Spirit Photography, Spirit Portraiture, and other Rare but Allied Phenomena* (L. N. Fowler & Co.; London, 1911)

Crawfurd, George *The History of the Shire of Renfrew* (Alex. Weir; Paisley, 1782)

Crichton-Browne, Sir James "Report of a Co-Cognitive Dream" in *Journal of Society for Psychical Research* Volume 12, 1905–1906 (November 1905)

Crowe, Catherine *The Night-Side of Nature, or, Ghosts and Ghost-Seers* (T. C. Newby; London, 1848)

Dalyell, John Graham *The Darker Superstitions of Scotland: Illustrated From History and Practice* (Waugh and Innes; Edinburgh, 1834)

Dash, Mike "Buddy, can you spare a stamp?" in *Fortean Times* September 1991

Davis, F. Hadland *Myths and Legends of Japan* (Thomas Y. Crowell; London, 1913)

Dennistoun, James & Alexander Macdonald (eds) *Miscellany of the Maitland* Club Volume 1 (Maitland Club; Edinburgh, 1833)

Dewar, Peter Beauclerk (ed.) *Burke's Landed Gentry The Kingdom in Scotland* (Burke's Peerage and Gentry; Wilmington, Delaware, 2001)

Downie, Anne *The Witches of Pollok* (Capercaillie Books; Edinburgh, 2010)

Fodor, Nandor *Encyclopedia of Psychic Science* (Arthurs Press; London, 1934)

——— *These Mysterious People* (Rider; London, 1936)

Forman, Joan *The Mask Of Time: The Mystery Factor In Timeslips, Precognition and Hindsight* (Macdonald and Jane's; London, 1978)

Fraser, Mark (ed.) *Big Cats In Britain Yearbook 2006* (CFZ Press; Woolfardisworthy, 2006)

——— *Big Cats In Britain Yearbook 2007* (CFZ Press; Woolfardisworthy, 2007)

Frazer, John "A Brief Discourse concerning the Second Sight" in D. Webster (ed.) *A Collection of Rare and Curious Tracts on Witchcraft and the Second Sight; with an Original Essay on Witchcraft* (Thomas Webster; Edinburgh, 1820)

Goodare, Julian (ed.) *The Scottish Witch-Hunt in Context* (Manchester University Press; Manchester & New York, 2002)

Grant, James *The Mysteries of All Nations: Rise and Progress of Superstition, Laws Against and Trials of Witches, Ancient and Modern Delusions Together With Strange Customs, Fables, and Tales* (W. Paterson; Edinburgh / Simpkin, Marshall, & Co.; London, 1880)

'Hafed' [David Duguid (ed. H. Nisbet)] *Hafed, Prince of Persia; his experiences in Earth Life, being spirit communications being recited through Mr. David Duguid, the Glasgow Trance Speaking Medium, with an Appendix, containing communications from Spirit Artists Ruisdale and Steen, illustrated by Facsimiles of forty-five Drawings and Writings, the direct work of the Spirits* (James Burns; London / H. Nisbet; Glasgow, 1876)

——— *Hermes, a Disciple of Jesus: His Life and Missionary Work; also the Evangelistic Travels of Anah and Zitha, two Persian Evangelists, sent out by Hafed; together with Incidents in the Life of Jesus given by a Disciple through Hafed* (Hay Nisbet; Glasgow / E. W. Allen; London, 1888)

Harrison, Ted *Stigmata: A Medieval Mystery for a Modern Age* (HarperCollins; London, 1994)

Hector, William *Selections from the Judicial Records of Renfrewshire: Illustrative of the Administration of the Laws of the County, and Manners and Condition of the Inhabitants, in the Seventeenth and Eighteenth Centuries* (J. & J. Cook; Paisley, 1876)

Hickey, Sally 'Fatal Feeds? Plants, Livestock Losses and Witchcraft Accusations in Tudor and Stuart Britain' in *Folklore,* Vol. 101, No. 2 (1990)

Hobbs, Sandy & David Cornwell "Hunting the Monster with Iron Teeth" in Gillian Bennett & Paul Smith (eds) *Monsters with Iron Teeth: Perspectives on Contemporary Legend* Volume III (Sheffield Academic Press; Sheffield, 1998)

Holder, Geoff *The Guide to Mysterious Glasgow* (The History Press; Stroud, 2009)

———— *Paranormal Dundee* (The History Press; Stroud, 2010)

Inglis, Brian *Natural and Supernatural – A History of the Paranormal* (Prism Press; Bridport, 1992)

Kendall, Charles & Henry Kendall *Strange Footsteps; Or, Thoughts on the Providence of God* (Bemrose and Sons; London and Derby, 1871)

Kenna, Rudolph & Ian Sutherland *They Belonged to Glasgow: the city from the bottom up* (Neil Wilson Publishing; Glasgow, 2001)

Kennedy, James *Folklore and Reminiscences of Strathtay and Grandtully* (The Munro Press; Perth, 1927)

Lang, Andrew (ed.) *The Violet Fairy Book* (Longmans, Green & Co.; London, 1901)

Larner, Christina *Enemies of God: The Witch-Hunt in Scotland* (Chatto & Windus; London, 1981)

Laurie, Peter 'Pig-ignorant' column in *New Scientist* 23 March 1978

Law, Marion "The Sounds of Iain" in *The Paranormal Review* July 1999

Law, Robert (ed. Charles Kirkpatrick Sharpe) *Memorialls; Or, The Memorable Things That Fell Out Within This Island of Brittain from 1638 to 1684* (Archibald Constable & Co.; Edinburgh, 1818)

Mcclelland, Robert *The Church & Parish of Inchinnan* (Alexander Gardner; Paisley, 1905)

McConnell, Brian *The Possessed: True Tales of Demonic Possession* (Brockhampton Press; London, 1997)

MacDonald, Hugh *Rambles Round Glasgow: Descriptive, Historical and Traditional* (John Smith & Son; Glasgow, 1910 – originally published 1854)

McDonald, S.W., A. Thom, & A. Thom, 'The Bargarran Witchcraft Trial: A Psychiatric Re-assessment' in *The Scottish Medical Journal,* Vol. 14, 1996

Macdonell, A.A. *Vedic Mythology* (Karl J. Trubner; Strasbourg, 1897)

Macgeorge, Andrew *Old Glasgow: The Place and the People, from the Roman Occupation to the Eighteenth Century* (Blackie & Son; Glasgow, 1880)

Macintosh, Hugh *The Origin and History of Glasgow Streets* (Hedderwick; Glasgow, 1902)

MacKinlay, James M. *Folklore of Scottish Lochs and Springs* (William Hodge; Glasgow, 1893)

McLachlan, Hugh V. (ed.). *The Kirk, Satan and Salem: a history of the witches of Renfrewshire* (Grimsay Press; Glasgow, 2006)

McLachlan, Hugh & Kim Swales "The Bewitchment of Christian Shaw: A Reassessment of the Famous Paisley Witchcraft Case of 1697" in Yvonne Galloway Brown & Rona Ferguson (eds) *Twisted Sisters: Women, Crime and Deviance in Scotland Since 1400* (Tuckwell Press; East Linton, 2002)

Macpherson, George *Highland Myths and Legends* (Luath Press; Edinburgh, 2004)

Maxwell-Stuart, P.G. *An Abundance of Witches: The Great Scottish Witch-Hunt* (Tempus; Stroud, 2005)

Mijatovich, Elodie L. *Serbian Folk-Lore* (The Columbus Printing, Publishing & Advertising Co.; London, 1899)

Mitchell, J. and J. N. Dickie *Philosophy Of Witchcraft* (Murray and Stewart; Paisley, 1839)

Mort, Frederick *Renfrewshire* (Cambridge University Press; Cambridge, 1919)

Napier, James *Folk Lore: or Superstitious Beliefs in the West of Scotland within this Century* (Alex. Gardner; Paisley, 1879)

Nickell, Joe "Spirit Painting" in *Skeptical Enquirer* Volume 10.1, March 2000

Pearsall, Ronald *The Table-Rappers* (Michael Joseph; London, 1972)

Pepys, Samuel *Diary and correspondence of Samuel Pepys, F.R.S.* Volume 4 (J.B. Lippincott & Co.; Philadelphia, 1855)

Podmore, Frank *Modern Spiritualism. A History and a Criticism* (Methuen & Co.; London, 1902)

Prentice, Rev. George *Church and Congregation: A History of the Congregation of Martyrs' Memorial Church of Scotland, Paisley*, 1835-1978 (Gleniffer Press; Paisley, 1978)

Pride, David A *History of the Parish of Neilston* (Alexander Gardner; Paisley, 1910)

Robbins, Rossell Hope *The Encyclopedia of Witchcraft and Demonology* (Spring Books; London, 1967)

Rogers, Charles *Social Life in Scotland from Early to Recent Times* 3 Vols (The Grampian Club; Edinburgh, 1886)

Rose, H.J. "Folklore Scraps" in *Folklore* Vol. 45, No. 2 (June 1934)

——————— "Unlucky Goldfish" in *Folklore* Vol. 62, No. 3 (September 1951)

Ross, Dorothy "Letter" in *Psi Report* April 2001

Scott, Sir Walter *Letters on Demonology and Witchcraft* (Wordsworth Editions; Ware, 2001 – first published 1830)

Sharpe, Charles Kirkpatrick *A Historical account of the belief in Witchcraft in Scotland* (Hamilton, Adams; London / Thomas D Morison; Glasgow, 1884)

Sharpe, James *Instruments of Darkness: Witchcraft in England 1550-1750* (Hamish Hamilton; London, 1996)

Sidgwick, Henry, Alice Johnson, F.W.H. Myers, Frank Podmore & E.M. Sidgwick "Report on the Census of Hallucinations" in *Proceedings of the Society for Psychical Research*, Volume 10 (1894)

Spenser, Edmund *The Fairie Queene* (Penguin; Harmondsworth, 1978 – first published 1590-1609)

Spottiswoode, Archbishop John *The History of the Church of Scotland* 3 Vols (The Spottiswoode Society; Edinburgh, 1851)

Stevenson, David *The Beggar's Benison: Sex Clubs of Enlightenment Scotland and their Rituals* (Tuckwell Press; East Linton, 2001)

Taylor, J. Traill (ed. Andrew Glendinning) *The Veil Lifted: Modern Developments of Spirit Photography* (Whittaker & Co.; London, 1894)

Thomas, Keith *Religion and the Decline of Magic* (Peregrine; Harmondsworth, 1978)

Underwood, Peter *Gazetteer of Scottish Ghosts* (Fontana/Collins; Glasgow, 1975)

Wodrow, Robert *Analecta, Or, Materials for a History of Remarkable Providences; Mostly Relating to Scottish Ministers and Christians* 4 Vols. (Maitland Club; Edinburgh, 1842-1843)

Wright, A.R. and E. Lovett "Specimens of Modern Mascots and Ancient Amulets of the British Isles" in *Folklore*, Vol. 19, No. 3 (Sep. 30, 1908)

Yeoman, Peter *Pilgrimage in Medieval Scotland* (BT Batsford/Historic Scotland; London, 1999)

HANSARD

HC Deb 22 February 1955 Vol 537

NEWSPAPERS

Airdrie & Coatbridge Advertiser 17 September 2008

Barrhead News 7 August 2004

The Bulletin 24 September 1954

Caledonian Mercury 2 May 2010

Daily Record 9 March 2001; 14 November 2003

Evening Times 29 March 2005

The Herald (formerly *The Glasgow Herald*) 12 November 1979; 1 April 1995; 12 January 2003; 1 April 2005; 26 October 2009

Kirkintilloch Herald 17 August 2007

Liverpool Daily Post 2 July 1964

Milngavie & Bearsden Herald 4 & 10 February 2010

News of the World 14 March 1999; 4 July 1999

Paisley Daily Express 6 July 2002; 18 February 2003; 20 & 29 May 2003; 12, 18 & 19 November 2003; 11 December 2003; 7 June 2004; 16 August 2004; 24 & 25 March 2005; 18 July 2006; 4 September 2007; 1 October 2007; 29 May 2008; 3 June 2010; 16 June 2010

Paisley Gazette 30 June 2004

The Sun 19 August 1971; 25 February 1983; 19 October 2009

The Sunday People 25 October 2009

Weekly News (Glasgow) 29 November 1903

WEBSITES

BBC News: www.bbc.co.uk/news

Big Cats in Scotland: www.bigcatsinbritain.org/scottishsightings.htm

The Ghost Club: www.ghostclub.org.uk

Glasgow Zoo: www.glasgowzoo.co.uk

The Horrors Of It All: thehorrorsofitall.blogspot.com

Scottish Society for Psychical Research: www.sspr.org.uk

Survey of Scottish Witchcraft: www.shc.ed.ac.uk/Research/witches.

INDEX